THE INTER-AMERICAN HISTORICAL SERIES

Edited by JAMES A. ROBERTSON

A HISTORY OF CHILE

Pedro de Valdivia, conqueror of Chile, founder of Santiago. Courtesy Instituto de Cinematografía Educativa, Universidad de Chile.

A HISTORY OF
CHILE

By LUIS GALDAMES

Translated and Edited by

ISAAC JOSLIN COX

NEW YORK
RUSSELL & RUSSELL · INC
1964

TO THE PEOPLE OF CHILE

ON THE FOUR-HUNDREDTH ANNIVERSARY OF THE

FOUNDING OF THEIR CAPITAL

PREFACE BY THE GENERAL EDITOR

NOTE: *This preface is as Dr. Robertson wrote it, before his death on March 20, 1939.*

THE PRESENT VOLUME is the fourth in the Inter-American Historical Series. Preceding it were the translations made and edited by Professor William Spence Robertson of Ricardo Levene's *Lecciones de historia argentina;* by Professor J. Fred Rippy, of J. M. Henao and G. Arrubla's *Historia de Colombia;* and by Professor Percy Alvin Martin, of João Pandiá Calogeras' *A formação histórica do Brasil.* These volumes have related the history of Argentina, Colombia, and Brazil as written by nationals of the three countries respectively. In this fourth volume Professor Isaac Joslin Cox gives to English-speaking people the history of Chile as narrated by a Chilean.

Señor Luis Galdames, leaning on the older histories of Barros Arana, but with many supplementary interpretations of his own, has written a narrative that comes well within the designs of this series. He has produced an interesting volume, as is attested by the eight editions of it that have already appeared in Chile.

Not only does this volume in the original represent a sane and solid piece of work, but Professor Cox's translation has carried over into English the meaning and spirit of the original. The general editorial policy of preceding volumes has been followed in the present one. Notes have usually been supplied by Professor Cox. Those supplied by the general editor are signed "J.A.R." The translator and editor has added a biographical appendix of persons mentioned in the narrative, the data for which have been taken, so far as those connected with the history of Chile are concerned, from well-known national sources. This will add interest to the author's work.

Professor Cox has long been familiar with the history of Chile and has several times visited that country. He has, therefore, more than a mere academic interest in it. To have known the great bibliographer, José Toribio Medina, is in itself an achievement.

Those connected with this series hope that this volume, as well as all those which have preceded it and those which will follow it, may draw closer the intellectual and cultural bonds between Anglo and Hispanic America.

JAMES A. ROBERTSON

INTRODUCTION BY THE TRANSLATOR AND EDITOR

CHILE IS A LAND of contrasts. The phrase, often repeated, cannot be too thoroughly emphasized. The long and narrow country, hemmed in by the Andes and the ocean, stretches from the desert area of Atacama southward to the bleak rain-drenched and forbidding slopes of Tierra del Fuego. From its eastern mountain barrier rises Aconcagua, the highest peak of the Americas, while relatively near its western shore line may be found some of the deepest of the Pacific's submerged areas. From barren area to dense forest, from mineral region to fertile valley, luxuriant in subtropic vegetation, the little country shows a wide variety in climate, in production, and in natural advantages.

Likewise varied are its population elements. In the pre-Hispanic period its aborigines exhibited marked cultural variations between those groups in the north which accepted the sway of the Inca Empire and the Araucanians of the south-central portion, ready to put up a stiff and lasting resistance to the Spanish conquest, or the miserable denizens of the extreme south. To this remote land the conquering Spaniards at different times sent representatives of sunny Andalusia and of the stormy Cantabrians, together with stubborn Aragonese and energetic Catalonians. To these varieties of Spanish forebears, the period of independence and subsequent years gave a British tinge, while recent decades added French, German, Italian, and Slavic elements. From these divers sources there is developing an ethnic stock that is gradually acquiring national consciousness. Even today it exhibits less evidence of divergent origins than its neighbors to the northward. For the future it gives promise of prolific fecundity.

The history of Chile, as might be inferred, likewise reveals striking contrasts. Its conquest partook of the features that marked the occupation of Mexico and Peru, but with scant material reward to its ruthless conquerors. During the colonial period the region developed much as did other Spanish colonies in America, but in most respects life there seemed more isolated and drab than elsewhere. Churchmen and civil administrators were of the usual Iberian type, but they wrought in a more remote field where good work was less appreciated or poor performance ignored. Rebellion, reconquest, and final victory marked its struggle for independence, bringing forth, as did the contest in other parts of the

Spanish dominions, both farsighted civic leaders and overambitious militarists. Under the direction of a dominant aristocracy—determined, if not always enlightened—it emerged more rapidly than they from the anarchy that closed the struggle and adopted a stabilized, if repressive regime of law and order. Changes in government, once the system was well established, have been very few. Its material progress has been consistent, although not equally shared by all classes. Its general development has been many-sided, emphasizing cultural features as well as material gain. Literary efforts have kept pace with mineral production. As in all other nations of Latin origin, political expression seems to require numerous party divisions, but proceeds through fairly regular channels. Even in the economic and social upheaval of recent years, Chile has suffered less disturbance than many of her sister republics.

The present work aims to set forth this complex yet unified story. For more than thirty years the *Estudio* of Luis Galdames has been used in the schools of Chile. During that period it has also become favorably known outside the country as one of the leading texts of its type. For this reason it has been selected to represent Chile in the Inter-American Series. The first edition of the book appeared in 1906. The present translation was first made from the sixth edition, which appeared in 1925, but was revised and compared with the seventh edition which came out three years later, and finally with the eighth edition which was published in 1938. The translation represents a faithful attempt to reproduce the author's interpretation of his nation's history, but it has been deemed advisable to omit the elaborate table of contents which the author published at the end of his last edition and the separate parts repeated at the head of each chapter. A few of the chapters as given in the last edition have been combined, but those are the only changes in the chapter headings. The translator and editor has likewise adopted more concise wording for the chapter subheads, and he hopes this will give the book a better appearance and at the same time present adequate subdivisions to the text. In view of the fact that the last edition of the author has just appeared, it has been deemed unnecessary for the editor to add a final chapter covering recent events. He has, however, noted a few important developments in the text or in footnotes, as may be observed in chapter nineteen.

A word with respect to the author of this work. Luis Galdames graduated in 1906 from the Instituto pedagógico, now a part of the national university. Following the customary procedure in higher education, he completed a law course and was licensed as advocate in 1903. His thesis on this occasion was "La lucha contra el crimen" (The Struggle against Crime). Still following the usual procedure, he practiced law for a time and then took up teaching as his life work. Before studying law Galdames had conducted classes in private schools. In 1905 he began work as a state teacher in history and geography in the Commercial Institute. Combining instruction there with similar work in the Liceo Barros Borgoño, in 1913, he became rector of the Liceo Miguel Luis Amunátegui. Here, through his ability as a teacher and organizer, he increased the enrollment of the school to one thousand students. In 1912 he became editor of *La revista de educación nacional* and in 1917 took on another educational review, *La vida nacional*, at the same time holding various offices in pedagogical organizations. Besides press work, he published in 1904 *El decenio de Montt* and in 1911, *Geografía económica de Chile*, as well as numerous monographs on educational and economic topics. In 1926 appeared the first volume of his monumental work, *La evolución constitucional de Chile, 1810-1925*. His writings are the fruit of persistent application, of intimate and accurate knowledge of his sources, of good judgment in the selection and treatment of topics, and of literary skill of no mean order.

Señor Galdames has not held aloof from civic activities. In 1918 he helped to organize the *Partido nacionalista* (Nationalist party), which its founders hoped would develop in keeping with the name. He acted as secretary of this group until directed by the minister of education to resign. In that same year he was the unsuccessful candidate of his party for the post of deputy in the national congress. He took an important part in the educational reforms attempted in 1928 and was chiefly responsible for the *Reglamento general de educación secundaria* which he fathered as director of secondary education for the country. Although his stay in that position was brief and his report is as yet disregarded, it will serve as a model for possible future reforms. Believing as he does in applying education to practical needs, Señor Galdames has made extensive studies abroad in pursuit of his ideal, and in 1935 assisted in reorganizing the educational system of Costa Rica, and in 1938 that of the Dominican Republic. At present he is dean of the faculty of social sciences, including the Instituto pedagógico, a part of the University of Chile.

Señor Galdames did not find the history of Chile an untrodden field. Its contributors, as the select bibliography of the present work will attest, are many. The annals of the country up to the middle of the nineteenth century were in a peculiar sense the province of Don Diego Barros Arana. From one point of view, the *Estudio* of Galdames is an epitome of the score or more of volumes produced by that great annalist. The younger writer has not merely abridged the older man's work and that of divers others for the later period, but he has given to his volume a life and force that make it in a very real sense his own. The fact that the book has passed through eight editions in the course of more than thirty years is sufficient proof of its originality and of its worth as a secondary school text. He has other rivals in this field, but his text holds first place for fullness, interpretation, style, and objective treatment.

The Spanish edition of the work contains no biographical or other notes. This was natural for it was intended for Chilean students and for general readers who would be reasonably familiar with the names mentioned. Readers from other lands, however, might require further explanation. Hence it has been deemed desirable to sketch briefly in an appendix, alphabetically arranged, the careers of the persons mentioned in the text, so that those interested may readily find them. A few brief biographical sketches are given in footnotes.

My wife, Grace Elizabeth Cox, made the first rough draft of the translation and helped to prepare the index. The line maps in the volume were prepared by my son, Walter Yost Cox. The illustrations are presented by the University of Chile, through the courtesy of Señor Raul Ramírez; Sr. Alberto Cabero, Chilean ambassador to the United States; and W. R. Grace and Company. In preparing the copy for the press, the editor has had the assistance of Mrs. Pearl Hoose Doughty, Mrs. Kathryn Sanders Fisher, Mrs. Miralotte Sauer Ickes, and Miss Lorraine Ellison. He wishes also to express his appreciation for the patient assistance rendered by the late general editor and by the director and members of the editorial staff of the University of North Carolina Press, especially Mrs. Catherine G. Anderson.

ISAAC JOSLIN COX

Northwestern University
November, 1940

CONTENTS

ILLUSTRATIONS

A HISTORY OF CHILE

CHAPTER I

THE NATIVES

THE PRIMITIVE POPULATION

VERY LITTLE IS KNOWN of the first inhabitants of Chile. We are ignorant of their origin, their appearance, and their customs. Some of their implements, which have been found in the lower strata of the earth, enable us to form an idea of the degree of culture they had attained and the means of livelihood at their disposal.

These native remains consist of rudely wrought stones, the bones of animals, and sea shells. They have been discovered accidentally in opening up mines, in cutting through mountains to build canals and railroads, and in digging for the foundations of buildings. Wherever it has been necessary to excavate to a moderate depth, these remains have been found by the thousands. The most common are those of stone, and their classification is not difficult because the uses for which the natives intended them were much the same— war, hunting, fishing, and whatever related to the food supply, nothing more. The following are the principal types:

1. *Bored Stones.*—These are cobblestones polished by friction in the beds of rivers. Some are round and flat, like a disk; others are compact, like a sphere. The perforation is usually conical, like two funnels united at the narrow opening, with the tops outward. The natives apparently used them to hold down the sharpened prongs of a kind of fork with which they scraped the earth in order to pull up roots and tubers.

2. *Hatchets.*—These stones are generally small. They were provided with a thick handle and were probably used in skinning animals, in cutting up the bodies of war captives, in separating shellfish from rocks, and in other ways.

3. *Arrowheads.*—These are pointed like the leaves of trees and are of two kinds—serrated and smooth-edged. It is thought that the serrated arrowheads were used in hunting, because they would stick in the wounds of the prey and prevent flight, or make it difficult. The others seem especially adapted to fighting and are much more numerous than the serrated variety.

Since these implements are found in deep strata of the earth, at a depth of from twelve to twenty-five feet, and since near them in similar soil are found also the bones of extinct animals like the mastodon, it is generally agreed that they belong to remote antiquity. From this we conclude that the primitive population of Chile dates from an epoch which must be reckoned in thousands of years, perhaps from the earliest time that it was possible for human beings to exist on the earth.

This information is the first gain derived from our study of these prehistoric remains; and, by comparing them with similar implements used by peoples who live today in a stage of culture about equal to that of these primitive aborigines, one can deduce the purposes for which the prehistoric implements were designed and the living conditions of the peoples who used them. Chile, then, like other countries, had a very remote Stone Age.

Remains of buildings of these prehistoric times are lacking, but on the seacoast and in almost all of the central zone there are sites where vestiges of huts and burial grounds of this distant age have been found, along with utensils of stone, baked clay, or wood, the bones of animals, and even petrified bodies. There are no other traces of primitive man. Rude and poor he may have been, but he was the forerunner of civilization in Chile, as other men of the same kind and condition were the forerunners of civilization in other countries.

GEOGRAPHIC DISTRIBUTION OF THE ABORIGINES

Another advantage is gained from the discovery of the native remains. By means of them we have been able to determine the geographic distribution of the primitive population and the general conditions of climate and production in Chile in the remote past. It is obvious that the men of the Stone Age could not have lived except in those places where the means of livelihood were readily available, and we observe in this connection that almost all of the native relics are found near the coast, lakes, and rivers, or in those places where vegetation, up to recent times, has been most developed. From this we may conclude that living conditions in Chile have varied little in the long course of the centuries.

The abundance of primitive remains and the unchanging nature of the climate and products make it easy to determine the first centers of population. It must not be thought, however, that permanent establishments are meant, or even towns more or less permanent. The savage is a nomad not so much by nature as by necessity. He has to go from place to place, following atmospheric changes and the seasons most favorable to him in his search for food and shelter.

The coast is his most hospitable refuge because its climate is not subject to such sudden changes as the rest of the continent, nor is it so severe. The ocean also provides him with its inexhaustible supply of fish and mollusks. Therefore primitive natives frequented the Chilean shore. The almost straight coast line from Tacna to Chiloé offers sheltered sites where dwelling places can be established under favorable conditions. Each of these sites is today a harbor or a fishing inlet.

On the eastern side, along the slopes of the Andes, there are many fertile valleys with abundant water and numerous animals. In the central zone especially, these valleys occupy the mountain gorges from which spring the torrents and rivers crossing the territory to the west. On each side the great cordillera presents an extremely varied aspect. On its summit lies perpetual snow, which pressure little by little transforms into ice; on its slopes grow forests of different kinds of trees, which become more and more impenetrable as they approach sea level; and at the foot of the slopes stretch meadows perennially covered with grasses which grow spontaneously, like the rest of the vegetation. In the cordillera region of central Chile there were in former times, just as there are now, lands well adapted to the easy sustenance of man. It is not strange, therefore, that a relatively numerous population dwells there.

Nor did the Patagonian Andes lack inhabitants. The topography of this zone on the Chilean side does not permit the concentration of a very large number of people, but at any rate the Patagonian did not lack food. The irregular distribution of the mountain ranges which cover western Patagonia to the sea permits many rivers to pierce the ranges through winding valleys and form great lakes of moderate depth. These accidents of topography guard the lowlands from the cold winds characteristic of that latitude and in some places are propitious to vegetation and colonization.

Parallel to the Patagonian region extends the insular zone. It was formerly, as now, almost uninhabitable. Beaten constantly by snowstorms and the strong winds from the Antarctic Ocean, its wide expanses present a spectacle of utter desolation. The severe temperatures make the development of vegetation difficult and almost prevent it. Not all these islands are alike, however, in climatic conditions. The archipelago of Chiloé, which is the most northern group, does not have the rigorous climate of those farther south. It shares the temperature and vegetation of the mainland. For this reason it sheltered an abundant aboriginal population. The real insular zone begins with the Chonos Islands and therefore these islands, like those which continue southward as far as the Strait of Magellan, had only a very sparse population composed then, as now, of aborigines.

Farther south, and on the other side of the Strait of Magellan, extends the large southern island of the American continent, Tierra del Fuego, which belongs about equally to Chile and Argentina. It is surrounded by many other islands of less importance. The latitude in which it lies shows at once that living conditions there are not favorable; rather, constant freezing temperatures and winds from the south and west laden with snow discourage vegetation. Even fish and mollusks are scarce. Nevertheless, man has been able to maintain himself there and, although a savage and few in number, he continues to do so successfully. Toward the center and northeast of the island conditions of life are better.

Two mountain ranges, the Andes and the coastal range, form the base of the topography of Chile. In the central belt, lying between the ranges and stretching from Azapa to the Strait of Chacao, one notices an almost invariable correspondence between natural products and primitive population. In the north are the deserts, which extend from Arica, across the provinces of Tarapacá, Antofagasta, and Atacama, to the capital of the last named, Copiapó. This vast region was almost wholly unpopulated in primitive times. In spite of its being very rich in minerals of all kinds, the scarcity of water and, consequently, of plants and animals makes life there extremely difficult even now. The savage aborigine, who was not in a position to profit from the mineral wealth, could not inhabit it to any considerable extent except in its few oases, among them the valley of Azapa and that of Loa.

Continuing southward from Copiapó, the outlook changes. The climate is temperate, vegetation increases, the rivers are permanent, rainfall begins and tends to become periodic. Between the cordilleras of the coastal range and of the Andes a series of mountain spurs cross the territory in various directions as far as Aconcagua and form the so-called transverse valleys. This belt of country today has many mines and produces choice grains and vineyards. In primitive times it was peopled by numerous tribes.

But the primitive population was most abundantly concentrated in the region which is now called the central valley, which extends from the slope of Chacabuco south of the Aconcagua River to the Gulf of Reloncaví, fronting the island of Chiloé. This region was and still is extremely abundant and varied in flora and fauna because periodic and copious rains, as well as numerous rivers, water it. Enclosed between the slopes of the eastern cordillera and the coastal range, it forms a tongue of very fertile soil. The river systems that cross it from the Andes to the sea have such a decided fall that, with a few irrigating canals, the layers of soil are reached and kept moist for a long time. A mild climate, without very sudden changes, and a warm sun in spring and summer encourage natural growth. This part of Chile was in early times a vast forest, broken only by meadows on the banks of the rivers. But since then civilized man has for various reasons destroyed this rich natural treasure. Consequently, the rains have diminished, and the climate has lost much of its regularity. From the Maipo to the Biobío the trees have been almost entirely cleared, and the last traces of this primitive forest are to be found only in the ravines of the Andes. To the south of the Biobío destruction continues rapidly but has not yet succeeded in completely destroying the virgin forests in the valleys of Imperial and Toltén, heart of ancient Araucania.

From north to south within this central valley there existed a notable increase in the numbers of the primitive population. We can be sure that the most populated section was that which extended from the south of the Biobío to the Maullín. This is a zone of large lakes and big rivers. It is also a zone of more abundant rains and of a more humid climate. Therefore, its flora and fauna were, and continue to be, the most abundant in the country.

It is evident, then, that the primitive population of Chile grew denser from north to south as vegetation increased, until it reached the insular and Patagonian zone, which, like the extreme northern part of the country, could not maintain man easily because of its intemperate climate, nor can it do so even today.

THE NATIVE RACE OF CHILE; THE ARAUCANIANS

Regions as distinct as those which are observed in that long stretch of territory harbored diverse races and groups of natives. But the only race of real importance in the history of Chile, the race which has contributed to form its nationality, is the one that inhabited the valleys extending from Taltal to Aconcagua and the great central valley as far as Chiloé. The innumerable tribes scattered throughout this zone were divided into various groups, which are designated by distinct names taken from the geographical localities in which the tribes were found. The most important were the Huilliches (people of the south) from Valdivia to Reloncaví; and the Pehuenches (people of Pehuén) between the Biobío and the Copiapó. All the rest of the native groups are included in the common name of Mapuches, that is to say, natives, or men of the soil.

In addition to this race were the Chonos, who dwelt in the south on the archipelago of that name; the Patagonians, in Patagonia; and the Fuegians, on Tierra del Fuego, who have never mixed with the population of the rest of the country. In the north lived the Changos and the Atacamians, grouped along the coast in the fertile spots of the deserts. These Indians of the northern region in all probability belonged to the aboriginal race of Bolivia and northwest Argentina, and only in certain periods united with the tribes of the central region.

Among the natives of the central zone toward the south the Araucanians deserve special attention as the most numerous type and the most characteristic of the native races of Chile. For some unknown reason the Spaniards gave the name Araucanians to the tribes living south of the Biobío. It may be derived from *auca*, a Peruvian word meaning free, or from *ragco* (clay water), a word used to designate the place where the first Castilian fort on the left side of the river of that name, the fort of Arauco, was erected.

The Araucanian type is as follows: of medium height, with well-proportioned limbs, large head, round face with narrow forehead, small eyes usually black, short and flat nose, large mouth with thick lips and white teeth, thin, short beard, pronounced cheek bones, medium-sized ears, and, completing the whole, a grave, sober manner, at times mistrustful but showing resolution and commanding respect. The complexion varies from mulatto to white but ordinarily it is copper-colored. Such, in its characteristic features, is also the national native type, which is still not difficult to recognize in the mass of the people.

The Araucanian had very few means of livelihood. His clothing was light. Some woolen fabrics and the skins of animals, like the guanacos, foxes, and mountain lions, some vegetable barks, and woven straw constituted all his apparel. The arms, the legs below the knees, and the feet were unprotected. The head was adorned with some animal skin, surmounted with feathers; the face was painted in black and red streaks, with colors extracted from trees.

The principal garment was shaped like a shirt without sleeves, made of two pieces, one in front and one behind, fastened together on the sides and on the shoulders with wool cords or strips of rawhide. It was called a chamal, and was used by both men and women. Later, when textiles came into common use, the men joined the chamal between the legs and drew it in at the waist. Thus worn it was called a chiripá. The women tightened the chamal at the waist with a belt or girdle and wrapped a full square scarf over their shoulders. They also adorned their heads, necks, and arms with rings, necklaces, or bracelets made of strings of beads, snail shells, sea shells, and sometimes tiny green stones. The last representatives of that people still preserve today features of that clothing.

The dwellings were very simple. The natives built them in sheltered places, frequently in ravines, on the banks of streams, or in the midst of forests. They consisted of a few forked poles or posts planted upright in the ground and joined at the top with sticks placed crosswise, forming in this way either a rectangle or a circle. A roof of straw or of cattails (totora) gathered from the marsh, descending like an inclined plane, and a fence of the same material or of *quincha* (reeds mixed with clay) completed the work. Such was the *ruca*. The farmhouses of today still imitate it.

This poor dwelling was, to the Indian, a valuable acquisition. Within it he ate, slept, and in the months of winter was protected from the rain and cold. The bed in a corner on the floor was only a heap of straw, and the pillow was a thick log or a tree trunk. In the center of the hut a fire burned constantly. It was lighted by means of two sticks, one of which fitted into the other. By pressing the former into the latter with a rotary movement, a spark was produced which was fed with tow or dry leaves and carefully guarded to keep it from going out.

Few foods were cooked, however. It was the custom to eat meat and fish half boiled. For this clay pots and dishes were used, as well as utensils formed by hollowing out the center of trunks of such trees as laurel, cypress, or oak to form a large cavity. The meat and fish were put into such a receptacle, with water and a few vegetables. Stones were heated in a fire made for that purpose. When they became red-hot, or nearly so, they were thrown into the receptacle and stirred with the contents.

For fishing the Araucanians used a kind of wooden or bone fishhook. They ventured out on the rivers or along the shores of the sea in little boats of rushes, reeds, and straw. Sometimes a canoe was hollowed out, with the aid of fire, from a trunk of laurel, oak, or some other large tree, until it was given the shape of a trough.

The weapons most used in hunting were the *boleadoras* and the arrow. The former was composed of two or three stones tied to the ends of strips of strong leather. Taking one of these stones in his hand, the hunter swung the others over his head and threw the missile at the legs of the pursued animal. Tangled up in the cords, it fell to the ground and remained motionless. The arrows, fastened to a slender shaft about twenty inches long, were shot from a wooden bow, strung with a firm leather thong.

In hunting birds, traps smeared with some resinous substance drawn from trees were frequently used. The revolving traps of wood placed on the ground and today called *guari-palos* are also of primitive origin. Besides the weapons described, the hunting Indian took with him his dog, an indispensable aid. This animal was small and was generally spotted. It had slender legs, a sharp nose, and large ears. Very quick in its motions, it rarely lost its prey.

But the most common food of the Araucanian consisted of vegetables, which were the natural products of the country—roots and wild tubers, like potatoes, and beans. Fruits he not only ate in abundance but also made from them alcoholic drinks of various kinds.

ARAUCANIAN SOCIETY AND CUSTOMS

The social organization of the Araucanians was very rudimentary. It consisted of the patriarchial family and the tribe. Relationship was the foundation of the former; regional life, of the latter. Relationship began with marriage. This act was celebrated after the groom had bought the bride from her father. The price paid for her was in animals, liquors, fruits, utensils, and ornaments of different kinds. Each individual lived with as many women as he bought. He was considered married to them all. Polygamy then existed. The ceremony of marriage was nothing but a feast for the married couple among relatives and friends of the tribe.

The woman did all the work of the home. She prepared the food and made the clothing for herself, her husband, and her children. She even had to follow her husband when he went on a campaign, carrying provisions for him. Moreover, she cultivated the soil, wove woolen cloth, and made clay utensils. The Indian, notwithstanding all this, treated her badly. Since he had bought her, he considered her his slave, whom he could, in turn, sell. The family was much neglected. During a boy's infancy, the father took no notice of him. Only when he was eight or ten years old did the father show him how to shoot an arrow and brandish the lance and the club. When a boy learned this he was considered a man.

However, the Araucanians wished their sons to develop into vigorous men. For this reason they accustomed them from boyhood to play the same games that the men played. Their favorite sports were those that required bodily agility, such as hockey and handball. In playing hockey, they formed two sides, which lined up at regular intervals. Amidst confused shouting each individual, armed with his own club curved at the point, tried to knock toward the opposite team the wooden ball with which his team played. In handball they also used a wooden ball, which they threw from one to another in the wide circle which they formed for the purpose. Besides such exercises, they used to bet on the one who could lift the greatest weight—tree trunks or stones, for example—or on the one who could first break a very strong bit of wood. With the same idea of preserving strength and health, they almost always took a bath in the river or in the nearest brook at daybreak.

Many families, who came, perhaps, from a distant common ancestor, but whose strongest tie was the locality in which all were grouped, constituted a tribe. This tribe frequently occupied a valley, living on the banks of a river or an inlet, or in the shelter of a forest. It had the character of a free association. It recognized no chief except in time of war. In time of peace the father of the oldest family or the individual who was the most valiant was the most respected. He was called *gulmen* or cacique. Later, the richest person generally occupied this position.

In spite of the distrust with which one tribe regarded another, it happened frequently that many had to ally themselves in order to carry on war against a common enemy. Then all who united for this purpose elected a chief, called a *toqui*, whose authority lasted during the campaign and whose duty it was to direct military operations. These federations greatly helped to unite the natives and persuade them of their racial unity.

In other respects the Araucanians never constituted a nation with an organized government. Their only institutions of a public character were military assemblages. These always took place when the tribes discussed the undertaking of a war. It devolved upon the cacique of each tribe to summon them. But if the question were one which affected many tribes against a common enemy, any one of their chiefs called all the chiefs together. First he assembled his own tribe, and, if it decided on war, the initiating chief sent an emissary to the neighboring chief. An arrow stained with the blood of a guanaco served as an emblem for the emissary. The bloody arrow was delivered to the nearest chief, who, in turn, called together his tribe and sent the same arrow on to another chief, and so on until the arrow reached the last tribe. This proclamation of war was called *correr la flecha* (sending around the arrow). The general assembly was commonly held in a level, isolated field, half hidden among the woods and ravines. After vigorous speeches, one man was chosen as supreme chief for the campaign. He, the *toqui*, was almost always the one who had shown the greatest muscular force or the greatest eloquence, or he was the chief most renowned among all the allied tribes for valor and energy.

Their weapons were not many—the arrow, the pike or lance, the war club or macana, and the *boleadoras*. The arrow, already described, was the least powerful and served more for hunting than for war. The lance, or pike, was formed of a shaft twelve to sixteen feet long with its point reinforced like that of an arrow. Handled with skill and vigor, it could easily pierce a man's body. But none of these weapons was more terrible than the war club (*maza* or macana). This consisted of a piece of hard and heavy wood[1] about five feet long and as thick as the wrist. In its lower part, for about a fourth of its length, it had an elbow or bludgeon, which narrowed toward the end, where it terminated in an edge. The *boleadoras* was used as a war weapon in the pursuit of fugitives after combat, in order to entangle their legs and make them fall.

THE CULTURE AND CHARACTER OF THE ARAUCANIANS

Aside from war the native Araucanian showed no great activity. His life was lazy and quiet save when assailed by some of the many superstitions and omens which made up his religious system. He knew the Supreme One of the gods by the name of Pillán. He believed this god to be an unknown power who managed the clouds and winds, who produced thunder, tempest, lightning, and earthquake. The heights formed his abode. The Araucanian also believed in the existence of other divinities or higher forces: one, evil, who occasioned misery and sickness and death; the other, good, who made the fields produce, brought abundance of birds and fish, and presided over human joys. In order to put the evil god to flight and to reconcile themselves with Pillán, when in some way he showed his anger, they were wont to burn the cinnamon, their sacred tree.

---

[1] In the original text, Galdames mentions the following: *Luma,* the *Myrtus luma,* a native hardwood of Chile; *boldo,* a Chilean plant of the *Lauraceae* family; *espino,* the hawthorn; *huayacán,* the common name in Chile for the *Porliera hygrométrica.*

Their superstitions were innumerable. They believed in ghosts, which appeared at different hours of the night, and in the shades of the dead, corresponding to our idea of souls. They spoke of colocolos, underground lizards, which caused death when one drank their saliva; of *chonchones*, animals with human heads, and with ears so large that they acted as wings to bear them through the darkness in order to suck the blood of the sick; of *pihuchenes*, winged serpents, which bled those who slept in the depths of the woods.

Besides these and many other superstitions, the Araucanians believed in omens. Sometimes the direction of the clouds, the flight of a bird, the sudden step of a beast—these things that seem so natural to us were sufficient to make them suspend a campaign or a feast, convinced that the happening augured disaster for them.

This confused mixture of superstitions and omens also required a priesthood. The ministers of their cult served both as soothsayers and physicians. The *dunguves* and *machis* were reckoned the most important. The *dunguve* was properly the soothsayer who discovered thefts and secret crimes. A witness who was present at a ceremony conducted by a *dunguve* described it in this way: "He leaves his house by itself and from the outside, addressing it with various conjurings, he makes inquiries of it, and from within the house they reply firmly in a high though mellow voice, where the thing is that he asks for." The *machi* was the healer. The native could not conceive of a person's being sick or dying of his illness. Sickness to him was punishment by an offended deity or some injury caused by an unknown enemy making use of magic means. He must then chase away the evil hidden in his body, and for this he sought the *machi*.

The cure consisted in a very showy ceremony called *machitún*. The relatives of the sick person gathered together with him in a hut. They put him on the floor and formed a circle around him. The *machi* planted a cinnamon tree branch by his pillow. He had a guanaco brought in, quartered it, took out its heart, and sprinkled the branch with its blood. He burned some herbs and filled the dwelling with smoke. Then he approached the patient, pretended to search the part of the body where the suffering or wound was, spit red, and at a given moment, amid general wonder, showed those present a lizard, spider, or some similar object—the cause of the mischief. During these operations the women sang in a mournful voice and accompanied their song with a disagreeable noise produced by dried gourds containing small pebbles, which they shook in rhythm. This was their music.

But there were times, in spite of everything, when the sick person showed no change for the better. Then the witch doctor excused himself, saying that the sick one had hurt his "most noble vitals." All believed him. If the patient died, the *dunguve* was called in to discover the culprit, which the *dunguve* did, usually designating some destitute Indian—a poor devil who had no one to protect him. This did not prevent the infliction of punishment upon the victim. He was burned alive, for such was the penalty for wizards. Centuries afterward there were women who exercised divination and healing. Even today among the last of the Araucanians, the *machi* is known as a witch.

The Araucanians also believed in a future life and, consequently, held worship for the dead. They did not believe in reward or punishment in the other world, but they thought that the individual would enjoy life beyond the cordillera or the sea according to the occupation he had performed in this life. The warriors would keep on fighting in the clouds against the same enemies that they had had on earth. Therefore, when the wind stirred up heavy cloud masses, the people were filled with wonder as they watched the clouds, and they uttered great cries to urge on their own dead. The chiefs, they believed, continued to live in the tribe, but only spiritually, or transformed into bumblebees or other insects. From this came the custom of throwing a portion of their drinks into the air during the feasts, in order to slake the thirst of these spirits.

Their funerals were very ceremonious, especially when some chief was to be buried. Forming a long double line, the men carried the body to the nearest hill. They opened a grave and built in it something like a niche of stones. There they placed the coffin, together with the objects that had been most used by the dead, such as weapons, household utensils, ornaments, and even drink and food for the long journey he had to take. Then they sang long and solemn choruses, eulogized his acts in a discourse, and drank in his honor as at any feast of rejoicing. A year later they made a pilgrimage to his tomb, told him what had happened in his family and tribe since his death, again uttered a eulogy, celebrated a final feast, and left him forever in peace.

The exact knowledge of the Araucanians was very limited. It was with difficulty that they counted up to a hundred, and many of them could count only to ten or twenty on the fingers of both hands. The only measure they had was the *jeme* (distance from the end of the thumb to the end of the forefinger extended), the *codo* (ell), the foot, and the pace. It was not until a late date that they learned the Spanish league. They were guided in reckoning time by noting the movements of moon and sun. They knew the medicinal virtue of some plants and used them somewhat as they are used today. For example, *pichoa* and *pircún* were purgatives; *huévil* cured fever; *chamico* served as a narcotic; *palqui* was sudorific; *cachanlagua*[2] furnished excellent refreshing beverages.

We cannot say what literature the Araucanian had. Undoubtedly he had a decided taste for oratory and poetry. In his popular assemblages he preferred eloquence to force. In his own festivals it pleased him beyond measure to have a singer celebrate in verse his acts, and later he even ostentatiously paid such a person. But as the singer did not write down his songs, it is impossible today to form much of an idea of them.

It is clear, however, that the Araucanian language—or Mapuche, as it is also called—was admirably adapted to harangues and verses, because it is both harmonious and flowing. Thousands of its words[3] are incorporated in the language of Chile today, including most of the geographical names. There is less to be said of the Araucanian's artistic productions. He did not paint. His carvings in stone or wood are too coarse to deserve the name of sculpture. As to his pottery, only a few vases and jars of baked clay tinted with colored stripes are worthy of notice. His music was sad and monotonous, and he lacked the more delicate instruments. Wood flutes, fifes, and gourd tambourines were all that he had.

It is not difficult to determine the outstanding features of the character of the Araucanians if one takes into account their means of livelihood, their customs, and their beliefs. Three admirable qualities were outstanding: they were patriotic, brave, and vigorous. But they also had three grave faults: they were cruel,

---

[2] *Pichoa,* the *Euphorbia portulacoides; pircún,* the *Anisomeria drastica; huévil,* the *Vestia lycioides; chamico* (a Quechuan word), the *Datura stramonium,* related to the hemlock; *palqui,* a plant of the family *Solanaceas* (used in Chile as a remedy for ringworm); *cachanlagua,* feminine form for *cachanlahuén,* Araucanian word for *Erythraea chilensis,* a reed plant.

[3] Those named in the original are: *calcha,* name applied to the clothing or bedding of a workman; *chancho,* the hog; *chape,* applied to a peasant's costume; *chercan,* a thin porridge; *choco,* name applied to hollow in a tree, hence to the round section of a tree trunk used as a wheel or roller; *echona,* sickle or reaping hook; *huira,* bark of the *maqui,* used as a cord for binding; *humita,* a cake made of fresh corn similar to the tamale; *luche,* a seaweed, the *Ulva latissima; llalli,* a fruit similar to a persimmon, eaten as a vegetable; *poncho,* blanket; *rulo,* a roller used to move heavy objects; *trola,* a fib; *ulpo,* a Chilean drink prepared in sugared water with flour.

superstitious, and drunken. Their patriotism and valor led them
to prefer war above all other occupations; in everything else they
were incurably lazy. War and superstition changed them into a
cruel, vengeful people.

It is well known that all barbarous peoples are, or have been,
handicapped by the same defects as were the Araucanians; no
other barbarous people have surpassed their good qualities or
have shown valor or more warlike tenacity in defending their land
and their liberty. And for this reason they deserved being im-
mortalized in *La araucana*,[4] the epic which the poet Alonso de
Ercilla wrote in spite of the fact that he was among those who
fought most bitterly against them.

THE DOMINATION OF THE CHINCHAS AND OF THE QUECHUAS

The native Chileans who dwelt north of the Biobío belonged
only in part to the same race as the Araucanians. The so-called
Picunches or Mapuches extended to Copiapó and were divided
into numerous groups. From the eleventh to the fifteenth centuries
they suffered first the invasion of the Diaguitas, coming from
northeast Argentina, then that of the Chinchas from southern
Peru, and finally that of the Quechuas, who at the arrival of the
Spaniards formed part of the vast empire of the Incas, extending
from Ecuador to Bolivia and Chile, with its capital in the city of
Cuzco. None of these invasions went further than the Maule
River and the first especially did not reach farther south than the
Maipo; but from them came the culture of Chilean natives who
inhabited the north and center of the country.

Of those three invaders, the Chinchas were the most progressive
and the ones who imposed their material civilization and many
of their beliefs and customs on Chile. They were shepherds, agriculturalists, miners, and industrialists. Their most useful domestic
animal, the llama, provided the wool for their clothing. They cultivated potatoes, corn, and peas. They distributed running water
by means of long canals. They exploited copper, silver, and gold.
They manufactured all kinds of articles, and utensils of wood,
metal, and baked clay. They built cities containing temples and
palaces. They constructed roads on which houses or inns were
located at intervals for maintaining a postal service, and they
carried on an active trade with other sections of the country.

The Chinchas were conquered by the Quechuas, an aggressive,
dominating people who appropriated to themselves all the elements

4 See pp. 49, 84.

Caupolicán, chief Indian leader at the time of the Conquest. Courtesy Instituto de Cinematografía Educativa, Universidad de Chile.

Santiago. *Above:* Academy of the Fine Arts in Parque Forestal. *Below:* Flower market, center foreground; church at the right; Cerro of Santa Lucía, center; Cerro of San Cristóbal, left background. The National Library is directly in front of Santa Lucía. Courtesy Grace Line.

of the Chinchas' culture and who, with their rulers, the Incas, formed the most extensive and prosperous state of America. Two of these rulers made an expedition against Chile in the middle of the fifteenth century and conquered the country as far as the Maule. In the territory they crossed, they did not find a completely barbarous population, but one already semicivilized by the influence of the Chinchas, a condition which had prevailed for more than two centuries.

For a long time it was thought that the level of material progress at which the Spaniards later found the Chilean natives of the northern zone was due to the beneficial influence of the Quechuas. The latest archaeological discoveries have corrected this opinion, which did not account adequately for the Chilean state of culture, since the Incan domination had lasted only until the date of the expedition of Almagro, 1536, a little more than eighty years—a very short period in which to raise a people from complete barbarism—and were engaged only in effecting the administrative organization of the conquered territory in order to exact an annual tribute from its inhabitants.

However, the Chilean natives continued to develop their incipient culture under the rule of the Quechuas. The northern and central zones of the country were crossed by roads. There was a postal service carried on by Indians on foot, with inns every fifteen or twenty miles. The *curacas*, or governors, were engaged in developing the prosperity of the hamlets and villages where the natives gained their livelihood and in encouraging productive activities.

For cultivating the fields, the natives opened irrigating canals or ditches in places where the soil best permitted it. Among the canals constructed in the Incan epoch and still existing somewhat on the same plan is the one that descends from the hills of the Salto in the vicinity of Santiago and irrigates the neighboring farms. It is called the Vitacura Canal,[5] after the name of the governor who ordered it opened. From the time that canals were opened, the crops of squash, corn, beans, and potatoes, which were native to this country, became more abundant. The production of fabrics made from the wool of the guanaco, vicuña, and llama also increased. The llama had been bred for centuries in Chile. The manufacture of articles of baked clay, also practiced for a long time by the natives, now received a new impetus. Vases, jars, and pitchers of clay became of prime importance in the household of the Chilean Indian.

---

[5] See pp. 282, 343.

But the work to which the subjects of the Incas gave the greatest impulse was the exploitation of mines. Gold, silver, and copper were found and were capable of being exploited in Chile just as in the country of the Incas. They concentrated their attention principally on gold, however, because this metal made up the tribute that was sent to the emperor. Among the gold washings where exploitation was then carried on, those of Marga-Marga, near Quillota, are especially noteworthy. Gold and silver pins and chains were painstakingly made in gypsum and clay molds. Numerous remains of these ornaments have been found in native graves of that period, because the Chinchas and Quechuas interred their dead at the foot of a hill, gathering about them the utensils they had used in life; but, unlike the Araucanians, who placed their corpses in the graves lying down, the former placed them in a squatting position, with arms crossed and knees almost in front of the breast.

The influence of the Chinchas and Quechuas was felt also in the intellectual development of the Chilean Indian. Idolatry was introduced into his religion and this meant progress in comparison with his former condition. In figuring, he learned to count up to a thousand without confusing quantities. He added to his vocabulary many words of the Quechuans, which still are incorporated in the national language. *Apa, cacharpa, callana, cancha, locro*[6] are among the several hundred words derived from the Quechuan language.

THE NATIVE PREHISTORIC CIVILIZATION

During the fifteenth century and at the beginning of the sixteenth, the customs of the Chilean Indians improved considerably. In their towns, in which population increased, ties of family and of tribe were more closely drawn. The cultivation of the new land, the development of clay pottery, the exploitation of metals, and the diffusion of wool clothing provided for them better food and wearing materials. The eating of cooked meat and vegetables became general; corn and potatoes served as the principal ingredients of many cooked dishes; and, in time, the bean became the most common and nutritious food.

As for clothing, shirts of wool, ponchos, girdles for the waist, and ribbons for the hair—which the women wore in the manner of

---

[6] *Apa,* an expression meaning to raise up or put on one's back; *cacharpa,* name given to the ordinary equipment of a trade; *callana,* an earthen baking griddle; *cancha,* an open space suitable for sports, applied to a cockpit; *locro,* a kind of stew.

braids—were owned by the greater part of the population. From some plants, principally the *quintral*,[7] they extracted different colors to dye their clothes. The feet were shod with sandals of leather. The head was covered with a *chupalla*.[8] Streams and marshes were commonly crossed on stilts.

The advance of civilization in the midst of barbarism was noteworthy. The transformation wrought during the rule of the Incas did not cost more than the payment of an annual tribute to the sovereigns in large stamped blocks of gold, through the *curacas* (governors) as intermediaries. Nor do we know of any shedding of blood in persecutions or battles.

At the end of some eighty years of tranquil submission the natives of north and central Chile virtually recovered their liberty. At the beginning of the sixteenth century scarcely any traces of the Incan rule remained. A little while afterward the Inca, Huaina Capac,[9] died and civil war arose in Peru between his two sons for the succession to the throne. For this reason the garrisons maintained by the Incas in Chile were weakened and the *curacas* and caciques were left almost independent.[10]

The civilization which the Chinchas and Quechuas helped to develop in the north central part of the country likewise spread, through the frequent contacts among the indigenes of both zones, to the south central part, as far as the region inhabited by the Araucanians. But in the first half of the sixteenth century

---

[7] The common name for the *Phrygilanthus tetandrus*.

[8] A coarse straw hat.

[9] His rule lasted from 1488 to 1526, up to the eve of the Spanish conquest. See Sir Clements R. Markham, *The Incas of Peru* (New York, 1910), pp. 95, 198, 241; and his *History of Peru* (Chicago, 1892), p. 53.

[10] For further information relative to the Indians of Chile, consult among others, the following books: Domingo Amunátegui Solar, *Las encomiendas de indijenas en Chile* (Santiago, 1909); Diego Barros Arana, *Los antiguos habitantes de Chile* (Santiago, 1874); Agustín Edwards, *Peoples of Old*; Joaquín Edwards Bello, in *Imágenes de Chile* (Santiago, 1933), pp. 1-63. The material in this volume was selected from contemporary travelers of the eighteenth and nineteenth centuries by Mariano Picón-Salas and Guillermo Feliú Cruz; Capt. Allen F. Gardiner, *A Visit to the Indians on the Frontiers of Chile* (London, 1841); Tomás Guevara, *Historia de Chile: Chile prehispaño*; Ricardo E. Latcham, *La alfarería indígena chilena*, and *La prehistoria chilena* (Santiago, 1928); Francis J. G. Maitland, *Chile: Its Land and its People* (London, 1914); Carl Martin, *Landeskunde von Chile* (Hamburg, 1923); José Toribio Medina, *Los aboríjenes de Chile* (Santiago, 1822); Juan Ignacio Molina, *The Geographical, Natural, and Civil History of Chile* (London, 1809); *Publicaciones del museo de etnología y antropología de Chile* (Santiago, 1917-1922); and Agustín Venturino, *Sociología primitiva de Chile indiana* (Barcelona, 1927).

even the influence it exercised over these last was not sufficiently strong to unify their type of living with the tribes located more to the north. Thus we have a situation in which the population in all the central part of the territory was becoming more dense and the forest vegetation more abundant while the degree of material progress in the same direction decreased, although not in very marked proportion.

Such was, briefly, the social, economic, and political state of the people who inhabited the territory of Chile in the era in which they were first brought into contact with Europeans coming from Spain. Their prehistoric civilization was now to be recast into the fully historic civilization to which "the conquerors" belonged; and with them Chile's own history begins. Not only will both civilizations be intermingled, but at the same time both races will be fused in order to give rise to a new race which will without doubt inherit the characteristics of its ancestors. Therefore the prehistoric period which we have sketched has a fundamental significance for understanding the formation and the spirit of the Chilean people.

---

[7] The common name for the Phrygilanthus tetrandrus.

[8] A coarse straw hat.

CHAPTER II

THE SPANIARDS

THE DISCOVERY OF AMERICA

DURING THE LATTER part of the fifteenth century the two nations which occupied the extreme southwest of Europe—Spain and Portugal—were engaged in a great enterprise—that of finding a maritime passage to India and neighboring countries. The regions of Asia and Oceania were much coveted because they produced articles of great value: spices (such as nutmeg, vanilla, cinnamon, pepper, cloves), pearls, diamonds, and ivory; and from China, adjacent to India, perfumes, porcelains, and silks were obtained.

Before this period Europe had carried on commerce with the Indies by way of exceedingly long and dangerous routes. Numerous caravans of merchants crossed the Mediterranean or the Bosporus and, passing armed through Syria, Mesopotamia, and Iran, or through Asia Minor, Armenia, and Caspian Turkestan, succeeded in descending the valleys of the Ganges and the Indus. Others crossed the Red Sea or the Persian Gulf in sailboats and, after touching at the shores of the Indian Ocean, continued toward the marvelous Orient.

It is easy to imagine the sacrifice and risk that those caravans of adventurers endured on so long a voyage, and easy also to calculate at what a great price they sold the products they brought into Europe. But at the end of the fifteenth century no one was able to use these routes because the Turks had made themselves masters of western Asia and of Egypt and were hostile toward Christians who ventured through their dominions.[1]

Such being the situation, with the European people lacking the valuable articles of the Indies—as all the eastern part of Asia was called at that time—it requires little reflection to see how profitable it would be to reëstablish this commerce. Portugal was the first to undertake the enterprise, and from the middle of the fifteenth century this project attracted the major attention of its kings. The western coast of Africa was selected as the route,

---

[1] For a contrary opinion, see Albert H. Lybyer, "The Influence of the Ottoman Turks upon the Routes of Oriental Trade," in *Annual Report of the American Historical Association*, I (1914), 127-133; and in *English Historical Review*, XXX (October, 1915), 577-588.

for it was necessary to go around that continent in order to reach the desired Indies.

Many mariners were sacrificed on these expeditions; but from year to year advance was made along the route sought. A Portuguese, Bartolomé Díaz, had already reached the southern end of Africa (the Cape of Good Hope) in 1488, and it seemed certain that Portugal was very near to attaining its goal when a poor mariner, a native of Genoa, presented himself at the court of Spain and proposed to the sovereigns the same plan of finding the Indies, but by a route quite opposite to that which the Portuguese were following. This mariner was Christopher Columbus. His project was founded on a scientific truth up to that time generally unknown—the rotundity of the earth—and it consisted in going to the Indies by sailing westward over the Atlantic Ocean.[2] But Columbus did not foresee the possibility of encountering en route distinct regions that would impede his passage, because he supposed the earth to be much smaller than it really is.

When he arrived in Spain no one was thinking of embarking on voyages of discovery. All the resources of the country were concentrated on a national war. The attempt was being made to oust the Moors or Mohammedans from the last stronghold they held on the Peninsula, after having occupied it for eight centuries —the kingdom of Granada.

The Catholic rulers, Ferdinand of Aragon and Isabella of Castile, were so preoccupied with the war that they had no desire even to hear about the project, the consummation of which was offered to them. But the wise men of the court studied it and decided that it could not be realized. When, however, Granada was taken by the Spaniards and when the war was thereby concluded, Isabella of Castile accepted the propositions of Columbus and lent him funds for manning three ships.[3] In these he sailed westward from the little port of Palos at the beginning of August, 1492. After many sufferings, on the twelfth of October of the same year, the squadron touched an island of the Bahama Archipelago which its commander called San Salvador. Then, changing his course toward the south, he coasted among the Greater Antilles,

---

[2] For a discussion of the purpose of Columbus, see Cecil Jane, "The Objective of Columbus," in *Select Documents Illustrating the Four Voyages of Columbus,* I, xiii-cxxii, "Publications of the Hakluyt Society" (2d series. London, 1929), Vol. LXV.

[3] See Robert Bigelow Merriman, *The Rise and Fall of the Spanish Empire in the Old World and the New* (4 vols. Vols. I and II, New York, 1918; Vol. III, 1925; Vol. IV, 1934), II, 194, 195.

disembarked on them, and finally began the return journey to Spain in order to give an account of his discovery. He firmly believed that he had found the Indies, and everyone else believed the same.

Three more voyages by the intrepid explorer, in which he discovered the rest of the Antilles, the northern coast of South America, and the coast of Central America, simply confirmed him in his first idea. He died in 1506 still persisting in his error. Meanwhile, a Portuguese, Vasco da Gama, during his voyages and eight years before his death had reached India in 1498, after going around Africa by way of its western and eastern coasts. The voyages to the country discovered by Columbus did not cease, however. All of the explorers thought they had come to the Indies, until two of them demonstrated that these lands were in reality a great continent. These men were Amerigo Vespucci and Vasco Núñez de Balboa.

The former was a native of Florence, Italy. A mariner like Columbus, he made four voyages to the recently discovered regions. He explored the northern and eastern coast of South America, as far as Puerto Santo in Brazil.[4] He afterward published a narrative of his voyages and a rough geographical draft of the regions over which he had traveled, and in this narrative he was the first to maintain that the discovered territories were not the Indies but another continent. This opinion was based on the fact that the products of these territories differed from those of India. The other discoverer, Balboa, at the head of the government of Panama,[5] started from the Gulf of Darién, crossed the isthmus, and discovered an immense ocean which, from the direction in which it extended, he named the South Sea. This was in 1513.

From then on it could not be doubted that what Columbus discovered was not the Indies but a continent of whose existence the rest of the world had been ignorant. Spain called it the *Indias Occidentales* (West Indies), in contrast to the others, and its inhabitants, *indios* (Indians). But men of learning in Europe afterward gave it the name of Land of Americus, or simply America, from the fact that a German geographer, who published in Latin a description of these regions based on the narrative of

---

[4] Whether Vespucci actually made all the voyages for which he put forth claims is still a moot question. On the tendency of present-day belief, see Edward Gaylord Bourne, *Spain in America* (New York and London, 1904), p. 103.

[5] Balboa was the leader of the colony at Darién, but technically a rebel and usurper.—*Ibid.*, pp. 108-112.

Vespucci, placed at the foot of the corresponding map two words which constituted its baptism: *Americi Terra* (Land of America).[6]

DISCOVERY OF THE STRAIT OF MAGELLAN

The Spaniards looked with displeasure on the discovery of the new continent. They wished for only the Indies, with their spices, their diamonds, their ivory, porcelains, and perfumes. The Portuguese had already succeeded in reaching the Indies and, when the Spaniards saw rival boats return to Lisbon laden with riches from the Orient, their ambition was redoubled because of their envy. America, in their opinion, was worth very little compared with the Indies, to which it was necessary to go in order to compete with the Portuguese for the commercial monopoly of all their products.

It would be exceedingly easy to realize such an ambition today; by sailing in the same direction around Africa as did the Portuguese, not only any country, but any individual, would be able to reach it. But it was impossible then for the Spaniards to go to the Indies by that route.

The Catholic countries of Europe considered the pope the sole proprietor of the regions where infidel and barbarian peoples lived. The kings of Portugal had obtained the express concession from the pope over all the lands which they might discover and conquer on their voyages to the east. When Columbus and his companions found new lands by sailing in an opposite direction, the sovereigns of Spain asked for and obtained a similar grant from another pope; but the latter, in order to avoid conflicts, was careful to fix a limit between both concessions. This limit was soon modified by common accord between the two nations thus benefited (by the Treaty of Tordesillas in 1494) and, as agreed upon, definitely remained as follows: an imaginary line (meridian) that cut the planet from pole to pole, 370 leagues west of the Azores. The regions discovered, or to be discovered, west of that line should belong to Spain; those to the east, to Portugal.[7]

The Spaniards, then, did not have any other way of reaching the coveted Indies except by passing through some part of America and keeping on to the westward. Some passage must exist between

---

[6] For the naming of America see Bourne, "The Naming of America," in *The American Historical Review*, X (1905), 41-51; and his *Spain in America*, pp. 90-102.

[7] *Idem*, "The Demarcation Line of Pope Alexander VI," in *Essays in Historical Criticism* (London, 1901), pp. 193-217.

the Atlantic Ocean and the recently discovered "Southern Sea." The Spaniards now devoted themselves to finding this probable strait which might unite the two oceans. The first expedition failed. A famous mariner of Castile named Juan Díaz de Solís commanded it. Skirting the coast of South America, he came to the estuary of La Plata, which he thought an arm of the sea and therefore called *Mar Dulce* (Fresh-water Sea). Believing that the passage he sought went through here, he entered this estuary and landed on an island, where the Indians attacked him, took him prisoner, with many of his party, and killed all whom they captured. Those who escaped returned to Spain to give an account of the disaster.

Four years after this event, in 1519, a new expedition left Spain with the same object as that of Solís. A Portuguese named Ferdinand Magellan commanded it. With five ships, following the same route pursued by Solís, he reached the estuary of La Plata, or *Mar Dulce*. Recognizing it for what it was—not an arm of the sea but a river—he approached the coast more to the south and was detained in the Bay of San Julián during the winter months of 1520. It was here that the sight of some tall muscular natives who walked around wrapped in skins made Magellan and his companions think they were a race of giants. Because they wore leather sandals, they left large tracks on the sand. The men, therefore, called them *patagones* or *patones* (clumsy-footed), and the region they inhabited, Patagonia. Advancing toward the south, they rounded Cape Virgins and Dungeness and finally, on March 1, 1520, entered the strait. On the day he discovered it, Magellan bestowed upon it the name *Todos los Santos* (All Saints), but posterity has justly given it the name of its discoverer.[8]

Magellan realized that he was in the southernmost part of the continent and that the region he saw toward the south must be

---

[8] The numerous narratives of Magellan's voyage are based upon the text of Antonio Pigafetta. A translation of this by Lord Stanley of Alderley was published as Vol. LII of the Hakluyt Society publications under the title *The First Voyage Around the World by Magellan* (London, 1871). On page eight of this translation, Pigafetta says, "They made a stay in this strait from the 21st of October to the 26th of November, which makes thirty-six days of the said year 1520." A more recent scholarly publication is Antonio Pigafetta's *Magellan's Voyage Around the World* (Cleveland, 1906), translated and edited from the Ambrosian manuscript by the late Dr. James A. Robertson, in two volumes of text and an index volume. In Vol. I, p. 65, of this edition occurs the first intimation of the presence of this strait on October 21, 1520. The strait was given the name "All Saints" (p. 240) on November 1, but later received that of the explorer.

an island. He named it *Tierra del Fuego* (Land of Fire) because of the lighted fires which he saw on it from afar. Arriving at the extremity of Brunswick Peninsula, he rounded Cape Froward and continued northwest until he emerged into the open sea, which he called "Pacific" because of its tranquil waters. Thus the southern part of our country was discovered.

Believing that the ocean was much smaller than it is, Magellan decided to follow the route to the west until he should completely cross it and arrive at the Indies. The scarcity of provisions at first, and later their absolute failure, made this passage extremely painful. The greater part of the crew died from hunger and thirst, and those who survived were compelled to eat the rats and the leather on their ships.

After some months the surviving portion of the expedition reached the Philippine Islands. Magellan and his companions landed on one of them in order to obtain food. Attacked by the Indians, the Portuguese commander fell dead with some of his men. The pilot, [Juan] Sebastián de Elcano, with only one ship (the *Victoria*), continued westward; he passed by the rich "Archipelago of the Spices" and in front of the continental Indies, and, after traversing the Indian Ocean and rounding Africa, reached Spain in September, 1522.

Of the two hundred and fifty men who composed the expedition, fifty had returned to Spain in a ship which was separated from the fleet in the strait; and, of the rest, only eighteen returned, so emaciated and thin that no one would have recognized them, if they had not identified themselves. But they had succeeded in discovering the strait which united the two great oceans; they had reached the Indies, just as Columbus had thought, by sailing westward; and they had, for the first time, circumnavigated the earth, thus proving its sphericity. The glory of these discoveries belonged principally to Spain.

THE CONQUEST OF PERU (1532-1533)

At the time that Ferdinand Magellan discovered the strait which bears his name, none of the countries of South America bordering on the Pacific knew of the Spaniards. On the other hand, the islands of the Antilles and the adjacent regions, washed by the same sea from Mexico to Venezuela, were already active centers of conquest. Not many years were to pass, however, before the regions bordering on the Pacific also were traversed by the Spaniards and conquered for their kings.

On the Isthmus of Panama a colony had been founded shortly

after the discovery of the so-called South Sea. This was the point of departure for those who undertook the discovery and conquest of the Incan Empire. Here also the first reports of its existence were received. After some explorations, which confirmed the information relating to the wealth of that empire, three men of the city of Panama formed an association to undertake its conquest. The priest of the colony, Fernando de Luque, and two Spanish adventurers, Francisco Pizarro and Diego de Almagro, were associated in this enterprise. The first risked only his capital; the other two, their lives.

In 1532 Pizarro, with fewer than two hundred men, in a surprise attack seized the person of the Inca in the city of Cajamarca in the north of Peru. This ruler, called Atahualpa, had just obtained the throne after a bloody civil war against his brother, Huáscar. Through the captivity of the Inca and his execution soon after, the conquest of the whole empire was completed. A year later Pizarro and Almagro entered Cuzco, the capital city. The northern and the central part of the empire were thus subjected to the conquerors, and, if the south—Bolivia, Tucumán, and Chile— did not also render obedience to them, it was not because the conquerors lacked the spirit to rule the entire country, but because they did not yet have either the time or the forces for the necessary scouting.

Very soon, however, they had all that was necessary. At the report of a new conquest, a great mass of adventurers landed in Peru. So much gold had been taken from the Incan treasury that the empire was everywhere reputed to be a country of fabulous riches. One can understand that there were many who desired to make their fortunes here. The two conquering chiefs, already enormously enriched, were anxious to divide authority in the conquered territories, just as they had divided the Incan treasure. The other associate, Luque, could take nothing, because he was already dead when the riches were found.

Pizarro was the leader of the enterprise and ought, by rights, to be the governor of the conquered empire. Almagro also wished to have his own domain and communicated his desire to the king. The latter thought this a just request, and divided administration of the territory. That of Pizarro was called New Castile and extended from a point near the line of the equator, two hundred and seventy leagues to the southward, reckoned along the coast. That of Almagro was called New Toledo and extended from the limit of Pizarro's grant two hundred leagues farther to the south, reckoned in the same way as the former. The eastern limits were not defined but might extend as far as the shores of the Atlantic, since no one yet knew the breadth of the continent.

The conquering leaders disputed hotly for the possession of Cuzco, the richest city, each one claiming that it lay within his domain; but finally they agreed that, until the king should settle the conflict, Almagro should leave to conquer a country to the southward, which the Peruvian Indians said was very rich in gold and which was undoubtedly within his New Toledo. This country was none other than Chile.

THE FIRST SPANISH EXPEDITION TO CHILE

In reality the Peruvian Indians who exaggerated the wealth of Chile lied knowingly, with the deliberate purpose of ridding their country of the greatest possible number of Spaniards. They secretly planned a general uprising for the purpose of restoring the native monarchy in the person of the Inca Manco,[9] a prisoner of the Spaniards in Cuzco. Excited by their good reports, Almagro prepared for his campaign into Chile. He spent on his equipment all the gold and silver that belonged to his share of Atahualpa's treasury, an immense fortune of a million and a half Spanish pesos, equivalent today to more than thirty million pesos of Chilean money.[10] Horses, weapons, equipment, and outfit for the campaign had reached fabulous prices in Peru because they were scarce, and those who could buy them had to have plenty of money. Even so, Almagro could equip five hundred Spaniards, to whom he added thousands of auxiliary Indians (*yanaconas*, as they were called) to carry the provisions.

The army set out on the march in the middle of the year 1535. This great mob of expeditionaries not only bore weapons of war against the Indians but also weapons to fight against nature—picks, axes, shovels, and other implements. The route followed,

[9] Manco Capac II (d. 1563?), put in power by Pizarro, who sought to rule through him, after the execution of Atahualpa, aided Almagro in his expedition to Chile and in 1535 escaped from captivity and supposedly was later assassinated.—José Espasa, *Enciclopedia universal ilustrada* (70 vols. Madrid and Barcelona, 1905-1930; appendices, 1930-1933; supplement, 1934), XXXII, 702; Manuel de Mendiburu, *Diccionario histórico-biográfico del Perú* (8 vols. Lima, 1874-1887), V, 127-134.

[10] The peso in Chile during the national period varied in value from thirty-five to forty-five English pence until the era of paper money following the War of the Pacific. See Daniel Martner, *Estudio de política comercial chilena e historia económica nacional*, Vol. II, *passim;* and Frank W. Fetter, *Monetary Inflation in Chile.* Galdames reckons the Spanish peso as equal to twenty-four Chilean pesos of six pence. See n. 11, p. 25.

on leaving Cuzco, was the Bolivian plateau amid the ranges of the Andes. After some weeks of travel they crossed the high plateau of Collao, bordering on Lake Titicaca, continued to the east of the Desaguadero River, which carries the waters from Lake Titicaca to Poopó and, at the end of a long trail in the midst of lonely mountains, they halted in Tupiza. It was now four months since they had left Cuzco and they had traveled a third of the route, but this part was the most hospitable. Wherever they passed, however, they devastated the fields and crops of the defenseless Indians and forced them to enlist in their ranks as *yanaconas*. This meant they would be treated worse than beasts. Fastened together in files by chains about their necks, they proceeded in separate groups, bearing provisions for the campaign or carrying on stretchers the Spanish soldiers and their horses when these became tired on the march.

After a long rest in Tupiza they struck their tents and advanced southward until confronted by the San Francisco Pass, where they had to ascend the Puna de Atacama, some thirteen thousand feet high. Amidst untold suffering they had crossed burning deserts, high mountains, and swollen rivers. But the worst part of the route still remained, the crossing of the Puna. Because of the altitude, the cold during the night is so unbearable in these regions that water freezes, and in the daytime strong winds from the west beat in the face of travelers. There is almost no vegetation, and the ground, formed of sharp shifting pebbles, draws blood even from the hoofs of animals. The *soroche* or *puna*, a suffocating sickness produced by the rarity of the air, causes nausea and painful convulsions.

In this heartbreaking region, the dead bodies of some ten thousand Indians were left. Most of the horses also perished, and, if many of the Spaniards did not meet with the same fate, it was only because of the special care they bestowed upon themselves. There were few, however, who escaped severe bruises. Numerous flocks of condors and vultures surrounded the expedition and carried off, almost before they fell, the corpses of the Indians and of the beasts of burden.

At last, however, the expedition was able to cross the cordillera and descend to Copiapó. The soldiers reached there in such a wretched condition that they looked like an army of specters. But, after all, they were now in Chile. In spite of the feeble appearance of the strangers, the Indians were greatly amazed at beholding these rare foreigners, white, bearded, and mounted on animals of a kind they did not know and so dextrous that rider and beast seemed like one person. So imposing was the invading host that they never tried to resist it; on the contrary, they helped it with whatever they possessed. This was in the early months of 1536. For some weeks Almagro and his men remained there, resting from the fatigues and sufferings of the journey. Then they advanced southward and, crossing by slow marches the valleys of Huasco and Coquimbo, established their general headquarters in Aconcagua.

On leaving Cuzco, Almagro had prepared and left ships in Callao to bring him provisions. Sailing with difficulty, only one arrived at its destination with provisions for the army and equipment for the animals. The *Santiaguillo*, as the ship was called, had navigated along our whole northern coast and seems to have unloaded its cargo in the cove of Los Vilos and then continued its exploration of the coast as far as the Bay of Valparaiso.

After renewing the shoes of his horses and arranging the equipment for the campaign, the commander of the exploring expedition thought the moment had arrived to begin the examination of the territory. He sent four exploring parties in as many different directions. The most important was the one that crossed the country as far as the banks of the Maule River and returned bringing lamentable reports. These explorations were carried on during the most severe months in Chile, June to August, and it seems that the winter of 1536 was exceedingly severe because the Spaniards then saw only swollen rivers and swamps, impassable under very heavy rains. The inhabitants lived in extreme poverty; they wore almost no clothes, their food was scarce, and their shelter consisted of some miserable huts of branches and straw. Worst of all, gold was nowhere to be found. Impressed by what they saw, the explorers concluded that Chile must be uninhabitable; and, although Almagro seems not entirely to have shared the same opinion, his officers induced him to return. They coveted gold above everything else and they found none in this country, while Peru abounded in the precious metal. On the other hand, Almagro had spent all that he possessed without profit, and it was necessary for him to go back to Peru to repair his fortunes. The return was immediately decided upon, and Copiapó was designated as a general concentration point toward which all were to travel.

The Spaniards did not fail on this occasion to commit every possible atrocity against the defenseless Indians whom they thought they were leaving forever. Fastening them in great droves with chains and thongs around their necks, they loaded upon them all of their food and clothing. They scarcely covered the naked bodies of their captives; they gave them only a little parched corn to eat and forced them to walk long journeys without stopping. If one became ill, they did not release him from the chain; his companions had to drag him along. If he died, they cut off his head rather than detach the chain.

At the end of 1536 all the exploring parties had assembled at Copiapó. They now decided to make the march through the desert of Atacama, a much less painful route than that over the cordillera. In the first months of 1537 all were in Arequipa. The energetic commander was now approaching the end of his career, where a disastrous fate awaited him. On returning to Peru it was found that the country had risen in rebellion and that Cuzco was in the possession of the brothers of Francisco Pizarro, but besieged by rebel Indians under the command of the Inca Manco. Almagro, after one battle, made him raise the siege but, in order to make the Pizarros deliver up the city to him, he had to go to war against them. One of these, Hernando, hated him exceedingly, and, when he took them prisoner after a brief fight, the other escaped while Almagro at once gave Hernando his liberty, under oath not to return and take up arms against him. Hernando failed to keep this oath; aided secretly by Francisco Pizarro, who lived in Lima, he organized an army, and advanced against Cuzco. The battle, fought on the plains of Salinas in view of the city, went against Almagro. The conqueror started proceedings against his rival and condemned him to death without allowing him any appeal. Almagro was executed at once in his dungeon and his body decapitated on the principal plaza of Cuzco.

For a few years more, however, civil war continued. Almagro's captains took his son for their chief, whom they called Almagro, *el mozo*, and their enemies dubbed that faction "men of Chile," a burlesque nickname because it recorded a failure.

THE FORMATION OF THE SPANISH NATIONALITY

In the years during which Chile was abandoned by its discoverers, all the countries where the Spanish language is spoken today, from Mexico to Argentina, had been widely occupied by the Spaniards. In this way Spain, through its dependencies, now possessed the most extensive territory that any nation of the earth had yet ruled and was, at the same time, one of the most cultured and influential countries of Europe. Spain was a monarchy that had to its credit more than ten centuries of existence

and had been organized as such by the purest branch of the
Germanic race—the Goths. However, these were not the first who
had populated the Iberian Peninsula. When they conquered it in
the fifth century of our era, a numerous population made up of
various elements was distributed over it.[11]

First of all, in the extreme north near the sea and in the mountain spurs which unite the Cantabrians with the Pyrenees lived
the Basques. Distributed through the Peninsula and thoroughly
intermingled were the Iberians and Celts (Celto-Iberians). The
Greeks and Phoenicians had left perceptible traces of their existence on the coasts of the south and east and even in an interior
region of Andalusia. Finally, the Romans, who ruled them all,
had founded many settlements in different parts of the country.
As the principal language spoken was that of the last-named,
or Latin, the people who occupied the Peninsula previous to the
coming of the Goths have generally been called by the common
name, Latins. This does not include the Basques, whose origin
is unknown.

As the Gothic monarchy was thus composed of a variety of
ethnic elements, the Goths predominated by force rather than by
culture. Once both races were in contact, the Goths ended by
adopting almost all the laws of the Latins, many of their customs,
and even their language, although the last was modified considerably by their own. At the end of the sixth century they were
also converted to Christianity.

During the first three centuries of their dominion in the
Peninsula, their progress was slow because, always addicted to
war, they did not know how to exploit the natural wealth of the
country. The Spanish territory is, moreover, largely unproductive.
The central region, or the two Castiles, was and is difficult to
cultivate and has a dry and irregular climate. The outlying
zones of less extreme temperature, although warm in the south
and with regular and even abundant rains in the north, had fine
lands that are today very rich; but then, in order to make them
productive, it was necessary to open roads, canals, and wells, and
even to drain swamps. All of this work required great concentration
of activity and the semibarbaric Goths were in no condition to

---

[11] A useful account of the development of Spain up to the sixteenth century
based on the well-known work of Rafael Altamira is C. E. Chapman's *History
of Spain* (New York, 1918), chaps. i-xxi. Briefer accounts are to be found in
Merriman, *op. cit.*, Vols. I, II; and Mary W. Williams, *The Peoples and Politics of Latin America*, chap. iii.

undertake it. To this should be added the fact that the work of irrigation in Spain has always presented difficulties. The country is a very mountainous plateau and the rivers that cross it in the greater part of their courses run at a considerable depth below the common level.

Because of all these circumstances most of the people in Spain during this period were poor and ignorant; but, in the centuries that followed, different racial elements were added to those already existing. First came the Arabs in the eighth century. They entered for the purpose of conquest, after crossing the Strait of Gibraltar, following the conquest of all of North Africa. Only the northern region of Spain, included between the Cantabrians and the sea, escaped conquest at their hands. Later the Moors also established themselves in the Peninsula. They were Mohammedans like the Arabs, but natives of North Africa. Finally, many Jews settled there peacefully.[12]

These three peoples (Arabs, Moors, and Jews) notably transformed the Gothic and Latin civilization which prevailed at their arrival. They were, in the main, agricultural and industrial, rather than warlike, peoples. Under them agriculture made advances of great importance. They cultivated almost all the productive land that they conquered. Among the plants introduced by them into Spain were rice, hemp, the palm, sugar cane, and cotton. The Arabs especially were more noteworthy than the others in this kind of activity. They established also many factories for the making of carpets, gauze, muslins, steel weapons, paper, leather, and other manufactured articles. After the Arabs the Moors kept up this agricultural and industrial progress. Commerce also received a tremendous impetus, thanks particularly to the enterprising spirit of the Jews.

Almost all the sciences from philosophy to mathematics and medicine, and almost all the arts, especially architecture, were cultivated among the Mohammedans.[13] They founded several notable universities in Spain, among which that of Córdoba sur-

---

[12] The Jews were there before the Arabs and seem to have contributed to the ease with which the latter overran Spain. See R. Dykes Shaw, "The Fall of the Visigothic Power in Spain," in *English Historical Review*, XXI (April, 1906), 209-228, especially p. 214.

[13] See Edgar Allison Peers, *Spain* (London, 1929-1930), pp. 38, 39; and H. D. Sedgewick, *Spain* (Boston, 1926), pp. 28-42, 47. For a contrary view see Louis Bertrand and Sir Charles Petrie, *The History of Spain* (London, 1934), pp. 82-94.

passed others, and many schools. They built wonderful edifices like the Alhambra of Granada, and finally, thanks to such great efforts, after eight centuries of contact with their invaders the Spaniards found themselves more civilized than all the neighboring peoples.

Never, however, did the Spaniard tolerate with good grace the dominance of the Mohammedan in the Peninsula. From the beginning of the eighth century to the end of the fifteenth, constant warfare was carried on by the Spaniards against the Arabs and the Moors. A handful of Gothic patriots who opposed foreign domination took refuge in the Asturias, and that fragment of soil, never overrun by the invaders, served as a place of refuge for the warriors who began the reconquest of Spain.

This struggle partook of a double character, national and at the same time religious—a war of the invaded against the invaders, of Christians against Mohammedans—and it lasted for the same eight centuries that the Moorish and Arabian domination continued. While there was a spot of land or a city anywhere on the Peninsula under the Mohammedan banner, the Spaniards never laid down their arms. During this long struggle they founded various kingdoms, among which the most important were Aragon and Castile.

In the last third of the fifteenth century the king of Aragon, Don Ferdinand, and the queen of Castile, Doña Isabella, married and formed a single realm of their kingdoms, and put forth greater effort to eject the Moors from their last stronghold, Granada. At the beginning of 1492 this enterprise achieved complete success, and the sovereigns could congratulate themselves upon having completed the Christianizing of the whole Iberian Peninsula. At the beginning of the sixteenth century, all this, with the single exception of Portugal, formed only one kingdom—Spain.

But those two monarchs, who for their religious piety were called the Catholic kings, were not satisfied with this and wished all their subjects, without exception, to profess the same faith. With this end in view, the same year in which they conquered Granada they expelled from Spain the Jews, a peaceful and industrious race, and deprived the subjected Moors of the public worship of their religion and antagonized them so much that hundreds of thousands also left the country. In addition, they established a tribunal, known as the Inquisition, which was to persecute all those charged with not practicing the Catholic doctrine faithfully. This was such a terrible tribunal that in the first sixteen years of its existence it ordered hanged and even burnt alive about eighty thousand persons.[14]

The prestige of the sovereigns was enormously increased by the discovery of America. This, as is known, was believed to be the rich Indies. All regarded this act as a reward given by God to the final victors over the Mohammedans and the implacable persecutors of heretics. The power of the Spanish sovereigns grew so strong because of this prestige that they exercised absolute authority. Before this time rich men, the masters of great estates who constituted the Spanish nobility, acted on their own properties as if they were petty kings, disobeyed royal orders, and revolted against the sovereigns. Now things changed; the Catholic kings imposed their authority on them, and those who did not accept it with good grace paid for their temerity with their lives. The monarchs became absolute.

When the Catholic kings died, a grandson succeeded them, who was even more powerful than they. Besides being king of Spain, he was emperor of Germany and master of many other dominions. This ruler, who in Spain was called Carlos I, and as emperor was called Charles V—a name by which he is generally known in history—tightened even more the reins of absolute monarchy and governed until the middle of the sixteenth century. During this last period Spain constituted a united and powerful nation, notwithstanding the varied elements which entered into the composition of its race.

THE CHARACTER AND CULTURE OF THE SPANISH PEOPLE IN THE SIXTEENTH CENTURY

The constant strife in the midst of which the Spanish nation was developed, the warlike and aggressive habits of the Gothic element, and the difficult conditions of labor in a great part of the Peninsula imprinted a special stamp on the character of the Spanish people. Of course, these circumstances made them long-suffering and stimulated their natural valor, and at the same time imbued them with a marked spirit of adventure. The frequent plundering of the fields during invasions and the pastoral life pursued by the greater part of the people, with the necessary moving of their flocks from place to place in order to be free from persecution and hunger, helped very clearly to develop this spirit

---

[14] This number is greatly exaggerated. See Henry Charles Lea, *History of the Inquisition of Spain* (4 vols. New York and London. Vols. I and II, 1906; Vols. III and IV, 1907), IV, 516-528.

—a spirit which more closely affected the Spaniards who emigrated to America, because almost all of them came from the Castiles, where the barrenness of the fields and the irregularity of the climate helped to emphasize this national characteristic here more than in any other section of the Peninsula.

Another distinctive feature of the Spanish character was the unsurpassed fidelity, a kind of idolatry, which Spaniards professed for their kings. Since during so many centuries the latter had guided them to victory for religion and for country, the people felt that their sovereigns had the right to exact the greatest sacrifice for them. The king was sacred, a representative of God on earth.

But nothing better distinguished a Spaniard from individuals of any other nationality than his extreme religiosity. He saw the hand of God everywhere, even intervening in his least acts. During his battles he believed that he had the aid of the Virgin, of the saints, and especially of the Apostle St. James, the patron of his armies. These he imaged in shining visions, trooping with him to battle and annihilating in an instant the enemies of his faith and of his race. The Spaniard's religious exclusiveness also made him intolerant and fanatical. His excessive preoccupation with supernatural intervention engendered in him many superstitions. He believed in sorcerers, spirits, demons, and other supernatural beings. Wars, pestilence, famine, hunger, earthquakes, which frequently attacked his country, were stimulating reasons for this disposition of his mind.

But there was no quality more powerful than his own ignorance. Even when Spain became a civilized nation, its culture was not general; only the higher classes of society, in which the higher and the lower nobility figured, possessed culture in proportion to their resources. The lower classes, farmers and villagers, were all rude people, lacking the most elementary education. But such was the case in the rest of Europe.

The firstcomers to America were certainly not of the higher nobility; these only came afterward as governors. The lower nobility (hidalgos) also came at first in small numbers. The majority of the discoverers and conquerors came from the lower class and were completely unlettered. In them the spirit of adventure was much more developed because of the very precarious condition of their existence. All, however, were tenacious, valorous, arrogant men, faithful to their king and scrupulous in observing the practices of their religion. But their fanaticism, their superstition, their cruelty, and their greed formed a combination of faults which in no little degree dimmed their character.

In spite of such defects, their degree of culture was much higher than that of the Indians of America, even the most advanced, and they presented a wonderful contrast to them. White—some with red hair and light eyes—with long beards, they were usually rather stout, of vigorous muscular strength, dextrous in the management of the horse; well clothed, and better armed, these conquerors necessarily were aware of their own superiority to the barbarous and unorganized tribes that peopled the new territories.

The clothing of the Spanish soldier was simple. It consisted only of short pantaloons reaching to the knees, where they were tied with a cord; a top coat belted at the waist; sandal-shaped shoes with soles of leather; and sometimes wool stockings covering the leg and joined at the knee to the pantaloon. Some, better clothed, used a kind of gaiter buttoned in front which was called a buskin, and on the calves of the legs jambes of leather, like our leggings. The Spanish soldier covered his head with a casque or helmet of steel, which protected him from the blows of his enemies. It was padded inside and provided with straps, which hung down both cheeks and, uniting under the beard, left merely the front of the face free. Commanders and officers were accustomed to use this same helmet with a wire cover which permitted them to see and breathe only through convenient openings.

But greater than the difference between the Spanish and the Indian clothing was the difference between their weapons. The conquering soldier used defensive and offensive weapons. The defensive arms were the casque already mentioned: the coat of mail or cuirass of steel, or simply of leather, which was belted in at the breast and shoulder; the shield or buckler of leather, oval-shaped, which was attached to the left arm in order to ward off the enemies' blows. The offensive weapons were, in the first place, the harquebus (equivalent to our musket), which was loaded with powder and projectiles of lead or pebbles through the muzzle and was fired with a fuse applied to a special vent that opened where the barrel joined the stock. Then there was the short sword with a sheath ordinarily of leather, like the bayonet of today.

The infantry used these arms. The cavalryman carried, besides a sword, a lance or pike of wood from ten to twelve feet long, with a point of steel. Attached to the saddle of the rider and to the breast of the horse with strong cords, this was a terrible weapon in a well ordered charge. The soldier also added to his armament a battleaxe or war club tipped with a ball of steel set with spikes. There were a few pieces of artillery or culverins, very heavy and fitted on wheels, which completed the war equipment of a good army. These culverins were charged with great difficulty, because their projectiles were commonly of stone. It was precisely these cannon and harquebuses, and firearms in general that caused most terror to the Indians; but the horse was the most effective aid to the invaders.

The superiority of the Spanish civilization over the American was thus shown principally in better and heavier offensive equipment. Each Spaniard equaled at least one hundred natives in battle, and that superiority had consequences other than military. The Spaniards brought to America all their ideas, their beliefs, their arts, their customs—in a word, all their civilization—and this, together with the power of their arms, triumphed over the native barbarism. They brought with them, moreover, a political organization and a social discipline much more advanced than any on this continent, and these they also imposed with strong hand and steadfast will.

CHAPTER III

THE CONQUEST

THE CONQUERING EXPEDITION

ONE DAY WHEN Francisco Pizarro was inspecting some of the distant parts of his territory, one of his officers, named Pedro de Valdivia, disclosed to him a desire to conquer Chile and asked to be officially named his lieutenant there. Great was Pizarro's surprise at this request. Chile had lost so much prestige after the expedition of Almagro that, according to public opinion in Peru, it could not feed fifty Spaniards. It must be understood that "to be fed" meant to make oneself rich. But Pedro de Valdivia was the most distinguished officer and the highest in rank in Pizarro's government. He was Pizarro's favorite officer and bore the title "field master" (*maestro del campo*), or, as we should say today, "chief officer of staff," and he owned an encomienda, or estate, with many Indians, and even a silver mine in the south of Peru—all granted to him by the governor.

But Valdivia was not merely a notable warrior. In that multitude of rude and, for the most part, illiterate adventurers, he was conspicuous for his learning and character. He regarded the men about him, and perhaps even Pizarro, as inferior to himself and he aspired to an independent position and a territory of his own. All the objections Pizarro raised against it were therefore useless. In the end he had to grant him the authority he sought and in 1539 named him his lieutenant-governor in Chile.

Born in La Serena of Extremadura, or in some neighboring village, Valdivia at this time was some forty years of age. Although very energetic in all his undertakings, what he was now going to attempt required additional qualifications—above all, money—and he possessed very little property. Since the commander of an expedition at that time had to pay all the expenses that it entailed, it could be foreseen that the force which would accompany Valdivia would be very small, which really happened; there were very few soldiers who wished to follow him. If his personal prestige encouraged them to do it, his limited resources, on the other hand, and the bad reputation of the country for which he was bound, held them back. He managed to muster barely a hundred and fifty men.

All difficulties were overcome, however, and the expedition was about to depart, when there arrived in Peru a bold Spaniard named Pedro Sancho de Hoz. He bore a royal seal, by virtue of which he was authorized to make conquests in the southern extremity of the continent. On the basis of this concession he pretended to have a better right than Valdivia to lead the expedition against Chile. A conflict in interests arose between the two men. Francisco Pizarro induced them to make an agreement according to which the two would make the conquest together. Valdivia would contribute to the partnership the elements that he had already brought together; Hoz, other new ones—horses, equipment for the campaign, and two vessels. Since it was desirable not to delay the course of the enterprise, it was agreed that Valdivia should leave immediately and that Hoz should join him en route.

Thus it came about that in January, 1540, Valdivia's expedition was able to start southward from Cuzco. Only fifteen men composed it. The rest, to complete the one hundred and fifty enrolled, were to join their commander on the march. After passing through Arequipa and Moquegua, Valdivia reached Tarapacá, at the entrance to the desert. Most of his companions had now joined him. The route selected was the same over which Almagro had returned to Peru. After four months of marching, they found themselves half way through the desert zone. Here they rested in a native settlement near the Loa River.

The encampment seemed more like a migrating settlement than an army. The expedition carried the most useful materials for colonizing the country toward which it was going—European grains, principally wheat; domestic animals, especially pigs and fowls; and a collection of tools for cultivation. Some three thousand *yanaconas* carried all this luggage. Women and children also went along with the expedition, but there was only one Spanish woman among them. This was Inés Suárez, who accompanied the commander.[1] While they tarried in the midst of the desert, Hoz arrived and joined Valdivia, but with the manifest purpose of assassinating him. He had complied with none of the agreements of their partnership, nor was he now able to achieve his fell purpose.

Advancing toward the south, they halted, one hundred and fifty strong, at Copiapó, seven months after their departure. They were in the first fertile valley of Chile. Valdivia there took possession of the country in the name of his king.

The Indians received them with displeasure. Almagro had

---

[1] See Stella May Burke, *The Conqueror's Lady* (London, 1930).

treated them so ill that they were not disposed to receive as guests these compatriots of the men who had scourged them. They hid their provisions and appeared almost naked, in the most miserable aspect, in order to see if they could make the conquerors give up their enterprise. But Valdivia saw through their stratagem and violently took their provisions from them. All the while subject to hostilities from the natives, the host continued the march until, at the beginning of 1541, it pitched camp in the valley of the Mapocho, at the foot of a wild solitary hill which the Indians called Huelén and Valdivia called Santa Lucía.

THE FOUNDING OF THE FIRST CHILEAN CITY

In contrast to Almagro's men, Valdivia and his followers formed a very good opinion of the country. The blue transparent sky, the woods and fields covered with grass and flowers, the climate mild and temperate in that transitory season from spring to summer during which they had partly surveyed it, made them think that these regions ought to be the most beautiful and fertile in the world.

A few days after his arrival on the banks of the Mapocho, Valdivia called together an assemblage of Indians, and to this body he reported that he had come to establish himself in the country in the name of God and by command of the king of Spain, just as his compatriots had done in Peru. He promised that, if they offered no resistance, he would treat them as friends; if otherwise, as enemies, and would even exterminate them. The Indians understood nothing of all this except that he wished to enslave them, but they went away apparently satisfied. They were waiting to gather their harvest in order to prepare themselves for resistance.

Valdivia then laid the foundations of a city which he called Santiago of New Extremadura in honor of the patron apostle of the Spanish army and in memory of his native province. He wished also to make people forget the bad reputation of the country by blotting out the name of Chile. But the second part of the name was soon dropped. As the limits for his government he designated Copiapó in the north, the Strait of Magellan in the south, and to the east and west both oceans. The date of the founding was February 12, 1541.

The site for the new city was admirably chosen, especially from a strategic standpoint. At that time the Mapocho was divided into two branches, a little to the east of the Huelén. One ran in the same direction as the present river, but through a much broader channel than the canal of today; the other flowed through the broad avenue which is now called Delicias. The two joined about a league to the west, leaving between them an island which at the western foot of the hill was only about five or six squares (*cuadras*) in breadth, but which grew larger toward the west.

It was precisely at this point that Valdivia began to locate Santiago. The hill was a fortress and the arms of the river were like walls. Parallel streets stretched from the foot of Huelén from east to west, for a distance of fourteen blocks. There were six streets at first; then three others were added to make nine in all. Some fifteen other streets cut these at right angles from north to south. Thus the original plan of the city of Santiago had an extension of fourteen squares measured from east to west.

The width of the streets was to be twelve yards (varas). As these streets were cut at right angles, the space of a square intervening between each, they formed rectangles enclosed within four streets. These plots were called "manzanas" (squares). The number of these squares exceeded 100. They measured not more than 138 yards each way, rather than 150, because from each side six yards were taken to form the street—six yards united to another six from the neighboring square to compose the twelve of the street.

Each one of the manzanas was subdivided into four lots (*solares*) by being cut in the middle with perpendicular lines. Having done this, Valdivia assigned to each of the soldiers and officers who were to become residents a lot on which to build his house. Half of his force was settled here.

One of the central manzanas was destined for the plaza (the Plaza de Armas of today). On the western side of this plaza was located the church and parish house, and on the north the government palace and prison. Then the first dwellings were erected, with walls of wood and mud and roofs of straw only. The Indians, of course, did the work. The first conquerors were installed in these houses, and not even the church in which Valdivia placed an image of the Virgin of Perpetual Succor, which he carried with him, contained better materials.

Before a month had passed after the founding of the city, Valdivia formed a *cabildo* or *ayuntamiento*, or as we would say today, a municipality. This corporation was composed of two alcaldes, six *regidores*, a *procurador* who represented it, and a secretary who certified its acts. The Extremaduran chief himself named the persons who were to constitute the *cabildo*. A short time after its establishment that body insisted that Valdivia should make himself governor of Chile, not simply as lieutenant of Pizarro but in the name of the king, and its request was granted. For this purpose Valdivia convened for the first time an open *cabildo*, an assembly of all townspeople, in order to deliberate on the question.

The conquering chief at once began to seek the most adequate means for exploiting and extending his dominion. He started work in the gold washings of Marga-Marga and ordered the construction of a vessel in the Bay of Concón, in order to communicate with Peru; but the work had scarcely been started when the Indians showed signs of hostility. Overnight all the Indians in the entire valley of Aconcagua, headed by the cacique, Michimalonco, declared themselves in rebellion. They killed the soldiers who guarded the *yanaconas* working at the gold washings and on the boat. They tore to pieces what had been done on the latter and threatened to extend the movement through the valley of the Maipo and farther south.

In spite of the efforts of the Spaniards to scatter the Indian bands and put down the uprising, they could not prevent an assault on the city and its complete destruction, barely seven months after its building had begun. The Indians set fire to the straw huts, killed four Spanish soldiers and a score of horses, and caused the almost total loss of baggage and provisions. Of the animals they had brought for food and propagation, the Spaniards saved only three hogs and two chickens; and of the grain, only a few handfuls of wheat. Even the records of the *cabildo* were burnt. It was a complete disaster. This happened in September, 1541. The Indians, on their side, had perished by thousands during the assault and had to retire in confusion to the mountain ridges of the vicinity. They had not succeeded in recovering either lands or dwellings. The city was rapidly reconstructed, however, with the aid of enslaved Indians or prisoners. Its buildings were now made of adobe and tile to prevent their burning easily; and since it was necessary for the Spaniards to live with weapon in hand day and night, it seemed much like an encampment.

In this way, the conquerors had to pass more than two years, devoting themselves to exploring the territory at no great distance from the city in order to break up the bands of Indians, seeking gold washings, and exploiting some of them, sowing small patches of grain and corn, and procuring provisions in whatever way they could. In spite of all their efforts, they suffered from hunger and nakedness until new supplies brought from Peru enabled them to renew their provisions.

THE FOUNDING OF OTHER CITIES

Hardly was the city of Santiago destroyed by the assault of the Indians, when Valdivia sent emissaries to Peru in search of more men and resources; but it was not until the end of 1543 that he succeeded in getting help. His supplies were sent in a vessel from Callao to Valparaiso and one hundred men arrived by land. These emissaries also brought reports of recent events in Peru, which were serious and had been the cause of their delay for two and a half years. The faction called "the men of Chile," whom Almagro the younger had headed, had instigated a revolution in Lima and had killed Francisco Pizarro. They then had taken control of affairs, and Almagro had refused to recognize an emissary of the king as governor of Peru. When Almagro's faction and that of the royal governor resorted to arms, the former was defeated and Almagro made a prisoner. Finally he was beheaded in the plaza of Cuzco, in the same place where years before his father had suffered death. These events suited Valdivia because they freed him from discharging his duties to his chief, Pizarro, whom he had begun to forget since his arrival in Chile, and left open the way for his aspirations to obtain from the sovereign confirmation of his title as governor.

With the new funds Valdivia thought only of consolidating the conquest. He ordered the founding of the city of La Serena in the north of the country in order to assure a road to Peru. Its founder was Juan Bohón[2] and the number of its citizens, thirteen (1544). In person Valdivia advanced through the region as far as the Biobío. Here the Indians severely assaulted him, making him realize that he was face to face with very different men from those he previously had known among the natives of America. He saw also the towns which made up those regions. Convinced that he needed still more reënforcements in order to dominate them, he returned to Santiago in order to send to Peru for them. His emissary to Callao, Juan Bautista Pastene, delayed two years in bringing them. The delay was explained as being due to the

---

[2] Bohón, a native of Rioseco, Spain, appeared in Lima in 1536, accompanied Valdivia to Chile, and returned to Peru with that leader. After the founding of La Serena he was put to death by Indians in the valley of Copiapó. See José Toribio Medina, *Diccionario biográfico colonial de Chile*, p. 135; Diego Barros Arana, *Historia jeneral de Chile*, I, 213-214.

alarming situation which Peru was again going through. There had been another revolution against the viceroy, headed by Gonzalo Pizarro, a brother of Francisco. The revolution triumphed and terror kept its opponents subdued.

Valdivia then prepared to go himself to Peru to get orders from the viceroy and to bring forthwith the men and funds that he needed. He wanted to take the greatest possible amount of gold in order to make a favorable impression concerning the wealth of his government. Since what he had was not enough, he despoiled various of his companions of what they had succeeded in gathering, although promising to restore it when he returned. He appointed Francisco de Villagra as his lieutenant; and, in the same ship in which Pastene had arrived, he embarked at Valparaiso for Peru in 1547. There were attempts at rebellion among his own soldiers and officers in Santiago. They were led by his former partner, Pedro Sancho de Hoz, who now sought to ignore Villagra's authority; but the latter seized him and hanged him with some of his accomplices; and all remained peaceful.

Once in Peru Valdivia, in order to suppress the rebellion, put himself at the service of the king's envoy, the cleric Pedro de la Gasca. He thus broke the bonds of friendship and gratitude that united him to the family of the rebellious leader, Gonzalo Pizarro, in order to embrace the cause of his king. The battle of Jaquijahuana,[3] which he directed and in which Pizarro was definitely routed, so accredited him with the royal envoy that the latter saluted him on the field of battle itself as "governor of Chile" (1548).

With Peru pacified, Valdivia easily acquired supplies of all kinds for his colony. He dispatched a company of more than one hundred men to Chile and after one and a half years' absence followed them himself, with more men and resources. The governor was now able to take a brief rest from his activity. Some five hundred Spaniards already peopled Chile. The city of La Serena had been destroyed by the Indians and Valdivia immediately ordered his captain, Francisco de Aguirre, to rebuild it in 1549. He himself went as far as the Biobío with two hundred soldiers. Reaching the banks of the river without adventure, he remained, during his explorations, in a place called by the Indians Andalién, which was covered with lagoons and was located where Concepción stands today. Here the Spaniards encountered the Araucanians

---

[3] This battle was fought near Cuzco. See W. H. Prescott, *Conquest of Peru* (2 vols. New York, 1848), II, 415-432.

a second time. These people surprised the invaders in a night attack of such energy and resolution that for the moment Valdivia and his men thought they were lost. Only after a fierce fight did they succeed in repelling the assault, and this was because of the aid which was given them by the Indian *yanaconas*, or auxiliaries, whom they had brought with them.

Notwithstanding his triumph, Valdivia understood anew that he had to deal with Indians braver and more warlike than those he had encountered elsewhere. For this reason he resolved to found a city near the Biobío River. He selected a splendid location near the sea, on the tranquil Bay of Talcahuano, and gave the name Concepción to the new town on March 3, 1550. The present port of Penco occupies the site of the first Concepción.

Shortly after this Valdivia penetrated into the Araucanian territory. In two successive campaigns he reached the banks of the river which today bears his name and founded two other cities: Imperial, called thus in honor of Emperor Charles V, situated on the borders of the river Cautín, where Carahue is today; and Valdivia (1552), more or less on the same site which it occupies at present. From Valdivia he sent Captain Jerónimo de Alderete toward the cordillera, and the latter founded a new city which he called Villarrica, near the lake of that name and at the outlet of the Toltén River. There were now six Spanish cities in the territory of Chile.

The chief of the conquest then went to establish himself definitely at Concepción in order to carry on from there the occupation of the territory in the extreme south. He soon founded a seventh city in the center of Araucania, which he called Los Confines, or Angol, situated a little east of the place which today bears that name. Three forts now guarded the hostile territory: Arauco, near the coast; Tucapel, on the western slope of the cordillera of Nahuelbuta; and Purén, on the eastern side of this same mountain chain. The towns which now bear these names are situated very near the ruins of those encampments.

The Indians did not keep up a continuous resistance to this occupation of their soil, seeming resigned to it. Thus passed the last months of 1553. In thirteen years of exploration and strife the entire country had been conquered by the Spanish expedition, which numbered at that date about one thousand men. The greater part were engaged in exploiting the gold washings they had discovered, in sowing grain, and in rearing livestock. The governor had divided the land and the conquered Indians among them, in order that the Indians might carry on the heavy labor of farming and mining. The conquest seemed, then, definitely accomplished. But it was not.

One day in December, 1553, a soldier arrived at Concepción hurriedly seeking Valdivia. He came from the fort at Tucapel to advise the governor that the Indians in the neighborhood clearly showed signs of revolt. Valdivia was not greatly alarmed but sent word to Tucapel that he would despatch reinforcements at once. Then he learned that three Spaniards on the way to that fort from Arauco had been murdered by the Indians. At this he resolved to go himself to punish the rebels. He selected forty of his best soldiers and set out with them.

He traveled slowly and with much precaution. On December 24, 1553, he reached a point near Tucapel. The following morning he continued the march. His troops moved forward with some apprehension, but nowhere saw any Indians. These, however, were hidden in the woods near by, carrying out a plan of attack arranged by their chief, Lautaro. This Indian, some twenty years old, had served as head groom to Valdivia but, months before this, had fled in order to join his rebel compatriots. The Araucanians, knowing that they would be attacked, had gathered in an assembly. Lautaro had made a fiery speech and proposed a plan which all approved. This plan consisted in forming different groups that would engage in battle, one after the other, until they wore out the Spaniards and, above all, their horses.

When Valdivia reached Tucapel he saw with much surprise that nothing remained of the fort but smoking ruins, for the Indians had destroyed and burnt it. As he found no Araucanians on the road, he believed that all had hidden themselves to escape the punishment which he was bringing upon them. But suddenly, on climbing the last little hill on the approach to the fort, a company of Indians came to meet him, brandishing their lances in defiance.

In a moment the fight was on. The first band of Indian warriors, repulsed and almost totally destroyed, cast itself down the hillside. Immediately a second band took its place, and, cut to pieces like the first, followed its example. A third band followed this; and thus the fighting continued as if it were to have no end. Finding it impossible to resist that brave rabble of barbarians, the Spaniards who were left alive decided to retire, along with their leader; but a multitude of pursuers harried them from the rear. Exhausted, covered with wounds, and with their beasts of burden hardly able to move, they were easily taken by their captors. Not one escaped. There the first governor of Chile ended his days.[4] No definite details concerning his death are given.

When the news of the disaster of Tucapel reached Concepción, the *cabildo* of the city hastily called on Francisco de Villagra to take command of the country and organize resistance. Villagra was in the south near the present city of Osorno, taking the necessary steps to found a new city. When he arrived at Concepción and learned all that had happened, he ordered Villarrica and Angol to be evacuated and their citizens to be transferred to Valdivia and Imperial, because of the difficulty he would have in defending the former cities. He then prepared a company of more than one hundred and fifty men and with it crossed to Araucania to avenge the death of the governor and to quiet the revolt.

After passing the Biobío, the expedition went south over the ridges nearest the coast until, on a height called Marihuenu, the enemy appeared suddenly as at Tucapel, led by the same Lautaro. Great was the surprise. The broken condition of the ground and the lack of knowledge of it prevented the Spaniards from maneuvering with certainty. After some hours of fighting, Villagra's men were defeated and about ninety of them were left lying on the field. Since then the height of Marihuenu has been named after Villagra.

The fugitives who arrived at Concepción caused so much alarm that no one thought of resisting. Someone reported that Lautaro was passing the Biobío, and everyone hurried to remove his possessions from his home and load himself with all that he could in order to emigrate to Santiago. The alarm, however, was false, but after some days Lautaro and his victorious troops actually entered the abandoned city, sacked the houses, and set fire to them. Of the five cities founded in the south of the country by the first conqueror of Chile only the two near the coast, Imperial and Valdivia, remained standing, and, of the three forts of Araucania, not one remained.

After a long march the citizens of Concepción arrived at Santiago, with them Governor Villagra himself. He equipped a new army and once more started for Araucania to help the cities of Imperial and Valdivia and to fight the Indians, who were so weakened after their triumphs that they did not even try to fight. Since they had not cultivated their fields, so that the enemy would find no provisions in them, they suffered from starvation,

---

[4] For a detailed account of the tortures to which Valdivia supposedly was subjected, see Barros Arana, *Historia jeneral,* I, 434-437.

and to this another calamity was added—an epidemic of typhus fever, which took thousands of lives.

Therefore, Villagra did not have much to do in Valdivia and Imperial. He then tried to rebuild Concepción; but the indefatigable Lautaro reorganized as many of his bands as he could, fell on the hardly begun buildings, and a third time completely routed the Spaniards. The citizens of that city who had come to settle in it anew had to flee in confusion to Santiago in 1555. Here the panic that seized the population was indescribable. The colony was believed lost; and, when it was reported that the intrepid Araucanian chieftain was advancing northward to take the capital, dragging along all the Indians he found en route, a retreat to La Serena or a return to Peru was considered.

Lautaro really did not stay in Concepción. The greater part of his army refused to follow him on his campaign against the central country because it judged it had done its duty with the maintenance of the line of the Biobío and aspired only to take the two southern cities that were left standing. But he was not disheartened by this opposition. With only a few companions helping him, he won, by his speeches, the Indians of the region between the Biobío and the Maule and, improvising a new army, he passed the Maule with his men. There was no doubt as to his purpose: he was about to aim his offensive at the heart of the Spanish colony.

Triumphant in several battles, he reached the banks of the Mataquito and crossed it. Here, for the first and last time, his natural skill as a warrior failed him. He stopped when he could have advanced much farther and perhaps crushed all resistance from Santiago. He stopped, no one knows why, and fortified himself on the northern bank of that river in a place which seemed impregnable. On the south, the river defended him; on the west, the high ridges of the Caune; and on the north and east, besides the thick woods which covered the land, were deep ditches and formidable stockades of tree trunks which he had constructed.

Villagra made a surprise attack on Lautaro's encampment. A certain Indian traitor pointed out to him the unknown road behind the hills. He led his troops up toward the west; they passed over the road and, at the dawn of an April day in 1557, fell on the native camp. The contest was desperate. Lautaro made a supreme effort to organize resistance, but he soon fell wounded and died among his men. The battle became more bloody still because the Indians did not give way in spite of the loss of their chief. All was useless; the Spanish horsemen and the *yanaconas* whom they carried with them inflicted terrible slaughter and inevitably dispersed the Indians.

With the surprise at Mataquito the reconquest of Chile by the Araucanians was frustrated. With Lautaro, who was its very spirit, gone, the attempt was never renewed.

THE LAST CAMPAIGNS OF THE CONQUEST

Francisco de Villagra had hoped that his sovereign would confirm his appointment as governor of Chile as a reward for his valiant services, but he was mistaken. The viceroy of Peru named his own son to the governorship of that colony. This son was Don García Hurtado de Mendoza, a young man of twenty-two years, whose family belonged to the highest Spanish nobility. Because of his youth and his family he was a strange contrast to the fighting captains of the colony. He knew Chile only as a name and had never served in any of the armies that fought in America. He was already, however, a distinguished officer. He brought an army of more than four hundred men, powerful war material, great quantities of provisions, and three vessels.

In the winter of 1557, Hurtado de Mendoza landed with his army on the island of Quiriquina, before ruined Concepción. He did not yet dare touch the continent because he was waiting for his cavalry, which was marching from Santiago, and remained on the island some months before he decided to land. He then erected a fort at a site somewhat farther south than the one occupied by the ruined city, on a hill overlooking the plains, and established his camp in it. The fort was very well constructed, having solid walls and broad ditches. The Indians had not shown signs of alarm until then; but, when they saw him proceed to land his troops and noted that the powerful invading army was trying to open a new campaign, they attacked the fort vigorously, under command of another chieftain called Caupolicán. The attackers marched forward over the trenches with desperate courage. They leaped over the ditches with breasts bared to the lances and shots of the defenders. They fell by hundreds; but, driven by heroic temerity, they persisted in the attack. They went so far as to seize the muzzles of the cannon by hand in order to overturn them. Mowed down by shot and blown into a thousand pieces, they finally were defeated and had to retreat in the greatest disorder.

After this triumph, Don García Hurtado de Mendoza made preparations to take possession of all the territory of Chile. He began without delay his great campaign into the interior of

Araucania. The Spaniards had hardly passed the Biobío when Caupolicán again attacked them. They engaged in a pitched battle in the middle of a swamp area called Lagunillas, on the present road from Concepción to Coronel. The rout of the natives was complete.

From Lagunillas on, the conquering army encountered no appreciable resistance. Don García ordered the fort of Tucapel rebuilt and Concepción resettled. He also founded a new city, Cañete, somewhat south of Tucapel. Then he marched as far as Imperial and Valdivia, and from there he went to Villarrica, which its former inhabitants were just beginning to resettle. He continued the march from Villarrica, keeping near the ridges of the cordillera of the Andes and always going toward the south.

Impenetrable forests and very dense thickets often compelled the Spanish host to spend the greater part of the day in opening a passage. Deep ravines succeeded the plains, and there were great lakes, small rivers, and muddy places, in which the horses were buried up to their breasts. The rain and cold and the cloudy and stormy days filled the souls of the explorers with despair. The Indian guides fled, leaving them lost in these solitudes; the *yanaconas* did the same; they were incapable of resisting nature in a form which, though magnificent, was so repellent.

But none of these obstacles, not even hunger or the exhaustion of the animals, could make these strong fighting men retreat. At the end of some weeks of such difficult travel, they reached the Gulf of Reloncaví and the ocean. They visited the numerous islands which extend southward and form the archipelago of Chiloé. Don García ordered an exploring company to cross the Channel of Chacao to the large island of that archipelago. Some ten Spaniards did it in an Indian canoe and then returned to rejoin their comrades. Among the ten was the poet, Alonso de Ercilla, who had already begun to compose the cantos of his celebrated poem *La Araucana*. From the shores of the Gulf of Reloncaví the expedition decided to return, and this was done through the center of the longitudinal valley. As the governor did not wish to leave those rich territories unclaimed, he founded the city of Osorno. The march northward presented no difficulties of importance; the Indians did not disturb them. As the winter of 1558 approached, the expedition stopped in Imperial. Don García now believed that the Araucanians were subdued and that, in consequence, all Chile was definitely conquered. This belief was strengthened when he received news in Imperial of the execution in Cañete of Caupolicán.

As military governor in that city Don García had left Captain

Alonso de Reinoso, a veteran of the native wars from the time of Valdivia. It was the duty of this chief to fight continually with the neighboring Indians, while Don García traveled through the south. At one time it was known that these Indians were meeting in a neighboring ravine for the purpose of combining in a new attack against Cañete. Reinoso at once ordered one of his officers to leave for that ravine with fifty soldiers. It was a harsh season of intense cold and torrential rains, and the Spaniards had to cross open prairies and marshes; but these men were not deterred by any obstacles.

The Indians, meanwhile, were unprepared. They believed a surprise impossible, both because of the hidden nature of the place where they were assembled and because of the state of the weather. The Spanish assault was completely successful. The Indians who did not take to flight were killed; only a few were carried as prisoners to Cañete. Among them was Caupolicán.

In Cañete Reinoso prepared a horrible death for the Araucanian chieftain. He had a stage resembling a theater raised in the public plaza and on it placed a sharp pointed stick. Then he ordered the victim to be brought in, and Caupolicán came, loaded with chains and with a rope about his neck. In the midst of the general anticipation, the Indian was seated upon the sharpened point of the wood so that it passed through his entrails. As a greater insult a group of archers, natives like himself, shot at his body until he died.

Don García returned to Concepción in January, 1559. The campaign had lasted fifteen months. In that space of time he had reconnoitered the country as far as the region of the islands; he had ordered the abandoned cities repeopled and had rebuilt the destroyed forts; he had also personally founded two more cities (Cañete and Osorno). Thus seven settlements arose in the previously rebellious territory from Concepción to Osorno. He had the right to hope for a reward from his sovereign for such activity. The king, however, had disapproved of his appointment and had decreed his dismissal in order to designate Francisco de Villagra as governor of Chile in his place.

Villagra had served from the beginning of the conquest at the side of Valdivia as one of his most forceful captains. He had been his lieutenant general much of the time until the last days of the conqueror. And it was the opinion among all his companions that he should definitely replace Valdivia, both because Valdivia himself had so declared on different occasions and because of Villagra's positive merits. But Don García, when he came to take charge of his government and found Villagra temporarily filling it, had treated him most contemptuously. He had afterward arrested him and sent him to Lima to be tried there for supposed crimes. So now, in his turn, Don García was promptly subjected to the humiliation of giving Villagra his post.

For the first time Don García hurried to install himself in Santiago in order to bring about order in an administration in which, during the campaigns in the south, he had used arbitrary and unjustifiable violence, especially in the division of the Indians and lands. He had deprived the greater part of the settlers of the cities of Concepción, Imperial, and Valdivia of their concessions, as he had done in the other cities that were depopulated and afterward repopulated in the interior of Araucania, to grant them to the men of his expedition, who had run no risks and had not undergone the suffering of the previous campaigns. He had imposed punishment and ordered capital executions without any process of law and for insignificant causes. Neither had his father, the viceroy of Peru, Andrés Hurtado de Mendoza, respected the rights or the lives of the early conquerors of that country. Therefore, the king of Spain, doing full justice on this occasion, had removed father and son from their posts and, in replacing the latter, had named the most meritorious among the associates of the first leader in the Chilean conquest.

Don García returned to Peru at the beginning of 1561, after the death of his father in Lima. He went from there to Spain in order to present to the court the merits of his services in the colony of Chile. He conveyed the belief that he had definitely consummated the conquest of this country by means of his campaigns and measures of internal administration; and, although those who were prejudiced by his acts as governor started a long suit which finally ended in severe penalties being imposed on him, it is certain that the sentence was never executed. Through his influence at court he made the services he had rendered weigh more than the errors he had committed; and in the course of years he became, like his father, viceroy of Peru.

As a matter of fact he was not wrong about the consummation of the conquest in Chile. This period of twenty years of exploration, of fighting, and of extraordinary suffering, during which the efforts of the Spaniards reached heroic heights in comparison with the no less admirable heroism of the natives of Arauco, is a period which closed with the rule of Don García Hurtado de Mendoza, for from that time the Spanish domination was unalterably fixed in all the country and a new epoch opened in the development of civilization in this extremity of the world.

THE FIRST BOUNDARIES OF CHILE; GEOGRAPHICAL EXPLORATIONS

The first boundaries of Chile were very different from the present ones. La Gasca, when naming Valdivia its governor, fixed the extent of the country that the conqueror was to command. Chile, according to this document, extended between twenty-seven and forty-one degrees south latitude (bays of Caldera and San Pedro) and embraced one hundred leagues from west to east, measured from the coast and following all its curves. Formerly a hundred leagues was longer than it is today; it was equivalent to one hundred and fifteen of the modern leagues. If we compare the area within such lines with that which Chile actually has, we shall find that the difference between them is not very considerable; what the country has gained in length it has lost in width.

Valdivia, however, always entertained the hope that his territory would extend to the lands of the strait. He insistently asked the king for it, and the king agreed, but not till after Valdivia had died. During the rule of Hurtado de Mendoza, the southern limit of this colony was effectively extended to the Strait of Magellan and, as it preserved a hundred leagues' breadth on the east, the result was that Chile at that time possessed a great part of what is now the Republic of Argentina, and its extent was about double the present area. Almost all of Patagonia was included in it; in the Gulf of St. George it extended to the Atlantic, and from there south all the extremity of America belonged to it, comprising 1,400,000 square kilos, more or less.

The governor of Chile did not take possession, however, of the Atlantic coast, nor did he found any settlement in the Patagonian zone of the Pacific. Only the region of Cuyo, north of Patagonia, from which the Río Negro separated it, and the region of Tucumán, north of Cuyo, as far as the twenty-seventh degree were really governed by him, and then constituted the trans-andine provinces of Chile. The first to take possession of the eastern and southern regions was Francisco de Villagra, in the name of Valdivia.

On his return from a journey to Peru, where he had gone in search of resources (1550-1551), Villagra traveled through the Bolivian tableland by the route Almagro had followed in his campaign to discover Chile. He continued through the territory of the present Argentinian province of Salta and, as he knew the eastern boundary of his chief's territory, he went toward a city called El Barco, recently founded by Spaniards from Peru. Villagra obliged them to recognize the authority of Valdivia and advanced toward the south. After exploring a great part of the region of Cuyo, he and his soldiers crossed the Andes opposite Santiago, through the Uspallata Pass, and joined the governor.

A year later Valdivia sent Francisco de Aguirre from La Serena to Tucumán because he received word that his authority had not been recognized there. Aguirre arrived at El Barco, moved the city a little more to the east, to the banks of the river Dulce, and called it Santiago del Estero (1553); but ten years later the province of Tucumán became part of the viceroyalty of Peru.

García Hurtado de Mendoza also sent an expedition to the eastern side of the Andes. This expedition left Santiago, crossed the cordillera through Uspallata Pass, and descended into the region of Cuyo. Pedro del Castillo,[5] who had reached Santiago a short time before, commanded it and in 1561 founded a city which he called Mendoza, in the name of and in honor of his chief.

In the twenty years of the conquest, then, the Spaniards became acquainted with the greater part of the country, even the regions on the other side of the Andes—not thoroughly, to be sure, but at least in their general outlines. A double impulse drew the conquerors to the different zones of Chile: the desire to find gold, Indians, and fields for cultivation; and the satisfaction of presenting to the king the whole country occupied by their efforts as an expression of their loyalty.

Nor were they less eager in exploration by sea. After the Almagro expedition, whose single vessel reached the Bay of Valparaiso, the ships that traveled the route between the colony and the viceroyalty surveyed the greater number of the ports and inlets of northern Chile. They sailed near the coast, fearful of being lost at sea. The voyage from Valparaiso to Callao lasted at least a month, but the return took much longer—at least three months. The cause of this disparity is easily explained. The Humboldt Current, which passes near the coast of Chile, runs toward the north; aided by it, the vessels which went from Chilean ports to Peru made the journey in much less time than those which came from Peru, because the latter had to sail against the same current.

The most celebrated pilot of those voyages during the conquest was the Genoese, Juan Bautista Pastene, who also, by Valdivia's orders, extended the survey of the Chilean coast as far as the

---

[5] Castillo escaped from the forces of Gonzalo Pizarro, joined the enemies of the latter, and helped to overthrow that rebel. He came to Chile with Hurtado de Mendoza and under the latter's orders founded the city named after his leader. See Medina, *Diccionario biográfico colonial de Chile*, pp. 192-193.

Channel of Chacao. He accomplished this exploration from Valparaiso in the course of a year (1544-1545) spent in going and coming. Landing at the various bays and river mouths he accomplished the survey in some detail. The roughest part of the coast, the insular zone, remained to be surveyed. Valdivia also sent an expedition in charge of Francisco de Ulloa[6] to explore as far as the strait. Ulloa fulfilled his task, but his voyage did not have the desired result because, when he returned in 1554, Valdivia had just died and no one thought of anything except the suppressing of the Indian uprising. The immediate practical end pursued in these explorations was to establish direct communication by sea from Peru and Chile to Spain. The idea was held that the strait could not be navigated from west to east, but only in the same direction in which its discoverer navigated it—from east to west—because of the supposed existence of a very heavy current from the Atlantic to the Pacific.

García Hurtado de Mendoza later entrusted exploration of the strait and adjacent territories to the pilot, Juan de Ladrillero, who took with him as second in command another mariner called Francisco Cortés Ojea,[7] who was familiar with these regions through having formerly accompanied Ulloa. In 1557 they left Valdivia in two vessels. At first navigation was easy; the north winds bore the bark along with relative ease. They visited the archipelagoes of Chiloé and Guaitecas, somewhat distant from the coast but, after several days of sailing, a tempest surprised them in the Gulf of Peñas, south of the peninsula of Taitao. This obliged them to enter the Channel of Fallos, which separates the islands of Serrano and Prat from the island of Campaña, and to anchor in a cove of the latter. On continuing the voyage, the flagship of Ladrillero was separated from that of Cortés Ojea because of another storm, and they did not again come together. In spite of having no news of his chief, Cortés Ojea kept on toward the south.

---

[6] Ulloa returned to Chile with Hurtado de Mendoza and later settled in Concepción. At the time of the exploit mentioned in the text he was about fifty years of age. One of that name in 1539-1540 assisted Cortés in exploring the Gulf of California and another accompanied Orellana on the Amazon. It is not possible to determine any relationship among the three. See Medina, *Diccionario biográfico*, p. 880. For a different point of view see Barros Arana, *Historia jeneral*, I, 328, 417.

[7] Ojea, an experienced cosmographer, prepared a formal report of his voyage, during which he encountered greater difficulty than his chief. In 1594 he appears as an encomendero of Indians in Osorno. See Medina, *Diccionario biográfico*, p. 220.

Innumerable were the dangers and the suffering that he ran. Among the intricate labyrinth of islands and channels he often seemed completely lost. Finally, in the spring of 1558, he returned to Valdivia. His voyage had lasted a year.

Cortés Ojea's news of the separation from Ladrillero created the impression that that mariner and his companions were definitely lost. It was not until another year had passed that it became known that the audacious enterprise had achieved success. In the middle of 1559 Ladrillero and his companions entered Concepción on their return.

Ladrillero had sailed from the Channel of Fallos to the south and crossed the strait which today bears his name, between the Esmeralda and Angamos Islands. Running from isle to isle and channel to channel, he finally penetrated into the strait and after several months arrived at Primera Angostura, its eastern mouth. He passed through the full length of the strait in both directions and also explored the maritime contours of the extreme south of the country.

TAKING POSSESSION OF THE SOIL; THE SYSTEM OF ENCOMIENDAS

Because of their distance, the trans-andine provinces remained a government apart; and Chile proper, the Chile of today, was populated and occupied by the conquerors only in the territory that extends from the valley of Copiapó to the Gulf of Reloncaví. However, this narrow strip of land which some have said could not feed fifty Spaniards, now at the end of the conquest harbored more than a thousand of them and fed them all. Nine cities had arisen in it, and beautiful cultivated fields yielded abundantly throughout its entire extent.

The Spaniards had to cultivate the soil and breed animals in order to live, and to work the mines in order to make themselves rich. As they were not accustomed to these occupations, since they were, above all, military men, they made the enslaved Indians work for them. Each of the conquerors wished to own his portion of soil and enough Indians to work it. The land which was assigned to a conqueror was called *repartimiento* and the Indians who lived on it and who were also assigned to him, encomienda, because he had them in his care ("commended" to him, according to the language at the time), and he made them work.[8]

The governors were authorized to give these concessions to their

---

[8] See Helen Douglas-Irvine, "The Landholding System of Colonial Chile," in *Hispanic American Historical Review*, VIII (November, 1928), 449-495.

more deserving companions, but only provisionally; the king reserved the right to approve them or not. The king of Spain was master of all the territories and conquered inhabitants, the only and absolute master, in virtue of the authorization given him by the pope to discover and occupy lands in the western part of the world. But, if his faithful vassals went to such distant and unknown regions and conquered nature and men at the cost of heroic sacrifices, it was because they were in pursuit also of their share of immediate benefits. As the sovereign possessed no other means than the conquests themselves with which to remunerate their services, scarcely any part of the territory was occupied before the chief of the conquering enterprise divided the lands and Indians among his men in order to ease His Majesty's conscience of such debts.

The concessions approved by the king gave the recipient the right to enjoy the *repartimiento* and encomienda during his lifetime, and at his death this right descended to his oldest son, who enjoyed it also while he lived. After the completion of these two lives, the territory and Indians assigned returned to the power of the sovereign, and he, or his governors for him, disposed of them in favor of another person.

It must not be understood that all the conquerors received this grant. It was attainable only by the strongest; but, under the protection of these, the rest made their fortune. It must also be taken into account that the "two lifetimes" were almost always nominal, because the heirs gave proof of services which made them eligible to the same concession, and thus this concession was converted into an indefinite heritage.

For the first time, in 1544, Pedro de Valdivia made the division of Chilean land and Indians in the conquered section from Aconcagua to Biobío, forming sixty portions, usually separated from each other by some river or range of mountains. In this way some of the captains fell heir to whole valleys, extending from the sea to the cordillera, with their corresponding Indians. Valdivia's own allotment was assigned the same way. It was situated between Valparaiso and Quillota and, fronting on the sea, contained the mines of Marga-Marga.

But two years later Valdivia modified these concessions. He reduced the sixty allotments to thirty-two, because the Indians were constantly becoming scarcer. While the governor was in Peru, those who had been dispossessed by this reform accused him before La Gasca and asked for the return of their allotments. La Gasca ordered Valdivia to give the *repartimientos* and encomiendas not to his friends but to the most meritorious, but Valdivia made no change.

Later, when the Extremaduran conqueror extended his dominion to the banks of the Bueno River, the concessions of land and Indians were much more numerous and the number of discontented was considerably lessened. Then Don García came and gave and took away the *repartimientos* at will. This drew on him the hottest wrath of those affected, but the system remained as established and served as the foundation for the acquisition of agrarian property rights in Chile.

The conquerors, thus provided with lands to be cultivated and Indians to work them, devoted their efforts first of all to working the mines. Gold was what they coveted most, because with it they enriched themselves at once and because 20 per cent of the production of the mines went to the king (the royal fifth). The more fifths the governor sent to the court, the more he, as well as the country from which they were taken, was appreciated.

At first little gold was found in Chile. A few streams contained it, and in these "washings" were established, but the return was not abundant. Valdivia received regular returns from the washings of Marga-Marga, already mentioned, and of Quilacoya, near Concepción, which he had taken as his share. But not all possessed the facilities that he had for exploiting mines, the innumerable Indians for the tasks, and the many soldiers to guard them. Only at the end of Don García's government were other gold mines discovered—in Choapa toward the north and near Valdivia toward the south. Silver and copper, especially the latter—metals so abundant in Chile—were not found by the conquerors, nor were they yet sought with interest.

Busied with the exploitation of gold, they did not spend much time on the tasks of agriculture and cattle raising, whose products, however, they needed daily; but they soon made a beginning in these labors. When the Spaniards first came, the Indians were harvesting potatoes, corn, beans, and squashes. The principal grain added to those already known was wheat. The Spaniards also introduced grapevines and at that time made wines. A great impulse was given to the indigenous crops, as well as to the cultivation of those recently introduced, by the opening of new ditches in which water was easily drawn from the rivers. Since all the central zone of Chile was a great forest, it had to be cleared to a great extent, above all in the vicinity of the cities, where fields for cultivation, called *chacras,* were situated; and these lands, never sown before, were of a luxuriant fertility. Fowls, pigs, goats, sheep, horses, and cattle were propagated with the greatest rapidity, to such an extent that, during the years of Don García's government, the cattle were counted in herds.

THE INDIANS IN SERVITUDE

In cattle raising, as well as in mining and agriculture, the Indian was the most indispensable element. He had to do everything, closely watched by his master. And as the latter's interest depended on drawing the greatest profit possible from the earth, the conquered race was reduced to the most cruel and severe slavery. The condition of the subjected Indians was, then, equivalent to that of the slave of olden times and the serf of the Middle Ages. They were exempt from no kind of labor, from domestic service to mining. The latter was the hardest for them because they had to pass a great part of the day in the washings with their legs in water. Neither women nor children nor the aged were exempt. All were obliged to devote their personal service to the masters. Overseers armed with whips watched and directed them in their labors. At the least sign of languishing the lash fell on their shoulders. Blood reddened the streams. A niggardly ration of parched corn was their whole food supply. Not a single farthing did they receive for the day's wages. At times during the campaigns in which they had to serve as beasts of burden to carry the provisions, hundreds of these unfortunates, weakened by weariness and hunger, fell dead along the road.

It was natural that, as they were accustomed to a free life, they should try to escape the suffering imposed by such severe treatment. They did try, but almost always without success, because it was with difficulty that they could change masters; from one encomienda they passed to another. The masters would then be involved in litigation over the ownership of the Indians because the latter were not easily distinguishable from one another. For that reason, and to escape vexation, they undertook the task of marking their slaves with a red-hot iron, like any beast. Each owner stamped his sign on the shoulder, cheek, or forehead of the Indians, where it could best be seen, and from that moment he could say "my Indians." The least fault of any of them was punished with one or two hundred lashes. If anyone stole an animal, his hand was cut off, and such were the punishments applied for other crimes, even of less weight. One can understand that the native race would diminish rapidly.

It was the general belief among the Spaniards that the Indians did not belong to the human race, that they were not worth more than a horse or a dog. Nevertheless, they ruled them in the name of religion and under the title of heretics. But generous voices were raised in Spain to condemn the idea that the Indians were beasts and to ask consideration for them. Public authorities were moved, and the king himself was disposed to protect the American race, which was, however, in his own interest, since the Indians worked the mines and from them was taken the fifth part for his treasury. If the Indians diminished, the king's fifths diminished also.

García Hurtado de Mendoza, obeying the instructions of the court, charged his legal adviser, Licentiate Hernando de Santillán, to devise measures to prevent the extinction of the enslaved natives. The legal adviser logically found the only means to be the suppression of the causes which began the evil, which could be reduced to two: excess of work, and very bad treatment. He elaborated an ordinance which Don García ordered to be carried out, which was called the "measure of Santillán" (1559).[9] It contained the decision that all Indians need not give personal services to the Spaniards, but that the head of each encomienda should deliver to the encomendero one Indian for every six of his tribe for work in the mines, and one for every five, for the fields. This personal tribute was called *mita*. It also was settled that the Indians should enjoy remuneration equivalent to a sixth of the production of his labors, that the encomendero should feed him with meat at least three times a week, and that he should give him the needed tools. He should excuse the women, the males less than eighteen years of age, and the aged over fifty from all obligation to work and should forbid the Indian to be treated like an animal.

The encomendero was obligated to sow lands sufficient for the feeding of his workers; to minister to them in sickness; to teach them the Catholic religion; and, lastly, to protect them on all occasions and to treat them with gentleness. This law for the protection of the Indians displeased the encomenderos, even if it did please the king as well as the Indians, because, in lowering the number of workers, it lessened the production of the fields and mines. Therefore, they were not disposed to comply with it. The Indians, for their part, were as little disposed to labor willingly for their masters. Accustomed to liberty, they fled to the woods

---

[9] This ordinance does not exist in its original form but in summaries given by the chroniclers Diego de Rosales and Suárez de Figueroa. See Barros Arana, *Historia jeneral*, II, 223, n. 19. See also Lesley Byrd Simpson, *The Encomienda in New Spain* (Berkeley, 1929).

in order to escape the *mita*. In this way the Spaniards, by their greed, and the Indians, by their indolence, brought about the failure of the measure of Santillán. It was never applied and did not alter the status of slavery in which the native race was held.[10]

---

[10] Many additional details regarding the system of encomiendas and the general relations between the Spanish and Creole proprietors of Chile and its Indian population will be found in Douglas-Irvine, *op. cit.*

CHAPTER IV

THE COLONIAL ORGANIZATION

GOVERNMENT AND ADMINISTRATION

During the first half of the sixteenth century the Spaniards conquered America from Mexico to Chile, and during the second half they organized it as a colony. Just as it fell to the lot of the Catholic kings to preside over and stimulate discoveries, and to Charles V to make conquests, so it fell to the lot of his son, Philip II, to preside over and direct the organization of the colonies.

It is well known that Philip II is the most absolute monarch that Spain has had and at the same time the most popular and beloved. Endowed with average intelligence and a cold, energetic character, he succeeded, without resistance of any kind, in impressing the characteristics of his personality on the government of all his dominions. Religious to the point of fanaticism, he adopted as the rule and mission of his life incessant warfare against Protestantism and in favor of the Catholic Church.

During his whole reign, which lasted about half a century (1556-1598), he waged wars with various European countries for reasons that were more religious than political. The extension of the territories which he ruled and the enormous income of his treasury made him the most powerful king of his time. Spain, Flanders, and a great part of Italy and North Africa, as well as half of America, belonged to him. He used to exclaim proudly: "The sun does not set on my kingdoms." Fortune, however, frequently did not favor him; in war he suffered many defeats which completely annihilated his squadrons; in peace he always lived in need of money, in spite of all the gold America sent him.

He firmly believed that the colonies of the new continent were his own personal property, which he could dispose of at will; and he believed that to draw from them the greatest pecuniary profit possible should be the principal aim of his administration. His subjects most eagerly supported him in the organization of the colonies. They and the king had a common interest. The one as much as the other strove by choice to exploit the conquered countries. Those who came to America thought only of enriching themselves in order to return home and enjoy their fortune. There were very few who carried with them the firm resolution to establish themselves perpetually on the new continent.

Under such circumstances, from the time they began to explore these regions, the sovereigns of the Peninsula wished at all costs to isolate them from the rest of the world and to prevent anyone not a Spaniard from establishing himself there; and the Spaniards themselves who desired to go had to give proof of their status, religion, honesty, and industry in order to obtain the required permission. This was certainly not a system exclusively Spanish. Portugal, France, England—all the colonial powers of the six-teenth and seventeenth centuries—introduced it as a colonial prac-tice of the period.

The representatives of the royal authority—viceroys and cap-tains general—were also isolated completely within their respective colonies. They could not contract marriage in them, nor be god-fathers, nor receive gifts, nor assist at private celebrations, except in an official character. They were even more definitely prohibited from having any private business whatever. The ecclesiastical authorities, bishops and archbishops, and the judicial authorities, *audiencias*, were to watch the governors, take care of each other, and give account to the king of what they observed and considered worthy of his knowledge. In this way a permanent rivalry was stimulated between the two groups.

The Council of the Indies[1] acted for the king in all American affairs. It proposed the names of the persons who should occupy public offices in America and took note of all the complaints and news that arrived in Spain. It proposed, furthermore, the laws which ought to be issued.

The highest colonial authority in Chile was the governor and captain general appointed, on the recommendation of the Council of the Indies, by the king as his representative in the colony. His most immediate ranking superior was the viceroy of Peru, but the governor could communicate directly with the king when he thought it necessary. His duties were as follows: to command the army; to appoint and remove the other public functionaries except those who received appointment directly from the king; to administer civil and penal justice as a supreme judge, either in person or through his deputy (*teniente general*); to direct the administration

---

[1] See Merriman, *The Rise and Fall of the Spanish Empire*, III, 619-623, for an excellent résumé of the establishment and functions of the Council of the Indies. Merriman places the "first definite and legal existence [of the Council] by the emperor in August, 1524." William Spence Robertson also points out in his *History of the Latin American Nations*, p. 97, that the council had existed in a rudimentary form "at least as early as the second decade of the sixteenth century."

of cities, designating the members of the first *cabildos*, with either himself or his subalterns presiding over the sessions of these bodies; to exercise the right of ecclesiastical patronage for the king and, under the title of vice patron of the Church, to name the parish clergy; to divide lands and Indians provisionally among the individuals whom he thought most deserving.

But these powers had two important limitations: In the first place, whoever was injured by his administration could apply for justice to the viceroy of Peru or to the king himself; and, in the second place, he was subjected to a public hearing (*juicio de residencia*) before a lawyer when his office ended, to which all those came who had grievances against him. Their charges being reviewed in the hearing itself, the king, in the last instance, decided on whom the responsibility should fall, after the Council of the Indies had, of course, passed on the preliminary proceedings. The governor was a salaried officer. Valdivia received two thousand pesos annually; Don García was given twenty thousand. Afterward this amount varied until it was settled at ten thousand pesos annually.

Aside from the governor, political authority resided in his deputy; in the corregidores, or governors of cities and subdivisions called *partidos* (today provinces or departments); and in the high constables (*alguaciles mayores*), with authority equal to that of prefect, whose duty it was to execute judicial and governmental resolutions. In addition, there were royal officers: three functionaries charged with watching over and administering public revenue, its records, and the pay of the employees. One was called treasurer (*tesorero*); another, accountant (*contador*); and the last, overseer, or rather, reviser (*veedor*). These men received appointment from the king.

Besides the corregidores, the local administration of the cities was in charge of the *cabildos*.[2] Each of these corporations was composed of two alcaldes, six *regidores*, a secretary, and a *procurador*, who represented it before the other authorities. On founding a city, the governor selected the members of the *cabildo*; these men afterward named those who should replace them each year; but, by order of the governor, three *regidores* were irremovable; later, these offices were sold at public auction. At any rate, the *cabildo* enjoyed a certain autonomy, and, as members were reeligible to these posts at the beginning and as the posts were afterward purchasable even for a lifetime, the result was that the same persons occupied them for many years.

[2] See W. W. Pierson, Jr., "Some Reflections on the Cabildo as an Institution," in *Hisp. Amer. Hist. Rev.*, V (November, 1922), 573-596.

The functions of the *cabildo* were exceedingly varied. Some of the more simple duties of administration consisted of looking after public improvements, cleanliness, and health. Other duties were judicial in character, as shown by the fact that the two alcaldes administered justice in private affairs. Others were legislative, such as dictating local ordinances and tariffs on the prices of certain articles and handwork. Lastly, some functions were political. When a public danger or other important affair was to be considered, it brought the people together in an open *cabildo* (*cabildo abierto*), an assembly so called because all the residents of the locality could be present and deliberate in it, in order to determine such measures as would save the situation. When a governor died without having designated the person to fill his place temporarily, the *cabildos* might likewise ask the king to name such an individual. In spite of its humble character, this institution frequently provoked difficulties for the leaders of the colony, especially when the latter imposed extraordinary contributions (*derramas*) on the neighborhood, or committed some forceful act.

During the colonial period there was nothing more complicated than the administration of justice. The governor had the right to judge certain civil and penal cases; the alcaldes were also judges of the courts of first instance in the same or other cases. An attorney, appointed as the governor's deputy, the corregidores of the cities, the constables—all had the character of judges in certain specified cases. There were also military judges, treasury judges (*jueces de hacienda*) who heard matters of taxation, judges of mines, judges of commerce, judges of water, and ecclesiastical judges who heard religious affairs and civil or criminal cases in which priests were involved.

But the superior tribunal in Chile was called *real audiencia*, a kind of court of justice composed at first of four members, or judges, appointed by the king. It was established for the first time in 1567, in Concepción, but was suppressed after seven years, to be again established in 1609. The governor presided over it and so this officer afterward bore not only the titles of governor and captain general, but also that of president. The *audiencia* greatly limited the action of the governors because in many cases the latter had to proceed in accordance with it. The organization of this tribunal was later somewhat modified.

The administration of criminal justice was very complicated, but the penal punishments inflicted on delinquents were exceedingly severe: the stocks, or *barra*, as it is called today; chains, like the fetters of today; the gallows, erected in a public plaza; the pillory, put in the same place, to fasten the hands of the culprit; and, lastly, the roller, located in the plaza also, to whip the criminals in public. Torture, or *tormento*, as it was then called, was the means most used for drawing out confessions from delinquents.

The legislation was the same as in Spain, save for the variations introduced by the ordinances of the king, especially for his colonies.[3]

THE AUTHORITY AND PRESTIGE OF THE CHURCH; THE INQUISITION

Political and ecclesiastical authority in Chile were almost the same, because the king made them both serve the ends of his government. The union of both powers originated in the first place in the belief that the powers of kings proceeded from God; and, in the second place, from the authorization that the pope gave the sovereigns of Spain to determine the ecclesiastical dignitaries of the new continent—an authorization that was equivalent to naming them, known as the right of patronage (*derecho de patronato*).

Side by side with the political and administrative organization, then, was the Church. Fervent Catholics that the Spaniards were, their first care in founding a city was to select a site for a church and accumulate materials for its erection. The construction of the Cathedral of Santiago was begun in the time of Hurtado de Mendoza, and this structure, a plain parish church during the years of the conquest, became in 1561 the seat of a bishopric, subordinate to the archbishopric of Lima. Its first bishop was Rodrigo González Marmolejo. Two years later, the church at Imperial was raised to the category of bishopric, subordinate also to the see of Lima.

During this same sixteenth century religious communities were established in the country; first, those of the Dominicans, Franciscans, and Mercedarians; afterward, those of the Jesuits and the Augustinians.[4] All these orders at once attained great prosperity

---

[3] Another brief account of the political organization of the Spanish colonies is in Merriman, *op. cit.*, III, 647-648. An excellent résumé is given by Charles Wilson Hackett (ed.), *Historical Documents Relating to New Mexico, Nueva Vizcaya, etc.* (4 vols. Washington, 1923-1937), I, 19-28.

[4] The Dominican order was founded in 1215. Members of this order were in Santo Domingo as early as 1510 and an ecclesiastical province was established there in 1530. A Dominican province was established in Chile in 1592. See *Catholic Encyclopedia*, Vol. XII, "Order of Preachers," p. 368E; Crescente Errázuriz, *Los orijenes de la iglesia chilena, 1530-1603*, pp. 97-102. The Franciscan order, founded in 1209, was identified with the Spanish conquest of America from the second voyage of Columbus ("Order of Minor Friars," *Cath. Ency.*, VI, 281, 298), and with Chile from 1535. See Barros Arana, *Historia jeneral*, I, 373, n. 89; Errázuriz, *op. cit.*, p. 103. The Mercedarians, founded in 1218

and possessed extensive properties through legacies of wealthy persons and through royal concessions. The first orders of nuns to be established were the Clares and the Augustinians.[5] The founding of monasteries, convents, and churches became so common and they became so numerous in Santiago that, at the beginning of the seventeenth century, this city was called the Rome of the Indies.

The number of persons consecrated to the monastic life became, a little later, relatively numerous in proportion to the general population. Different causes produced this great affection for the religious life. In the first place, preparation for the priesthood did not then involve long study or much training; further, the priesthood meant exemption from military service in the army, which was so dangerous in Chile because of the eternal warfare with the Araucanians that many, after serving in the army, abandoned this career in order to enter upon the ecclesiastical life; and lastly, the priesthood carried with it social considerations and the unencumbered existence which the charities of the parishioners gave it.

By its prestige, fortune, and numbers, the ecclesiastical authority was, in the early days of the colony, as influential as the political authority; and, little by little, by virtue of the privileges that it enjoyed and because of the moral influence it exerted, it came to be superior to it. Since it constituted the firmest pedestal of the monarch's absolute power and had for its principal mission the defense of the monarchy's divine origin, special prerogatives were bestowed upon it, among which the most important were the so-called civil jurisdiction and ecclesiastical privilege (*jurisdicción civil y fuero eclesiástico*). By the first, it had under its control the judging of all questions raised among laymen that related in any manner to religion; and, by the second, every question of civil and criminal character arising among ecclesiastics was to be judged before its tribunals. When anyone, whoever he might be, even the governor himself, resisted the mandates of the bishop, the latter fulminated

---

(*Cath. Ency.*, Vol. X), are said to have accompanied Columbus on his later voyages. They first arrived in Chile with Valdivia himself.—Errázuriz, *op. cit.*, p. 50. The Jesuits, organized in 1539, carried on their first American activities in Brazil (*ca.* 1549) and arrived in Chile in March, 1593.—Barros Arana, *Historia jeneral*, III, 215. Their arrival preceded by two years that of the Augustinians, the "Black Friars," whose organization dates from the first half of the century. —*Ibid.*, p. 217; Errázuriz, *op. cit.*, pp. 439, *et seq.*

[5] The "Poor Clares" (*Clarisas*) were members of the second, or female, order of the Franciscans, which was founded by Ste. Clara, a contemporary and most devoted follower of St. Francis. The first formal establishment in Chile, however, seems to have been made up of those belonging to the third or "tertian" order. It was located at Osorno before 1573.—*Ibid.*, p. 233.

his excommunication against him—a weapon stronger than a whole army, because it left the rebel outside the Church and isolated from society. This was the principal element that gave the ecclesiastical authority predominance over the political. More than once the bishop thought it necessary to excommunicate some governor, or at least threaten him with that penalty, because, in spite of the fact that both ought to act in accord, they did not always do so, but, on the contrary, frequently engaged in controversy. Among the various cases that might be cited is the following: the encomenderos paid the parish priests for their services, a payment which was many times the object of bitter discussions. Governor Rodrigo de Quiroga, on petition of the encomenderos, issued an ordinance reducing such payments; the bishop of Santiago, Friar Diego de Medellín, required the revocation of the ordinance under penalty of excommunication, and Quiroga had to give way.

Besides this, the tribunal called the Holy Office, and more commonly merely the Inquisition,[6] was charged with pursuing and punishing with severest penalties those individuals suspected of religious transgressions. There was only a commissioner-general of this institution in Chile, who depended on the tribunal of Lima and did not come until the last third of the sixteenth century. In 1562, however, the first "offender against the faith," a certain Alonso de Escobar, was prosecuted for having said of a respectable priest that when he preached only the letter of the Gospel he heard him with pleasure, but that when he undertook the moral application, he closed his ears, and "other words of like effect." The good man proved that he had said it once for a joke, without evil intention, but he had to pay the costs of the trial, bear a long imprisonment, and be transferred to Lima for the revision of the proceedings. When the inquisitorial commissioner arrived, these causes were followed up more strictly and were not unusual.

The customary proceeding of this tribunal was really terrible. One accusation, made verbally or in writing by any person whatever, was sufficient to open suit. The supposed criminal was seized and held *incomunicado*. Witnesses were called to testify, without excluding any—friends or enemies, servants or patrons, relatives, children, or spouse of the accused. They were solemnly sworn to maintain absolute silence about what would be asked them and warned to speak the truth. The accused did not know who these

---

[6] For the history of the Inquisition in Chile, see Henry Charles Lea, *Inquisition of the Spanish Dependencies* (New York, 1908), pp. 406-412; and José Toribio Medina, *Historia del tribunal del santo oficio de la inquisición en Chile* (2 vols. Santiago, 1890).

witnesses were and was ignorant of the plot woven round him to prove his guilt. His defense was impeded. On his first appearance he was flattered with a pardon, in order to make him confess his crime and afterward, if this method failed, he was subjected to atrocious torture. If no success was gained by any of these methods of forcing a confession from the accused, he was declared acquitted; but suspicion of the crime always hung over him. It frequently happened that the unfortunate man died in prison because of the torture. Then he was buried secretly and the process continued. If nothing was finally proved against him, absolution was read to his effigy and the site of his grave was told to the family. But if, on the contrary, he was found guilty, his body was disinterred and burned, and his ashes thrown to the winds.

When the accused was declared guilty, while still alive, he was counseled to reconcile himself to the Catholic faith. If he did this, he was hanged and his body burned. If he did not, he was thrown alive into the flames. This was called auto-da-fé. This act was executed with the greatest solemnity in the presence of the civil authorities, the ecclesiastical corporations, and the public. Although people in Chile were devout, the processes instituted by the commissioner-general of the Inquisition were not rare. But the auto-da-fé took place in Lima.

TAXES AND PUBLIC INCOME

In their communications to the king, the governors frequently dwelt on the beauty and natural wealth of Chile, but the treasurers or royal officials always mourned the poverty of the treasury; and the *cabildos* and private citizens, at every opportunity, were full of similar complaints. On the one hand, the constant warfare with Arauco made attention to agriculture difficult and caused excessive expenses; and, on the other hand, the limited development of industries and the occasional paralysis of labor in the mines considerably reduced the receipts.

There were two classes of taxes: those of a special nature, which taxed definite services in each community and which belonged to the *cabildos;* and those of a general nature, which taxed the production and business of the country in its different forms and which belonged to the king. The former constituted the local revenues; the latter, the royal treasury.

The *cabildos* preferably taxed the establishments of commerce and of industry, the exercise of manual arts, and that of the professions with definite fees, much like present-day licenses. They were further supported from the fines which were imposed on those who disobeyed their ordinances. The income which they thus received was, however, so slight at the beginning that the *cabildo* of Santiago, which was the most prosperous, had neither its own building in which to function—until, by order of the king, it purchased the house of Pedro de Valdivia—nor chairs to sit on, nor the means to pay a single employee.

The receipts of the crown were much more certain and plentiful. The following were the principal sources of revenue:

1. The royal fifth, 20 per cent of the production of the mines or washings of gold. This was collected from the proprietor of the extractive works at the time that the gold was stamped in the royal foundry established in Santiago. The circulation of gold dust was for that reason prohibited under penalty of confiscation.

2. The ecclesiastic tithe, the tenth part of the agricultural and cattle products of each year. It was levied also on garden products, fruits, and domestic fowls. The religious character of this income arose from the fact that it was destined for the maintenance and embellishment of public worship. Since early times the Roman popes had settled it on faithful Catholics, in consequence of the right of patronage enjoyed by the kings of Spain, and it continued to be collected by them, with the obligation of devoting the income to the sustenance of the Church.

3. The tariff (*almojarifazgo*), a customs duty of 5 per cent on merchandise introduced into the country or sent out of it. It was paid in each port where the merchandise was landed.

4. The excise tax (*alcabala*), an impost on the sale or transfer of goods, moveable or immoveable, in whatever form, at the rate of 2 to 6 per cent of its value.

5. The sale of papal bulls for eating meat on days when the Church prohibited it;[7] and of public offices, such as those of secretaries, defenders of nonresidents, and *regidores*.

There were, moreover, other taxes of minor importance and some receipts that eventually reverted to the crown, such as the income from judicial fines, a part of which belonged to the "Chamber of His Majesty," according to the expression used at that time. The extraordinary tax called *derrama* was also imposed on the colonists

---

[7] In 1509 Pope Julius II issued the bull "Santa Cruzada" which, followed by subsequent decrees, permitted the faithful to be relieved of certain forms of abstinence during fast days. The king could sell this privilege to his subjects, but they were obliged to renew it every six years. The proceeds were to be used in war against the infidel. In 1529 Charles V was empowered to extend this bull to America, but it was not so extended regularly until 1573, when it was used as a new source of revenue. See Barros Arana, *Historia jeneral,* III, 158.

on certain occasions, and these were very frequent in Chile. It was an arbitrary tax which the governors prescribed each time they thought the exigencies of war required it. The colonists hated it more than anything else because, aside from its being prescribed suddenly, each individual had to pay from his meager resources, according to the quota that the governor himself fixed.

The incomes resulting from all these taxes were always small, but the king knew how to indemnify himself. He authorized the governors to contract loans in his name when urgent circumstances required it; of course the king did not repay such loans. At other times he took possession of all the gold that any of the merchant fleets brought from America to Spain and gave a receipt in his name in favor of the person despoiled. His needs were such that there is no record of his ever returning these sums, though they frequently were the aid sent by the conquerors to their destitute families.

At the end of the sixteenth century, the poverty of the royal treasury in Chile was changing into misery. It lacked money to pay the numerous public functionaries, from governor to lowliest porter. And, further—a terrible menace—the soldiers were not punctually paid. Utter demoralization was on the point of dissolving the army, while the rebellious Indians were triumphing in the south. The king then ordered the treasury of Potosí to send to Chile an annual subsidy whose value changed frequently, but almost at the beginning amounted to 300,000 gold pesos. This subsidy was called a royal annuity and it was brought to Chile for the first time in 1600.

THE COMMERCIAL MONOPOLY OF THE MOTHER COUNTRY

From the beginning commercial isolation was added to the political isolation of the colony. It was without communication with the rest of the world and without immigration from any European country. Furthermore, the interchange of its products could be effected solely with neighboring colonies or with Spain through them as intermediaries. It was the system established by the sovereigns for the whole continent. It is fitting to remember that the other colonial powers of the period implanted the same system in their respective dominions. No one who was not a Spaniard could trade with America, and only one Spanish port was designated for this purpose—Seville, on the Guadalquivir River. A kind of customhouse and at the same time a tribunal of commerce, Casa de Contratación,[8] was established in the port to reg-

---

[8] It was founded in Seville in 1503. See Merriman, *op. cit.*, III, 623 ff.

ulate this commercial monopoly and was charged to intervene in whatever related to traffic between Spain and its colonies.

But Chile could not maintain direct relations with the Peninsula. As a general rule, a merchant fleet came once a year to America from Seville. Because of European wars and the incursions of the corsairs, however, these voyages often were delayed from two to five years. In compensation, some years two fleets would come. These were composed of various kinds of sailing vessels: some, called galleons, were of large tonnage, armed with heavy artillery to defend themselves from the corsairs. The irregularity in the voyages produced serious disturbances because, as the Americans could neither buy nor sell to anyone except the merchants of those fleets, there were years during which they had no opportunity or means to procure the European articles they needed, much less sell what they produced.[9]

The Chilean colonists were in a worse situation than the rest of the continent; no fleet came to their coasts. The following were the only definite ports in America for mercantile traffic with Spain: Havana, for the Antilles; Vera Cruz, for Mexico; Cartagena, for Venezuela and Colombia; Portobelo, for the rest of the South American colonies, Chile among them. Portobelo was situated in Panama near the Caribbean Sea.

The Chileans, therefore, had to go to Panama and cross the isthmus on muleback to meet the merchants of Spain; and, as this journey was long and difficult and not lacking in danger, one can understand that very few—or none—ventured to make it on their own account. Nor could the route from Buenos Aires across the cordillera, nor that of the strait be followed; they were closed to all traffic by order of the king.

In such isolation there was no other way than to send Chilean products to Callao, the merchants of Peru frequently bought, which, perhaps to sell them again in that country or to carry them to Portobelo on their own account. Here a kind of fair was held every time a Spanish merchant fleet arrived. As there was no competition, the merchants of the fleet dictated the standard of prices. They sold for their own satisfaction and bought the same way. They were not satisfied with gaining 100 or 200 per cent; they must gain fivefold on their capital, and such was the abuse that gains of 900 per cent seemed easy.

---

[9] For the general subject of trade and commerce in the Indies, see Clarence H. Haring, *Trade and Navigation between Spain and the Indies* (Cambridge, 1918); A. G. Keller, *Colonization* (Boston, 1908), pp. 226-241.

There were two results from this order of things: first, the enormous prices charged for European articles in Chile, so that very few persons were in a condition to acquire them; and second, the very low prices at which the national products were quoted, so that almost no one devoted himself to their production on a large scale. Thus, while a fanega (about 1.6 bushels) of wheat was worth two pesos, a cow the same, and a sheep one real, a packet of paper cost more than one hundred pesos, a sword, three hundred, and a cloth cape, not less than five hundred. Under such circumstances the colony was condemned to poverty. It must sell cheap and buy dear. There never was a commercial monopoly more rigid and more irritating.

With reference to production itself, on the other hand, the royal prohibitions against planting vineyards, olive trees, tobacco, and other industrial plants in order to prevent commercial competition with similar productions of Spain caused disturbances of no little consequence. It is true that those prohibitions were almost never respected, but nonetheless they showed clearly to what extremes the Spanish government tried to carry the exploitation of its colonies and restrain the development of their wealth. If to these obstacles are added the regulations and tariffs dictated by the *cabildos* for professions and manual trades, which placed bonds on free labor, and the ordinary and extraordinary levies, it will be seen how heavily burdened was the productive activity of the industries established by the colonists.

The plan followed by the kings of Spain in this system tended to enrich the royal coffers and those of their peninsular subjects, and one would believe from what has been said that they profited by following it. Nothing, however, was less true. It is a fact that because of the customs taxes which the crown collected and the fifth of the yield of the mines in America, its treasury was considerably increased; but the money left the royal chest as easily as it entered it, in order to maintain the ostentation of the court and the interminable European wars.

It is true also that numerous private fortunes grew out of colonial commerce but, to put it briefly, those fortunes did not remain in Spain. They went to England, France, and Holland, which were, in fact, the most inveterate enemies of Spain, and left Spain in a manner as inevitable as it was natural. The mother country was not an industrial power, and after the wars of the sixteenth century and the expulsion of the Jews and the Moors —who were the most industrious of its people during that century—Spain was left without industries of importance and with much less capacity than the maintenance of the colonies required. Since England, France, and Holland were really industrial nations, the Spanish merchant had to go to them to buy the necessary merchandise. The Spanish merchants were converted, then, into agents for the French, English, and Dutch producers. They loaded their ships with merchandise which they carried to America and sold at exorbitant prices, without real profit to themselves and at an enormous sacrifice to the Americans. This situation, created and exploited in the sixteenth century, lasted during the seventeenth and almost all of the eighteenth century.

THE ELEMENTS OF COLONIAL ECONOMY

Meanwhile the Spaniards living in Chile were forced by necessity to lay the foundations of national production, in all its various forms, within a narrow framework. Although gold was the product most esteemed by them, yet they were forced, even during the closing of the sixteenth century, to endure a scarcity of it. Among the weighty reasons for limiting the exploitation of gold fields were the imperfect methods employed in the extraction of the precious metal, and the rapid dying out of the native race on account of the severe labor in the washings.

Whether they liked it or not, they had to concentrate their attention on the tasks of agriculture and cattle raising and industries derived therefrom in order to produce anything. It is true that they always continued to force the Indians to perform all the work. Particular attention was paid to the cultivation of the vine, wheat, and maize. Hemp, which they used so extensively in making fuses for their arquebuses, ropes for their packs, and rigging for their vessels, was cultivated with careful attention also in La Serena and valleys farther south. All fruit trees and garden plants which had been introduced from Spain found here a region adequate for their propagation. The same may be said of domestic animals (cows, horses, asses, goats, sheep, pigs, and other animals), and fowls (turkeys, hens, ducks, geese, and others). Both climate and soil favored considerably the cultivation of all these plants, as well as the pasturage of animals. At first, however, none of this was done on a large scale.

The only manufacturing industries which were established during the earliest years of the colony were flour mills, looms or workshops for weaving cloth from the wool of the sheep, and tanneries; and almost all such industrial establishments were located in cities or in their immediate vicinity. Other industries, such as the making of rigging or cordage and the building of vessels, were set up in suitable localities. Oil and wine were also manufactured. From animals, in addition to the wool and hides, the dried meat or *charqui*, and the fat and tallow, occasionally made into candles, were utilized.

These very limited productive activities, in industry as well as in agriculture, had only one outside market—Peru. Exportation was carried on with great difficulty, as was also importation from that region. The vessels sailing between Valparaiso and Callao took a long time to make their voyages—one month in going and three in returing was common. Not until 1583 was this situation bettered a little. In that year the pilot, Juan Fernández,[10] coming from Peru, left the coast and sailed on the high sea. He discovered en route the islands which bear his name and, to the great surprise of his sailors and even of himself, he reached Valparaiso after sailing only for a month.

This discovery, which gave him great fame and which was of very great importance for the furtherance of mercantile relations between Peru and Chile, is easy to explain. Since most of the sailors at that time sailed only within sight of the coast, the ocean current which runs close to the coast of Chile, flowing toward the equator from the south polar zone, was contrary to and retarded the journey of those sailing from Callao to Valparaiso, while on the other hand it favored those sailing from Valparaiso to Callao. When Fernández left the coast, he escaped the force of this current and the northern winds drove his ship onward without great effort.

Although it is a fact that voyages were made more frequently when the sea route between Peru and Chile was shortened, it is also true that at the beginning this meant little to the colony of Chile. The colony exported at that time only wine, wheat, hides, tallow, and hemp, to which were added gold and some dyeing and medicinal substances. In exchange it imported rice, cloth, linens, silks, weapons, pig iron, paper, fine furniture, porcelain, metalware, and perfumes; but these transactions afforded little development because of the commercial system established by the mother country which obliged the colony to sell its products at very low prices and buy outside products at very high prices.

---

[10] A name applied to three pilots of the sixteenth century. One was master of the fleet which in 1534 bore Pedro de Alvarado to the port of San Miguel in Peru. Another, mentioned in 1546 as residing in Lima, was a native of Palos, Spain. A more likely person is the pilot who, in 1574 and 1586, is represented as voyaging along the west coast of South America. By some, a pilot of that name is credited with a sixteenth-century voyage to Australia. See Medina, *Dic. biog.*, pp. 288-290.

Internal commerce was as yet but little more active. There were not even roads for easy transportation. The principal traffic carried on between Santiago and Valparaiso was by mule or horseback in journeys of several days' duration. The cities thus remained commercially almost isolated. Besides this, the private persons engaged in trade had to submit to many impositions in order to continue in business. Aside from the tax similar to a license, which they had to pay to the *cabildos*, they were obliged to sell merchandise coming from a distance at cost during the first nine days of its public display, but this did not keep them from selling it at high prices. Merchandise and the products of the country were subject to tariff. The trade in foodstuffs was carried on in the public plaza, in a kind of fair or market called *tiangue*.

Among the difficulties with which trade at that time also had to contend was the instability of weights, measures, and coins. The *cabildo* of Santiago legislated for the whole country with respect to measures and weights, fixing them exactly, but its ordinances in this matter were never strictly observed. The quart, bushel, pound, and yard were then the conventional measures.[11]

The conquerors brought no money. They did not need it, since they came for the very purpose of seeking exclusively its raw material, gold, and did not have anyone with whom to trade. For this reason transactions were made at first by exchanging one article for another or by paying for goods with gold dust, and for that purpose some traders went around with their small scales in their pockets. Only in his last years did Valdivia establish in Santiago a smelter for evaluating and stamping gold. A little later there were also smelters in La Serena, Concepción, and other cities of the south and the circulation of gold in dust was prohibited.

The best-known money of that epoch was the gold or "Spanish peso," the value of which depended on its weight. Then came the real, which was worth from an eighth to an eleventh part of a peso, according to conditions; the maravedi (a peso generally equaled four hundred and fifty maravedis) ; and the ducat, which was worth a little more than peso. Besides these, there were many other fractional coins of silver. In order to determine values as compared with the coins of today, one must remember that the average Spanish peso was equivalent to twenty-four Chilean pesos of six pennies gold.[12]

---

[11] The measures and weights mentioned, with approximate equivalents, are: *almud*=quart; fanega=bushel; *libra*=pound; *vara*=yard.

[12] See *supra*, this chapter, n. 9.

To the instability in the value of measures and coins was added other difficulties for the exercise of commerce and industry, and even for professions and trades. These were the ordinances fixing the rates and tariffs, prescribed and enforced with great strictness by the *cabildo* of each city. The price of labor was fixed for artisans. For instance, a blacksmith in Santiago had to make a pair of horseshoes for three pesos and a pickax for five, neither more nor less. The making of a cloak by a tailor cost thirteen pesos, and the rest of the garments according to the style. The artisan must post the rate ordered by the *cabildo* in plain view in his shop, and the *cabildo* reserved the right to revise and alter that rate. The fee for doctors was also fixed—a peso at night, and four reales during the day. The price of drugs was determined, as was that of clothing and bread. Failure to observe these ordinances was severely punished, either by a fine for the benefit of the public works of the city, the informer, and the treasury of the king, or by confiscation of merchandise, if the culprit were a trader, or by work performed without pay for the general welfare of the community if he were an artisan.

In this way the economic activity of Chile was organized and started on its development during the first half century of Spanish domination. Under strict isolation it had to produce only for the benefit of the kings of Spain and their peninsular subjects. The colonists settled in Chile were not able to profit by the wealth wrested from the soil by the sweat of the Indians, except by going back to Spain. The whole system established by the mother country seemed calculated for men who kept moving and must shortly return to their native land. The colonists did not appear to be inspired by any distinct purpose. Their first forms of production and labor, just like their local ordinances of trade and industry, left the impression that they dwelt in encampments rather than in cities and that, instead of living in families, they always lived in campaigns, fighting at the same time against nature and men. Their necessities were not yet more than those of soldiers.

THE FORMATION OF SOCIETY; EARLY SOCIAL CLASSES

Chilean society had its origin in the union of the native race with the Spaniards, beginning in the earliest days of the conquest. The Spanish population was always small in numbers compared with the native population of the country. At the end of the sixteenth century, there were not more than five thousand Spaniards in Chile—men, women, and children.

Although sickness and bad treatment caused a rapid dying out of the native race, the fusion of the two continued extensively. The Spaniards had come to these countries without families, and it was not until after some years had passed that a few did bring over their families. During the second half of the century, therefore, the number of Spanish women in Chile was very small. They arrived in appreciable numbers only in the following centuries. This fact is explained, furthermore, by the circumstances that most of the men who at that time came from Spain to Chile were military men and came to fight the wars of Arauco and to make a fortune with their swords. A family in such a case was a hindrance.

So they took Indian women for their wives and in this way, on the encomienda as a foundation, and within the domestic service itself, a social class arose intermediate between the Spaniard and native, composed of mestizos (mixed bloods). Their physiognomy reproduced the European type, but their customs and character approximated more the native type of the country, since they continued to live with their mothers and received from them not only their language and first education, but also the characteristics of the race. These mestizos greatly exceeded the Spaniards in numbers before the end of the first half century after the conquest.

One more element soon came to be added to the population—the Negroes brought from Africa and sold as slaves. Some wealthy colonists bought them in Peru especially for use in domestic service, without implying that they were not also at times destined for the fields and mines. They were liked for their fidelity and submission. A Negro was worth from 300 to 500 pesos, according to his age, and a Negress from 200 to 300 only. Not many were brought into Chile because, among other reasons, there was no great need for them. There were mestizos and native women who could give the same service. The Negroes were also intermingled with the Indians, although in smaller proportion, still less with the mestizos, and rarely with the Spaniards. The children of Negroes who bore the blood of other races were called zambos[13] and mulattoes.

To summarize, the first elements of our society may be divided into five categories: Spaniards, Indians, mestizos, Negroes, and zambos and mulattoes. The first formed a privileged group who by their culture and force ruled the rest and placed a very different value upon each of the other groups.

The subjected Indian—*yanacona* or *mitimae*, according to the terminology of the time—bore all the burden of labor. Baptismal water had not yet bettered his condition; it made him a Christian

---

[13] Zambo: a name given to the issue of a Negro and an Indian woman, or of an Indian and a Negro woman.—J.A.R.

but did not give him civilization. His condition continued to be equal to or worse than it had been in the first years of the conquest.

The mestizos, generally looked down on by the Europeans, also worked in the fields with the Indians. But the principal occupation for which they were destined was war. As soldiers in the Spanish ranks their bravery and fighting power were commendable. The cruelty with which their least fault was usually punished incited them more than once to rebel and to swell the army of the natives. These then became chiefs to be feared; and their more thorough preparation for war and their better developed intelligence gave them many chances for victory. In the early period, the mestizo, Alonso Díaz, was the most renowned of all the chieftains. Under the name of Painemancu and holding rank as an Araucaniau chieftain, he devastated the regions of the south in several campaigns.

The treatment the Negro slaves received was also very severe. An ordinance of the time provided the following penalty for them:

Any person, whether he is a constable or not, who shall catch any male or female slave who shall have run away from the service of his master for more than three days or less than twenty, shall be entitled to receive ten pesos, to be paid by the master of said slave, and to such slave will be given for the first offense two hundred lashes in the public streets, and for the second, two hundred lashes and his foot shall be cut off.

The penalty for the third time was so severe as to be equivalent to death. It is to be noted that many of the most warlike natives taken prisoner with weapons in their hands were reduced to a condition of slavery. The zambos and mulattoes ordinarily followed the status of the mother, that is to say, they were slaves also and their treatment did not differ much from that given the rest of their class.

Intermingled among themselves, these varied elements formed the foundations of Chilean society and of the future nationality. The Spaniards, lords and masters of all those social groups, lived in the camps, where the mineral and agricultural works of their encomiendas were carried on, and in the cities. The life in the country was nothing but a continuous and violent exploitation of the soil and the Indians, and social relations developed there in all their barbaric rudeness.

CITY LIFE AND CUSTOMS

It was in the centers of population called cities that European civilization began to manifest itself, adapted to the circumstances of the time and the nature of the country. There were already twelve cities in Chile at the end of the sixteenth century—eight south of the Biobío and four north of it, not counting those on the other side of the Andes. But in addition to those already mentioned must be added the city of Castro in Chiloé, founded in 1567, and that of Chillán, founded in 1580, both by Governor Ruiz de Gamboa. None had a numerous population. Santiago, the largest, did not yet shelter more than five hundred inhabitants of European origin; each of the rest, scarcely a hundred. It is not possible to calculate the Indian, mestizo, and Negro population employed in family tasks and in the services of each locality. The king had conceded to some cities the distinction of using a coat of arms, with accompanying privileges, in spite of the small number of their inhabitants. Santiago, for example, had a coat of arms on a silver background. On it was painted a lion with an unsheathed sword in one paw and eight emblems of the Apostle Santiago around him. Above were the insignia of the king and the image of the apostle. The monarch also gave Santiago the right to call itself "a very loyal and very noble" city.

The urban population of the cities was divided into three categories: proprietors (encomenderos), indwellers (*moradores*), and transients. The first two received the common name of citizens (*vecinos*). The last was composed almost entirely of military men. The encomenderos constituted the richest class. The indwellers were the traders and artisans—those we call today the common people.

The right of residence was easily conceded. He who desired to become a resident had only to present himself before the proper *cabildo* and prove that he followed an honorable occupation and that he observed good habits. He then received a lot (*solar*), which he was obliged to enclose with a mud wall within a fixed time and to build his home on. The "letter of residence" that the *cabildo* authorized thus conferred a kind of local citizenship on the individual. From that time he could be elected *regidor* or alcalde and was subject to the imposts corresponding to the ordinances.

These towns and villages presented a poverty-stricken appearance. The low buildings had walls of adobe or plastered mud, and roofs of tile or straw—one to three rooms at the most. The narrow muddy streets were crossed by open ditches which carried off all the waste. They resembled our country lanes of today. Some of those of Santiago were already paved with round stones from the river and also had sidewalks of stone. At night there was no traffic through the unlighted streets after a certain hour. At the stroke of the curfew, given by a bell or drum, everyone had to go home. The curfew sounded at dusk for Indians and Negroes and one or two hours later for the rest, according to whether it was winter or summer.

The furnishings of the houses were very simple: tables, benches, chairs, cots, and bedsteads of wood or hides—all rudely made, the floor uncovered, of rough earth or brick. The walls were generally covered with a coat of lime. At night this dwelling was lighted with tallow candles and little oil lamps.

The common dress of the men was composed of a coat or jacket to the waist with a greatcoat for the richest; pantaloons to a little below the knee, held in at the bottom with garters; wool stockings or silk in some cases; and shoes like pointed slippers or simply like buskins (*borceguíes*), laced up in front. For protection a long cape of fine wool was used, which is still known by the name of "Spanish cloak." This costume was completed by a hat with broad brim and crown ending in a point like a bonnet, or perhaps a *chupalla* of straw, nothing more.

The women's costume was made of a saya, a kind of wrapper which covered the body to the ankles. It was girdled at the waist with colored ribbons and fitted the breast closely. The well-to-do used light coats and hooped overskirts, plain or plaited and gathered at the hips, which fell to the feet. An embroidered collar or ruff, a mantilla for the head in place of a hat, and shoes finer than those of the men and sometimes made of cloth completed their apparel.

The food generally consisted of vegetables, pork, and fish, eaten three times a day: in the morning, breakfast (*almuerzo*); in the afternoon, dinner (*comida*); in the night, supper (*cena*). Drinking water came from the ditches, but already in Santiago, at the end of the sixteenth century, pure water from the springs of Tobalaba and Apoquindo was brought by means of a narrow canal of brick and mortar to the plaza of the city where a pool was constructed. The first wines, grape cider (*chicha*) and light wines (*chacolíes*) made from the native grapes, were already abundant on the table.

There was little social activity. Large affairs, political and diplomatic, were lacking. Amusements were also few. There was neither theatre nor circus. The bullfights which Spaniards so much enjoyed occurred only now and then, and cockfights were almost always private. Instead, money was wagered on handball, cards, and dice.

On great occasions, when a king came to the throne, or a prince was born, or a member of the royal family was married, festivals of a public character were held, where, beside the bullfights, games of canes and rings were played in the presence of large crowds.

The game of canes consisted in breaking one of them as if it were a lance upon the breast of an opponent while riding at full tilt. The ring game consisted in inserting a lance into rings hung from wires while the animal was going at full speed. These last games were first celebrated on the ascension of Philip II to the throne of Spain.

The annual holiday celebrated in Santiago with the most pomp was called "passing of the banner." It took place on the eve of the day of the Apostle Santiago, patron saint of the city, and was continued on the days of the saint himself (July 24 and 25). This celebration consisted in carrying the royal banner and escutcheon of the city through the streets, accompanied by a great procession of people on horseback, among whom were the governor and members of the *cabildo*. A certain person called "royal ensign" was appointed to carry the banner and this position was one of great honor. The residents also had especially large fine-looking, high-spirited horses for the parade. In the afternoon of the twenty-fourth, the royal ensign, on horseback, accompanied by the governor, the other authorities, and a great concourse of horsemen consisting of the most distinguished men of the city, took the standard from the house of the *cabildo*, carried it through the streets, with cries of "Long live the King" shouted by the multitude, and placed it in the cathedral. At night there was a banquet in the governor's residence and on the next day, a religious ceremony in the church in honor of the apostle. During that day the standard was veiled. This ceremony ended, it was paraded in the same way as the day before, and returned to the *cabildo*, this act ending the celebration.

Other festivities of importance were religious in character. Practically no one was excused from daily attendance at morning mass; the same was true of the processions which took place frequently. Those in honor of the Apostle Santiago, the Virgin of Socorro (patroness of the conquest), and Corpus Christi were particularly solemn. All classes of artisans, with their respective standards and insignia, had to attend the latter. They also paraded to the shrines of various other saints: St. Lucas, the protector against locusts; St. Isidro, patron of rain; St. Antonio, the protector against floods; St. Saturnino, the protector against earthquakes; St. Sebastian, the protector against pests, and others. For the rest, the piety and devotion of the faithful were shown in legacies to the convents and parishes and in the founding of shrines or hermitages that later became churches.

This life, peaceful and free from interruptions other than the wars of Arauco, was not exempt, however, from vexation and disorder. The home life among the small number of Spaniards that experienced it was impaired by a certain harshness in the treatment of the family by its head. The wife and children were in an exceedingly subordinate position, under the severe authority of the father, who frequently resorted to blows to compel obedience. The morality of the people also was not very edifying. Law suits, quarrels, murders, and executions on the gallows, among Spaniards and mestizos, were so frequent in the lax state of the country and within the cities that they offer indisputable testimony to the lawlessness of customs among those whose numbers were still so small and whose life, therefore, should have been of great value in the engrossing tasks of ruling and developing the country.

INTELLECTUAL MANIFESTATIONS

The Spaniards of that period reckoned the morality of a person by the degree of his observance of religion. The one who confessed the most and heard the most masses was the best. They never were friends of any but religious enlightenment, because they believed all study not entirely in accord with the precepts of the Church harmful for society. In order to prevent the perversion of moral feeling among their colonial subjects, the sovereigns prior to Philip II, and especially Philip II himself, denied any encouragement whatever to public instruction and the free cultivation of literature and science and prevented the publication and entrance of books without previous permission from the representatives of the Inquisition. The intellectual progress of the colonists, moreover, was considered undesirable in Spain because, if instructed, they might aspire to take part in the government and perhaps even to make themselves independent. In consequence of such beliefs there were no public colleges or printing presses in Chile during the sixteenth century.

The first conquerors who came to Chile, and those who followed later, had little culture—not so little, however, but that most of them could sign their names. As their principal occupation was war, they did not consider the education of their children important. Nor did they think that teaching amounted to much; they were accustomed to the fact that little was taught in Spain, especially to the lower classes of society. In Spain also it was believed that instruction was harmful for this class of people because it gave opportunity for excessive ambition and might menace the stability of the social order. A like conviction existed in regard to the teaching of women, which, it was thought, would corrupt their morals.

The first efforts to found educational establishments were due here as much as in Spain to the religious orders; but the first form of teaching was individual instruction. The father who wished his sons to learn to read and write put them in the hands of parish priests and conventual priests, who taught them as much as they could besides, especially prayers and the miraculous lives of saints.

However, schoolmasters who wished to devote themselves to primary teaching were not lacking in Santiago; but the lack of interest on the part of the residents and the scant resources of the *cabildo* did not permit them to exercise their profession regularly and constantly. Meanwhile, the juvenile population increased considerably, especially among the mestizos. There were more than enough children for schools; but only the richest succeeded in learning merely to read and write.

The first primary schools date from the last third of the sixteenth century.[14] The religious orders founded them and held them in their convents, the nuns as well as the friars, principally for the purpose of making novices for their profession. The Dominicans were the first to distinguish themselves in this kind of activity, and later the Jesuits. Seminaries for the clergy also date from this period, one in Imperial and another in Santiago, founded by the bishops of these dioceses. The first Chilean clergymen were educated in their halls.

But there was no place where the mestizos could be educated, nor did the colonists who wished to give their sons a moderately good education have a place where it might be provided for them. These people had to send their sons to colleges in Lima in order to give them this kind of education, but the length and peril of the journey, the price of board and room, and the lack of vigilance under which the pupils were forced to live there kept many from taking that step. The number of Chileans who were educated in those halls, therefore, was very small.

But in spite of its poverty and ignorance, Chile had the good fortune to have, at that time, men of renown who made the country known in Spain and even in other parts of Europe because of the excellence of their writing about its history, its geography, and its inhabitants. The literature of the conquest and of the first half

---

[14] José Toribio Medina, *La instrucción pública en Chile*, I, xx. Señor Medina devotes a thick volume to his historical sketch on colonial education in Chile and follows this with a thinner volume of documents.

century of the colony is scant, but valuable—for Chile at least.

The principal documents that one ought to read in order to follow the advance of the Spaniards in Chile from its first steps are the five letters of Pedro de Valdivia to the king,[15] written for the purpose of giving the king an account of his campaigns and the results that the conquest promised. Valdivia certainly did not hesitate in those communications to exalt his own merits; but neither does he restrain the manifestation of the profound love that Chile inspired in him, praising it highly as a privileged land because of the mildness of its climate, the fertility of its soil, and the abundance of its natural products. Written in a pleasant, colorful style, these letters are at times real literary documents. The first conquering chief of Chile is, therefore, also its first chronicler and its first patriot.

Another of the notable works of the conquest is *La Araucana* by Don Alonso de Ercilla y Zúñiga. No other American country inspired an epic poem more famous than this. Designed to celebrate the heroism with which the native race of Arauco defended its land and to exalt the sacrifice which its conquest required of the Spaniards, it reflected better than any other style of writing the grandeur of that struggle and the real character of the Chilean Indian.

As a consequence of his grave displeasure with Hurtado de Mendoza, Ercilla did not praise the share of that leader in the conquest. Later, when Mendoza became viceroy of Peru, he encouraged certain writers to prepare the story of his campaigns in the south of Chile.

Among works written for that purpose is one in verse—another poem tending to supplant *La Araucana*, called *Arauco domado* (Conquered Arauco). Its author was Pedro de Oña, who was born in Angol during the conquest and educated in Lima. He is the first of the poets born in Chile, but only in chronological order, because his epic did not have the importance of *La Araucana*, nor does it possess the literary merit of the latter. Devoted exclusively to extolling Don García, Oña disregards the reality of happenings and frequently descends to the ridiculous.

Besides these works in verse, there is one in prose written by one who took part in the conquest and in affairs in the colony. This is *Historia de Chile* by Captain Alonso de Góngora Marmolejo,

---

[15] The letters appear in "Colección de historiadores de Chile y documentos relativos a la historia nacional" (eds., Mariano Picón-Salas and Guillermo Feliú Cruz), I, 1-62. See also R. B. Cunninghame Graham, *Pedro de Valdivia, Conqueror of Chile*, pp. 127-220.

a native of Andalusia, who took part in the wars of Arauco during the time of Valdivia and spent the rest of his life in that manner until his death in 1575. His chronicle extends from the earliest times up to that year. He wrote simply and impartially, without pretension of any kind; he is worthy of credit, therefore, when he tells what he saw.

All these works measure the intellectuality of those times, and for Chile they have the merit of having been the first inspired by its nature and its men. They certainly are not the only works that might be mentioned, but the rest do not have the same literary and historic value as these. The warlike atmosphere which prevailed in Chile during the sixteenth and a great part of the seventeenth centuries was not propitious to peaceful intellectual production.

CHAPTER V

THE GROWTH OF THE COLONY

THE WARS OF ARAUCO

DURING THE TWO and a half centuries following the period of con-quest—called the Colonial Period (1561-1810) because the country remained under the rule of Spain—war against the Araucanians was the absorbing interest of the population and the government. This was a struggle of three centuries between the European and the native, for it did not end even with the Spanish rule, but much later. It was interrupted for some years, at times for long periods, only to start again and again with the same fury.

Different procedures, some peaceful, others more violent, were put into practice by the Spanish governors in order to bring about the definite submission of the Araucanian Indians; none was suc-cessful. There were two general causes for this: the insatiable greed of the Spaniards, and the invincible laziness of the natives. The Spaniards, who came from Spain dreaming of fabulous riches, thought only of exploiting the conquered races; the Araucanians, accustomed to liberty and the indolence of barbaric life, could not resign themselves to work for the benefit of the invaders; and so a conflict between the interests of the one and the habits of the other was inevitable. Added to this was the unfortunate idea the Span-iards had formed of the natives, whom they considered incapable of assimilating the most rudimentary civilization and treated, there-fore, with the most wanton brutality, capturing them in times of peace in order to allot them as slaves among their encomiendas, and robbing them frequently of their women, provisions, crops, and domestic animals. The natural bravery of the Araucanian was aroused by these cruel abuses and this explains the endless wars with which this barbaric people have always defended their inde-pendence.

It will be recalled that Hurtado de Mendoza handed over his post to Francisco de Villagra in 1561. He had scarcely left the country, satisfied at having pacified "all the territory of Chile," when the *yanaconas* of Purén killed the captain and the soldiers who guarded them and aroused all their fellow countrymen to revolt. These obeyed the call, and in a few days all Arauco was in arms. Perse-cutions and sacrifices to pacify them were employed in vain. They lived up to their reputation for indomitable courage. Finally, after severe reverses, the Indians saw a chance to win. Knowing that Captain Pedro de Villagra,[1] son of the governor, had left Arauco with a body of troops and had to cross over the hill of Marihuenu, which had formerly been so fatal to him, they decided to make a surprise attack on him in that place. They met with such good fortune that in a few moments they destroyed the enemy's host. Villagra and some forty of his men were left dead on the field of action. The victor took possession of arms and horses. The evacuation of Cañete and Arauco was the immediate consequence of this deed of arms and the war continued with inhuman slaughter. Catastrophes produced by severe earthquakes accompanied by tidal waves came to the aid of the Araucanians. One such disaster destroyed Concepción in 1570; another which occurred five years later leveled the rest of the cities of the south as far as Valdivia.

The governors who came to Chile did not, however, try to understand the difficult status of affairs which had come about in the colony. They came with the most flattering illusions as to the immediate pacification of the territory. Disillusionment soon showed them their error; then they tried to invent new methods of combat in order to achieve their purpose. The most curious was that of prosecuting the natives in accordance with legal formulas in order to declare them rebels and traitors to God and the king and to condemn them to the penalty of death and confiscation of property.

This strange expedient was first put into practice during the government of Villagra and had its origin in the preachings of a Dominican priest called Gil González, who maintained that death ought not to be inflicted upon Indians and that whoever did so would be sent to hell, because the Indians "defended a just cause, that is their liberty, homes, and property." These preachings caused much alarm among the encomenderos, who feared lest they be deprived overnight of their laborers in the fields and the mines. They fought the doctrine of Father González vigorously and procured a lawyer to try the Indians with all the rules of penal procedure; and then, when the Indians were declared rebels and traitors and pen-

---

[1] The son, Pedro de Villagra, who perished in this combat, is to be distinguished from the cousin and successor ad interim of Francisco de Villagra. See Barros Arana, *Historia jeneral*, II, 301, n. 5, and 328. The time and place of the battle mention in the text (see above) are uncertain, but it probably occurred at the end of January or the beginning of February, 1563. See *ibid.*, pp. 313-316, especially p. 315, n. 23. The narrative of Barros Arana is based on Pedro Marino de Lóvera's *Crónica del reino de Chile*, Bk. II, chap. xvii, in "Colección de historiadores de Chile," VI, 270-274; and Alonso de Góngora Marmolejo, *Historia de Chile desde su descubrimiento hasta el año de 1575*, in *ibid.*, II, 99-102. See also Medina, *Dic. biog.*, p. 962.

alized with death and confiscation of their goods, an army was organized to execute the sentence.

Another method, less specious, but much more cruel, consisted in transferring the Indian prisoners, taken in general harvestings or "field days," to the northern districts, in order to replace the *yanaconas* there, who had perished by thousands in recent epidemics. Having been apportioned among the encomenderos who most desired them, these unfortunate captives had one foot cut a little above the toe joints in order to make them incapable of flight. This was called "disjointing" (*desgobernar*) an Indian; but neither these outrageous cruelties, nor the executions en masse of the chieftains who started the revolts wrought the desired effect. The gallows or a holocaust incited them, on the contrary, to new and more implacable vengeance.

The governors were gradually convinced of the uselessness of such violence, and, reversing their policy, they tried to subdue the natives by peaceful methods. One of the governors, Martín Ruiz de Gamboa, tried to win them with kindness. He issued an ordinance which, like the "measure of Santillán," imposed a tribute in money on the Indians as the price of their liberty. They had to pay that contribution in return for the privilege of tilling their fields. Such an ordinance was, like that of Santillán, absolutely ineffective. The Indians, lacking industry and habits of work, were unable to comply with it. Neither did it suit the encomenderos any better. It could not be applied in any way and was revoked. This method is known as the "measure of Gamboa."

After many alternations of triumph and defeat, the Spaniards at the end of the sixteenth century suffered a misfortune of such proportions that the stability of the colony itself was endangered. The year 1598 had passed, but not even the Indians of Purén, who had struck the first blow in rebellion at the departure of Hurtado de Mendoza, had ceased their hostilities. The governor, Martín García Oñez de Loyola, had taken charge of his post a short time before. Determined on pacifying Araucania at any cost, he had attempted several campaigns in this territory but with results no more profitable than his predecessors had obtained. Finally the Indians made a surprise attack on him in a field called Curalava, on the banks of the Lumaco River, on the road from Imperial to Angol. Completely surrounded by the assailants, the governor and some fifty of his men perished. Among them were captains, lawyers, and priests. A few days later the rebellion became general; the seven cities on the continent south of Concepción were destroyed and their inhabitants, if not killed, were obliged to take to precipitate flight. Thus the sixteenth century ended in the midst of a struggle without quarter, in which no kind of atrocity was lacking.

Impressed by these facts, a Jesuit named Luis de Valdivia, in the first years of the following century, resolved to take up as his burden the defense of the Indians. He showed that the cruelties of war and the bad treatment which the encomenderos inflicted on the natives were the only causes of their resistance to submission. According to his belief the Spaniards should entirely abolish the personal service to which the Indians were subjected and allow them freedom to work on their own account. Then, by preaching the gospel to them in their own language, they might be led to accept the Spanish rule. An army should be maintained only as a matter of precaution, in order to compel the respect of the Indians, rather than to attack them, and, in case of revolt, this army should be limited to defending the land acquired. This plan of pacification has been called defensive warfare. Father Valdivia went to Lima in order to influence the viceroy to put his plan in practice. He took it so to heart that, although he found that this official gave him decided mental support, he went to Spain for the purpose of convincing the court itself that it was expedient and necessary to adopt his plan.

His triumph was complete. The court agreed to suppress the personal services of the Indians and to abolish the encomiendas; it pardoned the prisoners and fixed the Biobío as a boundary to Spanish territory, leaving the Araucanians in peaceful possession of the regions farther south. In 1612 the plan was put into practice by mandate of the king, and Father Valdivia, in company with some missionaries of his order, took up his residence in the territory of Arauco. He gathered the Indians together in a conference, made the exchange of some prisoners, and explained to them the scope of the new situation. The Indians seemed enthusiastically disposed to accept; but very soon the self-sacrificing Jesuit experienced the futility of his efforts. Three missionary priests were assassinated in Araucania. General rebellion broke out all at once. Defensive warfare had failed, and in 1626, by order of the king, Philip IV, Luis Fernández de Córdova proclaimed in Santiago a cessation of this form of warfare. For fifteen years more, then, there was a return to offensive warfare, without the Spaniards' gaining any favorable result. In the alternations of victory and failure, they had the worst of it, losing hundreds of men; but the military men themselves were interested in keeping up the campaigns because, as the prisoners were reduced to servitude, they sold them as slaves and thus obtained a good income.

Later, however, a governor tried to reëstablish the defensive warfare. This was Francisco López de Zúñiga, better known by his title of nobility as Marqués de Baides. A friend of the Jesuits and an admirer of Father Valdivia, he thought, from the time of his arrival in Chile, that instead of warring with these Indians it would be better to "treat these rebels kindly, trying to attract them by good means and convert them to friendship." Disembarking at Concepción, he began his relations with the Araucanians by making them presents of clothing, glass beads, little mirrors, and other trifles. When he thought that those whom he had favored with these presents had represented him to their fellow countrymen as a man of peace, he invited all the chieftains to a solemn conclave. This assembly took place in the valley of the Quillín River (today Quillén), a branch of the Cholchol, in February, 1641, and its result was a cordial agreement between natives and Spaniards to suspend hostilities. Before separating, presents were exchanged.

The Pact of Quillín, as this act was called, was very much praised by the colonists but were of short duration. Scarcely a year had passed after the celebration, when the marquis had to start a campaign to put down new Indian uprisings. But afterward, during periods of peace, the governors celebrated new conclaves with the Araucanians, and one governor, Tomás Marín de Poveda, obeying express orders from the court, succeeded in 1692 in getting the Indians to accept the introduction of priests into their territory, in order to convert them to Christianity. This system of pacification was called that of the missions, and Jesuits and Franciscans rivalled each other in apostolic zeal to carry it out.

They did not have to wait for the fruits of their labor. A multitude of native children gathered to hear the gospel preached. They were baptized and learned and recited some prayers without understanding them, but nothing more was gained from them. After returning to their families, they forgot all they had learned and relapsed into the same barbarism. After a few years the futility of this system was apparent. Nothing demonstrated it more clearly than the frequent assassination of Spanish soldiers when they ventured into the Indians' territory. Therefore, in 1700 the Spaniards began to abandon the system.

The natives, however, experienced greater peace during the eighteenth century, not because of preaching or violence, but because of the suppression of abuses and of the severe methods that the Spaniards had hitherto made use of in order to terrorize them. The governors were careful to keep up the celebration of conclaves with the principal chieftains, in which the pacts that were agreed to previously were confirmed with the customary solemnity and exchange of gifts. Only two general uprisings took place in that century—one in 1723 and the other in 1766. A peaceful agreement had been brought about between Spaniards and Araucanians, since the former had begun to give up the attempt to rule them by force and had left them in peace on their own lands.

Meanwhile, such a prolonged and dreadful struggle had ended by imprinting very special characteristics on the political and social life of the country. During the frequent periods of warfare in the sixteenth and seventeenth centuries, people lived amidst the most despairing apprehensions, and under a strictly military regime. Labor was paralyzed, but the colonists had to obtain money to pay and equip the troops. The hard times bred discontent in the cities and gave rise to fiery protests every time an extraordinary contribution or *derrama* for continuing the war was imposed.

The troops, on the other hand, were discouraged because of the futility of their efforts. Being convinced that Chile was not the land of gold that they coveted, and that they risked their lives in it without result, the soldiers deserted, although desertion was punished at the gallows, and went to work in other lands where profit was easier to obtain. Some sought security and repose in a convent. In this way the colony was impoverished and depopulated, the government was hated, life was uncertain, and domestic customs were impaired by the rigidity of camp life. In spite of all, the growth of the colony was not retarded and the fact that a large permanent army was maintained there stimulated the active exploitation of the soil.

THE CORSAIRS AND PIRATES

The wars of Arauco were not the only events that terrorized the colonists during these centuries. They were also greatly worried by the frequent maritime expeditions which subjects of Holland and England—national enemies of Spain—undertook to the Pacific coast. These expeditionists, called corsairs, came at their own expense but were authorized by their respective governments to assail Spanish vessels and ports for the purpose of robbing them of the merchandise which they found in them. The alarm produced by their incursions arose not so much from their robberies and violence as from the religious creed to which they belonged. They were Protestants, and Spanish Catholics considered them "heretics." The forays of the corsairs, therefore, were looked upon in Chile from the religious viewpoint as a punishment of God, and helped to exalt the devout zeal of the colonists as well as their military impetuosity.

The corsairs, on their part, professed a profound hatred for Spain. The king, Philip II, self-declared protector of Catholic Europe, had made stubborn war against the English and oppressed the Dutch, who formed part of his monarchy, and he drove the latter to rise in rebellion because of purely religious differences. For such reasons the English considered the Spaniards irreconcilable enemies and the Dutch regarded them as more than enemies, indeed as scourges, from whom, after a long and bloody struggle, they had succeeded in emancipating themselves. Both were disposed to do the greatest possible damage to Spain and thought even the most common pillage lawful. Their ill will was aggravated by the fact that the kings of Spain had closed the Pacific Ocean to navigation and to the commerce of all the countries of the world. These monarchs considered themselves, in good faith, masters of this ocean as well as of America, because their subjects had discovered it and had taken possession of it in their name.

The first nation to prove to Spain that she was not powerful enough to rule all the ocean was the English. A sailor of this nation, Francis Drake, began his piratical expeditions in 1578 and was the first foreigner to traverse the Strait of Magellan. Entering the Pacific, he proceeded northward and reached Valparaiso. Here he captured a vessel anchored in the bay ready to sail to Callao with a cargo of hides and tallow and a considerable amount of gold. He ransacked the warehouses of the port, which was then no more than a poor village formed by some ten huts, and set sail, continuing again toward the north. After additional very profitable incursions against the other Spanish colonies, he returned to Europe by sailing toward the west. Thus he made the second trip around the world in 1580.

He left open the route of plunder in America to other sailors possessed of the same audacity. The route was tempting because from it he had returned enormously rich. Scarcely eight years had passed when a new corsair, Thomas Cavendish, entered the strait. Here a distressing spectacle met him. After the return of Drake, Philip II had ordered two military colonies to be founded in the strait for the purpose of keeping the heretics from sailing through it to attack his colonies. In compliance with his order there was founded near the Atlantic entrance the port Nombre de Jesús, and farther west, on the eastern shore of the present Brunswick Peninsula, one called Rey don Felipe. The hardships that the men had to endure in these establishments were unspeakable. Separated altogether from the rest of the world, they were soon without the most necessary supplies. When Cavendish arrived at Nombre de Jesús, hardly fifteen of the original four hundred settlers were alive, and they seemed more like skeletons than men. The corsair wanted to save their lives, but, when he was about to take them on board, an east wind blew up and he sailed away, taking only one of them. On anchoring at Rey don Felipe, they found only skeletons and dead bodies. Hunger had destroyed them. The English named this site Puerto del Hambre, and not without reason.

Cavendish rounded the Peninsula and, always keeping toward the north, finally halted at Quinteros, the bay nearest to Valparaiso. On landing here, he experienced the ill fortune of being attacked by Spaniards. Four of his sailors were killed and eight taken prisoner. The latter were taken to Santiago and six were condemned to the gallows. The corsair chief, however, obtained very rich booty along the other coasts of America.

In the seventeenth century the situation between England and Spain changed—from enemies to allies.[2] The English government could not now authorize piratical expeditions but neither could it hinder some of its venturesome subjects from going to the Spanish colonies on incursions of simple pillage. To these sea bandits was given the name of "filibusters" or pirates.

The most famous in this century was Bartholomew Sharpe. After crossing the Isthmus of Panama with several companions, he provided himself with vessels, taking on board some Spaniards. Then he began a series of raids along the Pacific coast. When he arrived at the Bay of Coquimbo, the Spaniards of La Serena fled. The corregidor of the city was left alone to treat with the Englishman —more to gain time for arranging a surprise attack than to arrive at an agreement. This official was obliged to ransom the city for a hundred thousand pesos; but this arrangement was ineffective because the residents had no way to raise that sum. As the intrigue wore on and Sharp saw that he was being deceived in order to make a surprise attack upon him, he decided that it was better to retreat; but before doing so he sacked whatever of value he found in the city, and then set fire to the buildings in 1680.

Years later, at the beginning of the eighteenth century, England

---

[2] In 1604 James I reëstablished peace with Spain which lasted until November 5, 1624, when war was declared by Charles I. Six years later the Treaty of Madrid was signed. The next break came in 1656 when Spain declared war on England. Although a treaty was signed in 1670, war really continued until 1688 when Spain, England, and Holland were allied against France until the war was ended in 1697 by the Peace of Ryswick. See Ramsay Muir, *A Short History of the British Commonwealth* (2 vols. London, 1920), I, 359-606.

was again engaged in war with Spain, and new piratical expeditions descended upon the Pacific coast. This time they were encouraged and even equipped by the English government itself for the purpose of observing commercial conditions in the colonies and of finding a way to establish traffic with them. The first of the corsairs of this century was William Dampier. He did not stop on the coast of Chile and merely touched the large island of Juan Fernández. What made this corsair particularly famous were the adventures of one of his sailors, called Alexander Selkirk, who, abandoned by his companions, lived five years on Juan Fernández entirely alone. His only companions were birds and wild goats. He made two huts of the branches of trees, one for sleeping and praying and the other for preparing his food. They were located on the banks of a stream in the midst of a wood. His appearance took on a strange aspect, with his skin weather-beaten by the sea breezes, his beard and hair very long, and his clothing of sealskin. When another English vessel picked him up, his fellow countrymen did not recognize him as a man of their own race. The singular situation of this sailor provided material for an admirable English novel, *The Life and Strange Surprising Adventures of Robinson Crusoe*, a person who was supposedly in the same situation as Selkirk.

The fleet most feared in America was that commanded by Admiral Lord Anson, whom the English government sent to the coast of America in 1740. Almost completely destroyed by storms in doubling Cape Horn, he had to go to the island of Juan Fernández for repairs. There he established a kind of general headquarters from which he often sallied forth to assault the merchant vessels which carried on traffic between Peru and Chile. Thus enriched, he returned to England by way of the Asiatic seas, without the Spaniards ever being able to surprise or overtake him.

The expeditions of the Dutch assumed a different character from those made under the flag of England. The latter had no other aim than robbery. The former were guided principally by the desire to open new paths of commerce for their nation, and, if they also robbed, it was more because of hatred than of a desire for money. Therefore, the permission granted the English corsairs and all the preparations for the affair were arranged with the greatest secrecy. The Dutch expeditions, on the contrary, were made openly, patronized by rich capitalists or by reputable commercial companies of the country.

The Magellan Company, founded in Rotterdam to carry on commerce with the Indies by navigating the strait of that name, sent a fleet which made the passage under Simón de Cordes. Storms scattered the ships of this fleet, and each met a different fate. The one commanded by Baltazar de Cordes, a brother of the commander, anchored in the Bay of Castro in Chiloé, tried to gain possession of the island, and incited the Indians to rebel against the Spaniards. He succeeded in his purpose and the garrison stationed in the city, powerless to resist him, surrendered. The Dutch treated the Spaniards with the greatest cruelty; they killed as many men as they could lay hands on; a few escaped by fleeing to the woods to hide (1599). As soon as the latter received aid they were able to take the offensive and rid the island of its invaders.

Even in the middle of the seventeenth century, Spain still maintained war with Holland, refusing to recognize its independence. The Dutch East India Company, founded to carry on commerce with the new Dutch colonies of Oceania, equipped an expedition to explore the extreme south of America, commanded by the capitalist, Jacob Lemaire.[3] He entered the Pacific through the strait which today bears his name—in the extreme southeast of Tierra del Fuego —and then sailed around Cape Horn, called so then in remembrance of the Dutch city, Horn, where that expedition was organized.

Another Dutch fleet for exploration only was directed by the pilot, Jacob l'Hermite, who was making hydrographic maps for several months on the archipelagos south of Tierra del Fuego, one of which today bears his name. The geographical importance of these explorations was considerable, and they did not molest the Spanish colonies in any way.

Very different, however, was the expedition commanded by the pilot, Hendrick Brouwer,[4] who was reputed to be a brave man in Holland. He crossed from the Atlantic to the Pacific in 1643 through the Strait of Lemaire, arrived at Chiloé, and from there passed to the continent. He intended to provoke an uprising among the Indians and influence them in his favor. He destroyed the fort

---

[3] Jacob Lemaire was born in Egmont, Holland. With another Dutchman, William Cornelius Schouten, he passed the Strait of May (Lemaire) in 1615 and sighted Cape Horn on January 29, 1616. The two voyagers continued to Batavia where they were seized by representatives of the Dutch East India Company for infringing on the latter's trade monopoly. Lemaire died that year on his way back to Holland. See *La grande encyclopédic,* XXI, 1118; and Barros Arana, *Historia jeneral,* IV, 151-156.

[4] Brouwer discovered a short route to Australia from the Cape of Good Hope, which Dutch commanders thereafter followed, and served as governor-general of the Dutch East Indies for three years after 1632. In the spring of 1643 he visited the coast of Chile and during that year died on the island of Chiloé. He was buried in Valdivia.—Espasa, *Enciclopedia,* IX, 1006. See also Robert Southey, *History of Brazil* (London, 1817-1822), chap. xix.

of Carelmapu and the city of Castro but died shortly after. His companions tried to take possession of Valdivia; but as they did not find any of the Indians willing to aid them and as their situation would have been very difficult, owing to the scarcity of provisions, they gave up the idea of settling there and set sail for the Atlantic, never to return.

Immense was the alarm produced by the coming of Brouwer both in Chile and in Peru. It was believed that Brouwer's fleet carried a large landing force. The viceroy of Peru sent his own son with a powerful war vessel and nearly two thousand fighting men to defend the plaza of Valdivia. When these defenders arrived, the Dutch had already been gone for some time, but nevertheless the son of the viceroy ordered fortifications built near the site of the city and stationed a body of troops there. From that date, 1645, began the direct dependence of Valdivia on the viceroyalty of Peru.

The raids of the corsairs and pirates caused grave consequences in the colony. Although it is easy to understand that three or four foreign vessels did not threaten the rule of the king of Spain, yet their presence produced extraordinary alarm. What was hated more than any other thing in the corsairs and pirates was their religious belief, since it was a crime to treat with "heretics." Bodies of troops were rapidly improvised and armed in any manner whatsoever in order to resist them. The churches opened their doors, calling on the faithful to pray that the enemy might retire as soon as possible from the coast. All tasks were suspended. The governor also suspended the military operations of the war in Arauco and hastened to advise the viceroy of Peru. Commercial navigation between Chile and Peru was suspended, to the consequent detriment of shipowners and traders in merchandise for ordinary consumption. The raids, therefore, caused a complete economic upheaval, both in commerce and in production.

THE GROWTH IN POPULATION; NEW CITIES

Just as the sixteenth century had been the period of Spain's grandeur and dominance in Europe, so the seventeenth was one of decadence, but so harassing a decadence that it seemed more like exhaustion. The expensive and unfortunate wars of Philip II, the expulsion of the Jews carried out previously, and of the Moors effected afterward, in 1609,[5] were the three things that had the most fatal consequences for the agriculture, mining, industry, and commerce of Spain. All these sources of wealth suffered such serious

---

[5] The author refers to the expulsion of the Moriscos in August, 1609, by Philip III. See Henry Charles Lea, *The Moriscos of Spain* (Philadelphia, 1901), p. 315.

shrinkage and such grave disaster that the mass of the Spanish population shortly found themselves without work or sustenance. There was a dreadful economic crisis during the whole century. In the cities, in the towns, and in the country, literally hundreds of thousands of people died from hunger.

In this situation the vessels that came to the colonies were almost literally boarded by whole families anxious to leave Spain in order to free themselves from the general misery. "The Indies," as they said there, were the refuge and salvation of all the abandoned. Although Chile was the farthest distant of those colonies, it too received its contingent of idle persons who came to "seek a livelihood" in its territory. While Spain was drained in this manner, the colonies increased their population at her expense. The military men also contributed to that increase. They came to no colony in greater numbers than to Chile, in order to participate in the wars of Arauco and in the defense of the coast from the corsairs. To these were added the employees and public officials, who generally brought their families along, and a multitude of the religious of the different orders already established in the country.

The mestizo population increased also with great rapidity, and the considerable number of them already living in the cities gradually grew greater. The cities of Rere and Talca date from the end of the seventeenth century and were founded by Governor Marín de Poveda in 1695. At that time, a century and a half after the settlement of the Spaniards in Chile, the European and mestizo population already numbered one hundred thousand persons. Santiago, the capital, had more than twelve thousand.

But the eighteenth century gave the greatest impetus to the development of the European population. Until the end of the previous century almost all the people coming from Spain had come from the several regions of Castile, and to these had been added some Portuguese and French. During the eighteenth century there came also an abundant Biscayan immigration, belonging to the Basque provinces of northern Spain, situated between the Cantabrian Mountains and the sea. Wholly industrious and active, coming from a territory which had much in common with central Chile in topography and climate, they constituted an element that made for rapid progress in the colony and established numerous families who later on became of considerable influence because of their wealth and culture.

Some governors of this century have left their names linked with the founding of many new cities. Such were José Antonio Manso and Domingo Ortiz de Rozas. The miserable, rude life of workers in

the country, the violence of their customs, shown especially in robberies and in an unparalleled number of assassinations, and the difficulty of improving their well-being and culture because of their isolation counseled those governors to establish the workers in organized groups in villages, which would soon become populous communities. Between 1740 and 1745 Manso founded San Felipe and
Copiapó in the north; Melipilla, Rancagua, Curicó, San Fernando,
Cauquenes, and Los Angeles in the south; and he also refounded
Talca a little farther west of the site where Governor Marín de
Poveda had founded it a half century earlier. It was these accom-
plishments that particularly made him worthy of promotion to the
viceregency of Peru and gained for him the honorable title of Conde
de Superunda, which his sovereign conferred upon him. Ortiz de
Rozas added to the towns already founded those of Quirihue, Coel-
emu, and Florida, near Concepción; those of Casa Blanca, Petorca,
and Ligua, near Valparaiso; and another on Juan Fernández in order to put a stop to the coming of corsairs, who had established
the center of their operations on that island.

But these initial measures of progress were not executed without
serious difficulties. In the first place, encomenderos and proprietors
near those villages complained to the king that they were left without peons, because all the laborers preferred to live in cities where
they were given sites for their own dwellings, and so the encomenderos resisted the governor's projects to the uttermost. They believed that their personal interests should be preferred to the well-
being of members of that class who, from being merely their servants, were transferred at little cost into proprietors.

Another obstacle was a severe earthquake which was felt on May
25, 1751, and caused enormous damage throughout the whole colony. This was not the only one that Chile suffered from in the eighteenth century; in 1730 a similar disturbance had caused incalcu-
lable damage in all the cities. That of 1751 was, like the former,
accompanied by tidal waves. All the towns along the coast felt the
force of this catastrophe; Santiago and Chillán also felt it seriously; but this time no city suffered more than Concepción. The
shock of 1730 had entirely destroyed it, and that of 1751 again destroyed it. Ortiz de Rozas had it rebuilt but changed the site. From
the coast where it was located (the present Penco) he transferred
it a little farther in, near the Biobío, where it is today.

He also had to rebuild Chillán, which the floods from the river of
that name, together with the earthquake, had completely wiped out.
Nor did he leave this city in its former location, but transferred it
to the spot which Chillán Viejo occupies today, some distance from

the river which had flooded it. The zealous executive had the misfortune, however, to see several of the cities which he had just established destroyed, among them Juan Fernández, where the great shocks of the earthquake and the tidal wave had wiped out almost the entire island. The king compensated him for these afflictions by granting him the title of Conde de Poblaciones (Count of Settlements). Later, at the end of the century, the most celebrated of the governors or presidents that the colony ever had, Ambrosio O'Higgins, also contributed to the development of urban life in the country by founding new centers. From that time date Santa Rosa de los Andes (Los Andes today), San José de Maipo, Nueva Bilbao (Constitución today), Parral, and Linares.

Thus, when the colonial period ended at the beginning of the nineteenth century, Chile contained thirty or more cities, although because of their poverty the greater part of them hardly deserved the name of village. Santiago, the principal one, did not have more than forty thousand inhabitants. Concepción, following next in importance, had only some five or six thousand. Before the earthquake of 1751, when it occupied the site of the present Penco, its population had risen to more than twenty thousand persons, and the fact that it was the general headquarters of the southern army had given it an exceptional prosperity; but after the earthquake had destroyed it, and it had been transferred to the site which it now occupies, and especially when the wars of Arauco were followed by a prolonged truce, it deteriorated greatly.

In the north, La Serena was the leading city, with a population about similar to that of Concepción. Valparaiso, the commercial port, Valdivia, the military outpost, and Chillán and Talca, each with three or four thousand inhabitants, completed the number of centers that deserved the title of city.

The appearance of such cities was still dreary and monotonous. Along their narrow streets ran streams of dirty water in open ditches. Their buildings were uniformly low and even in their very centers straw huts spoiled their general appearance. Unpainted walls made them still more unattractive. At night darkness and absolute silence reigned in them. There were no street lights; in the doorway of an occasional house a lantern with a wax candle shone until nine or ten o'clock. Persons that had to be abroad at those hours were preceded by a servant who lighted the road with a little street lantern carried in the hand.

In winter such streets were made impassable by mud, and the residents who lived some distance away disappeared with the first rains and were not seen again until spring. Santiago alone succeeded in having some of the streets and sidewalks paved with round stones from the river. Here also a few buildings were important and possessed a certain magnificence: the cathedral, the mint, the custom house (today the tribunal of justice), the consulate (now torn down), and the portals called Sierra Bella on the south side of the Plaza de Armas. In Santiago, moreover, as in the other cities, such buildings as the *cabildo*, the government house, the jail, and the principal church surpassed the others. They were all located around the central plaza, where there were no gardens, only a few trees.

CLASSIFICATION OF THE INHABITANTS

Distributed among the cities or villages and in the country districts from the valley of Copiapó to the island of Chiloé were a half-million inhabitants at the end of the eighteenth century. They occupied the territory at that time controlled by the Spaniards, with the exception of the interior of Araucania, where the native population preserved its independence and its peculiar usages and customs and was estimated at not less than one hundred thousand persons.

Less than two fifths of that half million were of European descent. This part of the population was made up of Spaniards born on the Peninsula (not more than twenty thousand) and of Spaniards born in Chile, called "Creoles" (something like one hundred and fifty thousand). The remaining portion, three fifths at least, was composed of mestizos of native and Spanish blood. This does not signify that the majority of the Creole population did not also have, in varying proportion, some admixture of Indian blood. What most distinguished the Creole from the mestizo, however, was that, while European blood, culture, and customs predominated in the former, in the mestizo the blood, culture, and barbarous customs of his native ancestors predominated.

About twenty thousand slaves, Negroes or mulattoes, and two or three thousand Indians, freed a few years before from the service of the encomiendas, completed the picture of the population. The foreigners settled in the country scarcely numbered a hundred and were mostly French.

The two or three thousand Indians represented, at the beginning of the nineteenth century, the last vestige of a race conquered and reduced to servitude in the middle of the sixteenth century. They were now almost totally exterminated under the lash of their masters in the labor of fields and mines. They were the survivors of a tragedy of three centuries, a tragedy in which a people of superior civilization had brought about the extinction of a conquered people by dint of exploitation and maltreatment.

In 1791, during the governorship of Ambrosio O'Higgins, the king, at his instance, had ordered the complete abolition of the encomiendas and the restitution to the royal patronage of the lands they occupied. Royal decrees to the same intent had been issued several times before, but the governors were neither willing to execute them nor the encomenderos to comply with them. They were too much in need of the subjected Indian—*yanacona* or *mitamae* as they called him—in the work on their lands to free him from servitude. But this time Governor O'Higgins, impressed by the bad treatment accorded to the Indian, resolved, in spite of all resistance brought to bear on him, to force obedience to the royal orders. It was not now so difficult, however, to execute this work of reparation and of justice for the repressed race because there were hardly two or three thousand natives then surviving in encomiendas throughout the whole country. O'Higgins settled these Indians in different villages or new settlements, where he gave them small parcels of land on which they might build their houses and labor freely. Even today, after the lapse of a century and a half, it is not difficult to recognize the survival of the type and their native customs in the population of those places—Pomaire, for example, near Melipilla.

When the Spaniards settled in Chile for the first time, in 1541, it was calculated that the native population was not less than five hundred thousand individuals. At the time of the abolition of the encomiendas—after exactly two and a half centuries—about one hundred thousand of them still kept their independence in the interior of Araucania, and of the rest only some two thousand remained. On the other hand, they were replaced in almost equal number by the mestizo race in which the Indian continued to survive. The ancient *yanacona* was replaced by the *inquilino* on the farms and by the wandering peon in the cities. The condition of either was certainly not so painful as that of their Indian grandfathers, but they had not on that account become much freer or more civilized.

PRODUCTION AND COMMERCE IN THE EIGHTEENTH CENTURY

The Spaniards who arrived in Chile in the sixteenth century always found plentiful means of subsistence and even prospects of wealth. It is clear that an accidental situation of scarcity and suffering had been created in the country during the early years of that century because of the wars of Arauco, but conditions shortly returned to normal and, along with the growth in population, the general wealth also increased.

Apart from the very nature of the territory, two circumstances in that century favored the economic development of the colony: first, the royal aid which supplied circulating capital to Chilean encomenderos and merchants, to the extent of three hundred thousand Castilian pesos annually; and second, the creation of the permanent army for the wars of the Arauco, which allowed labor to go on normally in the assurance that it would not be interrupted for levies or enforced conscription.

Chile had begun by being a cattle-raising country and it kept on being so. The growth in cattle raising and the introduction made at the beginning of the century of large herds from Argentina through the gaps of the cordillera lowered the price of meat. Although this importation was prohibited, it was, nevertheless, carried on clandestinely. The price of cattle was reduced from two to one and a half pesos per head; horses also were sold at much lower prices than in the previous century; and the breeding of mules, which greatly developed in this same period, now permitted their exportation to Peru. Sheep and hogs maintained their prices (a real a head) because consumption increased proportionately, in spite of their great abundance. The culture of bees was still more prosperous. All the species known today were brought from Spain and propagated so rapidly that they soon had no value.

Agricultural production also increased equally with cattle raising. The potato was grown abundantly in this century, as were also fruit trees—the apple south of the Biobío, the peach, olive, and almond north of Santiago; but no product was cultivated in greater quantity than wheat, especially in the last years of the seventeenth century. An earthquake that occurred in Lima in 1687 demolished that city and laid waste the fields in its environs. Then the exportation of Chilean wheat to Peru increased extraordinarily. Its value tripled in the country itself (from two to six pesos a fanega), and in Peru the price fluctuated between twenty and thirty pesos; but this sudden jump, which stimulated cultivation so much, lasted only a few years.

Mining did not keep up with those two factors of wealth in their progress. Gold was scarce and the methods of extraction too imperfect to make the mines pay; moreover, competent operators were lacking. Silver, which was found in some mines, also gave small promising returns. Copper was the only metal produced on a more considerable scale because of its abundance and easy exploitation. It was found in almost all the hills from Aconcagua to Copiapó; and, as it was used in Peru and Spain for the manufacture of cannon, bells, and other articles, its extraction for export to those countries created an excellent business.

Neither did the small colonial industries remain stationary in the seventeenth century. Ironworks and spinning mills multiplied. The carpets and blankets of Chillán and Concepción became famous. The carpenter shops of the Jesuits, in which furniture was made, also became well known, as did their dockyards, in which large barges were already being constructed. In Santiago there were silversmiths who made rough silver table service and jewelry. The clay pottery industry increased greatly throughout the whole country. If to these occupations were added the other industries immediately derived from cattle raising and agriculture, like tanning and milling, one will have a manufacturing movement, routine in character, but in every case progressive.

Commerce developed in spite of the obstacles which hindered it greatly. Besides wheat and copper, Peru received from Chile dried fruits, wines, and, as before, grease, leather, dried beef, flour, and tallow; and in return it sent weapons, articles of clothing, rice, and especially sugar. Of course this importation was slight because of the excessive price that European articles attained in Chile. These were the times when a silk dress or a Spanish cloak was handed down from generation to generation, from father to great-grandson, like a house or a farm. The value of all exports fluctuated around half a million pesos annually.

An improvement in the means of transportation corresponded to this mercantile development. Broad roads were opened and carts introduced, all of wood and pulled by oxen. There was also improvement in the postal service which had previously been carried on, from time to time, between cities of the north and the south when military communications had to be made, and nothing more. The same official that carried the correspondence of the government now carried the private mail. Something of the same sort occurred with maritime correspondence, which went to Peru and from there to Spain by way of Panama in merchant vessels, and which came from those countries after having made the same voyage.

THE ECONOMIC MOVEMENTS OF THE EIGHTEENTH CENTURY

During the eighteenth century commercial movements and all means of production became much more active. New circumstances in this period favored their development. In 1700 Charles II died. He was the last representative of the dynasty called the House of Austria. At once the dynasty of the House of Bourbon entered upon the government of Spain in the person of the French prince, Philip V—the name he was known by as king. This change in dynasty was of considerable advantage to Spain and to the colonies as well, in all forms of activity; and even the armed conflict to which it gave rise did not harm the latter. The ascension of the French prince to the Spanish throne really occasioned the war in which France and Spain were united against those European powers which did not accept the family alliance between those two countries because they considered that it would tremendously increase the prestige of France. Among those powers was England, whose government sent fleets and corsairs, as in the sixteenth century, to commit depredations on the commerce of the Spanish colonies.

Spain lacked even a halfway powerful fleet and had to trust the defense of its dominions to the French, who were stronger on the sea. But the French sailors, on coming to the colonies, took advantage of the occasion to establish a commercial interchange between the industrial producers of their country and the American merchants. This traffic was prohibited, but that did not hinder its being carried on clandestinely. Their merchandise, exempt from payment of custom duties and acquired in France at cheap prices, could be sold at a great profit in the American colonies at a much less cost than that which came from the Peninsula; the trade under those conditions was certain. It was also convenient for the colonists, because it permitted them to acquire European merchandise 50 per cent cheaper through legal channels and to sell some of their own products at a much greater price.

Along the extensive and unguarded coast of Chile this contraband commerce was easily carried on from the beginning because it was looked upon with favor by the people of the greatest social influence and, moreover, because there were governors who, up to that time, either aided it directly or ignored it. The regime of isolation to which the colony was subjected in matters of trade was, then, destroyed by contraband and, with the introduction of this new element into colonial life, commerce tended to free itself. The kings of Spain did not fail to observe this; but, not daring to bring about a complete modification in that regime, they introduced a reform which somewhat overcame its inconveniences.

Such a measure was the establishment of registered ships to carry on the mercantile traffic which had been previously carried on in the so-called "galleons." This sea commerce had its center in Cádiz—a much more suitable port than Seville, from which its privilege was transferred—and consisted in granting permission to certain outfitters of ships to exercise at their own risk and in designated colonial ports the interchange of merchandise of Spain with the products of America. As they had to "register" the permission granted for their trading with the authorities in these ports, in order that they might be permitted to land their goods, commerce carried on in this way took the name given above. The Pacific was opened to vessels which carried on this traffic by the route around Cape Horn; and the ports of Concepción and Valparaiso regarded the visits of these ships as important events. In this way direct commerce was established between Chile and Spain and the same was true of Peru. Commerce did not now have to cross the isthmus and go to the fairs of Portobelo, which now had no reason for existence and were closed. Moreover, at this time commerce developed with Buenos Aires across the great cordillera and was linked to that of Paraguay and Uruguay. Chile sent wines, flour, dried fruits, tallow, and copper ore, and in return received principally cattle, yerba maté, and some European articles.

In this way, during the first half of the eighteenth century, Chile added three new markets to the market of Peru, the only one opened up to that time: France, by means of the contraband trade; Spain, by means of the registered ships; and Buenos Aires, through the cordillera. The commercial impetus that these markets supplied rapidly outran all Chile's productive activities. A half century afterward, and up to the beginning of the nineteenth century, the contraband practices which had opened commerce with France to the colonies also opened to them commerce with England and the United States. The last-named had declared its independence in 1776. Ships of both countries cruised all along the coast of South America laden with goods manufactured by their factories, in order to exchange them as a contraband for the natural products of the colonies. They frequently traded on the Chilean coast where they were tolerated by the authorities and were very well received by merchants, farmers, and miners.

The court of Spain, meanwhile, impressed by the necessity of giving greater economic expansion to the colonies, conceived the idea of furthering direct commerce between them and the Peninsula, but always retained a complete monopoly of the traffic. This was the end that inspired the "Ordinance of Free Commerce between Spain and the Indies" promulgated by Charles III, in 1778. It qualified for this commerce several ports of Spain—not Cádiz alone, as previously—and also several in America, both on the Atlantic Ocean and on the Pacific. In Chile Valdivia, Talcahuano, Valparaiso, and Coquimbo could now receive vessels direct from Spain under normal conditions and were not, as before, subject to the irregularity with which the registered ships arrived. So-called "free commerce" was not free, however, except in respect to Spain; the rest of Europe always remained shut out from mercantile relations with America; but the contraband trade carried on by the French and the English and, shortly, by the North Americans continued as before to break in on the isolation of the colonies.

INSTITUTIONS FOR THE REGULATION OF TRADE

Other reforms of an economic nature were also carried into effect in Chile from the middle of the eighteenth century. One of these was the creation of the mint for coining gold and silver and increasing the circulating medium within the country. The first pesos and coins were made there in 1750, and from then on this coinage began to facilitate the interchange of Chilean products and to give greater activity to internal commerce. At first this mint was administered by a private concessionaire, but in 1772 the king changed it to a public service in charge of a high official named by himself, who bore the title of Superintendent of the Mint. The first to serve in this office of confidence and honor was Mateo del Toro Zambrano, Conde de la Conquista (Count of the Conquest), a Creole of extensive social ties who was later to play a most significant public rôle.

Another reform of the middle of the eighteenth century relating to commerce was the establishment of the monopoly on tobacco in 1753. According to this ordinance only the government could sell this article. Since the preceding century other articles had already been monopolized by royal order, such as playing cards and dice, but these commercial restrictions were not planned to limit consumption but to procure income for the royal treasury. In this respect they were financial measures rather than institutions of an economic character.

One of the fiscal reforms of this period had much more commercial importance—the reorganization of the customs (*aduana*). Until then the collection of the duty on exports and imports was made by private persons to whom the right of collection was auctioned at a fixed price. As can be seen, such a system lent itself to abuses. By royal order this now became a public service, and a public functionary, the administrator of customs, was appointed to collect that impost for the king's treasury. As the excise tax (*alcabala*) was subjected to a similar system, a like reform was introduced into it, and it was put into the hands of the same official.

Another of those reforms was the incorporation of the postal service with the crown in 1772. This service had formerly been carried on under the most deplorable conditions, entrusted as it was to private parties eager to get as much profit as possible from it. The irregularity with which correspondence was transported between Spain and the colonies was the principal drawback. The king appointed a general administrator of post offices, who dispatched the mail every two months from Spain to Buenos Aires and Chile in a special "packet boat," which on its return carried mail from those colonies. Later this trip was made every month. One can readily understand the great benefit this measure represented, especially for commerce. The internal postal service of Chile, however, was not regulated until later by the establishment of a monthly mail between Santiago and Concepción, and another each week between Santiago and Valparaiso. The Commercial Tribunal (*Tribunal del consulado*) was also established in Santiago in 1795. Its principal object was not only to ascertain and render judgments in commercial matters, but to promote improvements in this branch of economic activities, as in industry, agriculture, and mining.

In this way, by means of the administrative reforms indicated above and through the initiative of persons interested in the exploitation of the natural wealth of the country, the colony found itself at the beginning of the nineteenth century in an economic situation of relative prosperity as compared with the backwardness of former times.

COLONIAL ECONOMY AT THE BEGINNING OF THE NINETEENTH CENTURY

In agriculture, wheat continued to be the chief product and was cultivated throughout most of the territory. Next came barley, maize, kidney beans, and lentils; then potatoes, peas, and fruit trees. The olive and grape were among the cultivated products. Previously hemp had constituted an appreciable source of wealth, but at the beginning of the nineteenth century its cultivation had been almost abandoned. These activities, however, developed only to a limited extent. Flour, wheat, grain, dried fruits, grapes, and brandy were the only articles of export in this branch of trade; the rest hardly sufficed for ordinary consumption. The preparation of timber in the southern zone and of charcoal in the central zone was already very important.

The excellent fields for pasturage with which the country was provided now fed great herds of cattle and droves of horses and mules. Sheep, goats, hogs, and fowls were no less numerous. Cheese, tallow, hemp, dried beef, wool, and cured hides were articles of export. Fishing along the coast came to be a profitable industry, which even left a surplus for some export of dried fish as a sort of preserve.

The colonists continued to pay special attention to mining, and their returns therefrom were usually good. Even when imperfect methods were used in the extraction of gold and silver, and when the scarcity of capital and the difficulty of communication were weighty drawbacks, appreciable profits were obtained; but copper continued to constitute the most precious source of wealth and, although the price was low, it was not sent in large quantities to Peru and Spain or given in payment to smugglers.

The manufacturing industry had improved very little. It was occupied exclusively with the ordinary transformation of the products of agriculture and stock raising. Without factories adapted to the purpose, and without technical preparation for running them, such industries as flour mills and tanneries were still rather primitive. Looms for fabrics of rough flannel, with which the countryman clothed himself, and for blankets and carpets had not advanced much, and an experimental textile mill with European machinery, which was erected in Santiago, never attained a large output. The native clay pottery industry had greatly developed and had reached a moderate degree of perfection. The large earthen jars (*tinajas*) in which wines were kept in the warehouses, and which are still to be seen in some old vineyards, formed the most striking exhibit of this craft. Another industry was shipbuilding, which at some points on the coast, as at the mouth of the Maule, was developed to a high degree.

The volume of exterior commerce had become considerable. The mercantile lines of Chile during that period were still the same four as at the middle of the eighteenth century: with Peru on the Pacific; with Buenos Aires over the cordillera; with Spain through the Strait of Magellan; and the contraband trade through this same strait and around Cape Horn which linked the country with markets of the United States, France, and England. The total amount of interchange arose to an annual value of five million pesos.

The market with Spain was the most favored: about two fifths of the commercial movement belonged to it. Chile sent principally coined gold and silver and copper bars, and in return received silk and cotton goods, linen thread, porcelain, articles of hardware, a few agricultural implements, paper, and some printed books which related especially to law and religious matters. Peru exported sugar, cocoa, tobacco, idigo, and ordinary wool and cotton cloth to Chile. In exchange for these articles were sent tallow, dried beef, salted fish, dried fruits, and large quantities of wine, copper, and wheat. By way of Buenos Aires came yerba maté from Paraguay, soap from Mendoza, wool blankets and carpets, herds of cattle, and many European articles; and in return Buenos Aires received cured hides, copper bars, gold coin, and wines; but this interchange did not represent more than an amount equivalent to half a million pesos, while the trade carried on with Peru reached a million and a half annually. The contraband trade consisted of all articles of European origin and the greater part of the national products. It was evident that European articles had diminished in value, but those of the country had not advanced because there was always an abundance of them.

This commercial movement was hampered by many disadvantages. If the establishment of registered ships and the ordinance of free commerce had favored it during the eighteenth century, these factors did not, however, satisfy the aspirations of the colonists. The obligation to buy European articles exclusively in Spain, whence only five or six vessels came every year; the risks to which contraband trade was exposed, in order to provide the same articles at less cost; the difficulties of transit over the cordillera in winter; and the abuses committed by the shipowners of Callao, whose ships were the only ones that carried on traffic between Peru and Chile— all these represented impediments very prejudicial to commerce. All intelligent Chileans understood it well, and the conviction was born in them that there was only one way in which the country could fully develop its wealth—freedom of trade of a sort that could be practiced with any nation of the world.

URBAN PROGRESS; ROADS AND FORTIFICATIONS

Local progress of recognized value corresponded during this period to the gradual increase in wealth and population. It would not have been possible to make this progress without the economic advancement of the territory, which already was evident in the last century of the colonial era. The communities which were being established in the country from the sixteenth century on did not gain appreciably in construction, living conditions, and communication until the eighteenth century. Special attention was bestowed on Santiago, the capital, as may be easily understood. Almost completely destroyed by the earthquake of May 13, 1647, it was rebuilt little by little, with the restoration of all its public buildings, from the cathedral to the jail. We have already mentioned those which were regarded as the more valuable.

To the calamities caused by the earthquakes, there was added, a century afterward, the floods of the Mapocho, so frequent that every year the residents of this capital were liable to see their houses destroyed beneath the debris of the river. That of 1748 was particularly severe. The dikes, as the protective walls were called, were made and remade almost every year, but the river did not respect them. Each governor, then, had to do this work more than once. The same thing happened with the bridge of masonry previously built. The flood of 1748 carried it away completely and left only its lower piling. Many years were to pass before it could be rebuilt in a permanent form. Only after the great flood of 1783 did Governor O'Higgins order its complete reconstruction.

Moreover, the city had been expanding from the beginning of the eighteenth century. Its northern suburb (La Chimba) was rapidly populated and its suburb east of Santa Lucía (Providencia) was built up at the same time; but a feeling of insecurity still continued among its inhabitants. Assaults by armed bands and robberies—often the result of drunken carousals in the outskirts—grew with alarming persistency. The surrounding country was no better. The most daring banditry prevailed everywhere. One of the presidents of the middle eighteenth century, Manuel de Amat y Junient, was famous for the determination and energy displayed during his government in repressing such great disorders. His most notable work was the creation of the first police organization for Santiago and all Chile in 1758. It was composed of a squadron of fifty men, which had quarters behind the governor's palace, was paid with funds from the royal treasury, and was called the Queen's Dragoons.

Dating from 1756, Santiago also had a college for higher studies, which was called the University of San Felipe,[6] in honor of King Philip V, who had authorized its erection. It opened its classes two years afterward and had its own building, partly paid for by the residents, where the municipal theater stands today. The construction of the Maipo Canal, which put the rich land south of the city under cultivation, was a century-long task. Constructed by sections, it was begun about the middle of the eighteenth century, in 1743, and was concluded only during the following century.

The opening of broad, safe wagon roads was another task of the eighteenth century. The road uniting Santiago with Valparaiso was finished only in the closing years of the century during the government of Ambrosio O'Higgins, as was also the road over the cordillera through Uspallata Pass, which united Santiago with Mendoza and permitted commerce with Buenos Aires. Furthermore,

---

[6] The detailed story of the beginnings of this university is given by Medina in *La instrucción pública en Chile,* Vol. I, chap. xiv; the documents in *ibid.,* II, 244-261. See also Barros Arana, *Historia jeneral,* VI, 167-170, 197-198; VII, 493-499.

the road to Chillán and Concepción was improved, and in the south Valdivia and Osorno were also connected by not very ample, but easily traveled, routes.

Valparaiso had some fortifications, and storage warehouses for the shipping of goods were constructed and regulated in the port. Coquimbo, the port of La Serena, was also fortified, and a house built for its *cabildo* and jail. Valdivia, which by the middle of the seventeenth century had been fortified at its port, Corral, and had passed under the direct control of the viceroy of Peru, was in 1787 again placed under the authority of the captain general of Chile, and at the same time the island of Chiloé became a dependency of Peru. The chief of its fortifications, however, and also later the military chief of Valparaiso, continued to receive royal appointment and to communicate directly with the king or the viceroy of Peru. But, in their civic functions, their administration and public works were in charge of the presidents of Chile. Concepción, as previously stated, had been rebuilt on the banks of the Biobío after the earthquake of 1751, and since then Talcahuano had become its port. It took a long time for it to recover its ancient rank as the most important city of the south, but its local progress at the end of the eighteenth century was considerable. In all parts, then, the increase in population and wealth contributed to give these old villages the appearance of cities where conditions of life resembled those prevailing in like communities of Spain.

CHAPTER VI

COLONIAL GOVERNMENT AND SOCIETY

THE GOVERNORS and captains general of the colony were commonly called presidents because, from the time the royal *audiencia* was established in Santiago in 1609, they presided over this supreme tribunal of the country. Their duties varied little from the sixteenth to the nineteenth century; on the other hand, their moral authority and their prestige were subject to many fluctuations in that long space of time, because of the attendant circumstances by which their actions had to be governed, as well as the personality, not less distinct, of each one.

The governors of the sixteenth century were almost all military men and had no time for anything but the war in Arauco. Those of the seventeenth century were of a different type; some were military men and some were civilians, but all were equally interested in making a fortune in office at the expense of colonists and Indians. They were representatives of a weak, incapable government, managed in Spain by unworthy favorites, and of a society such as that of the Spaniards of that period—a society much exhausted by wretchedness and discouragement.

There were many types among these colonial presidents of the seventeenth century who were without refinement and were morose or greedy, caring only for their personal enrichment; but we shall mention only three. The first governor of this kind who arrived in the middle of the seventeenth century was Antonio de Acuña y Cabrera. Old, infirm, and lacking in character, he believed his government might prove a copious fount of wealth for himself and his brothers-in-law, two officials named Salazar. In spite of the fact that the country was in profound peace, this pair, who saw a means of making a fortune in war, decided to undertake a campaign against the Indians south of the Bueno River. They planned to lead this in person in order to punish the savages for having murdered some shipwrecked sailors from a Spanish vessel. The campaign was actually made and proved a military disaster of greater proportions than had up to that time ever been experienced in Chile. Half the army was lost in crossing the Bueno River, because the pontoon bridge constructed for the crossing broke while the soldiers were passing over it and no less than a hundred men perished. Some were drowned, while others fell into the hands of the Indians.

A general insurrection of Araucania was the first fruit of these blunders. As one of the Salazars, who was in the fort of Nacimiento, believed himself powerless to resist, with nearly two hundred and fifty soldiers at his disposal, he started hurriedly toward Concepción and while crossing the Biobío in 1655 he and his men fell into the power of the Indians, who massacred all of them. The enterprise advised and directed by the Salazar brothers thus cost three hundred and fifty lives. Meanwhile, the governor, Acuña y Cabrera, awaited in Concepción the result of their operations. When the people of the town learned of the disaster, they arose with cries of "Long live the king!" "Death to the bad governor!" Acuña y Cabrera was forthwith deposed.

Other governors, more prudent than he, succeeded him for some years and tried to put down the Araucanian uprising; but it was not long before a new adventurer, one more inept and more shameless, took charge of the colony. This was Francisco de Meneses, who had been a morose, turbulent military man. His subalterns nicknamed him Barrabas. He began his administration by quarreling bitterly with Bishop Diego de Humanzoro[1] because the latter had not received him at his arrival with that formality of etiquette which, in his opinion, his high position merited. Soon he was engaged in very noisy persecutions of his predecessor and the religious orders that had favored the latter. He later married secretly and without permission; he publicly established business undertakings of his own; he monopolized the sale of tallow, the most important article exported to Peru; he demanded that very valuable presents should be made to him, which he paid back in his own way; he converted into a source of wealth for his own use the confirmation and renewal of concessions of encomiendas; he sold military posts and some civilian positions and made those promoted pay him in gold; he took in charge the provisioning of the army, in order to make a profit from it; he imposed a heavy tax on vessels carrying on commerce between Valparaiso and Callao before allowing them to leave port, with the exception of those carrying his own goods. In short, there was no

---

[1] Fray Diego de Humanzoro was a native of Guipúzcoa, where he assumed the Franciscan habit. He was a man of some prestige at court, held important posts of his order in Peru, and took charge of the diocese of Santiago in 1661. In both provinces he insisted tenaciously on the prerogatives of his office and had already passed through serious disputes with the *audiencia* at Santiago before beginning his more heated quarrels with Meneses. See Barros Arana, *Historia jeneral*, V, 55.

public service that he did not reduce to his own personal profit, and all this openly and without the least prudence. His abuses and acts of violence against private persons knew no limit. The colonists in the greatest alarm wrote to the viceroy and to the court urgently begging that they be freed from the tyrant. He intercepted the correspondence and persecuted its authors. Finally the colonists succeeded in getting a hearing at the court and Meneses was dismissed in 1668.

Such unheard-of excesses taught the Spanish government that it was not possible to keep on entrusting the colony to this class of adventurers. In 1670 Juan Henríquez came to Chile in the capacity of governor. His honorable antecedents served as a guarantee of prudence, and his official labors in behalf of the material progress and security of the colony met with great approbation during his term of office. Among the important public works in which he definitely participated were the construction of the first dikes in the Mapocho, now confined to its actual bed, to protect the city of Santiago from its overflow; the erection of the masonry bridge over the same river, to assure the introduction of the fruits and foodstuffs with which the surrounding farms supplied the inhabitants; and the bringing in of a supply of clear water from the slopes of the cordillera to the Plaza de Armas of Santiago. He also coöperated efficiently in the building of new churches and convents. In another field of activity he fortified Valparaiso and Concepción and created a little "military park" in Santiago, in which numerous arms were collected.

After governing for twelve years, Henríquez was relieved from command. He did not leave behind favorable memories, in spite of his initiatory activities. He had lived in permanent conflict with the royal *audiencia*—the fiscal tribunal of the governors although composed at times of individuals of the same class as the latter. Moreover, what was worse, Henríquez had performed many acts of doubtful honesty. The following is particularly recalled and is only one of many of the same kind. In the frequent campaigns or incursions into Arauco, he took some eight hundred Indians prisoner; and these he later sold as slaves to several agricultural encomenderos, the buyers paying for them at the rate he himself set—five hundred fanegas of wheat per Indian, each fanega being valued at fifty centavos only. In this way he gathered four hundred thousand fanegas of wheat, all of which he sold to the contractors of his own army at two pesos per fanega, and was paid from the royal treasury. Thus he gained eight hundred thousand pesos.

The administration of justice also had been so completely relaxed that it depended only on the selfish caprice of members of the *audiencia* or other subordinate officials. The slow procedure and contradictory laws ordinarily made the exercise of private right a fiction. Among the multitude of cases which show the state of affairs, one is worth mentioning. There lived in Chile during the first half of the seventeenth century a very rich family called Lisperguer,[2] related to all the best families of the period. Among its members were some judges of the *audiencia*. A woman of this family, Catalina de los Ríos, committed so many murders that she never could keep count of them, and yet she always remained unpunished. When old and ill she was imprisoned for trial and the heaviest penalty imposed on her was the payment of an indemnity to the poor victims of her perfidy, but the payment was not to be effective until after she died. Nevertheless, the vulgar nickname of "La Quintrala" by which she was called is still a hateful and legendary memory of a vampirish monster whose crimes neither moved greatly the society of which she formed a part nor the judiciary called upon to restrain her.

In order to systematize the labyrinth of legislation which prevailed in America, the Spanish government published in 1681 *Recopilación de las leyes de los reinos de Indias* (Compilation of the Laws of the Indies),[3] which complicated that labyrinth even more, for it was so badly made that many of its provisions were contradictory; and, as no method was observed in its arrangement, it was exceedingly difficult to find the legal provisions applicable to a given case. Its best regulations were devoted to the protection and defense of the subjected Indians, but were never carried out.

From the beginning of the eighteenth century, the administrative personnel of the colony improved in quality as it also did in Spain. The new Bourbon dynasty, initiated by Philip V, in the Peninsula in 1700, was surrounded by coworkers of more intelligence and greater ability in the exercise of authority. In Chile nearly all the presidents of that century were respectable and industrious men

---

[2] The founder of the Lisperguer family in Chile came to that colony from Worms in 1557 with Don García Hurtado de Mendoza. Barros Arana (*ibid.*, III, 400-1, n. 10) characterizes as doubtful some of the accusations against the earlier members of this family, although acknowledging the impunity with which many of them flouted the laws and the authorities. For reference to "La Quintrala," see *ibid.*, IV, 236. See also Catalina de los Ríos, biographical notes, *infra*.

[3] The first edition of this great work, after earlier partial attempts at codification, appeared at Madrid in three volumes in 1680 under this title. The fifth edition, in four volumes, was issued by the Spanish government in 1841, but a later private edition has the approval of the government. See Espasa, *Enciclopedia*, XLIX, 1223, 1224.

who always deserved not only the royal confidence, but also consideration from those they governed. Several of them—such as José de Manso (Conde de Superunda), Manuel de Amat y Junient, and Ambrosio O'Higgins (Marqués de Vallenar)—well merited their elevation to the office of viceroy of Peru. Taking advantage of the relative peace enjoyed by the colony during that period, they founded cities, undertook to execute important public works, promoted local improvements of no little significance, and carried out with skill and honesty the administrative and economic reforms ordered by the royal court.

During the last quarter of the eighteenth century under the reign of Charles III the boundaries of the colony were modified. On the creation of the viceroyalty of La Plata in 1776, there was incorporated with it the province of Cuyo, which had belonged to Chile from the time of the conquest. This province, like Tucumán, which had been incorporated two centuries before into the viceroyalty of Peru, was settled by order of the governors of Chile but maintained a separate existence almost completely foreign, indeed, to that of Chile. The mountain gaps of the Andes, which thus separated it, remained impassable for several months a year; but commercially and socially the cities of Mendoza, San Juan, and San Luis kept in touch with Santiago.

In completing this change years later, in 1787, the archipelago of Chiloé passed under the charge of the Peruvian viceroyalty, and Valdivia was reincorporated with the government of Chile. At that same date, and under the presidency of Ambrosio de Benavides, the first territorial division of the colony was effected, which consisted in the establishment of two divisions (*intendencias*)—that of Concepción, which extended from the Maule to the Araucanian border; and that of Santiago, which extended from Copiapó to the Maule.[4] It was then decided that the intendant of Santiago should also be the governor of the colony, while the intendant of Concepción should be a special official, subordinate to the other but appointed directly by the king. Thus the first intendant of Santiago was the

---

[4] The creation of the viceroyalty of La Plata in 1776 afforded opportunity for reforms in colonial administration, which were incorporated in the Ordenanza de intendentes. The system under this ordinance was gradually extended to the other Spanish colonies, with some modifications. By decree it was to apply to Chile in 1784 and was actually introduced in 1787, but it was modified in 1802. See Vicente Fidel López, *Historia de la república argentina, su origen, su revolución, y su desarrollo político* (10 vols. New ed. Buenos Aires, 1913), Vol. I, chap. xxi; Bernard Moses, *Spain's Declining Power in South America, 1730–1806* (Berkeley, 1919), p. 246; Barros Arana, *Historia jeneral*, VI, 457-460.

governor himself, Ambrosio de Benavides; as for Concepción, the one favored with the nomination was the Irishman, Ambrosio O'Higgins.

Conjointly with this action each *intendencia* was also divided into departments (*partidos*), as we would say today. There were eight for Concepción and fourteen for Santiago—a total of twenty-two. At the head of each was placed a subdelegate, an official who filled the place of the old corregidor, this office being abolished. By these reforms the colonial administration was regulated as much as possible.

Presidents and governors now attained their greatest authority. Chiefs of the army, chiefs of the highest tribunal of justice, vice-patrons of ecclesiastical dignitaries and of the university and other institutions of learning—they became powerful officials. Moreover they enjoyed a good salary—ten thousand pesos a year. The governor and the intendant of Santiago as well as the intendant of Concepción had an advisory counselor (*asesor letrado*) or lawyer, whom they consulted when making their decisions and settling lawsuits in which they still took part as judges. The "judgments of *residencia*," to which they were subject, were now merely forms, in view of the integrity with which almost all of them acted.

From the beginning of their administration they were surrounded with all the prestige possible to such a degree that one of the best attended and most solemn public colonial holidays in the capital and in the most populous cities was the reception of the governor. The governor, on coming to take over the command, made his entrance into Santiago with great pomp. He was introduced into the city by a delegation of the *cabildo* that had gone to meet him in Valparaiso or Concepción or Los Andes, according to the way he journeyed. He and his family, in government coaches, accompanied by the members of the *cabildo* and the members of the *audiencia* and followed by the other public functionaries and distinguished persons on horseback and in carriages, entered the Plaza de Armas by way of the Street of the King to the chiming of bells, and between the double file formed by the people. Each instant could be heard cries of "Vivael rey!" "Viva el señor gobernador!" Once in the palace there was a banquet lasting three days. It was customary also for the governor to have a theatrical performance presented at the palace by improvised actors. Shows and fireworks were also given for the public. Afterward came the visits, called *besamanos* (the kissing of hands), of prominent persons and the special receptions in the *cabildo*, in the *audiencia*, and in the university. During the reception offered by this last body, one of the doctors read the discourse in praise of the governor, whom he extolled in most flattering verse.

THE ADMINISTRATION OF THE LAST COLONIAL PRESIDENTS

None of the colonial presidents better represented Spain in Chile than Ambrosio O'Higgins, whose eight-year term of office (1788-1796) was the most active and fruitful of the eighteenth century. Irish by birth, O'Higgins enlisted in the Spanish service and came to Chile as engineer of fortifications. As a reward for his work, he received promotion after promotion; he was colonel of militia, then intendant of Concepción, president of the colony, and finally viceroy of Peru and Marqués de Vallenar, a title with which his sovereign ennobled him.

With his name have been linked public works of great benefit for that time, such as the wagon road from Santiago to Valparaiso, the road to Argentina through Uspallata Pass, the reconstruction of the "dikes" of the Mapocho, and other projects; and, apart from the founding and refounding of numerous cities, such significant reforms as the abolition of the encomiendas of Indians and the creation of the Commercial Tribunal (*tribunal del consulado*). There are not, however, many who can compare with him. The last of these colonial presidents was Brigadier Francisco García Carrasco, a coarse, obscure military man under whose administration began the struggle for emancipation (1808-1810).

But if, in general, the quality of colonial governors had notably improved during the last years of Spanish rule, the same could not be said for the administration of justice, which had scarcely acquired a more serious status than formerly. Its ancient complexity still persisted, and lawsuits lasted ten, twenty, and even a hundred years. The alcaldes and subdelegates of each locality always had judicial functions. The Commercial Tribunal heard commercial suits; the Tribunal of Mining (*tribunal de minería*), recently created, passed judgment on matters indicated by its name, both with more rapid procedure. The president also used to hear petty cases, such as blows received in a fight, or bad deportment on the part of a son of some prominent family.

The "ecclesiastical tribunals," "military tribunals," and the "judges of water and forests" also continued to try cases involving their special jurisdictions; but the superior tribunal of justice was still as it had been for the past two centuries, the royal *audiencia*, composed of a "regent," four judges (*oidores*), and two attorneys (*fiscales*).

The strength of these officials lay in the permanent army, which amounted to about fifteen hundred men, distributed among the three branches of the infantry, cavalry, and artillery. Their principal cantonments were Valdivia and Concepción. In spite of being well disciplined and well equipped, they were not sufficient for the security of the inhabitants of the country. Almost all the cities that did not have the services of urban police would have remained completely unguarded if they had depended only on the army. But this lack was supplied by the militia (or national guard) which was organized upon a social basis during the last third of the eighteenth century. At the beginning of the nineteenth century it comprised some sixteen thousand men. All males able to bear arms had to take part in it and were instructed by officials of the regular army, principally on Sundays. When, in case of danger, they were called into service and went into quarters, they received a small compensation.

The officers of the militia were composed exclusively of young Creoles who were enthusiastic both about their uniform and their rank. The rank and file of the militia, as well as of the regular army, was composed entirely of Chilean mestizos, no less enthusiastic for military service than their officers. Although the pay of all was very low (a soldier received eight to twelve pesos a month according to his branch of service), the expenditure that the armed force necessitated exceeded 250,000 pesos, an equivalent of two fifths the total receipts of the colony. Because of this expenditure, it had no navy.

In reality, the public revenues scarcely reached 600,000 pesos a year, and the monopoly on tobacco, the *alcabala* and *almojarifazgo* or customs duty were the ones that brought in the most returns; but the revenue just about equaled the budget of all administrative services. In this way Chile, which had always cost more than it produced in taxes, at the end of the colonial period had come to be self-supporting.

Local administration, entrusted to the *cabildos*, had gained very little in efficiency. Those corporations, the only ones in which Chileans could acquire representation, had experienced many changes in their organization since they had been established at the founding of the first cities of Chile. They had extensive and varied duties which made them powerful; but the court, seeing a menace in their popular origin and action, had little by little restricted their functions. Early in their history it had taken from them the political power of designating the person who was to exercise the functions ad interim of the colonial governor; and instead of the election of residents who were to succeed them in their position, which the *regidores* held each year, it decided that membership in the *cabildo* should be perpetual and should be sold at public auction. The minimum price fixed at first for what was called the *regidor's* "emblem of authority" (vara), a cane with tassels, was three thousand pesos; but few were disposed to pay that sum in order to have the pleasure of occupying a seat in the hall of the *cabildo*, and as a result several places were left vacant. In the middle of the eighteenth century, when that sum was lowered to three hundred pesos, the *cabildos* were filled. The number of members varied according to the importance of the city, that of Santiago being composed, during its last years, of twelve *regidores*, who, furthermore, annually elected two alcaldes. An attorney (*procurador*) and a secretary, as before, formed part of the corporation.

Although the popular origin of the *cabildos* had disappeared, since any person could become a member by paying the auction price, they had, however, one especially important feature. They were composed, ordinarily, of men who loved their country—of Creoles who had been born in it—and they always tried to represent the aspirations of their fellow countrymen. When the idea of independence was spread abroad, it was these *cabildos* that best embodied it and defended it until they made it triumph.

THE CHURCH AND THE CLERGY

The profound religious spirit of the first conquerors of Chile lasted through the whole colonial period and always formed the basis of individual conduct in society. The importance of the clergy and the veneration they enjoyed among the faithful had, nevertheless, decreased somewhat. After the opening of the University of San Felipe, the monopoly in learning which they had held until then commenced to decline and a greater knowledge came to be the civic inheritance of many people. On the other hand the increase of wealth made study easier for some and they very soon realized that they could be taught without the necessity of wearing a habit. Furthermore, the expulsion of the Jesuits[5] and the disrespectful attitude toward religion and the clergy in the second half of the eighteenth century, of which King Charles III had given so many proofs, showed that it was not the priests who shaped the policy of the government. But if, in the judgment of some persons, the clergy

---

[5] See *ibid.*, chap. xi; Moses, *op. cit.*, pp. 131-141. See also Herbert Ingram Priestley, *José de Gálvez, Visitor-General of New Spain, 1765-1771* (Berkeley, 1916), pp. 211-233, for an account of the contemporary expulsion of the Jesuits from Mexico.

had lost a little of its early influence, it had, in exchange, gained generally in morality and culture, and this should have made it still more respected.

The most extreme act against the Church and the clergy during the colonial period was the expulsion of the Jesuits, which was executed in 1767 by royal edict. These priests formed the most influential order or congregation among all the religious orders in the country. By the end of the sixteenth century, they had succeeded in gaining, little by little, a decisive influence in society and in government. The zeal with which they practiced their pious duties, the reputation of being the most learned of all the orders, and the mortality and tranquillity that reigned in their cloisters had gained for them the favorable influence they exerted. Neither the failure of defensive warfare, which they had fostered with such generous effort, nor the poor results of the missions in Arauco, which they also had decided to create, had any part in overthrowing their influence. Furthermore, they were united to the wealthiest class of the colony by extensive commercial and industrial ties.

The enormous wealth represented by their fifty haciendas, all well cultivated, gave them great power. They had acquired them through pious effort as donations from the faithful; through their influence over the governors, who had also authorized some donations for them; and through the sale of the produce of these very estates. These "temporalities," as they called them, constituted an "ecclesiastical province," governed by a provincial chief and divided into eleven "colleges," or convents, each in charge of a rector.

The exploitation of the estates of those colleges was carried on with great activity and skill. No one produced with more profit than the Jesuits the principal articles of internal and external trade—wheat, tallow, dried beef, wines, and brandy. Their European connections facilitated the acquisition of better tools for farming than those in general use. Their workers, subjected to a strict, watchful system, became capable and expert, and their thirteen hundred Negro slaves made a producing power superior to any other known in the country.

The industries resulting from these labors were looked after with equal faithfulness. Their tanneries; their shops for the construction of furniture and small ships; their factories of clay vessels, pots, and table ware; their mills, bakeries, and even their apothecary shops—the only ones in the Chilean settlements—made the order virtually indispensable to the people. Numerous foreign artisans, whom they brought over clad in Jesuit robes, allowed them to display to common gaze fine embroideries, paintings, chalices, cups, candelabra, and even bells for their churches, such as no others possessed, and, furthermore, they polished delicate jewels which the rich competed for at high prices. This vast network of business involved the whole colony, from private persons to the governing groups, and gave the Jesuits a powerful influence, material as well as spiritual. Therefore, the economic disturbances produced by their expulsion were in proportion to their activity, and the sumptuous celebrations of the Church, the grand sermons, the rigorous course of exercises—all the worship, indeed—suffered when they left.

Their expulsion reverberated also in educational and cultural circles because they maintained schools and colleges, the most important of which was the Convictorio[6] de San Francisco Javier (St. Francis Xavier) in Santiago, and because among their priests were men of outstanding learning. One of them, Juan Ignacio Molina, a Chilean by birth, later wrote in Italy the *Historia de Chile*, the most complete of all histories published up to that time.

The administration of the Church was maintained until the end of the colonial period without much variation. The country remained divided into two bishoprics: Santiago and Concepción. It should be remembered that there was a bishopric formerly in Imperial, but this is the same as that of Concepción, to which city it was transferred at the end of the sixteenth century when the Indians destroyed Imperial. Just as in the seventeenth century the Church had considered Monseñor Gaspar de Villarroel of Santiago a bishop of faultless virtue, so also in the eighteenth it had another no less respect in Monseñor Manuel de Alday.

Each of the bishoprics was divided into numerous "curacies" or parishes. The number of persons consecrated to the service of worship is not exactly known, but it is believed that the clergy did not exceed three hundred in number, and the regulars, or friars living in convents, fluctuated around a thousand. If these figures are compared with those for the end of the seventeenth century and further compared with the total number of the civil population, it is evident that at the beginning of the nineteenth century a considerable diminution had been effected in the religious personnel, while the population had increased. The number of nuns, however, had not diminished.

The situation of the priesthood was good in the cities but bad in the country. The income on which the parish priests, canons, and bishops lived was the tithes and the first fruits or the part collected

---

[6] A *convictorio* is the section in the Jesuit College where the boarders live and receive instruction.

from the first crops gathered; but because the bishops generally had little to do with the country parish priests or because of difficulties in communication or what is more probable, because of greed, which would prevent many farmers from paying those imposts justly and promptly, it is true that country ministers of worship were found almost everywhere living in the greatest poverty. Morality was relaxed among them and as those least competent or of the least influence were sent to the faraway parishes they soon began to forget what they had learned and to neglect their charges. As for the religious communities, the chaplaincies or fields mortgaged to them, from which they reaped the advantage, the alms given them, and the properties that they owned allowed them to live comfortably.

But not only did the religious diminish in numbers and in the importance of their functions, but at that time devotion also began to lessen among the people. The festal days continued to be magnificent, and the masses and processions were especially well attended; but, as for confession, it usually happened that many of the faithful did not comply with the precepts of the Church during Lent—an act usually looked upon as so sinful that if it became known it was enough to bring persecution on the offender and even the withholding of customary greeting.

There was a custom in the parishes of giving a paper or ticket to the one who observed Lent, that is to say, who made confession and partook of his "Easter communion." Afterward a priest collected these papers, going from house to house. The house where he did not find one could be punished with some penalty by ecclesiastical authority; but usually the names of all those who rebelled at that sacrament were merely posted on a chart at the entrance of the church, which was equivalent to exposing them to public shame. There were few, however, who did not show this token, although many of those who did show it had not confessed or received holy communion, for they usually avoided complying with the precept of the Church by buying the ticket from some sacristan, or from some pious friend who consented to commune four or five times and could in this way save from going to confession three or four sinners in addition to himself. But, however that might be, what was both evident and well known was the social influence exercised by the Catholic Church in Chile during the three centuries of Spanish colonization.

Doctrinal teaching of the natives was little less than useless because it did not bring peace and civilization to the Indians as it pretended to do. Among the mestizos, on the other hand, the effectiveness of preaching was much greater, for it constituted the only form of culture and the only standard of morality that this mass of the population was capable of receiving, for they had hardly advanced a step from primitive barbarism. The violence of their character and the rudeness of their sentiments and customs were softened by the Church in order to accustom them to live in society and to incline them to satisfy their wants by labor.

In the Creole and Spanish society, also, cast as it was in the mold of European civilization, the influence of the Church was seen in the correction of hereditary vices, which the conditions ruling in those times and the life of the country stimulated rather than opposed. It is true that the crimes committed among these social classes, from grave offenses against personal dignity to treacherous murders by means of poison or dagger, were not rare either among men or women, and that evangelical preaching was powerless to restrain such violent manifestations even among the most fervent spirits. It is also true that impotency was shown, too, in the failure to correct drunkenness and gambling which had developed to lamentable proportions since the seventeenth century. But it must be remembered that everything contributed to favor these vices among uncultured people lacking ordinary distractions, governed by greed, and having control over large numbers of slaves. Without the counterpoise of religion, social relaxation would assuredly have had no limit.

Undoubtedly the Church went further than was fitting in its endeavor to regulate private customs and even the clothing that should be worn, in order to correct excesses of luxury among the women of the seventeenth and eighteenth centuries. It is also true that it overstepped its authority in the obstacles it put in the way of the free acquisition of culture by preventing the introduction of European books; but these mistakes did not menace the civilizing and moralizing influence that began to spread in the colonial society, although they may have restricted it.

COLONIAL EDUCATION AND CULTURE

The educational organization of the colony advanced very little during the seventeenth century. It did not immediately affect the mestizos, the popular mass of Chile, who were in complete ignorance. It is not possible to calculate the number of schools in existence at that time, but it can be affirmed that there were very few, and those were designed exclusively for the descendants of Spanish blood.

On the other hand, there were the two conciliary seminaries

(*colegios*) of the bishoprics, which were founded in the sixteenth century, and two other colleges that acquired the title of pontifical universities because, according to the special concession of the pope, they could confer the degree of doctor of theology. One of these belonged to the Dominican friars and the other to the Jesuits. The most important of the four was the last, called Convictorio de San Francisco Javier. Studies in these establishments were divided into three successive courses: Latin, philosophy, and theology. According to the Laws of the Indies, the individuals who graduated here had to swear that they believed and would teach that the "Virgin Mary had been conceived without stain," and that they would obey the kings, viceroys, and *audiencias,* in the name of God. The number of students who frequented these halls and were graduated from them was always very small.

In the middle of the eighteenth century, there was established in the colony its principal institution of learning. This was the University of San Felipe, called thus in honor of Philip V, who, as mentioned above,[7] issued the royal order for its erection in 1738. Because of difficulties concerning its location, it could not be dedicated until 1756, and its teaching began two years later, that is to say, exactly twenty years after it was created.

There were to be ten professors in the university, all of whom were not invariably present. The subjects taught were lay and canonical law, medicine, philosophy, theology, Latin, and mathematics. All these branches were divided into four departments that conferred respectively the degrees of doctor in theology, jurisprudence, and canonical law (advocate), medicine, and mathematics (engineer). All instruction was given in Latin. From the first, the departments of theology and jurisprudence were the best attended. Very few studied medicine and mathematics, because physicians were little esteemed in society. Their profession was hardly considered decent; they continued to be the old "bloodletters." The same thing happened with respect to engineers or "surveyors," as they were called. Those who won the greatest consideration were theologians and lawyers but, as the profession of theology belonged to the ecclesiastical status, those who wished to have a good, lucrative, civil profession devoted themselves merely to the study of law. For that reason the University of San Felipe was principally a law school. The number of its students did not exceed one hundred in any year.

All things considered, the University of San Felipe represented

---

[7] See p. 110, n.

great progress. No university yet existed in Argentina, Uruguay, or Paraguay, and those who aspired to university degrees in those countries had to go to Chile, which actually occurred, because it was the nearest. It freed Chile from the intellectual tutelage of Lima, where some Chileans had had to go to study and be graduated. In the country itself it filled a general desire for instruction which had been making itself felt for a long time.

Until then the papal universities had graduated only ecclesiastics, since they had no authority for anything else. The seminaries had done the same; they had prepared only those who were going to devote themselves to a religious career. The conventual schools for men and women gave scant primary instruction to a small number of rich pupils. Higher civil teaching now was to be given but the curriculum of the University of San Felipe did not differ in any way from the papal universities and other religious educational establishments—the same pious discipline, the same oath of faithfulness to God and the king, the same official language, Latin. Even the professors were essentially priests because there were no others capable of teaching. It cannot be denied, however, that this university at once began to exert a considerable influence on the very limited development of the lower branches of education.

Its company of a hundred students, which kept renewing itself with the years, belonged for the most part to the wealthy Creole society; and, although the knowledge it imparted to its members lacked scientific character and in reality was not worth a great deal, it at least served to impart love for study and learning and served to fortify the intelligence with that kind of mental gymnastics which involved the comprehension of Latin and of casuistical philosophy. This body of young men, then, devoted to study, formed in time a small intellectual group in the country. It favored primary instruction, which was now given not only in the conventual schools but also in the parochial schools—one for each parish—and it fostered the aspirations for culture that in the eighteenth century were germinating in the colonial society.

A general reform in education was desired more in extent than in content. No attempt was made to take from the Church the predominance it had always exercised over institutions of learning, but an effort was made to extend primary instruction in such a way that all social classes might profit by it; to embody the studies of physical and mathematical science in secondary instruction, with freedom from religious dogma, just as was already the case in the most enlightened countries of Europe; to permit the free introduction of all kinds of books, especially those devoted to the applied sciences such as those treating of agriculture, mining, and the other branches; and, lastly, to establish a printing press in the country, on which the productions written by Chileans could be published. But the ideas of the governing social class continued to prevail. Its members believed that learning to read and write was dangerous or of no advantage for the poor or for women, even rich women, because it might corrupt their religion and morals. Aspirations of the sort described above, therefore, were not immediately realized or even discussed.

Instruction in the schools was paid for by the students, and the teachers were generally priests. The salary received would not permit one to devote himself exclusively to teaching. Each child who went to school paid his preceptor fifty centavos a month. He had to carry his seat also and supply books and implements for writing. He was taught to read and to "spell," that is, to pronounce each word letter by letter and afterward to repeat it as a whole. Besides reading, he was then taught writing and the four arithmetical operations, although it was the rare student who passed beyond addition, some idea of grammar, Latin, and, most important of all, the catechism.

It will be noted that only the children of families who could pay went to these schools, but some were admitted free when their poverty and good habits were proved. In the classrooms they were separated into two groups, according to their means; one formed of the richest to whom the preceptor gave the title of "don" and whom he addressed as *usted* (you), and the other formed of the poor, whom the master addressed simply as *tú* (thou). Once or twice a week they had contests which were called *mercolinas* (Wednesdays) and *sabatinas* (Saturdays). They were separated into two groups to which they used to give the names "Carthaginians" and "Romans," or "reds" and "blues." When one of the group did not answer the question proposed by a member of another group, the questioner gave to the one questioned "gloves" (*guantes*) or strokes with a ferrule (*palmetazos*). The glove was a cord which had several knotted strands at the end, with which punishment was applied on the palms of the hand. The ferrule was a slat, oval-shaped at one end and with a handle at the other, with which the palms were struck. The professor himself used these same instruments frequently as well as a lash (chicote) of braided rawhide which he applied to leg and shoulder when the pupil did not know the lesson. Sometimes he drew blood, but it was a common saying and thought very reasonable that "the letter enters with blood."

There were no schools for girls. In some convents of nuns, daughters of rich families spent two or three years, where they learned particularly to pray. Some studied at home. The teaching of girls was judged so demoralizing that respectable priests denied absolution in confession to a girl guilty of learning French.

Until the end of the eighteenth century, there were no schools of secondary education (*colegios*), except the two conciliary seminaries and the Convictorio Carolino (which the Jesuits called San Francisco Javier), and teaching in them was hardly advanced beyond what had been received in the schools. The Convictorio, like the others, was of a monastic character, and for the greater part of the day, which was devoted to pious exercises, it seemed to be only a branch of the seminaries designed to prepare the clergy. In all of them Latin and religion had the preferred place.

Special or technical teaching was represented in Santiago by the college called the Academy of San Luis, where instruction was given in arithmetic, geometry, and drawing, with a section in practical mining. This institution, the only one of its kind in the colony, began to function in the last years of the eighteenth century. Its founding was due to one of the most scholarly and patriotic Chileans of that time, Manuel de Salas. As in the Convictorio Carolino, attendance did not exceed a hundred students.

LITERARY PRODUCTION AND ITS TRAMMELS

Such was, *in toto*, the intellectual preparation that young people received during the last years of the colony; petty, certainly, in extent and in content, but even poorer because of the extreme scarcity of books which restricted its perfection and diffusion. As Latin was the scholarly language, almost all books were in that tongue. The master works of Castilian literature were found only in the hands of a small number of Chileans. Foreign works which had acquired fame in Europe were read even less, because the Church prohibited them and did not yet permit their shipment to America. However, scholarly men who traveled in Europe introduced these latter works by contraband, read them secretly, and lent them only to members of their own family or to those in whom they had much confidence. Novels of knighthood and pious manuals furnished the common reading, together with a few treatises on the laws of Spain and the Indies. Not even the *Don Quijote* of Cervantes had a vogue in the colony. It is fitting, nevertheless, to point out an exception with respect to Plutarch, the agreeable but severe ancient moralist whose *Parallel Lives* was widely distributed throughout

Chile and constituted profitable reading, chiefly for its civic character.

José Antonio Rojas was among those men who, by means of their voyages to Europe, succeeded in forming for themselves a small library for their personal use. Moreover, this scholarly Creole of the eighteenth century introduced chemical substances into the country for experiments and apparatus for physics, and for that reason simple-minded people called him "the wizard." In 1780 he, with two Frenchmen—Antonio or Antoine Gramusset and Antonio or Antoine Berney—conspired together to make Chile independent of Spain. This unsuccessful attempt was called the "conspiracy of the three Antonios." However, it was a fruit of the higher culture of the epoch and a forerunner of emancipation. Gramusset was an illustrious merchant, and Berney a professor of classical languages.

Since nothing could be printed in Chile, even secretly, because there was no printing press[8] and since it was necessary to send manuscripts to Lima or to Madrid for publication and to obtain permission of the inquisitorial tribunal, it is easily understood that the literary production of national authors in the seventeenth and eighteenth centuries was simply nonexistent. Writers were not lacking, however, among the religious orders and the military men who came to Chile and settled in the country, and likewise among the foreigners who visited it, but not all had the good fortune to see in print the works they wrote.

The principal author of the colony in the seventeenth century was Bishop Gaspar de Villarroel, a defender of the liberty of the Indians and a man of high culture for the time and for the country. The most important of his works was entitled *Gobierno eclesiástico pacífico* (*Peaceful Ecclesiastical Government*). The works of the Jesuit, Diego de Rosales, and of Captain Francisco Núñez de Pineda belong to this same century. To the former is due the very thorough *Historia general del reino de Chile* (*General History of the Kingdom of Chile*), written after forty years of residence, which extends to the second half of the seventeenth century. To Núñez de Pineda we owe a valuable book entitled *Cautiverio feliz* (*Happy Captivity*), in which he treats principally of the character and customs of the Araucanians, with whom he had an opportunity of becoming acquainted at first hand because he was their prisoner for six months. These books were not published in Chile until the

---

[8] See José Toribio Medina, *Bibliografía de la imprenta en Santiago de Chile desde sus orígenes hasta febrero de 1817* (Santiago, 1891); see also p. 173, *infra*.

nineteenth century—some two hundred years after they were written.

To the eighteenth century belong the historical books of Abbot Juan Ignacio Molina, the Chilean Jesuit expelled in 1767. They were written and printed in Italy, were well circulated throughout all Europe, and helped to make the country known to the outside world. Another Chilean author who lived and wrote in Chile, a priest of the Dominican order and a man reputed for wisdom, was Fray Sebastián Díaz. He filled the highest position of his order in Santiago, and had a professorship in the University of San Felipe, from which he graduated also as doctor of theology. His principal work, *Noticia general de las cosas del mundo* (*General Knowledge of Worldly Things*), merited publication in Lima and serves to give an idea of what the university learning of that time was like. In his work he treats of angels and their nature—whose number he fixed at 6,666—of ghosts and different classes of miracles, and then he discusses the stars, the atmosphere, and the "three heavens," as he understood them, which he supposed were peopled with invisible spirits.

But the national writer of greatest merit in the century is without doubt Manuel de Salas. Especially versed in economic matters, as syndic of the *Tribunal de consulado* he wrote numerous *exposiciones* to the court. They are worthy of notice not only for the material they contain but also for their literary form.

Very valuable, too, for Chile, are the works of some travelers and voyagers from Europe who, after visiting the country, wrote complete accounts of the manner of the social life of those times. Among the best were the Frenchmen, Frézier and La Pérouse, and the Englishman, Vancouver, who published in their respective countries at the end of the eighteenth century the narratives of their travels. Their books afford most interesting information on colonial society.

From this point of view the works of the Spaniards, Jorge Juan and Antonio de Ulloa, also have importance and value. They traveled through America in the middle of the century on a special government mission. The *Relación histórico del viage* (*Historical Story of the Voyage*) and *Noticias secretas de América* (*Confidential Information about America*) are works in which they give exact information about the government regime and the social conditions of these countries and among them, naturally, of Chile. These same European travelers record the backward cultural state existing in the colonies during the eighteenth century. Chile certainly figured among the most unfortunate, for it had no adequate colleges, no modern books to read, no printing press, no theater, no arts of any kind; its little nucleus of learned people absolutely lacked the opportunities, means, and stimuli to leave any trace of their intellectual capacity.

SOCIAL CLASSES AND LIVING CONDITIONS

In colonial society, during the eighteenth century, three social classes came to be defined, each with well-marked characteristics:

1. *The Spaniards.*—This name was given to the natives of the Peninsula, purely Europeans, who had settled in the country. Afterward they were nicknamed "Goths." Their number, relatively few, did not exceed twenty thousand. They were composed of the officials of public administration with their families—presidents, judges, and other members of the *audiencia,* royal treasurers, and others—chiefs of the army, ecclesiastical dignitaries, big merchants, and another group of people who had come to seek their fortune. The relations which this social group enjoyed at court, the authority and power they held in their hands, the ostentation displayed by them in clothes and customs—more in keeping with European usage—were motives that led them to treat with disdain those who did not belong to their class. In every case, as they enjoyed public authority, they constituted the privileged, dominating element of the colony.

2. *The Creoles.*—These were Chileans by birth but Spanish by blood and not always free from some native mixture. Descended as a general rule from the former conquerors, they formed a much more numerous group than the Spanish—about one hundred and fifty thousand—and, if they did not enjoy authority, they possessed, on the other hand, the stable wealth of the country. They were usually merchants, industrialists, agriculturalists, or miners. Some were owners of large estates or exploiters of valuable mineral lands; others were proprietors of farms or of extensive landholdings. Proud of the services of their ancestors, they had aristocratic leanings. Some established entails of their lands (*mayorazgos*); that is, they provided that their properties could not be alienated after death but were to pass into the possession of the oldest son, who, in turn, was also to leave them, when he died, to his oldest son, and so successively in order, with such possessions, to maintain to the end the luster and position of the family. Some of those same Creoles, moreover, acquired titles of nobility, buying them from the court, and had themselves called "count" or "marquis" and put over the doors of their houses escutcheons which indicated the insignia or heraldry of their rank. Several of them had also be-

come men of learning, either in Lima or in Spain; and, after the University of San Felipe was founded, not a few graduated as doctors, principally in law.

The wealth, pride, and learning that some Creoles attained made them feel aggrieved with the court because it conferred the public offices of greatest influence and honor not on them but on individuals of the mother country. Of all the governors in Chile during the colonial period, only two were Chileans and they merely served in an ad interim capacity. On the other hand, there were several native bishops of Chile, because the king felt sure of the fidelity of the clergy and did not exclude them from office with such systematic strictness.

Where the Creoles had a great deal of public influence was in the *cabildos*, which were composed for the most part of that element. This, however, did not satisfy their ambition, as the importance of these institutions had lessened considerably. Their love for their country, which they thought the most beautiful in the world, inspired in them a desire to serve it in a wider capacity; and to see themselves pushed aside and governed by individuals—oftentimes unworthy—by vulgar adventurers, whose only merit consisted in having been born in Spain, incited their souls to rebellion. In this way a mute but deep-rooted rivalry was established between them and the Spaniards. The above-mentioned travelers, Jorge Juan and Antonio de Ulloa, observed this fact very clearly.

3. *The Mestizos.*—This social group, the most numerous—more than three hundred thousand—had been formed slowly through the centuries by the union of native women with Europeans or Creoles. All manual work was done by them. Whether as domestic servants in the cities, peons or renters on the farms, or diggers and pickers in the mines, their life was a perpetual sacrifice. Absolutely ignorant, addicted by inheritance to gambling and drinking, superstitious in the extreme, like the former natives, and also violent like them, they indulged in frequent quarrels and lived in the deepest poverty. However, they constituted a vigorous, hardy race, frugal in eating, capable of all kinds of work, including warfare, which aroused them more than anything else. From sun to sun they carried on without aspiration of any kind.

The majority of them were occupied in the fields, and the system of work to which they were subjected there was severe. The master gave to each head of a family a little plot of ground on the estate, which he might cultivate for himself and where he might raise some animals, such as sheep, hogs, cows, and horses. In return, this tenant was obliged to supply one or two peons when the proprietor (*señor*) needed them, during the season of sowing and harvest or at any other time. Usually the proprietors treated the farm hands badly, nor were they better treated by the administrator, overseer, and herdsman, who were the upper employees; but the proprietor lived little on his estate—two or three months a year only—because country life was very insecure and absolutely unprovided with resources in case of illness. His customary residence was in the nearest city, preferably Santiago.

In those different tasks, the tenant received a small wage, about a real per day. The free time left to him he occupied in cultivating his small plot, or *cerco*. As he usually lacked tools, work animals, and seeds, he could ask the owner or administrator for all these, which were given to him in return for a half share of the produce. This was called "planting on shares." But the poor man, together with his family, needed to be fed during the winter, and if anything was scarce with him it was money; so he frequently found it necessary to sell his crops ahead of time to the owner himself or to the upper employees, or to some traveling merchants who carried on this kind of business. This was called "buying green." The price of this sale was a third and at times a fourth of the real value of the produce after it was harvested, so that the interest on that loan rose to no less than 200 or 300 per cent of the value delivered. It is easy to calculate the miserable profit that remained to the farmer for his year's work.

The house in which he lived was a small hut of mud bricks mixed with straw, of only one room in which all the family ate and slept in the massed confusion. The native *ruca* was very similar. The bed was frequently nothing more than a heap of straw. On winter nights the winds and rain filtered through the chinks in the clay with which the walls were daubed. Food consisted of vegetables, garden stuff, and, above all, kidney beans, potatoes, squash, and black bread. Very rarely were they lucky enough to eat the flesh of the flocks which grazed before their eyes.

When bad treatment obliged anyone to leave the hacienda, his sufferings had no limit. He was asked to stop nowhere, for the person who changed masters was considered a poor worker and a bad tenant. All the country people did not succeed in finding employment, however, and therefore formed themselves into wandering gangs of day laborers who gravitated by preference to the cities to work and there constituted a dangerous rabble, because when they found nothing to do they lacked the means to obtain food and inevitably devoted themselves to robbery. The aged day laborer who was incapable of working was forced to become a beggar. The nickname of *roto* (ragamuffin, literally, "broken one") which came from the ragged condition of his clothing, began to be used at that time.

4. *The Negroes.*—This class included the offspring of the Negroes mixed with zambos and mulattoes. The offspring of Negro and Indian blood was called "zambo," and the descendant of white-Negro blood, "mulatto." They were the slaves for whom there was no legal or human protection. Ordinarily they led a secure life, since, hard as the heart of the master might be, it was to his own good to keep them in health and strength sufficient for the tasks to which they were assigned. Generally they were domestic servants and were clothed with the castoff apparel of the family. As is known, the Jesuits brought them from Peru in great numbers to toil in their fields and workshops, but they never exceeded more than twenty thousand, zambos and mulattoes together. Due to the rigid laws guiding their conduct, they mixed very little with persons of different stock, nor did the climate favor them.

CUSTOMS, CLOTHING, AND AMUSEMENTS OF THE
UPPER CLASSES

Only the first two of these social classes—the Spaniards and the Creoles—formed the cultured society. Their most important center, the axis of their life and activity, was always Santiago, although Concepción had at one time considerable importance as the military city of the country; but Santiago fixed the standard of social life and the customs of all the other cities, and the highest social group imposed them also on the others.

The colonial house was usually of not more than one story and consisted of three patios. The first, which faced the street, was entered by a broad passage or paved entrance hall (*zaguán*) in which there almost always stood a bench of stone or wood. On one side of the hall was the room of the porter or key keeper, and on the other side, the parlor where a high-backed bench was also frequently seen. Here the mistress of the house looked after those who provided for the family, the outside servants, the beggars, and the rest of the people who entered and left. In the center of this first patio stood one or two posts to which were fastened a pair of mules which drew the carriage (*calesa*), a small cart on two wheels. Rarely were there any rooms on the side walls of that patio, and when there were they were used for storerooms or for servants' bedrooms.

On the side at the rear was a room or salon where visitors were received and where the family gathered at night to take maté, or sometimes tea, and to pray. Some stools, "tabourettes" or square wooden seats, several chairs with backs, a sofa, some mirrors and small tables, a brazier, and above all, the platform (*estrado*), a kind of bench covered with floor carpet or matting on which the master of the house sat, formed the household furniture of this room. Off this opened the bedroom of the master and mistress of the house, in which were wooden beds, screens of painted cloth, chairs, and washstands. In the more pretentious houses the hall or reception room, and the boudoir or dressing-room were placed in front of the parlor.

In the second patio were found the rest of the family rooms— surrounded by corridors and vines—the garden, and the dining room. In the third patio were the kitchen, the bread oven, the tubs for washing, and the guardians of the house—the dogs, often numerous. The floors of the principal rooms were paved with brick and the walls, although hardly ever plastered, were painted white or rose-color. The eaves and spouts projected over the street. The only means of illumination were tallow or wax candles (*mecheros*) and small oil lamps (*velones*). In place of phosphorous matches paper lighters were used, or twisted cotton fibers, which when frayed were lighted by contact with a flame or live coal. The patios were almost always dark at night, as was the entrance hall, whose door of two panels guarded by enormous bolts was closed and securely fastened. Houses where a little street lamp with its tallow candle shone under the eaves were rarely found. Slight attention was paid to illumination. The same was true of ventilation and light; doors and windows were few.

In this dwelling the head of the family spent his time in the following manner: He rose very early with the sun, took maté, smoked a cigar, and went to mass. On his return he attended to some of his business, gave orders, and at ten in the morning drank a cup of chocolate with bread, which he called breakfast (*almuerzo*). Another period of attention to business followed and then a quiet siesta. The streets at that hour were deserted. After the siesta, between two and three in the afternoon came the dinner (*comida*) ; afterward some other occupations were carried on and at eventide the residents of the town gathered to converse in shops or in house entrances. Between eight and nine the curfew (*queda*) sounded, and all shut themselves up in their houses. They supped and slept. This was their ordinary life.

The women did not leave the house except to go to mass or to make some purchases. On clear summer nights they took the fresh air seated on the bench in the entrance way (*zaguán*). Some of the boys went to school and, until down appeared on their lips, they did not speak to their parents unless the latter spoke to them, and then they had to address them by the term "your honor." Young men up to the age of twenty-five could do nothing without their parents' permission and, when they wanted to smoke, they had to seek the consent of the father. Their first shave was a reason for a celebration. Their marriage was generally arranged by their parents, who selected the bride from among their family relatives or friends, in accordance with pecuniary interests. There were occasions when the bride did not know her fiancé, or even how he looked. Only rarely were betrothals spontaneous.

Among poor people farm life was a jumble of misery. Those better off were the domestic servants in rich houses where they numbered eight or ten men and women, comprising Negro slaves and mestizo servants of both sexes. Although these latter got very small wages, from eight to ten reales a month, they ate regularly and clothed themselves in the castoff garments of their masters.

Already, at that time, groups of boys filled the streets of Santiago and embarrassed passers-by with their talk and quarrels, with their throwing of stones, and with their tops, kites, or games of hockey (*chueca*). They were insultingly called "street urchins," the *palomillas* (young pigeons)[9] of today.

In spite of this simple life, men and women displayed unreasonable luxury in their clothing. This practice had already attracted attention in the seventeenth century and was the object of angry sermons on the part of some of the religious who saw motives for sin in it. The display of expensive apparel was, furthermore, in striking contrast to the general misery of the people. It was not possible to correct it, however, then or afterward.

The most costly cloth and jewels of gold on the men; the short silk skirts of the women, cloth from Flanders bound with gold and silver thread, and the multitude of jewels and their immoderate use were the preferred themes of those religious sermons. In the midst of the greatest calamities through which the colony passed, the wealthy class continued to display its expensive tastes. Some houses were also furnished with great luxury. In the salon or *cuadra* were rich European tapestries, costly mirrors, and stools or tapestried chairs with brocades worked in picturesque designs. The silver table service of the dining room was equally costly; and if the high price of imported articles is taken into account, together with the general poverty, the great expense represented by these acquisitions

---

[9] *Palomilla*, thus translated, is the name of a species of destructive night moth which lives in granaries. In America the name is applied to the lowest class of people; in Chile, to a group of young vagabonds. See Espasa, *op cit.*, XLI, 497.

will be understood.[10] This disproportionate luxury was attributed
to the governors and members of the *audiencia* who, accustomed to
the showy Spanish life of the time, brought to Chile their passion
for expensive and frivolous decorations.

During the eighteenth century high colonial society was no less
ostentatious. In the second half of that century, the ladies had
stopped using the old-style petticoat and dress skirt as street apparel or for holidays. Instead, the fashion of dresses of very fine
fabrics made with trains was introduced, with stays underneath. A
boy beautifully dressed as a page bore the train of the dress, and
if he held it by the plaits, so as to allow one to see above the foot,
the clergy preached in the pulpits against the practice, declaring
it immodest. Finally, Bishop Alday prohibited it as moral sin; but
then came dresses with short skirts (*faldellín*), even above the
ankle. The ecclesiastical authority judged this another immorality
and, although he prohibited it also, no one stopped wearing it until
the first years of the nineteenth century.

The *faldellín* consisted of a kind of hoop skirt, tight in front and
spreading out below the waist in such a way that the bottom was
widened at the edge. Gold and silver tissue, velvet, and other cloth,
according to the station in life, were the fabrics generally used.
Under the *faldellín*, and longer at the bottom and showing through
in front, went the *justán* or underskirt, with ruffles of fine fabric
also edged with lace trimmings. Stockings of white silk and open-
work showed through this finery. Shoes of kid edged with gold or
silver were another valuable belonging of the lady. A woolen bodice
girded the bust. A little jacket with sleeves above the elbow and
generally of lace allowed the arm to be uncovered. Rings, breast-
pins, earrings, and gold chains with pearls and diamonds completed
the apparel. The hair was dressed in braids and was arranged on
both sides like a covering over the ears; natural flowers and ribbons
of gold and silk of different colors held this arrangement in place.
A muslin scarf was sometimes used as a head covering. A custom
that was very much criticized by foreigners, although it was the
mode at that time in Europe, was the use of rouge and make-up
(*manito de gato*, "cat's paw")—a practice which no lady omitted.

As for the men, the old-style coat and cloth cape had not
changed. But the use of the frock coat and the dress coat had
already begun at that time, and the shoe with silver buckles, the
three-pointed hat for grand celebrations, and the high flat derby.

---

[10] The following passage has been left out of the seventh edition: "The poor
people, on the other hand, continued to use the national rough woolen garments,
the table service of clay, and wooden spoons."

Among the poor the former costumes, made of shirtings and flannel, with sandals (*ojota*) and the big straw hat, still prevailed.

The wealthy class frequently rode in carriages. These conveyances consisted of the four-wheeled coach covered with an awning; the large coach (*carroza*) like our victorias, drawn by four horses which only the grand potentates—*mayorazgos*, governors, and bishops—used; the gig (*calesa*), a two-wheeled vehicle drawn by a pair of mules, which the ladies preferred to occupy; and the single gig (*calesín*), something like the present tilbury drawn by one mule only.

The most common amusements of society people were private calls, during which the finest courtesy reigned and confections and beverages[11] were served. Of the public festivals, in addition to the church processions, the parade of the royal standard, the reception of the governors, the solemnities with which births and marriages of princesses and princes of Spain were still celebrated, the frequent bullfights, the cockfights, the horse races, and carnival festivities, in which confetti was merrily thrown, were also very well attended.

MORALS, DELINQUENCY, AND DISEASE

This tranquil and indolent population showed, however, many faults in its organization and common life. Its social morality was in an undeveloped stage. The mestizo, lacking culture, still semi-barbaric, without occupations in which decent livelihoods could be gained, kept the rude and violent character of his ancestors. The Creoles themselves, like the Spanish adventurers, were by no means models of equity and justice in their relations with others.

Crime reached enormous proportions. Not only were robberies and severe wounds received in assaults and quarrels the subjects of constant complaint; there were frequent murders on central streets of every city. In the completely unguarded country districts, an unbridled vandalism reigned. There were places, like the hills (*cerrillos*) of Teno, famous for the groups of bandits that made their dens in the vicinity. During some years it was estimated that there were twelve thousand wretches infesting the roads in the center of the country. No punishment—not even the most severe— was sufficient to check them. The stock, the whip, the gallows, enforced labor—all were useless. The most implacable persecutions, such as those ordered by Governor Amat y Junient in the middle of the eighteenth century, and those drawn up by the corregidor of

---

[11] *Mistelas* is the name mentioned in the text. It is a beverage made of wine, water, sugar, and cinnamon.

Santiago, Luis de Zañartu, also failed. The evil had deep roots; misery and ignorance kept the mestizo in barbarism and prevented him from developing social ideas. Religious principles, taught with difficulty, might hold the great majority through fear of eternal punishment, but they did not penetrate into the less capable souls, except in the form of superstitious practices. Lack of foresight, due to the same intellectual backwardness, claimed many of the indigent as its victims. Society had not succeeded in remedying this condition except to a limited degree. Charity was very little developed. Only the most important cities had hospitals and they were always poorly organized and poorly kept.

The absolute lack of cleanliness and of hygienic habits occasioned much illness. Appallingly fatal epidemics frequently occurred. Smallpox, particularly, caused disastrous effects nearly every year. In the second half of the eighteenth century a priest named Chaparro[12] had introduced vaccination, but only at the beginning of the nineteenth century did the practice extend to all social classes, owing to the initiative of the Spanish doctor, Manuel Julián Grajales, who earnestly advocated it. This remedy, however, scarcely lessened at all the effects of the scourge and by no means stamped it out.

The extraordinary mortality of which the poor especially were victims made this situation even more difficult. Families left in poverty had to beg in order to live and, if to this cause of general misery one adds the rest, he will come to the conclusion that begging was then one of the most common social customs. Useless were the ordinances repeatedly issued by the governors to prohibit and regulate it; those who needed bread overruled the laws. And in this land, so beautiful and so rich that it is a "veritable paradise"—to quote Salas—was seen the spectacle of an emaciated and half-nude mendicant begging for alms on every street corner. The long-delayed but at all events beneficial founding of the asylum by this self-denying philanthropist remedied somewhat the mournful impression produced by the sight of abandoned misery.

In this dark picture the higher groups of society also had their place. The militant spirit, so fully developed in them through many generations, continued to impress on their familiar customs an irreconcilably hard character. The excessive authority exercised

---

[12] Friar Pedro Manuel Chaparro graduated from the University of San Felipe in 1770 with degrees in theology and medicine. In 1802 he gained the chair of philosophy in the same institution. He introduced the practice of inoculation in Chile in 1764, but it did not then come into general use. See Medina, *Dic. biog.*, p. 231; Barros Arana, *Historia jeneral*, VII, 470.

by the father over his children gave rise to frequent scandals. The aristocratic prejudice that condemned wealthy families to idleness developed in them habits of intemperance and gambling that at times resulted tragically. As among the mestizo element, drunkenness and gambling were the favorite vices of many distinguished people. It was impossible, however, to avoid those extremes since there was no other way for them to spend their time and energy, nor should one forget the heritage of centuries which impelled them in that direction.

Such a society, then, was that of the colony—a society whose imperfections in all their aspects attracted attention. It had been formed by violence and for only one of its groups, leaving the great mass of the population abandoned to its fate. The portion blessed by that state of things (Spaniards and Creoles of fortune) appropriated to itself the European civilization and lived in conformity to it, but the great mass (the mestizos), who also bore their blood and whose sacrifices afforded them well being, continued to vegetate materially and morally in a semibarbarism that differed very little from that of the native period.[18]

---

[18] For brief sketches of Chilean social life during the eighteenth century, see Edwards Bello, in *Imágenes de Chile,* pp. 105-142, 191-200, 221-230.

CHAPTER VII

THE MOVEMENT FOR SELF-GOVERNMENT

ANTECEDENTS OF THE MOVEMENT

DURING THE first eight years of the nineteenth century there was no thought of changing the political regime of Chile, but the better-educated Chileans formulated many well-founded complaints against the mother country which may be summarized as follows:

1. In the *economic system* the lack of commercial liberty was criticized. This condemned the country to poverty, and prohibited it from coming into relations with the rest of the world and increasing its production. It made of the colony a mere trading post (*factoria*) for gathering supplies for Spain, whose decadent industries were not sufficient for its sustenance. Besides this monopoly, the heavy imposts that burdened commerce, agriculture, mining, and, consequently, the mass of the population caused complaint.

2. In the *intellectual system* the court was reproached for maintaining the mass of the colonists in ignorance, for not creating schools and colleges in sufficient numbers for their needs, and for not permitting in any way the free introduction of books of general information.

3. In the *administrative system* there was criticism of the preference which was given to Spaniards over the natives of Chile in filling the high positions of government, however well prepared some of the latter might be and however great was the public influence of their intelligence or wealth.

4. In the *moral system* the misery of the lower class was regarded as a grievous wrong, which, together with ignorance, led to drunkenness, beggary, and crime.

5. In the *juridicial system* protests arose from the complexity of the laws, the delay of judgments, the arbitrary processes, the venality of some of the judges, the unequal consideration with which different groups of society were treated before tribunals—all of which often made illusory the right claimed by litigants and nullified the guarantees to the individual against being dragged to prison without cause.

Some influences from abroad encouraged those criticisms. In the first place, there were certain books of English and French philosophers and writers who hated the Spanish colonial regime and who presented, as an ideal, liberty and equality of rights for all men in respect to their private relations and to the government. Prominent among those philosophers and writers were Robertson, with his *History of America,* and Rousseau, with his *Social Contract.* These works, although prohibited, were read in Chile by certain distinguished men after having been passed secretly through the customs of Spain and the colony. In the second place, the colonists were considerably influenced by the independence of the United States, declared in 1776 and won a few years later with the support lent by Spain itself.[1] In the third place, ideas of independence were inspired in the colonists by the French Revolution of 1789, which had put into practice the theories of its thinkers, had formulated the "Declaration of the Rights of Man"—not absolutely unknown in Chile at that time—and had beheaded a king. In the fourth place, the defense of Buenos Aires against the English, carried on in 1806 and 1807 with forces assembled by Argentinian Creoles, showed the colonists that they were as capable of forcing respect for the integrity of their territory as the Spaniards, and gave impulse to the still confused idea of nationality.

This idea, in fact, began taking root in the heart of the enlightened colonists in an unconscious, almost intuitive, manner during the last three decades of the eighteenth century. Added to the philosophical readings of that time and the suggestions arising from events in France and the United States was the regionalist or local tendency inherited from Spain—a tendency toward which the social groups that originally had dwelt in isolated mountain fastnesses, extending only to surrounding heights, seemed to lean. There were born the usages, customs, and institutions which endured for centuries, under the protection of persistent tradition. Such was one of the predominant elements of society in the ancient provinces and first kingdoms of Spain.

In Chile, as in other colonies of America, local individualism lived on in the descendents of the conquerors, aided by new social conditions, by the characteristics of the indigenous race—which the mestizos reproduced—and by the geographic structure of the territory. In no other part was there a more active battlefield, nor

---

[1] Spain's part in helping win the independence of the United States was substantial, but by no means a voluntary or definitive one. Juan F. Yela Utrilla, in *España ante la independencia de los Estados Unidos* (Lerida, 1925), Vols. I, II, narrates the diplomatic events connected with Spain's intervention and accompanies his account with a substantial volume of documents. See also E. S. Corwin, *French Policy and the American Alliance of 1778* (Princeton, 1916); and F. E. Chadwick, *The Relations of the United States and Spain: Diplomacy* (New York, 1909), chap. i.

COLONIAL CHILE

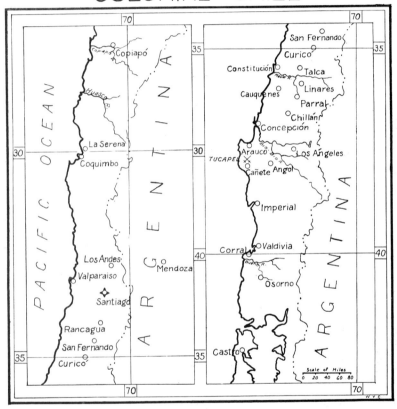

REVOLUTIONARY · CHILE

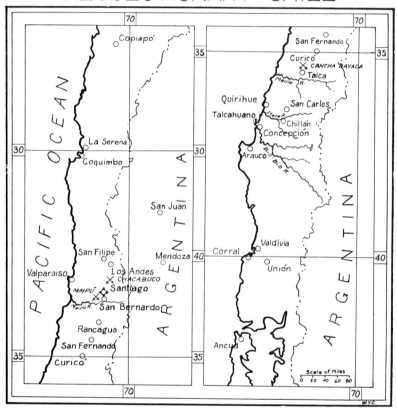

were there more indomitable men than those of Arauco. In no other colony did greater order, discipline, and enterprise exist to assure domination. In no other country did misfortune so test perseverance and develop constructive initiative. Warlike devastation, the destruction of cities, earthquakes, floods, plagues, famines, and droughts—all had to be resisted and remedied, and above all they had to be overcome. Periods of calm were prosperous and amply compensated for losses. Thus, there was being formed through three centuries an enterprising and long-suffering people, capable of overcoming the greatest obstacles—a people differing in certain measure from others of the same origin, and the traditional Spanish regional sentiment left with them the germs of future nationality.

Nature—in other terms, the geographical medium—conspired to the same end. As the territory was explored and became better known, the people were persuaded that the subsoil contained enormous riches and that the cultivated soil had unlimited possibilities. The gentle climate, the absence of poisonous reptiles and insects, the abundance of forest vegetation, the fertility of the cultivated fields, the stimulating yield of the mines, the landscape of the forests and mountains, the well-defined demarcation of the country —between the deserts of the north, the great cordillera, and the sea—all stimulated regional pride among the Creoles and furthered a patriotic restlessness, as was shown by their love for their native land and their desire for progress. The very isolation of the colony, at the extreme south of the continent, provided another element favorable to the spirit of nationality; and the name "kingdom of Chile," by which from early times the country was always designated in the chronicles and official documents, revealed the concept that this country constituted a geographic unity, separate and distinct from any other, where a considerable population could support itself from its own resources. At the beginning of the nineteenth century, the conviction aroused by these factors was already axiomatic. It was shown not only in the *historias* of the Abbé Molina, of Robertson, and of Raynal, but in numerous writers of that and of an earlier period.

The state of mind of the colonists, fruit of the internal, external, and traditional factors referred to, definitely expressed itself in new aspirations. Nevertheless, these did not yet go beyond obtaining from the mother country several reforms which might lessen the evils from which they were suffering. No one dared to speak, in public or private, of making the colony of Chile an independent nation by rising up in arms against the king. To reveal by a single word the thought of such a revolution would have been a crime worthy of the gallows. Criticisms against the existing regime were uttered in conversations around the hearth within the home, and with the utmost fear, as if one were plotting; and so few were those who commented upon these matters that they did not constitute the least danger. But, all in all, revolutionary thought, as the logical outcome of experience, had already unconsciously taken root in some spirits. All that was lacking for its manifestation was opportunity or what is usually called in history an immediate cause; and that opportunity was not long in coming.

FRENCH INTERVENTION AND COLONIAL REACTION

In the middle of 1808 mail from Buenos Aires brought the news of grave events occurring in the Peninsula. The French emperor, Napoleon I, had usurped the Spanish throne just as a short time before he had usurped that of Portugal. In order to effect that usurpation, he had taken advantage of an uprising of the Spaniards against Charles IV, and his minister, Manuel Godoy. The people hated the latter and accused him of treason against the country which he was trying to deliver up to the French.

As a result of this uprising Charles had had to abdicate the crown in favor of his son, Ferdinand VII, who was very much admired and beloved by most of the Spaniards; but, as the former could not reconcile himself to that abdication, he had entered into relations with the French sovereign in order, with his aid, to find a way of restoring himself to the throne. Napoleon I, then master of Europe, had caused Charles IV and Ferdinand VII to come to Bayonne (a French city situated very near the Spanish border). In a conference held there, he had obliged the two to renounce the throne of Spain and then cede it to him. This was the reported usurpation.

The news of such events produced consternation in Chile. But shortly arrived other news of greater gravity. Napoleon had elevated his brother, Joseph Bonaparte, to the Spanish throne, and he was already in Madrid supported by a hundred thousand French bayonets. The highest nobility of the kingdom had formed the court of the usurper; but the people, suffering a revolt of every patriotic sentiment in their souls, had arisen en masse against the invader. A governing committee established in Seville directed the national reconquest in the name of Ferdinand VII.

Overwhelmed by such events, the colonists of Chile were disposed to coöperate in the defense of the mother country and the restoration of the legitimate king, to whom with great pomp they swore allegiance in all the cities and whose effigy they carried through the streets to the cries of "Viva Don Ferdinand VII!" "Death to the usurper!" But at the same time that they performed these acts, it occurred to certain Chileans to ask themselves what would happen if Spain definitely remained subject to the French usurper. Should they submit to him also? Or should they resist and form an independent state?

Napoleon had sent emissaries to the American colonies to demand their peaceful obedience. The Queen of Portugal, a sister of Ferdinand VII, called Carlota—who was exiled in Brazil after the French invasion of her kingdom—had herself written to several persons in Chile, offering her protection to the colony in case the legitimate dynasty of Spain should remain conquered; and this fate was greatly to be feared because, in spite of some notable triumphs obtained by the Spanish people, the emperor in person had immediately led an expedition to the Peninsula and conquered the greater part of its territory.

Under such pressing circumstances the colonists had to take some action. Time was passing rapidly. Such events had been brought about in the course of little more than a year (from 1808 to 1809). Thus it was that at the latter date there were in Chile two political tendencies: one which aspired to the independence of the country, if the French definitely triumphed in Spain, and the other, uncompromisingly monarchical, which did not wish to hear the loss of the mother country mentioned and confined itself to fighting the enemy, keeping itself free to define its attitude when the war should be concluded.

The first of these groups had no organization or recognized leaders, but the principal point of support was the *cabildo* of Santiago, and it was logically made up of the most cultured Creoles. The second group was composed of the high officials of public administration, together with the rest of the European Spaniards, and naturally the governor of the colony, García Carrasco, headed it. The men of this affiliation dubbed the others "revolutionists," although their acts were inspired by the most submissive fidelity to Ferdinand VII; and the others called their opponents "Carlotinos" and "Frenchified," because they said that, if the French finally conquered the Peninsula, they would submit to Napoleon or to Queen Carlota of Brazil, provided they kept their privileges and offices. Intrinsically the two tendencies were only an expression of the deep rivalry that for some time had divided the Chilean Creoles from the peninsular Spaniards; the former, concerned especially for the fate of their country, deserved for that reason to be called patriots;

and the latter, especially preoccupied with the cause of the mother country, might simply be called Spaniards.

The dissensions produced because of happenings in Spain were not the only ones. There were others, of which not only the mother country was a target, but the governor of Chile himself.

In order to control the difficult situation created in the colony there was needed at the head of the government a man of great political tact; but the president of Chile was lacking in this quality. Francisco Antonio García Carrasco, an old military man of little education, had obtained the command of the country by mere chance. At the beginning of 1808, Governor Luis Muñoz de Guzmán died suddenly. Two years before, the king had decreed that, if in such an event the government were left without a head, the vacancy should be filled in the interim by the official of highest rank in the colony, provided he was not lower than colonel. García Carrasco found himself in a position to meet this ordinance. He was briga-dier general in the army and the only one qualified to perform the duty of the vacant governorship. He lived in Concepción, com-pletely removed from governmental councils. His life had been spent in encampments.

A stranger to the affairs of public administration, he had brought from Concepción, as his private secretary and counselor, Juan Martínez de Rozas, a Chilean lawyer, who was the person who had induced him to take over the command and had offered him his aid as a person experienced in such weighty matters. Hence, every-body believed that the secretary was going to be the real governor. Martínez de Rozas at that time figured among the very few really educated persons in Chile. Born in Mendoza in 1759, when the prov-ince of Cuyo for which this city served as capital was still Chilean, he had acquired his first education in the pontifical university of Córdoba and had been graduated as a lawyer in Santiago, after having studied law in the University of San Felipe. Years later, when Ambrosio O'Higgins occupied the *intendencia* of Concepción (1786-1788), Martínez de Rozas was his legal adviser (*asesor letrado*), and, when O'Higgins himself assumed the governorship of the colony, he left Martínez de Rozas in charge of the *intendencia*, with the rank of provisional intendant. Afterward, when O'Higgins was promoted to the vice-regency of Peru, Martínez de Rozas also became legal adviser to the new president. But, as the court would not confirm him in this office, notwithstanding the excellent recommendations that his superiors gave him, he had been obliged to return to Concepción after years of service. Aside from his profession, he possessed considerable fortune, belonging almost entirely to his wife.

Martínez de Rozas did not stay with García Carrasco more than a few months. He had tried to guide the president into the realization of certain reforms that would preserve the peace of the colony, and, as he did not succeed, he returned to Concepción, resolved now to put himself in contact with the most intelligent people of the south and of Santiago, in order to prepare for a complete change in the political regime. Meanwhile, García Carrasco went from one blunder to another and soon had alienated the wealthy classes of the colony, the royal *audiencia*, the clergy directing the Church, and the *cabildo* of Santiago.

After a year of his government, in 1809, there were already evident signs of a revolutionary movement, hostile to Spanish rule and to himself. Then he began to adopt methods of severity, the immediate effect of which was to arouse still more hostility. He issued decrees prohibiting conversation even about the affairs of the mother country; he persecuted certain persons charged with talking about these things ; and, in obedience to orders from Spain, he tried to expel the few foreigners who lived there, considering them propagandists for revolutionary ideas. As his unpopularity increased, the power of the Spanish group that he led diminished, and the revolutionary propaganda of the patriotic group prospered, aided by the crisis through which Spain was passing and by the fact that it was a protest against bad government.

As a result, at the beginning of 1810 the patriotic group already looked upon him as an adversary and was organizing to fight him. It represented a combination of vague aspirations for reform which certain educated men defined better than others, and which were still contradictory, since they involved, on the one hand, complaints against the existing regime, and, on the other, the swearing of fidelity to the king. It did not yet affect the people, not so much because the poorer classes were not considered, but because it would have been impossible to interest them in a revolt, for their ignorance kept them from understanding what was going on. The householders of a city formed the only class then called the people. Public propaganda, therefore, was not carried on ; nothing was printed, because there was no printing press, and open-air assemblies were unknown. Conversation and private letters served as the only means of spreading revolutionary aspirations. But leaders were not lacking; among the most respected were José Antonio Rojas in Santiago and Juan Martínez de Rozas in Concepción, both in constant correspondence.

Already well known were the revolutionary movements which had broken out in Quito and Chuquisaca in 1809. In Buenos Aires, where popular opinion was being prepared for the coming struggle, as in Chile, the authorities had news of what was going on in the latter country, and the viceroy of that jurisdiction informed García Carrasco that conspiracies were being formed against his government. The president was inclined to put down by any method whatever the least effort to revolt; but, however much he investigated what was going on, he succeeded in finding out nothing.

Finally, after many false alarms, he believed that he had found the thread of the conspiracy in the house of José Antonio Rojas in Santiago. He obtained the information through a secret investigation, based on certain denunciatory conversations referring to the establishment of a junta of government in Chile. The principal authors of the plan were the *procurador* of the *cabildo*, Juan Antonio de Ovalle Silva,[2] the Argentinian lawyer, Bernardo Vera Pintado, and Rojas himself, in whose parlors they met. The house of Rojas was then entered on the night of May 25, 1810, by agents of the authorities and in it were arrested the three conspirators. These were the first seizures made by the government among the patriotic group. Early in the morning of May 26, the offenders were taken to Valparaiso in order to send them to Peru.

Great was the excitement produced in Santiago by their imprisonment and exile, without any sort of legal proceedings. The three men were of high social standing: Rojas and Ovalle, now old men with extensive family and friendly connections, enjoyed universal esteem within the country; and Vera, although young, also aroused almost unanimous sympathy. A native of Argentina, he had pursued his law studies in the University of San Felipe and had married a lady high in Chilean society.

As soon as the news of the arrest became known, the families of the culprits besought the governor to revoke the order of exile, and their petition was espoused by the *cabildo* of Santiago, the tribunal of the bishop, the leading businessmen, the most representative citizens, and even the royal *audiencia*. The order was revoked and a

[2] Ovalle Silva, after pursuing his legal studies in Lima during the middle of the eighteenth century, returned to Santiago to practice his profession. By 1810 he had acquired a wide reputation for his public services. See Medina, *Dic. biog.*, p. 635.

member (*oidor*) of this tribunal was sent to Valparaiso to formulate the regular process against them.

But at the end of June news came to Santiago, and was rapidly spread about, that a popular revolt had broken out in Buenos Aires on May 25, the very day on which Rojas, Ovalle, and Vera were arrested. The viceroy had been deposed and a national junta of government established. This news determined the president to use more severity. It was not difficult for him to suspect a certain connivance between the conspirators in Argentina and those that he thought he had discovered in Chile. Since, with the knowledge of that revolutionary event, the spirit of restlessness might grow, and even more because of the delay in the lawsuit brought against the presumed conspirators, he gave a private order to put them on board ship without further delay, and on July 10 a frigate raised anchor in Valparaiso and sailed toward Peru, carrying on board Rojas and Ovalle. Vera remained for the moment in Valparaiso, ill of a fever which threatened his life.

On the morning of the following day, there arrived at the capital two messengers, panting with weariness, despatched by Ovalle and Rojas from the port at the moment of embarkation. The news fell on the populace like a thunderbolt. In two or three hours everybody knew it. People of the most diverse conditions and ages assembled at the plaza and paraded the streets, a prey to the greatest indignation.

The *cabildo* met in extraordinary session which by its own action was converted into an open *cabildo*, because the multitude thrust itself into the room, demanding that the governor be asked to revoke his order immediately. In the midst of the tumult which was almost a riot, and by means of the intervention of the *audiencia*, García Carrasco revoked it; but it was already too late. Two days afterward it was known that, when the messenger who had carried that communication to Valparaiso with the greatest haste arrived at his destination, the prisoners had for many hours been sailing the high seas. This time the excitement came to a head immediately. It is said that García Carrasco, who maintained a troop of soldiers ready armed and strictly quartered, was preparing to revenge himself on the populace and principally on the members of the *cabildo* who had taken prominent part in the events of July 11. A special guard of residents was formed which, accompanied by the people of the lowest status, patroled the streets night after night in spite of the rigorous cold of the winter season.

No one neglected to arm himself against the vengeance that

public rumor foretold. The popular tumults that broke out continually were not, however, checked by the governor. The capital seemed like an encampment. It was in open insurrection. The people began to discuss also the deposing of the president from office and the creating of a purely Chilean junta of government. To this end certain chiefs of the army pledged themselves, and mounted men from the neighboring farms were enlisted to strengthen the movement for revolt.

The royal *audiencia,* noting such maneuvers, considered it wise to settle the question in a peaceful way. In consequence, it approached García Carrasco and asked him to resign the command and, compelled by circumstances, he decided to do so. On July 16, at noon, it was announced to the populace that the president had resigned the command in favor of the Conde de la Conquista, Mateo de Toro Zambrano, by virtue of the latter's rank as brigadier of the royal armies—a title bestowed the previous year by the governmental junta of Spain.

THE ESTABLISHMENT OF THE FIRST NATIONAL GOVERNMENT

The elevation of the Conde de la Conquista to the command of the colony could not solve the conflict between Chileans and Spaniards, because the movement was not simply a change of presidents but the overturning of the governmental system. The group of patriots aspired to "nationalize" authority; and, if some of their most advanced men understood that this nationalization logically involved the independence of the country, others—the majority no doubt—thought only of remaining loyal to Ferdinand VII. What all patriots agreed upon was that Chile should create its own government, as the provinces of Spain and other colonies of America had done—among them, for example, Chile's nearest neighbor, Buenos Aires.

The *cabildo* of Santiago headed by its *procurador,* José Miguel Infante, was the most active center of the revolutionary movement and Juan Martínez de Rozas, accompanied by Bernardo O'Higgins, a son of the colonial governor of that name, was equally untiring in his propaganda at Concepción. The rich and ardent youth of the country served as the agency to further the ideas of reform. The group of Spaniards, on their side, did not spare means to hinder or pervert that propaganda. The royal *audiencia* was their support and their bulwark and the upper class of merchants followed its lead. The army and the clergy were divided into two parties: one, which adhered to the liberals; the other, which helped to resist them. Those figuring in the patriotic group were the officers of the civic militia together with some chiefs of the regular army who resided in Santiago; and, among the clergy, several priests of the ecclesiastical court. In the Spanish group other permanent officials of the regular army and the most prominent secular ecclesiastical authorities had a place, followed by the religious orders.

In the main, the struggle between Chileans and Spaniards seemed headed respectively by the *cabildo* of Santiago and the royal *audiencia*. From the beginning of his administration, the provisional president, appointed during the riots of July, felt buffeted about by the two opposing currents, and he vacillated between them. Mateo de Toro Zambrano, eighty-five years of age, was absolutely incapable of carrying on government in such difficult circumstances. He was born in Santiago, and a great part of his life had been devoted to private business. His public activity had been spent in filling the offices of corregidor and alcalde of Santiago and of superintendent of the mint. His being also an army official gave the governing junta of Spain occasion to appoint him brigadier in 1809, for the purpose of attaching him to the mother country. When the *audiencia* considered the resignation of García Carrasco, it determined that by virtue of that promotion the command ought to belong to the count—just as it had belonged to his predecessor two years before in accordance with the law; and as the count was a Chilean, the *audiencia* thought the agitation of the reform party would be pacified by seeing a fellow countryman elevated to the post of governor.

Events soon showed the supreme tribunal that it was mistaken. The *cabildo* of Santiago, which had accepted the new situation only as a truce, did its utmost to control the weak spirit of the president. Through their influence, two members of the patriot group who inspired confidence were placed beside him, Gaspar Marín, as adviser (*asesor*), and José Gregorio Argomedo, *ex-procurador* of the *cabildo*, as secretary.

The state of equilibrium between the two forces did not last more than two months. At first the count seemed to favor the *audiencia*. With the greatest solemnity he recognized the council of the regency, installed in Cádiz as a substitute for the former junta of government in order to keep up the fight for the independence of the Peninsula and the rights of King Ferdinand VII; but the propaganda and agitation of the patriotic party, far from ceasing, continued with more alarming characteristics.

The council of regency had sent to the Americas a proclamation which implied the most explicit condemnation of the dominant regime. In it the colonies were asked to appoint deputies to the

Cortes of the Peninsula, and, after declaring equality of rights between them and the provinces of the mother country, it said to them: "From this moment, Spanish-Americans, behold yourselves elevated to the dignity of free men. . . . In the act of selecting your deputy, it is necessary that each elector should say to himself: This man is the one who has to expose and remedy all the abuses, all the extortions, all the evils caused by the arbitrary and useless action of the chieftains of the ancient government. . . ."

Encouraged by this frank recognition of the necessity for political reform, the patriots displayed the most lively efforts in hastening the formation of a governmental junta, for which they had long been agitating. During the month of August their activity never ceased. Private meetings were daily held in the homes, on the estates, and at the countryseats of the richest people. The most active young men of the Creole aristocracy were sent in different directions, principally to the farms near the capital, to bring together groups of horsemen who should be ready for the moment of going into action. They circulated written proclamations from hand to hand and posted revolutionary placards at the corners of intersecting streets.

Among the most notable writings that were read during those days, the *Political Christian Catechism* (*Catecismo político-cristiano*) was conspicuous. Its author, hidden under the pseudonym of José Amor de la Patria,[3] distributed this "for the instruction of free people in South America." A long document, rational and strong in its language, it was at bottom an attack against the colonial regime and a brilliant apology for the system of republican government; and because of its simplicity it was within the intellectual range of all kinds of readers. Never had anything yet been written in Spanish America as vigorous as the contents of this piece of work—a truly admirable product for the time.

In the political argument set forth in its lines were such utterances as these, based on the proclamation of the council of regency:

Americans! Restrain the irritation in your breasts! In another age the declaration of a pope was necessary in order that the primitive inhabitants of these countries should be regarded as rational beings. Today the declaration of a government is necessary in order that you may be esteemed as an essential and integral part of the Spanish empire, that you may consider yourselves as elevated to the dignity of free men, and that you may no longer be what you have been, that is, wretched slaves. . . .

---

[3] José Amor de la Patria (1786-1868) was actually Antonio José de Irisarri. See biographical notes, *infra*, p. 483.

You have been colonists and your provinces have been colonies and wretched trading posts. It has been said that is not so; but this vile condition is not effaced by beautiful words, but by a perfect equality of privileges, rights, and prerogatives. By a wicked procedure and eternal injustice, the power, authority, honor, and income have been the patrimony of Europeans. . . .

The mother country has monopolized commerce and has forbidden foreigners from coming to sell or coming to buy at our ports and us from being able to negotiate in theirs, and with this eternally iniquitous and unjust prohibition we have been reduced to the most terrible misery.

Every year the mother country sends out swarms of employees who come to devour our substance and to treat us with insupportable insolence and arrogance; flocks of ignorant, greedy, lazy, unjust, barbarous, vengeful governors, who make their depredations without check or fear, because court appeals are most difficult, because the supreme government is three thousand leagues away, because they have relatives and protectors there who defend them and participate in their thefts and because they are Europeans and we are Americans.

The mother country burdens us daily with duties, taxes, contributions, and imposts without number, which in the end ruin our fortunes, and there are no means nor measures to prevent them. The mother country permits us to have no manufactures nor even vineyards, and desires us to buy everything from it at exorbitant and ruinously scandalous prices. . . . The whole plan of the mother country consists in not wanting us to try or think of anything but working mines as good slaves and as Indians of encomiendas, which we are in every sense, and they have treated us as such. . . .

The employees and Europeans in general come to the Americas very poor and leave rich and powerful. We go rich to the Peninsula and return plucked without a copper. How are these miracles wrought? Everybody knows. The mother country abandons the people of America to most frightful ignorance, not mindful of its education or of useful institutions for its prosperity; mindful, yes, to destroy them as much as possible and when they have drained and destroyed the provinces with taxes and exorbitant contributions and with the monopoly of commerce, they even desire charitable institutions and as much as possible of everything else to be carried on at the expense of these wretched peoples; for the treasures wrested from us by means of fiscal exactions must be used only for endowing European employees magnificently, for paying soldiers who oppress us, and for enriching the mother country and its favorites. . . . This has not been the work of two or three wretches who have abused their office. It has been the system invariably followed by the nation and the government. . . .

Americans! The Central Regency and Junta make fools of us! They want our money, they want our treasures and lastly they want us to nourish a serpent that has devoured our entrails and will continue to devour them while it exists. They want to keep us asleep in order to dispose of us as they please at the end of the tragedy. . . .

Generous Chileans! The inept despot who oppresses and tramples on us has snatched from the bosom of their families three of your most worthy citizens simply because they were not mute and stupid and did not keep silent like slaves. Let us remember the eleventh of July and try to understand that oppressors can do nothing when the people do not wish them to. . . .

No doubt there was passion and exaggeration in all this tirade; but there is as little doubt that in the existing state of mind such language could not be more inspiring. Although the *Political Christian Catechism* maintained that the republican form of government would result in more happiness for the country, it did not ask for such a creation in Chile. In the first place, its author understood that such an advanced demand would find no echo except among a few persons; secondly, he was not ignorant of the fact that the country lacked'preparation for accepting a republic; and third, such a complete change of regime, under the above circumstances, could do no less than fail.

Furthermore, it expressed the belief that after their independence all the Spanish colonies of South America would join together to form a single nation just as in the United States. Therefore, it pointed out a more conciliatory proceeding as being convenient and opportune. It counseled the Chileans as follows:

Convene an open *cabildo;* form a provisional junta as soon as possible to take charge of the superior authority, and call together the deputies of the kingdom to make a constitution and provide for its well-being. The national representation of all the provinces of South America should reside where all agree. . . . *Form your government in the name of King Ferdinand, so that when he comes to reign among us. . . .*
But for the immediate future, no intrusive kings, no French, no English, no Carlotas, no Portuguese, no other foreign domination. Let us all die Americans, before suffering or bearing the foreign yoke!

Those accusations as well as these projects reflected perfectly what the most advanced men of the patriotic party were thinking and doing. There was a reason for such qualifying terms as "insurgents" and *juntistas,* which the Spaniards gave to their adversaries, just as there was significance in the nicknames "Goths," "Carlotinos," and "Frenchified," with which they were paid back; but, just as the campaign to realize such vast aspirations was sustained and energetic, no less powerful and untiring was the campaign made against it by the Spanish group. To the efforts of the *audiencia* were added the manipulations of Vicar Rodríguez Zorrilla and of the bishop of Concepción,[4] and the violent preachments

---

[4] The diocese of Concepción was then under the control of Don Diego Antonio Navarro Martín de Villodres (1758-1820), a native of the province of Granada and a doctor in theology of the University of Salamanca. He was appointed to the see at Concepción in 1807 through the influence of Godoy and brought to his

of the clergy. The vicar sent a protest to the parish priests to be signed by the parishioners, in which the spirit of the rebellion was most severely condemned and in which the signers were urged to be "constant, loyal, and faithful to their much loved king and lord." The bishop also issued a pastoral of the same sentiment. The monastic clergy used all sorts of measures to second their prelates.

An intelligent priest of La Merced in Santiago sounded the highest note in a sermon which he preached in his church at that time, and which in comparison with the *Political Christian Catechism* represented exactly the way the Spanish party was thinking with regard to the crisis through which the mother country and its colonies were passing. After condemning as the greatest scandal of the day the revolutionary spirit of many Chileans, he added:

> Let us speak clearly: nothing can threaten our salvation more than this nor bring greater evils upon us. But how can Christians think of their salvation when they are stirred up and agitated with that new plan of government which is against the laws and precepts of God?—Because of so consequential a contempt, we have no order on the Peninsula.
>
> The constitution of the governments of America already has its being. . . . No order has been given us to alter it; we have not been told that we can govern ourselves by and at our own will; on the contrary, we know that the junta which represents the authority of the monarchy has given its orders. . . . To think, then, of resisting these orders is to desire to resist ordination, as the apostle says: *"qui potestati resistit, Dei ordinationi resistit"* (he who resists authority resists the orders of God).
>
> In Spain, there is no other authority recognized by the nation than the junta that Providence has given us. Say clearly that you do not wish to subject yourselves to nor obey the precepts of God; that you do not wish to obey the authority of the kings of Spain whom God has given us since the conquest and who have mercifully kept us until today; say that you think you can govern yourselves alone better than you can be governed by the authority on high; and then you will not wonder at our declaiming in the pulpits against such devilish disobedience and against such a lamentable ambition, which not only degrades our kingdom from the concept of faith, obedience, and submission in which nations have held it, but which excites the justice of God to discharge upon us all his thunderbolts and anathemas.

The "anti-junta" propaganda did not limit itself to the above. The clergy established missions and made supplications, so that with the help of Heaven the formation of the projected national government might fail. The statement was spread abroad by the

charge an "invincible hatred of free, representative government." He was especially disturbed by the activities of Martínez de Rozas and the latter's adherents. See Barros Arana, *Historia jeneral*, VIII, 191; Medina, *Dic. biog.*, p. 566.

Spaniards that, if that government was organized, the nuns would be dragged from their cloisters, and assassinations, sackings, and a thousand and one outrages committed.

All was in vain; the Chileans definitely recovered their influence over the Conde de la Conquista. They intimidated him with the spectacle of a violent overturn, the result of factional strife, and finally succeeded in making him decide to convene a great open *cabildo* in which would be represented as many as possible of the most respectable elements in the capital—civil and religious bodies, wealthy residents, and professionals of prestige—in order to discuss what ought to be done in the difficult circumstances through which the country was passing.

Having prepared this assemblage six days beforehand, the eighteenth of September was fixed upon for bringing it to a head. During those days invitations to the number of about four hundred and fifty were sent out and, of course, the persons to whom they were directed were for the most part favorable to the new ideas. The agitation of the patriots was now incessant. Armed patrols were organized among the people from the country and the most ardent residents of the capital to watch over the populace because it was feared that the regular troops and the leading men of the Spanish party would try to strike a blow which would cause the assembly to fail.

Thus the seventeenth arrived, and the excitement felt in the city showed very clearly that it was on the eve of a great event. At night there was a preparatory meeting among those most interested in the venture to make final agreements for the following day, and all separated at a late hour, resolved to persist in their design.

September 18, 1810, was a spring day radiant with sunshine. The site selected for the assembly was in the center of the community; it was the great hall of the commercial tribunal (*consulado*). From an early hour regular troops, directed by a sergeant major belonging to the Chilean party, guarded all the side streets that gave access to the small square that stretched in front of the Plaza de Armas and even beyond. In order to pass through the cordon of troops, each person invited had to show his ticket of invitation to the officers who headed the pickets of the guard.

At nine o'clock that morning, the hour fixed for the meeting, the room of the *consulado* was full; in it were some three hundred and fifty persons, with powdered hair, and ceremoniously dressed in frock coats, three-pointed hats, short pantaloons, silk stockings, shoes with silver and gold buckles, and wearing small swords. About one hundred of those invited were absent—almost all belonging to the Spanish party—among them the regent of the *audiencia*. This tribunal had no desire to be represented there.

Some minutes later the Conde de la Conquista made his entrance, accompanied by the secretary, Argomedo, and the adviser, Marín. The three took seats on the platform or dais, and the others gathered around on wooden benches placed there for that purpose. The aged president soon addressed his expectant audience. Arising he said, showing his badge of authority: "Here is the staff, dispose of it and of the command." Then turning to his secretary he added: "Announce to the people what I have prepared for you," and again he took his seat. Argomedo then arose and in a firm voice pronounced a brief discourse in which he confirmed the resignation offered by the count and asked the *cabildo* to propose "the most certain means of keeping them the assured, defended, and eternally faithful vassals of their most adorable monarch, Ferdinand." Then the *procurador*, José Miguel Infante, spoke in behalf of the *cabildo*. His discourse was long and unimpassioned. He showed how desirable it was to create a governing junta, similar to the one that existed in Spain, in the name of Ferdinand VII, as a means of securing his interests. He made an effort to prove that it was right for the Chileans to take this step, basing his argument on the declarations of the Royal Council of the Regency, and ended by showing that the junta would not be a menace to anyone because all elements of the country desired only union and harmony.

Notwithstanding the conciliatory terms of this proposal, the Spaniards present gave signs of rejecting it. Two of them, one after the other, endeavored to speak against it; but the murmur of disapproval and protest that spread through the room with their first words silenced them. Unable to continue, they had to retire from the assemblage. Almost all those present then stood up and in a loud voice began to repeat, "We want a junta!" The suggestion from the *cabildo* was at once approved by general acclamation and the *procurador*, Infante, nominated the persons who should compose it. At each name the assembly burst into applause.

The junta was constituted as follows: president, Mateo de Toro Zambrano, Conde de la Conquista; vice president, José Santiago Martínez de Aldunate, bishop elect of Santiago, who was abroad; members, Fernando Márquez de la Plata, Juan Martínez de Rozas, Ignacio de la Carrera, Juan Enrique Rosales, and Francisco Javier Reina,[5] a Spanish colonel, who, if not connected with the patriots,

---

[5] Francisco Javier Reina entered upon a military career in 1761 and was transferred to Chile in 1804, with the rank of lieutenant colonel of artillery. He was placed on this junta against his will, but seemingly lacked the courage to

at least did not openly oppose them; secretaries, Gaspar Marín and José Gregorio Argomedo. There were nine in all; but of these the count was merely a figurehead and, because of his age, had no influence. His death occurred four months later. Martínez de Aldunate never became a member of the body. Thus only seven of the members were in a position to serve.

The open *cabildo* was dissolved at three in the afternoon amid great signs of rejoicing. The ringing of bells announced to the populace the advent of the first national government. At night the city was illuminated, and a band of musicians was improvised to serenade the Conde de la Conquista and other members of the junta. Two days later a public proclamation of the new government was made from a stage erected in the main plaza for this purpose; three salutes of artillery were fired, the oath of obedience was administered to the army and to the administrative bodies, and money was thrown to the crowd that had gathered there out of curiosity.

In Santiago no one opposed the recognition of the junta except the *audiencia*. In Concepción recognition also called forth a special ceremony. The intendant retired from his post and Martínez de Rozas, who took it over as a member of the junta, increased the rejoicing of the popular celebration. In the following month the enthusiasm of the patriots was augmented by the return of those exiled to Peru—José Antonio Rojas and Juan Antonio Ovalle. They were received with a veritable ovation.

THE WORK OF THE FIRST JUNTA OF GOVERNMENT

The work of this first Chilean government was determined by the attending circumstances. It had to prepare for its own defense against the probable reaction that its adversaries might attempt and to institute some of the more desirable reforms in which there was unanimous accord to satisfy, in some measure, the aspirations that had produced it. The moment was not one for discussion but for action. Arms and money were lacking. Money was obtained in different ways; namely, by increasing the taxes on the tobacco monopoly, by lessening the salaries of public employees, and by soliciting private contributions. But weapons were more difficult to get.

---

resign. Hence he had to agree to many acts that he really condemned, including the death sentence imposed on Figueroa (see p. 161). During the Spanish restoration he sought to "purify his conduct" and to show that he had really been faithful to his king. See Barros Arana, *Historia jeneral*, VIII, 317, n. 27; Medina, *Dic. biog.*, p. 728; Virgilio Figueroa, *Diccionario biográfico de Chile*, IV, 613.

The relations that the *cabildo* of Santiago maintained with the junta of Buenos Aires helped greatly in this matter—relations which were closer as soon as the installation of the junta of Chile became known there. The reception of the news at Buenos Aires had been saluted with a salvo of twenty-one guns, which was followed by other demonstrations of sympathy. Moreover, that junta sent to the one in Chile a representative, a kind of diplomatic agent, so that both governments might work together in the reforms they undertook as much as in the armed defense which they saw would certainly have to be made in behalf of their rights and their territory. This mission had fallen to the Argentine lawyer, Antonio Álvarez Jonte.

After some months of labor they succeeded in organizing some fifteen hundred men—armed in whatever way possible, and worse clothed than armed—who, together with as many of the regular troops as were in the entire country, were to form the first army for the fatherland. This force was intended to repel whatever aggression might be attempted from Peru, because in that colony the old regime, with the viceroy at its head, continued without change. The junta of Buenos Aires, in coöperation with that of Chile, was to look after the defense against any attack from Montevideo or from Europe. The guiding spirit of the junta of Santiago during these preparations was Martínez de Rozas, who, when he had barely arrived from Concepción to take his place as a member of it, had, to a certain extent, assumed the exclusive direction of the government.

The most outstanding reform instituted by the junta in February, 1811, one designed to increase the public revenue and raise the country out of economic prostration, was freedom of trade. From then on the principal ports of Chile remained open to all the world, which was an old aspiration, one most eagerly demanded by intelligent colonists, and it meant a complete overturn in the existing economic system. However, its benefits in the first years were not very apparent, because the distance that separated the nation from the commercial centers of Europe, and the practice of contraband, which was exercised even in the most remote inlets of its coast, prevented any great development in the legal movement of trade. At any rate, the customs duties doubled at the end of the first year, and in the following years kept increasing at a steady rate. This reform, aside from an increase in revenue, was a most obvious demonstration of the revolutionary spirit which animated the new government. The duration of the latter, however, was limited to the time that would intervene until the election of a national congress, the legitimate representative of the interests and ambitions of the country.

At the beginning of 1811 everything showed that revolutionary ideas were gaining ground among the most educated Creoles—among other things, written placards nailed on street corners, frequent quarrels between Spaniards and patriots on the streets, and other similar demonstrations. Prominent among the writings that produced the greatest impression at that time was the proclamation of Quirino Lemáchez.[6] In this document the patriots were urged to declare complete independence. He said: "Nature made us equal, and only by virtue of a free pact made spontaneously and voluntarily, can another man exercise just, legitimate, and reasonable authority over us."

From these affirmations he drew the conclusion that, as neither the ancestors of the patriots nor the patriots themselves had agreed on a pact, the new government of Chile ought to be established by absolutely ignoring Spain. In high-sounding, burning language he painted the horrors of colonial domination and arrogantly added that "some day one would speak of the republic, the power of Chile, the majesty of the Chilean people." This proclamation, printed abroad many times, had a continental echo, because in Europe it was taken as the truest expression of the aspirations of the Spanish American people.

Its author, meanwhile, was unknown, for his signature was a plain anagram. Quirino Lemáchez meant Camilo Henríquez. Born in poverty in Valdivia in 1769, this agitator had been educated in Lima under the guardianship of relatives and in the convent of the friars of Buena Muerte. After finishing his studies he became a priest of this order. He was fond of reading, and, beside mystic books, he had others not of that kind, principally those of French philosophers. Although he read these prohibited works secretly, he was discovered and in Lima subjected to trial by the Inquisition. When liberated he was sent to Quito to found another convent of his order. The patriotic uprising that took place there in 1809 found him at this task and, as it was suspected that he had taken some secret part in the events, he was called to Peru. From there he determined to go to Chile and actually was in that country at the end of 1810. When he sent out the proclamation at the beginning of the following year, no one had even thought of him; but from that day he became one of the most popular and active personages in the revolution.

---

[6] The pen name of Camilo Henríquez González (1769-1825).

To the exaltation produced by that propaganda there was added in the following months a serious dilemma, which deepened the rivalry between Chileans and Spaniards. Word came from Buenos Aires that a new viceroy, Francisco Javier Elío, had been appointed for that colony, and that he had arrived at Montevideo with a thousand men and was attempting to take possession of his government by force. At the same time, the junta of that city asked the Santiago junta for men and munitions. Under the impression that Viceroy Elío would take Buenos Aires and would be able to proceed to Chile, the Argentine representative in Chile made use of every possible method to recruit men and send them to his country. The junta, on its side, also ordered a supply of gunpowder to be sent, and enlisted a body of regular troops to cross the Andes to aid the revolutionists of La Plata. The defeat of Viceroy Elío made this aid unnecessary.

In the midst of such anxieties, the junta decided to hold the election for deputies to congress. Preparations for that event were being made in Santiago, where the representatives of the district were to be elected on April 1, 1811, when, on the morning of that very day, the capital was aroused by a revolt among the troops which had as its object a counterrevolution in order to restore the fallen regime. It was what had been feared from the first.

The Spanish lieutenant colonel, Tomás de Figueroa, headed the movement and, although it consisted only of the force under his command, it produced great alarm. The revolt of Figueroa, however, was put down the same morning, after a brief exchange of shots on the main plaza between the rebels and the zealous patriot forces, formed almost entirely of recently incorporated recruits. The leader of the revolt, taken at nightfall in the convent of Santo Domingo where he had hidden, was tried and condemned to death that same night and executed in the public jail at dawn the next day, without being allowed any other personal privilege than to confess to the priest Camilo Henríquez.

This reactionary movement had more serious consequences than the death of the lieutenant colonel, Tomás de Figueroa, and some soldiers. The complicity of the royal *audiencia* being proved, the junta decreed the dissolution of that high tribunal that very month (April) and sent the members who did not voluntarily leave the country to places at a distance from the city. The junta took similar precautions with the ex-governor, García Carrasco, who still lived in Santiago and who was transferred to Valparaiso, from whence two months later he was sent to Lima.

The junta did not stop functioning until congress had been installed; but, after putting down the reactionary revolt, it could flatter itself that it had opened up and cleared the road to revolution. It had proceeded as a *de facto* government, assuming all public power, even forming its own army and, by introducing freedom of trade, reforming an economic system which had existed for centuries. It dissolved the highest secular court of justice in the colony and finally endowed the country with a national congress, as if it were already acting as an independent state. The responsibility for such acts was terrifying because of the consequences they must carry with them, but it had no terror for the men of the junta, among whom Martínez de Rozas was leader and continually guided that body toward the constitution of the new state.

THE INSTALLATION OF THE FIRST NATIONAL CONGRESS

A serious concern of the governing junta was the constitution of the national congress. Through the measures taken by it, almost all the deputies composing it were elected by the second fortnight of March, 1811. According to the regulations issued by the junta, the *cabildos* were to direct the elections in each province or *partido*. They were to make a list of the most honorable men in their jurisdiction and summon them to vote on a set day in its hall. The candidate obtaining the majority of votes was to be declared elected. Only one deputy was appointed for each district, but in some cities of importance two were allowed—Concepción, which was given three, and Santiago whose *cabildo* claimed twelve. The whole congress would thus be composed of forty-two deputies.

This simple mechanism functioned everywhere without hindrance, except in Valdivia, where the Spanish royalists ruled without opposition, and in Santiago, where the revolt of Figueroa held up the election on April 1, which was to be the final election; nor was it possible to effect it during that month.

The first of May came, the date set for the opening of congress, and the representatives of the capital were not yet chosen; but the deputies of the provinces, who were present and ready to exercise their functions and desirous of doing so, were not content to remain inactive until Santiago should elect its deputies, and asked the junta on that day to admit them into its sessions. The junta, led by Martínez de Rozas, granted the request and from that moment it was converted into a deliberative assembly. Without doubt the instigator of that maneuver was Martínez de Rozas himself, who, continually meeting strong resistance in the junta from certain moderate colleagues and counting on the majority of the provincial deputies, had to avail himself of that means in order to maintain his superiority.[7] Desiring at all costs to assure the advance of liberal ideas, he had used his influence so that the recently organized army should be entirely attached to him, and had not hesitated to place his personal friends, and even his nearest relatives, in command of the forces. These acts had aroused bitter hatred against him and had given occasion for his enemies to show him up daily in comic lampoons as a vulgar, ambitious man.

The *cabildo* of Santiago had declared itself against him and, when this body realized the importance of the party he had gained by incorporating the provincial deputies with the junta, it started an active campaign to hasten the election of the representatives from Santiago, and a week afterward they brought about the election and obtained a splendid victory—the twelve deputies elected by the capital were in opposition to the southern leader. They entered the junta and constituted a majority by which Martínez de Rozas lost his dominating influence in the government and withdrew from congress. Certain as he was of being elected in Santiago, he had not consented to enroll himself among the deputies for Concepción.

Congress and the junta, thus united into one body, constituted what they called the executive directorate. This new supreme power lasted until the formal opening of congress, and its work was principally concerned in opposing the policy of Martínez de Rozas. It filled the vacant offices with conservative men who would not help demolish the colonial regime as quickly as he had tried to. It created a court of justice to take the place of the defunct *audiencia* and filled it with lawyers of like affiliation; and lastly, by various means, it tried to persecute the most important followers of Martínez de Rozas and of his policy.

Conveniently prepared for by the executive directorate, the opening of the first national congress took place on July 4, 1811. At ten o'clock on the morning of that day the troops from the garrison were formed on the plaza and adjacent streets. At the same hour the deputies, the members of the junta and of the *cabildo*, the university doctors and residents of high birth left the governmental palace and with great solemnity entered the principal church. A mass was sung there, and from the pulpit Father Camilo

---

[7] The following sentence, omitted from the seventh edition of Galdames' work, appears in the sixth edition: "The cause of that resistance lay not only in the conciliatory spirit of the members of the junta who still retained sympathy with the past, but also in the excess to which Martínez de Rozas had carried his control."

Henríquez preached a commemorative sermon in conservative terms. The oath of the representatives was then administered, to the effect that they would protect the Catholic religion, obey Ferdinand VII, and defend the country and its recently founded institutions. After responding in chorus, "Thus we swear to do," they filed two by two before a crucifix surrounded by four lighted candles. This ceremony over, all left the church in due order; then they went to the session hall, which was the one the *audiencia* had used, and celebrated there the inaugural session of congress.

Juan Martínez de Rozas, in his rôle of provisional president of the governing junta of 1810, delivered a patriotic address to the deputies upon their duties and left the hall declaring that from that moment the junta established on the preceding September 18 ceased to function. Continuing the session, the oldest member among those present, Juan Antonio Ovalle, assumed the presidency and read another address in which he expressed his hopes for the intellectual and material grandeur of the nation. The session then adjourned. The city was illuminated that night and there was a display of fireworks. One of these represented a captive woman breaking her chains and regaining her liberty. It was the symbol of the country. Likewise there was by chance an allusion to the celebrated document of the United States of North America, whose anniversary of independence was the day on which the congress opened its sessions.

THE MEN, THE PARTIES, AND THE WORK OF THE FIRST CONGRESS

The session of the first national congress was one of controversy. All the interests and aspirations of the country were represented in it, except those of the lower classes of society, who witnessed such important occurrences merely as spectators.

From the beginning, three distinct currents of opinion made themselves felt in the assembly. These might be considered as corresponding to as many political parties. Men of quiet, conservative ideas, midway between those of the colonial regime and the one recently established, formed the majority. They did not wish to change the former completely and would have been disposed to remain dependent on the mother country, provided they were assured of certain reforms like free trade and the right to elect deputies to the Spanish Cortes. That faction of the patriotic party of 1810, influential because of its numbers, called itself "moderate," although it would have merited better the name "conservative." Its apparent leaders were the president of congress and José Miguel Infante. United to this faction and increasing its ranks because of affiliated tendencies was the "reactionary" or royalist group, which desired to reëstablish the fallen regime. Its deputies did not number more than three.

Opposing these dominant groups was another faction of the patriotic party, less numerous, but making up for lack of numbers by its boldness, for it attempted to end the colonial system and form the country into a republic; they were the *exaltados*, or radicals. In spite of the fact that certain men of the moderate party cherished ideas identical with those of the radicals, they did not attach themselves to the group because of their aversion to Martínez de Rozas, its chief, whom they continued to regard as the inspiration of this group, although he had remained out of congress.

Nevertheless, there were other men in congress itself of just as marked personality as Martínez de Rozas, who were among the most cultured inhabitants of the country. They now came forward to head the radicals in the first parliamentary debates. One of them was Manuel de Salas, the learned economist and philanthropist, whose activity had been so brilliant in the last years of the colony. Another man, still little known but soon to acquire chief prominence among the directors of the revolution, was Bernardo O'Higgins.

This leader was at this time thirty-three years old. He was born in Chillán on August 20, 1778, of the union of Ambrosio O'Higgins, who was governor of Chile, with Doña Isabel Riquelme.[8] He was educated in a Franciscan convent of Chillán and then in a seminary at Lima, and he had gone to England in accordance with his father's orders, with the idea of studying for some honorable profession. He was left there without any supervision whatever and without resources. His period of study was limited to two years and he shortly after returned to Chile when his father died in 1801, in order to look after his inheritance.

During his stay in England, O'Higgins had had occasion to ally himself with some distinguished Americans who happened to be living in London, who were already forming projects for the emancipation of the colonies. Among these was the Venezuelan general, Francisco Miranda, the greatest forerunner of Hispanic American independence. After fighting as a leader in the army of Washington for the emancipation of the United States[9] and striving

---

[8] The parents of Bernardo O'Higgins were not married. See A. U. Hancock, *A History of Chile;* J. J. Mehegan, *O'Higgins of Chile.*

[9] This is not quite exact. William Spence Robertson in his *Life of Miranda* (2 vols. Chapel Hill, 1929), I, 32-33, says: "By his service under the Spanish banner against outlying English colonies Miranda promoted the cause of the American Revolution. His relations with soldiers who won the independence of the Thirteen Colonies, however, extended little farther than a participation with

with no less courage in the ranks of the French revolutionists of 1789, Miranda emigrated to England with the idea of interesting the king in a project for Hispanic American independence.

In 1798 O'Higgins, a young man of twenty years, knew Miranda and was an intimate acquaintance of his in London. He became imbued with his ideas and enthusiastic over his emancipation plans and joined a lodge organized by Miranda in order to realize them—a lodge which was afterward called *Lautarina*,[10] whose aims he represented in Chile. Moreover, being a master of English and French, young O'Higgins read many revolutionary works which were published in those languages at the end of the eighteenth century. His connection with Martínez de Rozas and Concepción had finally convinced him that some day it would be necessary to found a sovereign state in Chile; and, when news of the upheaval in Spain arrived, all his thoughts were governed by that purpose. Rich, educated, brave, of handsome presence, he possessed admirable qualities for leadership. Once in congress, he and Salas assumed direction of the radical party.

Spanish troops in the conquest of English posts near the Gulf of Mexico. With French Allies who took part in these operations presumably he became acquainted. Available records of his coöperation with American patriots demonstrate that during the Bahama campaign he had unpleasant experiences with Carolinian insurgents. An entertaining legend long cherished by South American historical writers that he was a comrade of Lafayette and a soldier of Washington in the American Revolution is thus consigned to limbo."—J. A. R.

[10] *La logia lautarina,* introduced into Chile in March, 1817, was a branch of the one established by San Martín and Alvear in Buenos Aires, on the arrival of the former from Europe in 1812. Much uncertainty surrounds this "lodge" and its forbears. Some writers have sought to connect its origins with Miranda. That leader was, indeed, early interested in the Masonic order and possibly was initiated therein during his first visit to the United States. South American revolutionists gathered about Miranda in London during his stay there between 1800 and 1810, but it is hardly likely that they were ever formally initiated into a lodge to work for independence. The relations between O'Higgins and Miranda during that period were, however, very close. Freemasonry seems to have been a force among the Spanish patriots who resisted Napoleon and later opposed the reactionary government of Ferdinand VII and from Spain the movement evidently spread to South American centers. Among the autographed papers of O'Higgins was found what purports to be the statistics of a lodge which Vicuña Mackenna connects with the adjective *lautarina.* See his *Ostracismo del Jeneral D. Bernardo O'Higgins* (Valparaiso, 1860), pp. 269-283. See also Robertson, *Life of Miranda,* I, 199; and Benjamín Oviedo Martínez, "La Logia lautarina," in *Boletín de la academia nacional de la historia* (Caracas), XII (October-December, 1929), 436-451. See also López, *Historia de la república argentina,* Vol. VI, chap. v.

For about a month they succeeded in maintaining their position as radical deputies. But when the nomination of an executive junta was attempted, which was to have charge of public affairs while a national constitution was being prepared, twelve of the members of congress retired as a frank sign of protest because in that junta, which was composed of three members, they were not to have representation. The junta was named, nevertheless, and the radical group was ignored; but the junta did not last long because, in the first days of September, a military *coup d'état* occurred in Santiago and overthrew its influence.

The radical elements, deprived of power, saw the failure of their aspirations for political liberty in the course pursued by the conservative majority. Aided by the favor with which the latter party viewed the colonial past, the royalist group gained strength and plotted in secret the restoration of the fallen system. Martínez de Rozas had left Concepción to stir up the districts of the south, with the purpose of arraying them against this assembly. In Santiago itself there was a conspiracy of the same sort.

Under these circumstances, a bold young Chilean officer, recently come from Spain, made himself interpreter and executor of the radical proposals. This man, José Miguel Carrera, was born in Santiago on October 16, 1785, of one of the wealthiest and most influential families of the country. His father, Ignacio de la Carrera, had been one of the members of the first junta of government. His brothers, Luis and Juan José, had been among the most enthusiastic agitators in the popular movements of 1809 and 1810. At that time Carrera was in Spain. He had been sent there by his father to devote himself to trade and to the completion of his education, because his bold and arrogant character had early given much trouble to his family. However, he enjoyed the open sympathy of the young men of his time because of his vivacity, his intelligence, and his generous character.

When the French invasion occurred in the Peninsula, he abandoned his mercantile tasks, for which he felt little attraction, and joined the army that was defending national integrity. He fought in many battles until he was seriously wounded and had to remain in bed and be carefully treated. He now ranked as sergeant major of cavalry and, on recovering from his illness, he received news of the events in Chile and at once went to take part in the struggle which was beginning there.

His ideas were frankly revolutionary. He was associated in

Spain with Americans distinguished for their culture and he had formed, in intercourse with them, the belief that it was necessary to make the old colonies independent of the mother country, as the only way of achieving their prosperity. Upon reaching Santiago and observing the condition of affairs, he took his place without hesitation among the most advanced patriots and, counting on the prestige of his military campaigns and the high position of his family, he planned the movement which should snatch control from the moderate faction of congress. As his brothers were officers of high rank in two bodies of troops, it was not difficult for him to win proselytes in the army. The more radical deputies refused to coöperate in the projects of the new leader; so on September 4, 1811, at noon, two battalions assembled at his orders, arrested Colonel Reina, chief of the garrison of Santiago, disarmed other companies, and laid siege to the hall in which congress was in session.

The military *coup d'état* was carried out in a few hours, without resistance. The deputies from Santiago were reduced to six; others were dismissed; and new deputies, adherents of the radical party, were added to form a majority. The membership of the *cabildo* was modified; certain members opposed to the new regime were removed, and their places filled with others who were favorable to it. Lastly, the most substantial modification introduced was the formation of a new executive junta, composed of five members, of whom at least four, if not all, were radical patriots.

The junta thus formed, as well as the congress thus modified, was recognized throughout the country. In Concepción where a similar movement had been brought about through the influence of Martínez de Rozas at almost the same time as in Santiago—September 5—but by a civil element imbued with the separatist tendencies of the congress, the new junta was also enthusiastically recognized; but the provincial junta, created and maintained there by Martínez de Rozas, was still continued. Even in Valdivia a reaction shortly after occurred which gave the patriots predominance and incorporated the city in the reformist movement. In this way, the liberal party was entirely in control of the government and was able to celebrate the first anniversary of the installation of the junta of 1810 with a solemnity that foretold independence.

From that moment congress was very active—it formulated the greater part of the reforms which was afterward promptly carried out, and brought reforms of really patriotic scope to a successful conclusion. If unfortunate circumstances had not soon involved the State in civil and external disputes, without doubt the first representative assembly of Chile would have realized a more effective and enduring work.

From the beginning, with regard to administrational matters, it improved the local governments and the judiciary by inaugurating many suitable measures. Among others were the nominating of subdelegates by the central authority and the forcing of inferior tribunals to consult trained lawyers when they judged and sentenced criminals for serious crimes. It created the province of Coquimbo, which, like that of Concepción, was to be ruled by an intendant, and established a supreme court of justice in place of the tribunal in Spain, called "Council of Indies," just as the executive directorate had a while before created a court of appeals in place of the *audiencia*. Furthermore, in the principal cities it suppressed the sale of certain municipal offices or those whose incumbents served without pay—such as members of the *cabildo* or other municipal posts—and made them elective.

With regard to moral and religious matters, it suspended the remittances of money sent to Peru to pay the inquisitorial agents in Chile. This, in fact, was equivalent to closing that tribunal. It suppressed the parochial fees which were paid to parish priests for christenings, marriages, or burials, and established a fixed salary for these priests—a reform which raised many protests, greater no doubt than were caused by the abolition of slavery, a reform that alone would have been enough to immortalize that congress.

It is well known that there was a multitude of Negro slaves in Chile who had been brought from Africa—some ten thousand; and that, although their treatment was not so severe as had been accorded the Indians under the encomienda system, still the mere condition of slavery constituted an affront to humanity, according to the later view of all civilized nations. Therefore, the congress of 1811 declared that the children of slaves born in Chilean territory should be free and that all who should come in as slaves from the outside should also be free after six months' residence there. They did not emancipate those already in the country prior to the enactment of the law, in order not to injure the interests of their owners, who would have been able to inaugurate too strong a campaign in opposition to the government; but there were some people who, in keeping with the spirit of that resolution, freed their slaves of their own accord. Up to that time no country in America had taken such a step.[11]

Congress also enacted various economic measures tending to facilitate the interchange of national products with foreign countries. It established in clear terms the right of fiscalization[12] over acts of government that concerned each citizen and decreed publicity of its sessions by means of placards.

In regard to foreign affairs, it definitely broke off relations with Peru, whose viceroy had threatened it, and sent to Buenos Aires a diplomatic representative with instructions to make even closer the alliance existing between its government and that of Chile. It was the young lawyer, Francisco Antonio Pinto, who filled the post.

Conspicuous among the projects were the census of the national population; the creation of secular cemeteries in the environs of the city, and not within the churches or parochial churchyard, as had been permitted thitherto; the formulation of a constitution, for which task congress appointed a special commission; the extension of public education from the elementary school to the creation of a great establishment of secondary and higher education; and the general militarization of men within the country who were able to bear arms. But this congress was not continued much longer. It came to an end before the close of 1811.

CARRERA AND THE CONSTITUTION OF 1812

The military revolt of September had assured the most liberal patriots of their predominance in congress and had enabled them to urge the country on toward the rebirth of its political and social institutions; but the men of the new government had not been careful enough to flatter the young chief who led it or to use him in a way that would satisfy his ambitions. José Miguel Carrera and his brothers, alienated from governmental councils, then prepared a new military coup, this time with the design of taking upon themselves the direction of the country. They thought that in this way they would be able to improve the ideals of political reform already initiated.

---

[11] Through their own efforts during the last decade of the eighteenth century the people of color in Haiti had virtually abolished slavery and the equality of all races was recognized in the constitution promulgated by Toussaint l'Ouverture. For a discussion of the action in Chile, see Alcibíades Roldán, *Las primeras asambleas nacionales,* pp. 210-214.

[12] The "right of fiscalization" implies the right to censure or review the acts of another; hence, to call officials to a public accounting.

Not having reasons powerful enough to make a change in governmental personnel justifiable, they took as a pretext the fact that the national government, as constituted up to 1811, had no popular foundation because only certain persons designated and invited beforehand had taken part in the elections. In their opinion, therefore, the elections were illegitimate and congress itself was not free from that fault. The lower class, who did not understand anything at all of this, lived, according to Carrera, in a state of dissatisfaction with the authorities established in this manner; and from similar premises they inferred that the army, making itself the interpreter of the popular will, should reëstablish the principles of representative government, which required the direct participation of all citizens, without distinction of class or fortune, in the appointment of the governing class.

The revolt, which took place on the basis of these principles, after secret preparation, on November 15, 1811, was ostensibly led by Juan José Carrera, sergeant major of the regiment of grenadiers, but he was really acting on the incentive of his brother, José Miguel. Like the preceding outbreak, this movement triumphed without resistance. Its leader obliged congress and the junta to convene a great open *cabildo* to which could come not only those invited as before, but all those who desired to come; and this assembly, which was carried out under pressure from the revolting troops, appointed a new junta of government, composed of three members to represent the three provinces of the country. José Miguel Carrera was named for Santiago; Gaspar Marín, for Coquimbo; and Juan Martínez de Rozas, for Concepción. But Rozas was not in Santiago; so it was agreed that Bernardo O'Higgins should act as substitute for him until his arrival.

That situation did not last long. Marín and O'Higgins accepted membership unwillingly, claiming that it was the duty of the provinces to elect their representatives and that Santiago could not take upon itself the powers of the three. They maintained indifferent relations with their colleague, Carrera, and shortly, at the end of November, a conspiracy against the three brothers was discovered. Carrera then broke off relations with congress, considering it the instigator of the assassination that had been plotted against him. Marín and O'Higgins, seeing themselves subordinate to their colleague who had control of the military force, resigned their offices. This time Carrera assembled a third military mob and with it he dissolved congress on December 2, 1811.

Forgetting now those "principles of representative government," in whose name he had led the revolution in November, and declaring that the division of public power into legislative and executive was prejudicial to the state, Carrera assumed all authority and declared himself dictator. His military dictatorship, however, was not acknowledged throughout the whole country. The principal resistance occurred in the province of Concepción, where the local junta, directed by Martínez de Rozas, declared that it could not recognize his authority, since it did not constitute a representative government. Thereupon, Carrera organized several bodies of troops and sent them south, locating them near the Maule River, the southern boundary of the province of Santiago, for the purpose of making them march to the province which refused to recognize him as chief of the country and force its junta to respect and obey him.

Concepción took similar action, and even sent a more powerful army to defend the line of the Maule. Civil war seemed imminent; but Martínez de Rozas, leader of Concepción, was opposed to opening hostilities and entered into negotiations with Carrera. There was a conference on the banks of the river, and a long exchange of notes; in the end they did not reach an agreement. They merely decided that the troops of each province should return to their quarters. Martínez de Rozas for that reason lost prestige among his fellow provincials, who were sure of the superiority of their military units and come what may desired to strike an armed blow against Carrera. They accused their leader of lack of power for having opposed the fulfillment of their wishes.

As a consequence of such mishaps, relations between the two rival provinces were interrupted, commerce between them was paralyzed, and the agriculturists of the south suffered considerable loss. The army of Concepción could not be paid, for lack of funds; their salaries up to that time had always been met from Santiago from the general funds of the country. Soon the unpaid soldiers started a revolt in Concepción; they deposed the provincial junta and formed a new one, composed of army officers, and attached themselves to Carrera.

The principal victim of these deplorable dissensions was Juan Martínez de Rozas. Seized by the rebel officers of the province, he was turned over to Carrera, who confined him on a farm near Santiago, and shortly after exiled him to Mendoza. Weak and already ill, the famous leader, initiator of national independence, became exhausted in crossing the cordillera of the Andes; and after a few months' residence in the city of his exile, which was also the city of his birth, he died in 1813 at the age of fifty-four years.

Meanwhile, the revolutionary spirit was spreading so widely that a few people now thought of again being subject to the old mother country. In various public documents the name of Ferdinand VII appeared as a mere formula. In 1812 Carrera sanctioned a constitutional ordinance which is generally known as the Constitution of 1812 [13]—the first put in force in Chile—by which the country was organized almost wholly on a republican form, although recognizing by courtesy the legitimate sovereignty of His Majesty, the captive king. The supreme power continued to be vested in a junta composed of three members, each representing one of the provinces. A senate was also created. Carrera, however, remained in his position of military dictator, for, though he was only called a member of the junta, his other two colleagues, whom he himself appointed, lacked personality.

On the other hand, the arrival at the capital in the same year, 1812, of a North American consul, Joel Roberts Poinsett,[14] officially received by the government, led the patriots to entertain the hope that the United States would give aid to the colony that was trying to gain its independence. If to this is added the fact that the consul showed from the first decided leanings toward revolutionary ideas, one can easily understand that his assignment to Chile was celebrated as a victory for those who desired emancipation. Very soon also a national flag was created by decree, the first Chilean flag, which was to consist of three bands—one yellow, one white, and one blue. At the same time, it was ruled that the army and all the citizens should wear a badge of the same colors.

But these were not the only acts of the kind that showed clearly that the government directed by Carrera was leading the colony toward absolute independence. The impetus given to general education by various measures showed it better than anything else. Very soon, through the efforts of this leader, the first newspaper of the country appeared in Santiago on February 13, 1812, under the title *La aurora de Chile* (*The Dawn of Chile*). It is a fact that up

[13] For a summary of this document, see Galdames, *La evolución constitucional de Chile, 1810-1925* (1 vol. to date. Santiago, 1926), I, 320-335; Ramón Briseño, *Memoria histórico-crítica del derecho público chileno, desde 1810 hasta nuestros días,* pp. 56-57. The text is to be found on pp. 276-279.

[14] For the official status of Poinsett, see W. R. Manning, *Diplomatic Correspondence of the United States concerning the Independence of the Latin American Nations,* I, 6, 11; Barros Arana, *Historia jeneral,* VIII, 564. See also W. M. Collier and Guillermo Feliú Cruz, *La primera misión de los Estados Unidos de América en Chile;* and J. Fred Rippy, *Joel R. Poinsett, Versatile American* (Durham, N. C., 1935), pp. 41-49.

to that date printing was unknown in Chile. But the other American colonies possessed printing presses, which, although small, gave valuable service. Chile, so far removed from Europe, and poorer than other Spanish colonies, had not succeeded in introducing the press despite the strongest efforts made by the *cabildo* of the capital.[15] Finally, the North American merchant, Mateo Arnaldo Hoevel, settled in Santiago, and, being a constant partisan of the patriots, sent to the United States for a printing press—the first in Chile—and all its materials, even including typesetters. It had scarcely arrived when the government of Carrera bought it and, as soon as it was set up, took steps to publish a newspaper in order to support his policy. Camilo Henríquez was put in charge of it, as editor and, on the day and under the name mentioned, the first edition appeared on the street.

The newspaper—which was to be published once a week—consisted of four pages only, printed in two columns, and was the size of a sheet of official paper. However, its appearance created a great feeling of novelty and enthusiasm in the public mind. A contemporary relates that "men ran through the streets with an *Aurora* in their hand detaining as many as they met and read and reread its contents, expressing congratulations for such happiness and prophesying that, by this means, the ignorance and blindness in which they had lived until then would be banished."

In this work of diffusing the ideas of independence and self government in all directions, Camilo Henríquez was not the only one who distinguished himself. The old philanthropist and economist, Manuel de Salas, the learned and esteemed jurisconsult, Juan Egaña, and the young patriot, Manuel José Gandarillas, also collaborated with him on the *Aurora*. These four eminent Chileans have deserved the honor of being celebrated as the first national writers, and, in reality, their work of that period is admirable for its liberal policy and intelligent foresight.

They saw, though imperfectly, Chile converted into a democratic and prosperous republic, and exerted themselves to make their colonial compatriots, who had been accustomed to passive obedience to the monarch, understand the desirability of advancing along the road leading to the formation of a new political entity in the company of nations. To these men, this road was public education, free labor, moral customs, and patriotism—a civic virtue that demanded of each individual the giving up of many personal interests and even the sacrifice of life to the service of his fellow citizens.

---

[15] See p. 129, *supra.*

They went even further—they enlarged the national horizon to take in all of the Spanish American portion of the continents, at least all that of South America. Through its unity in race, language, religion, customs, and historic memories, this continent was called to make one country only, the American country. Some official documents and various publications of the period testify to this generous spirit of "continental fraternity," which from the first movements for emancipation was shown among the intelligent men of the country, and also in other Spanish colonies. These, then, were the pioneer writers who guided the generation of that time toward emancipation and toward the republic; and not a few of their ideas were already being practiced.

Public education was also an object of active attention. According to those patriots and many others, it was the supreme necessity of a people that aspired to govern themselves by the rule of liberty. Under the inspiration of this doctrine, numerous methods were attempted to establish primary schools in all towns and a large seminary for secondary and higher instruction in the capital. The difficulties that surrounded the national government prevented their immediate success. In 1813, when the political situation became somewhat normal, the junta over which Carrera presided sanctioned a new plan of primary instruction, according to which each place where more than fifty families lived was to have a school for males and another for females. Moreover, each convent of nuns must have a school for girls. Teaching was to be absolutely free. They also tried to create the profession of schoolmaster and to raise his social level, for the calling was still exercised by any person whatsoever, and often by those lacking essential knowledge and even morality; hence, this public servant was then considered as no more than a domestic servant.

As for secondary and higher instruction, the founding of the National Institute, inaugurated in August, 1813, was a work of that government. In order to give life to this establishment it was necessary to fuse together the three seminaries in Santiago at the end of the colonial epoch; namely, the Convictorio Carolino, the Academy of San Luis, and the Conciliar Seminary, to which was added also the University of San Felipe.

In the institute not only the teaching of the humanities and free professions was to be offered, but also primary instruction, for which purpose a school was annexed; and not only was civil teaching to be offered but also religious instruction for clerical preparation, so that the Conciliar Seminary was included without losing its identity. The place selected for it was the square that congress occupies today, in whose buildings the Jesuits had held their boarding school in the middle of the eighteenth century. In order to complete this educational work, provision was made for the creation of a public library, which was accomplished by taking as a basis the collection possessed by the University of San Felipe and adding books through private donations.

Such a vast work thus contemplated needed internal peace in order to flourish. The country did not have it because scarcely were the political dissensions in which it found itself involved at an end, than it had to sustain a war against a royalist invasion directed by the viceroy of Peru against Chile. Therefore, some of the reforms that had been inaugurated, like the creation of the institute, could not be made permanent in the midst of the perils of war. Nevertheless, the spirit that animated them continued to survive, until they were established afterward in permanent form.

At all events, in the three years of propaganda, of reforms, and of internal strife, the idea and purpose of being definitely free from Spain had possessed the major part of the educated population of the old colony. Martínez de Rozas first, and after him, Carrera, were the men who had best understood the real trend of the revolution and had given it its logical impetus.

CHAPTER VIII

THE MILITARY STRUGGLE FOR INDEPENDENCE

INVASION FROM PERU ; TREATY OF LIRCAY

FROM 1810 to 1813 the course of the patriotic revolution had been relatively peaceful. Besides the victims of Figueroa's revolt and others killed in the military mobs of Carrera, the country had no occasion to mourn the shedding of blood. It was, however, evident that, sooner or later, the new institutions would have to prove their stability on the field of battle. The Spanish government and its representatives in America were not at all reconciled to the loss of this colony; but the peril seemed far away to men of the revolution, because of the crisis in which the mother country was involved; and, although they had the foresight to organize some military forces to look after the defense of the country in case of need, they did not succeed in overcoming all the difficulties in obtaining arms and money. This worked against their purpose, which, indeed, they did not think they should make too great an effort to realize.

Notwithstanding, there were grave reasons for anxiety. In the midst of the revolutionary agitation which shook the whole Hispanic American continent, and while colonial governments fell, the viceroyalty of Peru remained undisturbed although some threats of overturning it had been felt there. Its viceroy, Fernando Abascal, an energetic man and a confirmed royalist, had taken extraordinary pains to uphold the cause of the crown, and the many resources at his command had permitted him to succeed in his effort. His intervention in Chile was greatly feared; he had even sent threats to the rulers of the new government; but not even then had they hastened to gather means of defense.

The viceroy very soon confirmed his threats. Not satisfied with maintaining Spanish sovereignty in Peru, he put into execution a plan of attack against Argentina and Chile, with the object of reducing them to obedience to the mother country. The plan consisted in invading simultaneously the territories of both countries. A division of his army crossed Upper Peru (today Bolivia) in the direction of Buenos Aires; and another division, formed in Chiloé, was sent toward Santiago from the south. The first to arrive at its destination was to cross the Andes and help the other.

In accordance with that combined campaign, at the same time that the army of Upper Peru advanced against Tucumán, General

Antonio Pareja, proceeding from Callao, disembarked on the island of Chiloé with a group of instruction officers and subofficers. As this island constituted a military province dependent on the viceroy and no revolutionary manifestation had made itself felt there, Pareja organized a body of troops composed of its garrison and its inhabitants.

He embarked this force in the same boats which had brought him from Peru and reached Valdivia without any trouble. A short time before, an antirevolutionary movement had occurred in that city, which had replaced the patriot authorities with royalists. The place was at once taken at the order of the invading general, who, without loss of time or men, increased his army with new material and went by sea to Talcahuano. Landing his men a little south of this port, in the Bay of San Vicente, he attacked the garrison of the place and, after a short fight, forced it to surrender.

From Talcahuano, the general suggested surrender to Concepción, and the city capitulated under certain conditions, because of a military revolt that had prepared it for surrender. In succession the principal towns of that province as far as its boundary at the Maule swore fidelity to Ferdinand VII and made mockery of the national government. Half of Chile was in the power of royalists at the end of the triumphant march of the general's army. This was at the end of March, 1813.

Santiago was completely ignorant of what was occurring in the south. News of such grave events arrived only at the beginning of April, and the sensation they caused was enormous. The most important people congregated at the doors of the junta and the senate, vehemently insisting that the most resolute measures be taken to defend the country. These authorities at once started to billet all soldiers and provincial militia, to form new bodies of troops, and to send them forward to preserve the line of the Maule. José Miguel Carrera, named general in chief of the campaign, hastened to Talca, followed by some officers and soldiers, and began to assemble there all the patriotic contingents which were scattered about, while the forces at Santiago were being brought together.

In a few days the frontier of the Maule was protected from invasion; as Pareja advanced to the vicinity of the river, the two armies at the end of April faced each other with about equal strength—four thousand men on each side—but, while the patriot soldiers consisted only of poorly armed and poorly equipped platoons, the royalists had numerous squadrons of veteran troops, whose superiority to the enemy appeared evident. Nevertheless, in this first campaign of the Chilean army there prevailed the most ardent enthusiasm and determination. Their principal leaders, the three Carrera brothers, O'Higgins, and Juan Mackenna, forgetting old quarrels as all patriots had forgotten them in the common peril, were determined to fight to the utmost in defense of national integrity and the new institutions.

The early encounters took place on the hills of Yerbas Buenas near the town of San Carlos. The first was a surprise attack delivered by a party of patriots against the royalists at night, when, because of the darkness, great disorder prevailed during the assault. The second was a battle in which both sides suffered heavily, as a result of which the patriots were scattered and forced to retire, while the royalists moved forward to entrench themselves in Chillán.

Carrera, with his army considerably augmented by new contingents sent him from Santiago, permitted Pareja to reinforce himself in Chillán and advanced toward the south. Without much trouble he took Concepción, Talcahuano, and other cities in which there were Spanish garrisons. Then he turned back to besiege Chillán. This was in the winter of 1813, from July to August. The siege was a failure. The patriot soldiers, weakened by cold and rain and obliged to fight in the midst of impassable swamps, were defeated and had to retreat.

Lieutenant Colonel Juan Francisco Sánchez took command of the royalist forces on the death of Pareja, which occurred in the same city. That commander celebrated the calamity of the patriots as a great victory and thought all resistance was at an end. Great religious festivals were celebrated in Chillán in honor of the king, and sermons were preached in all the pulpits against the "wicked insurgents."

The rout of the Chilean army was, however, not so complete. Though the commanders had seen many of their squadrons reduced and the spirit of the army languishing, they maintained confidence in the outcome. Taking Concepción and Talcahuano, they entrenched themselves near the Itata River. There they were making ready to undertake a new campaign against Chillán, when one night a Spanish detachment made a surprise attack on the patriot camp situated near a ford of the river Roble. The confusion produced among the Chilean recruits was indescribable. O'Higgins, exhibiting the *sang-froid* and activity that had always distinguished him, succeeded in uniting the scattered ranks and in repelling the attack.

Meanwhile, on both sides, the war acquired characteristics of unspeakable cruelty. The enemy was robbed, sacked, and killed without compassion. Many people wanted to make an honorable peace with the invader. The junta which governed Santiago during the campaigns of Carrera finally made itself the interpreter of this desire for peace and went to Talca for the purpose of contacting the Spanish leader of Chillán and of depriving Carrera of the command. The disasters of the latter were attributed to lack of skill and his conduct was severely criticized for having put all the army under the control of his brothers. The tentative plans made by the junta did not succeed because, shortly after their arrival at Talca, a new Spanish commander, General Gavino Gaínza, arrived with more reinforcements and greater determination to attack. The junta, indeed, carried out its first purpose, deprived José Miguel Carrera and his two brothers of the command of the patriot army, and appointed Bernardo O'Higgins, who was in Concepción, as general in chief. But its members had scarcely returned to Santiago in March, when they received the news that Talca had fallen into the power of the enemy and that José Miguel and Luis Carrera had been seized in Penco by the royalists and sent to Chillán, in March, 1814.

The capture of Talca by the royalists aroused the most dire fears in Santiago. The capital, unguarded, was left open to the invader. An open *cabildo* then met and asked the governing junta to resign its command because, under such dangerously critical circumstances, it was necessary to concentrate authority in one man. The junta resigned and Colonel Francisco de la Lastra, who was governing Valparaiso, was at once named supreme director with dictatorial powers. O'Higgins had received news of the fall of that city and immediately advanced toward the north.

Colonel Mackenna with another body of troops found himself in El Membrillar, a farm situated near the Itata River, a little west of its confluence with the Nuble, and entrenched himself there to wait for O'Higgins to join him. The royalist general, Gaínza, who remained in Chillán, aware of these movements, flanked Mackenna and moved to a position south of the two patriot commanders. Near the left bank of the Itata, in a place called El Quilo, the troops of O'Higgins defeated the royalist division sent to stop them. Gaínza then returned to El Membrillar, attacked Mackenna, and suffered a new defeat, which obliged him to fall back on Chillán. Mackenna and O'Higgins joined forces at El Membrillar, as had been planned.

Notwithstanding the two former defeats, the royalist army with its commander advanced toward the north. O'Higgins and Mackenna, noting that this movement meant nothing less than an attack on Santiago, followed them. Both armies then hastened their march in parallel lines, knowing that the first to pass the Maule would possess the capital. On the way O'Higgins learned that the division sent to recover Talca had been conquered at Cancha Rayada. But, undismayed by this bad fortune, he continued the parallel march that he had undertaken and succeeded in crossing the Maule almost at the time that Gaínza did, by an exceedingly uncomfortable ford (that of Las Cruces), with water up to the horses' necks. Going forward rapidly, he cut off the royalist advance and fortified himself in Quechereguas, on the right bank of the Claro River. Gaínza attacked him, trying to open a way to the capital, but in vain. Repelled in two attacks, he had to fall back to Talca. Santiago was saved; but Concepcíon, in April, 1814, again fell into the hands of the royalists.

After a whole year of warfare the situation of the two armies was not greatly changed. The province of Concepción and the cities of Valdivia and Chiloé were in the possession of the Spaniards; the provinces of Santiago and Coquimbo, in that of the patriots. Talca alone had been wrested from the latter and was the only advantage the royalists had obtained since the opening of the campaign; but both armies were tired, and peace was the common hope of both parties. The damage that agriculture and commerce suffered from the depredations of war and the forcing into service of men devoted to those occupations caused a general protest. Up to a certain point, however, the struggle was a civil war, because the army of the king had been formed of Chileans from Chiloé, Valdivia, and Concepción.

In such circumstances, a commodore, or English naval commander called Hillyar arrived in the country. He was sailing the Pacific in command of some of his country's ships and after visiting Peru he had to go on to Chile. He tendered Viceroy Abascal his services in arranging a negotiation between the belligerents, and his proposition was accepted. Hillyar had scarcely arrived at the Chilean coast when he entered into relations with the authorities and was soon accepted by Director Lastra in his character of mediator. He gained a like acceptance from Gaínza in Talca, and after many conferences a treaty was agreed upon and signed in May, 1814, on the banks of the Lircay River, a tributary of the Maule; for this reason it is known as the Treaty of Lircay.

In this agreement it was stipulated that: first, Chile was to recognize the sovereignty of the king of Spain just as when it formed a province of that monarchy; second, hostilities were to be suspended and prisoners exchanged; third, the Spanish army was to leave the country at the end of a month and Talca after a few hours; fourth, while the deputies were being elected to be sent to Spain, and until the Cortes should decide what ought to be done, the authorities of Chile were to remain at their posts.

At first both parties showed a disposition to comply with the pact. Gaínza gave up Talca and retired to Chillán; and Director Lastra suppressed the national flag that Carrera had had the army adopt two years before, together with the patriot badge, and replaced them with the Spanish flag and badge. But a lively discontent was not long in making itself felt in both the royalist and Chilean camps. Gaínza's troops felt they had lost an opportunity for victory, and the troops of O'Higgins thought the same.

In reality the patriots suffered the greater loss, because, in recognizing themselves anew as vassals of Ferdinand VII, they completely perverted the spirit of the revolution, and because they had lost the chance to impose on their adversaries by force any resolutions they might have desired. The disbandment of the royalist troops had actually begun in Talca to such an extent that Gaínza would not have been able to resist a well-coördinated attack. To sign such a treaty, then, while in such a situation, meant humiliation and disaster to the national cause.

THE NEW DICTATORSHIP OF CARRERA; THE DEFENSE OF RANCAGUA

The hope of the most ardent patriots was now personified, as on former occasions, in José Miguel Carrera. This leader, captured by the royalists in Penco, together with his brother Luis, shortly after having been deprived of the command of the army, had been transferred by Gaínza to Chillán. According to the treaty they were to be liberated; but in a secret clause of this agreement it was stipulated that they should continue as prisoners since, their irreconcilable ideas being well known, Director Lastra feared lest they provoke a popular military insurrection against the treaty. The Spanish commander wished nothing better than to find any pretext at all for not complying with the clause which obliged him to evacuate Chilean territory. Calculating that their activity would produce important disturbances, he gave them a chance to escape. As a result the Carrera brothers fled from Chillán and reached Santiago, where they were pursued by the government of Lastra as agitators of the people. They soon effected a military *coup d'état* and assumed command. They replaced the supreme director by a governing junta composed of three persons, among whom

Don José Miguel took his place, occupying the presidency, and hurriedly banished to Argentina those persons who might offer resistance to them. Prominent among those banished was Juan Mackenna, the most outstanding officer in the army of O'Higgins. The purpose of this revolution was to continue the war at all hazards.

The new dictatorship of Carrera was threatened by extraordinary opposition. O'Higgins, who was in Talca with his army, did not recognize the other leader and marched on Santiago in order to disperse his troops. He had no sooner passed the Maipo than he was met by a brigade under Luis Carrera and was obliged to retreat. From this moment the country was in open civil war. O'Higgins, a little south of that river, was in the midst of preparations for a new attack, when he received news of greatest importance. The viceroy of Peru had disavowed the agreement of Lircay and was sending a new contingent of troops in charge of General Mariano Osorio, who was empowered to force the submission of Chile.

Osorio had landed at Talcahuano and had reached Chillán. From this place he sent an official letter to Santiago addressed to "those who command in Chile," asking for the surrender of all revolutionary forces. It was the official bearer of that arrogant demand who, while on his way to the capital, notified O'Higgins of what had occurred. That leader then decided to change his policy and wrote to Carrera proposing that they forget all that had passed and unite the two patriot armies in order to repel the new invasion. Carrera accepted. O'Higgins recognized the junta on September 4 with only one condition—certainly a very generous one—that he should be permitted to form with his troops the vanguard of the army that defended the national integrity, and he went to take his advanced post in Rancagua near the Cachapoal River.

Osorio, meanwhile, advanced from Chillán toward the north with five thousand soldiers. On the last day of September, 1814, the two armies came within sight of each other at a distance from either bank of the river. In the night Osorio moved to Cachapoal, as if to make an attack on Rancagua. When O'Higgins saw that it was impossible to fight in the open country with an enemy that had such superior forces, he fortified himself with seventeen hundred men in the plaza of Rancagua. This plaza, situated in the center of the city, faced then, as today, the four streets which intersect its four sides. The entrances to the side streets, therefore, were a block apart. It was exactly at the intersections of these four streets, where they gave access to the plaza, that O'Higgins constructed adobe trenches with which he fortified himself and his troops.

These forces, of course, did not constitute all the army of the country. José Miguel Carrera, in his capacity of general in chief of the campaign, had given the command of the other two divisions to his brothers, Juan José and Luis, and he remained about a league north of Rancagua with more numerous but much less disciplined forces than those of O'Higgins.

On the morning of October 1 the Spanish troops attempted to blockade the fortified plaza. The struggle lasted all day; three consecutive assaults were repelled by the defenders. The cannon placed in the trenches and the gunfire from roofs and windows of buildings that surrounded the fort caused much bloodshed in the rank of the besiegers. The flag of the country flew from each trench and from the tower of the church. There the flagstaff was crowned by a black streamer, a sign that the garrison would fight till death. Night separated the combatants. From time to time desultory shots filled the air and raised alarm in the silent encampments.

As the Spaniards gradually apprehended disaster for themselves, the patriots grew more spirited in their vigorous defense of the plaza, but they realized that their situation would soon become indefensible if they did not receive help from the outside. The arbiter of the campaign at that moment was José Miguel Carrera, who with fresh troops was holding himself ready a league away from the place of combat. Consequently, O'Higgins sent a message to the general in chief—a message which was carried by an intrepid soldier who leaped over the walls and scaled the buildings. Written on a sheet of paper, it simply said: "If munitions come and the third division attacks, all is accomplished." By the same carrier Carrera replied: "Munitions cannot leave except at the point of the bayonet. This division will make its sacrifice tomorrow at dawn."

In the early morning of October 2 Osorio renewed the attack and the contest continued with terrible carnage. The defenders of the plaza confided blindly in the aid of Carrera. At eleven o'clock in the morning the watchman situated in the tower of the church at Merced announced that a cloud of dust was visible on the roads to the north. A cry of "Viva la Patria" greeted the happy news because that cloud of dust could be raised only by the approaching forces of Carrera. Soon, however, this cry of triumph and hope was changed into a despairing lament. The same watchman began to cry: "They are already fleeing." The division of Luis Carrera, meeting with the first royalists who had advanced to check it, scattered and retreated in the direction of Santiago.

In spite of all, resistance in the plaza did not cease. The royalists cut off the water in the ditches that entered the encampment of the defenders and the latter, with munitions almost exhausted, perspiring under the hot sun, and hungry and weary after more than thirty hours of fighting, had no water either to drink or to use in cooling the cannon. In the latter the powder took fire before the charge could be rammed home. The defenders saw no way of continuing the fight. Even the bodies of the fallen served as trenches.

Moment by moment the steady assault, skillfully directed, became more intense. The decisive instant finally approached. The buildings on one side of the plaza were set on fire by the besiegers. A spark that fell on the powder supply of the patriots caused an explosion that sent it flying. Protected by the confusion and the smoke, the enemy then entered from different sides. O'Higgins, still serene and comprehending that further resistance was useless, now ordered as many as were able to mount and flee. About five hundred men followed him and opened a way through the trenches amid a rain of bullets. A third of them remained lying on the field, but the general saved the banner together with the remainder of his army. Meanwhile, the conquering soldiery took possession of the plaza and attacked with savage fury the wounded, and the women and children who had taken refuge in the churches. When the column of O'Higgins from afar cast a last look back on the destroyed plaza, the sun was just sinking and they could still perceive on the horizon the smoke arising from its ruins.

With that day's events ended what was called "the Old Fatherland" (1810-1814). The period was marked by institutions and reforms that a small but energetic minority succeeded in implanting. It was also characterized by the failure of the revolutionists through indecision to follow frankly the way of independence, and by civil dissensions and disturbances that brought about the final catastrophe of Rancagua.

THE RETURN TO THE COLONIAL REGIME

With the taking of Rancagua, the way to Santiago lay open to the royalists. In fact, three days later the advance host of Osorio entered the capital to the pealing of bells, the discharge of skyrockets, and the applause of the multitude. On the next day the streets were trimmed with banners, while the troops stationed in them awaited the arrival of the victorious commander, who was received late in the afternoon in the midst of great manifestations of joy. From that moment the colonial government was reëstablished and the Spanish reconquest consummated.

While this was going on, the remaining hosts of the patriot army, with O'Higgins and Carrera in their ranks, together with many of the foremost residents from the capital began the emigration to Argentina and about three thousand crossed the Andes through Uspallata Pass. Without other than ordinary clothing they were fleeing from persecutions to come and from the disordered and wretched populace which had given itself up to looting almost as soon as news of the national disaster reached them. This emigation did not halt until it reached Mendoza, where it was kindly received by the governor of the province of Cuyo, José de San Martín.[1]

In Santiago Osorio at first showed himself amiable and merciful toward the conquered people. Many persons of rank approached him and offered their assistance in the work of government, and many of them certainly had not figured in the royalist group, which seemed to have greatly increased with victory. Little by little, however, Osorio showed the real tendencies of his spirit—tendencies directed toward the establishment of a severe and watchful regime of obedience throughout the country, although without exaggerated abuses or shedding of blood.

But reaction against the work of the national government was energetically begun. Ferdinand VII had months before entered Madrid, in May, 1814, restored to his throne, thanks to the decline of Napoleon's power in Europe, and had undertaken a similar campaign on the Peninsula. He had disavowed the acts of the government of the Regency which in his name had directed the reconquest of Spain during his captivity and dissolved the Cortes which gave a liberal constitution to the monarchy, because he aspired to reëstablish, by any and every means, the absolute system in force at the date of his abdication at Bayonne in 1808. This reactionary effort against the ideas of liberty, which was carried out in the political institutions of the kingdom, must necessarily be completed with the reëstablishment of the same regime in the colonies. The "insurgents" of the latter corresponded to the "liberals" of the former. The royalist policy in America as well as in Spain was in-

---

[1] The standard work on San Martín, the publication of which did much to fix that general's reputation, is Bartolomé Mitre's *Historia de San Martín y de la emancipación sud-americana*, in three volumes. A later edition appeared in four volumes in 1890. Based upon this is William Pilling's *Emancipation of South America*. For San Martín's plan, with reference to his earlier and later career, see chap. vii, *infra*.

spired by the same idea: a return to the past. And because of this Osorio also considered himself obliged to obey that policy.

The first repressive act that served as a basis for starting serious persecutions was the establishment of the tribunals of adjustment, created in Spain by order of Ferdinand VII, and established also in Chile. The *cabildos* of each locality composed these tribunals, and all persons charged with having in any manner failed in their duty of loyalty to their king had to appear before them; but it should be understood that it was not the *cabildos* that gave definite sentence in these causes, but the chief or president of the colony.

Shortly afterward, Osorio had more than forty of the principal patriots left in the country seized and deported to the island of Juan Fernández, where they had to endure a life of poverty, far from their families and from all centers of appeal. Among those deported were the old patriots José Antonio Rojas, Juan Antonio Ovalle, Juan Enrique Rosales, Ignacio de la Carrera (father of José Miguel), Manuel de Salas, and Juan Egaña. Nor did the North American who introduced printing into the country, Mateo Arnaldo Hoevel, escape this fate.

Such punishments immediately brought on the inevitable result —the creation about Osorio of an atmosphere of hatred, which continually became heavier. Although this general in taking such measures was only complying with the mandates of his king and of the viceroy in Peru, it is certain that some of his subalterns exercised a terrible espionage. The Regiment of the Talaveras, to which was entrusted the policing of the city, committed so many and such cruel arbitrary acts against individuals accused as patriots that it acquired an unsavory reputation. Its captain, Vicente San Bruno,[2] became particularly notorious among the implacable and bloody persecutors of the vanquished patriots.

There were other acts that contributed to make the government of the reconquest more hateful and at the same time weaken it. An unjust distinction was very soon established between the troops brought from Peru or Spain, like the Talaveras, for example, and those organized within the country, principally from Chiloé. The former received good wages punctually, the others, miserable pay, much delayed. The rivalry thus introduced into the army assumed a very grave character. Only the influence of the priests, who incited the soldiers to fight for the faith, succeeded in keeping these

---

[2] San Bruno's bloody reprisal in the prison of Santiago in February, 1815, is detailed in Barros Arana, *Historia jeneral*, X, 41-48. His energetic resistance on the battlefield of Chacabuco is noted in *ibid.*, p. 605, n. 18.

resentments from developing into an uprising. Furthermore, as the maintenance of the armed forces required increased expenditure, extraordinary contributions were levied on the inhabitants of the whole country, and these payments gave rise to insuperable resistance. Nor was the sequestration of the goods of the patriots, which was also decreed and produced no little rancor, sufficient to meet the large deficit that the financial situation continued to create.

To those violent measures, employed to assure the restoration of the old regime, was added the reëstablishment of almost all the former institutions that the revolution had abolished. The royal *audiencia* and the university again arose, and, as a result, the courts of justice created by the revolutionists were suspended and the National Institute was closed. The Inquisition was again introduced, to which was added the Order of Jesuits, who reappeared after their dissolution in 1773 and were summoned by Ferdinand VII to establish themselves in his dominions; and finally, liberty of trade was suppressed and the monopoly of the mother country again ruled. An official newspaper was founded in order to favor this reactionary work, under the title of the *Gaceta del gobierno de Chile*, which carried "Viva el Rey" for its motto.

RIGOROUS REGIME OF MARCÓ DEL PONT

When Osorio was most busily engaged in making secure the colonial institutions, he received notice that he was relieved from command and that his successor was on the way. Although he deemed this act an injustice, because it meant that his services were not recognized, and was profoundly depressed by it, he prepared to deliver the power to the new president and actually did give it up at the end of 1815, after governing for a year and some months.

The successor of Osorio was a Spanish general of not very worthy military antecedents, but of good social connections, by the name of Francisco Casimiro Marcó del Pont. The imposing ceremonies with which he was received and the peaceful conditions observed in the country made him and the royalists think that the reconquest was finally accomplished. The new governor brought quantities of trunks full of clothing and jewels which he showed little by little, to the great astonishment of the colonists; he also brought special coaches and costly furniture. All this luxury led them to look upon him more as a man of society than as a soldier and ruler.

But this man, who would have been inoffensive outside of government, when endowed with power became a tyrant. The numerous proclamations issued by him, threatening with the severest penalties, even death, those who were caught in any radical conversation, those who left Santiago without his permission, those who did not wholly pay the extraordinary contributions imposed by Osorio, those who gave shelter to any deserter from the army, those who did not give up the arms they had, and so on are still famous for their lack of consideration and their uselessness. At the same time he showed a cold, implacable cruelty. He established a tribunal of vigilance and public security, charged with judging by means of a very speedy proceeding—"brief, summary, and secret," according to the legal expression—all those who in any way might constitute a menace to the established order and to the monarchical cause. It thus constituted a kind of "court-martial" over which an army officer was to preside. He bestowed the presidency on the very notorious Captain San Bruno, who exercised it with the diligence and inflexibility that only he knew how to use in these cases, and the tribunal soon made itself so abominable to certain social classes that it became the symbol of the most ominous tyranny.

In another way the energy that Marcó del Pont put into pushing the proceedings against prisoners exiled to Juan Fernández, his disobedience to royal decree that conceded them the pardon they asked for, his prohibition of popular diversions—among them the *chaya* (confetti or water throwing), and the carnival—and a forced loan that he obliged them to subscribe to, ended in his incurring the hatred of almost all the people of the country. That system of terror, with its implacable persecutions and very severe levies, brought to mind the worst days of the colony and popularized an aversion to the king and his followers among the lower classes of society. The idea of revolution took firm root among all the people.

The Spanish reconquest in this way wrought its ruin by its own actions; for, if the prisoners on Juan Fernández could not attempt revenge, and those of lesser rank shut up in the jail of Santiago did not have enough influence to start a new revolution, the emigrants to Mendoza, on the other hand, were necessarily led to attempt an attack against that unpopular and arbitrary government for the purpose of restoring the institutions buried in the disaster of Rancagua.

Various events made Marcó del Pont and his counselors understand the reality of this danger and led them to believe the people of Chile themselves were disposed to support a patriotic restoration. Among the clearest warnings were uprisings in different parts of the country incited by Manuel Rodríguez against the government of Marcó del Pont during 1816 and the beginning of 1817. There was no man more popular in Chile during the last months of the reconquest than Rodríguez. About thirty years old, graceful in appearance, and of easy speech, he had graduated as a lawyer from the University of San Felipe and had taken part in the opening events of the revolution as a public agitator. When Carrera came to the dictatorship, he had been his secretary. He emigrated to Mendoza after Rancagua, but recrossed the cordillera, like many other patriots, to prepare public opinion against the Spaniards, so that the expedition fostered there against the government of reconquest might find opinion in Chile disposed toward a general uprising.

He fulfilled his mission better than anyone else. Entering into relations with all classes of people, even bandits, he improvised guerrilla bands with which he made numerous assaults on the royalist parties who guarded the different towns in the center of the country. He diffused everywhere news of the expedition that should come from the other side of the Andes to free Chile. He revived hope of a definite patriotic restoration. He so alarmed Marcó del Pont that the latter put a price on his head—a thousand pesos— and was obliged to divide the troops into many parties in order to pursue and break up Rodríguez' bands. Especially noteworthy was the capture of Melipilla and of San Fernando, with only a few men and in only a few minutes. Using the inexhaustible resources of his cunning, Rodríguez entered the first of those cities, in the midst of confusion and in full daylight, to the cries of "Viva la Patria," "Kill the Saracens!" Followed by some eighty horsemen, he instantly took possession of the garrison and of the public authorities, distributed the public funds among his own men, and then began his retreat. He did the same in San Fernando, where he succeeded in terrorizing the garrison with a few bundles of skins filled with stones and dragged by horses, bundles that sounded, during the night of assault, like pieces of artillery.

Hundreds of such exploits are recalled, but nothing was more curious than the means he used to introduce himself everywhere, to collect whatever information he wanted, and finally to communicate it himself to the emigrants at Mendoza. A historian relates:

Taking fictitious names, on occasions dressing in the habit of a Franciscan friar, the poncho of a countryman, or of a servant, or carrying the pack of a traveling merchant, he entered garrisons and houses that the officers of the Talaveras battalion frequented, prepared tricks to make them lose their reputations, and craftily incited soldiers to desert the service. It has been related that one day wishing to see the president, Marcó del Pont, at first hand, he had the singular boldness to place himself at the entrance of the palace and open the door of the coach, feigning the most respectful submission.

A personage like Manuel Rodríguez could do no less than become extremely popular with the multitude and exert an enormous influence on the revolutionary spirit of the people, but he was not the only one. With him at the time were a hundred young patriots who stirred up mobs and disorders in various towns and caused the greatest alarm to the government. The perturbation of the president increased to such an extent that he issued absurd proclamations in order to find a way to put down the revolutionary movement he saw spreading throughout the entire nation. One may judge of them by the following, issued at the beginning of 1817:

No person, of whatever class or condition, shall henceforth travel the road from Maipo to Maule on horse or mule, nor in any other manner ride on these animals within the limits comprised in the territory between the sea and the cordillera. Any individual, whether soldier or countryman, is authorized to seize any one who goes mounted on the above animals and may take for his own the mount which the transgressor shall lose, his person being subject to penalty of death, which I impose in this case and which shall be infallibly applied.

But this decree was issued during the exigencies and afflictions in which the governor saw himself involved, in order to make headway against the patriot invasion, which, according to announcement, would at any moment pass the Andes, and it could not be carried out for lack of time.

SAN MARTÍN AND THE RESTORATION OF THE NATIONAL GOVERNMENT

While throughout the territory of Chile the Spanish authorities were trying to blot out completely rebel ideas—ideas that were, however, kept alive by patriots from the other side of the Andes—Chilean emigrants in Mendoza were being organized to undertake the restoration of the rule of liberty that began in 1810. After the disaster of Rancagua, the persecutions of Osorio, and the violence of Marcó del Pont, conditions had so changed that now no patriot thought of respecting Ferdinand VII as his legitimate sovereign; absolute independence had come to be the inmost aspiration of all Chileans.

Formerly, as long as the captivity of the king lasted, there could be diversity of opinion in the national party concerning him; now these differences could no longer exist, since the king had already been reëstablished on the throne and revolution had necessarily to go against him. Under these conditions the emigrants of Chile had planned the problem of national restoration.

José de San Martín, an Argentinian by birth, although a son of a Spanish captain, was then governor of the province of Cuyo, with his residence in the capital, Mendoza. He was born in 1778 in a village near the Uruguay River, known by the name of Yapeyú, in the territory of Misiones. While San Martín was still a boy, his father took him to Spain and entered him in the best institution of military instruction in Madrid. The young San Martín left there as an officer in the Spanish army and served in it with bravery during those unfortunate days of the Napoleonic invasion, until he attained the rank of lieutenant colonel.

Becoming acquainted in Cádiz with some prominent Americans, he consented to their proposal that he return to his native land in order to lend to it the coöperation that circumstances might require. On arriving at Buenos Aires, he placed himself under the orders of the revolutionary leaders and was entrusted with organizing a regiment of horse grenadiers and in several campaigns distinguished himself with this regiment. He found himself in Tucumán, where he had been detailed to hold back the troops of the viceroy of Peru, which, after winning two battles, were advancing toward the interior, and he conceived the plan of warfare, the execution of which has given him his renown. Ignoring the plan of the viceroy, according to which the army that was marching against Buenos Aires must work in conjunction with the one marching on Santiago, he discovered what was precisely the most effective method to defeat or curb it.

In his opinion the defense of northern Argentina against the soldiers of the viceroy was entirely useless in insuring the success of the revolution, because the viceroy could continue sending more and more troops without fearing loss of his government, even if these troops should be defeated. It would be more convenient, first, to free Chile; then, to send from there a squadron with an army in it against Peru and to attack the viceroy in his own territory. The Peruvian patriots would then take up arms and help the invasion. Once the viceroy fell, not only would Argentina remain free but all South America, since the center of royalist power on the continent rested in Lima. Such was San Martín's plan. His best strength was devoted to its realization.

Feigning illness, he requested that he be retired from Tucumán and granted the governorship of Cuyo. In Mendoza, according to his statement, he would regain his health, and meanwhile he would peacefully continue to drill recruits. His request was granted. The arrival of emigrants from Chile in search of refuge confirmed him in the necessity of putting his plan into practice, which, aside from sentiments of fraternity that inclined him to receive them kindly, was another reason why his courtesies bore marks of special interest.

At first the emigrants did not respond worthily to such marked favors. The civil discord in Chile which had caused the loss of the country followed them even here. The partisans of Carrera and those of O'Higgins made mutual recriminations, throwing the blame for the past disaster in each others' faces. Carrera, furthermore, tried to maintain on that foreign soil the same rank and preëminence that he had enjoyed in Chile, and conducted himself before the governor of Cuyo with arrogance very inappropriate to his condition as a mere guest. Such imprudent conduct obliged San Martín to take energetic measures against Carrera and his more influential partisans, going so far as to send them out of his jurisdiction so that the central government of Buenos Aires might take what action it wished. But even after they had been transferred to that city, dissensions did not cease. Many other Chilean emigrants had gone to establish themselves in that center for the purpose of gaining a livelihood in any manner. Carreristas and O'Higginists again found themselves in discord there; and the scandal came to its climax when Luis Carrera, because of such disagreements, killed Juan Mackenna in a duel.

But these emigrants who showed themselves so deaf to conciliation and misfortune did not for a single instant lose sight of their country. José Miguel Carrera, assured that he could do nothing in Buenos Aires, went to the United States in order to find a way to arm a company there with which to undertake the reconquest of Chile. The O'Higginists, on their side, labored with the revolutionary government of Buenos Aires to assume the expense of the patriotic expedition that was being prepared. O'Higgins in person had gone to settle in that city. In perfect accord with San Martín, he was wholeheartedly ready to second the latter's plan. When the greater part of the obstacles were overcome, O'Higgins returned to Mendoza to take his post in the army of San Martín. Finally, in the middle of 1816, the expedition against Chile was definitely determined on, through the vigorous support of the supreme director of Buenos Aires, Juan Martín Pueyrredón,[3] who was in accord with the general in chief.

The declaration of Argentine independence, made July 9, 1816, revived still more the enthusiasm of the troops enlisted for the campaign. The "Army of the Andes," as it was called, reached the number of some four thousand men by the end of 1816, and its organization had taken San Martín more than two years. Many of the emigrant Chileans were also incorporated in its ranks. Finally, at the beginning of January, 1817, the army started on its march from Mendoza. It was separated into five divisions, which were to cross the Andes at the same time at as many different points. One, in charge of Ramón Freire, a brave soldier in the former army of O'Higgins, was to cross the cordillera through the Planchón Pass in order to fall on the district of Talca, Curicó, and San Fernando; another was to cross the "gate of the Piuquenes," in order to slip quietly into the valley of the Maipo; a third, very superior in numbers to the two mentioned, led by Colonel Gregorio las Heras, was to advance through the Uspallata Pass and then descend upon the city of Los Andes; and finally the bulk of the army, distributed in two divisions—one of which O'Higgins commanded—with the general in chief at the head, was to pass through the Garganta de los Patos (Ravine of the Ducks) and establish its camp in Putaendo. Still two more platoons of troops, which did not number a hundred men each, were ordered by San Martín to march, the first from Rioja toward Copiapó, and the other from San Juan toward La Serena. In this way the Argentine general would simultaneously occupy the north and the center of the country.

By the beginning of February all those divisions and groups came within sight of the territory of Chile. The passage of the Andes had been most dangerous; the altitude, which in those passes varies between 10,000 and 15,000 feet, caused among the soldiers the strange vertigo called *puna*. The changing terrain, the length of the routes, the intense cold at night would, it seems, have presented an insurmountable obstacle to the methodical advance of the troops. However, no considerable disaster occurred, and the divisions of Las Heras and San Martín, following constantly the itinerary as planned, arrived at their respective destinations after several small skirmishes with royalist parties. San Martín went

---

[3] For a description of the government of the Platine provinces under Pueyrredón as supreme director and of the director's relations with San Martín, see López, *Historia*, Vol. VI, chap. v. See also Mitre, *op. cit.*, Vol. I, chaps. xi-xiii, and pp. 608-628.

forward from Putaendo with his army to San Felipe and from there to Curimón, continually pressing toward the south in the direction of the capital.

Meanwhile the governor of Santiago sent more and more troops to meet the invaders. Completely stupified, Marcó del Pont did not know what to do in face of the peril that was threatening him because he had dispersed his powerful contingent of forces to different points of the country and did not know how to unite them in order to give battle with probability of success. Thus it was that the troops he succeeded in bringing together to face San Martín did not number half of the latter's force—fifteen hundred men against three thousand. General Rafael Maroto, put at the head of the royalist army, determined to fight on the hill of Chacabuco, at the northern entrance to the valley of the capital; and, as was to be expected, he lost the battle. In the early hours of the morning of February 12, 1817, the encounter took place, and two charges of the division commanded by O'Higgins were enough to disorganize his forces completely; soon the rest of San Martín's army was added to that attack and midday had hardly passed when the victory of the patriots was complete. The execrable San Bruno was numbered among the prisoners.

The authorities of Santiago received the news of the defeat late in the afternoon but tried to hide it from the people, and the town went to sleep, a prey to the greatest uncertainty. However, on the same night, Marcó and his subalterns abandoned the capital, going toward Valparaiso where they had several ships on which to take refuge. At dawn on the thirteenth no one could doubt the patriot success, since Santiago was left without authority and completely unguarded. The populace arose and sacked the houses of the royalist merchants, but on the same afternoon the first vanguard of the victorious army arrived to restore order in the town.

On the next day, the fourteenth, San Martín and O'Higgins entered the city with their troops and were received with delirious manifestations of joy. The most powerful residents, united in an open *cabildo*, offered San Martín the command of the state, but he refused to accept it, giving as an excuse his position as general in chief and the necessity of executing the war plans which his government had put in his charge. Then O'Higgins was proclaimed supreme director of Chile.

The fugitives of Chacabuco, however, continued to wander secretly through different parts of the central region of the country. Many of them, and among them Maroto, had succeeded in embarking for Peru on the ships at anchor at Valparaiso; but others, among them Marcó del Pont, had been taken prisoner in the days immediately after the victory. The unfortunate president was lodged in Santiago and shortly after sent to Argentina, where he died. The prisoner, however, who did merit being treated with no consideration was San Bruno, the chief of the Talaveras, on whom principally fell all the wrath of the people. Two months after the battle he was executed in the capital.

Meanwhile the other divisions of the Andean army, which at that time had entered Chilean territory through the different northern and southern gaps of the cordillera, had subjugated the rest of the country from Copiapó to the banks of the Maule, the region in which, at that time, the control of the patriots was made permanent. One of the first acts of Governor O'Higgins was to release the Chileans confined on Juan Fernández. The *Aguila*, a boat seized in Valparaiso, sailed to get them and all were restored to their homes. The return of these patricians was celebrated in that port and in Santiago as a triumph. They had suffered so much during the two long years of their captivity—because of the copious rains and the flooding of the ravines and because of the scarcity of food —that the stay in that desolate place seemed like a horrible nightmare.

But the greatest activity exercised by O'Higgins was in the organization of a national army, since he could not help foreseeing that the royalists who ruled the province of Concepción would attempt an attack and that, if they did not, the viceroy of Peru would not hesitate to send a new contingent of troops to join them. Moreover, he had to suppress stoutly the counter-revolutionary attempts of many Spaniards who, believing that all had not been lost, secretly plotted to revolt. The sequestration of the goods of the royalists, the exile of Bishop Rodríguez Zorilla, and some of his canons, were among the many repressive methods which were put into effect immediately.

San Martín betook himself to the Argentine capital in order to plan with Director Pueyrredón the best method to begin the campaigns that were to follow. O'Higgins, meanwhile, did not delay in sending against Concepción a body of troops to take possession of the province. That body, in charge of Colonel las Heras, fulfilled its mission, but the royalists of Concepción concentrated their forces in Talcahuano and firmly entrenched themselves there. O'Higgins himself left shortly after with new troops to support Las Heras and succeeded in gaining control as far as the south bank of the Biobío. General Freire, on the other side, took the plaza of Arauco; but in Talcahuano, the royalists, reinforced by the remnant of the army of Chacabuco, which the viceroy of Peru had forced to return to that plaza, offered effective resistance to the patriots and their positions could not be taken. At all events the national government and the patriotic regime, begun in 1810, were restored until the hazard of arms should again decide their fortune.

INDEPENDENCE—PROCLAIMED AND ACHIEVED

Just as was foreseen, at the end of 1817 news was received in Chile that the viceroy of Peru was sending a new army under command of General Osorio, the conqueror of Rancagua. It was then resolved to raise the siege of Talcahuano and concentrate all the army north of the Maule, and this course was actually followed. The patriotic population of Concepción also evacuated the city and at the beginning of 1818 Osorio with his new army landed at Talcahuano without being molested. Active war was to begin once more.

While O'Higgins was returning from the south, San Martín, who was in Santiago on his return from Buenos Aires, was working without rest, under the patronage of the provisional government located there, to place the army on a footing for defense. O'Higgins had halted in Talca in order to assemble there all the army of the south. In that city he then put his signature to a memorable document which meant the boldest challenge launched at the enemy —the act declaring Chile's independence. Some days after this act, on February 12, 1818, the first anniversary of the battle of Chacabuco, the proclamation and oath of independence were made effective with extraordinary solemnity in all towns of the country from Copiapó to Talca. The country's cause was from that moment the only concern of all. People without being forced handed over as much money as they were able to give in order to meet the expenses of war, and even the women gave their most valuable jewels.

The beginning of the campaign, however, did not meet popular expectation. Osorio left Talcahuano and crossed the Maule, while O'Higgins, abandoning Talca, joined San Martín, who brought up troops from Santiago and was to take the chief command of the whole army. The royalist camp was then situated in Talca, with five thousand men, and the patriot army, seven thousand in number, moved to occupy the broken plain of Cancha Rayada, a league northeast of Talca. In view of the inequality of forces and the weariness of his troops, Osorio considered himself lost, but suddenly, on the night of March 19, taking advantage of the Chilean army's being in motion, and confident that he would not be noticed, he fell upon it by surprise and completely routed it. In the confusion caused by the assault most of the troops were scattered.

O'Higgins was wounded by a ball in the right arm and with difficulty saved himself from being left on the field or from falling into the hands of the enemy. San Martín remained unhurt. Only one division of three thousand soldiers commanded by Colonel las Heras was able to retreat in order from the field of battle toward Santiago. Many of the fugitives were with him. On the following day when the first news of this great disaster reached the capital, it produced the deepest dismay and grief. Many began to prepare to emigrate once more to Mendoza. The rumor became current that O'Higgins and San Martín had perished or were prisoners. Other rumors affirmed the report that the royalist army was coming against' Santiago by forced marches and that the patriot forces, completely annihilated, could not anywhere offer resistance to it. Measures of the provisional government tending to revive the spirit of the people, to appease the terrible unrest, and to unite some elements of defense were all in vain.

When three days of anguish had passed, more complete reports began to show clearly that the defeat was not of such magnitude as was supposed. At this time that energetic and astute man who had directed the guerrillas of the reconquest, Manuel Rodríguez, betook himself to the public plaza, held an open *cabildo*, harangued the multitude and, exhorting them to persist in the defense of the territory to the uttermost, succeeded in arousing anew the hope of salvation. The popularity of this leader then reached its height and the legend that formed about him still recalls the celebrated apostrophe with which it is said he electrified the multitude: "Citizens! We still have a country!" For one day he exercised in Santiago the power of a virtual dictator. He distributed arms to the people and formed a battalion of two hundred men to which he gave the name "Hussars of Death," because they were to carry as a device a skull painted white on a black background.

If his authority did not last longer, it was because O'Higgins soon entered Santiago and resumed command as supreme director. San Martín also arrived shortly, and both leaders again received the felicitations of the entire city.

THE BATTLE OF MAIPÚ

After the disaster of Cancha Rayada the work of the moment consisted in uniting all the forces that were still on foot to defend the capital against Osorio's army, which was advancing slowly toward the north. A battle that would decide the fate of the Chilean, and even of the American, revolution was to occur. If it were lost, perhaps Argentine independence would be endangered; and, if it were gained, the liberating expedition to Peru which San Martín had resolved upon would become a reality.

Days of unheard-of anxieties were these for the two men who had taken over the responsibility of the expedition. O'Higgins, recovering from his wound, did not rest, however, in the task of preparation, and San Martín, tenacious beyond all others, drilled and maneuvered the troops with surpassing activity. With the division of Las Heras as a basis, the patriot army was reorganized in a little more than a week, and in the first days of April established its quarters a league south of Santiago on the plain of Maipú. On April 4 the army of Osorio already had passed the Maipo River and taken its position facing San Martín.

Meanwhile, the most desperate anxiety reigned in Santiago. The women went to the churches to ask for divine protection, in behalf of the country. The few men who had not taken up arms to meet the enemy now grasped them to guard the people. Some merchants, fearing the excesses of the suburban mobs, barricaded the doors of their stores. Orderlies on horseback came and went at a gallop and kept the whole city in a state of most intense alarm. O'Higgins, nervous and restless, unable to be present on the battlefield because of his wound, took whatever precautions he thought necessary in order to guard the capital or to undertake a retreat to Coquimbo. The night was passed wholly without sleep, each one imagining from moment to moment that he heard the gunfire announcing battle.

Thus dawned April 5, 1818—a clear, mild day. The armies passed the morning in observing each other, and now and then the advance guards of one or the other exchanged shots. The plain of Maipú, the site on which the battle was to take place, is not entirely level, being divided by numerous chains of hills generally called the "Cerillos." On a series of these toward the north, extending almost directly from east to west, San Martín developed his line of battle. On another series of hills toward the south, which formed a sort of triangle, one of whose sides paralleled the other army, Osorio developed his line. Between the two was a space of lower ground as long as the whole line of attack and varying from five hundred to a thousand meters in breadth. This was the distance that separated the combatants. Their forces were equal, about five thousand men on each side,

A little before noon, the patriot army began the firing that started the battle. The Chilean artillery functioned from the first with rare precision; the cavalry wrought havoc. There was an instant, however, when the infantry retreated in order to flank the right wing of the royalists, which was resisting with terrific force. That resistance, however, did not last very long. Bodies of fresh troops, despatched by San Martín to reinforce the infantry thus driven back, reëstablished the superiority of the patriot army. Following these movements there was a sharp attack on the Spanish line, which was extended out farther and farther and forced to make up in discipline and bravery for the number who had fallen. At two o'clock in the afternoon it was already exhausted and then had to retire in defeat and fortify itself in the houses of Lo Espejo, about a kilometer farther south.

At that hour the bells of Santiago started to ring. People embraced on the streets, giving vent to the most intense emotion and mingling their cries of "Viva la Patria" with the peals sent forth from the bell towers. The din of the battle caused an indescribable anxiety among the population. Emissaries came and went reporting at intervals the varying events of the day. Finally one messenger, in a voice choking with emotion, gave news of the patriot victory, now openly declared.

At that moment, O'Higgins was not in the government palace. He had departed in the direction of Maipú with the troops that guarded the vicinity and with a number of townspeople. He had not been able to resist the impression made on him by the boom of cannon and the odor of powder that the wind brought to the city. Popular legend recalls him as pacing through the town on his war horse with his right arm bound and in a sling, amid the acclaims of the multitude, especially of the women. He is supposed to have said before leaving: "Only one arm is left me but with it I shall decide the fate of the country." Reaching the tent of San Martín at the very moment when the royalists were dispersed, he embraced him, exclaiming, "Glory to the savior of Chile!" And San Martín replied, "Chile will never forget the name of the illustrious invalid who today presents himself on the battlefield."

The fact is, however, that O'Higgins, in spite of his wound, repaired to the plain of Maipú with a considerable reinforcement and arrived there when the battle was already decided in favor of the patriots. But as it was renewed in the houses of the hacienda of Lo Espejo, where the entrenched royalists made a heroic resistance, he was able with his men to contribute to the victory. The most horrible part of the battle was that very attack on the redoubt of

Lo Espejo, because the successful soldiers were enraged and gave no quarter, in spite of their leaders' exhortations for moderation.

Meanwhile Osorio, with a portion of his guard, had taken flight, when he barely saw that the day was lost. In spite of the quick pursuit made after him, he succeeded in escaping. Some days later he shut himself up in Talcahuano and months afterward embarked for Callao. In this manner the last cannon shot of Maipú, discharged at sunset on April 5, 1818, meant for Chile the decisive moment of emancipation and the advent of "the new country" three and a half years after the end of "the old country," which Osorio himself had buried in Rancagua.

THE POLITICAL CHARACTER OF THE WAR FOR INDEPENDENCE

The situation of Chile on the date of the battle of Maipú was that of a country affected by a revolution lasting eight years (1810-1818) ; that is to say, it was an irregular situation in which all classes of society were disturbed and all public services disorganized. The disturbance had been so profound that it could not be limited to a simple change of political rule. It must necessarily transform many of the existing social habits and institutions to adapt them to a new form of government to be established in place of the one that had been overthrown. But it is a fact that up to that time colonial society had been only slightly modified, and for that very reason there were serious obstacles to the republican organization which the government tried to give to the former colony. A slight examination of the situation then existing will give a more precise interpretation to those difficulties.

The military spirit, atavistic because it was the inheritance of the two races that here mingled their blood, and because the long-drawn-out Araucanian war had stimulated it much more, still had an influence on popular custom through its qualities of powerful leadership and its very barrack-room firmness, and it led people to regard each pretentious swordsman as chieftain in his own right. The campaigns for independence had only accentuated this kind of respect for force which was at the same time the most visible manifestation and the most solid foundation of authority; and this respect for men of arms was justified by their intervention in former events, which had been effective, disinterested, and brilliant.

The same lack of initiative and of public action, the same old passivity, accustomed to hope for all that was good and to fear all that was evil from the omnipotence of a master—whether he be called king, captain general, supreme director, president, or master —continued as before to dominate the character of the masses, the educated as well as the ignorant. The prejudices of nobility, blood, and fortune still caused productive labor and the laborer to be looked upon with contempt and learning, with compassion. Those who bore the titles of count and marquis, the old primogenitive aristocrats, continued to exhibit their parchments and to make their superiority prevail over other social classes and even over men of their own class.

The extreme piety of former times, still very little tempered in spite of the adherence of the majority of the clergy to the conquered colonial regime, always inclined the people to consider the priest not only as the guardian and support of Catholic faith, but as the depository of all truth. The absolute absence of civic culture caused men of slight education to misinterpret the noble struggles for the common good and frequently to attribute them to petty motives of personal interest. This interpretation scattered the seeds of discord over any attempt to unite for the common good.

The good qualities of the period were of a private nature and were confined to home and to business, not to public life. This last, as a matter of fact, since it had never existed, lacked traditions and doctrinaire precedents. Only from the nascent patriotism, from that spirit of social solidarity that had been developed in the conquering class during the recent battles and persecutions, could one hope to triumph over the mass of obstacles that stood in the way of the new order.

The attempt to organize a democratic republic on a popular representative basis was being made; but the people had not been prepared for the exercise of sovereignty and consequently were unable to make their representation effective in the government. What we now call the "people"—the proletariat group of society, which occupied the most subordinate rank in the life of the nation and was composed of the mestizo class, formed by the crossing of Indian with Spaniard—was to be converted into a power through its numbers, for in the new organization of government it was summoned to be the legitimate sovereign, and upon its vote was established the election of the higher authorities.

If at first the adherence of the masses to the revolutionary movement had been feeble and of no consequence, after the disaster at Rancagua and the arbitrary course of the reconquest, and above all, during the campaigns for national restoration, when they saw their blood flow in defense of free institutions, they were converted into firm supporters of independence and became entitled to the consideration of the public powers. But their lack of culture and their misery kept them from comprehending the importance of and participating in the benefits of the recently created situation, and they continued to occupy the same servile rank as formerly. It is understood that a republic with such a social foundation can be a republic in name only. In this way only the rich, educated class of Chileans had the privilege of exercising political power. From that moment, through force of circumstances, the wealthy Creoles constituted a dominating oligarchy, and the republic was to be organized in disregard of the people.

The social class of Creoles had made the revolution, and by its aid independence triumphed. It had overthrown the authority of the king, together with the traditional respect which until then had been yielded to him. It had overpowered the privileged class of European Spaniards, which it had expelled from the country or had assimilated, annihilating it completely; and now that the popular mass could do nothing, the Creoles themselves concentrated in their hands all public power. Among them were three influential elements—the colonial aristocracy, the clergy, and the army—which had to form the government and organize the republic. For the moment the colonial aristocracy could do little or nothing, because it was principally occupied in recovering from the material losses suffered in behalf of the movement for emancipation. Not all its men were formerly patriots, but now all were, because the patriots had triumphed. Under the circumstances, neither could the clergy aspire to be the directing force, since they had scarcely recovered from the unfavorable opinion occasioned by their adherence to the monarchy. Only men of the sword and men of civil prestige, such as writers and thinkers, remained to face the situation. The military element then prevailed and the country continued under its command. Aside from this, the war could not yet be considered finished, since a great part of the territory, from Chillán to Chiloé, was still held by royalist troops; and the center of colonial power in South America, the vice-regency of Peru, remained intact.

To organize a republic under such difficulties was more than difficult—it was impossible. On the one side, colonial society was not adapted to the new political form; and, on the other, the constant menace of war prevented the completion of tasks of that kind. Consequently the people would have to live under a provisional military regime before constituting a political state. Accordingly they lived in that way.

The only thing in which there was unanimous accord was in adopting the republican form of government, now that the establishment of a national monarchy was in no way acceptable. No one was in a position to become king, and the hatred fostered against Spain extended to the whole monarchical system. The ideas of liberty and equality which had given form to the revolution were irreconcilable with the absolute power represented by a king; and the example offered by the English colonies of North America, which had won independence from their motherland and had formed a prosperous federation, seemed to the revolutionists conclusive proof that the only system possible in America was the republican.

So, if it was feared that the prevailing military power might abuse governmental faculties, in no case could the thought of a monarchical reaction be entertained. Briefly, emancipation had a character almost exclusively political. It substituted for the monarchical and colonial form of government a republican one and transferred the predominance of the Spanish social group to the purely Chilean Creole group; but in no respect did it affect the institutions on which such things as property, family, labor, religion, and law were founded. The revolution had, however, to strike little by little against those social institutions until it modified them profoundly.

CHAPTER IX

THE MILITARY DICTATORSHIPS

THE PERIOD OF O'HIGGINS (1817-1823)

THE MAN on whom had fallen all public power in Chile since 1817 was an illustrious and serene spirit of indisputable superiority among the best of his contemporaries. Bernardo O'Higgins formed a rare combination of warrior and statesman; he was at the same time a general and a thinker; the swordsman in him did not make him less the man of ideas; nor as such was he less the man of practical judgment. From the first, however, he seemed enveloped in the most serious difficulties. The directing politicians were divided into two personal parties; namely, the friends and partisans of José Miguel Carrera and those of Bernardo O'Higgins. It was chieftainship in action.

It has been mentioned that the former, displeased with San Martín in Mendoza, had considered it necessary to settle in Buenos Aires and then had journeyed to the United States in order to organize a company with which to return and attack the royalists of Chile. Now this enterprise, almost inconceivable on account of its impetuous character, was nevertheless realized. Carrera succeeded in interesting in his own behalf in the struggle for the independence of Chile some North American shipowners and merchants and in equipping three ships, with which he started for Buenos Aires.[1] He arrived at that port during the very days when the army of the Andes, after crossing the cordillera, was occupying its first position in Chilean territory and was preparing to engage in battle at Chacabuco.

Supreme Director Pueyrredón was not disposed to let him pass on to Chile, fearful of the disturbances that he might provoke there; and, as he might try to flout the vigilance that the Argentinian executive maintained about him, he was seized and shut up on a vessel from which he took flight for Montevideo. His brothers, Juan José and Luis, shortly after also tried to cross the Andes, and start a new revolution in the name of Don José Miguel, in order to snatch from O'Higgins his recently inaugurated government, but the provincial authority in Mendoza seized them. An odious

---

[1] For an account of Carrera's mission to the United States and of his relations with prominent individuals there in 1816, see Collier and Cruz, *La primera misión de los Estados Unidos de América en Chile*, chaps. xi, xii.

trial followed, and finally, three days after the victory of Maipú and when the news of the same had not yet reached Mendoza, they were condemned to death and executed in that city. The sensation caused in Chile by so cruel a deed, which was attributed to the secret orders of San Martín and O'Higgins, was stupendous, and from that day the friends of Carrera were united in opposition to the supreme director.

That execution was followed in Chile by the assassination of Manuel Rodríguez, the notable warrior and popular agitator. As he was numbered among the ringleaders of the movement hostile to the government which broke out after the death of the Carreras, and as he committed the imprudence during those days of entering the governor's palace on horseback at the head of a multitude of people, O'Higgins ordered him arrested and sent to Quillota. On the way, near Tiltil, where today rises a monument commemorative of his sacrifice, the officer who guarded him had him assassinated by some soldiers on the pretext that he had tried to escape but, in reality, in obedience to the instructions of his superiors. This occurred at the end of April, 1818.

José Miguel Carrera, exiled in Montevideo, thought only of avenging his brothers; and, putting into play his insuperable activity and audacity, he scattered to the four winds from that capital numerous printed proclamations in which he attacked the reputation of the authorities of Buenos Aires and of Chile, employing the harshest kind of epithets, even going so far as to call them mere "assassins and robbers." Later he was mixed up in the civil disputes among the Argentinian provinces. He organized a terrifying mob composed of the Chileans who were living in that country and who wished to follow him, and later of the barbarous Indians of the pampas. He gained the favor of a new supreme director at Buenos Aires, raised to power after the fall of Pueyrredón and then threatened Mendoza and Chile. Becoming the terror of the neighboring republic, he finally fell into the power of the governor of Mendoza in 1821, after two years of most exciting conflict and after many encounters, and was executed in the principal plaza of the city. As a greater disgrace his head and arms were ordered nailed to the trees along the roads. Thus this man, famed for his many merits, ended his life in the same place and manner as had his two brothers—all victims of their ambition and pride, but victims also of a noble desire to free their newborn country.

Such tragic occurrences could only embitter men's minds against the rulers of Chile and create troublesome obstacles in the development of their political plans. Even though some of these events took place outside the country, it was well known that an alliance existed between the governments of Chile and Argentina, whereby all that was done in Argentina against Chileans received beforehand the tacit approval of O'Higgins, if not his express order. There really was such an alliance; not only were the ruling men of Chile bound to those of Argentina by official relations, but also by an intimate secret pact, contracted within a revolutionary association called *Logia lautarina*.[2]

This society, secret alike in its constitution and in its proceedings, had been established by San Martín in Buenos Aires, shortly after his return from Europe. It was similar to the one founded by Miranda in Paris, from which it was derived. Its object was to fight against Spain everywhere possible; its very name, derived from Lautaro, was a symbol. Only certain persons of influence and social connections joined it under the strictest oath of secrecy, any violation of which was punished by death. This same lodge was introduced into Santiago by San Martín shortly after the victory of Chacabuco and was brought into intimate relations with that of Buenos Aires, being, indeed, almost a part of it. Pueyrredón, the director of the Argentine Confederation, and O'Higgins, the director of the Republic of Chile, figured with San Martín among its principal members. Thus is explained the invariable accord with which the governments of Buenos Aires and of Santiago proceeded while those men ruled over them; and, as the lodge was secret and so much mystery was made of its transactions, it was always accused of the death of the Carreras and of Rodríguez and even of the most insignificant extortions of the dictatorship, until it was given all the appearance of a bloody tribunal.

But it was not only the violent ill will shown by the friends of Carrera for the friends of O'Higgins that disturbed the administration of the supreme director; the financial situation of the country was just as serious, or more so. The former military campaigns and those that would have to follow until the territory was completely occupied by patriot arms called for resources in money much larger than those the government had received up to that time, and the public finances were in a woeful state. The methods worked out by the director and his minister, José Ignacio Zenteno, to increase the revenues consisted, aside from the seizure of royalist property, in the complete reform of the system of taxes established up to that time—above all, in employing stamped paper, customs

---

² See p. 166, n. 10.

tributes, and the tobacco monopoly—and in the imposition of new and heavier tributes on the towns and territory subject to the patriot arms, such as gifts and forced loans, requisitions of animals and forage for the army, extraordinary monthly and annual contributions, and other payments. With all these changes the annual revenues increased to more than two million pesos; and, if one recalls that at the close of the colonial period collections had not reached six hundred thousand, he will understand that the growth of national wealth had advanced rapidly in just ten years, notwithstanding the state of war; otherwise it would have been impossible to bear such heavy burdens.

In spite of the evident increase in revenues for the public treasury, the obligations to be met by the State were so increased that the taxes were not enough to meet them except in a very limited way. The situation with respect to agriculture and mining, the two constant sources of production in the country, was getting worse because of the very war disturbances and of the routine methods used in exploiting them; and, even when the government enacted different laws in their behalf and even some protective tariff customs, which made the importation of similar products harder, very little benefit resulted from them. In addition, two earthquakes during these same years, one in 1819 which destroyed Copiapó, the mining center of the territory, and another in 1822, which destroyed Valparaiso, the commercial center, brought inevitable economic disaster.

In the midst of the poverty of the treasury and the general tribulation, under the dictatorship of O'Higgins, the domination of the patriots, nevertheless, extended to the extreme south in the central valley of Chile; the first national squadron was formed; and Peru was liberated with the help of a Chilean force. The war in the south lasted during the whole administration of O'Higgins. The leader directing it for the patriots was Colonel Ramón Freire; and, for the royalists, Captain Vicente Benavides.[3] The remains of the army defeated at Maipú retreated to Chillán, whence it soon went to Concepción and from there to Valdivia; but Benavides stayed behind with a respectable body of troops which carried on a fierce war of plunder and extermination that deserved to be called a "war to the death."

This strange personage was a Chilean born in Quirihue, who joined the national army, deserted, and fled to join the royalist

---

[3] Vicente Benavides, born in Quirihue about 1785, was a ferocious guerrilla leader who filled his page in Chilean history "with blood and grief." For details of his tempestuous career, see Barros Arana, *Historia jeneral*, XII, 98-102, n. 5.

army, in which he reached the rank of captain. Taken prisoner and twice condemned to die, he was shot on the last occasion after the battle of Maipú; but it happened that the charges were blanks and he was saved without receiving more than a saber blow, which was given him as a *coup de grâce*. A short time afterward, as he had shown much ability and activity, San Martín wished to make use of him and sent him as a spy to the royalist army to incite the troops to mutiny, but he enrolled in it and later became a dreadful enemy of his country.

Defeated in numerous encounters, he went to rally forces among the Araucanians and, with a group of Indians added to his guerrillas and supplies sent by the viceroy of Peru—who also made him a colonel—he renewed his filibustering and plundering campaign from Chillán to Araucania. Some bandits, the Pincheira brothers, seconded with their depredations the work of the royalist colonel. Even when Freire broke up his bands in various encounters, he did not succeed in taking him, until one of his own friends betrayed him when he was hidden on a lighter coming from Peru and delivered him up to the government. Benavides was hanged in Santiago in 1822, and with him ended the most vigorous royalist resistance in Chile.

THE FIRST NATIONAL SQUADRON

While the war of the south lasted, the first Chilean squadron also was organized. The men of the revolution, O'Higgins among the first, understood very well that the struggle for independence would be completely fruitless if it were not maintained on sea as well as on land; and the day after the encounter at Chacabuco they began to consider ways of constructing a squadron to rule the Pacific. Before the reconquest they had succeeded in gathering some small vessels but, as there were not enough to form the basis of a fleet and as the disaster of Rancagua occurred so soon, nothing was salvaged of the results of those first attempts. There was urgent need, then, to begin the work anew; O'Higgins and his minister, Zenteno, undertook it.

Despite the seemingly insuperable difficulties proceeding from the scarcity of resources in the treasury, an English merchant frigate was purchased, manned for war, and named *Lautaro*.[4] This and the brig *Aguila*, captured in Valparaiso after the triumph of Chacabuco, served as a basis for the first national squadron.

---

[4] For a contemporary description of the initial exploit of the *Lautaro*, see John Miller, *Memoirs of General Miller in the Service of the Republic of Peru* (2 vols. London, 1828), I, 182-184.

With the purchase of three more boats this squadron of Chile included five vessels by 1818, and was able to sally forth in search of the enemy. Four of those vessels actually went that same year from Valparaiso to the south, under the direction of Manuel Blanco Encalada, captain of the navy, now promoted to chief command. O'Higgins, watching the boats from a hill at the port as they spread their sails in the distance, said to those accompanying him: "Three tiny craft gave the sovereigns of Spain possession of the new world; those four are going to take it away from them."

The supreme director was not mistaken. This first campaign gave happy results. The capture of the Spanish frigate *María Isabel* in the Bay of Talcahuano and of some maritime transports of the same nationality established at one stroke the mastery of Chile on the ocean. After its capture the *María Isabel* was called the *O'Higgins*. Chilean corsairs helped to carry on the maritime war successfully. In several craft they traversed the Pacific coast, committing hostilities against the commerce and navy of Spain, and in a short time seized about thirty boats of the enemy. The shore line of Chile was now almost completely swept clear of Spanish ships, and the growing squadron was able to undertake an enterprise of greater proportions, which would have seemed beyond reason if in that period all things were not thought possible—nothing less than an attack on the fleet of the viceroy of Peru, for the purpose of preparing the way for the liberating expedition.

To direct this campaign, they engaged Lord Cochrane, a mariner as wise as he was daring. This Englishman [Scot] made Chile his second fatherland. A former chief of the English fleet, he had a reputation which without doubt made him the leading mariner of his time. Son of a peer of that country, he was born in 1775 and became a member of the British parliament, after having comported himself valorously in many naval combats. Involved in a troublesome lawsuit as a result of certain stock speculations, he thought himself condemned and persecuted there, and this induced him to seek another field of action outside his own country. Moreover his extreme ideas—he was an uncompromising radical in his politics—disgusted him with most persons of his rank. Thus it was that, after entering into relations with the agent of Chile in London, he decided to lend to this new republic all the force of his intelligence and valor.

At first the results did not come up to general expectation. The two expeditions conducted by Cochrane to Peru in the same year, 1819, failed. The viceroy's squadron shut itself up in Callao under the protection of the forts which defended the port and did not offer to fight. But Cochrane sailed as far as Guayaquil, effected some landings, and seized some Spanish merchant vessels, which was a good deal, although he did not accomplish the principal object of his enterprise—the destruction of the viceroy's squadron. On returning to Chile, he tried to wipe out the bad impression produced by this relatively fruitless expedition by performing a deed scarcely conceivable in its boldness.

With only one vessel, the *O'Higgins*, he appeared in 1820 before Corral, the port of Valdivia. After seizing a Spanish ship he found there, he landed a body of troops and at the point of the bayonet by a surprise assault took the fortifications of that place, which unconditionally surrendered. The capture of Valdivia was a military feat, almost inexplicable, since the stronghold of Corral was defended by more than seven hundred soldiers and more than one hundred cannon, and Cochrane did not muster more than three hundred musketeers.

With this act all Spanish resistance ceased in that part of the country and, once the bands of Benavides were defeated, Chilean control was extended as far as the Channel of Chacao. The admiral attempted a similar enterprise in the plaza of Ancud in order to conquer Chiloé, but he was repulsed. Only this island, then, remained unsubdued by the patriots, and at that time there was no other opportunity to attempt to capture it because the whole attention of the navy and army of Chile was now to be concentrated on Peru.

THE LIBERATING EXPEDITION OF PERU ; THE INTERVIEW AT GUAYAQUIL AND ITS AFTERMATH

The plan conceived by San Martín years before when he occupied the government of Cuyo had not in 1820 been completely realized. Chile was liberated, but the viceroy of Lima continued to maintain the colonial regime in America. The revolution triumphed in all the former dependencies of Spain except in Peru. On the Peninsula, Ferdinand VII was struggling with a formidable revolt against his absolute rule. The movement sponsored by the liberal Spanish element started at Cádiz where an army of twenty thousand men was almost at the point of embarking in order to put down American independence, and in the bosom of that very army. Colonel Rafael de Riego headed the insurrection on January 1, 1820, in behalf of the reëstablishment of the liberal constitution of 1812. The most profound fear took hold of the court, and the expedition against the American insurgents was frustrated.

San Martín's plan against the royalists of Peru was thus made more workable and from that moment the government of Chile devoted all its activities to carrying it out.

The liberating expedition of Peru, it might be said, had really been in preparation since the day following the battle of Maipú. The difficulties opposing its organization are not to be told here. It had been thought possible to count on the wholehearted aid of the government of Buenos Aires in view of the alliance that San Martín had established between Argentina and Chile, but the internal disturbances in which the former confederation found itself involved and the frequent changes of government and of policy in the government itself, which that situation made necessary, finally obliged the supreme director of Buenos Aires to stop lending San Martín Argentine aid. He was even ordered to return with all the forces that he had in Chile. The expedition to Peru was deemed impossible in view of the scarcity of resources in the Argentine treasury and the supposed poverty bordering on bankruptcy of Chilean public finance. Then San Martín, seconded by all his officers, disobeyed this order and O'Higgins decided that his administration should assume entire charge of the equipment and cost of the enterprise. It seemed an act of folly. Chile was the most distant and obscure of the former colonies of Spain. Yet it was assumed to have not merely ambition but resources enough to undertake the work of deposing the viceroys from their century-old throne in the richest American colony. However, it was not impossible.

Accumulating funds largely by means of forced loans, and in many other ways, concentrating all the energies of the nation on that single object, with unvarying constancy, O'Higgins and his supporters succeeded in suitably equipping an army of forty-five hundred men and a squadron of twenty-three boats and armed transports of war, with a crew of two thousand men. In addition to the necessary provisions for the maintenance of this force, they shipped equipment and armament for organizing fifteen thousand soldiers among the patriots of Peru. In the middle of August, 1820, that entire force was assembled in Valparaiso ready to embark.

Almost all the troops and the greater part of the officers were of Chilean nationality. The two chief leaders, San Martín, commander of the army and of the entire expedition, and Lord Cochrane, in command of the navy, if not Chilean by birth, were such at least in devotion. The treasury of Chile was left without a single cent and burdened with debt. The country had left nothing undone for such a vast undertaking. Hitherto, the Pacific Ocean had not borne a more powerful fleet.

The troops embarked on the eighteenth and nineteenth of August.

The port of Valparaiso presented a wonderful spectacle. The ships, dressed with the national colors, awaited their contingents of men. The populace, as on a festival occasion, assembled on the shore to take leave of their relatives. There were tears on many countenances. Some wept for fear that they would never see their loved ones again and others because of patriotic emotion aroused by the magnitude of the enterprise undertaken by the republic. The music of military bands softened this sensation of sadness and revived enthusiasm.

The embarkation was performed with surprising order and regularity; and on the morning of August 20 a salvo of twenty-one guns saluted the anniversary of O'Higgins' birth and announced that all was ready for departure. Shortly after noon a south wind filled the sails; the convoy raised anchor for the journey north-ward. Exclamations of "Viva Chile!" uttered by the crew drew similar cries from the shore. The women waved their handkerchiefs in the air. O'Higgins, following with emotion the gentle movement of the ships, murmured to those around him: "On these four bul-warks hang the destinies of America." [5]

In Peru the liberating army began the campaign by taking pos-session of Pisco and next by blockading Callao. Here Cochrane took the Spanish frigate *Esmeralda* by boarding it, in spite of its being protected by the fortifications of the port; but the latter did not capitulate. San Martín, on his side, placed his encampment some thirty leagues north of Lima and entered into negotiations with the viceroy, Joaquín de la Pezuela. These negotiations led to no results; meanwhile the army remained inactive. San Martín had thought that all he had to do was to arrive with his troops and the Peruvian patriots would rise up against monarchical despotism. His disappointment was great; no one stirred in Lima, and only one or two places in the viceroyalty gave signs of insurrection. Neither did the viceroy, certain of the inferiority of his own force, risk battle.

Finally the invading chief resolved to approach Lima and then the royalist army, wearied of Pezuela's passivity, which it regarded as cowardice, rebelled and deposed him and named a new viceroy.

---

[5] For the quotation see p. 210, *supra*. For a general account of this expedition, compare the following: Hancock, *A History of Chile*, pp. 181-194, *passim;* Mark-ham, *A History of Peru*, pp. 241-251; and Pilling, *The Emancipation of South America*, chaps. xxvi, *et seq.* A contemporary narrative is afforded by Miller, *op. cit.*, Vol. I, chaps. ix-xvi, *passim.* See also Mitre, *Historia*, Vol. III, chaps. xxvi, *et seq.;* and Barros Arana, *Historia jeneral*, Vol. XII, chap. ix, and Vol. XIII, chaps. ii, *et seq.*

The latter, however, evacuated the capital in a little while, and San Martín entered it peacefully. The people of Lima now declared themselves in favor of the patriots on July 28, 1821; solemnly proclaimed the independence of Peru; and named San Martín chief of the country with the title of "Protector." Following the conciliatory attitude that he had resolved to observe, the general ordered the division which he had sent to the towns of the interior (*la sierra*) to return. Thanks to this movement, the royalist army was able to reorganize and recruit its force in that same region and to pursue and harry all persons that had declared for the patriot government.

At the end of a long siege and blockade Callao had to surrender; but a severe controversy almost made fruitless the gains of the liberating expedition. Cochrane and San Martín could not agree and broke relations. There seems to be no other reason for their disagreement than that the leader of the squadron, finding himself without means to pay his sailors, had taken upon himself the responsibility of compensating them from the funds of the viceroyalty against the orders of San Martín; but at bottom there was something more. The impetuous and dominating character of Cochrane had not been able to tolerate the passive course of San Martín in Peru and this general, on his part, had not been able to suffer without anger the other's impetuosity and violence. However this may be, Cochrane left Peru with his squadron and coasted along the Pacific as far as Mexico, a foray during which he seized many Spanish ships. In the middle of 1822 he returned to Chile without having become reconciled or even on speaking terms with San Martín.

Meanwhile, the situation of the liberating army in Peru became difficult. Ill-treated by the climate and decimated by illness and strife, it showed itself powerless to resist royalist attacks. San Martín then sought help from Chile and Argentina. Chile alone made a new sacrifice and sent him provisions and troops. The star of the celebrated warrior seemed eclipsed; he lost prestige even among his officers; but, at the very time that San Martín declined, in Venezuela, Colombia, and Ecuador, north of Peru, arose a new military genius—Bolívar the Liberator.

After overrunning those nations in triumph, he offered to San Martín a plan for combining to liberate Peru and asked for an interview with him. San Martín accepted joyfully, writing him: "America will not forget the day on which we embrace." And they really did embrace on July 26, 1822, at the city of Guayaquil. For several hours the two most influential Americans of their time tarried there, conferring behind closed doors and entirely alone, but they did not reach any agreement. It is known, however, that they discussed the way to assure Peru's independence and the most suitable political regime for South America, whether monarchy or republic. San Martín preferred the first and Bolívar the second. The former then thought it would be preferable to withdraw from the military and political scene.

San Martín did not remain much longer in Peru. After having installed the first Peruvian congress and resigning to it the command which he had exercised as protector, he moved to Chile. The army which he had led, however, remained in Peru, except for a few officers who returned with him. That army was later dispersed, but almost all the soldiers enlisted with the troops of Bolívar, who came to consummate the independence of Peru; and, under other banners and without their proper identity, and distributed among the different regiments of the Liberator, they fought bravely in the great and decisive battles of Junín and Ayacucho. And so, no matter how it came about, Chile could flatter itself that it contributed effectively to make Peru a sovereign state.

In spite of this, the end of the liberating expedition was not satisfactory, since it had not succeeded in realizing the mission which had been entrusted to it; and this was all the more to be regretted since the means put into the hands of the leaders had been sufficient and had cost untold sacrifices. Activity and assurance in directing the campaign were lacking on the part of one leader; and the spirit of accord on the part of the other.

It was not strange, then, that the prestige of San Martín and of Cochrane should suffer greatly. Furthermore, the predominance of O'Higgins was also approaching its end and a civil struggle of considerable proportions was proclaimed against him. Rather than see himself enveloped in the overturn which threatened Chile, San Martín retired from the country to Mendoza; and, without further participation in politics, he passed on to France, in one of whose cities (Boulogne) he died in 1850, in very modest circumstances. Cochrane also left Chile for the same reason as San Martín and only a few months after; but he did not refrain, like his rival, from undertaking new campaigns; on the contrary, he went to lend his naval services to Brazil and then to Greece, fighting in the same cause of liberty for which he had fought in Chile, always brilliantly and boldly. It was not till 1860 that he died in his native country, after having written the *Memoirs* of his agitated existence.[6]

---

[6] Some of the documents connected with the departure of San Martín and Cochrane are to be found in Miller, *op. cit.*, App. G and H, pp. 386-389.

THE SOCIAL POLICY OF O'HIGGINS

The motive which started the agitation in Chile against the supreme director was not only the unflattering conclusion of the campaign against Peru; there were others of a much more important nature which arose from his administrative and political career. It should be noted at once that the dominant tendency of his course was social reform; that is to say, it had as its object the modification of society with respect to the revolution and the republic, with the idea of adapting it to the new political regime. When he came into power the revolution was as yet no more than a simple change of government from which the Spaniards had been eliminated and the Creoles substituted. O'Higgins believed that in order to organize a real republic it was necessary first to modify society, since it was not possible for the same social state which had served to support the colony on a monarchical basis to serve for the republic, which required a popular basis.

Nothing could contribute more, in his belief, to change old habits than the development of education; and few things occupied the supreme director so much as this. In 1819 the National Institute, founded in 1813 and closed during the Spanish reconquest, was reopened, and a year later, the Public Library also, which was entirely reorganized by the old patriot, Manuel de Salas. At the time this was done, there were founded also through official coöperation other educational institutions, such as the Liceo of La Serena in 1821 and the Lancasterian schools in Valparaiso and Santiago, called "Lancasterian" because in them was initiated a new method of teaching, whose author and promoter was an English educator, Joseph Lancaster.[7] This method consisted in the children's giving themselves mutual instruction just as was done later in the system of "monitors." In order to establish it they brought in some foreign teachers. Two of them were English Protestants, a circumstance which then could not be viewed with indifference.

In a broader sphere of action, the opening and upkeep of primary schools was relegated to the *cabildos* and to convents of the religious orders for men and women; and the government, desiring that each should have facilities for instruction, declared books, pamphlets, and periodicals free of customs duties and gave them free circu-

---

[7] See Webster E. Browning "Joseph Lancaster, James Thompson, and the Lancasterian Systems of Mutual Instruction, with Special Reference to Hispanic America," in *Hisp. Amer. Hist. Rev.*, IV (February, 1921), 49-98, particularly pp. 75-81.

lation through the national post offices. It likewise favored the
services of the press and, although its liberty was very much restricted in whatever touched on political comment, there were at
that time no less than two independent newspapers, besides the
government paper called *Gaceta ministerial* (*Ministerial Gazette*).

Another very strong interest of the supreme director was the
local improvement of the more important towns in the country. In
Santiago he founded a market for the sale of all food supplies consumed in the capital, on the same site where the Plaza del mercado
(Market Plaza) is located today. Up to that time its character
was indicated by the name given it—the *basural* (garbage pile).
With this measure the central plaza of the city gained in health and
cleanliness because it largely ceased to be what it had been, when
the sale of those materials took place on its eastern side and all the
waste was thrown into the open ditches. The general cemetery
which Santiago has at the present time was then founded against
the protest of the clergy who, in defiance of all hygienic prescrip-
tions, persisted in having the dead interred inside the churches or
near them.

The present Alameda de las Delicias was converted by O'Higgins
into a promenade; the avenues were lined with poplars; the drains
were made of brick; and the piles of stone and garbage scattered
about there disappeared. The illumination of the streets was also
decreed and this was to be done by having each resident place a
lantern in the principal doorway of his house and keep it lighted
until midnight. The urban and rural police were organized in the
best manner that resources allowed. From that time dated the
night watchmen (*serenos*) who for many years loudly announced
the hours and changes of weather. Street paving, public hygiene,
and local ornamentation since then have given Santiago the appearance of a modern city. Santiago was not the only city to enjoy those blessings; Valparaiso, Concepción, La Serena, and other
cities participated in them.

Valparaiso, especially, had developed rapidly as a result of
the foreign population which settled little by little in that port.
It already numbered more than three thousand individuals, and
there was increasing activity in business because of commercial
liberty. It ought rightly, therefore, to have merited the special attention of the government. One of the measures that raised a general protest because of religious sentiment was the creation of a
cemetery for dissenters, which O'Higgins ordered to be founded
there, for the purpose of avoiding trouble among the immigrants

of other religions than the Catholic. Had not the earthquake of 1822 destroyed the city, its prosperity would have become really extraordinary for the period.

New centers were also established at that time: Unión in the south, Vicuña in the north, and San Bernardo near Santiago. The founding of the last city, whose name was given it out of deference to the director, was joined to a very important event—the completion of the Maipo Canal in 1821—a half century's work which had just been finished, thanks to not less than twenty years of untiring labor and the constant protection that the government of O'Higgins bestowed upon it. Considering the tools for working and the capital that could be obtained at the time, this work, which was the cause of the agricultural wealth of the entire valley, appeared colossal to his contemporaries.

But O'Higgins thought that his administration could also modify some popular customs which had taken root throughout the centuries and were the result of ignorance or of atavistic prejudices. Among the most pernicious figured cockfights, bullfights, the celebration of the carnival (*chaya*), the festivities in the taverns of the suburbs, in which games of dice and the most offensive drunkenness prevailed, together with quarrels often of a bloody character. The director ordered all these prohibited under penalties of no little severity. He also prohibited processions at night which engendered many scandals, including the fetichistic adoration of certain images or amulets said to be miraculous, which were located in some churches and other public places. On the other hand, he encouraged the creation of a theatre in Santiago, an edifice of light material which was erected in front of the present palace of congress. For some time the first dramatic presentations that in a more or less permanent form were given in the capital took place there. This innovation of O'Higgins was very much opposed by the clergy and other persons who considered those spectacles immoral.

In another field of activity, the government of the supreme director had to carry on a most persistent struggle against banditry. As a consequence of the state of disorganization in which the country had been kept during the war of independence and the economic disturbances to which this situation had given rise, armed robbery in the cities and rural districts had increased enormously. Many parties of bandits overran the country roads, assaulting and frequently murdering passers-by and farm dwellers. At times they carried their excesses into the very centers of the towns. The alarm of the working people who lived in the midst of such insecurity was incessant. O'Higgins appointed special tribunals to

judge and condemn to death in less than forty-eight hours malefactors who were seized, and periodically sent parties of gendarmes
to patrol the farms and mountain ridges where they took refuge.
For some months these extraordinary methods produced the desired effect, but the plague revived again with equal vigor and
boldness.

The reforming action of the dictatorial executive was exercised
not only against the lower classes of society but against all classes.
Shortly after coming into power, he decreed the suppression of
titles of nobility conferred by the king on certain wealthy residents
and the distinctive "coats of arms" which in testimony of these
titles were placed on the front of their houses. Such "hieroglyph-
ics"—these were his terms—were "intolerable in a republic"; and
a little later he tried, although without success, to abolish the
mayorazgos, or privileges of primogeniture, which also were opposed to republican institutions. On the other hand, he created a
"Legion of Merit," a civic corporation, in which were incorporated
by favor of the director all those persons most distinguished in
public service.

Up to a certain point the relations of the government with the
dignitaries of the Church and the clergy remained friendly; but
enemies of emancipation as those dignitaries had been, if they
tolerated the dictatorship of O'Higgins, they did not accept it
with good grace. His attempt to transform colonial society met
with resistance, especially from the conventual clergy. But a
good part of the secular clergy had attached itself to the revolution and the dictator had been pleased to make use of them in
directing ecclesiastical affairs, assuming the same right as the
king of Spain over religious functionaries.

Many difficulties, however, presented themselves for relief,
which concerned the regulation and income of the clergy and the
naming of the bishops for Concepción and Santiago. These charges
were then vacant—Concepción, because the priest had been promoted to serve the diocese in Peru; and Santiago, because the
titular, Rodríguez Zorrilla, had been banished to Mendoza on account of his intransigent royalism. The government smoothed out
these difficulties as well as it could. It reinstated in his office as
bishop, Rodríguez Zorrilla, who at last showed himself disposed to
recognize the condition of independence created in Chile, and sent
the presbyter, José Ignacio Cienfuegos, to Rome in order to discover a way of arranging these questions directly with the Pope, who
still persisted in not recognizing the new states of America. Cienfuegos was a convinced and resolute patriot who had served in the

interim as bishop of Santiago. Nevertheless, there was much latent displeasure among the greater part of the clergy against the government of O'Higgins.[8]

FOREIGN AND DOMESTIC POLICY

The supreme director was much more fortunate in his foreign policy. He celebrated alliances with the governments of Peru and Colombia and maintained the former pact with Argentina, in spite of a marked coolness of relations which had made itself felt between that country and Chile during the internal discords of the confederacy and the campaign of San Martín in Peru. The recognition of independence was extended by Brazil, Mexico, and the United States. That act by the last-named country produced special rejoicing in Chile, although the United States did not particularly recognize Chile in 1822 but all the nations, formerly Spanish, created in America.[9] O'Higgins also kept a diplomatic agent in England, whose government, it was hoped, would recognize the independence of the states of the new continent. For the moment this hope was not realized but, on the other hand, it extended to Chile a very significant gesture: its agent, José de Irisarri—a notable Guatemalan who since 1810 had contributed his advice and his writings to emancipation—was able to contract there a loan of a million pounds sterling, the first that was extended to a rising republic. This act revealed the kind of confidence and prestige that Chile had gained abroad (1822).

But the dictatorship of O'Higgins was already threatened at its foundation. His internal policy was, little by little, arousing resistance, which continually became greater. There were intellectual people who regarded his government as a parody on a republican system. He himself did not have a much better opinion of it, but he believed that a long and painful transition period was necessary to reach such a system and that a dictatorship was indispensable during that time. For a people like the Chileans, who had recently come out from under an age-long despotism, it was necessary, ac-

---

[8] For the mission of Cienfuegos to Rome see J. Lloyd Meacham, "The Papacy and Spanish-American Independence," in *Hisp. Amer. Hist. Rev.*, IX (May, 1929), 160-165.

[9] For the message of President Monroe, suggesting this recognition, and the report of the Committee on Foreign Affairs of the United States House of Representatives, see Manning, *Diplomatic Correspondence of the United States concerning the Independence of the Latin American Nations*, I, 146-156. See also Henry Clay Evans, *Chile and its Relations with the United States*, p. 27. Heman Allen of Vermont was appointed first minister of the United States to Chile.

cording to his manner of thinking, "to confer good upon them by force," when they would not accept it any other way.

He had sanctioned a provisional regulation, which is known from the date on which it was promulgated as the Constitution of 1818.[10] Although he created in this document a legislative senate composed of five members with whom he should exercise command, and a supreme judiciary tribunal, charged with the high administration of justice, he retained for himself almost unlimited powers. He personally named the members of those bodies and set no limit to his own authority. It was true that he offered to convoke a constituent congress, when the whole country should be freed of royalist troops, but it was no less true that when that time had passed and not a royalist soldier remained on national territory, outside of Chiloé, such a body was not convened.

On the other hand the execution of the Carreras in foreign territory, the assassination of Manuel Rodríguez, the heavy forced contributions which he had exacted, his effort to overthrow the interests of the nobility, his slight respect for dominant religious ideas, the favor that he bestowed upon foreigners, the democratic temper of his relations—all these acts were severely judged in the circles affected by his course. Neither the glory of his campaigns nor the acts recognized as having won the country's independence—organizing the first national naval squadron and forming the liberating army of Peru—nor his undeniable learning and probity, nor his constant activity and consecration to public affairs were sufficient to keep his opponents from attributing certain features of despotism to his dictatorship.

Thus it happened that after breaking with his own senate he was obliged to convene a constituent assembly. The election of popular representatives throughout the republic aggravated the evil because it was done under the pressure of the government and at the exclusive will of the director. Such a counterfeit assembly sanctioned the Constitution of 1822. This code was never put into force because a revolution overtook him two months before it was promulgated. What caused the greatest dissatisfaction was that it extended for "ten years more" the authority of dictatorship that forced its approval.

At the end of 1822 Concepción arose in insurrection with its intendant at the head, and some days later La Serena also rebelled. The movement extended through the jurisdiction of both prov-

----

[10] For the text of this document, issued under the joint signature of O'Higgins and Irisarri, see Briseño, *Memoria histórico-crítica*, pp. 356-370. See also Galdames, *La evolución constitucional de Chile, 1810-1925*, I, 483-504.

inces in obedience to the juntas created in them, and Ramón Freire
was acclaimed chief of the uprising. At the beginning of 1823 the
country thus found itself in full rebellion.

THE ABDICATION OF O'HIGGINS

Before the disturbances of Concepción and La Serena, however,
O'Higgins did not believe that the agitation would take root in
Santiago and entered into negotiations with the rebels in order
to come to an agreement. The capital, in turn, arose in rebellion
and an open *cabildo* met to ask the supreme director to abdicate
the command. Shortly before noon on February 28 the hall of the
Consulado, which had served as a meeting place for the revolutionists in 1810, was invaded by a crowd of the most representative citizens of Santiago, numbering, young and old, more than two hundred.

A commission left that place and went to the government palace,
situated as formerly on the Plaza de Armas, to ask that O'Higgins
come to hear the complaints of the people. The supreme director
refused to take such a step, for he did not recognize the assembly
as one that was really representative, and ordered his guard to
resist. Learning that its leader was involved with the insurgents,
he entered the garrison full of wrath, seized that officer, and violently pulled the epaulets off his coat. He then faced the troops and
gave them the order to present arms, which they did with cries of
"Viva el Señor Director!" He went at once to the garrison of another corps, whose commander was also among those involved in
the revolt. He chided him as he did the former and forced the soldiers to obey him. He stationed the two regiments in the Plaza de
Armas and put himself at their head.

Meanwhile, the citizens assembled within the Consulado were uncertain what to do. At nearly five o'clock in the afternoon they had
not succeeded in getting the director to attend their assembly and
they feared that he would force them to disperse. Then they sent a
final delegation, which made the director understand that the people
there were not, as he thought, a crowd of irresponsible agitators,
and he decided to attend. Once at the table of the presidency,
O'Higgins asked: "What is the object of this assembly?" He was
told that its object was to ask him to resign, the only means of
exorcising the civil war threatening the republic. Three respected
citizens in turn gave utterance to this sentiment.

A tumult arose in the hall. O'Higgins, standing up, exclaimed:
"Neither seditious cries nor threats frighten me. I scorn death
today as I have scorned it on the fields of battle. I cannot allow the

discussion to continue in the form it has taken nor ought I to allow it." He added that if they desired to continue the discussion, they should name a commission to come to an understanding with him. The commission was named; the director at once entered into discussion with it behind closed doors; and he was convinced of the necessity of retiring from the government.

The resolution of the director was announced to the people, and it was what the people desired; namely, that he resign his authority. A salvo of applause greeted the announcement. The gathering again invaded the hall and with his approval a junta of government was named to assume provisional control in place of the director. The junta was composed of three members and a secretary, who were, respectively, the citizens Agustín Eyzaguirre, José Miguel Infante, Fernando Errázuriz, and Mariano Egaña.

Then O'Higgins arose and delivered over the command to his successors. Taking off the sash which he used as the distinctive mark of his authority, he said:

I am sorry not to deposit this sash before the national assembly from which I last received it; I regret that I must retire without having made permanent the institutions that have been thought proper for the country and which I have sworn to defend; but at least I have the consolation of leaving Chile independent of all foreign domination, respected by the outside world, and covered with glory for its deeds of arms.

After placing the sash on the table, he added: "Now I am a plain citizen." He begged them to accuse him of the crimes that he was believed to have committed and of all the misfortunes he was thought to have caused. He concluded by opening his coat with such haste that he tore off the buttons, saying: "Take such vengeance on me as you wish! Here is my breast."

A sonorous "Long live General O'Higgins" was the response. Then they accompanied him to the palace with acclamation. The night was spent in popular rejoicing. Some days afterward O'Higgins went to Valparaiso and, at the end of a "trial of residence" (*juicio de residencia*) that lasted several months and ended in a complete justification of his conduct, he embarked for Peru. No one then doubted that the patriot of 1810, the general of 1813, and the dictator of 1823 was also a great citizen.

THE DICTATORSHIP OF FREIRE

The governing junta which provisionally replaced O'Higgins was short-lived. The resignation of the supreme director was scarcely made known in Concepción, when General Freire with his troops went to Santiago. He did not recognize the powers of the junta to exercise the authority for the whole country, since it did not represent the three provinces into which the country was divided, and he had a new one named which was composed of three members, one for each province. This junta did nothing but elect a provisional supreme director until another general constituent congress should be convened, and the election fell on the only person who was in a position to take command, because he had a force at his disposal and had headed the rebellion—Ramón Freire.

The new supreme director was a young military man, thirty-five years old, who had performed very valuable service in the campaign for independence, fighting like a hero on different occasions. But if he possessed surpassing qualities as a fighter, he was not endowed with equal attributes as a statesman. Only his influence in the army could justify that designation. As his prime minister he selected Mariano Egaña, a son of Don Juan. Young Egaña was intelligent and energetic. Freire was also advised by a corporation called the conservative senate (*senado conservador*) composed of nine members, some of whom were individuals of exceptional intellectual attainment — among others José Miguel Infante and Camilo Henríquez.

Notwithstanding its provisional disposition, the government thus constituted showed itself as well disposed as the one preceding it and promoted several social reforms. It tried to abolish honorary titles with which individuals of public character were invested, such as "excellency" or "most illustrious señor," as well as the Legion of Merit created by O'Higgins. It tried also to abolish punishment by the lash which degraded criminals more than it corrected them, but in none of those attempts was it successful because of the opposition of Minister Egaña. One reform succeeded, although not before surmounting many obstacles; namely, complete abolition of slavery. It will be recalled that in 1811 the first Chilean congress had abolished this wretched institution, but such a measure had only affected sons of slaves born in Chile and persons who were enslaved when they arrived in the country. This time the resolution of the senate, in 1823, sanctioned by the executive, made it effective for all who were still held as slaves in Chile.

The democratic spirit of the corporation was opposed by the ministry of Freire; but Egaña and the senate were in accord with regard to the attention that should be given public instruction, and the diffusion of scientific knowledge among all popular classes. In this spirit they attempted to reform the plan of studies for the National Institute, giving a place in it for manual arts and trades.

A junta of education was created to take charge of the inspection and immediate direction of this service and to propose to the government the future studies that might be thought advisable; and this body founded a special university for the cultivation and propagation of science, called the Chilean Academy. As yet, however, these initial measures were not realized and existed only as aspirations.

The importance attributed to the constituent congresses, notwithstanding their previous failures, soon induced the educated class of the country to concentrate upon the election which was to be held. The election was freely made. The new assembly met in Santiago without hindrance and its first act was to name Freire permanent supreme director. Besides many projects which they did not adopt, congress passed the republican constitution, which they had gathered to discuss, and it was promulgated at the end of 1823. This fourth attempt at a fundamental code (the others are dated 1812, 1818, and 1822) is called the Constitution of 1823[11] and is the most curious political document of the period.

It was drawn up by Juan Egaña. It established three powers: executive, legislative, and judicial, already basic in public law. A supreme director exercised the first, closely associated with the second, which was vested in two houses—one, of the senators, which functioned permanently; and one, of the deputies, which functioned only by special summons. But the distinguishing feature of this constitution was its regulation of private as well as public life. It lasted only half a year. Freire, by a *coup d'état*, suppressed its operations and the senate accorded him dictatorial powers.

The gravest difficulty encountered by this and the preceding administration was the precarious state of public revenues. The disturbances that occurred at O'Higgins' fall and the same revolutionary movement that motivated them caused a decline of production in the country and an increase of fiscal expenditures. Moreover, the loan previously contracted in London, the interest on which had greatly increased, very seriously prejudiced the government. It was to have been invested in works of public benefit, but almost all of it had been spent to save urgent promissory notes which did not have that character.

Among the many measures then devised to meet that situation, the most important was the delivery to a private concessionaire of the tobacco monopoly and other similar monopolies (playing cards,

---

[11] For the text see Briseño, *op. cit.,* pp. 405-434. Briseño's comments on the document appear in *ibid.,* pp. 111-172. See also Galdames, *Evolución constitucional,* I, 600-658.

tea, and foreign liquors), under obligation to assume the payments on the loan. The monopoly of those articles which the State previously controlled now became the privilege of a mercantile association (1824), which carried on business under the firm name of Portales, Cea and Company, the manager of which was Diego Portales—a transaction that soon acquired widespread notoriety. This arrangement did not last more than two years, however. The enterprise did not make good, could not meet its obligations in regard to the loan, and had to abandon the monopoly and return it again to the State.

One more operation, not so complicated as this, but one which aroused formidable opposition against Freire, was the seizure of the possessions of the regular clergy, to which was added a complete reform in their regulations. These measures provoked the sudden rupture between Church and State, a rupture toward which affairs had been moving since the last years of O'Higgins' dictatorship. The solution of the different questions disturbing the harmony between Church and State had, in fact, deserved the constant attention of O'Higgins, up to the point of sending an emissary to Rome to treat personally with His Holiness. It will be recalled that this mission was entrusted to the presbyter, José Ignacio Cienfuegos. Notwithstanding the difficulties that he encountered there because the pope refused to recognize the sovereignty of the new American states, Cienfuegos succeeded in having an apostolic mission sent to Chile with the special purpose of normalizing the religious situation of the country.

The vicar, Juan Muzi, designated by the pope to undertake this mission, arrived in Chile in 1824, and he was in the country when the arrangements mentioned above were adopted for the reform of the regular clergy and the seizure of their goods. He was there also when the government removed from his post Bishop Rodríguez Zorilla, the celebrated priest and enemy of the revolution. The latter had returned from his exile in the last years of the dictatorship of O'Higgins, who had reëstablished him in the diocese, trusting in his avowal of adherence to the republican regime. But hardly had O'Higgins fallen, when the bishop began a new campaign against the government and, when he saw himself favored by the presence and friendship of the apostolic delegate, he redoubled his efforts. Freire then removed him from his office; but shortly after Infante, in charge of a provisional government, banished him.

This resolute act of the chief of state and the premonitory signs of the dominance he was just beginning to exercise against the Church induced Vicar Muzi to leave the country, declaring his mission a failure.[12] This very act aroused the religious prejudices of the majority of the people and placed the director in a very delicate situation, under the weight of general condemnation because his work of organization and his demonstrations of firmness in governmental acts were represented by his adversaries as signs of an irreligious attitude harmful to the faith.

Although surrounded by the difficulties mentioned above, the directors of the republic believed then that it was absolutely necessary to complete national control by incorporating the archipelago of Chiloé with Chilean territory. When Freire was raised to power, the general, Antonio Quintanilla, still maintained the Spanish flag in Chiloé. The director, who was above all a military man, directed two campaigns against the large island of the archipelago, in the last of which he triumphed over the royalist commander and the flag of Chile has remained hoisted forever on the fortifications of the port of Ancud (1826). With the taking of Chiloé, the long struggle against Spain in behalf of independence came to its final, irrevocable end not only in Chile but in all the former colonies of America.

King Ferdinand VII nevertheless continued to maintain a hostile attitude in respect to these states and refused to recognize their sovereignty; but any project whatever for Spanish reconquest in America now became merely a dream. Four of the larger European powers (France, Austria, Prussia, and Russia), which together formed what was called the Holy Alliance, had thought of offering their aid to Spain in order to recover these dominions. They purposed to restore to its former height the absolute power of all the European monarchs. The pope himself in an encyclical had fostered the initiative of those sovereigns, after condemning American emancipation.[13]

But these schemes had met with strong opposition from the United States and England, causing the plans to fail. Monroe, the president of the United States who had recognized the sovereignty

---

[12] Professor Mecham pronounces the mission of Muzi as significant because it marked "the beginning of a modus vivendi" between the American governments and the papacy. See his "The Papacy and Spanish-American Independence," in *Hisp. Amer. Hist. Rev.*, IX, 165.

[13] For a general discussion of the attitude of Spain and of the continental powers, including the pope, and of the United States, see Barros Arana, *Historia jeneral*, Vol. XIV, chap. xx. A supplementary discussion of value is Dexter Perkins, "Europe, Spanish America, and the Monroe Doctrine," in *American Historical Review*, XXVII (January, 1912), 207-218. See also H. W. V. Temperly, "The Later American Policy of George Canning," in *ibid.*, XI (July, 1906), 779-797.

of the new republics, was led by that presumptuous intervention to formulate in 1823 the celebrated international theory which is known as the Monroe Doctrine. According to this, his government declared that the American continents were "henceforth not to be considered as subjects for future colonization by any European powers," and, as for the nations newly constituted in it, "we could not view any interposition for the purpose of oppressing them, or controlling in any other manner their destiny, by any European power, in any other light than as the manifestation of an un-friendly disposition toward the United States." That theory, which has been synthetized in the formula "America for Ameri-cans," caused great alarm in Europe, except in England, which was itself in accord with the United States with respect to the recognition of the American republics, as in 1825 it actually did recognize some, although Chile was not among the number at that time.[14]

England and the United States acted thus because they were impelled in the first place by the liberal ideals of their governments; and in the second place by their economic interests, which made them comprehend that the recently formed republics would furnish excellent markets for their industrial products. But these republics did not at the time respond to such demonstrations of adherence and confidence as came to assure their independence in an un-changeable form. They had struggled stubbornly and heroically for fifteen years without the help of anyone, performing prodigies of energy. Thus their triumph became not merely a national, but almost a personal glory; but lack of traditions and political habits compatible with the liberty they had gained could not yet permit them the firm and enduring organization that they needed.

Everywhere the two principal tendencies shaping their organiz-ing purpose were in ceaseless opposition. One element wished to see a republic established in accordance with the logic of the revolu-tionary movement, a real republic, free and democratic, regardless of the popular elements that were necessary for it, which the col-ony had not bequeathed to them; and the other, taking this fact

---

[14] For Monroe's annual message containing these extracts, see J. D. Richard-son (comp.), *Messages and Papers of the Presidents of the United States* (10 vols. Washington, 1789-1897), II, 218-220. For the subject of general British relations with the South American republics during this period, see F. L. Paxson, *The Independence of the South American Republics* (Philadelphia, 1903), chap. iii. The correspondence between the United States and Chile during this period will be found in Manning, *op. cit.*, II, 1091, *et seq.;* between the United States and Great Britain in *ibid.*, III, 1474-1524. See also Evans, *op. cit.*, pp. 36-41; and Barros Arana, *Historia jeneral*, XIV, 368, 469-535.

into account, aspired to a system little different from the one over-thrown—a system which would not break completely with the past, which would not profoundly modify society, and which, in short, would result in a colonial republic. To accomplish all this, leaders came and went, rose and fell from power.

In Chile Freire, surrounded by these group complications, could not accomplish abundant profitable results. A new congress succeeded the one of 1823 and abolished the constitution issued by the latter but, amid the revolutionary plots that arose in different cities and, amid the stormy sessions for which congress itself was a stage, this was forcibly dissolved by the director. A third then followed, which met a like fate, until Freire, tired of this fruitless and seemingly endless political play, called together a fourth legislative assembly and to it delivered the public authority in 1826.

CHAPTER X

ANARCHY AND ORGANIZATION

FEDERALISM AND ITS RESULTS (1826-1827)

From 1826 to 1830 Chile lived in a state of constant disturbance. Different congresses and supreme directors succeeded each other and executed such measures of organization as they could and soon fell, defeated by revolts and military coups that had no more justification than the caprice of their leaders. The congress of 1826 decreed the federal organization of the republic, in accordance with the views of José Miguel Infante, who for years after devoted himself to an untiring campaign in behalf of this principle, because he believed that federation was the ideal of free and prosperous countries.[1]

The federation of the United States served as a model and example to the supporters of that policy. It was said that "unitarianism" benefited only the capital and was a detriment to the provinces, and that federalism, without prejudicing the capital, benefited all the regions of the country. Federalism, moreover, would give the people direct participation in their provincial and local affairs by means of an autonomous government, which each province would elect. In this way the republic would become really democratic.

Consequently, the federal system was established in 1826. The country was divided into eight provinces, each to be governed by an assembly elected in a popular manner and by an intendant, similarly elected. All the other authorities were also to be designated by the people, including the parish priests. The impracticability of this organization was seen at once. The debates stirred up throughout the provinces upon the determination of their boundaries and the designating of their capitals did not promise tranquillity; and shortly the election of the respective officials gave rise to numerous grave complications. The absence of the habit of exercising civic rights in the general mass of the population—now called upon to agree in the direct naming of their governing bodies—the ignorance and destitution among the people, and unlimited ambitions

---

[1] The text of this constitution is given in Briseño, *Memoria histórico-critica,* pp. 442-459. His discussion of the document is in *ibid.,* pp. 184-203. See also Galdames, *Evolución constitucional,* I, 671-738.

of many who judged themselves worthy of obtaining representative offices were determining causes of the more or less complete failure of that system, whose discredit began with its very initiation. It also had deplorable consequences—general disorders everywhere, including outrageously arbitrary acts at the elections and acute misery in city and country.

Such a state of things was bound to do tremendous damage to the financial development of the country. The national treasury was impoverished to such a degree that there were no funds with which to meet the most pressing requirements of public service. The employees of the administration did not receive their back salaries, nor did the representatives in congress, who were to receive pay for the period that they were in session, receive a single cent for their expenses in the capital; many who came from the provinces lived in deplorable poverty; worst of all, however, the army did not receive its pay, and the officers and soldiers were disposed to mutiny at every opportunity, with the hope of settling their accounts. Such was the most powerful cause of the revolts that occurred frequently, wherever there was an encampment of troops.

So critical a situation reached the height of its confusion when, at the beginning of 1827, a military revolt headed by Colonel Enrique Campino broke out in Santiago. On horseback this leader entered the hall in which congress was in session and ordered it to dissolve, threatening with the guns of his soldiers the representatives who scattered in all directions, a prey to the greatest confusion. But the triumph of the revolt did not last more than a few days because Campino's very companions abandoned him, and Freire was reëlected president.

Months afterwards, the congress which had sanctioned the federal organization was dissolved. Its system had failed and many of its former partisans had themselves turned against it. The task of organizing the republic had to begin anew. This task General Francisco Antonio Pinto, vice-president elect, now undertook and, by the resignation of President Freire, came to the highest representative position in the country. Pinto was a man a little over forty years old, who from his youth had given valuable service to the nation as a soldier during the revolutionary campaigns and the expedition to Peru, as a diplomat in Buenos Aires and London, and as a minister of state during the dictatorship of Freire. With advanced ideas in political matters, he was a distinguished member of the liberal group that aspired to transform the country into a democratic republic. One of the first acts was to suspend the working of the federal regime, which had thrown the nation into anarchy, and then to consult the provinces as to whether they would insist upon being governed in that form. The response was almost unanimously adverse to federalism. Then the chief of state convened a new constituent congress.

THE CONSTITUTION OF 1828

The situation of the political parties which were to take part in the elections was clearly defined. During the dictatorship of Freire, and principally in the congress of 1826, a movement of integration was taking place among them. The former personal parties of Carrera and of O'Higgins had almost entirely disappeared. The first of them had no longer any reason for existing after the death of its chief. The second had been disorganized with the settling of O'Higgins in Peru; and, if a few were still loyal and awaited his return and restoration to power, their influence was very limited.

On the other hand, the federal party had succeeded in rooting itself so extensively in public opinion that almost the whole congress of 1826 had been fervently devoted to it; but the ill success of the experiment had soon turned against it in the bosom of the assembly itself an opposition that was powerful because of the number and quality of its members; and, when Pinto was promoted to the presidency of the republic, none kept his belief in the system except its convinced apostle, José Miguel Infante, and one or two others among his followers.

Two currents of ideas now drew all public men together into vigorous groups, far removed from the former individualism. The reformist and democratic current, which aspired to change society in whatever way necessary in order to adapt it to the republican formula, had obtained a large majority, thanks to the activity of its leaders and to an ardent, youthful contingent that entered its ranks; and since Pinto, who was looked upon as its leader, arose to power, it had greatly increased its strength. This party called itself liberal, but its adversaries gave it the nickname of *pipiolo* (novice) in a tone of disdain because of the limited social prestige of some of its members. The other current was the moderate movement, which desired a tolerant political organization with colonial institutions. Counting on the decided aid of the clergy, it was for the most part made up of rich men, heirs of entailed estates, and family heads of ancient nobility. Therefore, its opponents nicknamed this party *pelucón* (bigwig), derived from the powdered wigs that the aristocrats of the colony wore on solemn occasions; but it called itself conservative;[2] and this was perhaps the name best fitted for it.

Conservatives and liberals, or "bigwigs" and "novices," then entered upon an electoral struggle at the beginning of 1828 for selecting deputies to the new constituent congress. The victory at the ballot boxes belonged by an overwhelming majority to the liberals, who hastened to discuss the constitution which was to be given to the country.

The sessions were begun in Santiago and shortly afterward were transferred to Valparaiso. The plan which served as a basis for discussion was prepared by a Spanish litterateur and educational leader who had resided for some time in Chile, José Joaquín de Mora. He was a man of marked liberal principles, which he had already diffused in his own country, and in Chile he had allied himself with the same party; for this reason, as much as for his well-known literary talents, the editing of the constitutional statute was intrusted to him.

Mora was fully equal to the trust which was placed in him, and his plan, which was approved with slight modifications, appeared the best of all that had been prepared up to that time, because of its clear and concise form. The oath to support the Constitution of 1828 was solemnly taken on September 18 of that year and a compromise resulted between those of liberal and federalist tendencies. Conservative theories did not enter into it except in one respect—the Catholic religion remained in a privileged condition as the religion of the State and "with exclusion of the public exercise of any other whatever," although it was declared that "no one would be persecuted or molested for his private opinions."

In other respects, the constitution established a legislative power composed of two houses, one of senators and the other of deputies, and of a permanent commission which should exercise this power during the recess of these houses. The executive power resided in a president of the republic, in a vice-president, in case of the president's illness or death, and three ministers, selected at the will of the president. The president was to remain in office five years but could not be reëlected until after one other term, at least, should elapse, reckoned from the end of his administration. The judicial power was directed by a supreme court.

Within this organization the legislative power was supreme, or

<hr/>

[2] For a discussion of political parties in Chile during the period covered by this chapter, see Alberto Edwards, *Bosquejo histórico de los partidos políticos chilenos,* pp. 7-28.

rather congress was the immediate representative of the people. It was the body which formed the budget, fixed the salaries of public employees, granted military promotions, and named the members of the supreme court. It also was the body that could censure the president and his ministers and hold them responsible for the acts of government. And, finally, it was congress that decided presidential elections in case none of the candidates should obtain an absolute majority in the colleges of presidential electors, whom the people appointed for each province. The choice for president was thus indirect or through a secondary election.

Everything up to this point appeared acceptable, although the liberals, wishing to avoid presidential omnipotence, would have placed supreme power in the legislative assembly and undoubtedly would have created a greater ill than they were trying to prevent; they would oppose the tyranny of one by the no less dreadful tyranny of many. But the Constitution of 1828 was fundamentally deficient in its provincial and local administration. Compromising, in this respect, with the federalism of Infante, it established provincial assemblies elected by the people, empowered to designate the respective senators and to propose three names to the chief of state for each post of intendant, vice-intendant, trial judges, and judges of letters (*jueces de letras*). In each department a municipality elected by popular vote appointed the governor.

Such a system was as impracticable as that of 1826, or more so, because it was not possible that, simply by reading this code, men of the provinces, most of whom were without culture, and the great mass of them destitute, should acquire the courage and independence which the practice of civic rights demanded. Briefly, the Constitution of 1828 labored under a fundamental defect; it was too far ahead of the society of the time. It trusted in the fallacy that political laws can mold people according to their will.[3]

THE REVOLUTION OF 1829

Thus it was that this constitution did not pass its first test. In 1829 the elections for congress were carried out and soon after, in the same year, the elections for president of the republic. In both elections the liberal party received an enormous majority. Pinto was again elected to occupy the presidency; but, in trying to elect the vice-president, a grave difficulty occurred. None of the candidates for whom the provincial electoral colleges had voted received

---

[3] A description of this constitution is given in Briseño, *op. cit.*, pp. 204-224; the text in *ibid.*, pp. 470-488. See also Galdames, *Evolución constitucional*, I, 739-783.

an absolute majority. Congress, which was in session in Valparaiso, proposed to make use of the constitutional provision for the case, which authorized it to decide the election. The candidates who had obtained the highest number of votes, but not the necessary number, were Francisco Ruiz Tagle (100 votes) and Joaquín Prieto (61 votes) ; but, as neither of them was a member of the liberal party, which had a majority in congress, this body designated a third person for vice-president, Joaquín Vicuña, a liberal who had obtained only a very small number of votes (48) in the electoral colleges.[4]

The opposition group energetically protested against what they termed a violation of the constitutional code ; because in their judgment this code ordered that in such a case the choice by congress must be restricted to one of the two candidates receiving the highest number in the provincial electoral colleges. Although the injunction of the constitution in this particular was not quite clear, it might at least be so inferred from its basic provisions, because such was the usage outlined for deciding the election of president. But, nevertheless, in the letter of the text it was not declared—perhaps through forgetfulness—that the same rule should apply in rectifying the election for the vice-presidency.

On the other hand, the provincial elections had been carried out with little regard for rules, which led the conservative party to call them null and void. Added to all this was the resignation of Pinto from the office to which he was elected. He based this action on motives of health, but in reality he was terrorized by the signs of revolution which were apparent throughout almost the entire republic. The conflict really ended in the revolution of 1829, headed in Concepción by General Prieto, in the name of the constitution that congress had violated.

The army of the south advanced against the capital and most of the towns favoring the movement revolted as it advanced. In Santiago, there was the most indescribable alarm. Congress had been in session at Valparaiso and declared itself dissolved by its own resolution. At the capital, a series of assemblies followed, which lasted several days and then stopped functioning, in the midst of general storm and tumult. Finally, when Prieto approached the city, the government troops were put under the command of General Francisco de la Lastra. A little south of Santiago,

---

[4] Barros Arana, in *Historia jeneral*, XV, 374, *et seq.*, discusses at some length the constitutional question involved in this election. Joaquín Vicuña is not to be confused with Francisco Ramón Vicuña who was then temporarily filling the office of chief executive.

in Ochagavía, a battle took place between the two armies; the action remained undecided, because both leaders agreed to a truce or armistice. Shortly afterward, a treaty of peace was signed in Santiago, and by it the provisional command of the country and the troops of both sides were placed at the disposition of General Freire.

All did not stop here, however. The conservative party, now dominating the spirit of Prieto and having acquired power in Santiago by means of a recently created governing junta, thought that Freire was not needed, but that, on the contrary, as commander of the army he was becoming a hindrance, because of the ties that bound him to the defeated liberal party. Then the junta schemed to displace the two generals and conferred the military leadership on Prieto. This was at the beginning of 1830.

Freire left Santiago, gathered some troops, and with them went to Valparaiso and embarked for Coquimbo to organize a campaign against the party that controlled the government and to restore the authority of the Constitution of 1828. In this way the country was plunged into a civil war, and curiously enough both parties represented themselves as defenders of the violated constitution. Freire sailed from Coquimbo to the provinces of the south and pitched his camp near the Maule River. The two armies finally found themselves face to face, a little to the north of that river near the Lircay, a branch of the Maule. The battle that took place there on April 17, 1830, decided at one stroke the fortune of war. Freire was totally defeated. About three hundred were left dead on the field and an uncounted number wounded. It was the last bloody struggle of that period.

PORTALES AND HIS FIRST DICTATORSHIP (1830-1831)

In the midst of the chaos of civil war, one man in the bosom of the conservative party had clearly excelled all others. He was Diego Portales. Born in Santiago in 1793 of a distinguished family, he had not taken part in the struggle for independence, or later mixed in politics under the dictatorship of O'Higgins. He had been a merchant from his youth, and had thus reached thirty years of age without attracting public attention. As he had pursued very haphazard and elementary studies, he was not thought fit for the proper discharge of public affairs, nor perhaps did he consider himself fit for them.

But it happened that in 1824 he had to enter into very direct relations with the government of General Freire as agent for the mercantile house of Portales, Cea and Company, which took charge of the monopoly of tobacco and other articles. This enterprise, as stated above, could not carry out its contract with the treasury, which stipulated that it must cover the payments on the English loan, in compensation for the monopoly over such sales. The transaction failed and the contractors did not make the payments. After two years the contract was annulled and the monopoly was again administered by the treasury; but the liquidation of accounts pending between the government and the company was long and complicated, and political passions accentuated the trouble. The question of monopoly was thus transformed into a political question, and Portales also became a party man. Around him there was gathered a group of citizens of no little importance, which was called by their adversaries the "monopoly party."

In 1827 the party published a new paper entitled *El hambriento* (*The Starveling*), which, according to its title page, declared that it was a "public paper without periodic or literary flavor, non-political, but useful and merry." And Portales, who effectively supplemented his scant learning with natural talent and gracious and satirical genius, made his jest in prose and verse a formidable arm of attack; and his paper, widely read, gained for him a vociferous popularity. Thus in 1828, when the conservative party began to resist liberal institutions, it counted the untaught editor among its most renowned associates.

During the revolution of 1829, Portales was active as a popular agitator. A little before the encounter at Lircay, José Tomás Ovalle came into power as vice-president. Portales was then called to the ministry, in which he filled simultaneously two portfolios, that of interior and foreign relations, and that of war and navy. The activity and energy that he displayed in those offices made him the real director of the government.

From Santiago he coöperated in the campaign of Prieto, taking whatever measures seemed conducive to its triumph; and, when success came, the prestige of the minister increased so much that his authority became omnipotent. Ovalle was a good man, as an individual, but he lacked the bravery and boldness that circumstances demanded. Portales, who possessed these qualities in the highest degree, overruled him from the first day of his ministry. Congress conceded extraordinary faculties to the government and the minister began to exercise a civil dictatorship more resolute and more vigorous even than former military dictatorships (1829-1832).

The one-time merchant, now dictator, continued to lack political knowledge. But the absence of theoretical preparation did not harm him; on the contrary, it seemed to favor him, because theoretical publicists were precisely the ones who had so greatly upset the country. Juan Egaña, with his moralistic constitution of 1823, and José Miguel Infante, with his federal organization of 1826, had merely produced the fruits of anarchy; and the middle road followed in 1828 by Pinto and Mora, other theorists, had not led to better results. The work of the moment consisted in giving the State an organization that would guarantee peace and working power. Portales thus understood the task and devoted himself wholly to working it out. The most urgent need, in his estimation, was to give peace to the country and stability to public administration. In order to do this it was necessary to put an end to the revolutionary spirit and to treat without pity those who disturbed public order and thus showed themselves implacable enemies of all progress.

Turbulent militarism, which had proved itself incapable of directing the republic, was the first to receive a mortal blow from Portales. On the very day that the battle of Lircay was fought, he issued a bold decree dismissing the officers and leaders of Freire's army and then included in this dismissal other leaders who, while not taking part in the civil war, did not show their frank and explicit adherence to the established government. Men like General Pinto and Las Heras fell, under the dictates of this measure. Freire was captured shortly after the battle of Lircay and exiled to Peru.

In order to guarantee political institutions against the frequent revolt of troops, Portales reëstablished the civic and national guard on an entirely new basis and distributed it in different corps under leaders of unquestioned adherence to the constituted authority. He subjected these corps to an active discipline and finally put himself at the head of one and began to attend public exercises on festal days in military uniform. A little later, moreover, he reëstablished the Military Academy in 1832, an institute destined for the technical preparation of officers. In this were to be enlisted young men of the aristocratic class, which was more inclined toward order than any other.

Having subjected to law the armed element, Portales did not show consideration of any kind toward the *pipiolo* or liberal party, against which he principally fought. Defeat left it at the mercy of the victor. There was no public employment, no matter how insignificant, that was not given to individuals of the triumphant party. Not a single opponent held the task that he had performed at the time of the revolution. These positions were held by partisans of the new system. Neither federalists nor the adherents of

O'Higgins shared or exerted any influence in the government. Infante was eliminated and likewise the partisans of O'Higgins, notwithstanding their favorable rally to the conservative party during the struggle. This exclusion reached such a point that, when O'Higgins desired to return to Chile, the will of one person was enough to keep him out. Portales closed the doors of the country on the exile, because his presence was considered disturbing.

The dictator was well aware that this severe policy, personal and absorbing, must arouse powerful resistance on the part of those whom it hurt. The military men who were dismissed and who thus lost their only means of livelihood would not easily reconcile themselves to a life of peaceful misery. The *pipiolos*, who exercised power during the government of Pinto, would neither resign themselves to their lot nor would they alienate themselves from public affairs. In the same situation were the followers of O'Higgins and the federalists who were not able to give up their ideal of government.

Portales did not risk the danger. As soon as various tentative plots became known he suppressed them with a hand of iron. On the other hand, newspapers of a revolutionary character, violently attacking his person, showed him that the spirit of rebellion was not asleep. Unterrified by their threat he gagged the press. Without modifying the laws that established their liberty of action, he procured juries that would condemn at his wish as "seditious" those publications that were against the government and, even without referring to such juries, the extraordinary powers with which he was invested allowed him to exercise his authority against the authors of adverse articles. Among other writers who for this reason were exiled from the country was José Joaquín de Mora, whose liberalism and fresh literary genius, shown in some guerrilla newspapers, truly annoyed Portales.

[It seemed incredible that one man alone should have been able to acquire such insuperable power in so short a time. But when one recalls that colonial society had been accustomed to receiving orders from abroad and without discussion; and bears in mind that no one had revealed more character than he, nor more activity, nor more disinterestedness in the exercise of his ministry; and when it is known that a long period of anarchy had already made itself insupportable and had even led some to despair of the fate of the republic, one should not express surprise at the preference for a master who could mold the government system with steel-like energy, rather than for a multitude of men without ideas of their own and without sufficient will to cause another's to triumph. The colonial aristocracy which now formed the political oligarchy needed one who could master unhealthy, disorganizing passions, and it found that master in Portales.][5]

THE CONSTITUTION OF 1833

Having reëstablished the peace of the republic, the new government determined to give it an organization more in accord with the tradition and habits of society than were those that had preceded it. Another constituent congress was convened in order to reform the Code of 1828, and that assembly, brought together in 1831, was able to finish its work two years later and present the new constitution of the republic for the sanction of the executive, which was definitely announced on May 25, 1833.[6]

This code began by fixing the boundaries of the Chilean state, which extended "from the desert of Atacama to Cape Horn and from the cordillera of the Andes to the Pacific Ocean, including the archipelago of Chiloé, all the adjacent islands and those of Juan Fernández." It continued by declaring that the government of Chile was "popular and representative," that sovereignty resided essentially in the nation, and that its exercise belonged to the legally constituted authorities. Then it established the Roman Catholic apostolic religion as the state faith, "excluding from public exercise any other whatsoever." Among succeeding resolutions appeared the rules relative to rights of citizenship and suffrage. To exercise the latter, one must be twenty-five years of age, able to read and write, and, moreover, must enjoy an income determined by a special law or must possess property.

Then the constitution went on to establish the fundamental principles of the republic: equality before the law; equal right to fill public office and employment, provided one met the condition demanded by the laws; proportionate division of imposts; liberty to leave the country and to change from one place to another in it; inviolability of private property, except for the right of expropriation for public use which the State reserved, but with consequent indemnity; right of petition to the authorities; and liberty to publish individual opinions in the press without previous censure.

---

[5] This paragraph, which appears in the sixth edition of the present work, is omitted in the seventh edition. It is a valid part of the author's discussion.

[6] The text of this document is given in Briseño, *op. cit.*, pp. 489-510. His discussion is to be found in *ibid.*, pp. 230-265. See also Barros Arana, *Historia jeneral*, Vol. XVI, chap. xxxix; and Ramón Sotomayor Valdés, *Historia de Chile durante los cuarenta años*, Vol. I, chaps. vi, vii; Galdames, *Evolución constitucional*, I, 863-970.

Then came the organization of the legislative power, which belonged to congress. This body was divided into two houses: one of deputies, elected popularly by departments every three years; and the other of senators, appointed by "special electors" who were chosen by the people for this purpose. The senators served nine years in their posts, one third being renewed every three years. Among the most important powers of congress were the approval or disapproval of the budgets and the authorizing of the president to make use of extraordinary faculties in specified cases and to suspend individual securities. This was equivalent to a temporary suppression of the constitution.

Continuing, the code took up the manner of making laws and then went on to treat of the executive power, which the president of the republic was to exercise. The president was chosen by special electors selected by popular mandate. He could be immediately reelected for five years, but no more, unless a new period intervened. Accompanying the president of the republic were his secretaries or "ministers," of which at first there were three: interior and foreign relations, war, and treasury. Moreover, he had a "council of state," which advised him, and with which he must keep in accord. Among the powers of the president was one which provoked opposition in the discussion of the constitutional plan. That high functionary could declare, in accord with his council, any province whatever or the whole republic in a state of siege. With this declaration the functions of the constitution would be suspended and the executive would be armed with extraordinary powers. He could go so far as to arrest any individual and confine him at any point in the country without process of law. But such a situation could continue only for a specified time and must cease in any case on the coming together of the houses, unless these bodies should agree to prolong it and should by law authorize the president to do so.

The judicial power was established in a supreme tribunal of justice, with the guarantee of permanent tenure and responsibility on the part of the judges. The judicial magistrates must be named by the president of the republic from the three proposed by the council of state. Provincial and local administration was entrusted to the intendants and governors, who were agents and direct representatives of the executive, and to municipalities, constituted by the vote of the people.

Among the last provisions were those involving individual rights, according to which no one could be arrested without an order from competent authority, or be judged by others than the tribunals established in legal form. Moreover, it was declared that public education should be a "preëminent attention of the State" and permanent systems of primogeniture should be reëstablished.

Such, in the aggregate, was the Constitution of 1833, which prevailed up to 1925 with modifications of greater or less consideration. The men who chiefly coöperated in producing it were Mariano Egaña, whose plan served as the basis for discussion, and Manuel José Gandarillas, a writer who had the most prominent part in the debates that preceded its adoption. The former represented the conservative tendencies and the influence of his father, shown in his efforts to increase the authority of the president of the republic. Gandarillas, on the contrary, represented liberal tendencies, translated into an earnest determination to restrict that authority and to strengthen the action of congress.

However this may be, it is certain that, notwithstanding the severe criticisms that for one reason or another have been made against that constitution, present judgment has come to be favorable to it. It corresponded to the social state of that time and did not do more than recognize its manifestations, such as they were. From this fact came its success and the accord that definitely brought about the organization of the republic. Finally, it recognized the Catholic religion as the religion of the state, simply because no one, save some foreigners bound to the country by business ties only, thought any other way in Chile. If it revealed a certain spirit of opposition to the clergy, it did not follow that this would extend to religion itself. That opposition arose principally from its action against the patriots during the struggle for emancipation; but, that struggle now being finished, the antagonisms that had thus been provoked began to disappear, and the great mass of the country remained as Catholic as before.

The preservation of the right of primogeniture, another of the points which deserved the most bitter criticism, was in obedience to an economic reason and a political motive of the time which it was not possible to disregard. Its abolition caused considerable harm to the first born of families who had placed their hopes on such entailed property and this, added to the lordly or aristocratic prepossession to which the right of primogeniture corresponded, must strongly arouse the implacable ill will of the injured individuals against the government—an ill will which at that time endangered its stability.

Ultimately, the wide scope of the powers granted to the president of the republic, which in some ways made that functionary a provisional monarch, finds its explanation in the ingrained habit of the people of that time of obeying sovereign authority; in the anarchic system through which the country had passed; and in the very object of the code, which General Prieto expressed in a proclamation of those days in the following terms:

The reform (or the new constitution) is nothing more than a means of putting an end to the revolutions and disturbances which arose from the confusion in which the triumph of independence left us. For this reason the system of government to which the republic was subjected under that constitution may be qualified as "autocratic," in view of the great authority or power which was concentrated in the hands of the citizen elected as president.

CHAPTER XI

CHILEAN SOCIETY IN 1830

LIFE IN THE CITIES

REGARDLESS OF THE form of government, republican society had changed but little in the twenty years which followed the beginning of the revolution; it continued to be almost the same as colonial society during the last years of Spanish control. Nevertheless, the population had increased considerably, owing, no doubt, to the development of wealth and to immigration, which commercial freedom had attracted. From half a million at the beginning of the nineteenth century, it had already reach a million in population at the beginning of the stable period of the republic.

Cities were also growing rapidly—Santiago had more than forty-eight thousand inhabitants, and Valparaiso about half that number. Toward the south, Talca, Chillán, and Concepción, and, toward the north, Coquimbo, La Serena, and Copiapó were prospering in similar fashion. But all kept their old methods of building with crooked, narrow streets, in the Spanish manner, and low adobe houses of uniform construction, with very few windows; and this gave the dwellings the appearance of great warehouses. Only the principal cities (Valparaiso, Santiago, and Concepción) had brick sidewalks and streets paved with round cobblestones. Police protection was known only in these same centers and public hygiene had progressed but little. The streets were rarely swept, and on the outskirts of the cities were disease-breeding heaps of refuse thrown from the dwellings. Lighting at night was so scant that the people had to suspend traffic soon after dark.

Just as before, Santiago continued to be the center of social life. Customs were still very simple. A curious person who proposed to become acquainted with the city, and who in the morning set out to explore it with that purpose, would, no doubt, have gone first to the *abasto,* or market square. Here his attention would have been attracted, not so much by the noisy going and coming of the maid servants with their large baskets and bright-colored skirts and kerchiefs, purchasing articles for the family consumption, as by the extensive refuse heap which stretched to the Mapocho. Then, going a little toward the east, he could have witnessed the stone-throwing fights which the idle boys of the district of Chimba carried on with those of the Santa Lucía district across the river, to amuse themselves.

Returning to the center of the town he would see young women of social position and a few men entering the churches to hear the daily mass. The ladies, wrapped in black cloaks, would be followed by their respective maidservants, who carried for them straw mats and colored foot carpets. The men would be attired in loose dark trousers, a short coat, and a shirt with collar crossed by a broad rose-colored cravat. A light woolen hat and pointed shoes completed this costume.

Once in the principal plaza, he would observe a new commotion among the people. Many sellers of shoes, sandals, shirts, parched corn, pancakes, and other articles might be scattered about offering their wares. Purchasers would dispose of some of their old possessions by throwing them into an open ditch, in order to provide themselves with the new. Boys would collect the abandoned sandals and throw them at one another's heads, thus devising a game for their amusement. Some prisoners from the jail (where today stands the municipal building) would perhaps be starting to clean up the streets a little with some broad branches of hawthorn. They made little impression.

Before midday, the inquisitive one might see the worshipers from the mother church go out to the porticos on the south side (today Fernández Concha) in search of merchandise, or simply to see something new. Certainly the buildings along those porticos were not at all like those of today. They had two stories but were so low that in the earthquake of 1822 many people who were in the upper rooms fell to the ground and suffered no injury. As midday approached there would be absolute silence; everyone would be at breakfast (*almuerzo*). Our traveler would also breakfast in one of the inns or hotels of the city, and then he might go out to examine other streets, taking care not to go far from the plaza, for the uncleanly environs of the city would cause him much discomfort. On the north side of the river there were only four groups of sheds or thatched huts of very forbidding appearance. This district of Chimba was merely a suburb to which swarmed many idle people who were wont to engage in games of chance and in excessive drinking. The same thing occurred on the south side of the Alameda, beyond which rose a few homes of artisans, followed, farther on, by somewhat extensive suburban dwellings and estates. The district now known as Providencia, beginning at the east of Santa Lucía, and that of Yungay, extending from beyond the street of San

Martín toward the west, were similar suburbs. As for the rest of the city, in the central streets activities were almost completely paralyzed from midday until three in the afternoon.

If our inquisitive visitor were traveling about on festival days or during Holy Week, he might come face to face with some penitents, barefoot, clothed only in a loose shirt and long white trousers, and wearing a crown of thorns on their heads. He would note that each was carrying a wooden cross on his left shoulder and a rope in his right hand. They prayed as they walked, groaning deeply, at the same time administering heavy blows to their own shoulders.

Our traveler might visit the capital in the spring. In the afternoon he would doubtless make his way to the Alameda de las Delicias to be present at the promenade of the girls and the young men of social rank. His attention would be called to the simplicity of the dress of the maidens: the short hoop petticoat, plain or with flounces, the little jackets with tight sleeves, the stayed waists, and the colored shawl on the shoulders. A few would be wearing gold brooches in their hair and at intervals one could catch a glimpse of their shoes with silver buckles.

In the shade of the poplars on the stone and brick benches, he would note some groups comfortably seated and engaged in pleasant conversation. It is very probable that he could even see there the most important public men of the time, who frequently showed themselves at the promenade and sat there to discuss their affairs. When it began to grow dark, all the promenaders would withdraw to their homes. Suddenly a bell would sound, at first gently, then more rapidly; it was the signal for prayer, pealing from the church towers. All would stop where they were, make the sign of the cross, and pray, while here and there could be heard the voices of acquaintances, saluting as they met:

"Good night!"

"May God grant the same to you!"

Night was falling. Possibly there would be a play at the only theatre of the city, where some comedy might be given, or where one could hear a concert of piano, harp, and guitar. Here the visitor could appreciate the luxury of the wealthy inhabitants of Santiago. The misses and matrons displayed their elegant fabrics, gauzes and laces; generous décolletés scarcely broken by a pearl necklace; fans of colored laces and fine kid gloves, so recently come into use; beautiful hair nets entwined with threads of gold and brilliants. The men wore Prince Albert dress coats of very ample proportions. Our visitor would not be able to stay long in the theatre. It was the custom to smoke there and, as the only light was that from tallow candles, the smoke and the accompanying evil odor might in a short time make him dizzy.

If there were no theatre, he might visit the home of an acquaintance. Very likely he would find the family in the vestibule seated on the bench there, taking the fresh air if the season permitted. On being shown into the reception room he would observe no little luxury. There would be in more or less profusion great mirrors of Venetian glass, rich tapestries from Flanders, draperies of rich materials, small tables, and chests of cedar or walnut. Perhaps, instead of paintings, he might observe on the wall the picture of some miracle-working saint. If he were well acquainted at the house and there were daughters, it is probable that they would play the guitar and sing. It is almost certain that they would not have a piano, because that instrument was not yet very common in Chile, and only a few wealthy families could boast of one. He would be invited to tea, and the table service of ornate silver would not fail to produce a good impression. He could also enjoy maté, sucking it through a silver *bombilla*.

He might chance upon a fiesta or family gathering on the occasion of the saint's day of some member of the household. On such occasions there would be dancing. The most aristocratic dance was the minuet; but, when enthusiasm reigned in the gathering, it was the custom to descend to the vigorous popular dances, such as the *cueca* and the *zamba*.[1] Often there were also rural excursions to the neighboring country houses and, as the only conveyance of any size was the *carretón*, a large cart, they made the journey in this. On the whole these expeditions were much enjoyed because they then treated one another with affability. In Santiago there was also a philharmonic society in which the young men who were fond of dancing and music met to entertain themselves and to organize public functions.

The tourist whom we have been following has not yet finished his excursion. He would have gone, no doubt, before leaving, to a café or wineshop, in which he would have been diverted with watching fifty or more idle men playing billiards or cards. It is worth while to observe that the very poor light in such places, tallow candles, did

---

[1] The *cueca* or *zamacueca* was a lively popular dance, supposedly originating in Peru, but it may have been derived from Andalusia. The performance was usually accompanied by the harp or guitar, with singing and handclapping on the part of the spectators. The *zamba* was a more moderate dance popular in Argentina and Chile. See Espasa, *Enciclopedia*, LXX, 915, 916.

not prevent the people from enjoying themselves until midnight in games of chance. After this last expedition, our traveler would go to sleep in a small room in some tavern. In order to go about the streets, he had to be accompanied by a *sereno* or night watchman, who, while keeping him free from any attack, guided him through the intricate tangle of streets, amid the darkness which was broken only by an occasional lantern.

But this life of the highest class of society was not the life of all; the poor, the great mass, almost.the entire populace, lived in a very different manner. In the suburbs of the city and even in some parts near the center were found their habitations—huts raised scarcely six feet above the ground, covered with thatch, surrounded by adobe walls, with earthen floors which were generally damp. Their food was beans and potatoes, and very seldom meat. Their utensils were earthern pots and dishes, wooden spoons, and some sort of steel knife. The clothing of the men consisted of trousers, a shirt, and a woolen blanket (*manta*), sandals, and a cap. The women wore a cotton sack like a large chemise, a kerchief about the neck, and sometimes sandals, when not barefooted. Clothing for the children was so scant that it scarcely covered the body. The system of tenantry in the country had not altered its program nor had living conditions changed since colonial times. Rural servitude continued to exist, attached like trees to the soil.

Popular amusements were not abundant; horse racing and cock fighting were the most common, and were attended by people of all classes, because they played for money in these sports. The peons and the artisans were not satisfied with these spectacles but must gather in small dramshops (*chinganas*) where they drank until they were intoxicated, sang and danced, played cards or *palitroque*,[2] and in settling up they were wont to resort to the bare dagger, even killing each other on the slightest pretext.

But the greatest enthusiasm usually prevailed at the patriotic festivals. On the twelfth of February and the eighteenth of September of each year came those celebrations which recalled the winning of independence. The cities were decorated. From the time of the dictatorship of O'Higgins, the tricolor banner of today has been used; the present coat-of-arms was adopted in the third year of the Prieto administration. In this way the symbols of national sovereignty were popularized before a quarter of a century had passed after the initial date of the revolution.

---

[2] *Palitroque,* a game played with cone-shaped sticks or pins, somewhat similar to bowling.

The names of the leaders of the revolutionary struggle, adorned with banners and coats-of-arms, were placed on great placards in the public square. Military maneuvers were held and these were especially attractive to the multitude. And to the *Te Deum*, as an act of gratitude, great solemnity was given. The people, without distinction of class, abandoned themselves to the most open expressions of pleasure, and various groups went through the streets huzzaing for the fatherland. A dance in the government palace or a pageant in the theatre recalling the events of independence was the rule. Military bands or some improvised orchestra would play the national song, which was not the same as it is today. It was composed by Don Bernardo de Vera in 1819, and of this there has been kept only the chorus. It contained very insulting references to Spain:

> Those monsters who bear within themselves
> A character ignoble and base,
> How can they ever be compared
> With the heroes of April the Fifth?[3]

There were also innumerable private gatherings to celebrate the glorious days of emancipation. It was the custom to have grand banquets at which were uttered patriotic speeches, to show the path of progress which the republic should follow. In all towns, even in those of lesser importance, similar fiestas took place, with a program in which merely the occasion was celebrated, although in some there was emphasis upon local color.

EXPANSION IN WEALTH AND CULTURE

There were reasons, indeed, for rejoicing over the work of the revolution. The prosperity of the country was an evident fact that showed itself chiefly in the development of wealth. Agriculture and cattle raising had advanced but little; but, on the other hand, commerce and mining furnished excellent returns. Under the protection of free trade, merchants from all over the world came to Chile to increase its production and particularly to secure precious metals. As a result of free trade, the northern district of the republic, a mine par excellence, was increasing its output of copper and gold. Silver, which had been until then scarce in Chile, became

---

[3] The original stanza is as follows:

> Esos monstruos que cargan consigo
> el carácter infame y servil,
> ¿cómo pueden jamás compararse
> con los héroes del 5 de abril?

a large source of wealth with the discovery of the mines of Arqueros, near La Serena, in 1825, and of those of Chañarcillo, near Copiapó, in 1832. This last discovery, by a simple woodcutter, Juan Godoy, yielded enormous quantities of silver and influenced in a most beneficial manner the general progress of the country.

Public education, the most constant concern of republican governments, was still in a very unsatisfactory state; but at any rate it was much above its former condition. In the primary grade the situation continued to be deplorable. The schools for the education of the people were very few; the town corporations maintained some; and, though Portales had commanded that one be opened in each convent, the order was only half obeyed and was without appreciable results. But in the secondary and superior grades considerable progress had been made. Three cities had *liceos*, or public high schools: Santiago, La Serena, and Talca. The most important was naturally the school in Santiago; namely, the old National Institute of former times that had been established in the capital as the center of public instruction.

Not less than ten private "colleges," or seminaries, for boys had arisen here under official sanction, by virtue of moderate subventions. The chief ones were the Liceo of Chile, founded by José Joaquín de Mora, and the College of Santiago, which was founded by a French educator, but which reached its greatest prosperity under the direction of Andrés Bello. These two establishments had, however, like the others, a precarious existence. The National Institute absorbed almost all secondary and higher instruction.

Education for girls continued to be in the care of the nuns in their convents and was very insignificant. But there were also in that period several private "colleges" for girls, which soon met the same fate as those for the boys, among which might be noted the one founded by the wife of Mora. In the field of professional teaching there may be mentioned the beginning of instruction in engineering and the establishment of the School of Medicine and Pharmacy in 1833.

But in order to achieve such progress, the government had to employ the services of many learned foreigners who had come to the country under direct contract. Among them Mora and Bello held first place. Mora is still known for his political activity. Andrés Bello was a native of Venezuela, in whose capital (Caracas) he was born in 1781. After having rendered valuable service as a statesman in winning the independence of his fatherland, he was sent to serve in a diplomatic post in England in the employ of

Colombia, the republic within which Venezuela was incorporated. There he also was entrusted with the post of secretary of the legation for Chile, and then he agreed to occupy a position in the country itself as chief of the ministerial section of foreign relations. In 1829, when he was about fifty years of age, he arrived in Chile.

He brought with him a considerable reputation as a litterateur and scholar, which he promptly and fully confirmed in Chile. In addition to the duties to which he was pledged, he took over the editing of the government periodical, *El araucano*, and, for a time, the direction of the College of Santiago. When this institution was discontinued, he began to give private lessons at his home, in law, Spanish literature, and philosophy. He exhibited such ability in this teaching and in his other occupations that soon he was considered the most eminent scholar that had ever been known in Chile. His prestige was established by the publication of his *Principios de derecho internacional* (*Principles of International Law*) in 1834, which was known throughout the civilized world.[4] [In politics he always tried to keep out of party struggles, as much because of his position as a foreigner as because of his lack of interest in that form of activity. He preferred the quiet of his study to the tumult of popular gatherings. Nevertheless, he contributed his modicum of talent to the service of the conservative party which was in control.][5]

Of the other scholars who served Chile also at this time, it is fair to mention the Spanish mathematician, Andrés Antonio Gorbea, the real founder of the school of engineering in Chile; the English physician, William Blest, to whose initiative is due to a large degree the establishment of the school of medicine; Lorenzo Sazie, another famous physician, who took under his care the direction of that school; and Claudio Gay, the naturalist, French like Sazie, who was commissioned by Portales to make a complete survey of the land and products of Chile. This was an investigation too large for the strength of one man, as Gay doubtless realized at the end of twelve years of hard and continuous work. His great *Historia*

---

[4] In addition to his earlier diplomatic experiences, Bello served as arbitrator in 1864 in a dispute between the United States and Ecuador and in the following year in a dispute between Peru and Colombia. His *Principios de derecho internacional* (Santiago, 1832), while an elementary treatise, was well received and widely quoted. Bello was the first to point out the insufficiency of principles in the work of Vattier and he serves as a precursor to Wheaton. See Carlos Calvo, *Le droit international* (2 vols. 2nd ed., Paris, 1870-1872), I, 85-86; also consult Calvo's index. For other editions, see Bello's *Obras completas* (15 vols. Santiago, 1881-1893), Vols. X, XV-XVIII.

[5] The portion enclosed in brackets is omitted from the seventh edition.

física y política de Chile (*Physical and Political History of Chile*), published in the middle of the nineteenth century, was the result of his unceasing industry in the discharge of the commission which had been entrusted to him. In other respects the country presented few evidences of a state of enlightenment. It may be said that the labor of the government in its effort to raise educated men in Chile through the diffusion of instruction resulted only in preparing the way for future intellectual development.

SANITARY CONDITIONS; MENDICANCY AND DELINQUENCY

The progress related above was not achieved without encountering definite obstacles. The sanitary condition of the country was one of them. Smallpox had become endemic, and in the years 1831 and 1832 a terrible epidemic of scarlet fever visited the entire country, and especially the cities of Valparaiso and Santiago, where the crowding of dwellings rendered more intolerable the uncleanly habits and the general lack of hygiene, particularly among the lower classes. In order to make headway against these scourges and improve the sanitation, a charity commission was created, entrusted with the direction of these services from the capital, with watching the hygiene in all public institutions, and with proposing to the government those measures which they judged conducive to public health.

But there were two other social evils which demanded no less attention: beggary and crime. The revolution and the republican regime were as far from having extinguished misery as from ending ignorance and crime. The entire social order suffered from the consequences. Beggars thronged the streets and highwaymen terrorized the countryside. The various measures adopted to end mendicancy had no other result than its regulation, which consisted in obtaining permission of a parish priest before taking alms. In Santiago the number of beggars continued to be almost as great as in the last years of the colony.

Assassinations and robberies by armed bands were all too frequent, not only in the rural estates but even within the towns themselves. In 1828 a deputy affirmed that during that year there had been eight hundred assassinations in the capital and no one denied it. There were districts like the Hills of Teno (*Cerrillos de Teno*) in the province of Curicó, and the Slope of the Prado (*Cuesta de lo Prado*) west of Santiago which could not be crossed without an escort of gendarmes.

The severity that Portales visited upon offenders had been of no avail in suppressing those crimes. He had sent several parties of armed men against them, instructed to shoot without mercy. The hard labor on public works to which he condemned those arrested for minor offenses also availed as little; crime continued to be a terrible plague. There were no prisons in which to guard felons securely; most of them escaped with ease. Not even the prison of Santiago, situated on the Plaza de Armas, offered conditions favorable for this purpose. Police protection was lacking. Portales created a body of "vigilantes" or day police who, added to the *serenos* organized by O'Higgins, made a more or less regular service. But, few in numbers, neither one nor the other satisfied the many demands of the situation. In the rural districts, no ordered or permanent police existed.

Crime in this period had, as its greatest representatives, two brothers who were popularly nicknamed the Pincheiras (scullions). Natives of the province of Maule and brought up there, they had devoted themselves from childhood to adventures of the lowest sort, and had served for some time among the royalist guerrillas. When Benavides sought allies among the bandits to maintain the cause of the king of Spain and to plunder at will, they enrolled themselves in his ranks; and, after his death, they continued their career of plunder and crime in the central provinces of the country, from Curicó to Concepción, always under the pretext of upholding Spanish sovereignty. The headquarters of their bands were located near the cordillera in the steep valleys which the mountain ridges form as they open out toward the west, and, assisted by the Pehuenche Indians of those districts, their depredations extended equally on both sides of the Andes. In one of their raids they even reached Mendoza and concluded with the governor a treaty of formal alliance as between powers, obtaining what they wanted.

They not only plundered but also assassinated, and in their band were individuals so bloodthirsty that they sacrificed the victims of their depredations through pure caprice. It had been impossible to surprise those merciless wretches, even though for twelve consecutive years the various national governments had despatched contingents of troops in pursuit of them. Finally, in 1832, General Manuel Bulnes, well acquainted with the difficult topography of the district in which the malefactors were operating, was commissioned by President Prieto to capture them at all cost and, after a long campaign, he did get them; but, in order to accomplish it, he had to make use of a veritable army and to employ a varied strategy. The crueler brother was executed the moment he was taken prisoner, together with many of his comrades.

In 1830, then, the reforms and social improvements which had been hoped for at the fall of the Spanish regime had scarcely made a noticeable impression.[6] Colonial society remained static, with its organization, with its virtues and defects, in spite of twenty years of agitation and upheaval. What improvement could be seen was the economic expansion which benefitted the upper classes—the landholders and miners and the traders and manufacturers. But the great mass of the people had to wait many years before obtaining their share in the advantages offered by the new order. However, it was then evident that education and culture, more widespread than before, were preparing the way for a greater collective well-being.

---

[6] For brief sketches of the social life at the beginning of the nineteenth century, see Edwards Bello in *Imágenes de Chile*. Cf. p. 140, n. 13.

CHAPTER XII

THE AUTOCRATIC REPUBLIC

PORTALES AND THE PRESIDENCY OF PRIETO

THE CONSERVATIVE PARTY, reorganized and invigorated by Diego Portales, immediately after the revolution of 1829 gave legal sanction to its power by electing, in 1831, General Joaquín Prieto as president of the republic, as has been related. Expanding very quickly, this group enacted the political code which definitively organized the State and governed the country almost without interruption for the next thirty years (1831-1861). The Constitution of 1833 was the most complete expression of its aims. It established a regime of authority and of force, exercised at the discretion of the chief magistrate with a minimum of fiscal supervision. All power rested in his hands. Congressional and municipal elections were to be directed by him and his immediate agents or deputies, his intendants, and the governors. The judges of all the tribunals would be named by him, together with the remaining employees in the public service. As generalissimo of the armed forces, on him alone would depend the army, the navy, and the police corps. During the thirty years to which we refer, this structure remained intact and functioned without lessening its rigor, except in times of political calm and relaxation. Therefore, this period customarily has been called the "autocratic republic" regime, which necessarily would have to pervade all national life.

By others that regime might be called "conservative," as much for the name of the party that introduced and supported it as for the determination which this very party always showed to maintain without change the continuity of the colonial spirit, or the mentality of the past. Others would rather call it "oligarchic," because a restricted social circle then controlled the government and took advantage of its influence. The great mass of the people meanwhile could not participate in the government because of the misery and ignorance in which it was submerged. But this type of oligarchy not only ruled the country in that period, but likewise, although widening its circle, in later periods. Therefore we do not apply to the period in question the term "oligarchic." The conservative spirit which became characteristic of it seems to us without doubt an important feature, but we consider the term "autocratic" more appropriate because it defines less vaguely the state of force in which that regime maintained the republic.

About 1831, when General Prieto initiated his government, the republican generation which assumed power differed very little from the last generation of the colonial period. It had no other general aspirations than for tranquillity and order, both propitious for the acquisition of wealth by means of peaceful and prolonged labor. These aspirations were represented and were always dominant during the ten years of this administration. Portales had made himself the interpreter and promoter of that tendency, and he had imposed it upon the ministries which he filled with dictatorial authority for about a year and a half (April, 1830-August, 1831).

The system of Portales meant an inflexible reaction against the aims which had animated the fathers of independence, who evolved the plan of a democratic republic, principally for the benefit of the dispossessed classes. These in a short time would elevate the level of their culture and enter into the enjoyment of well-being compatible with the political function which was reserved for them through the promising action of the new regime. Nevertheless, little or nothing had been done for them because of the vicissitudes and upheavals which followed the emancipating movement. Now the normalizing of the government of the republic restored a system which prevented the hearing of claims for the legal recovery of rights because such claims were thought subversive. The liberals then represented, at least to a certain degree, the logical consequence of an emancipating revolution in so far as they derived from it reforms of a social character designed to put the entire population of the country in tune with democratic institutions. But the twenty years of strife had not only conquered but crushed them and, under an authority which stifled by the aid of force the slightest manifestation of discontent, they no longer had hopes of renewing the struggle.

In spite of the vigor of the system legally introduced, the first period of the Prieto administration (1831-1836) was not entirely peaceful. There were several military conspiracies which proposed to overthrow the government; and, although unreasonable and illusory, they represented in substance a protest against the ruling reaction and against the spurious policy of social reform which had been sponsored since emancipation. The republic would not be a popular democratic regime, but an oligarchic and burgeois system directly beneficial to the propertied class.

In order to stifle those attempts at revolt, President Prieto was obliged to make use of the extraordinary faculties which the Constitution of 1833 bestowed upon the executive shortly after this was put into effect. Conspirators were punished with imprisonment and exile. In the following years the country enjoyed tranquillity and the government was able to devote itself without fear to the consummation of the work which it had begun.

THE ORGANIZATION OF THE PUBLIC TREASURY

Without doubt the most important work was the organization of the public treasury, which the preceding disturbance had completely upset. Because of these disturbances the total revenue receipts were not very great, scarcely reaching a million and a half pesos annually, notwithstanding the fact that under the dictatorships of O'Higgins and Freire receipts had fluctuated around two million. It was urgent, therefore, to devise adequate measures for increasing the revenue, lessening expenses, and regulating the collection of taxes. This last operation had, during the recent disorders, assumed the character of a scandal in many government bureaus. Portales, actively interested in that work, caused Manuel Rengifo to enter the ministry of the treasury in 1830. This man, versed in finance and of great probity, remained in charge of that office until 1835.

The first indication of the designs animating the new ministry was the establishment of the strictest economy in fiscal disbursements, this being made possible by the dismissal of useless or little needed employees and by careful inspection of the others. This measure reduced the budget in one lump to less than three hundred thousand pesos. Next Rengifo turned to the regulation of the revenues, consulting not alone the interest of the treasury, but also the welfare of those contributing. To this end, while discontinuing some levies, he imposed others upon a new and more equitable basis.

As the principal sources for revenue, he specified the customs duties, the monopoly of tobacco and playing cards, tithes, and the excise. Among these the branch of customs was given the preferred place. He ordered a new tariff on official appraisement; from all impost he exempted books which were not considered immoral or irreligious (if they were, he did not permit them to enter), scientific instruments, and industrial machinery; he transferred to the ports the customhouses located in the capitals of the provinces; and he ordered that coastwise trade should pay duty at one port, that of departure or of arrival, and that only Chilean vessels should engage in it. Consequently, the coastwise trade was reserved for many years for the national merchant marine which, because of this privilege, was able to organize itself and grow.

Taking advantage of its fine geographical position as a point of transfer in the movement of merchandise around Cape Horn and through the Strait of Magellan, he endeavored to make Valparaiso the foremost port on the Pacific. With this end in view, he established there extensive fiscal warehouses which, on the payment of a small fee, were to receive and care for the cargoes of ships from any part of the world, whether this cargo was destined for Chile or was to be sent to any other country whatsoever. This protective measure for commerce produced the desired result. Valparaiso saw floating in its bay the flags of all nations, and in a short time became the emporium of the Pacific coast of [South] America.

Under the direction of Rengifo, the government also interested itself in the protection of national industries and agriculture by means of customs duties, more or less high, upon foreign products that were similar to those of the country. For this reason, among other articles coming from abroad, ready-made clothing and footwear, and wheat and cattle from the Argentine that came through the passes of the Andes were taxed heavily. For a similar reason the fields intended for the cultivation of hemp and flax were exempted from payment of the tithe. Rewards were offered to those who introduced or adapted to the country industrial inventions for the greater use of those plants, and it was ordered that the vessels of the navy should be provided with rigging made in Chile.

The greater part of these efforts proved fruitless, partly because the contraband trade—as was the case in regard to cattle—evaded the customhouses of the Andes and partly because the country was not adapted for the cultivation of flax and hemp. One measure, however, which produced good results was the exemption of Chilean fishermen from taxation.

The department of the excise was also one of the sources of revenue which seriously engaged the attention of Minister Rengifo. This tax, like the others, dated from colonial times and had various forms. It was levied upon the products of agriculture and of industry, upon wholesale and retail trade, upon documentary deeds transferring real estate rights from one person to another. The first two forms were very odious because the right to collect them was sold to some individual at public auction—on this account they were called "auctioned excises"—and these persons practiced an unpleasant espionage over the business of the contributors in order to gain the greatest possible income from the levy. Besides, they injured the consumer because of the consequent rise in prices. These excises were abolished and were replaced by a more equitable tax which did not involve the inconveniences of the former and which was collected by fiscal employees. This tax was called *catastro* and consisted of a percentage on the valuation of the lands and their buildings, something like the present tax on incomes. The tax imposed on contracts was retained, but with lessened obligations; and no change was made at all in the tithe because of the religious origin of this agricultural impost.

All this work of reorganization gave the results for which Rengifo was hoping. If it did not increase the income of the treasury all at once, it did succeed in realizing this increase gradually, in such a way that in the period of five years (1830-1835) it amounted to about a million pesos and caused the public income to rise from a million and a half to two and a half million pesos. His greatest service, however, was not this but the stimulus which he gave to the development of the national wealth.

But the government had to face obligations in excessive amounts over and above the necessary expenses of administration. There was a public debt representing in the aggregate a sum of ten million pesos, which was classified in two divisions: domestic and foreign. The domestic debt consisted of the numerous obligations contracted by the state with individuals dating from the colonial period, such as loans, requisitions, unpaid salaries, and other obligations. During the struggle for independence and the succeeding revolutions, these obligations had considerably increased until they amounted approximately to four million pesos.

The external debt consisted of the loan contracted in London in 1822 for a million pounds sterling at 6 per cent annual interest with 1 per cent for a sinking fund. Little had been realized from this unfortunate transaction. Of the five million gold pesos that the country had immediately anticipated, there had been paid over but little more than three million because the certificates had been placed on the London Stock Exchange at a discount of more than 30 per cent, and the payment of commissions, reports, and other expenses had cost many thousands. Of those three millions, about one-half had been loaned to Peru, and Peru was not paying up. In order to meet the interest which the debt was drawing, the government found itself in such straits that it even had to grant the tobacco monopoly to a private company on condition that the company take care of the charges; but, as was seen above, the company could not fulfill that contract, and from then on this obligation was met with the greatest irregularity—a fact which discredited Chile in England and Europe. When Rengifo entered upon his ministry, several years' interest was due, and this raised the debt to six million pesos.

In order to meet such large obligations, the minister devised various kinds of measures; but he made it a point of general concern to satisfy first the accounts of Chilean creditors; that is to say, of those who had a part in the domestic debt and who might become dangerous to the public peace. Holders of the loan could wait, as indeed they did wait some years more, until 1842, when the same Rengifo, returned to the ministry of the treasury, agreed to a satisfactory arrangement with them.

The financial operations of Rengifo, however, were not accomplished very quickly; they aroused some irritating opposition and sharp criticism, especially the plan to pay the creditors of the treasury within the country. According to this plan, the notes against the State were designated as "overdue" and "current." Overdue notes were those made before the date on which the minister took his portfolio (1830), and current notes were those which had been contracted since that time. These last were to be paid from the general funds of the treasury on the date when they fell due; and overdue notes, in warrants against the customs duties. There was no difficulty about current credits; but the strange thing in the proceeding was that the creditor for the overdue debt, if he wanted to be paid, had to deposit in the treasury twice as much as the amount of his credit, and then to receive an order for the payment of the whole amount; that is to say, for three times the original amount. In this way an individual to whom the State owed five thousand pesos before 1830 had, in order to be paid, first to turn over ten thousand pesos; and when this was done, to draw against the customs for fifteen thousand pesos. So strange a form of settling accounts provoked well-founded protests. The sharp commentaries arose not only from the demand for the deposits—which represented an obligatory loan—but from the insecure proceedings which were employed to verify and examine the credits themselves.

The minister gave up his portfolio in 1835, not precisely because of those measures, but because of various other reasons which will presently appear; but in those five years he had completely reorganized public finances, introduced economy and order into the administration of the national revenues, increased the fiscal receipts, diminished the domestic debt of the State to half its former amount, and extended effective stimulus to the sources of production.

THE INTERNAL POLICY OF PRIETO'S GOVERNMENT

Already in 1835 the conservative party was not maintaining harmony in its ranks, and Rengifo was a victim of the discord that resulted. Little by little, various signs of division had become apparent. The heterogeneous elements which composed the party could not be reconciled, chiefly for two reasons. In the first place, the excessively restrictive policy in excluding their opponents— shown in the persecutions of which the fallen *pipiolo* party was made the victim—did not meet the unanimous approval of the members of the party. Men of liberal and tolerant spirit like Manuel José Gandarillas and Diego José Benavente found fault with this. In the second place, opinion was no less divided over the religious questions arising in this period, upon which the government had placed itself unconditionally at the service of the Church.

The predominance of the clergy had been noticeably increased after the earthquake of 1835, which destroyed all the towns of the coast between the Maule and the Biobío—for it was accompanied by a tidal wave—and wrought destruction even to Chillán and Concepción. Just as on other occasions, this catastrophe was represented by the priesthood as a visitation from Heaven, and the increasing devotion of the people gave evidence of the most passionate intolerance.

Within the cabinet itself the current policy, moderate and a little less submissive to the clergy, was at variance with the opposite view. The minister of the treasury, Manuel Rengifo, represented this spirit of conciliation and peace, just as the minister of the interior, Joaquín Tocornal, was the most resolute servant of the Church and of authority. The moderate conservative faction then took Rengifo for its leader and launched a newspaper called *El philopolita*[1] (*The Friend of the Common People*), for which the prolific and energetic pens of Gandarillas and Benavente began to write; and, as the presidential election drew near and the reëlection of General Prieto for a second term was almost assured, this group undertook to oppose it and craftily started the presidential can-

---

[1] For references to this periodical and its activity in opposition to the reelection of General Prieto, see Edwards, *Bosquejo histórico de los partidos políticos chilenos*, pp. 33-34, and the same author's *La fronda aristocrática en Chile*, chap. xii. See also Sotomayor Valdés, *Historia de Chile*, Vol. I, chap. xv, *passim*.

didacy of Rengifo. By a logical procedure, the *pipiolos* who had been defeated in the revolution of 1829 were shown to be in favor of Rengifo's candidacy; and round about the minister of the treasury was thus formed a more or less powerful nucleus of opinion. Rengifo did not aspire to the presidency and he had declared himself in favor of the reëlection of Prieto; but the fact remained that his name continued to appear as the standard of battle against the most irreconcilable "Bigwigs," and that in *El philopolita* religious prejudices were attacked with no little bitterness.

Meanwhile, Portales saw with sorrow that division had arisen in his political camp and prepared to intervene. At first he watched these disagreements from Valparaiso, where he had settled after leaving the ministry and where he had carried on the local government with his characteristic diligence. Then becoming impatient with such a commission, he resigned it and took up his quarters on a large estate near Ligua, which he acquired by purchase, and from here he continued to observe the political movement which was developing in the capital. He affected the most absolute abstention from party affairs, but he could not conceal from himself the danger which threatened his most diligent adherents and endangered his own rigid organization.

Among the *filopolitas* (a name which was given to the dissenting conservatives because of their newspaper), he saw acting as leaders men like Gandarillas and Benavente, who had never been his enthusiastic supporters and were now his personal opponents. In addition, the defeated liberals were also adhering to this group. Even if Rengifo were the friend of Portales, he would not be able to tolerate the latter's policy, should he achieve victory through those factions. On the opposite side, the president and his minister, Tocornal, better reflected the absent dictator's ideas and made clear his duty to aid them if they were in danger.

At this juncture exertions were beginning to be made to rehabilitate those military officers who were dismissed in 1830. This purpose, which was supported by the *filopolitas*, who were eager to attract to themselves the definite aid of the *pipiolos*, induced Portales to appear among his friends in order to defend an act, the execution of which had devolved on him, and a policy which he himself had guaranteed. In fact, between sunset and sunrise, when the patriotic festivals of September, 1835, had scarcely ended, he entered the palace of the government to take over the ministry of war, without public announcement of any sort. Rengifo was surprised and resigned. Then Tocornal was transferred to the portfolio of the treasury and Portales united the portfolio of the interior with that of war. In this way the formidable politician again found himself in the same position as in 1830, at the head of two ministerial departments, as powerful as before or even more so, "with a purveyor of funds, Tocornal, and a purveyor of signatures, the president." A new civil dictatorship was established from that moment. The reëlection of General Prieto was accomplished without difficulty; members of both the liberal group and the *filopolitas* refrained from going to the polls in almost all the provinces.

The constitution permitted the reëlection of the president to succeed himself for a second period of five years, and while this provision remained in force all the presidents availed themselves of it to have themselves reëlected. This meant then, ten-year presidential terms. Reëlection was achieved without difficulty, owing to the irresistible power placed by the constitution itself in the hands of the chief of state, who named the mayors and members of the municipal councils, the governors, intendants, and judges, and thus dominated the electoral system. According to this, individuals with the right to vote, who wished to make use of that right, had to enroll before their respective town councils, from which they received a certificate or ticket called "qualification." This qualification had to be presented by the citizen when voting.

The capacity to exercise that right as regulated by the constitutional code provided that, besides Chilean citizenship and the attainment of one's majority, one should know how to read and write. There was a further requirement of ownership of property or income, the amount of which was to be fixed by a special law, but this law had not been passed. Moreover, the government did not begin to apply the requirement of knowing how to read and write until after 1840. After that year the administration tried to make it effective, but congress declared that it should be applied only to citizens who enrolled themselves in the future; those already enrolled should continue to enjoy the right of voting until death.

The commanders of the civic forces in the cities had hastened to enroll in the national guard, and in the country the landowners had acted in a similar way with their tenants. So the former as well as the latter preserved the qualifications of their subordinates, that they might not be lost, as they said; and, when the elections occurred, they used such suffrages as they believed convenient. In this way the commanders and landowners controlled an enormous electoral power and, as almost all of them were supporters of the established government and conservatives from conviction, there was no need to ascertain who was to win any elections. Besides this, the governors and intendants (direct representatives of the executive) decided electoral complaints, and, although this function soon passed to trained judges, the government lost little thereby because these officials were no less its dependents. To the opponents was left nothing but to try to attract free electors, who played a large part also in conservative and governmental ranks, and to practice bribery, which, because of the scarcity of money, had not yet acquired significant proportions.

In practice, the intendants and governors controlled the elections of senators and representatives within their own jurisdictions. The chief of state and his ministers made lists of the people who were to make up each chamber for a constitutional period, and the elections were carried out according to these lists. It was rare that more than three or five opposition candidates succeeded in defeating the government candidates in the different departments. The orders of the minister of the interior to the agents of the executive were expressed more or less in these terms: "His Excellency instructs me to make known to you that Señor or Señores [here the names] should be chosen in your department for the post of [here the name of senator or deputy]." If any candidate of the opposition attempted to electioneer at any point whatever in the country, the respective government agent would receive from the minister of the interior a communication like this: "Manage to prevent Don . . . from coming to your department by advising him to refrain from presenting himself in it. If he insists you can have him arrested as a disturber of the public peace."

By these measures, and the effective forces upon which the party in power relied, the latter could almost always secure a loyal congress. But it is only fair to bear witness that, for the most part, the Executive did not abuse his great power in any venal manner. Reputable men generally appeared in the lists of congressmen, some even with ideas opposed to the government, who, because of their recognized intelligence and moderate character, deserved to have a place in the national representation. On the other hand, as there existed no incompatibility between the post of senator or deputy and the holding of public office, many of the most distinguished servants of the administration also entered congress.

A similar proceeding took place when the presidential election was held. The government took a candidate under its protection and caused him to win, making beforehand the list of "presidential electors." Thus is explained the ease with which each supreme executive was reëlected. When the election agitation took on a dangerous character and threatened to disturb public order, the executive still had one other recourse: to decree a state of siege and to assume the extraordinary powers which the constitution granted him. Against this no resistance was possible.

Such election management was not peculiar to the administration of Prieto. Certainly it began with the Constitution of 1833, but it lasted almost unaltered for more than half a century, although at times it lost much of its rigor. If it had serious inconveniences, if in reality it was neither popular or representative, if it trampled under foot all political liberties, it was, nevertheless, the only thing possible in a country which lacked a politically conscious people and civic education, and it had the advantage of permitting the government to make itself stable and continuous.

But the supporters of the liberalism which was destroyed in 1830, and a portion of the intelligent young men preparing to enter political life did not look favorably upon this situation. According to them, the country ought to rule itself freely, without the tutelage of the executive, and the elections ought to be held with the most absolute abstention on his part. The electoral intervention of the president, the extraordinary powers of which he made use when he declared one or more provinces of the nation in a state of siege, and the persecutions which his followers inflicted upon those who were not supporters of the government exasperated these men, and frequently led them to conspire and to form wild schemes for revolt.

THE NEW DICTATORSHIP OF PORTALES (1835-37)

We have earlier noted that in September, 1835, Portales assumed anew the ministries of interior and of war and initiated another period of rigid control. General Prieto was reëlected the following year under the auspices of the minister and he had scarcely begun his second presidency (1836-1841) when a threat of revolution arose to disturb the republic and to give Minister Portales the opportunity to make use of extraordinary powers for the second time.

General Freire returned from Peru with two ships and went to Chiloé to raise an army on the island, with which to overthrow the government. The enterprise failed completely. Freire was taken prisoner before he began operations and subjected to a council of war, which condemned him to death; but a higher tribunal, a court-martial, commuted that sentence to exile.

From that instant Portales became exceedingly exasperated. Several military conspiracies had been discovered during those same days, and the trials then instituted ended with severe sentences. He believed that the arch culprit was Freire and that the death penalty was the only one suited to him. He thereupon indicted the members of the court-martial, who had been of the opposite opinion, before the supreme court, which acquitted the accused; and Freire, along with many other political offenders, was taken to Juan Fernández, an island converted into a prison for that class of culprits. But he did not remain there long. He was exiled to Sidney, an English colony in Australia, and thither he was transferred.

In the opinion of the minister the most serious part of this was not, however, the expedition of Freire itself, nor the other complications, but the insult which Chile had received from Peru, because Freire had prepared the attempted revolution in its territory, with the complicity of its government. With this in mind, Portales broke off diplomatic relations with Peru.

For some time the relations between Chile and Peru had not been very cordial. The expenses of the liberating expedition led by San Martín and Cochrane and the sum of money which the Chilean government conveyed to that country from the English loan had given occasion for vexatious diplomatic negotiations. Then later it had been impossible to enter into a commercial treaty, and both countries were keeping up a struggle over customs duties which gave opportunity for mutual protests and recriminations. In Peru the importation of Chilean wheat was burdened to the absurd extent of three to six pesos a fanega. In Chile there was a similar tariff on Peruvian sugar, and to these commodities were added several others both in Chile and in Peru. Ill will in Peru reached such a point that the government some time before decreed a highly distasteful tax against merchandise from any source which might have been deposited in the free warehouses of Valparaiso for the purpose of lessening the prosperity which that port was acquiring, thanks in a great measure to this trade privilege.

Moreover, the frequent revolutions staged in Peru were giving an opportunity to a foreign power, well known as unfriendly to Chile, to intervene there and stir up both internal discord and international friction. This foreign power was none other than Bolivia, whose president, General Andrés Santa Cruz, was ambitious to incorporate the republic of Peru with his government, and with this purpose in mind he was secretly encouraging revolutions in that country. Fearing that Chile might be an obstacle to his plans, he tried to stir up another, equally great, in the latter country and this explains why he advised the revolutionary government at Lima to furnish the aid which it gave to General Freire. This government, however, did not last long. Shortly after Freire set out from Callao, Santa Cruz assumed the direction of Peru and Bolivia jointly, under the title of "Protector of the Peru-Bolivian Confederation." One campaign against the anarchistic Peruvians had brought about the realization of the fortunate general's most cherished aspirations (1836).

Such overwhelming success could not fail to attract the attention of the men governing Chile; and, although Bernardo O'Higgins, exiled in Peru, through letters to President Prieto and other friends tried to minimize the aggressive spirit which the men directing that country were showing toward Chile, Portales did not become over-confident; but, from the moment that he received the news of the revolutionary expedition of Freire, he determined upon war with the Peru-Bolivian Confederation.

Portales did not conceal from himself the seriousness of such a step. The confederation had an army inured to war in its revolutionary struggles and, in any case, larger than that of Chile. On the other hand, Chile, very recently emerged from revolutionary chaos, lacking resources and needing its energies to assure its progress, was not in a favorable condition for such an enterprise; but Portales believed that the aggrandizement of Santa Cruz was dangerous to the internal order of the republic—through the civil strife, which, like the attempt of Freire, he might continue to provoke—and a threat against the very independence of the nation. And he, who with such fortitude had assisted in establishing and giving vitality to this system, now believed that he was obliged to free it from all obstacles and to assure the stability of the national government. Hence he staked all the credit and the future of Chile solely on this warlike enterprise.

Seeking to take advantage of Santa Cruz and deprive him of his squadron, Portales sent two ships to Peru under the command of Victorino Garrido, a Spaniard by birth, who by mixing in Chilean politics had risen from a simple merchant to the rank of colonel and had held several public positions. A man very much esteemed for his good sense, Garrido fitted in perfectly with the mission entrusted to him. He captured by surprise the ships of the Peruvian navy at Callao; then he entered into negotiations with Santa Cruz, who left the ships in his possession in accordance with a treaty which they concluded, and returned to Valparaiso victorious.

The attitude of Santa Cruz was inexcusable from every point of view and is only explained by his fearing to see the realization of his plan thwarted by a war of such proportions. At first he had proceeded in a very different manner; he had imprisoned the chargé d'affaires of Chile in Lima, Ventura Lavalle, and had interpreted events as they in truth appeared—as a declaration of war. But finding it better, upon later reflection, to disentangle himself from the serious situation, he freed Lavalle and concluded the treaty by which Garrido received the vessels. Portales, however, was not satisfied with this result. On the arrival of Garrido at Santiago he disapproved of the treaty on the grounds that Santa Cruz had not given the explanations which he owed the Chilean government, and that he had committed a grave outrage on Lavalle, the chargé, by imprisoning him for a few moments. Portales, indeed, was not fair in his judgment; the blow inflicted by Garrido upon the Peruvian fleet practically precipitated hostilities and deprived the Chilean government not only of the right to ask but even to hope for any explanation. But, as in his own mind he was resolutely decided upon war, he judged the events in the light of this decision. Besides, there were in Santiago a number of Peruvian political exiles who professed a profound hatred for the protector, Santa Cruz, and they made Portales believe that a Chilean army scarcely could reach Peru before a formidable revolt would break out against the protector's authority, which, as they asserted, the Peruvian nation considered a most hateful tyranny.

The government then asked congress to authorize a declaration of war; it was unanimously granted. Mariano Egaña[2] was sent to Peru, accompanied by several ships from the national navy, with instructions to demand from Santa Cruz: (1) satisfaction for the injuries done to Lavalle; (2) the dissolution of the Peru-Bolivian Confederation; (3) the acknowledgment of the unsettled accounts pending from the loan with which Chile had earlier favored that nation and from the cost of the liberating expedition; (4) the payment of indemnity for the injury which had been caused by the expedition of Freire to Chile; and (5) the limitation of the naval armaments of Peru. Such exorbitant demands could not be accepted and they certainly were not. Egaña, in fulfilment of his instructions, formulated without delay the declaration of war. This was in November, 1836.

The declaration of war created an unusual situation for the government, or rather for Portales, who was directing it without any check. Unlimited extraordinary powers were conferred upon him, the entire republic was declared in a state of siege, and he was given

[2] See p. 467, infra. For Egaña's activities at this time, see Valdés, II, 236, et seq.

the means to conduct the war as he saw fit. This was, in truth, the most solemn moment in his life, and he knew how to meet it. His activities and his determination to carry on the war against Peru were manifold and immeasurable. But in the interior of the country hatred against him, held in check for a long time, broke out in all sections. Numerous conspiracies came to light and the dictator promulgated barbarous laws to punish those responsible for them.

Neither these extraordinary powers nor the state of siege were enough to restrain the spirit of rebellion which lay in wait for him. A law was decreed which threatened the death penalty to those political malcontents who would not remain where they were confined, or who broke away from their exile, a penalty which the officer who might arrest them should execute within twenty-four hours, without any appeal. Some special tribunals were created, called "permanent councils," which were to function in the capital of each province for the purpose of condemning without appeal within three days and according to military law those who disturbed public order or were guilty of disrespect toward the government. Many were banished and several executed. A reign of terror prevailed. The minister, the dictator of former days, had degenerated into a tyrant. The war, far from making him popular, made him most hateful in the judgment of many persons. The people did not feel patriotic exaltation at the call of martial music proclaiming the campaign because the motives of the conflict were not sufficiently explained.

Finally, at the beginning of June, 1837, the dictator went to Quillota to review a body of troops encamped there. Suddenly the officers in charge arrested him, kept him isolated, loaded him with chains, and declared themselves in open insurrection. Colonel José Antonio Vidaurre led the movement. The mutineers made their way toward Valparaiso and took Portales with them in a small carriage, or *birlocho*. The garrison at the port prepared to resist. At dawn on June 6 fighting began on Barón Hill. The minister, still loaded with irons, was a short distance away under the guard of an officer named Florín, who, when the first shots were heard, bade his soldiers force Portales from the open carriage, commanded him to kneel, and then gave the order to fire upon him. Two volleys sounded and the victim rolled over on the ground. The first light of dawn showed the shapeless corpse of the great statesman, before whom the republic for so many years had prostrated itself. It also revealed the complete rout of the assassins and rebels, who, promptly arrested, atoned for their crime on the gallows.

The death of Portales was regarded in those days as a tremendous national calamity, and the manifestations of grief and the splendid funeral accorded him had no precedent in Chile. The assassination was all the more hateful because the rebellion lacked any fixed purpose; it answered to no political movement or to any plan of reaction, systematically developed. The assassination bore to posterity the figure of the minister crowned with the aureole of the martyr. He died at the age of forty-four.

THE WAR AGAINST SANTA CRUZ

The war which Portales had prepared became popular with his death, because it was surmised that the assassins had been instigated and even paid by Santa Cruz, which was only a supposition. The first campaign, directed by Admiral Blanco Encalada in 1837, was a disaster. The exiled Peruvians had convinced President Prieto that a very powerful army was not necessary to destroy Santa Cruz, because the Peruvian people would rise in rebellion as soon as the Chilean troops disembarked on their coast. The small army which was sent as a result of reliance upon those hopes disembarked in Chilca and reached Arequipa. The city was seized and the exiles established in it a provisional government; but no one rose in rebellion. The same result, neither more nor less, had occurred in the case of the liberating expedition of San Martín. Blanco Encalada, surrounded by forces double his own, had to capitulate, and to save his army he concluded with Santa Cruz the Treaty of Paucarpata[3] —so named from the small village in which it was signed. By this treaty, Blanco recognized the Peru-Bolivian Confederation; the Chilean army withdrew from Peru and the ships seized by Garrido were to be returned. Santa Cruz, for his part, conceded to Chile only the amount of the government loan.

In Chile such a pact produced general indignation. It was disavowed by the government, and Santa Cruz was so informed. Then the ports of Peru were blockaded and a second campaign was prepared and departed in 1838, in charge of General Manuel Bulnes, a nephew of President Prieto and a soldier inured to war in the campaigns of the south, especially in the pursuit and capture of the Pincheira bandits. As before, numerous exiled Peruvians followed the army. Among them was Agustín Gamarra, who had been president of Peru and had fallen, through the intervention of Santa Cruz.

---

[3] Paucarpata, a Peruvian hacienda of the department of Ayacucho, province of Huanta.

The troops of General Bulnes were much more numerous than those that Blanco had collected. With them he landed to the north of Callao, in Ancón. This time the northern provinces of Peru rose in revolt. Bulnes was able, after several days of scarcity, to secure supplies and advance upon Lima. A battle opened to him the gates of this capital. Gamarra established here a provisional government of which he made himself president, and hostilities centered in the environs of Callao, a fortified place practically invulnerable. It was impossible to take it. To the difficulties of the situation was added the partiality manifested in favor of Santa Cruz by the diplomatic representatives of England, France, and the United States—nations which had ships in the harbor. Those representatives did not cease in various ways to thwart the invading general and to provoke conflicts, even to the point of refusing to recognize the effective blockade of Callao.[4] The determined and at times, haughty, action of Bulnes was necessary to make them observe their neutrality.

On the other hand, the army concentrated in Lima was being decimated through the effects of the hot climate and unhealthful surroundings. Santa Cruz withdrew into the interior, organized meanwhile a powereful defensive force, and held it there, while the Chilean soldiers were perishing in Lima, so that in the long run he might have better assurance concerning the outcome. Bulnes resolved at last to leave the capital, and, uniting with Gamarra, withdrew his troops to the north of the country. While the army to restore the liberties of Peru, as the Chilean army was called, was occupying the northern provinces, Santa Cruz established himself in the capital. Soon, however, he abandoned it; for, while the Peruvian troops could withstand the climate, the Bolivians suffered the same ills which had decimated the Chileans.

At the beginning of 1839 hostilities which had been manifest only in light skirmishes increased, and on the twentieth of January of that year a decisive battle took place on the banks of the Santos River near the village of Yungay. Santa Cruz suffered a complete rout, from which he barely escaped by flight. The battle of Yungay ended the domination of Santa Cruz and destroyed forever his confederation.

In November of that same year, the victorious army made its entry into Santiago amid the acclamations of the people. Gen-

---

[4] See Evans, *Chile and its Relations with the United States,* p. 63. Yungay, the decisive battle of this campaign, takes its name from a small town in the Peruvian department of Ancash (formerly Ancachs).

eral Manuel Bulnes became the idol of the people and the leading
citizen of that time. Military glory was then the highest of glory
and the people were right in their enthusiasm. The victory of Yungay and the destruction of the Peru-Bolivia Confederation gave
Chile a high place in America; and the European states began from
this date to consider it the strongest and best organized of the nations that had risen from the Spanish colonies. The people, too,
took account of this aggrandizement. Therefore, a year and a half
later, when considering the renewal of the presidency of the republic, the candidacy of Bulnes was irresistible and the victor of
Yungay received as a reward the highest magistracy of the state
(1841).

POLITICAL TRANQUILLITY AND ECONOMIC PROSPERITY

The death of Portales and the happy ending of the war against
the Peru-Bolivian Confederation resulted in a sound and stable
peace for the republic, founded not yet so much on the strength of
the government as on patriotic sentiment. After the expedition of
Yungay the constitutional regime was reëstablished, congress again
assembled, President Prieto divested himself of the extraordinary
powers which he had assumed, and the state of siege ceased. The
permanent tribunals were suppressed, and the greater part of the
army officers deposed in 1830 were restored to their rank and
honors. Special consideration was given O'Higgins. Besides being
reëstablished in the military rank which had been taken from him
before 1830, he was permitted to return to the country. The permission was like an invitation, but he could not take advantage of
it, for, when he was preparing to do so, he died in Lima in 1842.

The policy of conciliation and oblivion which sought to blot out
the hateful disagreements of the past, and to which the disappear-
ance of Portales gave free rein, exerted a healthful effect upon the
material development of the country. General Prieto was able to
conclude his administration under normal conditions and to deliver it in the same state to General Bulnes, chosen by an overwhelming majority of the suffrage in 1841. Following the same
course, the new government hastened to proclaim a law of amnesty
for all political offenders. Thereupon the republic entered fully
upon a life of peaceful and fruitful toil.

Aided by this situation there opened up forthwith an era of
business prosperity. Agricultural production acquired a very noticeable impetus through the introduction of modern machinery,
the opening of new roads, the founding of a national society of

agriculture in 1838 intended to encourage it, and various other factors. Foreign commerce increased rapidly and then acquired the benefits of steam navigation, the culmination of the unwearying energy of the North American sailor and merchant, William Wheelwright. After many years of effort, there was organized in Chile a limited liability corporation, the major part of whose shares were centered in London, with the object of establishing a line of merchant steamers between the American nations of the Pacific and Europe. In 1840 the first ships of this company entered Valparaiso amid enthusiastic acclamations.

On the other hand, the exploitation of the coal resources of Chile was begun at the same time in the mines near Talcahuano, whereby a new source of mineral wealth was added to the extraction of the precious metals. Mining, indeed, developed to a very flattering degree. Gold had declined, but in its place the exploitation of silver and especially of copper reached a very high figure. The provinces of Atacama and Coquimbo were centers where it abounded to such a degree that some years prior to 1840 Chile was the foremost producer of copper in the world.[5] Some eminent foreigners who had come to establish themselves in the country powerfully influenced the development of mineral wealth. Among them were the wise Pole, Ignacio Domeyko, who at this time initiated scientific instruction in mining in Chile; and the English industrialist, John Stevenson,[6] who applied new and more effective methods to the exploitation of silver. With the assistance of specialists of various nationalities, the development of copper also underwent a complete change in the methods of getting the greatest possible returns from the native veins.

The fortunes which were being accumulated because of this prosperous situation impelled the rebuilding of the principal cities with more lasting materials and with some regard for architectural style. Household goods were renewed and increased. The industries

---

[5] The production of copper in Chile reached an early maximum in 1876, when it equaled some 38 per cent of the total world production. From that point the percentage of production in Chile decreased to 3.62 per cent in 1906. See Alberto Cabero, *Chile y los chilenos*, p. 321. For references to coal, see Martner, *Estudio de política comercial chilena e historia económica nacional*, I, 37, 196.

[6] Possibly Robert Stephenson (1803-1859), a leading civil engineer, only son of George Stephenson. From 1824 to 1827 he was in charge of mining operations for the Colombian Mining Association of London. He was famous as a builder of locomotives and bridges. See *New International Encyclopedia* (New York, 1916), XXI, 508; S. Smiles, *Life of George Stephenson and of his son Robert Stephenson* (New York, 1868), pp. 303-308.

devoted to these tasks as well as the older ones of the country received considerable stimulus, and the guilds of artisans with personnels which increased daily brought to these same cities a numerous and active population. Everywhere greater well-being was extending from the highest social classes to the most humble. The year 1840 marked the beginning of an era of material prosperity for the republic.

THE INTELLECTUAL MOVEMENT OF THE FORTIES

The material progress of the country, under the order and peace which the republic enjoyed, was a most powerful agent in the intellectual movement which began in 1842. It had been in preparation for some time. The lessons of Mora and of Bello had not fallen on barren ground. An intelligent youth was being prepared to take advantage of them. It was the first republican generation which was entering into activity with a recognition of its responsibility for the future of the nation.

The teaching staff of the National Institute, believing that politics was not the only field of activity worthy of a man, was the first to display interest in the cultivation of literature in its various forms. The separation of the institute from the seminary in 1835 invigorated the former. It was foreign professors who gave the greatest stimulus to that enthusiasm, and their pupils were not slow in becoming infected thereby. Among the Chilean professors there were also some of marked distinction, among whom were Ventura Marín, the author of *Elementos de la filosofía del espíritu humano* (*Elements of the Philosophy of the Human Spirit*), a book which attracted attention in its time because of the unusual study developed therein; and José Victorino Lastarria, who taught classes in geography and general legislation and who soon made himself one of the leaders most respected by the studious youth of that period.

This movement also penetrated the press of the time. Until 1842 the only daily in the country was *El mercurio* of Valparaiso, which concerned itself merely with trade matters. In Santiago several periodicals appeared and disappeared, especially on the eve of elections, without leaving any noticeable trace. But in this same year of 1842 two literary periodicals were founded in Valparaiso, which, although they lasted only a few months, were of special importance. One was *La revista de Valparaíso* (*The Valparaiso Review*); the other was *El museo de ambas Américas* (*The Museum of Both Americas*). The former was conducted by an Argentinian,

Vicente Fidel López; the latter was directed by a Colombian, Juan García del Río. At the same time there joined the editorial staff of *El mercurio* Domingo Faustino Sarmiento, an Argentinian like López, who began to insert in the daily issue of the paper articles on literature. In the year 1842 Valparaiso also acquired another daily organ, *La gaceta de comercio* (*Commercial Gazette*).

These foreigners showed no little superiority of spirit over the native sons and on more than one occasion called attention to the poor quality of Chilean literary production and to the indifference of the young men toward the improvement of their minds. They were exiles from the civil discord in their native lands, seeking in Chile an honorable calling by which to gain a living. García del Río held a unique position because he was an adventurer in politics and in letters who had traveled through several South American countries and had held posts of high public influence in some, until it was forgotten that he was a Colombian. López and Sarmiento became purely literary men in Chile and belonged to a small group of talented men who had crossed the Andes, fleeing from the tyranny of the dictator, Juan Manuel de Rosas—a small group which called itself the "Argentine Immigration."

Whatever importance these men may have had and however influential their writings, it is a fact that the intelligent Chilean youth felt a certain shame at their own indifference and, through the quickening of their enthusiasm and by bringing together the information acquired in the institute or through private lessons in the house of Andrés Bello, they established in 1842 a literary society, with the object of initiating a national literature. Lastarria was chosen president and directed its course. Almost at the same time another group of young men was also starting in Santiago a literary periodical, *El seminario*, whose chief contributors were Antonio García Reyes, Manuel Antonio Tocornal, and Antonio Varas. That periodical devoted many of its columns to belles-lettrés.

From that vigorous beginning of the year 1842 many other national writers and poets arose who were later to achieve a distinguished position in the political and intellectual life of the country, among whom were Eusebio Lillo, Francisco Bilbao, Salvador Sanfuentes, José Joaquín Vallejo, the popular "Jotabeche" according to his pseudonym, and Juan Nepomuceno Espejo. In addition to this movement, toward the end of the same year the first daily of the capital, called *El progreso*, appeared; it was edited by Sarmiento. It is worth noting that this publication later had to be subsidized by the treasury in the same way as did other dailies. Without this subsidy it could not have lived.

Under the energetic stimulus of the national government activity in teaching paralleled that in literature. Already during the Prieto administration the branch of public instruction had been separated from the ministry of the interior and formed, with the departments of justice and religion, a separate and fourth ministry. And that same year, 1842, saw created the University of Chile. For some time past consideration had been given to the organization of this teaching institution to replace the University of San Felipe, which the colony had supported from the middle of the eighteenth century.

In spite of its feeble life and its almost exclusively monastic mold, this ancient institution had rendered services of no small value to public instruction; but when independence was accomplished and higher education, together with secondary education, was concentrated in the National Institute, there was no longer any reason for its existence and it was preserved only as a memento, or rather as an anachronism. In 1839 Mariano Egaña, minister of the department, issued a decree suppressing it and declaring that in its place should be established a "house of learning," called the University of Chile. This decree should have had the force of law, owing to the wide powers which the executive still held through his extraordinary prerogatives; but, although it sufficed to suppress this colonial institution after a century of existence, it did not succeed in organizing the new corporation. This could only be accomplished three years later by virtue of a law enacted in 1842.

The organization given to the university by this law was almost the same as it is today. There were five faculties (theology, the humanities, law, medicine, and mathematics), each one with its corresponding dean, rector, general secretary, and a council composed of these officers and two other individuals who were appointed by the president of the republic. But with regard to its attributes, the difference was considerable. When founded, it was no more than an advisory body, entrusted with watching over secondary and higher education and with proposing those measures for improvement which it judged fitting.

It had, however, one power which stimulated study and the results of which were of great benefit. This regulation provided that the university should hold annually a solemn meeting at which one of its members, named in due season by the rector, should read a paper on some period of national history. This gave rise to interesting studies which in subsequent years greatly increased the knowledge of the history [of the country]. In addition, the university inaugurated contests upon special themes, and the prizes incident thereto were also distributed at the same meeting.

As was natural, the president of the republic named the persons on the five faculties, and the officers who were to direct the corporation. Concerning these last, there was no hesitation. Andrés Bello was made rector, in spite of the efforts of the clergy to have a priest named in his place; but on undertaking to name the individuals for the faculties, it was found impossible to complete the number—thirty for each one—because, in spite of including among them all the able teachers of the defunct University of San Felipe who were still living, there were not enough men who were worthy of such a distinction. The opening of the University of Chile did not occur until September 17, 1843, in the same place which the ancient University of San Felipe had occupied (today the municipal theatre), and it was a solemn event, at which the most distinguished society of Santiago was present.

The zeal of the government for extending and improving instruction did not stop here. The creation of the Normal School for Teachers of Santiago (Escuela Normal de Preceptores de Santiago), the first in all the country, dates also from this time (1842). It was accomplished through the agency of the minister, Manuel Montt, and was placed in charge of the Argentinian who was writing so brilliantly for the press, Domingo Faustino Sarmiento. The new institution had a very special importance; it was the first step taken to raise primary education to the height of the great national need which it ought to satisfy. Theretofore it had been impossible to meet this demand because the disturbed state of the republic and the scant revenues would not permit it. Moreover, some of the government officials, though they might understand the importance of schools, did not consider the teacher of equal importance, for they thought that any person who knew how to read and write could teach this to others.

At the time of the founding of the normal school, in all Chile there were not above fifty primary schools for both sexes, poorly equipped, and worse served, in which one was taught only to read, to write, and to pray. A total of little more than three thousand children attended them, in a population which ought to have had not less than two hundred thousand of school age.

In continuing this work, the attempt was also made to diffuse technical education. To accomplish this there was created in Santiago a school of arts and crafts, and a school of agriculture, with land added for the practice of cultivation. The latter served as a beginning for the Quinta Normal. Still more was done—artistic culture was attempted in the foundation of the School of Architecture and Painting, and of the National Conservatory of Music. These educational plants represented progress up to then unknown in South America.

Not only did higher and primary, and artistic and technical instruction receive the attention of the public authorities; secondary education shared as well in this attention. In 1842 there were six institutions giving secondary instruction: the National Institute, and the high schools of La Serena, San Felipe, Cauquenes, Talca, and Concepción. A little later the high schools of Rancagua and San Fernando were founded. In the school at La Serena was first established a chair of chemistry and mineralogy to stimulate the development of the mineral district of the north by the technical preparation of young men from that section. With this class Ignacio Domeyko began scientific instruction in mineralogy in Chile, which was to be continued later at the University of Santiago.

Domeyko was a Polish scholar of wide attainments in matters of education, and he promoted a general reform in secondary studies, which the government accepted and in 1843 ordered to be put in practice in the institute. By this plan, six years were devoted to the study of the humanities and, at the same time, instruction was introduced in various branches of the same course of study; among these branches were history, the natural and physical sciences, mathematics, and a foreign language.

Through the activity of Antonio Varas, then rector of the Institute, this reform was established in that institution and changed almost entirely the trend of instruction, directing it into more scientific paths, based on the understanding of natural phenomena. But, since the lack of competent personnel prevented the extension of the benefits of the new plan to the provincial high schools, scholarships were provided in the institute for superior students from those districts, to the end that, when properly prepared, they might become instructors. This measure which, up to a certain point, gave the character of a normal school for instructors to the National Institute, was put into practice there, but it did not achieve the hoped-for results. At any rate it demonstrated that just as it was necessary to train teachers for the lower schools, there was a similar need for the high schools. In the institute itself this necessity was felt very promptly, since the new plan could be applied only partially through lack of teachers, and its advantages were not appreciated for a long time afterward.

The movement of 1842 had immediate consequences in the religious world, in the political world, and in general culture. Even though the motive which inspired young men to form a literary society and to found a periodical of the same character was far from leading them to abandon the Church in any particular, or to place themselves in opposition to it, they could not omit that issue completely from the debates which were agitating public opinion. *El seminario* was, during the months of its existence, a timid, but open, tribunal for liberal propaganda tending to promote social reforms.

Where the new spirit manifested itself more forcibly was in the contribution made to a periodical called *El crepúsculo* (*Twilight*) by Francisco Bilbao, a law student, then (1844) twenty-one years of age. This article was called "Sociabilidad chilena" ("Chilean Sociability") and its severe criticism of the past, in violent terms which included religion as well as politics, brought a formidable protest from the clergy, and soon its author was condemned by a jury on printing to pay a large fine for being "blasphemous and immoral." The numbers of *El crepúsculo* containing that study were to be burnt in the public square, according to the order of the supreme court; and, in order that nothing should be wanting to this condemnation, the council of the university expelled Bilbao from the National Institute, where he was pursuing his law studies. All this show of persecution produced an effect the very opposite of what was hoped for; instead of suppressing the hated young man who had so openly struck at many of the most fixed colonial prejudices, it converted him into something like a martyr for freedom of thought, gained for him great popularity, and his article, of but scant merit, became so celebrated that it is read even today,[7] or cited as an interesting episode in the struggle of ideas.

Different in form, but similar in effect, was another study to which the organic law of the university gave rise. This law provided for the presentation of an annual paper upon national history at the solemn session of the corporation by one of its members. The first of these sessions took place in September, 1844, and the required paper was presented therein by José Victorino Lastarria, previously appointed by the rector, under the title "Investigaciones sobre la influencia social de la conquista y del sistema colonial de los españoles en Chile" ("Investigation into the Social

---

[7] See Pedro N. Cruz, *Estudios sobre la literatura chilena*, I, 9-10.

Influence of the Conquest and of the Spanish Colonial System upon Chile").[8] A much larger work, more judicious, more methodical, and better written than that of Bilbao, it treated the history of the entire colonial period of the country from a critical or philosophical point of view, as was stated, and attributed to that period the vices from which the national society was suffering.

Whatever may have been the value of the essay, it undoubtedly called forth inspiring controversies relative to the manner of writing history: whether it was better to adopt this critical method or that of simple narrative. Andrés Bello used his powerful influence in favor of the latter, causing it to be noted that historical studies of a philosophical character could have importance only when the facts they were based upon had been proved and this was the purpose of narrative and documented history. It was time to philosophize only when this method should have exhausted the materials; to reverse the process was antiscientific and premature. However that may be, the intellectual ferment of 1842 was opening a new era in the development of culture in Chile—an era characterized by its effort to separate the republic from colonial traditions.

THE GOVERNMENT OF BULNES; INTERNAL PEACE AND ECONOMIC PROGRESS

Like Prieto, General Manuel Bulnes presided over the development of the country for ten years (1841-1851). It was a tranquil and productive period. His government busied itself more with strengthening the nation's credit abroad, with promoting wealth and culture, and with organizing administrative services than with political struggles.

Manuel Rengifo now returned to the ministry of the treasury and devoted himself especially to liquidating the loan of 1822 contracted in London. Interest on this loan had been suspended for several years and this suspension of payment had given Chile a bad reputation among English capitalists. By means of a direct arrangement with the creditors he succeeded in establishing an equitable form of cancellation, and, in the course of time, the debt was liquidated. Meanwhile its service was carried out with scrupulous punctuality and, as a result, the public credit of Chile became solidly established.

On the other hand, he issued a new customs regulation based on "free trade," that is to say, one that lowered imposts in order to

---

[8] Cruz claims with regard to this work that the author has ideas, but lacks the facts to support them.—*Ibid.*, pp. 77-81.

facilitate the importation of foreign merchandise. Although this measure produced at first a diminution of the customs revenue, soon the cheapening of prices on these articles increased their consumption, importation increased proportionately, and the customs revenue again mounted. There was also passed at that time (1843) a law of weights and measures. This regulated mercantile transactions to a great extent and provided for the decimal system which is in force today. Up to that time, the Spanish system of the colonial period was still in force. This was not based on any scientific principle, lacked accuracy, and lent itself to numerous frauds. It suffices to say that neither at that time nor up to the present has the law been applied with rigor in the entire country.

It fell to the Bulnes' administration, by taking possession of the Strait of Magellan, to extend the effective control of Chile to the southern coast of the Pacific. From the time of Pedro de Valdivia, what was then called the "Kingdom of Chile" was considered as extending to that strait, and it is known that Hurtado de Mendoza commanded it to be explored, in keeping with the express recommendation of his king and the declaration which the sovereign had made, with the idea of extending thus far the southern limit of the colony. It should be remembered also that he had founded two Spanish settlements on the strait, and that disaster had overtaken the settlers.[9]

Until the time of General Bulnes, no attempt had been made toward occupying those territories, and ships of different nationalities passed frequently through them on trading or scientific enterprises. In Europe such regions were considered important, and in France and England some began to think that perhaps it might be desirable to found colonies there after taking possession of the territory, on the ground that because of its abandonment it belonged to the first occupant. When this information reached Chile, the government ordered the strait to be occupied and the Chilean flag to be raised on it as a sign of actual dominion, in order to avoid any pretensions of other nations. In 1843 the schooner *Ancud* set out from Chiloé with a force for landing. After an unfortunate voyage it doubled the Brunswick Peninsula and established Fort Bulnes on its east coast upon almost the same spot where, at the end of the sixteenth century, had been founded one of the Spanish colonies which an English pirate called "Starvation Port." On the fort was raised the flag of Chile and by this act the territorial integrity of the republic was achieved. A few years afterward, in

---

[9] Cf. pp. 54, 93, *supra*.

1847, the founding of the city of Punta Arenas, later Magalianes, completed the work; but that territory and Chilean Patagonia, which extended toward the north, and all the adjacent islands had not yet been either peopled or explored.

Districts still nearer the center of the country, like Valdivia and Llanquihue, remained almost uninhabited. The government sought means to populate these last-named regions, since the others, because of their intemperate climate, did not permit easy colonizing. Foreign colonization was then initiated and an immigration agent was established in Europe to secure industrious families who might wish to find a new field of activity in Chile. This post fell to a German gentleman, Bernardo Philippi,[10] distinguished for his intelligence and good judgment. At the end of the Bulnes' administration, the first colonists had already begun to arrive. They were German laborers to settle in the region of the Valdivia River.

This introduction of foreign elements coincided with a Chilean emigration to California, owing to the reputation of the gold mines which had just been discovered in that territory (1848), which were said to have a marvelous production. Most of the people who left Chile in search of a fortune in California suffered there the most unheard-of hardships through lack of food, through constant quarreling with people of other nationalities, and through numberless circumstances which prevented their return to their native land. On the other hand, the wheat of Chile found a ready market in California, and its exportation, which grew to large proportions, caused it to bring very high prices. This stimulated the cultivation of much untilled land and these fields added their quota to the increase in national wealth.

Various administrative services were created or developed under the presidency of Bulnes. A bureau of statistics, a branch of administration then unknown in Chile, was established in 1843. The penitentiary of Santiago was founded in 1846, and with this were abolished certain old-time barred carts, or traveling prisons, which Portales had established, still in use. The police force was reformed and appropriations for the service increased. New roads and irrigation canals were opened by means of fiscal coöperation. The postal service, both domestic and foreign, was expanded and regu-

---

[10] Bernardo Philippi was a younger brother of Rudolfo Amando Philippi (see 504). He had established relations with Chile as early as 1831 and in 1845 acquired the estate of Bella Vista in Valdivia. He was named governor of the province of Magallanes and in 1852 was murdered by Patagonian Indians. See Miguel Luis Amunátegui, *Ensayos biográficos*, IV, 156, 162, 163; Virgilio Figueroa, *Diccionario histórico y biográfico de Chile*, IV, 505.

lated. Hygiene and public welfare received a new impetus.

In regard to international relations, the government of General Bulnes managed to strengthen friendship with all those countries, preferably the American, with which Chile was in most frequent communication. An agreement was secured between the Peruvian and Chilean governments through a final arrangement of the old debt which Peru owed to Chile. However, the disputes about boundaries with Bolivia and Argentina were already beginning in this period. But the event of most consequence was the celebration of a treaty with Spain, by which the ancient mother country recognized the independence of Chile in 1844. Cordial relations between the two nations were restored, the harsh feelings left by the struggle for emancipation were softened, and mercantile negotiations acquired greater volume.

The reëstablishment of this harmony was signalized a little later by an act which deserves to be remembered. The national hymn of Chile contained certain verses offensive to the motherland, and not infrequently insulting outbursts against Spain occurred when they were sung at the September festivals. After reiterated petitions from the diplomatic representative of that nation in Santiago, the government resolved to change the patriotic hymn for another more in accord with the situation which the recognition of independence had created; and the poet, Eusebio Lillo, then a youth of some twenty years of age, was actually commissioned to write the text of a new hymn. He accomplished his task and gave to the country the song now in use. From the old song, of which Bernardo de Vera was the author, only the chorus was kept. At the patriotic fiestas of 1847 the new hymn was sung for the first time with the music composed years before by the Spaniard, Ramón Carnicer.[11] With some slight changes it is still sung today.

Thanks to the intervention of the diplomatic agent of Spain and to the spirit of harmony which should inspire Spaniards and Chileans, the new song began thus:

> The bloody struggle has ended;
> Now is brother he who yesterday was invader;
> We have washed away the reproach of three centuries
> By fighting on the field of honor.[12]

[11] Ramón Carnicer y Batlle (1789-1855), born in the Spanish province of Lérida, early attracted attention by his musical ability, especially in connection with orchestral work and the opera. Among other compositions he produced *El Barbero de Sevilla*. See Espasa, *Enciclopedia*, XI, 1196.

[12] The original Spanish of this stanza is as follows:
> Ha cesado la lucha sangrienta;
> ya es hermano el que ayer invasor;

But for a long time the public did not become accustomed to hearing this song, and when their enthusiasm burst forth at patriotic festivals they would exclaim almost invariably: "The old song!" The new hymn was very superior in poetic emotion to that which had preceded it.

That policy of conciliation and of industry which inspired the acts of President Bulnes also had its vexations and those stirred up between the government and the clergy were not the least. The Chilean Church had reached a degree of development very gratifying to its faithful followers, owing to the protection which the governing party accorded it, to its tradition of dominance over all consciences, and to the zeal and virtues of the priests who were directing it. In 1840 the archbishopric of Santiago had been established with Manuel Vicuña as its first incumbent, and almost at the same time the bishoprics of La Serena and Ancud had been created. Foreign clergy had been brought in to direct the missions of Araucania and Chiloé, with which the administration attempted to civilize the still barbarous Indians. Among the new and wealthy churches that had been constructed was the mother church of Valparaiso.

Little by little, however, during the Bulnes administration the unfolding of general culture and at the same time the influence of Protestant foreigners had introduced ideas less in accordance with the state religion and even the daily *Mercurio* of Valparaiso once dared to speak of religious toleration. This produced a great scandal and under the protection of the archbishop *La revista católica* (*The Catholic Review*) was founded in Santiago in 1843 to undertake the defense of the Church, threatened by the movement, subversive to its dogma, which appeared to be breaking out among the intellectual youth of the period. Soon Bilbao and Lastarria, in their writings in 1844, confirmed the fears of the clergy.

But there were other incidents, though slight, which were enough to show that the predominance of the religious spirit was being weakened. Thus, for example, it was the custom of *serenos*, or night watchmen, when calling the hours and the state of weather, to add: "Hail most Holy Mary." This formula was suppressed by the administration of Santiago. Likewise, at the solemn procession of "Corpus Christi" it was customary for the flags of the battalions which had been gathered for the procession to be spread on the ground in order that the priest who was carrying the host might pass over them. This practice was also discontinued. Both inno-

---

de tres siglos lavamos la afrenta
combatiendo en el campo de honor.

vations gave rise to offensive publications and controversies.

However, acts of that sort were not the ones most disturbing to the harmony between Church and State; there were others, such as the law relating to the marriage of nonconformists, which excused non-Catholics from the obligation of celebrating their nuptials in accordance with the rites of the Catholic faith, and in such a case compelled the parish priests to serve as witnesses to the validity of the contract; the law relating to civil patronage, which granted to the agents of the executive, jurisdiction over the parish priests for the fulfilment of their duties; and the law relating to the religious profession, which fixed the age of twenty-five years as the minimum for entering upon major clerical orders.

The discussions upon those affairs became so violent, and so little was the ecclesiastical authority in harmony with the State's encroachment upon what is considered its absolute and private jurisdiction, that the prelate (José Alejo Eyzaguirre) who had occupied the archepiscopal seat because of the death of Manuel Vicuña, resigned before he had held the office two years (1843-1845). Rafael Valentín Valdivieso, a priest like Vicuña and Eyzaguirre and as virtuous as they but much more virile in spirit, succeeded him in this office. The new archbishop continued to struggle against the legal prerogatives which the State was exercising until the last years of the Bulnes administration, or rather against the right of the political authority emanating from national sovereignty to intervene in ecclesiastical affairs.

POLITICAL AGITATION IN THE MID-CENTURY

The period of President Bulnes, in general so tranquil and fruitful at the beginning, came to its last year in the midst of tumultuous agitation. After 1849 the political parties sharing public opinion suddenly became restless. On one side were the old *pelucones* who formed the most rigid nucleus of the conservative party, firm in their resistance to any innovation in the political system. They had succeeded in having two laws passed which strengthened their power considerably; namely, the law of internal rule, which gave new attributes to the governors and intendants and made of the executive a power still more irresistible than it had been; and the law of the press, a highly restrictive law which imposed heavy penalties on those who should publish opinions adverse to the established order, or should in any way arouse disobedience against the government, even if they should merely *intend* to commit such misdemeanors. Making common cause with this central group were young conservatives like Manuel Antonio Tocornal and Antonio García Reyes, who were less uncompromising than the *pelucones* and more open to the reforming tendencies of the age.

On the opposing side arose the new liberal party under the intellectual guidance of José Victorino Lastarria. This originated almost entirely from the literary movement of 1842, and with it had also been incorporated the ancient *pipiolos*. This group was attempting a series of reforms tending to weaken the authority of the executive, to liberate the press, to make the suffrage independent, and to make of Chile, in short, a true republic, "popular and representative." The European liberal revolution of 1848 had inspired this group of young reformers with its example, and the reading of that very eloquent book, Lamartine's *Histoire des girondins*,[13] in which those ardent republicans of the French revolution were praised and glorified, had greatly influenced them to throw themselves wholeheartedly into the struggle for the ideals of reform.

The congress of 1849 was the first battlefield between these two opposing currents. In it the liberal group, thanks to the support accorded by the ministry presiding over elections, had secured a numerous representation formed by men of a decided liberalism, although they did not belong to the militant faction. The sessions of that assembly were greatly disturbed, and its echoes were transmitted to the public through the formation of the Reform Club,[14] which was of short duration.

But in 1850 a new political element was added to those already known. It was that established by Francisco Bilbao in the Society of Equality. Bilbao, after his condemnation for writing "Sociabilidad chilena" (Chilean Sociability), had gone to Europe to study and during the revolution of 1848 had found himself in France. Sharing to a large degree the socialistic ideas which were developing in this movement, and possessed of a self-denying love for the poor, he believed that a democratic party, purely popular or proletarian, which should represent the interests of the working classes, might be formed in Chile. For that purpose it was necessary to enlighten the masses, and such was the aim pursued by him in founding the Society of Equality. For the propagation of his ideas he had

---

[13] Published in Paris in 1846. Although not a critical and scientific history, it is written in a vibrant style and contributed greatly to the overthrow of the monarchy of Louis Philippe. See Espasa, *op. cit.*, XXIX, 370-372.

[14] A loose organization of the opposition in congress that aimed to bring about certain constitutional reforms. See Alejandro Fuenzalida Grandón, *Lastarria i su tiempo* (2 vols., Santiago, 1911), Vol. I, chaps. xiv, xv.

The two leading figures of the War for Independence. *Left:* José Manuel Carrera. *Right:* Bernardo O'Higgins. Rivals for control of the revolutionary movement. Courtesy Instituto de Cinematografía Educativa, Universidad de Chile.

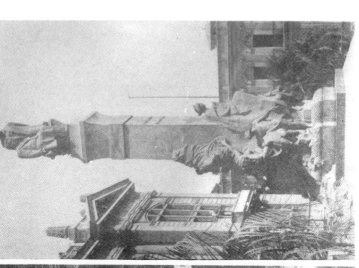

Outstanding leaders of the mid-century. *Left to right:* Diego Portales, founder of the system of government under which Chile continued for ninety years. Andrés Bello, leading intellectual figure of the first half-century of national history. Manuel Montt (seated) and Antonio Varas, president and chief minister of the 1850's, associates in power and leadership. Courtesy Instituto de Cinematografía Educativa, Universidad de Chile.

a periodical, edited by Eusebio Lillo, which was called *El amigo del pueblo* (The Friend of the People).

Soon, however, the new society, which had gathered together a respectable number of workmen, became a political club, and adhered, logically, to the group with whose ideas it had most affinity —the liberal party. The equalitarians and liberals then determined to carry on together the electoral campaign which was under way for a change in the presidency of the republic. Who was to succeed Bulnes? That appeared to be the principal question which they proposed to solve.

This question affecting the conservative party was already solved—their only candidate was Manuel Montt. His candidacy met very strong resistance in the groups opposing the government, because there was recognized in the candidate the same restrictive and autocratic spirit which Portales had exhibited. As Bulnes' minister he had shown unwearying industry, and afterward, in the chamber of deputies, a sober eloquence. But the fact that he appeared at the head of the conservative party and that it was he who had presided at the elections of 1846, when a state of siege existed in Santiago, provoked bitter hatred against him.

General Bulnes, having decided to make Manuel Montt the candidate of the government, summoned to the ministry of the interior the man most confessedly attached to the person of the candidate, Antonio Varas. This filled to the brim the wrath of the opposition. The Society of Equality became the center of the movement against the governmental candidate, and its press lifted up its standard with menacing violence. In the chamber it made similar demonstrations against the supervising intendants. The disturbance came to a head when one night in August, 1850, the Society of Equality, while in session, was attacked by a crowd armed with cudgels and led by some subordinate officials of the administration. The executive was thereupon accused of being the instigator of that riot and recriminations and protests continued with extreme intemperance.

The equalitarians, under the constant direction of Bilbao, now began public manifestations, which were actual meetings devoted to propaganda against Montt and the government. The intendant of Santiago then forbade those gatherings, and before the end of the year 1850 the society itself was declared dissolved by this officer and any other of similar character was prohibited, on the pretext that they constituted a danger to the social order. Such a measure had been taken by virtue of the state of siege which the government decreed. Also by virtue of those extraordinary powers which this suspension of individual guarantees gave it, the opposition dailies were closed and the leaders of the liberal movement, among whom were José Victorino Lastarria and Federico Errázuriz, were sent into exile. Bilbao also found safety in flight. In the meantime the Montt candidacy had been publicly proclaimed.

At the beginning of 1851 party enthusiasm increased. The restrictive measures taken by the authorities in prohibiting public assemblies, closing the opposition dailies, and arresting and exiling the ringleaders of the movement opposed to it had produced their inevitable result: greater exasperation of spirit and the conversion of the persecuted into conspirators. To the disorderly occurrences in the provinces, there was actually added on April 20, 1851, an attempt at revolution in the capital. This cost the lives of more than a hundred persons, after an armed struggle in the Alameda de las Delicias and in the neighborhood of the artillery quarters, situated at the foot of Huelén. Here the uprising itself was broken and the leader, Colonel Pedro Urriola, killed by accident. Peace was then reestablished.

Electioneering activity, however, was not checked. The liberal party, although disorganized, with its leaders in prison or in exile, had taken up the candidacy of General José María de la Cruz, intendant of Concepción and first cousin of General Bulnes. This candidacy was a complete failure. Montt, as was to be expected, was elected by an overwhelming majority. Only Concepción and La Serena gave their vote to Cruz; in all the other electoral districts Montt had an enormous advantage over his adversary.

The contest did not end here. The opponents, holding the election void—because, as they said, intervention had been pronounced —maintained that Montt was not the legitimate president of the republic, and gave clear signs of armed insurrection. And so it happened that, during the first fortnight of September, 1851, there broke out in La Serena and Concepción a revolutionary uprising which had as its leader the very candidate defeated at the polls, General Cruz. In this way President Bulnes, who had come to power on a wave of deserved popularity, who had been a pledge of tranquillity for the republic, and who had coöperated effectively in its progress, was leaving his high office involved in the vortex of a revolution.

CHAPTER XIII

THE DECADE OF PRESIDENT MONTT

THE REVOLT OF 1851

WITH THE CUSTOMARY preliminary ceremonies, the new president of the republic, Manuel Montt, on the eighteenth of September, 1851, ascended the steps of the Moneda (the palace to which the government house had been transferred shortly before). He was a man of forty-two years. He had been born in Petorca in 1809 and had completed no less than ten years of political life. He was poor as a boy and owed his rise solely to hard work and study. Educated in the National Institute, he graduated from it in law and was its rector for five years (1835-1840). The elections of 1840 raised him to the chamber of deputies; and scarcely had it opened its sessions, when it chose him as its president. In the same year General Prieto called him to the ministry of the interior, and in that position it fell to his lot to direct the presidential election of Bulnes.

During the first part of Bulnes' administration, Montt was the most industrious of his ministers, chiefly in the branch of public instruction, where he contributed effectively to the founding of the normal school, the school of arts and crafts, and the university. During the second period, as a member of the chamber of deputies and as an adviser to the government, he continued to act in an influential capacity. Therefore it was not strange that President Bulnes, when he confidentially recommended the candidacy of this public servant to the representatives of the executive in the provinces, should declare that he had been "his most active assistant in all the serious crises and difficulties arising during his administration."

But Montt entered upon the highest national magistracy in the midst of a revolution which was agitating both the northern and the southern parts of the republic at the same time. The revolution of 1851 had its roots in the desire for freedom of suffrage, advocated by many able men. They believed that the people were already prepared to judge for themselves upon matters of national expediency and they did not hesitate to take up arms in defense of that right which constituted the very basis of the republican system. But at bottom the armed protest was aimed at the entire "autocratic system" which the conservative party had brought upon the government and which they were now beginning to believe necessary.

The struggle was stubborn and imposed huge sacrifices upon the government. General Bulnes had already left his successor invested with extraordinary powers; and, not content with having taken upon himself the responsibility for this measure, he also took over the leadership of the troops destined to crush the revolution. After many minor skirmishes, the decisive battle occurred at Loncomilla on December 8, 1851. On the river of that name and near its confluence with the Maule, the troops of General Cruz and General Bulnes fought for several hours with a fury without precedent in the civil wars of the country. Upon the field remained about two thousand dead and not less than fifteen hundred wounded. Some days later the revolutionists of Cruz, not completely conquered but wholly demoralized, capitulated and delivered their forces to the government. Only La Serena held out in the north; but at the end of a rigid siege it was also taken in the last days of the year 1851. Thus, at the beginning of 1852 the administration, inaugurated three months before, was able to devote itself to its work.

ADMINISTRATIVE LABOR OF THE DECADE

Like the two preceding presidents, Montt was reëlected and governed during two constitutional periods, ten years. No administration had been more active than this since Chile became a republic. In the administrative department all the services were enlarged and organized anew according to plans better devised and directed. Valuable public works were continued or begun. Through the combined resources of the government and of the capitalistic company formed by Wheelwright, the railroad between Santiago and Valparaiso was extended to Quillota during this period. Work was also begun on another railway line which was to unite Santiago with Talca. At the same time a telegraph line was stretched between those same cities and the highways were improved.

It is characteristic of the culture of the period that there were in congress senators and deputies who were opposed not only to the government's assisting in the construction of railroads but even to permitting their establishment. They claimed that the railway lines were prejudicial to agriculture because they cut up large estates and occupied much land; that they displaced the muleteers and carters whose services would no longer be needed; in short, that all society would suffer because of the trains for, aside from the inevitable accidents, they would facilitate the flight of armed bandits.

On the other hand, the penitentiary in Santiago was finished, the insane asylum was built, the palace for congress was begun. In Valparaiso the customs warehouses were greatly enlarged, and at several points on the coast lighthouses were erected.

In the economic field the Savings Bank (*Caja de ahorros*) was established in order to encourage thrift among the working classes. In order to establish special credit and to stimulate agriculture, the Mortgage Loan Bank (*Caja de crédito hipotecario*)[1] was created in 1856, which loaned money to farmers upon the security of their property. The first public bank was also founded at this time. These efforts for the development of general wealth were followed by a regulation of the public treasury, beginning with a modification of the taxing system. The most important measure in this field was the suppression of the tithe, a colonial tax of ecclesiastical origin, which the State collected as a subvention for the budget of the Catholic Church. It had become a heavy tribute which profoundly affected agriculture and was replaced by a tax on the production of each piece of real estate. With the object of favoring subdivision of rural property, sales of estates which were made in favor of different persons were exempt from the payment of the *alcabala*.[2]

Besides these reforms, many others were undertaken in the same field; and they all added to the development of productive resources and of commerce by sea and land, and brought about a large increase in fiscal receipts—from four and a half million in 1851, they almost doubled by 1861. These receipts were not enough, however, to cover all the expenses of so active an administration and a loan of seven million gold pesos was contracted in London, intended especially to carry on public works which, like the railroads, had productive value. This credit transaction was the third which Chile contracted for with English capitalists, but under conditions very

---

[1] This institution was created for the purpose of making loans upon mortgages, to be repaid in installments, over a period of twenty-one years. It began to do business in 1855. Intended originally to aid the owners of small farms, its facilities have really been more thoroughly utilized by the owners of large estates. Its regular interest charge was not to exceed 8 per cent per year. See Martner, *Estudio de política comercial chilena e historia económica nacional*, I, 278-279.

[2] The *alcabala* was a local sales tax of ancient origin which was definitely planted in Spain by the fourteenth century and later extended to the colonies. Despite its irritating character, it survived in Hispanic America until the late nineteenth century. In some cases it has since been revived. See Espasa, *Enciclopedia*, IV, 205; see also n. p. 69 *supra*.

much superior to the others, particularly the first loan of 1822.

One reform of great importance, economic as well as social, was the final abolition of entailed estates. This colonial institution, which rendered impossible the division of the property of a man of rank and constituted an unjust privilege in favor of only one of his heirs, had victoriously resisted the harsh attacks directed against it from the early years of the republic. Now it was successfully abolished, transformed into an annuity or interest fixed upon the entailed property in favor of the person for whose profit the entail had been established.

Efforts were also made to develop the colonization of uncultivated lands belonging to the State. For that purpose the government tried to give the greatest possible extension to foreign immigration, especially of the Germans; and, besides encouraging the colony of Valdivia already founded, the district of Llanquihue was also colonized, and there the city of Puerto Montt arose. Soon these uninhabited regions were harboring an industrious population to which herds, tanneries, packing houses, breweries, and other industries gave employment and wealth.

Greater energy was also expended in the diffusion of culture. Between the years 1851 and 1861 more than five hundred public schools for both sexes were established in the nation and, added to those already existing and to the municipal and private schools, they formed a total of more than nine hundred institutions of that kind, which furnished instruction to about forty-five thousand children. The effective coöperation of the Society for Primary Instruction, a private association founded in this same period (1856), helped in bringing about those results. To complete the task of preparing teachers, the government created the Normal School for Women Teachers and gave considerable encouragement to the one for schoolmasters. Public libraries distributed in the different provincial centers afforded easy reading for the poor and helped to extend general intelligence. Along with primary instruction, practical instruction was developed. To the schools of arts and crafts and of agriculture were added those of mines in Copiapó, and of commerce in Quillota. The administration which had founded the asylum to take care of those mentally deranged could not do less for those deficient in speech and hearing, and the school for deaf mutes was created.

Secondary instruction improved in the same way, if not to the same degree as the primary (which demanded greater attention), yet at least appreciably. The National Institute was enlarged to such an extent that it could now accommodate more than a thousand students. The *liceos* of Chillán and Valdivia, added to institutions already in existence, brought the number of such schools up to ten, and the reform in the plan of studies begun in the second year of Bulnes' administration, which had been applied only to the National Institute, was now extended to all, to the degree that circumstances or rather the aptitude of the teaching personnel permitted. University instruction also received an impetus. Among other measures in its favor was the introduction of the scientific study of political economy in the law courses. Professor Courcelle-Seneuil was employed to teach this subject. He enlightened the nation with notable works in his field and left in Chile a whole generation of students to follow in his footsteps.

Chief among those who for many years coöperated in the general progress of national culture, in addition to Courcelle-Seneuil and Bello, were the chemist and mineralogist, Domeyko; the German naturalist, Rudolfo Amando Philippi; and the French geologist, Amando Pissis, to whom the government of Bulnes had entrusted the preparation of a topographic map of the republic. Pissis completed the greater part of this task, and from it resulted better maps than had been made in Chile up to that time. Later he completed the *Geografía física de la república de Chile* (*Physical Geography of the Republic of Chile*), the first coöperative work to be written about the country. In addition, Domingo Faustino Sarmiento, the first director of the normal school for men, published under governmental patronage his excellent work, *La educación común* (*Public Instruction*). He returned a little later to his own country, where he became one of its presidents. A Chilean professor, a youth trained through his own efforts and the most indefatigable study, Miguel Luis Amunátegui, published also with the aid of official patronage another pedagogical work almost as noteworthy as the one mentioned above. This was *De la instrucción primaria en Chile: lo que es i lo que debería ser* (*Concerning Primary Instruction in Chile: what it is and what it ought to be*).

Such efforts for intellectual progress gave Chile prestige abroad; but what most attracted the attention of learned foreigners was the government's maintaining an astronomical observatory when no other nation of Spanish America was yet concerning itself with the science of astronomy. The observatory was of North American origin, having been established on Santa Lucía Hill years before by an astronomical commission from the United States. The Chilean government acquired it and put in charge of it the German mathematician, Carlos Moesta.[3]

However, it was not merely this kind of effort which won prestige for Chile among foreign nations. There was something more which was the cause of deserved eulogies—national codification of the laws. The attempt was made to revise completely and to give coherence and unity to the ancient Spanish legislation which continued to rule in the republic. But only one body of laws, the most important, was finished in this period—the *Código civil* (Civil Code),[4] a monumental work whose entire compilation Andrés Bello carried through in the course of more than twenty years, in accordance with his own ideas and those of the various commissions appointed for the purpose. In 1855 it was published and was to go into effect the first of January, 1857. It was the most adequate and scientific legislation which had been established up to that time in America and served as a model for various other nations of the continent.

INTERNAL AND EXTERNAL POLICY

The administrative activity of the government was not carried on without opposition, the strongest arising from the clergy, where it should least be expected. The Church continued to flourish. The religious budget, increasing from year to year, permitted it to meet the needs of the faith in a fitting manner. Archbishop Valdivieso, an intelligent priest of rare energy, watched assiduously over its improvement. Besides, two religious orders had been added to those already in the country, the Capuchins and the Jesuits. But the good understanding which the Church maintained with the State was rudely interrupted at the conclusion of the first period of Montt's presidency (1856) by a circumstance, insignificant in itself. A sacristan of the cathedral was expelled from the service. In the ecclesiastical council, discussion arose as to whether the sacristan had been deservedly expelled. Two canons thought not and opposed the wish of the majority who thought otherwise. These canons were suspended from their duties, with the consent of the archbishop, for treating their hierarchical superiors with disrespect;

---

[3] Carlos Moesta (1825-1884), an astronomer of German origin, came to Chile in 1850. After taking part in the survey of the country, he was made director (1862) of the national observatory. He later returned to Europe and lived and died in Dresden, but acted there as consul general of Chile. See Espasa, *op. cit.,* XXXV, 1279.

[4] See p. 351 n.

but, not yielding, they made an appeal to the supreme court. That tribunal revoked the decision of suspension.

The archbishop then protested against this decision before the government, basing his protest on the fact that the civil authority could not interfere in matters purely spiritual, such as the prohibition against saying mass, confessing, and preaching, imposed on the disobedient canons.

From such a beginning followed a sharp exchange of notes between the minister of worship and the metropolitan prelate; and the question ended with the voluntary submission of the canons at the suggestion of the government; but, from then on, harmony ceased to exist between the executive and the head of the Church, and from every side very violent attacks were directed toward the government for having tried, it was said, to discredit the Catholic religion through its highest representative in Chile.

To those difficulties were added others proceeding from numerous diplomatic complaints laid before the government by the representatives of various foreign nations—chiefly England, the United States, and France. Such complaints were based on injuries suffered by the nations of those countries during the revolution of 1851 and certain other public disturbances.

Although unjust and contrary to the diplomatic practice of European states, they caused the government of that time serious harm and the nation no little expense. Nevertheless, the doctrine was then firmly maintained that, in order for foreigners to obtain indemnities for injuries suffered because of seditious movements, they must appear before the ordinary tribunals on the same conditions as the people of Chile. To this end a law was dictated called the "Law of Civil Responsibility," by which, in case of sedition, all those involved in mobs against individuals were held personally responsible for excesses committed. In other respects, the foreign policy of this period was limited to maintaining good understanding with the other states of America and Europe and to making several commercial treaties.[5]

Nor was this administration wholly peaceful in its domestic policies. Having begun with a struggle against an armed revolution which affected the entire republic, it drew to a close as another revolution started afresh with features as serious as the former. The nation reached a critical period, a period marked by changing ideas and by the development of liberal tendencies as opposed to the authority that had dominated for a quarter of a century. There

---

[5] Cf. Martner, *op. cit.*, I, 273, 284.

was severe criticism of the centralization of the entire government
in the president of the republic and there was an attempt to overthrow unlimited control of the legislative power by the executive.
For this purpose the critics tried to revise the constitution. The
president was accused of excessive suspicion against citizens who
were not entirely in harmony with his policies and of attempting to
prolong the authority of the regime under which he had risen to
power.

In all that there was really as much truth as falsehood. It is
certain that during his term President Montt had adopted the most
rigorous measures for suppressing even the slightest evidences of
the spirit of rebellion which still inspired certain groups of society.
The "extraordinary powers," with their train of imprisonment and
banishment, had been employed many times ; but one must take into
account that most of the people of position and fortune, who were
aiding and supporting the government, were so fearful of those
movements that at the least attempt at conspiracy, at the least
alarm of revolt, they even went so far as to run en masse to the
executive in search of security for their interests.

On the other hand, the president himself and his chief advisers
believed, in good faith, that the nation, because of its lack of general culture and because of the ignorance and poverty of the more
numerous classes of the population, was still not prepared for con-
sciously exercising a purely representative government. A form of
tutelage practiced by the executive over the people and over the
other powers of the State was still considered necessary. Consequently, it was thought in official circles that the reforms claimed
by liberalism—reforms tending to weaken the prerogatives of the
president of the republic and to strengthen those of congress—
were premature reforms which did not take into account the social
situation of the nation. However that may have been, the more advanced liberals could not bring themselves to recognize that the
government had considerable justice in its contentions and they
fought it both in the press and in public discussion.

To the opposition of this political group was added in 1857
that of the "reactionary conservatives," the supporters of the
tradition of the former *pelucones*. For the most part they were rich
and haughty landholders who had been angered by the dissolution
of the aristocratic bond of entailed estates and by the dispute in
which the executive had been involved with the archbishop of Santiago—a dispute in which they believed they saw unmistakable
signs of impiety in the president and his most loyal supporters. In

this way the powerful conservative party—which had raised Montt to the presidency, which had sided with him during the first period of his administration, and which had reëlected him in order to continue without interruption the political control which it exercised during the two preceding administrations—found itself divided over night into an intransigent faction, devoted to its political and religious principles with unvarying fidelity; and into a moderate faction, which showed itself disposed to accept in part the ideas of liberalism, and still more disposed to maintain the predominance of the State over the Church.

The intransigent conservative group came then to make common cause in the opposing camp with the still more intransigent group of the liberal party which embodied the tradition of the *pipiolos* of 1829. It was a strange thing: *pipiolos* and *pelucones* found themselves for the first time united, constituting the liberal-conservative fusion (later called "coalition"), and it was Montt who drove them to unite against him.

One faction of the liberal party, the less advanced, and a faction of the conservative party, the more moderate and conciliatory, united in their turn to support the president. Thus it was seen that, as one of the political groups which had fought him before with no less ardor, the moderate groups of both parties adhered to him, and in exchange the radical groups of both parties were united against him. Liberals and moderate conservatives, then, in the same year, 1857, formed a party of the government which called itself the national party, whose motto was "Liberty within Order." Their adversaries called it Montt-Varista because at the head of it was Antonio Varas, the chief of the ministry of Montt during his first term; and to his political formula they opposed their "Order within Liberty."

The personality of Varas is so intimately related to that of President Montt and to the work of his decade that it is not possible to omit his name in treating of that period. Antonio Varas was a native of Cauquenes, where he was born in 1817, of a modest family. Like Manuel Montt, he attended the National Institute and, aided by an elder brother who was a professor in the same institution, he studied with determined persistence. Soon he himself became a professor and inspector there and formed a close friendship with Montt.

Little by little, he continued to rise in the same manner as Montt, and in such a way that he seemed to fill the posts which the former left vacant. When Montt became rector of the institute, Varas was his vice-rector; when Montt became minister, Varas became rector; when Montt left the ministry of justice to pass to that of the interior, he was replaced by Varas; when Montt was a candidate for the presidency of the republic, Varas was the minister of the interior who presided at the elections; and finally, when Montt was president, Varas was chief of the cabinet and was his companion during the five years of his first presidential term. It is not strange, therefore, that, as Montt's second term neared its end, it was believed that Varas would like to succeed him.

But Varas aroused strong resistance and upon him was concentrated all the wrath of the opposition. The liberal-conservative fusion fought him resolutely because he represented the continuation of the dominant system of government, and nothing more. Looked at from another point of view, Varas was an intelligent and distinguished man. He held two professional titles; he was a lawyer and an engineer and both in the reviews and dailies of the time and in the chamber of deputies, to which for several years he belonged, he had shown excellent qualities as writer and orator (which his adversaries recognized), as well as a knowledge of the most pressing needs of the nation.

THE LAST YEARS OF THE DECADE

The vigorous personality of Antonio Varas had been impressed upon all. The "fusionist" liberals and conservatives, however, tried to prevent by all possible means his ascent to the presidency of the republic, on the grounds that his government would signify the continuation of the regime of force which it was necessary to do away with. In opposition to his candidacy and with the hope of obtaining the reforms that they desired, the "fusionists" prepared and brought on the revolution of 1859. Preliminary agitation was shown in congress during the previous year with the presentation of a bill of amnesty in favor of all of those indicted or involved in the revolutionary movements of recent times. This amnesty was finally granted only to residents in the country. Those who were in exile could not yet return to the country. Then the agitation continued with the publication of the periodical *La asamblea constituyente* (*The Constituent Assembly*), directed by Benjamín Vicuña Mackenna. The title alone of the periodical sufficed to point out the most important of the reforms sought. Collaborating in the publication were the brothers Manuel Antonio and Guillermo Matta and Justo and Domingo Arteaga Alemparte, also brothers—all exponents of a vigorous intellectual and political drive. Numerous meetings were held in the Union Club in order to mold public opinion for reform, and at the end of 1858 the propaganda was rapidly extended throughout the republic.

The executive and the provincial authorities tried to suppress those demonstrations against the government, for they considered them seditious and a danger to public order. In December of that year there were arrested some hundred and fifty people of social standing who had gathered in the Union Club, in violation of a prohibition of the intendancy, to discuss political matters together. Immediately a decree was issued which declared the provinces of Santiago, Valparaiso, and Aconcagua in "a state of siege." The armed struggle was seen to be approaching.

In January, 1859, the insurrection definitely began in Copiapó and then in San Felipe, Talca, Talcahuano, and other towns. The latter movements were promptly suppressed, but Copiapó did not yield. Far from this, its leader, Pedro León Gallo, a rich miner of the region, with an army of more than a thousand men, organized almost entirely at his own expense, overcame the government troops in the battle of Los Loros,[6] to the north of La Serena, and advanced upon that city, which he occupied in military fashion. In the provinces of Atacama and Coquimbo the great majority of the people seemed to share the revolutionary spirit, and the danger for the dominant political power was imminent. But in April, 1859, a new body of government troops routed the army of Gallo in Cerro Grande, south of La Serena. These two dates were the most important of the revolution and with the latter it may be considered as finally overcome.

New difficulties disturbed the Montt government as it approached its end. One of these was the insurrection of the Araucanians. As in 1851, some of the revolutionary leaders of 1859 went to stay among the semibarbarous tribes of the south and renew in their minds the century-old hatred against the Spanish power, of which they led them to believe the republic was the representative. Involving the old caciques, these agents caused a native insurrection to break out in the same year, 1859, and kept it up for two years by means of a series of guerrilla fights and ambuscades. Finally, when peace was again restored, the occupation of the Araucanian territory was begun by means of forts and cities founded each time farther in from the frontiers. But the heroic and ancient race held

---

[6] For a characterization of this battle, see Manuel Blanco Cuartín, *Artículos escogidos* (Santiago, 1913), p. 613.

on to a large part of its land and, defeated but not subdued, kept itself independent for a long time to come.

The other grave difficulty of the Montt government was the economic crisis of 1861. Among the causes for this might be counted the civil war with its supplemental Araucanian rebellion, a war which had killed and impoverished many people, had drawn away many from labor and produced a general unrest; the lessening of the output of the mines, which formerly had unexpectedly made great fortunes and stimulated excessive consumption; and the competition which Australia and California offered to wheat dealers of Chile, a competition which caused a fall as rapid as it was unexpected in the price of that commodity. The crisis was shown in many commercial failures, in the impoverishment of numerous families, and in the paralyzing of public and private works.

Otherwise, there were no new political difficulties. On the approach of the electoral contest of 1861 for the presidency, Antonio Varas voluntarily renounced the candidacy which friends offered him. Since they formed the majority of the government, and official intervention in elections was the rule, this renunciation amounted to that of the presidency itself. But as his candidacy aroused such strong opposition in the "fusionist" liberal-clerical group, it was feared that if he should assume power it would lead to a repetition of the revolutionary events that twice in ten years had disturbed the country. Varas preferred to withdraw his name from the list and retire to private life, an action which showed his enemies that he had the sentiment of a great citizen. The person then favored for the presidency was José Joaquín Pérez, another politician of the same national party, but acceptable to the opposition, which also gave him its support.

On September 18, 1861, Montt handed over to his successor the presidential insignia and withdrew forever from power.[7] For a long time his actions as ruler were severely discussed. With him ended in fact a regime of force, which sought to stifle every aspiration for social or political reform supported by force. However, that regime realized a work of organization and of culture which, although slow and restricted, had vast projections. Montt's government, in particular, left traces of lasting public benefit.

---

[7] Montt later became state councilor, deputy in congress, special envoy to the American congress that met in Lima in 1864, and its presiding officer. He was also the center of the bitter attack directed by the Chilean congress in 1868 on the supreme court, of which he was presiding officer. See Edwards, *Bosquejo histórico,* pp. 64–65.

COMMERCIAL DEVELOPMENT AND SOCIAL REFORM

The political movement, which had been in operation at the end of the Montt decade, had roots much deeper than the simple questions of election or amnesty. It was the result of a slow but sure social evolution which had been in process for many years past through the influence of culture and wealth. This evolution must, with time, modify profoundly colonial society, which on achieving independence completely lacked habits of liberty and self-government.

Now, after half a century of independent life, it was not the landed aristocracy, formed by the great proprietors, descendants of the entailed estates, which exclusively dominated the groups in the *pelucón* party. The commercial movement built up new fortunes and created new influences. Foreign commerce amounted to about fifty million pesos a year, of which more than half represented exports. The coastwise trade approximated twenty million. These figures represent a tripling of values in the space of fifteen years (1845-1860), which measured the rapidity of economic progress. Mining and agriculture increased in equal ratio. Thus, while the exportation of minerals amounted in 1845 to some four and a half million pesos of forty-eight pence and in 1860 equaled about nineteen million, agriculture, whose exportation in former years did not reach a million pesos, was in 1860 more than four and one-half million. The figures for the intervening years more than once exceeded those given.

Urban population was also increasing. Santiago became a city of 100,000 inhabitants; Valparaiso, of some 60,000; and, although the rural element still formed 70 per cent of the total population of the country, there is no doubt that there was a strong tendency toward "urbanization" and with it a more intense and conscious civic culture. Interior communications were being made more quickly and foreign communications were at the same time gaining in speed through steam navigation. Immigration was daily incorporating new elements of civilization.

General culture was now being developed in a more favorable atmosphere within cities relatively populous, in direct contact with European literary production, and in a public more impressionable and more attentive to higher culture. To some purpose there had been created, and were functioning, several hundred primary schools; the provincial *liceos* and the colleges of the capital exercised some influence; and credit must be given to the periodicals and the scientific and literary reviews which began to appear and continued to flourish.

All those factors and many others of a similar kind had gradually instilled into society new ideas, new aspirations, and a concept of the personal value of individuals somewhat different from what had heretofore prevailed. If wealth continued to be a power, culture, ability, and civic virtue were also becoming influential, and so a new aristocracy began about 1860 to supplant the old. Instead of an aristocracy of land and of blood, founded on traditions of family and on personal fortune which, with the abolition of entailed estates, had legally disappeared, there arose an aristocracy of business and of learning, founded sometimes on the large fortunes which speculation was creating for its chosen ones, and sometimes on the prestige which learning conferred.

So one saw the Gallos, rich miners of the north, rise against the government and direct a revolution, and soon thereafter, together with the Matta brothers, Manuel Antonio and Guillermo, lay the foundations of a new political alignment, the radical party. And thus one also saw several men like José Victorino Lastarria and Miguel Luis Amunátegui, who, without possessing goods or fortune, achieved political and social influence, thanks only to their endowment of intellect and character. Such a condition, which could previously have been seen only in the midst of the disturbed period of the revolution for independence, a transient period when it was necessary to take advantage of all the energies of the people, was now observed again in an entirely normal period of national life.

Another of the old-time powers of society, the clergy, also lost vigor and influence. To the narrow and uncompromising intolerance of former times which, in the name of religion, condemned or absolved men, books, and doctrines without protest from anyone, there succeeded now a tolerance, moderate and to a certain extent paternal. The religious dispute of the Montt decade had demonstrated this.

It was then the weakening of those old social classes—the colonial nobility and the clergy—which gave way to the rising liberal aspirations, so much opposed at first and so powerful later; and it was the development of wealth and culture which stimulated these same aspirations. Along with this evolution of ideas, the entire nation was modernized; the cities not only increased in population but also in beauty. Substantial buildings of brick and mortar, the paving of streets, public sanitation, and gas lighting date from that period. Evolution was at once moral and material.

Nevertheless, the relative well-being, which the upper classes of society were attaining together, extended only to a very limited degree down to the lower ranks, where poverty, gambling, drunkenness, and ignorance, leading to beggary, crime, or death, continued to work as much havoc as in the former period, or but little less. The wandering peon of the cities, without home or family, and the tenant of the country, without more resources than those necessary to keep him from starving, were social groups which did not yet participate in the benefits of the republic except to a limited degree.

Notwithstanding this, at the end of the first half-century of independent life Chile began to abandon the preoccupations and ailments of the ancient colony and fully take its rightful place in the activities of civilized nations. Whatever may have been the defects of the autocratic regime, imposed by a traditionally conservative society of the past, it was evident that this regime had permitted a slow but effective progress in all phases of national activity, and also that, in the hands of governors jealous for the future of their fatherland, it had coöperated effectively for progress.

When its mold became too narrow to contain the political aspirations of many of the most prominent men of the nation, then it yielded its place to a governmental ideal which was conceived to be more in harmony with social development; namely, the ideal of liberalism. For many years still, this conservative and autocratic spirit must continue to exert a powerful influence on the fate of the republic. The most effective change, was, then, more social than political in its nature, the reverse of what had taken place in the first quarter of the century. Although the doctrinal ideas of the government were about to take another direction, their administrative ideas would nevertheless persist, and it was that which truly counted in general progress.

Governmental coöperation in the general activity of the nation did not change in form or was it more accentuated, since from that piont of view liberals and conservatives did not differ greatly. It was only questions of moral and constitutional import that divided them. While for the conservatives political authority and religious dogma were the two fundamentals of well-being and of collective progress, for their adversaries liberty in politics and liberty in belief and ideas were conditions indispensable for social development. But in order to pass from one system to the other, from the autocratic republic to the liberal republic, there was needed a transformation in society itself which would permit it to make conscious use of liberty. Therefore the triumph of the liberal school of thought indicated that this transformation had been produced, or at any rate, was being produced, at least in the upper ranks of society.

CHAPTER XIV

THE LIBERAL REPUBLIC

PRESIDENT PÉREZ AND HIS GOVERNMENT

FEW STATESMEN in Chile had attained the position of first magistrate under more favorable circumstances than had José Joaquín Pérez. He formed his first cabinet with the aid of all parties and of all persons who longed for tranquillity in the republic. That body, therefore, reflected the state of calmness, conciliation, and forgetfulness that followed the ardent agitations of the past. All political groups had representation in it—liberals, conservatives, and nationals—and all praised it.

The personal qualities of the president in themselves constituted a guarantee of peace. He was a man of some sixty years: he had served the republic in different diplomatic and consular offices: he had traveled in the United States and Europe and had acquired a superior culture which, with his serene and moderate character, made him an extremely likable person. During the Bulnes administration he had several times been minister and, in the following decade, counselor of state. Although as a politician he had national affiliations, he had not been closely associated with President Montt as an ostensible participant in his government. One of his first acts was to approve the Law of Amnesty in favor of all those exiled for political reasons.

But this condition of harmony and good will was not long maintained. Questions of precedence in the bosom of the cabinet broke the formidable governmental bloc. The national party separated from him, and a group of the most advanced liberals, who desired constitutional reform at all costs, took the same step and from that moment began to call itself the radical party. The Matta and Gallo brothers were its leaders.

The government, then, rested on the same political combination which had so rudely fought President Montt in 1859, the so-called liberal-conservative fusion; and thus the nationals and radicals, who together represented strong parliamentary forces, remained in opposition. But in the elections of 1864 the complexion of congress was changed by the president, and the governmental alliance gained a considerable majority, to the detriment of the opposing groups. From that moment the opposition parties saw their influence in the government lost, but launched, in turn, a vigorous public campaign. The radicals, especially, began to organize throughout the country in order to spread their doctrines of constitutional reform. This, however, did not harm the government, which viewed the campaign only as a spectator. On the other hand, the inauguration of certain public works, undertaken in the former administration but finished in this, such as the railroad between Santiago and Valparaiso in 1863, gave it prestige at home as well as abroad.

In the midst of the tranquil political situation, a terrible disaster overwhelmed many respectable homes of the capital. On December 8, 1863, occurred the burning of the Compañía, a church situated in the most central part of Santiago. It had been destroyed years before by fire, but this time the disaster caused the death of more than two thousand persons. While the religious ceremony in honor of the Virgin was being celebrated with the greatest solemnity between seven and eight at night, one of the hangings of the church took fire from the flame of a candle that had just been lighted. The fire spread to other and still other hangings until the great arch was converted into a furnace. Meanwhile, the multitude which filled the church, principally ladies of the highest society, rushed madly to the doors, trying to escape, a useless attempt. Some fell over others and the exits became a horrible heap, a veritable human wall. Cries and lamentations rent the air and the flames in a few moments burnt all to a crisp. The alarm and despair that possessed the city was indescribable. Every attempt at rescue had been unsuccessful. General opinion has since then opposed rebuilding on the site, and it was converted into a garden (today that of congress) in which was erectd the image of the Virgin Mary as a commemorative monument.

THE CONFLICT OF PERU AND CHILE WITH SPAIN

The exceedingly tragic impression which this misfortune caused throughout the entire country was soon to fade because a serious conflict arose in the north between Peru and Spain in 1864—a conflict in which Chile judged that it ought to intervene in some way or other. Up to that time Spain had not recognized the independence of Peru and, ever since the mother country had suspended hostilities in the war which Peru waged to obtain its emancipation, Spain regarded its relations with its former colony as simply a condition of truce, tacitly agreed to on its part without any pact. From the battle of Ayacucho (1924) and the capitulation of Callao (1826), the last campaigns in behalf of the independence of Peru, until 1864, the Spanish court thought that the state of truce had been extended, and that in consequence it should still treat Peru only as a colony.

The Peruvian government, on its side, assured of independence and lacking revenue, had, unlike Chile, declined to recognize the accounts left unsettled by the colonial viceroys. Availing itself of this situation, Spain[1] sent to that country a "commissary," such as it used to send during the colonial period to arrange matters relative to such accounts and other affairs. This extraordinary envoy made the voyage accompanied by a small squadron in which sailed a commission of scientists who were to make certain observations and strengthen relations between the American states of the Pacific and their ancient mother country.

On such a pretext the ships passed by the ports of Chile without arousing any suspicion. When the commissary arrived at his destination, the government of Peru declined to treat with him, declaring that, as a sovereign state such as it was, it would negotiate only with a "plenipotentiary" and that it implied an offense to the dignity of the Peruvian nation that a "commissary" should be sent, as if it were still a Spanish colony. Without further parley, the commissary moved his squadron to the Chincha Islands and forcibly occupied them in the name of Her Majesty, Isabella II, queen of Spain at that time, alleging that the right of replevin empowered the former mother country to recover its lost viceroyalty or any part of it.

This act naturally aroused the indignation of Peru because the Chincha Islands produced guano, then the country's principal source of wealth, and because the act of occupation in itself constituted an unqualified abuse of force. New reinforcements, however, arrived from Spain, and the inability of Peru to defend its rights induced the government of that country to treat with Admiral Pareja, the commander of the Spanish ships. But the Peruvian people, led by Colonel Mariano Prado, arose in rebellion and overthrew the government, raised this leader to power, and aroused a national defense against Spain.

Meanwhile, the indignation caused by that act in Peru had spread to all of former Spanish America because it was judged a precedent of fatal consequences for the territorial integrity of the old colonies to permit such aggression from their ancient mother country. And

---

[1] For a brief account that presents this intervention of Spain on the west coast of South America in as favorable a light as possible, see Espasa, *Enciclopedia,* XLIII, 129.

although the words "truce" and "replevin" were revoked by the cabinet of Queen Isabella II, the gravity of the occurrence remained, since the Chincha Islands were retained as a pledge by those occupying them, until Peru agreed to pay what Spain asserted was due it. The sentiment of "American solidarity" that had been manifested with so much force in the struggle for emancipation was revived in all the countries on this continent that spoke the Castilian language, and they tried to ally themselves in order to repel the invader in any possible way.

In Chile, especially, all shades of public opinion cried out against Spain. Meetings were held in different cities, and in Santiago the populace violently attacked the Spanish legation. The government declared contraband of war the coal with which the invading squadron was supplied. These occurrences did not, however, cause an immediate rupture of relations, because official explanations were given the offended plenipotentiary, and a contract was made with him. But by September 17, 1865, when the people were engaged in the traditional ceremonies commemorating national independence, the squadron of Admiral Pareja appeared before Valparaiso. On the following day an ultimatum from him was received at the Moneda. According to that document, Spain refused to recognize the contract made with its representative in Chile, and Pareja demanded that within four days his flag be saluted with twenty-one guns. As the sole response, a declaration of war against Spain was sent the admiral. The declaration was made through a law which the president proposed and congress approved on September 24 by the unanimous vote of all its members in the midst of delirious, patriotic enthusiasm.

At once all parties suspended their doctrinaire struggles and put themselves at the disposition of the government. The latter attended to the defense of the coast as quickly as possible, made an offensive and defensive alliance with Peru, Bolivia, and Ecuador, and dispatched agents to Europe and the United States in search of armaments and fighting ships. The agitation throughout the republic was enormous because it lacked sufficient resources to carry on a maritime war against so powereful an enemy. There was only one moderately useful boat, the sloop *Esmeralda,* which had to take refuge from the squadron of Pareja in the channels of Chiloé.

However, that vessel left its anchorage one day and secretly started north under the direction of its commander, Williams Rebolledo. In front of Papudo Roads he surprised and captured the Spanish schooner *Covadonga* of the Spanish fleet. When Admiral

Pareja learned of this, he quietly committed suicide. His body was cast into the sea. Pareja had blockaded the principal ports of Chile. At his death the blockade was maintained by Commander Méndez Núñez, who succeeded him. Although this commander led his squadron on two expeditions to the south as far as Chiloé to recover the *Covadonga* and avenge the disaster to his arms, he was not successful.

Spain, tired of this fruitless warfare, ordered Méndez Núñez to retire from the Pacific but, before doing so, to bombard the ports of Valparaiso and Callao in reprisal for the offenses received. Méndez Núñez complied with the command, Valparaiso being the first port bombed. The port, being dismantled at the time, was unable to resist an attack of that kind. Therefore, almost as soon as the Spanish squadron was sighted, the representatives of foreign countries made all sorts of attempts to persuade the commander to forego a destruction as useless as it was unjustified, but they were not heeded.

On the morning of March 31, 1866, the assaulting ships coolly began to cannonade the town. The firing lasted four hours. The customhouses, other public buildings, and commercial centers were the preferred targets for the shot. Some fires occurred and caused destruction of merchandise to the value of fourteen million pesos. Satisfied with its action, the Spanish squadron went on to Callao; but the bombardment of that place, well defended with artillery since colonial times, was not executed with impunity. After a struggle of several hours, the ships of Méndez Núñez suffered serious reverses and retired and returned to Spain. The Pacific was cleared of Spanish vessels.

There was a long delay in making treaties of peace and friendship between the belligerent countries, but the attempt to replevin American territory in the name of a truce by which Spain pretended not to recognize the independence of the old colonies never was renewed. The consequences of this war were in a certain way very salutary for most of the American states. Besides reviving in all of them the same feeling of solidarity that had increased their strength during the struggle for independence, it showed them that by remaining united they would be able to resist effectively any project of conquest devised against them by European countries; and, in the future, it obliged them to be more foresighted in whatever concerned their national security. They ought to live in peace, but prepared for any disagreeable or dangerous emergency that might arise.

Chile acquired many implements of war with which to renew the material equipment of the army, and two new vessels which, together with the *Esmeralda* and *Covadonga*, constituted four regular units of sea warfare. In addition, the fortifications of Valparaiso were immediately begun and finished in four years. Finally, a political party, the "radical," adopted the idea of American confederation among all the former Spanish colonies, an idea which had interested many statesmen before, and preached it with enthusiasm, although without success.

MATERIAL PROGRESS UNDER PÉREZ

Hardly had the war ended when President Pérez was reëlected for a new constitutional period with the nationals and radicals in opposition. Like his three predecessors (Prieto, Bulnes, and Montt), he remained at the head of the republic for ten years (1861-1871). Although the first period of his administration occurred during the conflict with Spain, it was, nevertheless, fruitful in the development of public services in respect to police, roads, postal service, telegraphs, railroads, and education. During the second period, the government continued its effective work in promoting these services.

The telegraph line in the south was extended as far as Lota and from there to Nacimiento, on the Araucanian frontier. The railroad line uniting Santiago with San Fernando was extended as far as Curicó; operations advanced in the next section as far as Talca and then from Chillán to Talcahuano. In the north, the branch from Llay-Llay to San Felipe was also pushed forward; and, in the mining regions of the transverse valleys, railroads under private initiative were being similarly extended. Postal service gained in speed, and roads connecting the different regions of the republic from one end to the other increased in comfort and security in proportion as special attention was given to the rural police who protected the country and guarded the travelers from banditry.

Persistent attention was also given to public education during this administration. New public *liceos* arose in the provincial capitals which up to that time had not had them. The last founded were those of Los Angeles and Ancud. A reform in secondary education was inaugurated at the same time, beginning with the National Institute. This institution continued to take on greater vitality under the careful and invigorating direction of Diego Barros Arana, named for the post of rector in 1863.

The reforms consisted in requiring in the curriculum of the

humanities the study of physics, chemistry, physical geography, cosmography, botany, and zoology—all branches that were usually grouped under the general designation of natural sciences; in the development of historical studies, especially on America; and in the specialization of instructors, who from being teachers of entire courses became teachers of specific branches. Although the introduction of these studies into the fields of secondary education was not new—for they dated from the Bulnes administration—still, because of lack of suitable teachers and the slight value attributed to them by parents, and for other reasons, about twenty years had passed before they could really be established under regular conditions. The zeal and energy of Barros Arana were necessary to bring about a serious and orderly consideration of such studies. From that time on the rest of the *liceos* began to apply the programs of the Institute.

There was also a development in primary instruction that corresponded to that in secondary education, although to a more limited extent, and an evident improvement in higher and professional branches. The university was likewise endowed with more ample means than the law for its erection had contemplated, and it made considerable gain in the importance of its studies and in the selection of its faculty.

The accomplishment of this work, of interest to all, depended upon the increasing growth in public revenue, which nearly doubled itself every ten years. At the end of Pérez' administration, it amounted to about twelve million pesos. This naturally showed a flattering economic condition among the common mass of the population, to which the development of agriculture, mining, lumbering in the forests of the south, and commerce contributed. It was necessary to make over the laws that governed the last-named branch, which were almost entirely of Spanish origin, and in 1865 the *Código de comerico* (Code of Commerce)[2] was definitely promulgated, to go into force from 1867 on. Although it had been in preparation for some time, it appeared exactly ten years after the Civil Code.

Another manifestation of the economic movement of that time was the first national exposition of agriculture in 1869, in which acquaintance was made with numerous agricultural machines and systems of breeding for the advance of cattle raising. In fact, from

---

[2] The law for the promulgation of this code is dated November 23, 1865. See Ricardo Anguita, *Leyes promulgadas en Chile,* II, 208.

that time alone dates the general use of machinery in exploiting the soil.

Parallel to this unfolding wealth was the incorporation of new territories into the civilized life of the country. Colonization was extended from the regions of Llanquihue and Valdivia to those of Araucania. It was carried on not only with foreign elements but also with national, by means of concessions or sales of tracts of land located within those territories which had been Indian domains but which were passing little by little into the control of the republic.

Araucania continued to survive through all this troublesome time. In the beginning of Pérez' administration there appeared among the natives a French adventurer, who, after carrying on commerce with them, gathered them together, treated them kindly in a parley, and proclaimed himself their king. This French king of Araucania whose purpose, as he assured them, was to free his subjects from the tyranny of the government of Chile, set up his throne there under the name of Orelie Antoine I.[3] The self-made monarch did not, of course, continue many weeks in power because he was taken prisoner by the forces that guarded the frontiers, brought at once to judgment, declared insane, and expelled from the country.

An act of this kind, although ridiculous, made the government see the danger of delay in thoroughly incorporating the Araucanian territory with the republic. At this time was definitely put into practice the method of subduing the natives which certain colonial governors had tried to employ since the seventeenth century, and which had been started afresh at the end of Montt's decade. It consisted in surrounding the Araucanian frontier with forts, in having cities founded under the shelter of those forts, and in slowly advancing into the interior. In 1868 a new native uprising occurred which made clear the problem of Arauco. This insurrection lasted for three years. It was, however, only one more episode in the age-long struggle of the Araucanians to maintain their independence and the possession of their soil.

POLITICAL ACTIVITY UNDER PÉREZ

The political movement of the country, which was relatively quiet during the first period of Pérez' administration, took on the char-

---

[3] The Chilean authorities at first took this adventurer, Tounens by name, as a joke, but his activity soon caused them to apprehend him by strategy. See Hancock, *A History of Chile*, p. 239.

acter of active controversy during the second period. The parties opposed to the government had sacrificed their aspirations while the conflict with Spain lasted in order for the moment to lend their coöperation to national defense. Now, with the war ended, they returned to their fierce campaign of publicity and propaganda. Already in 1865 the more advanced groups had obtained a law explaining or interpreting the article of the constitution by which the Catholic religion was established as the religion of the State. By this law it was declared that non-Catholics could exercise their worship in private houses and keep up private schools for the education of their children, in conformity with their beliefs. With this action, the liberty of worship was established. Almost at the same time the law of "civil responsibility" was abolished. It had been issued at the end of Montt's administration against authors of uprisings and popular revolts. It will be recalled how bitterly this law had been resisted.

But these victories of the liberal elements of the country did not in any way satisfy such advanced groups as the radicals and young nationals. These groups were, indeed, the ones which had a great desire to reform many features of the constitution in order to weaken executive power. They founded the clubs of reform and thus kept alive and in permanent activity the enthusiasm for political doctrines in Santiago and some provincial capitals. The congress of 1867 had approved in general some proposals of reform which comprised almost the entire constitution, but upon which the congress of 1870 had to pass judgment.

Of all the reforms sought later by the advanced parties, the only one realized by the end of Pérez' administration was that prohibiting the president of the republic from being reëlected immediately after concluding his constitutional period of five years. From the operation of the constitution of 1833 until that time, 1871, the right of reëlection had always been exercised to such an extent that in forty years there had been only four supreme executives. In 1871, then, a law was enacted to the effect that any citizen who had been president of the republic for a constitutional period could be reëlected only after another period of five years had intervened. It was the first reform introduced into the text of the celebrated code suggested thirty-eight years before. The liberal-conservative coalition of the government was tenaciously opposed to other reforms. On the other hand, the executive did not abuse his constitutional privileges. Pérez governed without the need of extraordinary powers or "states of siege."

The one who was opposed to such methods and who exercised the most influence in his office was Manuel Antonio Tocornal, the leader of the conservative party of that period and of the coalition in power. He was minister of the interior for two years and president of the house of deputies for several years. An honorable politician, orator, and writer by profession, he largely directed the administration of Pérez, during whose term he died (1867), after twenty-five years of public life.

The contest over the election of a successor to Pérez was most active. The liberal-conservative bloc of the government, on one side, and the national-radical opposition on the other offered their respective candidates and worked ardently for them. The logical and inevitable candidate of the liberal-conservative coalition would have been Manuel Antonio Tocornal, but with his death the personality of Federico Errázuriz Zañartu came to the front almost unexpectedly. He had been among the liberals of 1848 and among the revolutionists of 1851 and had marshaled the coalition ranks of the Pérez administration, during which he had been intendant of Santiago and minister on more than one occasion. He was the candidate of the government and inevitably triumphed at the polls, in accordance with the electoral and political practices still prevailing. Nevertheless, he had a competitor. The opposition of independent nationals, radicals, and liberals raised the candidacy of the wealthy industrialist and financier, José Tomás Urmeneta, but he was far outdistanced at the polls. Likewise the candidacy of Errázuriz, as well as that of Urmeneta, had been proclaimed through "limited conventions," the greater of which did not reach one hundred persons, but among these three were departmental delegates throughout the country. The proceeding was going to take root, although on very broad democratic conditions.

CONSTITUTIONAL REFORM AND ECONOMIC CRISIS UNDER PRESIDENT ERRÁZURIZ

When Federico Errázuriz Zañartu arose to power in 1871, he was forty-six years old, a descendant of one of the most aristocratic families. His family had been of the greatest political importance in Chile from colonial times. Enterprising, active, at times irregular, he had left traces of his character both on the municipality and intendancy of Santiago and on congress and the ministries that he served. From his very youth he had attracted attention for his ardent liberalism, as an associate of Lastarria in the agitations that preceded the revolution of 1851, during which he was exiled to Peru. But the principal reward of his public life had been gained in the ministry of war during the unfortunate days of the conflict with Spain. He had then devoted all his faculties to the service of national defense.

Once in the presidency, he showed the same energetic qualities that had previously distinguished him. The extension of the railroads from Curicó to Talca, from Talca to Chillán, from Chillán to Talcahuano and Angol, on the Araucanian frontier, was his constant interest. The boulevard of Valparaiso, the congressional palace, the Quinta Normal School of Agriculture with its exposition palace of 1875, the university buildings, all of which he saw completed, as well as many other constructions, were public works consistently promoted by his government.

Benjamín Vicuña Mackenna, appointed intendant of Santiago, coöperated in these efforts by directing the modernization of the city. The hill of Santa Lucía, converted into a promenade, and Cousiño Park, ceded to the public by its proprietor, were turned over to the city. There were new streets and recently planted plazas. Urban tramways, drawn by animals, began to unite the widely separated extremes of the capital, thanks to the establishment of a private corporation aided by the State. With the impetus given by all those enterprises, Santiago continued to make progress as a modern city, and a more enterprising one.

Furthermore, with the entry of foreign capital and the contracting of English loans by the government for public works, business increased considerably. This was also evident in the exploitation of the mines of Caracoles, recently discovered in 1870, near Antofagasta (from which, for some years, poured a veritable stream of silver), and in the equally profitable exploitation of the nitrate plants of Tarapacá (Peruvian at that time), and of the guano deposits of Antofagasta, in Bolivian territory—enterprises undertaken by Chilean capitalists and workmen.

What better characterized the administration of Errázuriz Zañartu was not so much its earnest efforts in the field of public works or its feverish economic enterprises, but the fierce political struggle which took place during this period. Then began agitation in behalf of freedom of instruction. The conservative elements, which formed part of the government coalition, were not in accord with the prevailing trend of public education because, to their way of thinking, the preference given to natural sciences in public schools was contrary to religious belief and injurious to private morality. Moreover, there would no longer be a chance to monopolize the professional positions in the gift of the university since free competition of professional men would bring out the most competent. Intrinsically these ideas were tending to favor private seminaries, which had recently been founded and which belonged almost entirely to religious bodies. But if one considered the question from a higher point of view, he would be assured that, on that very account, it was advisable to allow freedom in the subjects studied so that everyone might receive the degree that was most in accord with his wishes.

Inspired with these ideas and with the determination to realize them, at least in part, the minister of public education, Abdón Cifuentes, a respected member of the conservative party, issued a famous decree at the beginning of 1872, by which he exempted professors of public schools from giving examinations to students of private seminaries, as was done at that time, and authorized the directors of the latter establishments to hold the examinations and confer certificates that would be valid in the university. It allowed them, moreover, to reduce studies to the curricula considered desirable, within the minimum required in the university program.

This decree produced immediate confusion. Veritable auctions for examination tickets were established, and the case is reported of young men who passed all the humanities of the entire law course in only one year, naturally without knowing anything of the studies for which they showed certificates—certificates bought, as if at a public market, for three or five pesos each. Such degradation of education and of professional dignity produced an immediate reaction. The minister resigned the following year (1873), the decree was annulled, and conditions reverted to their former state. By another decree, however, it was declared, a short time later, that teaching of religion was not obligatory in the public schools, and students whose parents asked for the privilege could be exempted from it. Meanwhile Barros Arana, supporter and instigator of scientific studies, had been obliged to abandon his post as rector of the National Institute. Although exonerated by the minister, he was not reappointed.

On the other hand, so-called theological questions which were being discussed at that time and which were making the government coalition futile induced the president of the republic to remove the conservatives from the Moneda, to constitute a ministry, based upon an entirely liberal parliamentary majority. Thus it came about that the powerful coalition which had been in control of the government for ten years was definitely broken in 1873, and the conservative party was thrust from power, not to recover it for twenty years.

The so-called theological questions were the following: the suppression of "ecclesiastical privilege" or the right of the clergy to be judged by their own tribunals, distinct from those for ordinary inhabitants in the national territory; the "secularizing" of the cemeteries, that is to say, the establishing of religious neutrality of these places in such a way that the dead belonging to any religion could be interred in them; "civil marriage," the celebration of marriage in the presence of public officials by a special contract, leaving the wedded parties at liberty to celebrate it religiously also, if their belief thus counseled them; and, ultimately, the "separation of Church and State," thereby converting the former into a society or private institution.

The liberal and national parties had not uniformly agreed on all these reforms. Only the radical party favored them without reserve, but it was not strong enough to enact them. The conservative party resisted them tenaciously; and the clergy, who looked upon them as a menace to faith and morality and a blow to their influence, spoke in the pulpits, in the press, in the home, wherever they could obtain a hearing, in opposition to everything they considered a sin against the conscience of the great majority of the population. The political struggle degenerated, therefore, into a religious struggle, and the conservative party was transformed into a clerical or "ultramontane" group, as its adversaries branded it, opposed to the other extreme party, the radical, or "red," as it was nicknamed.

An almost unlimited freedom of the press began to be the rule at that time. This freedom, acquired under the law enacted in 1872 to correct certain abuses of the press, contributed to foster the heated conflict. It was an especially benevolent law which, by retaining the old-time jury chosen by lot in order to judge such abuses, and by reducing penalties to fines more or less slight in case of guilt, made the daily press a tremendous power.

The liberal-radical bloc finally triumphed, but only in part. In the Penal Code promulgated in 1874, it succeeded in introducing numerous statutes that punished priests for specified crimes; and, in the organic law of tribunals, promulgated the following year, it obtained the abolition of the ecclesiastical privilege for all civil and criminal causes. In the question of cemeteries, it only succeeded for the time being in having a section of the Catholic cemeteries themselves opened for the burial of dissenters. Meanwhile the clergy, directed by Archbishop Valdivieso, continued to protest; and, when the articles of the Penal Code affecting ecclesiastics were debated in congress, the metropolitan see threatened solemn excommunication against the parliamentarians who fostered them, which was not enough, however, to keep the legislators from approving them. On the other hand, nothing could then be done in respect to civil marriage and the separation of Church and State.

In the no-less-difficult field of constitutional balance between the powers of congress and of the president of the republic, the struggle was also earnest and active. The campaign which the reform clubs had been making for a considerable time to broaden the powers of congress and to limit those of the executive now began to have the desired effect. In accordance with this purpose, many articles of the State constitution were revised in 1874. Inconsistencies were established between certain public employments and legislative functions; the extraordinary powers of the president were restricted; the house of deputies placed seven of its members on the "conservative committee," which represented congress during its recess, and the powers of that committee were broadened. The personnel of the council of state was similarly modified. Into it were introduced representatives from the two houses to constitute a majority, and with that change the advisory body, whose members had previously been selected by the president, came to have a more popular origin. In short, more effective measures were passed to insure the responsibility of ministers to congress.

The electoral system was reformed. Control of elections was taken from the municipalities, which then depended directly on the executive, and was transferred to "Boards [juntas] of the larger taxpayers." In place of the "general ticket" (*lista completa*) which was formerly used in electing members of congress, according to which each of the opposing parties voted for a number of electors equal to that of the representatives to be chosen in the respective jurisdictions, the "cumulative vote" was introduced, but only for the election of deputies. For senators the general ticket was retained; and for the municipal elections, the electors were permitted to vote for two tickets, one with two thirds, and the other with one third of the number to be chosen.

The cumulative vote was invoked to produce a considerable modification in the composition of the house. It represented an attempt to give to minority parties the representation that corresponded to each, according to the number of its qualified citizens. If, for example, a precinct of a thousand electors voted for three deputies on a general ticket, 501 of them were enough to elect the three deputies and the other 499 were left without any representative. With the cumulative vote, each voter had as many votes at his disposal as deputies to be elected in the precinct, votes which he could use in favor of one or more candidates.

None of those reforms disturbed the continuity of the government. The cabinet, controlled by the minister of the interior, Eulogio Altamirano, an emphatic liberal politician and vigorous parliamentary orator, remained in office during the five years of this administration. Consequently Altamirano was his most efficient collaborator.

The government of Errázuriz Zañartu was in its last stages in 1876. Except for the ardent political struggles, nothing had disturbed its tranquillity, neither revolutions nor external wars; but the country had passed through a most severe economic crisis. The public debt, which the last loans had increased, drew from the treasury much of its income, through interest charges and amortization. The treasury was burdened by a very heavy deficit. The mines of Caracoles gave out, as did many other mines, and numerous corporations formed for their exploitation went into bankruptcy. The nitrate plants of Tarapacá were recovered by the government of Peru, and the guano deposits of Antofagasta were burdened in various ways by the government of Bolivia. Consequently, the Chilean interests invested in one or the other suffered enormous losses. Capital fled, or hid itself. The rate of bank discounts rose. Commerce partly closed its doors. Fortunes irrevocably invested in costly buildings or employed in improvident luxury remained only as a memento of vanished wealth.

THE ECONOMIC CRISIS OF PINTO'S ADMINISTRATION

When Federico Errázuriz Zañartu gave up his office to his successor, Aníbal Pinto, the business crisis was passing through its sharpest period. The latter, elected as the official candidate, was in the very prime of life (fifty years old). Through family antecedents —he was the son of General Francisco Antonio Pinto—he belonged to the oldest historical liberal party, and because of his moderation he counted on the sympathy of all parties. Although a man of a solid reputation acquired during his long sojourn in Europe as secretary of legation, he did not have a long political record or a colorful one. He had served the *intendencia* of Concepción for ten years, under the Pérez administration, and had acted as a member of several congresses; but he derived his prestige rather from his exquisite culture and recognized talent. During the greater part of the preceding administration he had served as minister of war and navy and it was precisely this office that enabled him to aspire to the presidency of the republic.

His candidacy was somewhat unusual in that it was presented and furthered by a full convention of a thousand individuals. A new practice in the republican organism of the country, it was uniformly continued from that time on in each presidential election. In that convention, Pinto contended for leadership with Miguel Luis Amunátegui, famous historian and teacher who represented in politics the tendencies of a very temperate and tolerant liberalism. And then, at the polls, although counting on the aid of official intervention he had to overcome another of the most illustrious historians and Chilean publicists, Benjamín Vicuña Mackenna. The popularity of the latter had made it possible for him to organize in a short time a political group, called "liberal-democratic," which almost wholly disappeared the day following his defeat.

Perhaps no other president of Chile was destined to become more conscious of his responsibility in office than Aníbal Pinto. When he came into power, he had to meet the acute economic crisis that had arisen during the former administration; and, when the half of his term was hardly finished, he entered upon the greatest of all the conflicts that had threatened the republic. Argentina, Peru, and Bolivia, the three neighboring states, involved Chile in difficult discussions, which they were unable to solve in a fitting manner.

The government tried to check the economic crisis in matters affecting the treasury by creating new levies to increase its income and by adopting the greatest possible economies in order to cut down expenditures. Among these economies were such measures as the suppression of the bonus of 25 per cent on the salary of public employees which the former administration had granted in a moment of generosity, and the reduction of the army and the disarmament of several war vessels.

But if the fiscal assets were largely put in order by methods of this kind, private fortunes continued to feel the pressure of the economic crisis that shortly degenerated into a monetary panic. The circulating medium became scarce because of the exportation of gold and silver coins apparently necessary to cover commercial obligations in Europe. Interest on money increased, and international exchange became lower. In consequence, the cost of living rose to unprecedented heights. On the other hand, real estate and state bonds, together with banking credit, depreciated. There came a day when the banks could not convert their bills into specie. The government was intimately tied up with the banks because it had taken great quantities of their bills as loans in order to meet its obligations, so it then came to their assistance and succeeded in passing a law for the inconvertibility of bank bills in 1878, by which a set rate was given these in all transactions. By their value in exchange very soon diminished to 25 per cent of their normal value. From that time began the regime of paper money in Chile with its resultant inflation.[4]

Notwithstanding the grave and uncertain situation and international alarms, the government continued to enact highly important laws, such as the one that established the incompatibility of judicial with parliamentary and administrative offices, for the purpose of separating political from judicial affairs; the one that suppressed the tobacco monopoly, an old form of taxation that limited the cultivation of this plant in the country and gave rise to much contraband trade; and the one that reorganized secondary and superior instruction in 1879. There still remained to be solved the international questions to which, beginning with 1879, all the attention of the government was to be devoted.

THE INTERNATIONAL PROBLEMS OF CHILE

Chile had already carried on a half century of orderly constitutional life and it had maintained uninterrupted cordial relations with foreign countries except at long intervals. Only two conflicts had occurred during that time; that of 1836 with Bolivia and Peru, which had become allies under the leadership of General Santa Cruz; and that of 1865 with Spain.

The United States of North America had celebrated treaties of friendship, trade, and navigation with Chile under favorable reciprocal conditions, and so had several other nations of America and of Europe, among the latter being France, Belgium, England, and Germany. Postal treaties and pacts of other kinds had also been negotiated with almost all the countries of the world. The external credit of the republic could not be bettered and was superior to that of the other states formerly established by Spain in America.

Diplomacy in Chile had very little to do that was disagreeable. Although certain claims made by citizens of foreign nations were

---

[4] For a study of the rôle of paper money in Chile, see Fetter, *Monetary Inflation in Chile.*

pressed in Chile by their respective representatives, these were always satisfactorily settled.[5] But the foreign policy of Chile was, above all, American. It worked toward the "united solidarity" of all the republics of the continent, with no other object than to defend them from any aggression that threatened the independence or territorial integrity of any one of them. Because of the Peruvian-Spanish conflict and the resultant war that included Chile, the government made a beginning toward a realization of that ideal by making an offensive and defensive pact with Peru, Bolivia, and Ecuador in 1865. But from then on no advance could be made toward this ideal. On the contrary, Chile soon found itself involved in serious external complications. In order to give them due attention, it was necessary to create the ministry of foreign relations, by segregating it from the ministry of the interior in 1871. From that date cabinets were composed of five ministers.

Those complications arose from questions of boundaries, a situation that characterizes the reciprocal relations of all Ibero-American republics. The problem of frontiers has really been common to these republics. On separating from the mother country, they adopted the same boundaries for their respective territories as they had had when colonies. This is what has been called the *uti possidetis* of 1810, the year of the emancipation revolution. Those colonial boundaries were vague and undetermined because they passed through regions little known or absolutely unknown, in which the only population, if any, was a few savage nomad tribes. When these regions began to be populated and exploited, the question of sovereignty arose in them. It was necessary to mark the frontiers in order to know to which state the wealth of its soil belonged. Although Chile was bounded only by Argentina and Bolivia, it had to carry on boundary disputes with both of these republics.

The dispute with Argentina began first. In 1847, its government protested to that of Chile about the recent founding of the colony of Punta Arenas and the act of taking possession of the Strait of Magellan, effected four years previously. In the opinion of the Argentine government, Patagonia and the strait belonged to Argentina. From that time it carried on a series of diplomatic negotiations, at times interrupted and again renewed, without coming to any agreement. Thus more than thirty years passed. But in 1878 these negotiations were cut off and an armed break seemed imminent. The fleets of Chile and of Argentina were ordered to the strait.

---

[5] A perusal of Evans' *Chile and its Relations with the United States* would seem to confirm this statement, especially with respect to Great Britain.

Soon, however, a calmer spirit prevailed. A war between the two countries was considered fratricidal. They had made the memorable campaign of independence together. They had mutually aided each other in their subsequent difficulties. The negotiations were reopened, and in 1881 a boundary treaty was signed that for the moment solved all difficulties. Chile remained in possession of the strait; and Argentina, of eastern Patagonia. The dividing line on all the common frontier was to pass over the highest peaks of the cordillera of the Andes which divided the waters. Any cases of disagreement among the experts charged with the demarcation were to be referred to an arbiter named by common consent.[6]

While this settlement was being concluded, the dispute with Bolivia arose. Years before, some Chilean explorers, crossing the desolate desert of Atacama, had discovered on the shore near Mejillones rich deposits of guano, the exceedingly fertile excrement of sea birds. After exploitation was begun, Bolivia claimed the territory where the deposits lay. The diplomatic debate with Chile over this claim began at once and became a very heated one. In 1866 a boundary treaty was signed between the two countries. Chile recognized Bolivian sovereignty and fixed its northern limit on the twenty-fourth parallel of south latitude. Moreover, it was agreed that the product of guano deposits already discovered or to be discovered between the twenty-third and twenty-fifth parallels and the amount of customs taxes received on the exportation of minerals from that zone should be divided equally between the two countries.

Shortly after, other Chilean explorers found deposits of nitrate in the vicinity of Antofagasta, and others, later, found the Caracoles mines in the same region. The explorers petitioned for and obtained from the Bolivian government the right to exploit such wealth; but under very burdensome conditions which, nevertheless, they fulfilled faithfully. To that region, then, went Chilean laborers and capital. They founded the port and city of Antofagasta; they later caused Calama, Mejillones, Cobija, Tocopilla, and other cities to prosper. They performed enormous tasks in opening roads, creating watering places, and making the desert habitable. The first railroad in Bolivia was the one the miners constructed from Antofagasta into the interior.

Bolivia did not seem pleased to have the Chileans populate their desert and make it productive. A people still uncultured, shut in by almost impassable mountains and plains, Bolivians despised the

---

[6] See Paul D. Dickens, "Argentine Arbitration and Mediation," in *Hisp. Amer. Hist. Rev.* (November, 1931), XI, 469-472.

foreigner, whoever he might be, just because he was one. Therefore they hated both Chile and the Chileans of the plain (pampa). The Bolivian government never concerned itself about complying with the Treaty of 1866. Chile did not collect one cent of the duties from Mejillones and Antofagasta. And, not content with this violation, the Bolivian government committed hostilities in various ways, above all by imposing very heavy taxes on the producers of guano and nitrate. New diplomatic negotiations followed new Chilean demands. Finally, in 1874, Chile was persuaded to make one more concession. In a treaty signed that year, it gave up to Bolivia all its rights north of the twenty-fourth parallel upon the one condition that the industrialists of the desert should not be burdened with new taxes.

The intervention of Peru also greatly influenced the attitude of Bolivia. Notwithstanding its enormous wealth, Peru always appeared to have no revenues because it flung away all its assets in wild revolutionary enterprises. At the end of each of these, the victorious group, now become the government, had to remunerate its followers by keeping up an incredible number of civil employees and military chieftains. Peru's financial stringency reached such a point that it had to declare itself bankrupt and suspend payment of the interest on the public debt. It was then that it decided to lay hands on the nitrate deposits of Tarapacá. These, like those of Antofagasta, were being exploited by Chileans. Foreseeing that, if it despoiled these industrialists, Chile would make war against it, Peru decided to come to an understanding with Bolivia. In 1873, therefore, it signed a treaty of offensive and defensive alliance with that country, a treaty that was kept most secret.[7] From that moment Peru dared attempt anything. Its government passed a law granting a monopoly of the nitrates of Tarapacá to the State. Henceforth, the producers were to hand over all the nitrates they extracted to the Peruvian government at a price the latter itself fixed, a price that would inevitably ruin them. Having obtained this result, Peru issued a new law for the expropriation of nitrates. The proprietors must sell them to the State with all the equipment for exploitation. But the State did not have the means to pay for them. It advertised a loan in Europe that was not covered. Then it agreed to pay on time. The ruined nitrate producers could only yield. In 1875 they delivered their holdings, their machinery, their buildings—everything. Peru never paid what was due them; but the government of Chile, contrary to the prophecies of Peruvian states-

[7] For the text of this treaty see William Jefferson Dennis (ed.), *Documentary History of the Tacna-Arica Dispute*, pp. 56-59.

NATIONAL CHILE

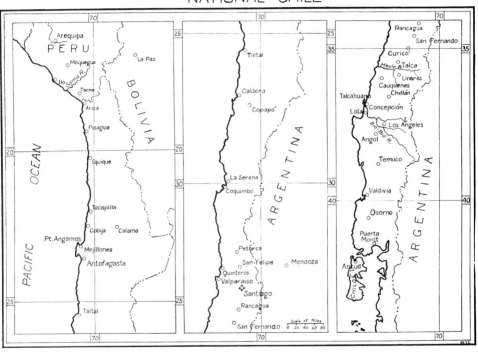

Chilean historians. *Upper left:* José Toribio Medina, bibliographer and historian, recognized as the leading man in his field in Latin America. *Upper right:* Diego Barros Arana, leading historian of Chile, prominent educator. *Lower left:* Miguel Luis Amunátegui (standing), prominent historian, minister of state, leading liberal politician and educator; Gregorio Victor Amunátegui, physician and writer, always associated with his brother. *Lower right:* Benjamín Vicuña Mackenna, orator, administrator, prolific annalist. Courtesy Instituto de Cinematografía Educativa, Universidad de Chile.

men, did not formulate any claim for that spoliation, since Peru, as sovereign of Tarapacá, could issue for that region those laws which might be most agreeable to the government.

Thus came the year 1878. The secret alliance of Peru and Bolivia continued unaltered. After one revolution—like so many others —an adventurous general called Hilarión Daza seized the government of Bolivia. Urged on by the Peruvian government, he resolved to give a finishing stroke to the Chilean nitrate industry. He would do in Antofagasta what had been done in Tarapacá.

Disregarding entirely the Treaty of 1874, the dictator Daza levied a new and heavy tax on the Chilean Nitrate Company of Antofagasta. That act brought to a climax measures of hostility which for a long time the Bolivian officials of the coast region had been adopting against the Chileans. It was useless for the Chilean government, in behalf of the company, to bring the Treaty of 1874 to the attention of Daza; useless also for it to propose arbitration as a means of settling the question. The dictator wished to drive the Chileans out of the desert and "regain possession of the nitrate plants," according to the language of his advisers.

As was hoped, the company refused to pay. Daza then resolved to embargo all its goods and sell them at public auction. The embargo was actually begun, work was suspended, and a date set for the auction. In this manner the policy of conciliation, of harmony, of almost unlimited compliance which Chile was practicing toward its sister republics of America suddenly came to a violent end. Its legitimate economic expansion was being checked in a shameful and humiliating manner. It was being cast out of those inhospitable deserts conquered by the brawn of its nationals at the cost of great hardship; and at the same time its most solemn treaties were being violated. To resist these wrongs there was no longer any recourse but war.

In the middle of February, 1879, and on the very day appointed for the auction of the nitrate plants, two hundred Chilean soldiers under the command of Colonel Emilio Sotomayor landed at Antofagasta, took possession of the city without any resistance, and hoisted the flag of Chile on the public buildings. The entire population, filled with great enthusiasm, gathered to acclaim these men as liberators. There were no Bolivians present except administrative employees and a small garrison. All were allowed to leave without hindrance. The occupation of Antofagasta, thus accomplished, marked the beginning of a war which was to keep the whole American continent in suspense.

CHAPTER XV

THE WAR OF THE PACIFIC

THE BACKGROUND OF THE CONFLICT

As soon as the occupation of Antofagasta was known in Peru, its government, then directed by General Mariano Prado, knew that it was also involved in the conflict. Not finding itself prepared for war, it proposed to gain time by sending an envoy to Chile to propose mediation. Should the Chilean troops retire from Antofagasta, said the envoy, all would be arranged in a peaceful manner. The government of Chile refused to accede to this. Meanwhile Peru mobilized its army rapidly, Bolivia declared war against Chile, and the press of those countries brought clearly to light the existence of the Peru-Bolivia alliance. The representative of Peru when questioned about that treaty replied that he knew nothing of it, but stated that he did not think it existed. On the other hand, the representative of Chile, in Lima, after many conferences with the Peruvian minister of foreign relations, obtained a declaration that the alliance existed.

When notified of this treaty, the Chilean government declared war on Peru and Bolivia in April, 1879, following the example of Bolivia. Peru responded to this declaration with the expulsion of all Chileans from its territory and the confiscation of their goods. Chile did not imitate, even as an act of reprisal, this conduct of its enemies. On the contrary, it was benefitted by the procedure, since the greater part of the Chileans thus expelled increased the ranks of their own army eventually and, knowing the region as they did, served later as important aids in the invasion of Peru.

The forces of the belligerents were very unequal. Chile, with a population of two and a half million inhabitants, kept up an army of barely twenty-five hundred men; while Peru, with a population of three million, maintained one of eight thousand; and Bolivia, with two million, one of more than three thousand. The allies, therefore, commanded a permanent army of eleven thousand, more than four times greater than that of Chile, and a population more than double that of Chile. In respect to a fleet their superiority was also evident. If Bolivia had no vessels, Peru counted on four cruisers, several transports, and sloops. Chile had only two cruisers and some frigates and sloops of little value. It was not strange, according to this showing, that in foreign countries the defeat of Chile should be regarded as certain. Only those near at hand, who knew the complete disorder that characterized the governments of the allies and the serious purpose of the Chilean government, could cherish hope of success for the latter.

Nevertheless, the War of the Pacific,[1] as this armed conflict was called, was from the first favorable to Chile. In the month and a half elapsing between the date of the occupation of Antofagasta and the last days of March, 1879, Chilean troops conquered almost without resistance the whole Bolivian desert as far as the boundary of Peru. The campaign of Antofagasta was, then, a triumphal march for the Chilean hosts. Bolivia could not take its army across the high chains of the Andes in so short a time for the defense of Antofagasta because the terrain presented insuperable obstacles. It preferred, therefore, to join its troops with those of its ally.

THE NAVAL CAMPAIGN

Meanwhile, relations with Peru were broken, and hostilities began on the ocean. The naval campaign was then undertaken with feverish activity. The Chilean admiral, Williams Rebolledo, took his squadron into Peruvian waters. He blockaded Iquique and then went to Callao, leaving in the former port only two old wooden vessels already too worn out for use: the *Esmeralda* and the *Covadonga*. The Peruvian squadron had departed from Callao southward in different divisions, and the Chilean vessels did not encounter it on the way. So it happened that the two most important cruisers of Peru, the *Huáscar* and the *Independencia*, in charge of the commander of the former, Miguel Grau, arrived before the harbor of Iquique and prepared to seize the two vessels blockading the port.

Then took place the memorable naval battle of Iquique on May 21, 1879. At dawn Captain Carlos Condell, commander of the *Covadonga*, was advised by the official watch of his vessel that two large ships had been sighted toward the north. He at once leaped to the bridge. From his observation it was not difficult to recognize those vessels as the *Huáscar* and the *Independencia*. While his crew was being put under arms, he betook himself to the *Esmeralda*, which lay farther within the bay, in order to give notice to its commander, the chief of the blockade, Capatin Arturo Prat, who immediately decided to resist to the utmost. He communicated this resolution to Condell and ordered him to follow his course. "All right" (*está bien*), replied Condell serenely. At the same moment, a shell

---

[1] See Diego Barros Arana, *Histoire de la guerre de Pacifique* (Paris, 1881-1882); Gonzalo Bulnes, *Historia de la guerra del Pacífico* (3 vols. Valparaiso, 1912-1919).

from the *Huáscar* fell shrieking into the sea between the two Chilean vessels, spattering their hulls. The firing had begun.

After an hour of active cannonading, during which the *Independencia* discharged its guns on the *Covadonga*, and the *Huáscar* its guns on the *Esmeralda*, the commanders of the two latter vessels, Grau[2] and Prat, found themselves face to face. As the *Esmeralda* was near land, a heavy musketry fusillade was also delivered from the port. It was evident that the Chilean vessel was losing the contest. It could hardly move; its shot fell in vain against the hull of its adversary. During a moment of calm, Prat assembled his crew and harangued them, saying: "Boys, the contest is unequal. Our colors have never yielded to the enemy. I hope they will not have to do it on this occasion. While I live, that flag will flutter in its place; if I die, my officers will know how to fulfill their duty." The crew uttered a "Viva Chile," and the duel continued with more vigor.

By the third hour of the struggle, the corvette had already been pierced by many projectiles and was leaking, but its fire did not lessen. Commander Grau, knowing that such an unequal battle could not last much longer, stopped firing and with his engines under full steam drove the *Huáscar* against the *Esmeralda*, caught it amidships, and pierced it with his ram. Prat, who was calmly waiting for that moment, gave one sharp command, "Board!" His men did not hear it; and he, only accompanied by Sergeant Juan de Dios Aldea, jumped to the deck of the enemy vessel. There both fell, riddled with bullets.

The struggle continued, however, directed by Lieutenant Luis Uribe. At the second ramming, another lieutenant, Ignacio Serrano, also jumped on board with a few sailors. All met the same fate as Prat and Aldea. A third blow of the ram finally overturned the *Esmeralda* and left its masts and hull a mass of splinters. A marine guard, young Ernesto Riquelme, then discharged a last salvo at the water's level and sank into the ocean with the remains of the old ship, its flag, still waving at the masthead, fluttering over the waves.

The midday sun illuminated that sacrifice. But the duel that had occurred in the roadstead of Iquique was not the whole of the fight. A little more to the southward the *Independencia* had also encountered the *Covadonga*. The forces of these adversaries were even more disproportionate than those of the first pair. The *Covadonga* was as much inferior to the *Esmeralda* as the *Independencia* was superior to the *Huáscar*. At the same hour, however, that the more

[2] For Grau see p. 479.
[2] For Grau see p. 479.

powerful vessel sank the weaker one at Iquique, the weaker of the Chilean vessels sank the more powerful Peruvian vessel at Punta Gruesa, a short distance from that port.

The *Independencia* with its formidable guns had pursued the *Covadonga* southward. The latter, drawing near the coast, kept up the fight while retreating. At the end of more than three hours of conflict, the *Independencia* had approached its adversary as if to cut it in two with its ram; but the *Covadonga,* a small ship of light draft, kept in the shallow sea among the reefs of Punta Gruesa. The *Covadonga* then advanced cannonading the *Independencia* to the point of yielding. Only immediate aid rendered by the *Huáscar* prevented the crew of the *Independencia* from surrendering. On trying to approach, the *Independencia* struck bottom, crushed in its prow, and keeled over, completely grounded. The *Covadonga* then escaped, pursued by Grau's powerful vessel; but, as the latter had shortly to abandon his pursuit because he feared to encounter a Chilean squadron, the other vessel proceeded to take refuge and repair its damages in the port of Antofagasta.

Such was the result of the naval combat of Iquique. Chile lost a poor and already worn-out bark which, however, was sunk in the water with almost all its crew and with its flag still flying. Chile also lost many men; of the two hundred that manned the *Esmeralda* only sixty were rescued by the *Huáscar;* but it gained a hero, Prat, whose act became for all Chileans the most glorious emblem of patriotism and whose name, from that day, proudly repeated on every lip in the battle, seemed to guide the armies to victory or to death. Peru, in exchange, lost its most formidable war vessel.

After the dead were buried in the city of Iquique, where Prat was also given honorable burial, the *Huáscar* betook itself to the south, and bombarded Antofagasta. It then returned to Callao in order to repair damages and, once more ready, returned to the south. On its course it seized, near Antofagasta, the Chilean transport *Rimac,* which was carrying a whole corps of the army and a large supply of arms and munitions. This deed produced in Santiago and in the principal cities of the country a great expression of protest against the naval leaders. The press and the houses of congress echoed this indignation. The blockade of Iquique was then raised, the squadron repaired to Valparaiso in order to prepare itself for a new campaign, and soon Admiral Williams Rebolledo presented his resignation. The naval captain, Galvarino Riveros, was substituted for him.

Meanwhile the *Huáscar* and other minor boats of Peru became the terror of the Chilean coast. For several months, Grau, astute and brave, had been able to frustrate pursuit from the enemy ships, but his success did not last. When the Chilean squadron reëntered the campaign, a plan was formed to hunt down the rapid, formidable Peruvian cruiser. In fact, Captain Juan José Latorre, commander of the Chilean cruiser *Cochrane*, encountered the *Huáscar* on its return from an excursion to the south, in front of Mejillones, at Angamos Point on October 8, 1879. Although the latter tried to flee, it did not succeed because the *Cochrane* was the speedier. At that very place, then, Latorre obliged the formerly terrible Grau to engage in combat. The action was not very long—an hour and a half. With the first discharges, Grau fell, torn to pieces by a shell which burst against the armored tower from which he was directing the vessel. Two officers, who successively occupied his post, fell also, swept by the fire. The *Blanco encalada*, a cruiser which Riveros directed, arrived to reinforce the action of the *Cochrane* and the great Peruvian vessel surrendered.[3] Shortly after, a Peruvian sloop, the *Pilcomayo*, also surrendered to its conquerors, and with this success the Chilean squadron remained mistress of the ocean. The remaining Peruvian vessels did not leave their ports. The *Huáscar* was repaired and incorporated in the Chilean navy.

Two campaigns were then completed, that of Antofagasta and that of the sea, in the course of eight months, February to October, 1879, and both resulted in a complete triumph for Chile. All was not ended, however, and a third campaign was begun immediately.

THE NORTHERN LAND CAMPAIGNS

The most energetic and sustained activity had been displayed in the three belligerent countries, while the maritime war lasted, in order to reorganize and increase their respective armies. Peru received, by way of Panama, arms purchased in the United States, and with them fitted out its army and that of Bolivia. Chile received arms from Europe by way of Magallanes and in a short time placed twelve thousand men in Antofagasta, where the Chilean general quarters had been established. It had not been necessary to resort to foreign credit in order to meet the extraordinary expenses of the war; internal credit had been sufficient. To assist in maintaining this credit, new issues of paper money were put out, administrative expenditures were restricted, the wages of public employees were temporarily reduced, and private donations were called for.

---

[3] See Hancock, *History of Chile,* pp. 285-288. The action was significant in that it was the first important test of ironclad vessels in warfare at sea. See also V. Figueroa, *Diccionario histórico,* III, 664-665.

Meanwhile, the allies, overcoming enormous financial difficulties, had established their general quarters in Iquique; and there, under the immediate inspection of Presidents Prado and Daza—the former stationed in Arica and the latter in Tacna—they had brought together fourteen thousand men. It was thought that Chile would not dare invade Peru through the southern desolate desert region. At the beginning of November, 1879, however, ten thousand Chilean soldiers landed at Pisague after a strenuous fight. They were, for the most part, vigorous miners of the pampas, commanded by General Erasmo Escala. The campaign of Tarapacá was opened. One battle only was all that was necessary to give the invading army control of that province.

Colonel Sotomayor left Pisagua with six thousand men to take possession of the rich and abundantly watered plain of Dolores, situated toward the southeast. Buendía,[4] the Peruvian general, in his turn, left Iquique with a division twice as large and marched northward to meet the enemy; while the president, General Daza, advanced from Tacna toward the south, in order to enclose the Chilean division between two fires. Before Daza could reach his destination, the army of Buendía was completely routed in Dolores by the troops of Sotomayor on November 19, 1879. On hearing this, Daza returned to Tacna without giving battle. The garrison of Iquique fled, as did the garrisons of other adjacent cities.

In a few days all the territory of Tarapacá was occupied by Chilean forces. But the defeat of the allies had a much greater result. On being informed of it, the populace in Peru and Bolivia were inflamed with anger against their presidents. Prado returned from Arica to Lima and was obliged to resign, after which he made a journey to the United States. The resignation of Prado gave rise to a revolution in Peru, headed by the celebrated popular agitator, Colonel Nicolás de Piérola. The revolution was a success and Piérola became dictator. A similar uprising occurred in Bolivia, where Daza was deposed and replaced by General Narciso Campero, a man of prestige and energy. Thus the year 1879 ended with the complete disorganization of the allies and the unconditional surrender of Antofagasta and Tarapacá to Chile.

At the beginning of 1880, Chilean troops began to invade a more northerly district of Peru. Thirteen thousand soldiers landed at Ilo and Pacocha, north of Arica, took possession of Moquegua, and opened the fourth stage of the struggle: the campaign of Tacna

---

[4] General Juan Buendía is mentioned and a different presentation of the Tarapacá campaign is given in Markham's *History of Peru,* pp. 380, 394. See also C. Reginald Enock, *Peru* (London, 1912), pp. 83-85.

and Arica. This time it was General Manuel Baquedano who directed operations. For the moment he met with no more resistance than was offered by a body of Peruvian troops, fortified on the heights of Los Angeles, slightly north of Moquegua. When this position was taken by assault, he hastened his march to Tacna. But he had to cross long deserts cut by steep mountain ridges and scarcely interrupted by two valleys—those of Locumba and Sama—where plantations of sugarcane and vineyards and fruit trees could furnish some refreshment to his army. In addition to the difficulties of the terrain there was added, for the rest of the way, the suffocating heat of the tropics.

All difficulties were overcome, however, and at the end of a two months' march, during which only one encounter took place with the enemy, the Chilean army came within sight of Tacna. The allied army, in charge of the president of Bolivia, General Campero, had fortified itself on the hills near the city, facing the so-called "Field of Alliance" on the southwest side. General Baquedano ordered an attack on their position. The battle of Tacna opened with horrible carnage. Nearly five thousand dead and wounded remained on the field. Of that number two thousand were Chileans, but the Chileans were victors, as before. The prisoners were very numerous, and the rest of Campero's troops were scattered when retreating into the interior. The city was occupied on May 26, 1880.

The port of Arica remained to be taken. It was blockaded by Chilean vessels but vigorously defended by fortifications provided with powerful artillery, by the iron-clad *Manco Capac* which had been converted into a floating battery, and by a numerous and warlike military division in command of one of the bravest and most capable of Peruvian leaders, Colonel Francisco Bolognesi.[5] This division was fortified on the Morro, a massive, flattop mountain overlooking the sea. This mountain was now encircled on its remaining sides by numerous dynamite mines. The assault of this fortress was successfully accomplished, however, twelve days after the occupation of Tacna, by a body of troops directed by Colonel Pedro Lagos. The brave Bolognesi died in action, and all of his subordinates either fell, dead or wounded, or were taken prisoner. The sailors of *Manco Capac* sank that vessel and surrendered to the blockaders.

Thus ended the campaign of Tacna and Arica, like that of Anto-

---

[5] Bolognesi (d. 1880), because of his sturdy defense of Arica against great odds, is one of the national heroes of Peru. For a description of the battle, in which he died, see Hancock, *op. cit.,* pp. 302-303.

fagasta and Tarapacá, with the complete conquest of the two Peruvian provinces. Meanwhile, the Chilean squadron blockaded the coast of Peru as far as Callao and also bombarded that port. The naval captain, Patricio Lynch, who had served many years in England, was put in charge of a military and naval division, which traversed the coast of northern Peru, imposing war taxes without hindrance and exercising acts of sovereignty. During that time military operations on land ceased, and it was thought that the war would come to an end. England offered the belligerents its friendly mediation to bring about peace. Chile accepted but Peru refused. The United States was more fortunate. The allies accepted the mediation offered them by the latter, with the secret hope of finding its government friendly. Chile also accepted the offer in good faith but without deceiving itself over the result of the conference.

In October, 1880, the North American plenipotentiaries and the representatives of the belligerent countries met in Arica, on board a North American cruiser, and held a conference generally known as the conference of Arica.[6] The Chilean representative, Eulogio Altamirano, laid down there the only conditions to which Chile could agree. Among these conditions was the definite cession of Antofagasta and Tarapacá to the victor. The representatives of the allies openly refused this condition, and the negotiations were ended.

THE LIMA CAMPAIGN AND THE END OF THE WAR

The friendly intervention of the United States was frustrated by the disagreement of Bolivia and Peru to the Chilean propositions. From that instant it was understood that a peace would have to be dictated at Lima. In Chile the press, congress, and the universal public opinion, as shown by meetings in various cities, demanded in no uncertain voice that the army advance against the Peruvian capital. "To Lima!" was the continuous cry. The government was forced to decide on the campaign against Lima. In the last two months of 1880 about twenty-five thousand Chileans, transported by land and by sea under the orders of General Baquedano, established their central headquarters on the banks of the Lurín River, about five leagues south of Lima. They had had to disembark at different ports, among which Pisco and Curayaco were the principal ones. Under a burning sun they had had to cross rugged mountains, desolate sands, and very fertile valleys, in which a multitude

---

[6] See W. R. Sherman, *The Diplomatic and Commercial Relations of the United States and Chile,* 1820-1914 (Boston, 1926), pp. 126-127. See also Evans, *Chile and its Relations with the United States,* pp. 102-104.

of Chinese who worked as slaves on the sugar and coffee plantations received them as liberators and accompanied them in the capacity of servants. Finally, they were separated from their fatherland by thousands of leagues, without other hope than victory or death.

On the side of Peru, Piérola, the dictator in Lima, worked miracles of patriotism and fortitude and was able to organize thirty thousand men to resist the Chileans. With surprising energy he fortified strategic positions immediately south of the city, especially the hills of Chorrillos and Miraflores. And so, in the first days of 1881, he had everything mined and entrenched there, ready for defense, but all in vain. On January 13 the Chilean troops with irresistible force carried the fortifications of Chorrillos at the point of the bayonet. On January 15 Miraflores also fell in the same way. After these battles, Baquedano received the unconditional surrender of Lima. Meanwhile, the populace sacked the capital as well as Callao, where the last Peruvian cruiser, *Atahualpa*, was converted into a bonfire and sunk. It was necessary for the Chilean army to make a hurried entrance into these cities in order to prevent the rabble from continuing its pillage.[7]

The events at Chorrillos and Miraflores marked the end of the war. Piérola, who escaped from Lima, tried unsuccessfully to raise the Indians of the interior in revolt and to organize resistance anew. Another leader, Colonel Avelino Cáceres, succeeded him, and others came later, keeping Peru for two years in a condition of complete anarchy, with guerrilla uprisings everywhere, which different bodies of the Chilean army had to oppose relentlessly. In one of those campaigns of the sierra, a Chilean detachment of seventy-seven men, under the command of Captain Ignacio Carrera Pinto,[8] was surrounded in the town of Concepcíon by Peruvian forces which numbered eighteen hundred—both Indians and regular troops. After fighting for twenty hours in the vicinity of the town plaza, all the Chileans fell under the banner that they sworn to defend. This was on July 9 and 10, 1882.

Meanwhile, a time came when it was thought peace was within sight. Shortly after the occupation of Lima, its military commander, the navy captain, Patricio Lynch, favored the election of Presi-

[7] For a contrary account of the events marking the capture and occupation of Lima, see Markham, *History of Peru,* pp. 410-417.

[8] Ignacio Carrera Pinto (1848-1882), born in Santiago, was a grandson of José Miguel Carrera (see p. 460). At the beginning of the War of the Pacific he entered the army as sergeant and was a captain at the time of his heroic death. See Pedro P. Figueroa, *Diccionario biográfico,* I, 304; V. Figueroa, *op. cit.,* II, 369.

dent Francisco García Calderón, who established his government in a town near Lima called La Magdalena; but, when a definitive treaty was about to be signed, the latter declared that he would not sign it on the basis of a cession of territory. He thought that the United States would intervene in favor of Peru; and the hope of that intervention induced him to refuse to come to any agreement. Ultimately, the Chilean army of occupation annulled his authority and sent him as a prisoner to Santiago. Not until 1883 could peace be mentioned, through the elevation of General Miguel Iglesias to the head of the government of Peru. He was an eminent man who succeeded in imposing a policy of peace and regeneration upon the anarchical chiefs.

The peace conferences took place in Ancón, a town situated north of Lima, and in October, 1883, the treaty with Peru was signed there. By the Treaty of Ancón, Peru ceded to Chile the perpetual ownership of the province of Tarapacá and the sovereignty of the provinces of Tacna and Arica for ten years, at the end of which time a plebiscite of its inhabitants should decide to which of the two countries they should definitely belong. The country with which the provinces should remain was to pay the other country ten million pesos.[9] Furthermore, an arbitration tribunal was created in order to pass on the claims of Chileans injured by the war, just as Chile had already covenanted with the governments of England, France, Italy, and Germany to recognize the claims of their respective citizens, injured by the same cause.[10]

Months later, a truce with Bolivia was signed in Valparaiso,[11] by which all the Bolivian territory included between the Andes and the Pacific, or rather, the actual province of Antofagasta, was definitely left under the sovereignty of Chile.

---

[9] For the text of the Treaty of Ancón, see Dennis, *Documentary History,* pp. 220-224. See also his *Tacna and Arica,* chap. ix.

[10] The covenant with France is dated November 2, 1882, and is given in *British and Foreign State Papers,* LXXIV, 128-132; for other covenants see *ibid.,* pp. 321-324, and LXXV, 495, 1102-1105.

[11] For the text of this truce, see Dennis, *Documentary History,* pp. 225-227.

CHAPTER XVI

THE PERIOD OF EXPANSION

SANTA MARÍA AND THE LIQUIDATION OF THE WAR OF THE PACIFIC

IN FACT, the War of the Pacific had ended with the occupation of the capital of Peru in January, 1881. Chile remained in possession of the rich nitrate and copper lands, whose development had given rise to the conflict. The production of those territories and the abundant incomes which thereby accrued to many private individuals, and more fully to the State at the same time opened up in the country a period of economic development whose swift progress was evident and was felt among all social classes. This period lasted ten years, until the unhappy revolution of 1891 interrupted it. But the national drive which it signified did not immediately cease. The political events of those years could not resist the influence of that powerful expansion.

In March, 1881, General Baquedano returned from Lima. His reception in Santiago was quite an apotheosis; and, as had happened forty years before with General Bulnes, there was a strong current of opinion in the country which desired to reward the skillful and valorous leader with the first magistracy of the republic. General Baquedano ought to have succeeded President Pinto that same year, but the liberal majority of the government did not accept his candidacy and he forthwith gave up the contest. The general was a conservative, and, moreover, it was felt that his presidency would signify the return to a regime of force which liberalism was unwilling to admit.

Another candidate then arose, aided by the main part of the dominant parties (liberal, national, and radical) and by President Pinto himself. This aspirant was Domingo Santa María, who, counting on official aid, was elected without competition and began his term of five years on September 18, 1881. Santa María had spent more than thirty years in public life and had been one of the revolutionists who had opposed Montt's administration. Having been exiled for that reason, he traveled to Europe and on his return again entered politics. He was deputy, senator, and minister. During a great part of the War of the Pacific he was at the head of the ministries of foreign relations and of the interior. When he became president, his partisans considered him an experienced and energetic statesman.

The government of Santa María had to devote much time to the settlement of the war. It was a tiresome diplomatic task. While the Chilean forces occupied Lima and fought the leaders in the Peruvian mountains, Piérola, Cáceres, and others, the United States government showed evident intentions of intervening against Chile. Argentina, at the instigation of Peru, tried to insure the meeting of an American congress at Panama (previously projected by Colombia) for the purpose of having the right of conquest condemned therein, or rather, the annexation of territory as compensation for war. On the other hand, the European powers annoyed the Chilean government with a multitude of claims for damages their citizens were said to have suffered in consequence of hostilities.

Many a grave question strained all the nerves of Chilean diplomacy. It finally succeeded in causing the United States to relinquish thoughts of intervention; [1] it also brought about the failure of the congress of Panama; and as for the claims, it formed treaties with European powers by which the pretensions of the claimants were submitted to arbitration. Thus all dangers were dissipated, the treaties of 1883 and of 1884 could be signed, and with these acts the conflict of the three republics ended.

At the same time the definite submission of the Araucanians was brought about. During the War of the Pacific, the troops that guarded the Araucanian frontier were greatly depleted, for entire companies were drawn away and transferred to Peru. Taking advantage of this situation, the natives rose in arms in 1880 and in their surprise attacks (*malones*) raided all the neighboring territory. The garrisons of some forts had to retreat, and the territory of the Traiguén, formerly occupied, saw its security endangered.

But when Lima was taken, the first of the returning troops were sent to put down that rebellion. Colonel Gregorio Urrutia, in command of the army of the frontier, gained control in two years of the lines of the Curacautín and of the Upper Biobío on the slopes of the Andes. New communities like Temuco, Carahue, and Nueva Imperial arose under the protection of the military operations, and new colonists of foreigners and nationalists furthered the occupation of the territories incorporated in the republic. The locomotive also shortly crossed these regions; the first lines over which it ran were those from Angol to Traiguén and from Collipulli to Victoria. The last remains of the brave Araucanian race thus were reduced to a small amount of territory and subjected to a protectorate under laws enacted by the national government (1883).

---

[1] See Evans, *Chile and its Relations with the United States*, pp. 112-118.

Great relief was felt in the country over the conclusion of this struggle and especially over the settlement of the war against Peru and Bolivia. Chile came to exercise supremacy in South America and increased its territory by more than a third. A new era of peace and labor was opened. The exploitation and exportation of nitrates, borates, and iodine, continuing to increase in Tarapacá and Antofagasta, went on constantly adding to private wealth and especially to the public revenues in a startling and unparalleled manner. From fifteen million before the war, the revenues grew five years later to more than thirty-six million and continued to increase in similar proportion.

With these abundant receipts, pensions were paid to the families of those who died in the war and compensation offered to those disabled in the same conflict; the wages of public employees were increased and new administrative positions were created; various public works were continued, and others begun; foreign immigration was encouraged; and, finally, effective assistance was given to the development of agriculture and mining by opening new roads, constructing bridges, and establishing technical instruction under European teachers.

Those revenues served for everything except for redeeming paper money. And such redemption was, notwithstanding, a duty, because the currency had been issued by the State and under its guarantee, as an extraordinary measure during the economic crisis marking the beginning of Pinto's administration and the end of the international crisis. It came about, then, that the paper peso depreciated to the value of twenty-five pennies while the gold and silver coin was worth forty-eight pennies or, at least, thirty-nine. Trade, which had to pay its European creditors in specie, exported metallic currency. This resulted in the shipping out of silver and gold and the triumph of the paper-money regime. But as this became worth about half as much as the former money, the merchants raised prices in even greater proportion. The cost of living suddenly increased, and transactions subject to fluctuations of international exchange were rendered unstable and insecure. The mass of consumers suffered the consequences of this depreciation in the purchasing power of the national coinage and did not fail to raise protests.

CIVIC REFORMS AND CONSTITUTIONAL CONTROVERSIES; BALMACEDA

More engrossing to the government than the economic and social problem arising from the paper-money regime was the election of a new archbishop. In 1878 Rafael Valentín Valdivieso, head of the

Chilean Church for thirty years, died in Santiago. No priest ever left in the country better memories for virtue and charity. His whole life had been a constant struggle not only in behalf of his faith but, more than that, in behalf of the poor to whom he always gave what he had, even sacrificing for them every comfort and pleasure.

But this humble and kindly man became harsh and unyielding when he thought the prerogatives of his Church were attacked. More than once, therefore, he saw himself enveloped in bitter conflicts with the civil authority, whose right of "ecclesiastical patronage" he accepted only under protest on every occasion when it was exercised. For this reason the government at his death desired to fill his place with a priest who would be a pledge of harmony between Church and State. It actually elected Canon Francisco de Paula Taforó, also an eminent churchman of blameless life but possessed of outstanding liberal ideas, and proposed him to the pope for appointment. The clergy of Santiago and the conservative party were alarmed; they opposed the selection and succeeded in having the pope withhold the nomination.

Once in power, Santa María asked the Vatican to hasten the affair; but the Vatican gave itself time to consider it and meanwhile sent Monseñor Celestino del Frate[2] as "apostolic delegate" to settle difficulties with Chile. Del Frate, learning in Santiago the previous history of the affair, advised His Holiness that the nomination of the prebendary Taforó ought to be rejected. The relations of the government and the delegate became strained, and the latter soon received his passport. Del Frate left the country, after having insinuated in a note directed to the minister of religion that he did not recognize the right of patronage exercised by the government of Chile (1883).

This insinuation made against a liberal government accused of being antireligious was somewhat dogmatic, as well as being very imprudent. It is not strange, therefore, that it was taken as a provocation. Congress, which also was liberal and almost entirely attached to the government, at once undertook to busy itself in the discussion of the so-called "theological reforms" which had so stirred opinion during the administration of Errázuriz Zañartu. Although it debated much concerning the separation of Church and State, it reached no agreement in respect to the status of the Church when it should once become free; and this and other differences caused the failure of the separatist project. On the other

---

[2] For an unfriendly view of the attitude of the Santa María government toward this mission, see Carlos Walker Martínez, *Historia de la administración de Santa María,* Vol. I, chap. vii.

hand, a law was passed creating secular cemeteries; that is, common cemeteries for individuals of any religious belief whatever; and by this law public and municipal cemeteries were of that type. As the clergy protested with passionate violence against the passage of the law, the president issued a decree prohibiting the establishment of private cemeteries of a religious character.

Laws concerning civil marriage and civil registry were also approved and passed. By these the clergy lost its ancient right of legally establishing the family. Since that time this has become a function of the State, with the Church absolutely cut off from its former practices. So great was the opposition made everywhere by the clergy against these laws, stigmatizing them as "sacrilegious," that the country seemed on the verge of a revolution. The year of these reforms, 1884, was also the year of the law of personal rights, which limited to certain determined cases the right of the judicial and administrative authorities to arrest private persons.

This was not all that was done by the reform spirit animating the Santa María administration. It also fought, as for some time liberalism had been fighting, to restrict the powers of the president of the republic. One law provided that every constitutional reform which the president of the republic might reject or veto should be passed, however, if congress insisted upon it, by a two-thirds vote of each house. Another law (1885), that of home rule (*régimen interior*), deprived the intendants and governors of many of their prerogatives; and, finally, a reform of the election law extended suffrage to every [male] Chilean twenty-five years old who could read and write, without the necessity of having the income required by the Constitution of 1833 as a condition for exercising this right. This was universal suffrage in full measure.

The government of Santa María was not, however, one of political liberty; far from it, indeed, for no president exercised to the same extent as he did the right of intervening in elections—the basis for all the other powers. In this way he made congresses and excluded his adversaries from the ballot box by all kinds of violence. The congress of 1885 had special interest because on its composition depended the election of the next president. This time, official intervention went to deplorable extremes, occasioning bloody disturbances. But although the government obtained an overwhelming majority, the disorganization now affecting the liberal groups immediately transformed the legislative assembly into a veritable camp. Many of the older liberals broke with their party and acted independently, thus swelling the ranks of the opposition. They were called "the unattached." Many radicals did the same with respect to their party; and thus was constituted a formidable opposing coalition composed of radicals and dissenting liberals, who united with the conservatives.

The motive provoking the want of harmony in the bosom of liberalism was none other than the discord into which their groups were thrown over the presidential candidate to succeed Santa María. The parties of the government (national, liberal, and non-dissenting radical) had as their candidate, José Manuel Balmaceda, who was also the candidate of the chief of state.

This politician at forty-five years of age had spent twenty years in public life. He had been an excellent student in the seminary at Santiago and had even shown a predilection for the priesthood; but, on leaving the hall of learning, literary and scientific reading drew him away from his faith. In the silence of the country, where he spent some time in agricultural pursuits, the rebellion of his spirit seemed to be strengthened, and, on entering politics, he became a liberal and a reformer. Rich, distinguished, tall in stature, he succeeded without the professional title that was almost necessary for those who aspired to leadership. He had a facility for words, and was graceful in delivery and brilliant in expression. During the administration of Errázuriz and Pinto, he was frequently heard in the house of deputies, in reform clubs, and in public assemblies. And finally, during the Santa María administration, he was minister of interior and an important, if not a principal, factor in the theological and constitutional reforms accomplished during that period.

When Balmaceda became official candidate for the presidency of the republic, the unattached liberals and conservatives opposed him stubbornly in the legislature. They tried to overthrow the cabinet that had been appointed to intervene in the presidential election, but did not succeed. Then they adopted an extreme measure. The term of the tax bill was to expire on January 5, 1886. In order to be able to make collections, the new bill had to be enacted on that day. If it were not, the government would lack funds to carry on the administration. The numerous minority, composed of influential men, unceasingly obstructed the passage of that bill in the house of deputies. January 5 arrived, and the bill could not be passed. The ministry would have to fall and the candidacy of Balmaceda would be withdrawn. The majority then convened the house in permanent session. Pedro Montt presided over that assembly. At daybreak on January 9, 1886, Montt declared the debate closed on the tax bill, in the midst of the most heated protests of the opposition, which tried to keep up its objection. Put to a vote, the bill was naturally approved. With this action of the majority, the ministry was saved and also the Balmaceda candidacy. The electoral struggle assumed a violent character. Again blood ran, but all resistance was useless. The intervening governmental force brought victory to the candidate whom it supported.

THE GOVERNMENT OF BALMACEDA; GREAT PUBLIC WORKS

The government of José Manuel Balmaceda was characterized from the beginning by extraordinary political and administrative activity. His first cabinet, headed by Eusebio Lillo, was formed of persons acceptable to the opposition minority. It was the purpose of the president to unite anew all liberal groups or, as he said, "to reconcile the great liberal family," leaving only the conservatives in opposition. That first cabinet at once partially revealed this purpose. It did not last, however, more than two months. It was then replaced by a ministry of reconciliation, as it was called, because in it were included two men of the liberal national opposition. But neither did this cabinet maintain itself in power very long, and after its fall there followed an unavoidable ministerial rotation, aided by the most confused political disorganization. Nevertheless, the president desired to carry on the government in peace with all factions, and even tried to cajole the conservatives by settling the archiepiscopal controversy that had originated in the former administration in accordance with the wishes of the papal court. With the naming of Mariano Casanova as archbishop of Santiago in 1887, harmonious relations with the pope were restored.

Meanwhile the public revenue kept increasing rapidly and afforded a relief never before attained by the national treasury. It rose from thirty-seven millions in 1886 to fifty-eight and a half million in 1890. The active exploitation and exportation of nitrate in Tarapacá and Antofagasta now began to bring into the State many millions of pesos annually through the operation of the customs tax which was levied on its exportation. This tax, together with the other duties levied on trade which increased with unusual rapidity (for annual imports increased from forty-four million pesos in 1886 to sixty-eight million in 1890), fostered by the prosperity of all the productive resources of the country, permitted the government to make considerable disbursements in undertakings and services of social importance, the necessity of which began to be manifest.

During this time great public works were continued or begun which were to give luster to the Balmaceda administration and to remain as testimony of its industrious and enterprising spirit. The mere enumeration of them is a long task in itself: more than a thousand kilometers of railroads; many safe bridges over rivers in the central zone; extensive wagon roads repaired or newly surveyed; the service of telegraph lines and the installation of running water in many cities; many large, commodious buildings for *intendencias*, government offices, jails, hospitals, and primary schools; the canalization of the Mapocho River in all its course through the city of Santiago; the construction of wharves in different ports and of the great breakwater at Talcahuano; and many other betterments. It was a veritable orgy of material progress and even a new department of state had to be created to look after it—the ministry of public works in 1887, which now made a sixth ministry.

On the other hand, public instruction also obtained favorable attention. Higher studies were revised, especially the courses in medicine. The Pedagogic Institute (*Instituto pedagógico*) was founded in 1889 for the purpose of forming a corps of teachers of secondary education. A new system called "concentric" was installed in this institution. New *lycées* for boys and girls and the first *lycées* for girls were founded. The National Dormitory (*Internado nacional*) with room for about a thousand students was built as a complement to the National Institute. Primary education was again regulated, standardized, and extended by the founding of hundreds of schools. In intellectual as well as in material effort, then, the administration of Balmaceda set itself to realize works that were enduring and of positive value for the country.

In a different department of governmental activity, that of financial administration, important reforms were also introduced. The taxing system was modified in an effort to make it more nearly equal for different social classes; and along with the ancient *alcabala* other imposts of minor importance were suppressed. Furthermore, there was created the tribunal of accounts, an office to inspect the expenditure of funds of the State. Part of the public debt was canceled; but paper money was not redeemed.

The army and navy also were considerably improved. The land forces renewed their equipment, changing it entirely for the more modern type in use in Europe; and, to increase the fleet, the construction of two new cruisers and two torpedo boats was ordered. Finally, colonization in the south and immigration were amply furthered by the State.

The republic seemed on the way to safe and rapid growth. However, a great calamity came upon the country during that period (1886-1887). This was the cholera, an epidemic that caused enormous damage and innumerable deaths; but at least it obliged the country to reform completely its charitable and health services.

On the other hand, the laboring class in the cities, now partly conscious of its right to a greater participation in the general wealth and to a freer and more cultured life, began to organize itself into societies and to show discontent by provoking the first strikes ever known in Chile. This agitation, among other causes, was brought about by the lowering of international exchange, which, lessening the value of paper money, cut down the day's wage, raised the price of food, and encouraged the immigration of foreigners, who, entering into competition with Chilean workmen, prevented the raising of wages. These movements were the origin and reason for the existence of the democratic party, a small but unruly group founded in 1887, which from that time on began to take part in electoral and political struggles under the intelligent and firm direction of Malaquías Concha, a lawyer of note, who founded and aided it for many years, until it became an important factor in the government. The seed then sown has borne even more fruit since his day.

Internal policy was complicated by all this. The old parties, more disordered than ever, broken up into different groups and almost dissolved, failed to come to an understanding with the executive. Ministries came and went. One after another, combinations were formed today only to fall tomorrow. As before, the president was the most powerful elector of congress. Although official intervention in elections during this period did not reach the frequently bloody character of the preceding period, it was not for that reason less effective. However, the president perceived that those who were friendly to him during the period of their candidacy became hostile to him when once elected. But above all else he wished to show himself liberal, and so he assisted and even took the lead in electoral reforms that congress was forced to sanction. A law was enacted declaring that the "majority" age for exercising the electoral right should be twenty-one years instead of twenty-five as fixed by the constitution; the position of "substitute deputy," created by the former law, was suppressed and the "cumulative vote" was extended to all elections. It will be remembered that in the constitutional reforms of 1874 senators were excluded from that type of election.

Those reforms, which broadened the right of suffrage, which offered to minorities an expeditious means of strengthening their representation in both branches of congress by the use of the cumulative vote, and which tended to democratize the government still more, were not put in force under the presidency of Balmaceda because, on nearing the end of his term, the extraordinary controversy concerning internal policy which arose did not permit him to develop any initiative but fatally brought him to revolution and civil war.

THE REVOLUTION OF 1891

During the year 1890 President Balmaceda found himself involved in the gravest constitutional conflict that up to that time had ever existed in the republic. The opposition had come to be a majority in congress. The political camps were marked off with great precision. On the side of the government there was only a narrow liberal nucleus, and on the side of the opposition, a real amalgamation of parties—unattached liberals, nationals, radicals, and conservatives. This majority criticised governmental acts with uncontrollable persistence. An abundance of paper money had introduced prodigality in administrative affairs, as shown in useless employees, exaggerated cost of public works, and pensions dispensed abroad. Here the opposition had its chance to lash the president.

The official candidate to succeed Balmaceda was now under discussion and for this honor Enrique Salvador Sanfuentes, then minister of the interior, had been designated. Parliamentary opposition was used at that point to break down the cabinet and the candidacy. The president, already greatly annoyed, maintained that congress had no more right to impose on him a minister of its choice than to prescribe for him the clothes he ought to wear and the food he ought to eat. The parliamentary majority then denied him authorization to collect the taxes. It was the same weapon that had been wielded against Santa María, with the difference, certainly essential, that on that occasion it was the minority that wielded it. The president finally gave way and named a new cabinet to the satisfaction of the majority. The tax measure was adopted.

But then came still more serious events. The "cabinet of conciliation" fell, and the president substituted for it another from the minority led by Claudio Vicuña. Congress had now closed its session; it could not, therefore, censure the act. But the appropriation bill for 1891 had not been discussed or approved. For this purpose the president ought to have convened congress in extraordinary session, but he did not do so. Thus January 1, 1891, arrived. The president issued a manifesto to the country declaring that the same appropriation bill would be in force for that year as for the previous year. The constitutional conflict came to an end. The president concluded by violating the constitution and assuming actual dictatorship.

In the face of such an attitude, congress answered immediately with revolution. At daybreak on January 7, 1891, the vessels of the national fleet anchored in Valparaiso Bay raised anchor and went northward to open the insurrection against the executive. The naval captain, Jorge Montt, was in command of the vessels with the title of commander of the fleet by appointment of the vice-president of the senate, Waldo Silva, and the president of the house of deputies, Ramón Barros Luco. At the same time there was published an act signed by a majority of the members of congress by which President Balmaceda was deposed for having violated the constitution of the republic. News of these events circulated throughout the country with the speed and force of lightning. The country was in full civil war. Of the fleet, Balmaceda had left only a few transports, but the army, which was determined to support the dictatorship without reflection, remained loyal to him.

The revolutionists established their government at Iquique. It was directed by a junta which was composed of Montt, Silva, and Barros. After several encounters they took possession of the provinces of Tacna, Tarapacá, Antofagasta, and Atacama, and organized an army, employing the most modern weapons that they could get in Europe and using funds obtained principally from the nitrate revenues. As the population of those provinces showed themselves almost entirely favorable to congress, it was not necessary to carry on cruel persecutions against them after the authorities were deposed and the garrisons conquered.

Balmaceda, in turn, augmented his army with prodigious activity. His agents formed levies of countrymen who were taken away from their work by force. He declared the whole country in a state of siege, deposed the revolutionary congress, decreed new elections, and constituted a new congress. He brought together a convention which named Claudio Vicuña as candidate for the presidency of the republic. Vicuña was elected in June without opposition. He issued paper money and made requisitions of crops and animals from the farms of his enemies. On the other hand, he deprived of office all public officials who opposed him, imprisoned all men that seemed dangerous, closed the opposition presses, and established a diligent espionage over all prominent homes.

The military operations were long and bloody, as were also the naval operations. Among these, the sinking of the cruiser *Blanco encalada*, the flagship of the constitutional fleet, was to be deplored. During the revolution there arrived from England the torpedo boats, *Condell* and *Lynch*, the construction of which had been previously ordered. Put at the service of the dictatorship, they waylaid the *Blanco encalada*, anchored in Caldera, and a torpedo from the *Lynch* sank it.

The revolution lasted more than seven months and its end was not yet in sight. Meanwhile, the great majority of the country declared themselves opposed to Balmaceda. Everywhere conspiracies were formed against him and guerrilla bands organized. The jails overflowed with political prisoners, and in them torture was a common means of drawing out confessions in regard to revolutionary secrets. Indignation reached its height when a party of young men of wealthy families were surprised while organizing a guerrilla band in Lo Cañas, a farm near Santiago belonging to the conservative leader, Carlos Walker Martínez. Troops attacked them unexpectedly and many were killed. The prisoners were executed on the spot.

Finally, in the middle of August the revolutionary army, composed of ten thousand men, landed at Quinteros, a little north of Valparaiso, under the command of Colonel Estanislao del Canto. Balmaceda now had forty thousand soldiers but could send only a fourth of that number against the enemy. The battle occurred at Concón, near the mouth of the Aconcagua River. The army of the dictator was routed. The prisoners took arms on the side of the conquerors on August 21, 1891. Seven days later a new battle took place at Placilla, near Valparaiso, which was a fresh victory for the revolutionists and this time definitive. The two battles cost the contenders a loss of eight thousand men, including killed and wounded. Among the first was the illustrious commander of the army, General Orozimbo Barboza.

Midday of August 28 had hardly passed when the result of the battle at Placilla, which occurred that morning, was known in Valparaiso and in Santiago. Valparaiso surrendered to the emissaries of the revolution; but it was the victim of a frightful pillage, inflicted by the rabble round about. The capital had no better fate. The houses of men well known to be in sympathy with the dictatorship and also many places of private business were destroyed the following morning in broad daylight. The same thing also occurred in adjacent suburbs.

But the pillage in Santiago was inexcusable. Balmaceda had abdicated power early on the morning of the twenty-ninth in favor of General Manuel Baquedano, a neutral in the contest, and had placed a whole military division at his orders to guard the inhabitants. The general intervened too tardily, however, in repressing the excesses.

Some days later, Jorge Montt and the other members of the junta of government arrived to install themselves in the capital. The revolution of 1891 was over. It had cost the nation ten thousand lives and more than a hundred million pesos; and it had cost private persons enormous sacrifices and losses. In return, the country gained a new political rule, that of parliamentarism, by which the executive power was made subject to congress. One could not make sure that this result was sufficient compensation.

Meanwhile, after his abdication, President Balmaceda had taken refuge in the Argentine legation. From here he could look upon the glorification of his adversaries and the manifestations of wrath and vengeance against his person and his friends. Nervous and disquieted, he awaited in his hiding place the day which should end the period of his presidency. He could have fled, putting the ranges of the Andes between himself and his avengers. In Argentina he could have found refuge, as so many of his partisans already had done; but he considered flight unworthy. He thought for a moment of giving himself up to his enemies and awaiting the hour to defend himself; but he feared he would not be respected by those who should judge him.

He formed then an irrevocable resolution—suicide. September 18 1891, arrived, the legal end of his period. He wrote several letters to members of his family and to his most intimate friends. He also wrote a kind of manifesto, his political testament, in which he explained and tried to justify his acts. On the next day he arose early and dressed himself in severe black; then lying on his bed, he took a revolver, pressed the barrel to his right temple, and fired the shot which instantly killed him.

CHAPTER XVII

CULTURAL AND SOCIAL PROGRESS

The fiery political struggles and the two international wars that agitated the liberal period considerably extended civic education in the country and aroused the sense of nationality. At the same time, they also gave an impulse to culture, awakening ambitions for the realization of which study was necessary. The steamship lines sailing to Europe continually brought Chile nearer the nations of greatest literary and scientific progress, permitted the wealthiest men to undertake knowledge-provoking journeys, and brought about a more frequent exchange in publications, while at the same time communication was accelerated. Although it already had fallen into disuse, the "censoring of books" established in the times of Portales and designed to forbid the introduction of those thought undesirable was suppressed at the end of Pinto's administration. Free reading, much less expensive than formerly, necessarily raised the average level of intelligence.

Further, the effort that the governments had put into developing public education in all its branches necessarily contributed its benefit to general culture. At the end of Balmaceda's administration there were already distributed throughout the whole country some fifteen hundred schools, government or private, which were attended by no less than eighty thousand children of both sexes. Although this number did not correspond to even a fourth of the scholastic population, nevertheless these schools for a long time had been creating a genuine foundation of culture.

The National Institute and the provincial high schools also seemed to be well attended; and, as the governing class of citizens had to come from them, special attention was devoted to these institutions. Normal schools for men and women, designed for the preparation of a corps of primary teachers, were other important centers of common learning. The seminaries of each diocese educated, likewise, a multitude of young men either for the priesthood or for ordinary life. Many private colleges—like those belonging to religious congregations and those supported by the government—under the direction of distinguished educators contributed to the same cultural ends. Higher professional instruction attracted a greater number of students every year; and every year also a large number of lawyers, engineers, doctors, dentists, and pharmacists, all active, trained young men, left their halls. The state university already felt the competition of the Catholic University, established in 1888 by the archbishop to give a religious basis to professional studies.

Moreover, institutions of other kinds, such as libraries, museums, scientific and literary societies, were exercising their influence on general learning. The "Circle of Friends of Letters" founded at the end of Montt's administration, and later the "Academy of Fine Arts" and the "Progress Club" were among these centers. Their contests, their public lectures, and their discussions stimulated scholarly pursuits and revealed a literary flowering of no small value. Almost all the men who at that time had any part in the intellectual or political activity of the country belonged to those societies.

Nothing, however, showed better this slow but sure development of national culture than the progress of the daily and periodical press. In 1860 there were only two substantial dailies in the country: *El ferrocarril* (*The Railway*) of Santiago and *El mercurio* (*The Mercury*) of Valparaiso. Thirty years later there were no less than twenty in the different cities of the republic. Seven were maintained in the capital alone. Half a hundred periodicals in cities of lesser importance made a chorus with these. With the War of the Pacific, sellers of "extras" appeared in the more populous centers, boys who satisfied the curiosity and eagerness of the public for events of the campaign by everywhere calling out the daily newssheets. Among the educated class, the daily was, from that time on, as necessary as food. Telegraph service with the outside world gave greater interest to its columns.

Among the most celebrated newspaper writers of that period were the Arteaga Alemparte brothers (Justo and Domingo), José Antonio Torres, Manuel Blanco Cuartín, and Zoróbabel Rodríguez. For the rest, the list would be innumerable, for scarcely any of the Chileans who left a name in politics or in letters refrained from entering journalism, at least for a number of years. Reviews were also maintained with an increasing number of subscribers. Besides those edited under the patronage of fraternities or of professional associations—like the *Revista médica* (*Medical Review*), the *Revista forense* (*Forensic Review*), and various educational reviews—there were others of a more general literary and scientific character. One of the first and most influential was *La Semana* (*The Week*, 1859-1860) of the Arteaga Alemparte brothers. In this publication they began to show their notable qualities of style—vivacity, conciseness, energy. But their merit rested principally on a later work entitled *Los constituyentes chilenos de 1870 (The Chilean Constituents of 1870)*, a fine volume of critical-biographical editorials.

Later came new periodical publications, among them the *Revista del Pacífico*, the *Estrella de Chile (Star of Chile)*, and the *Revista chilena*, in which almost all writers of the period collaborated. The variety and importance of the writings in these publications and their serious tone make all these reviews, even now, copious sources of information. The *Anales de la universidad* and the *Revista católica*—fruits of the literary movement of 1842—completed the picture of intellectual production in the world of periodicals.

LETTERS, HISTORIOGRAPHY, AND THE NATIONAL ARTS

The highest representatives of letters in the nineteenth century concentrated their efforts on valuable books. In 1865 the life of Andrés Bello, the wise publicist who had been something of a mentor for two generations of Chileans, peacefully came to an end. He died at the age of eighty-four when young men still sought friendly intercourse with him. His influence on literature as a critic and master of language who wrought with equal ability in prose and verse, as internationalist, and as jurist survived for a long time. [His poetry, among which the free translation of *The Prayer for All* by Victor Hugo is preëminent; his discourses, among which is considered best the one with which he inaugurated the university; his *Gramática de la lengua castellana (Grammar of the Spanish Language)*; his *Principios de derecho internacional (Principles of International Law)*; and, lastly, the *Código civil chileno (Civil Code of Chile)* which he edited, as well as many other pamphlets and articles, have formed for him one of the most enduring pedestals that any intelligent, industrious man has been able to acquire in Chile.] [1]

---

[1] The portion enclosed in brackets occurs in the sixth edition of Galdames' *Estudio* but was omitted from the seventh. Bello's *Gramática* appeared in Santiago in 1847 (2nd ed. Paris, 1874). A reprint was published in his *Obras completas*, Vol. IV (Santiago, 1883). His *Principios de derecho de jentes* was first published in Santiago in 1833 and reprinted under the title *Principios de derecho internacional* in Santiago in 1861. See his *Obras completas*, Vol. X. His *Proyecto de código civil* (Santiago, 1853) was edited and reprinted in 1865 (*Obras completas*, Vols. XI, XII). *Proyecto inédito de código civil,* based upon his subsequent corrections and annotations, appears in *Obras completas,* Vol. XIII (Santiago, 1890).

But shortly, with new men, new ideas prevailed in the country. José Victorino Lastarria, the aged professor of the institute and celebrated parliamentarian of the mid-century, was one of the guides of the new generation. Although politics absorbed the greater part of his time, it was not politics that gave him his solid reputation and his powerful influence on the intellectual development of the republic. Rather, it was literature—his books. Therefore he has been called, as was Bello, "master."

He carried his uncompromising liberal tendencies into his writings. Among his many works three are most important; namely, *Lecciones de política positiva* (*Lessons of Positive Politics*), a book with a philosophical purpose, although not very clear and hardly practical; *La América*, a work also political in tone, in which, after demonstrating the vices of the old Spanish organization, he tried to set up new principles so that true democracy might be realized on the continent; and *Recuerdos literarios* (*Literary Memories*), a long defense of his intellectual life in which he has at the same time written the history of Chilean literature during the first fifty years of the constitutional era of the republic.[2] Always struggling against the indifference of his fellow countrymen, Lastarria died after seventy years, in 1888.

Much less fortunate than Lastarria, however, was another of the liberal propagandists, whose personality has been the most discussed in Chile; namely, his disciple, Francisco Bilbao. Expatriated in consequence of the revolutionary movement of 1851, he lived in Peru and Argentina. He died in the capital of the latter country long before Lastarria (1866). Leading an unfortunate, outlawed existence, he issued from his exile numerous revolutionary treatises, principally anticlerical, such as *La América en peligro* (*America in Danger*), that were in no respect unworthy of the author of *Sociabilidad chilena*.[3] Although none of his efforts merit the name of "works" and leave much to be desired in the way of clearness and

---

[2] See p. 485. The first edition of the *Lecciones* appeared in Santiago in 1875. The first part of *La América* was written and published in Buenos Aires in 1865, the second and third parts in Santiago in 1867. The first edition of *Recuerdos* appeared in Santiago in 1878; a second edition, enlarged and illustrated, was published in Santiago in 1885. For an appreciative article on Lastarria, see Agusto Orrego Luco's "Don Victorino Lastarria: Impressiones y recuerdos," in *Revista chilena*, I (April, 1917), 5-47. See also Armando Donoso, "Sarmiento y Lastarria" in *ibid.*, X (May, 1920), 5-34. For a less favorable view, see Cruz, *Estudios sobre la literatura chilena*, I, 59-143.

[3] For a reference to Bilbao and his *Sociabilidad chilena* (Santiago, 1844), see p. 279. The secnod edition of *La América en peligro* was published in Buenos Aires in 1862.

correctness of language, it is a fact that the remembrance of his struggles as an agitator of the masses during the middle of the century and of his passion for the betterment of the workingman made of him for many years a gigantic moral figure. His name was taken by some exalted reformers as their battle emblem; and the polemics which were the subjects of his writings gave him considerable influence in the liberal society of the time.

But no form of literature in those days made greater strides than history. The past of the nation was investigated devotedly in the archives of Chile and of Spain by men of indefatigable industry. From the years when university memoirs had invariably to discuss some point in the history of Chile, studies of this nature followed each other one after another and came to compose a real library both abundant and select. But the greater part of those memoirs, such as the great work of Gay, soon were relegated to oblivion before the notable works of a whole generation of professional historians.

The first of them is Miguel Luis Amunátegui (1828-1888), who succeeded by his own efforts in distinguishing himself as a student at the National Institute, as a professor for nineteen years in the same institution, and then as an indefatigable writer. His first work, written like many of his other works, in collaboration with his brother, Gregorio Víctor, was *La reconquista española.* Later came others and still others: *La dictadura de O'Higgins* (*The Dictatorship of O'Higgins*), his most interesting work, according to general opinion; *El descubrimiento y conquista de Chile* (*The Discovery and Conquest of Chile*), the most pleasing and artistic; and *Los precursores de la independencia de Chile,* the most philosophical in range. Numerous works of various kinds and many other historical productions complete the picture of his vast literary effort. Strict documentation, the most scrupulous testing, simplicity of expression—such are the qualities of Amunátegui as a historian.[4] He was also a politician, but it is his literary labor that has made him most deserving of national gratitude.

At the time that Amunátegui wrote, Benjamín Vicuña Mackenna[5] (1831-1886) also cultivated history with a charming bril-

---

[4] *La reconquista española . . . 1814-17* (Santiago, 1851); *La dictadura de O'Higgins* (Santiago, 1853); *Descubrimiento y conquista de Chile* (Santiago, 1861); *Los precursores* (3 vols. Santiago, 1870-72).

[5] For Vicuña Mackenna see p. 531. *El ostracismo de los Carreras* appeared in 1857; *El ostracismo del Jeneral D. Bernardo O'Higgins,* in 1860; *Historia crítica y social de Santiago . . . 1541-1868* (2 vols. Santiago, 1869); *Historia de Valparaíso . . . 1536-1868* (2 vols. Santiago, 1869-72); and *Don Diego Portales* in 1863, reprinted in 1937.

liancy of language and a productivity that is surprising. He was a man of manifold activities. Revolutionist, journalist, politician, diplomat—he wrought in all these fields, but he left the great impress of his life on the cultivation of national history. His production is most varied and enormous, a hundred volumes, but his principal books are: *El ostracismo de los Carreras*, *El ostracismo del jeneral D. Bernardo O'Higgins*, *Historia crítica y social de Santiago*, *Historia de Valparaíso*, and *Don Diego Portales*. This last work has always been judged his most complete because of the abundance of his investigation on the subject. The War of the Pacific drew from him a dozen volumes to glorify the heroism of the race. [Brilliant and eloquent narration characterized Vicuña Mackenna; and, although his language was impaired by much carelessness and he did not always adopt the serious tone that his themes required, he is not only the most fertile of Chilean writers, but also the most charming of Chilean historians.][6]

Diego Barros Arana (1830-1907) follows next. Educated in the institute, he devoted himself from young manhood to historical reading and investigation and traveled in Europe and America, collecting data and documents for a vast compilation. While he was preparing this work, he published several others on such men as the guerrilla fighter, Vicente Benavides, on Freire, Valdivia, and Magellan, and some textbooks, such as his *Compendio de historia de América*. But his most notable works of that period were his *Historia jeneral de la independencia de Chile*, and his *Historia de la guerra del Pacífico* (*History of the War of the Pacific*). Finally, at the end of thirty years of patient and painstaking preparation, his great compilation appeared, the *Historia jeneral de Chile*, the first volume of which was published in 1884, and the last, twenty years later.[7] There are sixteen full volumes in which is told the past of Chile from primitive times up to 1833, the date of the constitutional organization of the republic. It is the most complete that could be asked for, both because of the abundant research which

---

[6] The portion enclosed in brackets is omitted from the seventh edition of Galdames.

[7] For Barros Arana see p. 316. His *Estudios históricos sobre Vicente Benavides y las campañas del sur, 1818-1822*, appeared in 1850; *Opúsculo histórico sobre el Jeneral Freire*, in Santiago in 1852; *Historia jeneral de la independencia de Chile* (16 vols. Santiago, 1854-1858); *Compendio de historia de América* (2 vols. Santiago, 1865. 9th ed., 1907); *Historia de la guerra del Pacífico* (2 vols. Santiago, 1880-81); *Historia jeneral de Chile* (16 vols. Santiago, 1884-1902). See Víctor Manuel Chiappa, "Bibliografía de Don Diego Barros Arana," in *Rev. chil. de hist. y geog.*, LXVI (July-Sept., 1930), 227-341.

enabled the author to prove each fact with scrupulous care, and because of the profound erudition that permitted him to treat all his material adequately. Barros Arana is justly considered the most finished of Chilean national historians.

Next to these three masters of historical literature in Chile come many other authors, who without having written special works on definite institutions or periods have contributed to a knowledge of national history. Such are the following: Crescente Errázuriz, formerly a Dominican priest, afterward presbyter and beloved archbishop of Chile and a famous writer, to whom we owe a series of interesting books on the origins of the Chilean Church, and the early period of the Spanish conquest; Ramón Sotomayor Valdés, author of an excellent *Historia de la administración del general Prieto, 1831-1841;* Gonzalo Bulnes, with his military histories on *Expedición libertadora led Perú (The Liberating Expedition of Peru),* and *Campaña del Perú en 1838 (The Peruvian Campaign of 1838);* and José Toribio Medina, a scholarly and extraordinarily persistent and productive investigator, who kept working to the end and who, in the time to which we refer, had already published his *Historia de la literatura colonial de Chile, Los aborígenes de Chile,* and two histories on the Inquisition, one dealing with that tribunal as it existed in Lima, and the other as it existed in Chile.

Light literature was also represented by important works and authors. Among the writers on national customs, one stands out above any of his compatriots—José Joaquín Vallejo, a popular writer under the pseudonym of "Jotabeche," who, although he died very young, left works of a fine quality, which were compiled after his death and published under the title *Artículos de Jotabeche (Articles of Jotabeche).* Then came Daniel Barros Grez, whose studies and national novels won no little reputation. Among these last, *Pipiolos y pelucones* is the best known. But the novel attained greater importance and interest in the hands of another Chilean writer, Alberto Blest Gana, among whose numerous productions of that period *Martín Rivas* surpasses all others.

In nothing, however, was the period which we are studying more prolific than in poets. Their names are well known and popular in the country and collections of their verse are very abundant. Among them are Eusebio Lillo, author of the "Canción nacional" (National Hymn) and many other poems; José Antonio Soffia, Guillermo Blest Gana, and Luis Rodríguez Velasco, the three who were outstanding in exquisite sentimental verse; Salvador Sanfuentes who died in 1860, and who cultivated history, the drama, and legends in verse; Guillermo Matta, philosophical and patriotic poet, rude, with little harmony in his compositions, but of extraordinary productivity; and lastly Eduardo de la Barra, who, to the qualities he possessed as a facile and at times arrogant versifier, added a rare knowledge of philology and notable qualities as a debater. He has left scattered but valuable works.

To the second half of the nineteenth century and especially to the period of liberal institutions belongs the rise of a Chilean literature, whose value, whatever it may be, makes it possible for one to appreciate the rapid expansion of culture within the country and with it the confirmation of a spirit without prejudice and free from traditional shackles.

Art had also its representatives by this time. Among various distinguished painters the following deserve to be noted: Pedro Lira, who was a real apostle of painting, among whose canvasses the best known is "La Fundación de Santiago" (The Founding of Santiago); and Rafael Correa, one of whose pictures, "El Puente de cal y canto" (The Bridge of Stone Masonry), brought him much of his fame during that period. Among the few Chilean sculptors who succeeded at that time in creating various masterpieces are Nicanor Plaza with his "Caupolicán," now famous; and Virginio Árias with his group, "Dafnis y Cloe," also of much artistic merit. From 1884 on were held annual expositions in the Salon of Fine Arts, constructed expressly for that purpose in the Quinta Normal of Santiago. Some deserving pupils pensioned by the government were also sent to Europe from the Academy of Painting and the Academy of Sculpture.

Only the National Conservatory of Music and Oratory was at that time unproductive; it did not produce a single lyric or dramatic artist. The number of cultured artists in the country was not really great, but those who are among that number may be justly considered as the founders of the national art of Chile.

CONDITIONS OF RURAL AND URBAN LIFE

The population of the country had for some time past been experiencing a considerable increase. In 1885 a census was taken, by which it was evident that there were more than 2,500,000 inhabitants in the territory of Chile. Six years later this population, in spite of the losses caused by cholera and afterward by the revolution, was computed at about 2,800,000. Those losses, however, had been partly made up by foreign immigration, which, although never very numerous, increased from year to year. The capital and suburbs contained about 250,000 inhabitants. There was still a considerable numerical inequality between the urban and rural population. The former included only a third of the total number. The other two thirds were scattered in the country districts.

Some changes were noted in rural life. There existed, as before, the tenant and his ranch, the wandering peon and his misery. But the absolute ignorance of the former began to be broken, if not everywhere, at least on those haciendas nearest the populated centers, thanks to the frequent intercourse imposed by commerce between the villager and the countryman. Furthermore, not a few landlords, as proprietors of their estates, provided a shed for school purposes, along with the chapel to which the worker went on Sunday with his family to hear mass, and the store in which he bought his provisions. Here for several months each year was the "master," teaching the alphabet, writing, and prayer to the children of the more favored tenants, who could take something from the day's wage and pay a monthly peso for the instruction. This was not common, but neither was it exceptional.

On the other hand, in the same measure that the purchasing power of money lessened, wages increased.[8] From the former real they passed to the *chaucha* (twenty centavos), and from the *chaucha* wages later increased to four reales (fifty centavos), the highest amount then reached as a daily wage by a tenant. The outside peon, who worked in the fields only in the months of sowing and harvest, could get as high as seventy or eighty centavos, "without rations," that is to say, by paying for his own food. The women, for their part, reaped and carried on other more or less simple field labors for a real or twenty centavos a day, when extra hands were needed. Of course the day's wages thus indicated were not fixed nor were they maintained equally throughout the whole country but they prevailed in the central part of Chile. They fell to half of those amounts in the south in the less populated agricultural and grazing regions; in the mines and nitrate plants toward the north they arose to double or triple. Nor were the coal miners governed by these wages.

The tenant farmer had the advantage over the wandering peon of possessing his dwelling place, a miserable hut of clay and straw but still his dwelling, and a plot of one or two hectares on which he cultivated some trees, sowed his crop, and even grazed his animals. It was customary, moreover, to allow him the privilege of sending his animals to the woodland or to the nearest hill, where

---

[8] See Fetter, *Monetary Inflation in Chile*, p. 18.

they ran wild until the spring "round-up," when the holiday of branding and sheepshearing occurred. The overseer, superintendent, administrator—all the hierarchy of upper employees—invariably enjoyed those privileges and an adobe house, at times "tiled," and a little plot of four or five hectares for their own crops.

Food was not expensive nor did it lack nutritive elements. There were fowls and their eggs for the countryman; the cow and its milk; the lamb, whose flesh, the "meat of Castile," frequently if not ordinarily was served as a stew; the pig or hog; and other foodstuffs. There were also at hand vegetables in the garden, cereals from the harvest, and firewood in the forests. The countryman sold his barley and potatoes for three pesos a bushel (a fanega); his corn for four; and his wheat for five; his heifers or colts for twenty pesos; his lambs for three—all small sums, but his necessities, which were few, did not require a very large outlay either. He wore only trousers, shirt, short jacket, blanket (*manta*) or poncho, big hat (*chupalla*) or cap (*bonete*), according to the season. The sandal (*ojota*) was enough to shoe him. Thus his life, in direct contact with nature, was filled with the bracing atmosphere of the earth and lacked the disturbances, the confusion, and the anxieties of the city, especially of the large centers; that is, it was a semi-barbaric rusticity. It had its fatigue, its pains, but also its joys.

When Sunday came the tenant who was not hurried in the work of his little patch was transformed into a genteel *huaso*.[9] He mounted his best horse, wore his best clothes, among which he would not fail to wear the beautiful belt of wool at the waist or the *huarapón* (panama hat) of straw, or the blanket of varied colors; he put on his finest shoes and his stanchest spurs—and then went to mass. There the men of the district met and talked together and arranged for races or bullfights in the afternoon. These amusements ordinarily began and ended with revelry, and not infrequently with quarreling and death. The spring "round-up" and harvest festival, and other holidays, used to have similar endings. Their spirit of barbarous combativeness was not yet completely dormant.

This picture of country life has not always been the same; but it is that of a few years back and is still very much like that of today. The same thing is true of urban life, which, forty or more years ago had, though not so much activity as now, the same characteristic features. Their clubs, theatres, walks, holidays, quarrels,

---

[9] The term for a Chilean farmer.

and luxury were, with little variation, what they are today. Their cost has increased, of course, and is from four to six times as great, while the cities have gained in beauty, comfort, and healthfulness.

The buildings of brick, the great palaces, comfortable hotels, broad paved avenues, drinking water, and other conveniences were general at that time, through abundant public and private incomes, which kept increasing with the better exploitation of agriculture and mining, along with new industries and trade furthered by the same economic urge. Companies of firemen, created by private initiative at the middle of the century in Valparaiso, Santiago, Valdivia, and then in almost all cities of any importance, now performed their valiant work of rescuing and saving, with generosity and efficiency. Through their organization, on a basis of gratuitous services rendered by their individual members, they were, as today, genuine national and civic institutions.

The War of the Pacific had opened an era of prosperity in national finances. In ten years the income of the public treasury just about quadrupled (from fifteen to sixty million). Such a rapid rise in fiscal power everywhere permitted a forcing of the economic expansion of the country in all its manifestations.

On the other hand, the principal productive sources developed to a remarkable extent. Mining, especially, after the incorporation of the nitrate region into the nation, achieved heights never before imagined. Copper maintained its production of the mid-nineteenth century and increased annually the national wealth from twelve to twenty million pesos; silver, although already declining, gave no less than ten million. Gold itself, now almost exhausted, rated from one to two million; and even manganese, under active exploitation at that time, produced a half to one million each year. The production of nitrate, which in 1880 reached an annual value not above twenty-five million, returned nearly eighty million in 1890.[10] Agriculture also increased its annual returns rapidly, devoting a greater area of land each year to cultivation and perfecting its implements and working machinery. Thus exportation, which was supplied almost exclusively from these products, rose from twenty-seven million—the figure which it reached in 1870—to more than fifty million in 1880 and to sixty-eight million in 1890. In its turn, the manufacturing industry, which, after a half century, had hardly begun to be represented, now began to furnish articles for outside trade. Economic prosperity was then

---

[10] See Martner, *Estudio de política comercial chilena,* II, 447, 493.

an evident fact that no one could deny. It flattered the patriotism of the rulers and of the men of affairs.

The working mass of the population also began to enjoy the benefits of the new situation, although on a much smaller scale than the upper classes of society. Urban salaries doubled in the large centers. The day laborer now collected as much as a peso for his daily wage, instead of four reales. The artisan of every kind was scarcely content with one and a half pesos daily. But this same working class was the one that kept supplying patronage for the tavern, the jail, and the hospital, and increased the amount of vagrancy and beggary. Alcoholism, an innate vice among the people, paralleled the progress in salaries, so that any excess of the latter above satisfying the most pressing necessities would inevitably stimulate drunkenness. The statistics published at that time began to show that, notwithstanding the favorable development of wealth in the country, crime considerably increased, and nearly half the criminals who entered the jails committed their crimes in a state of intoxication. The multiplication of hospitals on account of epidemics was not enough, however, to satisfy the demand for beds for the "sick without resources," who found it necessary to seek that sheltering charity; and the vagrant and beggar, far from disappearing, continued to be at least as numerous as before. They talked of curing these social diseases through encouraging savings, through education, and through public hygiene in its different branches. They talked also of vigorous repression; but at that time nothing or very little was attempted. Nor were they able to repress gambling, a vice that, in all spheres of society, economic progress itself was helping to develop.

At the end, then, of the period sketched above (1861-1891), Chile began to be a country of wealth and splendor. She transformed herself and prospered rapidly in different forms of activity; but she did not succeed in curing, except to a very small degree, the native vices of her people.

CHAPTER XVIII

THE PARLIAMENTARY REPUBLIC

BASES OF THE PARLIAMENTARY REGIME

THE REVOLUTION of 1891 was a serious incident in the constitutional life of the republic. With it there fell not only a president but also the presidential authority. It was an entire political system that collapsed. All parties helped to break it down, even the one that created it, the conservative party—the party that counted among its first and most glorious traditions the Constitution of 1833.

That code had made of the president of the republic a strong, invincible authority. In him were concentrated all the powers of the state. He not only directed the administration of the country, but controlled the congressional elections and appointed his successor. The courts of justice, the army and the navy as well, and all public functionaries depended directly on him; and the intendants and governors—his immediate representatives in the provinces—with the police and alcaldes of their jurisdiction, held the entire nation in one single net of authority.

As we have seen before, that authority, nearly omnipotent, suffered no curtailment while the government was directed by the conservatives. When the liberals came into power they weakened it not a little with several constitutional reforms. But in spite of the fact that in their program freedom of suffrage held first place, and in spite of the fact that the revolutions of 1851 and 1859 had been fought in their name, they did not deprive the president of the republic of his greatest power, that of intervention in governmental affairs. The liberal presidents intervened in elections just as did the conservatives whenever the opportunity presented itself. Thus conditions continued during the sixty years between 1831 and 1891.

But the ruling social class, whose culture and wealth continued to increase, thus opening new horizons to their ambitions, no longer accepted the tutelage of the executive. The conservatives abominated it, for since their fall from power they suffered from electoral intervention as much as they had formerly profited by it. The liberals, who, in their turn, enjoyed it as much as they had formerly disliked it, were divided: some sided with the government, others were against it. The latter now came to hate intervention, and they constituted that formidable majority in congress which, founded on constitutional rights, dared to resist the wishes of President Balmaceda.

The old principle of electoral liberty sprang up anew and was carried by the opposition as its standard of battle. To it was added the autonomous commune, which was to be its most solid bulwark, and the parliamentary system, which was to be its crown and guarantee. The old presidential regime was finally conquered on the fields of Concón and Placilla,[1] and there was no delay in applying the principles proclaimed by the conquerors.

At the end of the same year, 1891, the new Law of Municipalities[2] was passed. It divided the country into a number of communes, each of which should be administered by its municipal council whose members, or *regidores*, elected by popular vote, were to hold office three years. The powers granted to these corporations were very broad, more ample even than those that formerly pertained to the governors in their departments. The health, cleanliness, and embellishment of towns, the promotion of public education and of all industries, and maintenance of a standing police force were a part of their working program.

But no power was more important from the political point of view than the establishing of the electoral power. The enrollment of citizens, and popular balloting for their own municipal officers, for deputies, senators, and the president of the republic fell under its control. And as the municipalities were administered in absolute independence of the executive power, the latter, which had previously controlled elections by means of governors, intendants, and alcaldes selected for its convenience, from that moment lost all influence in determining the authorities of the State. The "autonomous commune," consisting as it did in that freedom of the municipality to manage the services and interests of each locality, thus put an end to the already worn-out official intervention in elections.

If to the above be added the Law of Parliamentary Incompatibility,[3] issued in the time of Balmaceda but only now put in practice, we have the complete annihilation of presidential omnipotence. By this last law, legislative offices were closed to all employees paid

---

[1] For Concón and Placilla, see p. 347.

[2] For the autonomous commune established by this municipal law, see Ricardo Anguita, *Recopilación de leyes por orden numérico* (11 vols. Santiago, 1900-1925), Ley No. 2960 in VIII, 111-150. Irarrázaval was active in this movement.

[3] For the law of parliamentary incompatibilities, see *ibd.*, Ley No. 2451, in VI, 129-131.

by the State; therefore no official could, from then on, enter congress and continue at the same time to hold his other office. The object of this requirement was to prevent the selection of any public employee by the president to defend his policy in either of the houses.

In this way, then, the parliamentary regime was firmly established. This meant that the president would either govern in accord with a congressional majority or not at all. The free election of congress and of the president guaranteed harmony between both powers. Thus was realized the old longing for electoral liberty, but not the balanced harmony which they wanted.

What followed in practice, though contrary to what had happened before, did not change the constitution of the republic in any fundamental way. In place of the old omnipotence of the president was substituted the omnipotence of congress. The situation may be explained very simply. When the chief of state caused the majorities of the houses to be chosen according to his desire, there rarely was a conflict between them and him because they were chosen for the express purpose of avoiding such conflict; and, if for any reason such a conflict occurred, it was settled almost always in accordance with his desire. In the parliamentary system, congress was chosen by popular election, independent of executive power, and its majorities were made up in an equally independent manner; and, as the president could not govern except in accord with these majorities, the result was that he had to submit to them in all his acts.

Majorities were dependent upon circumstances; more than that, they were generally composed of political groups of differing principles, which appointed their respective delegates to occupy the ministerial offices. These at once tried to superimpose the interests of their group on those of their allies; if the president yielded to their claims, ministerial solidarity was broken and the group that thought itself injured withdrew its ministers. The conflict thus presented between the parliamentary majority and the president then resolved itself into a fall of the ministry, an occurrence so frequent in the course of the years, 1892-1924, that the instability of ministries came to constitute the normal system of government. Ordinarily two or three months did not pass without the break-up of a cabinet. Cases were cited of cabinets that lasted a week or only a day. They were, to be sure, peaceful conflicts, but it is no less certain that through them public administration was disturbed and frustrated and that the most important affairs of national interest were subjected to delay and postponement. Under such a system, it was never possible to undertake methodical and continuous governmental work.[4]

With such a degree of instability, the functioning of government was seriously compromised. The real governors were not the chiefs of state, but the leaders of parties through whose committees must pass all public business. In this manner it was planned to make the presidency of the republic a purely decorative office, or at most a conciliatory element. The government lost its unity. There was no one man responsible for its operation. It was impersonal and divided. Private interests, under cover of this situation, tried to place themselves above the common interest and did so more than once. The yearly budgets were burdened with useless and enormous sums in order to pay electoral services with administrative offices or to meet binding obligations. There was financial waste and administrative disorganization. Members of congress intervened in public offices, intimidated the officials, wearied them with their demands. Even the parties came to contract their alliances on the bases of distributing high offices among their supporters.

POLITICAL PARTIES AND METHODS

The plethora of fiscal wealth, as we have noted, permitted the budgets to be inflated for electoral purposes. Moreover, the multitude of political parties into which congress, even more than the country, was divided, helped to aggravate the difficulties of the parliamentary regime. During the period of conservative control there were only two parties: conservative and liberal. During the liberal regime there were four: conservative, liberal, national, and radical. These last three frequently united and were considered as a single entity, "liberalism." From the revolution of 1891 to 1924, seven parties appeared. To the four mentioned above the following were added: the liberal-democratic, formed by a political nucleus that had favored President Balmaceda during the revolution; the democratic, created previously (1887), but whose parliamentary representation did not have any influence until long afterward; and the liberal-independent, a party without a popular basis, very small, and the only one in congress without a recognized program, holding the views which the individual judgments of its members considered opportune.[5]

---

[4] See article by Paul S. Reinsch, "Parliamentary Government in Chile," in *American Political Science Review*, III (November, 1909), 507-538.

[5] The standard work on political parties of Chile is Edwards' *Bosquejo*

The almost absolute predominance of the leaders tended to make those groups into personal parties, without much regard for their programs. In general, they preferred not to concern themselves with programs because among members of the same group it was difficult to agree on any point whatever. They acted for the most part only on matters of practical interest, such for example as economic measures. When, therefore, any one of those problems was carried to the houses, it would be declared an open question; that is to say, a question on which anyone could argue as he pleased without compromising his party or provoking internal divisions. What really happened was that all groups lacked coherence and unity of purpose in reference to the material interests of the country. In these matters parties have never existed in Chile, only men capable of understanding its material affairs.

"Moral interests" alone established clear lines of demarcation between the parties, and in these were centered educational and religious ideals. Considered from this point of view, there were only two parties that held definite doctrines—the conservatives and the radicals. The former believed that the State should educate as little as possible and this from the religious point of view, allowing private individuals full liberty to teach; the State, moreover, should protect the Catholic faith by all means in its power. The radical party held that the State must be, as far as possible, the only educator, and that instruction in the schools should be obligatory, free, and secular in all branches, without interfering with teaching by private persons if carried on under state supervision. As for religion, the State should maintain absolute freedom in belief, even to the separation of Church and State. To these questions, both groups applied the term "doctrinaire."

But none of the political groups had sufficient power to govern by itself alone. Every group had to unite with related or antagonistic groups in order to make a parliamentary majority. The two extreme groups, the radical and the conservative, were always enemies, in spite of the fact that they entered upon the revolution of 1891 together and on more than one occasion afterward were united in the government.

The liberal nucleus, called doctrinaire because it tried to maintain the traditions of the historic party, ordinarily remained united with the radical; in turn, the democratic liberals served as the party of the center; the side to which they adhered had the majority

---

histórico de los partidos políticos chilenos. See especially pp. 102-115. See also his *La fronda aristocrática en Chile.*

for several years. Radicals, doctrinaire-liberals, and democratic-liberals often constituted, and as often dissolved, the so-called liberal alliance. On the other hand conservatives, nationals, and democratic-liberals many times made up the so-called liberal-conservative coalition. Democrats and independents were incorporated in one or the other combination, according to the issue of the moment; that is to say, according to their electoral, political, and administrative preferences.

THE PRESIDENTS AND THE POLITICAL COMBINATIONS
(1891-1920)

The instability of the above party combinations was especially shown in the presidential elections. Those battlefields then were invariably shifted. Without taking into account the elevation of Jorge Montt, raised to power by the triumphant revolutionists of 1891, the liberal-conservative coalition, joined in the next election by men of other parties, gave the supreme magistracy to Federico Errázuriz Echaurren, son of the president of the same name, by so small a majority over his competitor, Vicente Reyes, if it was a majority at all, that congress had to decide the election (1896). But the liberal alliance, reinforced in like manner by men of all parties, took revenge in the following election of 1901 by elevating Germán Riesco to the presidency of the republic with a two-thirds majority over the coalition candidate, Pedro Montt.

In 1906 the political groups split up so much in trying to select a successor to President Riesco that the designations "coalition" and "alliance" disappeared. The so-called national union, composed of radicals, nationals, doctrinaire-liberals, and a dissenting group from the conservative party, backed the candidacy of Pedro Montt, the very statesman who was beaten five years previously by the same powerful radical-liberal alliance. "Administrative regeneration" founded on a "political truce" was the platform on which two thirds of the electoral body of the country grouped themselves and gave Montt a victory as great as his previous defeat. Fifteen years of futile party struggles, during which governmental instability and the disorganization of public services had come to deplorable extremes, justified that program and that change in opinion.

At this time, the son of the president of the ten years from 1851 to 1861 was looked upon as the representative of a vigorous political system, capable of carrying out a positive program of national interest. His candidacy, thus considered, meant a protest against the system installed after the late revolution. It was the desire, at his election, to restore to the office of president of the republic at least a great part, if not all, of its traditional influence.

All this was useless. From the first, President Montt's activity was hampered by parliamentary groups that scarcely permitted him to develop his program. Although he tried to impose and did impose his powerful personality on the government, in conformity with his well known energetic character, he only obtained from congress the passage of a few important laws, among them that for the "longitudinal railroad" which was to unite the country from Tacna to Puerto Montt.

As an example of the impotence which the authority of the chief of state had now reached, we may recall two acts of his administration. During all his political life, the president had been a fervid and unwavering supporter of a metallic system of money; yet he was constrained by congress to issue thirty million pesos in paper money, and afterward, when trying to put into practice the redemption of all paper money circulating in 1909, as the law of emission ordered, congress issued a new law postponing that financial operation until 1915. The president vetoed this last law, but was beaten by congress, which insisted upon it by more than the necessary two-thirds majority.

In the midst of the disappointments that beset his administrative tasks, the president contracted a serious illness, went to Europe for treatment, and had barely reached Bremen when he died there, in August, 1910, more than a year before completing his term of office. He was succeeded by Elías Fernández Albano, the vice-president, who also died at the beginning of September. Then the oldest minister in office, Emiliano Figueroa, assumed the chief magistracy with the title of vice-president.

The country was preparing to celebrate the first centenary of independence and almost all the foreign ambassadors who had come to attend the festivities were already in Santiago. The liberal convention, previously summoned to select a candidate for the presidency in Montt's place, met a few days later, and at the end of a week of prolonged voting nominated the old and illustrious statesman, Ramón Barros Luco. The conservative party concurred in this nomination and Barros Luco was unanimously elected at the polls. He assumed the presidency on December 23, 1910, and completed his normal term.

The sudden political transformation, brought about in the course of a few days with absolute regard for the provisions of the constitution, showed how profoundly orderly sentiment and respect for law were rooted among all the inhabitants of the republic, and caused the foreigners who were visiting the country to form a very favorable impression of its republican organization. They were right, no doubt, seeing that similar progress had not yet been attained by any other Hispanic American country. Nevertheless, had they been given an opportunity to see the functioning of the electoral system which served as a basis for that political regime, they would not perhaps have failed to make serious amendments to their reports.

In reality, the parliamentary system not only exercised powerful influence in directing public affairs; it modified also electoral habits in a way that was nothing less than deplorable. For the abuses of former governmental intervention with its imprisonments, its soldiers, and its executions, it substituted the intervention of money, the free purchase of the vote. Although prohibited and punished by law, bribery was a deplorable reality. The parties did not seek to send the most capable men to congress, but the richest—those able to pay for an election. If ability was united to fortune, good; if not, that also was good. In any case, money was indispensable. An election as deputy might cost from 20,000 to 100,000 pesos, and an election as senator, from 100,000 to a million. The amount depended on the location of the candidacy and was in proportion to the resources of the adversary.

The custom of selling the vote spread from the lowest social class to persons who qualified as "decent," and to such an extent that the case is told of villages where the rabble was incited to rise up and stone the houses of their best-known electoral agents because the parties there had made arrangements to avoid a contest and in consequence presenting only one list for their suffrages, leaving each free to vote without pay. The masses of people then became convinced that it was the "duty" of a candidate for deputy or senator to bribe his electors.

If there be added to this procedure the falsification of returns and records—a practice which was current, customary, and therefore unpunished—one will reach the conclusion that electoral liberty, for which so much blood had been shed was nothing, in practice, except liberty to indulge in fraud and bribery. The republic became a "free democracy" but a venal one which was weakening at its very source the most important law in its power.

This deplorable situation reacted harshly on civic spirit. There was a tendency to belittle the conception of "national solidarity," which led one to intervene generously in affairs of common interest. Few, indeed, were those who really seemed to preserve true sentiments of patriotism. If activity and enthusiasm were shown in electioneering periods, it was because a small group succeeded with great effort in stirring up opinion and because the general mass saw in the distance the fee for its vote. But men of that same group promoted more than one campaign through the "morality of the suffrage," and, although they succeeded in obtaining but little result, their efforts were not less valuable on that account.

During the presidential elections of 1915 and 1920, which so greatly aroused the mass of the people, one could see some progress in civic customs. The two great political forces into which public opinion divided, the alliance and the coalition, fought on the basis of a definite program that accorded with public needs; and, although those programs did not in practice go beyond good intentions, because circumstances of various kinds did not offer a chance to realize them, it is certain that they reëchoed profoundly throughout the electorate of the country, helped to fix its ideas on some national problems, dissuaded a great number of citizens from bribery, and aroused new aspirations of social welfare.

The election of 1915 bore Juan Luis Sanfuentes to the presidency of the republic on the arms of the coalition, after a most stubborn struggle with the opposing combination; and that of 1920 bore to the same office Arturo Alessandri, the candidate of the liberal alliance, at the end of a no less violent struggle, in which the resulting "tie" could be decided only by a "tribunal of honor." In the election of Sanfuentes, the partisans of stability in the prevailing social and political order conquered. They were, for the most part, men of fortune who believed that any marked change in existing institutions constituted a menace to public peace, religious faith, and the free development of business. In the election of Alessandri, the victory went to the advocates of a profound social and political change, in the sense of a broader "democratization" of national institutions. People of all conditions, but especially of the educated middle class and the working masses, adhered to the program of the candidate who announced the advent of a "new system" for the republic.[6] The status attained by the proletariat in some European countries as a result of the great war (1914-1918) was in keeping with the appearance and acceptance of those reforming tendencies whose efficacy in Chile was scarcely felt. At

[6] For speeches of Alessandri, especially to working men, see *El Presidente Alessandri y su gobierno* (Santiago, 1926), *passim*.

all events, it stimulated the civic spirit of the working element and strengthened its aspirations for greater political influence and a greater economic well-being, or, as they say, in their language, greater justice in the distribution of national wealth.

CHAPTER XIX

DEMOCRATIC ORIENTATION

ALESSANDRI AND THE CRISIS OF PARLIAMENTARISM

THE DESIRE for social reform became widespread among the masses of the people during the election of 1920. But this impulse was not to continue under its protagonist, Arturo Alessandri, without strong opposition. From the beginning his administration was an agitated one. It began December 23, 1920, and, after an interval of little more than six months, ended October 1, 1925. The president came into power with the unquestioned aid of the liberal alliance which had a majority in the house of deputies but not in the senate. The renewal of both branches of congress in the election of March, 1921, did not change that situation; the alliance had a more numerous majority in the house of deputies, but did not succeed in breaking the opposing majority of the senate, which was only partially renewed. This majority represented the tendency of the political combination called national union, which in 1920 had grouped itself about the illustrious citizen, Luis Barros Borgoño, in order to raise him to the highest magistracy in opposition to Alessandri, and which, in the following year, set itself rigidly to criticize the acts of the new government.[1]

Thus a difficult situation was created for the president: if in the house of deputies he counted on the unconditional adherence of a powerful majority, in the senate, on the contrary, he had to face a no less compact majority disposed to oppose or delay his governmental activity. For three years the two party combinations—the alliance and the union—continued in this position, with slight variations that did not change their views or modify their action. The parliamentary system forced the ministers to keep the confidence of both houses, expressed by their majorities, a course which, in this case, was impossible because, while one regarded them with favor, the other looked on them with misgiving, if not with frank hostility, and there was no constitutional measure that would permit a solution of the conflict. The ministries lasted only a few weeks or at most three months, because they encountered the censure of the senate and at times even of their own friends in the

---

[1] For a convenient summary of the political struggles of the period, consult Clarence H. Haring, "Chilean Politics, 1920-1928," in *Hisp. Amer. Hist. Rev.*, IX (February, 1931), 1-26.

other house. Moreover, this "ministerial rotation" was not new; it had already lasted thirty years since the beginning of parliamentary in the country but had seldom presented such grave characteristics. Ministerial changes of the former administrations frequently resulted from a lack of discipline in the parties, from the personal ambitions of some leaders, or the alteration in political majorities of the two branches of congress. Antagonism between the two houses had never manifested itself with such persistency and obstinacy.

The practices of the parliamentarians making up the governmental majority had not varied in respect to intervention in administrative services. As before, under the same system, they kept trying to procure employment for their friends, thus pleasing their most influential electors at the expense of the public treasury and inflating fiscal costs to an unheard-of degree. The president and, above all, the ministers were obliged to weaken their resistance in the face of this unlimited encroachment by members of congress on the state administration and had to compromise with them in order to maintain themselves in power and realize any of their aspirations for the public welfare. In the midst of these difficulties, the government of President Alessandri secured the approval of various laws of a financial character concerning loans and tax reforms—which would provide for better administrative service and carry out public works—and of other laws that were designed to protect industry, labor, and the working classes; and even approved of some laws of international importance, such as the protocol with Peru to submit to the arbitral decision of the president of the United States the final solution of the Tacna-Arica question (1922).[2]

But the president of the republic longed to go further along the road of economic and social reforms which constituted the foundation of his governmental program. In this he encountered the opposition of the senate, which did not permit these advances and limited itself to dispatching the laws that it considered most urgent. At the end of 1923, with the renewal of congress already approaching, an act that was to be verified in the elections of March, 1924, the conflict between the senate and the president of the republic took on more serious aspects. Fluctuations and crises in the ministries became more frequent and legislative activity was almost

---

[2] For a brief view of this arbitration, see Dennis, *Tacna and Arica*, chaps. ix-xiii. Selected documents on the negotiations will be found in his *Documentary History of the Tacna-Arica Dispute*.

completely suspended in order to make room for vexatious political debates.

Public agitation then arose in favor of modifying the prevailing constitutional system. It was proposed to deprive the senate of its political attributes, especially the power of deposing ministers by censure, and to establish a system of greater governmental stability. The president took upon himself the direction of the campaign, proposed constitutional reform in manifestos and addresses, and, in order to carry it into effect, asked the electorate of the liberal parties to give him a congress with a uniform majority in both houses.

The popularity of the president, which had not abandoned him from the time of his candidacy, favored this propaganda; and the liberal alliance in March, 1924, attained an overwhelming majority in both branches of congress. But the electoral campaign had been most bitter and had left an impression of disagreeable charge and countercharge, because in some departments and provinces the intervention of the executive, with the help of the army, had been openly brought to bear in favor of certain candidates. This was, really, a useless deploying of outside forces upon the electoral body, which was decidedly inclined to support the president's policy and which would, in any case, have given him the uniform majority in both houses that he wished to get.

The new congress began its sessions in June. Many projects of importance awaited its consideration, among them the appropriation bill for the same year (1924)—which was not yet settled—and several other measures of financial and social legislation. Its work of three months was futile; discussions of electoral policy absorbed almost all its activity. The lack of discipline in the majority parties reached deplorable extremes and further complicated their debates. At the beginning of September, congress was already burdened by a sense of loss of prestige, owing to its incapacity to discuss and dispatch laws so long planned and hoped for. In those days the head of the cabinet and principal co-worker in President Alessandri's government was Pedro Aguirre Cerda, a radical politician of recognized shrewdness. Nevertheless, his influence was not sufficient to bring congress to act upon the messages submitted to its consideration. The army was anxiously awaiting the approval of one of those projects designed to better its economic condition, which was becoming impaired every day by the depreciation in the value of money and the consequent rise in the cost of living. Meanwhile, instead of approving this and other urgent projects, congress passed a law for parliamentary compensation by which its own members were granted remuneration under the guise of indemnity for the time consumed in their legislative tasks.

This vote of congress produced a storm of astonished indignation throughout the country. It was not that the people rejected parliamentary compensation, which in general they considered just; it was the manifest unconstitutionality of the law, since the constitution expressly established the principle that legislative offices were gratuitous; it was a fact that members of this very congress voted pay to themselves from the time they began to function; it was the increasing deficit that existed in the public treasury while the very ones who were supposed to devise measures to diminish it added several millions to it; and, finally, it was the preference given to this project above so many others of more urgent financial character—it was all these considerations together that raised against congress that formidable wave of opinion.

The officers of the army corps that garrisoned Santiago thereupon decided to become the interpreters of that public sentiment and to intervene effectively to prevent the compensation act from being passed. Although in order to accomplish this the group had also to break, as far as its members were concerned, the constitutional provision prohibiting such meetings, it organized a military committee which won the adherence of General Luis Altamirano, inspector in chief of the army, and requested the president of the republic to veto that law. It asked, further, the coöperation of the executive for the immediate dispatch of various projects then pending in congress, among which was that relative to the economic situation of the armed forces. Thus was initiated the military movement of September 5, 1924.[3]

The president received the petitions of the officers and called General Altamirano to the leadership of the ministry. He obtained by act of congress the approval of all those laws without any debate; but the president well understood that, as he was subjected to military force, his situation as supreme executive was indefensible, and on the evening of September 8 he resigned his office. General Altamirano assumed executive power in his capacity as vice-president, and two days later appointed a military junta of government, presided over by himself and completed by another gen-

[3] See General Juan Bennett A., *La revolución del 5 de setiembre de 1924*, pp. 1-37; Enrique Monreal, *Historia completa y documentada del período revolucionario, 1824-1825*.

eral and an admiral. His first act was to dissolve congress, and the following day, September 11, he issued a manifesto to the country, explaining the reasons for his action. Then he appointed a ministry of civilians—except the minister of war and navy, who was an admiral—which was headed by the well-known university professor, Alcibíades Roldán. Meanwhile, President Alessandri, who had taken refuge in the embassy of the United States, went abroad by way of the cordillera. He was authorized by congress, before it was dissolved, to absent himself for six months from the country, but he really did not intend to return. The chief of the radical party, Pedro Aguirre Cerda, who had been the leader of the president's last cabinet, also very shortly followed him into exile.

PRESIDENT ALESSANDRI AND THE CONSTITUTION OF 1925

The junta of government presided over by General Altamirano maintained itself in power until January 23, 1925, or about four and a half months, when it was replaced by a new military junta composed of a general and an admiral and presided over by a citizen, Emilio Bello Codecido, a diplomat and politician of approved governmental experience. A military revolt directed by some of the officers of the garrison corps in Santiago brought about the fall of the government of General Altamirano. He was accused of violating the purposes of the movement of the previous September fifth and of developing a policy satisfactory to the parties of the national union, which shortly before had proclaimed the presidential candidacy of their leader, Ladislao Errázuriz, a brilliant and forceful parliamentarian belonging to the groups opposing President Alessandri. Moreover, charges were made against him for not having carried out the program of social and economic reforms included in the movement of September and for not hastening the organization of the constituent assembly that was to reform the political system.

In the manifesto of January 23, 1925, with which the second military revolution hoped to justify its action, a policy of complete change in national institutions on the basis of a new constitution was proposed, as well as the immediate return to power of President Alessandri, who was traveling in Europe. Meanwhile, with feverish activity, a series of "decree-laws" was issued by the different departments, which now numbered nine ministries, for the purpose of carrying out at once the economic and social reforms called for by the needs of the country. From these efforts there arose a whole new code of legislation,[4] the predominant tendency of which was to protect the laboring masses of the people and to introduce better conditions of public health. José Santos Salas, a military physician, was the soul of that movement as minister of hygiene and social welfare.

These frankly revolutionary political upheavals had not aroused violent resistance or caused any loss of blood. They had merely determined the deportation of several public men for conspicuous activity in connection with those very events. Thus, just as President Alessandri and his minister, Aguirre Cerda, had to leave the country after September 5, so Ladislao Errázuriz and some of his friends, accused of conspiring against the new order of things, were also obliged to go into exile.

President Alessandri, upon insistent summons by the junta of government, by labor committees, and by party directories to renew his governmental functions and put himself at the front of this movement for national reform, left Rome for Chile a few days after January 23, and in the latter part of March reached Santiago and resumed power. The great popular demonstration with which he was received was unprecedented.

Alessandri very promptly devoted his efforts to the reform of the constitution. He called together an assemblage of men from each political group and from each national activity in order to discuss the subject; and this assembly, called the "Grand Consultative Commission," after long deliberation by their subcommittees issued a project in July, 1925, for constitutional reforms, which was to have the sanction of a plebiscite.

The reform was an entirely new political constitution[5] and marked the end of the parliamentary system, which had prevailed for thirty-three years. It created a strong executive, with ample administrative powers, without diminishing public liberties and individual guarantees of long standing. It deprived the chamber of deputies and the senate of the power to depose ministries by means of censure, and authorized the first of these bodies to bring before the senate accusations against ministers and even against the president of the republic for various abuses of power. It increased to six years the term for the office of president; and established his election by direct vote. It made parliamentary offices

---

[4] See *Recopilación de decretos-leyes por orden numérico* (Santiago, 1925), Vol. XII. This volume covers the first three hundred decree laws issued between September 15, 1924, and March 9, 1925.

[5] For a complete commentary on this constitution, consult Guillermo Guerra, *La Constitución de 1925* (Santiago, 1929).

incompatible with those of the ministry; it provided for the improvement of public administration by entrusting it to special councils of experts, and it separated Church and State and guaranteed the fullest liberty of conscience in the practice of religious beliefs.

This last reform has been favored for more than forty years by a fraction of the advanced liberal groups, chiefly drawn from the radical party; but it has always encountered opposition among the conservative groups and among the clergy—opposition so stubborn that it was considered blasphemy merely to support it in principle. The slow but effective rise of culture in the country made possible, nevertheless, the definite establishment of religious tolerance and the archbishop, Crescente Errázuriz, proved no obstacle to its being included in the constitutional text. Thereupon all resistance ceased; and, as compensation during a transitory period of five years, an annual fiscal subsidy of two and a half million pesos was granted the Church.

The text of the pertinent constitutional provision is worthy of record. It reads as follows:

The Constitution assures all inhabitants of the republic . . . the expression of all beliefs, liberty of thought and the free exercise of all religions not opposed to morality, good customs or public order, permitting therefore the respective religious faiths to erect and maintain churches and their appurtenances under the conditions of security and hygiene fixed by the laws and ordinances. The churches, confessions and religious institutions of any creed will have the rights which the laws now in force authorize and recognize with respect to property; but they will remain subject within the guarantees of this Constitution to the common law for the control of their future property. Churches and their dependencies, destined to the service of worship, will be exempt from taxation.

The constitution likewise made declarations of a democratic character, within the socialistic concepts already widespread. Along with the guarantee of public freedom and individual rights, it naturally recognized ownership of any kind as inviolable; but it added:

The exercise of the right of ownership is subject to the limitations or precepts necessary for the maintenance and progress of social order; and in that sense the law will be able to impose obligations or services of public utility in behalf of the general interests of the State, the health of the citizens and the public well-being.

Moreover, it at the same time assured

protection to labor, industry and works of social foresight, particularly in so far as they refer to the sanitation of dwellings and economic conditions of life, so as to provide each inhabitant with a minimum standard of welfare, adequate to the satisfacion of his personal needs and those of his family. The law will regulate this provision. The State will take measures for the suitable division of property and the establishment of domestic common property.

Written expressions lead one to believe that the constitution in force permits the State to carry out, within legal procedure, all the reforms which are necessary to the economic readjustment of society and for the greater benefit of the wage-earning classes. The constitution has admitted at the same time the concept that property is not an inalienable individual right, to the exclusive benefit of its owners, but a social function which these same classes practice—a function capable of being subordinated to public interest and to the needs of common progress.

Under another set of topics, the new constitutional code likewise introduced important modifications. It suppressed the conservative commission and the council of state, integral corporations, the first of which was a component part of the legislative power and the second, of the executive. Neither had ever been very useful and now was no longer justified. In place of leaving the chambers, as hitherto, to pass on the electoral qualifications of their own members and of the president of the republic, it created for this purpose a permanent "qualifying tribunal," to be renewed each four years and to be composed of five members, elected by lot, from among the former presidents or vice-presidents of both chambers and from among the ministers of the superior courts of justice. By this means it was possible to save time and avoid the ill will which arose from discussing the legality of electoral acts in so far as they had to affect this or that candidate. All in all it represented the greatest guarantees of impartiality. The new code also tended toward the decentralization of administration by providing for provincial assemblies, which were charged with looking after and presenting the needs of their respective regions to the president of the republic. They were also authorized to dictate ordinances and even to impose local taxes in order to satisfy, entirely or partly, those same needs. Up to the present time, this reform has not been introduced because of failure to provide the necessary law. Finally, reform of the constitutional text has been made much easier by having its discussion and approval submitted to a single legislature, instead of two, as was provided for in the Constitution of 1833. Reform is to be accomplished through a law, but it will have to be approved in the first passage by the chamber of deputies and the chamber of senators, by an absolute majority of the members present in each. Sixty days later both chambers will meet in full congress with the quorum indicated above; and in this second step the bill will be voted upon without further discussion. In case there is no quorum, the full congress will meet the following day and will proceed to vote with such members as are present. The president of the republic cannot "veto" a reform bill so approved, but can propose amendments or modifications. In case of disagreement between the president and congress concerning all or part of the reform, it shall be definitely decided by popular vote.

The Constitution of 1925 bears the signatures of President Alessandri and of all the members of his cabinet, among whom the minister of justice and public instruction, José Maza, was the most active and efficient collaborator in the editing, phrasing, and arrangement of the approved text. It was promulgated and sworn to on September 18, 1925, in a solemn ceremony that took place in the salon of honor of the Moneda, in the presence of all members of the government, the diplomatic corps, high functionaries, and persons of distinction. Commemorative medals were struck off and distributed and its operation was begun under the most promising auspices. In conformity with it, parliamentary crises ended; the Constitution of 1833, which had ruled the country for ninety-two years, was replaced by a new fundamental code, which reestablished in another form the so-called "presidential" system.

As a matter of fact, that regime was not new in Chile. Without expressly saying so, the Constitution of 1833 had permitted its practice, with slight modification, until 1891. Only the conflict between the president and congress, started in 1890, and the revolution that accompanied it, cast doubt upon its legitimacy and definitely replaced it. But parliamentarism was not a deliberate creation of the conquerors of 1891. Political activity immediately conformed to this system through opposition to that just overthrown. If it had not been for the disgraceful, and oftentimes violent, electoral intervention of the government, it is probable that the power of the president would not have ended even at that time. The return to it, sanctioned by the Constitution of 1925, reestablished, then, a certain continuity in Chilean political life.

However, the leaders of the parties which had alternated in power before that date did not acquiesce in the new situation with good grace. Excluded from the immediate business of government, deprived of all influence in the management of public service, and reduced simply to the rôle of legislators, they showed little sign of vitality. Many of their members withdrew; and others were forced to abstain from taking part in public affairs. Aside from this, the policy of the next few years, until 1932, displayed the unforseen character of every period of transition and readjustment.

Scarcely was the Constitution of 1925 promulgated when a new congress had to be elected in place of the one dissolved the previous year. As President Alessandri ended his term at the end of the same year, it was almost necessary to hold the presidential election at the same time. The incidents arising from that state of electoral agitation led to the resignation of President Alessandri on October 1, when only about three months remained for the completion of his term. Colonel Carlos Ibáñez was then serving as minister of war and in that office represented the armed forces which had made the revolution of January 23. It had been proposed that the parties should present only one candidate and by this agreement avert an electoral struggle for the presidency of the republic. As this agreement was not brought about, a group of prominent citizens offered the presidential candidacy to the minister of war, who accepted it. President Alessandri told Colonel Ibáñez that his status as candidate disqualified him for continuing in office as minister of war. The colonel refused to give up this office and the president had to resign. In doing so, he surrendered the leadership of the cabinet to the very statesman who had been his competitor in the presidential election, Luis Barros Borgoño, who assumed power in the capacity of vice-president. Alessandri again went into exile.

THE REFORMIST DRIVE
(1925-1931)

Under the vice-presidency of Barros Borgoño the parties came to an agreement. Colonel Ibáñez resigned his candidacy; and then Emiliano Figueroa was proclaimed the only candidate for the presidency of the republic. He was an influential politician who in 1910 had been vice-president when critical conditions threatened the country and who, moreover, had rendered meritorious services as a diplomat. The election was won without difficulty and at the end of 1925 the new executive began his work. But he carried it on only a year and a quarter. From the beginning his policy was very similar to that of former presidents. He was surrounded by co-workers familiar with the party battles of the generation in which parties directed the government and exercised all the power. But he showed no appreciation of the considerable change that had been produced in national public life by the reform movements of

September, 1924, and January, 1925, whose ideology was frankly revolutionary.

From 1925 Colonel Ibáñez continued as minister of war and, acting in accordance with the intention of the revolution, sought to set the government on a different course—a course that should firmly establish the predominance of the executive over congress and allow him to put into practice the program of reforms favored by the army. By the first months of 1927 that policy of reform was resolutely inaugurated by the minister of war; and the president began to withdraw from the direction of public affairs and to yield his authority to the minister, who assumed it. A change in the cabinet then necessarily followed. Its head, Manuel Rivas Vicuña, a liberal politician of well-earned prestige, resigned. Colonel Ibáñez assumed the ministry of the interior and then the office of vicepresident, while the president availed himself of a permission to retire temporarily. Soon afterward, on the fourth of May, President Figueroa resigned. The country being thus summoned to a new election, Colonel Carlos Ibáñez, on the twenty-second of the same month, was chosen president of the republic without opposition.[6]

President Ibáñez, having arisen to the rank of general, was above all a man of the sword, distinguished for the vigor and rectitude of his character. In keeping with the revolutionary movement that raised him for the first time to the government as minister of war, he gave a vigorous impulse to the reform of administrative services and national institutions. Assisted by various efficient collaborators, he broadened the intervention and activity of the state in a manner until then unknown in Chile. Administrative reorganization and the introduction of new services demanded considerable expenditures. At the same time a vast plan of construction—railways, harbors, roadways, irrigation systems, canals and other public works—was completed. The credit of the country abroad and at home remained almost intact. In order to meet a mass of simultaneous payments it was necessary to contract loans to the amount of billions of pesos. Thus a budget was formed which was called "extraordinary," in order to differentiate it from the ordi-

---

[6] In a personal interview which took place in August, 1935, General Ibáñez assured the translator and editor that his purpose was to carry out the policy initiated by Balmaceda (see p. 342). Aquiles Vergara, in *Ibáñez, César criollo* (2 vols. Santiago, 1931), presents an unfavorable study of Ibáñez, his purposes and his methods. For a brief summary of political and economic conditions during his rule, see Charles A. Thomson, "Chile Struggles for National Recovery," in *Foreign Policy Reports*, IX (February, 1934), 283, *et seq.*

nary budget, which received the regular taxes and defrayed the ordinary expenses.

Not always were the payments from the extraordinary budget made with due economy. The contract, for example, for the services of the Foundation Company, a North American construction firm, proved a very bad transaction for the treasury because of the excessive cost and lack of care in respect to the works with which it was entrusted. The abundance of resources developed a certain spirit of extravagance in public administration, as was shown in the multitude of new employees, in the high salaries of their superiors and in the number of automobiles at their disposal, in expensive commissions abroad, and in other respects. All in all, a sensation of well-being pervaded the country, because, along with the opportunities for profit among the various social classes, consumptive power increased and money circulated in corresponding proportion.

Among the co-workers of the government of General Ibáñez, the minister of the treasury, Pablo Ramírez, had an important rôle. He was a politician who had figured in the radical ranks and whose financial operations aroused sharp criticism on the one hand and decided praise on the other. From his office he controlled all the public services and for some time came to be a sort of universal minister. Under his influence the public debt increased out of all proportion to the national resources; but he likewise brought about reforms and undertook enterprises which later were to be considered very honorable to that administration.

The services of public instruction were appreciably improved and became objects of laborious effort. The University of Chile became autonomous and enjoyed a sufficient budget. The branches of secondary, primary, normal, and technical education were completely reorganized; progress was made in school construction.[7] The police in their turn were reorganized and unified throughout the country, forming the *carabinero* corps, a much more efficient force and one affording personal security in the country and in the cities. The navy and the army, as is known, received preferential treatment and the aviation division secured its rightful place among the forces destined for national defense. Likewise the internal government was modified on the basis of a new scheme of geographic and administrative units, composed of sixteen provinces and two territories. This scheme was chiefly entrusted to Alberto Edwards, the writer

---

[7] For a personal account of educational conditions under the Ibáñez administration, see Mariano Navarrete C., *Los problemas educacionales* (Santiago, 1934).

and demographer, who was a conservative politician upon whose help President Ibáñez counted, especially during the last years of his administration. This scheme for redistricting the country has not been carried out, but it is worth while to remember that it helped give value to the territories of Aysen and Magallanes, whose cattle and lumber developments have opened up to the country an extensive field of prosperity.

In another field of activity the old problem of Tacna and Arica was finally settled by means of direct negotiation with Peru. The department of Tacna definitively remained in the power of the latter country and the department of Arica in the power of Chile. Likewise Chile had to pay Peru an indemnity and grant it other compensations. The treaty was signed in Lima in June, 1929, and it was put into execution at once, joint commissions of engineers fixing the boundaries.[8] This treaty was a great relief and a token of peace on the international horizon of South America. Participating in its immediate solution, aside from the president, were the minister of foreign relations, Conrado Ríos Gallardo, and the envoy extraordinary of Chile in Peru, Emiliano Figueroa Larraín.

By 1930 a sharp financial crisis became visible, which was then complicated by the lessened demand for Chilean products in foreign markets, and this brought with it a general economic depression. In this emergency the government determined upon the creation of the Nitrate Company of Chile, the so-called COSACH (*Compania del salitre de Chile*). This financial operation was widely discussed and censured in influential political circles. The capital of the company was evaluated at three billion pesos. Half of the shares were to belong to the treasury and the other half to the capitalistic enterprises which were exploiting the nitrate fields. In that same year, 1930, and in the three following years the company was to hand over to the state 660,000,000 pesos in quarterly payments.[9] The decrease in the consumption of Chilean nitrate abroad and some of the provisions of the law, which rightly held up its execution, did not permit the law to be wholly carried out; and its unpopularity contributed much toward undermining the prestige of the government.

In 1931 the monetary situation became acute, with the relative paralysis of business, the devaluation of mineral and agricultural

---

[8] See *The New International Year Book, 1929* (New York, 1898-1902, 1909- . . .), p. 183; also Dennis, *Tacna and Arica*, chap. xiii.

[9] For a reference to the formation of COSACH, consult the biographical sketch of Pablo Ramírez Rodríguez in V. Figueroa, *Diccionario histórico*, V, 603. See also *New International Year Book, 1932*, p. 173; Thomson, *op. cit.*, pp. 288-291.

products, and the almost complete closing of foreign markets to these products. There was discontent and dissatisfaction throughout the country. The government found itself obliged to suspend service on the foreign debt, which absorbed a great part of the ordinary receipts. In order to silence the censure of which it had been the object, it resorted by means of laws, or decrees with force of law, to measures in restraint of public opinion. In this sense the government did not respect constitutional guarantees. Imprisonment, banishment, and deportation were carried out without regard to legal formalities, freedom of the press, or parliamentary prerogative. In 1930 there was constituted by executive decree the so-called "Thermal Congress," because its members were appointed during a summer's sojourn of government deputies at the *termas* (hot baths) of Chillán. This strange method of setting up a legislative body was based on an electoral law which permitted parties in any department to avoid a contest in designating the candidates to be elected, provided there was an agreement to that effect. What could be done in one department could be done legally in all the departments of a province and in the entire country; so it came about that there were no elections in March of that year, thanks to the agreement of the representatives of the principal parties, whose agency, however, was very doubtful, and a supreme decree filled all the vacancies in both chambers. It is understood that the prestige of this congress was undermined by the basis on which it was selected and that the procedure itself was a very grave error.

Be that as it may, this congress as well as that which preceded it gave the executive every facility for doing his work. On more than one occasion that body vested him with extraordinary and most ample faculties to legislate in its name. Thus, while the years of prosperity lasted, the system of government had come to be a legal dictatorship, authorized by the legislative power, supported by the army, and consented to by the citizenry, and the impulse for reform which was to develop under such a system was totally obscured. Reproaches and protests arose from the civilian elements when the resources at the disposal of the government became scarce and exhausted, that is to say, when the financial and economic crisis clearly showed itself.

In a way unforseen by the public and after several abortive conspiracies, the political situation reached a crisis in July, 1931.[10]

---

[10] C. H. Haring, "The Chilean Revolution of 1931," in *Hisp. Amer. Hist. Rev.* (May, 1933), XIII, 197-203, gives details of the overthrow of Ibáñez, based on personal observation. See also *Current History*, Vols. XXXIII, XXXIV, *passim,*

In order to inspire confidence in the public and to give assurance that repressive measures would not be adopted against the discontented and that strict legal order would be maintained, there was brought to the ministry of the interior the well-known jurist and professor, Juan Esteban Montero, and to the ministry of the treasury the engineer and former railway director, Pedro Blanquier,[11] a man of upright character. In a few days they had to retire from office. Restlessness increased. On July 23, the university students resorted to an open strike against the government, accompanied by demands for real freedom of expression. A group took possession of the university building and made a fortress of it, thus giving the signal for public agitation which precipitated resistance. Their action was complicated by several unfortunate happenings, above all by the death of a student and a professor, both persons of wide and distinguished social connections. There followed confusion and suspension of work in industry and commerce. In the midst of that state of affairs General Ibáñez on July 26 resigned and fled the country.

THE GROWTH AND ACTIVITY OF THE ARMED FORCES

The intervention of the armed forces in the internal politics of the country, from 1924 until the termination of the government of General Ibáñez and even during a short period afterward, constituted an unaccustomed event in the republican practices of Chile. It was exactly one century since such a thing had occurred. The difficult era of institutional organization, which culminated in a period of anarchy between the years 1826 and 1830, after the dictatorships of O'Higgins and Freire, presented a case in which the army performed an active political rôle.[12] But from 1830 onward, only in the civil wars of 1851 and 1891 did the army and the navy assume a corporative rôle in action developed by the strife of civic groups. The conflict over and order reëstablished, those forces returned to their ordinary tasks and ceased to be preoccupied with exercising corporate control of the government. The Constitution of 1833 had prescribed that the public force was to remain "essentially obedient" and that no armed body could deliberate. The Constitution of 1925 reiterated the same prescription.

and especially Henry Grattan Doyle, "Chilean Dictatorship Overthrown," *ibid.*, XXXIV (September, 1931), 918-922.

[11] Blanquier had performed notable work in financing and organizing the railroads of Chile. For this purpose he floated a large loan in New York in 1928. See V. Figueroa, *op. cit.*, II, 226.

[12] See Chapter IX, *supra*.

All in all, from 1924 to 1932 the military forces set up and destroyed governments, often exercised power, counted upon the public confidence, and obtained the support of many well-known civilians, experts in political or administrative affairs. If we seek to explain the fact, we would find it above all in the social prestige of the sponsors and officers of the armed forces, a prestige derived from their organization, their discipline, and their culture, and heightened besides by the glory which these same institutions had gained in memorable campaigns. The people have always looked upon these institutions as their own and therefore the military profession has always enjoyed relative preëminence. Let us see how that situation has been maintained.

The frequent threats of war arising during the fitful negotiation of international affairs with Argentina and Peru at the end of the last and the beginning of the present century led to a great supply of warlike materials and a more or less complete reorganization of military establishments. The task has been an earnest and persistent one. In regard to the army, the reform first of the service of the national guard and next the establishment of compulsory service in 1900 brought a considerable number of men to the barracks, but in a somewhat irregular way. According to the Law of Recruits and Substitutes which this latter legislation created, all Chileans between eighteen and forty-five years of age were obliged to enroll themselves in military registers and to be incorporated in the army by lot and divided accordingly into active and passive, or reserve, contingents. Individuals from twenty to twenty-one years of age belonged to the active contingent and were the ones who must serve as soldiers for the term of a year or a year and a half. But at first it happened that after casting lots—and after those selected in conformity with it were called—only a few responded for service. The rest found exemption under the provisions of the law, always alleging important engagements. For that reason, therefore, the casting of lots was later omitted and it was decided that all the active contingents must join the ranks each year. The situation, however, was not greatly bettered, and those excluded from service were always numerous, especially as the system of casting lots had again to be employed on account of the impossibility of giving space in the barracks for the entire contingent of the year.

The regular army corps, amounting to a total of ten or twelve thousand men, form the instruction units, and, with the conscripts of each year who number about the same, make up the permanent army, which fluctuates around twenty thousand men of all classes of arms and equipment—infantry, cavalry, artillery, engineers, pontoon and aviation units. These forces are divided into four military zones, each of which has in charge the guarding of a determined number of provinces. With the force of *carabineros*, also militarized, the services have come to include more than fifty thousand men.

The first organization of this army was under General Emilio Körner, who bore the rank of captain in Germany, when engaged by the Chilean government, years before the revolution of 1891. The revolution, in whose ranks he acted as tactician, gave him prestige. Aided by other German and Chilean leaders, he introduced the Prussian regime into the army and the most modern armament of the Mauser and Krupp systems.

Beside the regular troops there are many other military establishments, namely, "directive," as the general inspection of the army; "administrative," as the department of military administration; "instruction," as the academy of war, the military school —this latter designed for the preparation of officers—and the school of subofficers. Moreover, the navy yards and arsenals have a separate personnel, charged respectively with the manufacture of projectiles and other military equipment and the preservation of arms and equipment.

The navy also has been increasing and augmenting its war equipment with new acquisitions until it includes about ten armored vessels and numerous submarines, torpedo boats, destroyers, and transports. These forces still lack unity in type so that the materials of one vessel cannot be adapted to another. The law of compulsory military service also applies here, but the number of "naval conscripts" has always been so few that it has not filled the personnel for the vessels and it has been necessary to resort to "enlistment" or voluntary contract.

The navy, like the army, has its own directive, administrative, and instruction departments. Within the latter are the naval school and the schools for pilots and cabin boys. The navy, moreover, has its health service, its arsenals, navy yards, and dry docks in Talcahuano. This bay, and that of Valparaiso, which are well defended, have become the fortified ports of the republic. The general direction of the fleet for many years was in charge of Vice-admiral Jorge Montt, president of the republic after the revolution of 1891. He obtained that rank when he gave up the supreme magistracy. Like Körner in the army, Montt inspired and executed reforms in the navy.

These institutions are maintained and directed with a certain autonomy. They are ruled by special laws and their investment of funds as well as their discipline and evolutions are in charge of their directing personnel; that is, under the inspection and care of the ministry of the respective branch to which they belong. The national defense made up of these elements has cost the treasury annually between one fourth and one fifth of its general income.[13] Laws for the protection of those invalided by the War of the Pacific, and insurance and retiring pensions, granted during recent years with great frequency, also enter into those budgets.

Aside from their own peculiar ends, the army and the navy render also positive cultural benefits to the country. The navy has several establishments devoted to meterological observations and designates vessels for hydrographic explorations, all of which contribute to the subject matter of national geography in a very appreciable form. Its *Anuario hidrográfico* (*Hydrographic Annual*) records those studies. Among those of greatest ability who have devoted themselves to this form of service are Captain Francisco Vidal Górmaz, author of the *Geografía náutica de Chile* (*Nautical Geography of Chile*), who is considered one of the most eminent of the geographers and sailors of the country; and Vice-admiral Luis Uribe Orrego, author of several works on naval history. In the case of the army, the preparation of topographical charts of different regions by the most competent officials has also greatly contributed to the exact knowledge of the country. One of the most learned leaders, General Jorge Boonen Rivera, wrote a *Geografía militar de Chile* of unquestioned value; and another, no less distinguished, General Indalicio Téllez, wrote the *Historia militar de Chile*.

The above exposition permits one to understand the passive and at times active adherence which public opinion lent to the *de facto* governments, depending as they did on armed forces, from 1924 to 1931. The government of General Ibáñez rested principally on the prestige of those forces; and the electoral act which brought him to the presidency in 1927 was like a reiteration of the confidence which the military organization inspired in the mass of the people. In various political sectors these marks of confidence seemed imposed by circumstances which the people were compelled to accept. But the spirit of a civilian regime that had been in practice for a century remained latent in many men, and once more in 1931 made itself felt.

---

[13] In the budget for 1935 the estimates for defense (war, navy, and aviation) were 284,872,950 pesos in a total of 997,301,053 pesos. See *Ley de presupuesto de entradas y gastos de la administración pública de Chile para el año 1935* (Santiago, 1934).

THE CIVILIAN REACTION
(1931-1932)

With the resignation of President Ibáñez there followed an agitated period during which civilian control was reëstablished. The general had turned over the command to the president of the senate, Pedro Opazo Letelier, who on the following day, July 27, 1931, appointed Juan Esteban Montero as minister of the interior and to him transmitted the command, making him vice-president in accordance with the constitution. Montero was popular, chiefly because of his upright civic attitude during the last days of the Ibáñez administration, and from the start proposed to adjust his actions strictly to legal norms. There were to be no more decree laws; in spite of the faults of its election, congress was to continue its functions; and the economic problems of the hour, accentuated by unemployment and popular misery, were to be solved through the orderly courses of government. On the other hand, it was necessary to normalize the political situation, for which purpose the free action of parties was to be reëstablished and presidential elections were to be called at once. These were set for October fourth.

Montero did not remain in the vice-presidency a month. In the middle of August a convention of professional men met in Santiago and, in spite of his insistent refusal to accept the appointment, proclaimed him candidate for the presidency of the republic. Feeling the candidacy to be incompatible with the vice-presidency, Montero transferred this office to the minister of the interior, Manuel Trucco, on the twenty-second of that same month.

The vice-presidency of Trucco, which lasted for three and a half months, was threatened in the early days of September by a revolt of the navy. The government was struggling to solve its financial difficulties when the crew of the *Admiral Latorre*, anchored in Coquimbo, revolted against its officers. The movement spread to other ships and extended to the naval stations of Valparaiso and Talcahuano. It appeared inspired by extremist tendencies, but within a week the army and the air corps stifled the revolt.

The election of October fourth gave a great majority to Montero over the opposing candidate, the former President Alessandri. A powerful political combination of the center, formed by the conservative and radical elements, under the name of Civic Union, brought victory to Montero. The candidacy of Alessandri was supported by leftist groups, of radical, liberal, and democratic affiliation. Montero assumed power on December 4, 1931.

The same criterion of strict legality was again in control of the government and was necessary in order to solve existing problems. Expenditures had to be reduced, salaries lessened, employees decreased—in short, a policy of the severest economy had to be adopted. It was necessary to reëstablish foreign credit by arbitrating for measures to meet the payments on the public debt, and at the same time to look after and secure places for more than two hundred thousand idle laborers who constituted a social menace. Nitrate sales had become paralyzed. The import trade resorted to the Central Bank in order to convert bank notes into gold with which to pay its creditors. It was necessary to ration the gasoline supply and for this reason to stifle the strike of the taxi drivers' union, in April, 1932. In the same month was dictated the law which created the Exchange Commission, in order to control the conversion of drafts into gold available for the creation of credits abroad. The same law ordered the conversion of bank notes into gold to be suspended for an indefinite time in order to maintain the specie reserve of the Central Bank, which already had decreased considerably. This policy was a return to the fiduciary regime which had ruled for more than half a century.

After the resultant devaluation of the peso there followed a rise in the cost of living and chaos in the domestic market and in commerce abroad. From all sides were heard complaints which demanded quick governmental action and instantaneous results. The enemies of the combination called CoSACH clamored for its dissolution and blamed it for the closing of the nitrate markets and for having placed this source of wealth at the mercy of foreign imperialism. Meanwhile, the government searched for solutions to this problem in Europe, but without hope of success.

In the midst of such a complex and difficult situation, both the civilian and military sectors of the population plotted to overthrow the government. The best known among the conspirators was Carlos Dávila, former Chilean ambassador to Washington during the Ibáñez administration and agile journalist of former years. In April, 1932, he had proposed a political plan of national economy to be directed by the State. The authorities sought him as a conspirator but failed to find him. On the other hand, Colonel Marmaduke Grove, named chief of aviation under the title of "Commodore of the Air," likewise harbored revolutionary proposals in order to implant a socialist regime in Chile. With similar purpose a lawyer of prestige, Eugenio Matte Hurtado, separated himself from another political group.

These representative men having been brought together, an insurrection of the armed forces followed. At midday on June 4, 1932, Commodore Grove gave the signal for the *coup d'état*. Airplanes, crossing the center of Santiago in all directions, scattered subversive proclamations and threatened the Moneda. After the uprising of the air forces came that of the School of Application of Infantry. Its commander, Colonel Pedro Lagos, was ready to support irrevocably the political plan of Dávila. In the evening of that day the rebels besieged the Moneda, demanding the resignation of President Montero and the surrender of command to a junta comprised of Dávila, Matte Hurtado, and General Arturo Puga. The president refused to resign, but under pressure he had to abandon the government and the country. The blow had been delivered without any counter movement among the remaining troops of the garrison. The junta started to function immediately and Commodore Grove assumed the ministry of national defense, whence he proclaimed the "Socialistic Republic of Chile."

In accordance with that plan, congress was dissolved and the government resorted once more to the despatch of decree laws. Through these decrees it was ordered, among other things, that the Bank of Popular Credit should return to its clients the articles of clothing, the sewing machines, and other implements given as security, and that the collection of pending commercial obligations should be suspended for thirty days. With respect to past obligations, the National Savings Bank (*Caja nacional de ahorros*) was ordered to give credit up to 50 per cent of its active funds to merchants and industrialists whose capital did not exceed two hundred thousand pesos, so that these might meet their obligations. With these and other similar measures the new regime seemed suddenly to become popular, and the meetings and parades in the capital, with radical mottoes and declarations, widely extended this popularity. Nevertheless, the junta lacked unity of purpose and agreement on active measures. It was a heterogeneous coalition. Echoing the indignation and alarm which that policy aroused among the upper classes, Dávila resigned; but in four days Colonel Lagos, with the forces at his command and with the aid of other regiments, again restored Dávila to power, displacing the rest of the members of the junta, and creating a new one. This occurred on the sixteenth of June; the socialist republic had lasted twelve days. Its leaders, Matte and Grove, were relegated to the island of Pascua and to utter their names in public was forbidden.

From that moment, Dávila's predominance in the government was admitted without contradiction. Several weeks later the junta, which had suffered modifications in its personnel, was dissolved.

Dávila himself then assumed complete power, with the title of provisional president. This change of front was not resisted by the higher social elements who expected Dávila to curb the advances of demagogical socialism, apparently becoming a serious danger. Besides, the improvised government counted upon obedience through the adherence of the public forces. Nevertheless, those same elements did not lend it active coöperation. The parties did not rally around it and the people showed no confidence in its course.

Meanwhile, the provisional government worked actively to ward off economic depression. It organized the development of the gold washings, mainly in the province of Coquimbo. It created the Amortization Bank for service on the foreign debt, an institution which later was perfected and enlarged; and it adopted other measures of relative merit. Nevertheless, deportations and other acts of violence continued. The Central Bank issued bank notes to defray public expenses outside the budget. Disorder in several divisions of the administration resulted from the haste or cunning with which measures were carried out. There was delay in determining the reëstablishment of normal constitutional conditions. These were obstinate factors which day by day increased the isolation of the government and finally precipitated its downfall.

With the purpose of silencing criticism arising from these conditions, Dávila in August dictated a decree law, summoning parliamentary elections for the end of October, 1932. This congress was to have a constituent character, and it was designed to discuss constitutional reform of an accentuated socialistic hue. The Constitution of 1925 already seemed to favor that tendency and permitted any measure in that direction to be put into practice by legal paths. The announced reform therefore appeared superfluous and well devised to distract public opinion from the problem that it was most urgent to solve; that is, the return to normality. Therefore, the determination of Dávila did not arouse favorable echo and was destined to fail.

In fact from early September it was observed that the provisional president was becoming increasingly isolated; that he was being abandoned by all sections of public opinion. Financial wastefulness led to a deficit of funds, thus leaving the public treasury in a critical state. The army no longer supported him unitedly and lost faith in his executive capacity. Thus it was that a slight military movement, headed by the air corps, was sufficient to force his resignation on September 13, which was scarcely one hundred days from that *coup d'état* which on the previous June fourth had brought him to power.

Dávila's government had marked the maximum point of disorganization in the political forces of the country. That such an ambiguous dictatorial regime, partly military and partly civil, could be maintained, even for a brief time, can only be explained by the chaotic state of public opinion and an ill-defined anxiety for social reform among the masses of the people. After him civilian reaction again made itself felt within a few weeks.

Dávila had surrendered the government to General Bartolomé Blanché and had embarked for the United States. Blanché had been one of the most loyal of the co-workers of General Ibáñez. In the last days of September, General Pedro Vignola,[14] at the head of the Antofagasta garrison, ignored the authority of Blanché and proclaimed a return to the constitutional system. In the south, the Concepción garrison followed him. Blanché, who was not particularly fond of power, yielded; and by constitutional procedure handed over the command to the president of the supreme court, Abraham Oyanedel, who took it over on October 2 in the capacity of vice-president. In order to fill the ministry of the interior, he called upon Javier Ángel Figueroa, who had been his colleague in legal affairs and, long years before, a liberal politician of the first rank.

Oyanedel, making valid former decrees, set the date of parliamentary and presidential elections for the thirtieth of October, when Arturo Alessandri, the same statesman who had already held the office during the years 1920-1925, was elected president by a tremendous majority. In the parliamentary elections, the traditionalist parties, styled those of the right or of order, won a majority of seats in both chambers. Alessandri commenced his second administration on December 24, 1932; and he made it from the beginning a return to constitutional and civic normality. Thus ended that turbulent period of nearly a year and a half which followed the resignation of President Ibáñez.

ALESSANDRI'S SECOND GOVERNMENT
(1932-1938)

It may not yet be the moment to appreciate the political development of recent years, under the second presidency of Alessan-

---

[14] A contemporary writer, quoting Col. Marmaduke Grove, says of him: "He was a good cadet, an excellent officer, but a bad chief." See *Hoy*, November 26, 1936, p. 22.

dri. But we shall complete our sketch of this aspect of national life by describing several facts of noteworthy importance. The situation under which the new government was inaugurated could not have been more disturbing. On one side, the unemployed, estimated at a hundred and sixty thousand persons, continued to present a very serious problem. The public treasury was in arrears and acknowledged a foreign debt close to four billion pesos (in gold of six pence), besides an internal debt of more than nine hundred million in current money. Service on the foreign debt had not been met during the preceding year, but it would have been imprudent to suspend service on the internal debt. The fall in the value of circulating money began to stimulate exports, but imports decreased, and this situation definitely disturbed the market. The sanitary state of the country, made more acute by unemployment and misery, had become deplorable. Typhus fever, the plague of lower civilizations, had already appeared in the capital as well as in the provincial towns; and in 1933 its prevalence became alarming. Lack of social discipline, fruit of so many fluctuations and upheavals like those which had just occurred, developed a tendency to discontent and encouraged peremptory demands for relief from existing evils. The government had to move in several directions at once and in the most rapid manner, in order to satisfy public clamor.

Alessandri's record decidedly shows his interpretation of the presidential regime established by the Constitution of 1925; and he set it up without condescension or vacillation. In filling the ministries, only the will of the president was to prevail, notwithstanding party agreements or even parliamentary majorities. The ministers were to remain in the government as long as they had the confidence of the chief of state, in spite of the censures of congress. There was no method other than that of accusation, constitutionally conducted, to remove them from office if the president should insist on keeping them and they decided not to resign. Such was the theory of the new regime.

Under that doctrine, ministerial stability, unknown in the country for half a century, has been achieved; and with it a certain methodical continuity in governmental operations. Ministers Gustavo Ross and Miguel Cruchaga Tocornal continued in office as ministers of the treasury and foreign relations respectively for more than four years. And the minister of national defense, Emilio Bello Codecido, had already (in 1937) served his ministry more than five years, from the very first day of the new administration. Other ministers have remained in their positions one or two years.

Leading executives of the last six decades. *Left to right*: Arturo Alessandri, president, 1920-1925, 1932-1938, popular leader, and later restorer of presidential power. Pedro Aguirre Cerda, present chief executive, important educational leader. Courtesy Sr. Alberto Cabero, Ambassador of Chile to the United States. José Manuel Balmaceda, upholder of the executive power in Chile's Civil War, 1891, founder of the party that still bears his name. Courtesy Instituto de Cinematografía Educativa, Universidad de Chile.

Above: Modern Araucanian woman, typifying the Indian element in the Chilean blood stream. *Below:* A modern "Huaso" made up for his part. Courtesy Grace Line.

Not always has the conduct of these secretaries of state been considered wise. There have been instances of bitter criticism or frank censure. But the presidentialist theory, in so far as the immovability of ministers is concerned, has remained unchanged. Not only, then, the text of the constitution but the practice of the government itself has firmly established the presidential regime, or, the personification of public power in the supreme magistrate.

To administer this order of things in a permanent fashion would not have been an easy task without the support of an organized civil force. Political uncertainty and opposition, arising from different sources, threatened new upheavals. In 1933, then, there was created the Republican Militia, a regular institution composed of armed and disciplined volunteers. Its organization began in 1932 and in the following year it already extended throughout the country, with over fifty thousand members. Its chief organizer and head was Eulogio Sánchez Errázuriz. The militia planned to prevent by armed force alteration of the legal order, and consequently it was to be at the service of every government conforming to normal constitutional standards. A whole century had passed since Portales reëstablished the "civic bodies" of the colonial era with a similar purpose; and since then the country had not resorted to such a forceful remedy. It happened, however, that in the two years of its existence the Republican Militia began to be transformed into a partisan corporation, with a perceptible tendency toward the right. This was due, of course, to the social status of the majority of its members—young men from the upper or the comfortable middle class. Its unpopularity then became manifest. From the parties of the left, attacks against it increased because it was thought to be illegally constituted and even a menace to the public peace. Its dissolution was brought about in 1935 not exactly because of that distrust but because it was thought that it was no longer indispensable to the ends for which it had been established. The constitutional government had strengthened its position.

The most arduous task of this government was unquestionably of an economic nature: to encourage by all possible means agricultural, mineral, and industrial production in order to absorb unemployment. The government had to find places for the one hundred and sixty thousand or more day laborers and artisans who eventually were thrown out of work because of the paralyzation of the nitrate plants and the general restriction of industry. It had to increase the capacity of the budget and balance public receipts and expenditures. This called for a financial reconstruction that Minister Ross undertook with resolute spirit. This reform had to be based upon the simultaneous increase of productive sources and the consumptive capacity of the population. For such purposes it seemed necessary for the Central Bank to increase the amount of paper money in circulation; and, from five hundred and fifty million pesos which this circulation had approximately reached in 1932, it rose to about one billion in 1937, while at the same time the metallic reserves of the bank decreased. This monetary inflation brought with it a maximum devaluation of the unit of exchange, the peso, and a resultant rise in the cost of living, from which the proletarian classes suffered grave harm. The increase in wages and salaries did not compensate them for the higher price of food, clothing, rent, and other individual necessities. The cost of daily and other periodicals measures this increase—in the last five years this cost has tripled.

Nevertheless, productive development has continued. With the aid of the banks of agricultural credit, industries, including coal and other forms of mining, have, on the one hand, greatly expanded, while on the other hand through the opening of foreign markets to many Chilean products, the sources of national wealth have experienced an effective increase. The amount of exports has been rising year after year. Nitrate sales have again expanded in the markets abroad. With the dissolution of the hated CosACH in 1933, the Corporation of Nitrate and Iodine Sales (*Corporación de ventas de salitre i yodo*) was established and entrusted with the propaganda and distribution of these products.[15] In centers of nitrate exploitation, production has been renewed since then, at least partially; and from the fiscal duties on the exportation of these products the government has decided to reëstablish abroad service on the public debt. Finally, thanks to economic expansion in the different phases to which we have been referring, unemployment disappeared almost entirely in the course of three years.

An increase in budgetary capacity has been another easily perceptible fact. From a billion in 1934, the budget reached two billion in 1938,[16] thanks to the reforms introduced principally in the customs tariffs and in the taxes on commerce and industries. Their

---

[15] This law passed the Chilean congress on January 3, 1934, and was signed by President Alessandri on January 8. Under the law, the private companies which had been absorbed in CosACH were reëstablished. See *New International Year Book, 1934*, p. 141; Thomson, *op. cit.*, p. 290.

[16] The ordinary expenditures for 1938 were estimated at 1,589,100,000 pesos. For the three years ending December 31, 1937, it was estimated that Chile had redeemed some 13 per cent of its total foreign debt with an allowance of 1.8 per cent interest. See *New International Year Book, 1937*, p. 149.

prosperity, which also is evident, has permitted these activities to withstand the taxes. This situation of comparative fiscal ease has favored the improvement or extension of administrative services in their various ramifications and the execution of important public works—above all, road construction, irrigation, and health. There have been complaints, nevertheless, with respect to deficiencies in these types of service, but they arise in large part from the contrast between what should be done in these directions and what could be realized only by counting upon extraordinary measures. Alessandri's government has not resorted to such means, and what he has been able to accomplish has been paid for out of ordinary receipts.

Social legislation for the direct benefit of the proletarian masses has since 1920 been one of the national aspirations furthered by President Alessandri. During his second administration, as during his first, the program he sponsored has been only partially realized because of opposition from the traditionalist parties, whose individualism is still their most distinguishing characteristic. Nevertheless, some additional legislation has been adopted since that date. This has been supplemented by the law dictated in 1937 on a minimum living wage for employees in commerce and industry—a far-reaching law among the measures demanded by the middle classes in recent times. It must be followed by a law of minimum wage for the dayworkers on farms and in cities. A bill to this end is still (in 1938) being held up in the legislative chambers. Aside from this, there have not been any serious labor conflicts in this period except for a railway strike in 1936.

Internal tranquillity also has kept pace with the policy of peace and friendship which the republic for many years has been practicing with all countries of the world and particularly with its neighbors. In that policy there has been stressed, through choice, a certain Americanist feeling or tendency to coöperate with the rest of the republics on the continent in preserving reciprocal harmony and understanding. Chile intervened amicably in 1935 together with Argentina to put an end to the "Chaco War" between Paraguay and Bolivia. Sincere good will has characterized relations between Chile and Peru since the Tacna and Arica dispute was settled. This was very satisfactorily confirmed in the same year with the signing and approval of a commercial treaty between both countries.[17] Similar pacts, although not of that same scope, have

---

[17] The United States Department of Commerce reported that 1937 was the most prosperous year for Chile since 1929. See *La Hora* (Santiago, Chile), June 6, 1938.

been made or are in the process of being made, with Bolivia, Ecuador, Colombia, Cuba, Brazil, and other countries. The Inter-American Peace Conference,[18] held in Buenos Aires at the end of 1936, permitted Chile to reiterate its proposals of continental cordiality and its willingness to coöperate in maintaining unity of purpose among all the republics of the continent. The minister of foreign relations, Miguel Cruchaga Tocornal, took part personally in this conference. His reputation as an internationalist, confirmed by the leading rôle he has taken in Europe and America, helped during four years to supply a certain tone of security and confidence to the conduct of Chile's foreign policy.

Alessandri's administration has not been above reproach and criticism, but this is not the place to examine it. Several reforms have not been realized because of the resistance of the parties which, through chance parliamentary majorities, have made up the basis of government. Several measures for the public good, particularly those destined to alleviate the misery of the lower classes, have not been adopted because of that same resistance or lack of sufficient funds; and other measures, such as the full application of the law of compulsory primary education, have suffered delays through various circumstances. The conservative forces have exerted the most influence in the government because they have succeeded in maintaining unity of action and a majority in both branches of congress. In the elections of March, 1937, they again obtained a triumph over the leftist parties, although resorting once more to the systematic buying of votes—a practice which appeared to have been abandoned.

Be that as it may, the president has not yielded to the extreme claims of the rightist parties which in 1936 armed him with full repressive authority against any demonstration by word or deed contrary to the established order. This was the so-called law of "internal security," which up to the present the government has applied only on rare occasion.[19] According to the declaration of the chief of state himself, it

---

[18] See Michael F. Doyle (ed.), "The Inter-American Conference for the Maintenance of Peace," in *International Conciliation,* Pamphlet 328 (March, 1937), pp. 193-289, published by the Carnegie Endowment for International Peace.

[19] The columns of *Hoy* for the issues from October, 1936, to February, 1937, are filled with references to this law, which was passed February 12, 1937, the anniversary of the declaration of Chilean independence. According to its opponents, the law was designed to repress freedom of speech and of the press and was passed in time to influence the congressional elections of March, 1937.

is limited exclusively to prosecuting crimes committed by those who want to substitute and replace the democratic régime of government by a dictatorship, be it of the proletariat or of any other kind. It seeks equally to defend the republic from red or white dictatorship. It does not prosecute those who criticize the government with the intention to better its methods, but punishes those who transgress against the republic and democracy, and try to destroy them.

[Thanks in part to the above law and to the activity displayed in government circles, the conservative forces secured a majority of the seats in congress in the elections of 1937. This result apparently led its opponents to seek greater unity among themselves. Accordingly, the various parties that were inclined toward the left —socialists, communists, a portion of the democrats, and the major part of the radicals—united in 1938 to form a left wing popular front, somewhat similar to the French model. In due time, after considering the claims of Colonel Marmaduke Grove, this combination selected as its standard-bearer Pedro Aguirre Cerda, a former associate of Alessandri in the latter's more liberal days and a prominent educational and social leader. The conservative elements, made up largely of the old conservative and liberal parties, with some recruits from the radical and democratic ranks, settled upon Gustavo Ross, who had headed the treasury during the first four years of Alessandri's administration and whose conduct of that ministry had done much to reëstablish the financial credit of Chile. Each of these candidates, it may be added, belongs to the group of Chilean millionaires.

[As a further disturbing element in what promised to be a bitterly fought campaign, General Carlos Ibáñez, who had returned to the country in May, injected his candidacy. The principles he espoused seemed nazistic in tendency. The faction that professed them had become increasingly noisy during the past few years and, in view of his own record as president, Ibáñez might seem a fitting candidate. Whatever strength the movement may have had was entirely dissipated when on September 5, 1938, a premature uprising led the government to repress the disturbing faction and to place its candidate under arrest. In the struggle to recapture certain buildings seized by the Nazis, about a hundred people were killed. Later, when the fascistic chief, Jorge González von Maree, assumed all responsibility for the uprising, Ibáñez was released, but withdrew his candidacy. A few of his followers voted for Ross, the conservative candidate, but most of them supported Aguirre Cerda.

[Much bitter discussion and a few minor outbreaks characterized the closing days of the campaign. When the result was declared, Aguirre Cerda was credited with some 212,000 votes, to 199,000 for Ross. The defeated party claimed that the actual majority was less than a thousand and had been obtained by fraud. The demand for a recount threatened to precipitate civil strife, and in November, Ross, upon being assured that the army would not support him, withdrew his demand. His action, plus the decision of President Alessandri to accept the leftist victory, meant that Chile was to have the first popular front government in South America. This triumph seemed to assure a continuance of the measures for social betterment that have characterized recent years of Chilean history. Public sentiment in the capital and in other centers indicated popular acceptance of this result.

[The new administration started promptly on its program for social betterment. It proposed to increase national production, improve the status of the common people, provide for internal security and internal defense, reorganize public instruction, reduce the prices of foodstuffs, and make extensive appropriations for highway construction, public housing, and other social projects.

[By-elections to fill vacancies in the Chamber of Deputies demonstrated the popularity of this program, but it was immediately neutralized by the great earthquake of January 24, 1939—the most disastrous in all Chilean history. Six of the richest agricultural provinces of the country, including such rich cities as Concepción, Chillán, and Valdivia, were laid waste, with the loss of nearly 50,000 lives and a property damage of $30,000,000 to $40,000,000. Without hesitation the new government faced the appalling task of giving aid to the sufferers and beginning the process of reconstruction—tasks in which it was assisted by help from Argentina and other neighboring countries, and from the United States and Europe.

[This calamity naturally checked the administration's policy of internal development and for a time stilled partisan clamor. In undertaking recovery, the government planned to combine its previous program for increasing national production with reconstruction of the devastated regions. The president asked congress to authorize loans of two and a half billion pesos to finance the combined program. This proposal called for an increase in taxes on incomes, inheritances, and corporations that would especially affect the more wealthy element of the population. For a time the rightist opposition in congress promised to neutralize the policy of President Aguirre, but in the end he secured substantial approval of these twin proposals, which were to be financed in part through a credit of $5,000,000 from the Export-Import Bank of the United States, later increased to $12,000,000, but depended largely upon an increase in internal taxes and control over economic enterprises of foreign ownership.

[Opposition to this program further heightened conservative discontent with the president and his supporters. An attempt to drive the minister of the interior from his ministry failed, but the warlike situation abroad threatened still further difficulties. The actual outbreak of war greatly reduced Chile's imports and exports, but its trade balance for 1939 was more favorable than that of the previous year. Nazi elements among the population, of both Spanish and German origin, while not numerous, had already become vociferous and difficult to control. The government, however, promptly suppressed these manifestations of unrest by weeding out the less dependable military and police officials and exiling agitators of foreign birth. In this way an incipient revolt of July, 1939, was suppressed and ultimately its putative leader, former President Ibáñez, was once more forced into exile.

[Meanwhile party division developed among the groups supporting the administration. In both the radical and socialist parties, its chief supporters, one faction veered more directly toward the left while the leaders of the liberal party sought to attract the more conservative elements of these parties to the right. These maneuvers, with some support from the communist element of the Popular Front, forced a reorganization of the cabinet in which, however, the controlling element still supported President Aguirre. In a measure these political changes reflected charges of fraud in connection with Jewish and Spanish refugees, brought against the administration. Furthermore, continued opposition from the right, in July, 1940, pointed toward congressional measures to suppress the communist party. On the other hand, the leftists charged their opponents with "flirting with the Nazis" and building up a private army, in order to bring themselves into power.

[In its foreign policy the new government brought about closer commercial affiliation with Argentina and the settlement of a minor boundary dispute. Uniformly supporting a wider Pan-American policy, including closer relations with the United States, Chile in common with other Latin American countries has accepted military and other missions from the United States and has further coöperated in defense of the Western hemisphere. The government,

however, refused to join other American nations in protest against
the Russian invasion of Finland, but its favor to Spanish Loyal-
ists threatens to lead to a brief diplomatic break with the Franco
government. Meanwhile it is taking measures to protect itself from
further Nazi infiltration.] [20]

So it is that Chile has come to be considered abroad as a regularly constituted democracy, which seeks the path of betterment
without violent disturbance. Chile is a democracy where one can
speak and write with the utmost freedom, where individual guarantees are respected, where refuge is offered to those persecuted elsewhere for the expression of their ideas, and where one is justified
in hoping for a better and more harmonious understanding among
all social classes.

---

[20] The editor has supplied the part enclosed in brackets from the files of the
New York Times for 1938-1940, and from contemporary Chilean newspapers.

CHAPTER XX

FOREIGN RELATIONS

EVEN THOUGH we have referred, on earlier pages, to various acts of international importance, something still remains to be said the better to emphasize certain aspects of Chile's relations with other countries, from the last years of the past century to the fourth decade of the present century.

When the revolution of 1891 ended, the country found itself involved in a serious diplomatic struggle with the United States. In the middle of October of that year a hundred sailors of the *Baltimore*—a vessel of the North American fleet anchored at Valparaiso—landed at the port. They were in search of amusement and in one of the cross streets met a group of Chilean workmen. For some unknown cause a quarrel started among them and shortly degenerated into a real fight with clubs, stones, and fists, which resulted in the death of two sailors and the wounding of several others. The North American minister in Chile immediately sent a note to the government asking explanations and claiming the logical indemnity. A judicial investigation, he was told, would determine the response to his note and the resolutions to be adopted.

From that moment, diplomatic efforts took a bitter turn, to such an extent, indeed, that the Chilean minister of foreign relations asked the department of state in Washington to recall its representative in Santiago, because he had become an "unacceptable person" to the government. This was not done. The situation was aggravated by the publication of a telegram by the minister of foreign affairs, directed to the representative of Chile in the United States, charging him to protest against certain assertions made by the president of that country about the *Baltimore* affair in his message to the North American congress. The telegram was worded in anything but cordial terms. When it was known, the government of the United States sent an ultimatum to Chile, demanding the withdrawal of such terms and the indemnity previously asked for, and threatening to cut off diplomatic relations if the demand were not acceded to. Before such a threat the government of Chile found itself in the dilemma either of acceding to the demand, thus sacrificing its national *amour-propre*, or of accepting war in order to satisfy that same sentiment. It preferred the former;

it acceded and paid the government of the United States an indemnity of seventy-five thousand pesos to those wounded and to the families of those killed in the affair at Valparaiso.[1]

That was not the only disagreeable affair in which Chile found itself involved with foreign countries after the civil war. Because of the military operations, and especially the pillage that followed them in Valparaiso and Santiago, citizens of several foreign countries, almost all merchants, suffered considerable damage. Their ministers in Chile brought up in their behalf numerous diplomatic claims for indemnity. These requests amounted to great sums— hundreds of thousands of pesos. But none degenerated into a violent quarrel like the dispute with the United States. On the contrary, they employed for their solution conciliatory proceedings—compromises and arbitrations—just as after the war with Peru and Bolivia.

The country most interested was England. Chile came to an agreement with that country by which there was set up an Anglo-Chilean tribunal of arbitration composed of a representative of each of the states and a third member. The tribunal functioned in Santiago and in a short time rendered a decision on the claims presented to it. For the most part, it declared them null; and those which it allowed were considerably reduced and thus paid.

In spite of the decisions and compromises arranged with other countries, questions of this nature remained pending for a long time. But the Chilean diplomatic service in these claims as in others presented later—caused by the popular riots into which strikes have at times degenerated—has sustained and continues to sustain firmly the same doctrine of international law practiced among themselves by European states; namely, "Governments are not responsible for injuries occasioned to foreigners because of any internal disturbance whatever, when the constituted authority has done its utmost to avoid them." The reason is simple: citizens are not paid in such cases, and it is not just to put foreigners in a privileged position, guaranteeing them from that class of risks, since they are protected by all the laws and courts of the republic equally with any citizen of the country.

---

[1] For an account of the *Baltimore* incident, see H. C. Evans, *Chile and Its Relations with the United States* (Durham, 1927), pp. 145-152. Consult also Osgood Hardy, "The Itata Incident," *Hisp. Amer. Hist. Rev.*, V (May, 1922), 195-226, and "Was Patrick Egan a Blundering Minister?" *ibid.*, VIII (February, 1928), 65-81.

BOUNDARY DISPUTES AND ARBITRATION WITH ARGENTINA

In furthering the diplomatic reclamations, the old question of boundaries with Argentina was renewed. The Treaty of 1881 seemed to be defined in clear terms, for it determined that the line marking the division of waters in the cordillera, the *divortium aquarum*, should serve as the boundary between the two countries and that whatever difficulty arose in the demarcation should be settled by arbitration. But it was not so in practice. Eleven years after, when the Argentinian commission began the work of fixing the landmarks, it maintained that the *divortium aquarum* of the Andes was not the principle expressed in the boundary, but the highest peaks, inasmuch as the Treaty of 1881 read textually, "the highest peaks that divide the waters."

As a matter of fact, both interpretations presented difficulties, but those arising from the "line of the *divortium aquarum*" were nothing in comparison with those connected with the "line of the highest peaks." Suffice it to say that in the Patagonian region, where the cordillera of the Andes is a confused labyrinth of scattered peaks, the Argentinian claim would have meant the extension of its territory to the Pacific, while the Chilean formula would in no case have extended its claim to the Atlantic, because the eastern coast of that end of America is a vast plain cut by rivers which rise in the Andes at a great distance from the ocean.

From that time on negotiations were confused and the question remained unsettled for several years, giving rise in each country to threats of war. The experienced leaders for marking the boundary, Francisco Moreno for Argentina, and Diego Barros Arana for Chile, maintained their respective lines with unalterable firmness. Finally, in 1898, when an armed crisis seemed imminent, a protocol was signed by the representatives of both republics, leaving the question to the arbitration of the king of England.[2] Almost at the same time an agreement was also reached to settle by arbitration another of the rough points in litigation: the delimitation of the Puna of Atacama, which was a separate question. In this matter, the arbitrator appointed was the plenipotentiary of the United States in Argentina, William I. Buchanan.[3]

---

[2] A brief reference to these boundary disputes is to be found in F. A. Kirkpatrick, *A History of the Argentine Republic* (Cambridge, England, 1931), pp. 206-208. For further references see *New International Year Book, 1898,* pp. 51, 184; *ibid., 1899,* pp. 62-63; *ibid., 1901,* pp. 170-171; *ibid., 1902,* pp. 154-156.

[3] See Paul D. Dickens, "Argentine Arbitrations with Reference to the United

To commemorate these agreements, designed to end at once all misunderstandings, the presidents of Chile and Argentina, Federico Errázuriz Echaurren and General Julio Roca, who had taken a very direct part in them, held a formal conference on board their respective war vessels, in the Strait of Magellan. The cordiality manifested by both executives resulted in their meeting's being called the "embrace of the straits."

Shortly after this ostentatious manifestation of friendship, the delegations of Chile and Argentina, composed of prominent politicians of both countries, met in Buenos Aires to discuss the dividing line of the Puna of Atacama, in the presence of the North American minister. The conference ended without agreement and the arbitrator made the demarcation. The greater part of the disputed territory fell to Argentina. This ended the litigation of the Puna (1899).

The result of this negotiation produced great discontent in Chile. It was said that President Errázuriz had "given up the Puna." A similar sentiment arose in Argentina because, as that country wished all of it, the piece assigned to Chile was judged a spoliation. Furthermore, the press of each country began to accuse the other of exercising acts of domination and even of diverting streams of water in the territories submitted to the decision of the British arbitrator, who had not as yet rendered his decision. He had appointed a tribunal of technicians to investigate the litigation and had resolved to send an exploring expedition to the disputed ground. A commission actually came, in charge of an English colonel, Thomas Holdich, a member of the tribunal of arbitration. It was said that by means of such unfounded reports each country tried to give a false impression to the explorers and to flout the good faith of the arbitrator.

The agitation spread from the press to the congresses, and from the congresses to the people. During the whole of 1901, war again appeared more threatening than ever. Military and naval armaments were assembled in such quantity and at such enormous expenditure that they were out of all proportion to the resources of the two republics. This created the impression that both were headed for destruction. Little by little passions were allayed. The mutual complaints were settled by new agreements, and finally, before His Britannic Majesty could give an opinion, Chile and Argentina celebrated two pacts that removed all fear of conflict.

States Participation Therein," in *Hisp. Amer. Hist. Rev.*, XI (November, 1931), 469-472. See also T. H. Holdich, *The Countries of the King's Award.*

They were the pacts of May, 1902, which are very explicit and worthy of note on more than one point.

By the first it was resolved to adjust all differences that might arise between the two countries by arbitration; by the second, agreement concerning armaments and naval equality was made in such a manner that for five years neither could acquire new war vessels by which it might outstrip the other. This pact, the only one of the sort known up to that time, attracted much attention throughout the civilized world. It was a tribute to justice and peace hitherto unknown. Furthermore, in a supplementary act, stipulations were made for the neutrality of Chile in the affairs of Argentina on the Atlantic and the neutrality of Argentina in the affairs of Chile on the Pacific.

Months later, when the echoes of the mutual demonstration with which those pacts were celebrated were not yet silenced, the arbitral opinion of King Edward VII was announced. Without giving the decision to either of the litigant states, this established a dividing line that was a median between the claims of both. In that way the decision of the king was a decision worthy of Solomon; it ordered the disputed area to be divided into two almost equal parts. Chile and Argentina concurred in it and considered as ended a litigation concerning boundaries that had lasted for half a century, from 1847-1902.

PACTS WITH BOLIVIA AND PERU

After the arrangements with Argentina, definite steps were also taken to harmonize relations with Bolivia, still subject to the state of truce that had been agreed upon at the conclusion of the War of the Pacific. After most laborious negotiations a Chilean-Bolivian treaty of peace and friendship was signed at Santiago, in 1904, according to which Bolivia recognized the absolute and perpetual ownership of Chile throughout the coastal zone which Chilean workmen had occupied before Chile had taken armed possession of it. In exchange it obtained from Chile valuable concessions, among which were the construction of a railroad between Arica and La Paz, designed to give a twofold outlet to Bolivian products by way of the Chilean coast; namely, that of Antofagasta, established for some time by the railroad that leads to Oruro; and that of Arica, which was constructed within a few years.

Chile, moreover, was obliged to offer a guarantee to foreign capital invested in the construction of Bolivian railroads and obtained as compensation a rebate on railway tariffs in favor of

Chilean commerce. Thus after twenty years of distrustful truce (1884-1904) there followed an era of mutual confidence. But fifteen years later, when it seemed that nothing could happen to alter that state of things, there arose in Bolivia a twofold hope cherished by some of its political groups. Claims were advanced, on the one hand, for the cession by Chile to Bolivia of a port on the Pacific which could be no other than Antofagasta or Arica (the only ones bound to Bolivian territory by railroad), while, on the other hand, Bolivia went still further and sought the recovery of the whole territory of Antofagasta, perpetually ceded to Chile by the Treaty of 1904.[4]

Founded as were those desires on the necessity of obtaining for Bolivia an outlet to the sea, the representatives of that country carried them to the European conference of the League of Nations and before the government of the United States, while negotiations between Chile and Peru were being transacted in Washington. Their petitions were not heard because the desire of Bolivia to have a port on the Pacific implied the revision of the treaty of 1904, which Chile could not accept, since it would have involved the renunciation of rights legitimately acquired with the consent of the very country making the claims. Direct negotiations, nevertheless, between Bolivia and Chile respecting the cession of a port on the Pacific were resumed, after the definite settlement was reached in the litigation between Chile and Peru respecting the sovereignty of Tacna and Arica, and are still pending.[5]

The dispute over those territories has finally been solved after long and unfortunate negotiations. By the Treaty of Ancón,[6] Peru, in addition to ceding to Chile perpetually and irrevocably the province of Tarapacá, had left Tacna and Arica under the latter's sovereignty for ten years, at the end of which time a popular plebiscite, by vote of the inhabitants, was to decide to which of those two countries they should definitely belong. The one with whom they were left was to pay the other ten million pesos. When the moment arrived, a special protocol was to establish the form for carrying out the plebiscite.

---

[4] Regarding definite arrangements with Bolivia, consult Dennis, *Tacna and Arica,* pp. 198-199.

[5] See *New International Year Book, 1922,* p. 90. During the summer and fall of 1921, the Bolivian government requested the secretary of the League of Nations to refer to the assembly some aspects of the Tacna-Arica dispute which concerned itself. In September Bolivia further requested the league to revise the Treaty of 1904. Because the matter was so thoroughly an American question, the assembly avoided action.   [6] For this treaty, see p. 335.

Ten years passed (1883-1893) and the Treaty of Ancón could not be carried into effect in this respect because Peru lacked funds to cover the stipulated indemnity in case it was favored in the plebiscite, and because it did not yet have a stable, responsible government. Moreover, the two countries could not agree on the manner of carrying out the vote. As Chile remained sovereign in Tacna and Arica until a contrary course should be determined, Peru contended that the representative of a foreign country should preside over the voting as intervener or arbitrator, assisted by agents of the interested countries. As thus stated, agreement on the question was impossible, in spite of the many negotiations undertaken to secure it during the interval. The government of Chile, strictly adhering to one single opinion, would not accept those conditions, still less those that the government of Peru put forth with respect to the persons who might take part in the voting.

Later, however, the government of Chile took a decisive step to put an end to the question. Through the mediation of the government of the United States at the end of 1921, it invited the government of Peru to initiate direct negotiation which should settle, once for all, the nationality of those territories. The proposal being accepted by Peru, the representatives of both countries met in Washington in 1922, presided over by the North American secretary of state and agreed upon the basis for a protocol, which the governments of Chile and Peru approved. According to this, the final solution of the litigation was left to the arbitration of the president of the United States, who was to decide whether the plebiscite stipulated in the Treaty of Ancón should be carried out or not; and, if his decision was affirmative, in what manner it should be effected; and, if negative what should be the further fate of the disputed provinces. His decision was made in conformity with the views sustained by the Chilean government; he declared that the plebiscite should be carried out (1925).

But that resolution, which was thought at first easy to execute, could not be realized in practice. The representative of the arbitrator, acting on the spot with the representatives of the two interested countries, was persuaded that it was absolutely impossible to determine in due manner the persons who had the right to vote in the plebiscite. The irritating incidents between Peruvians and Chileans to which the registrations gave rise roused their indignation and even provoked violence. Finally Peru refused to continue the registration of its voters and the plebiscite was declared a failure. However, the arbitrator continued to be interested in reaching a solution and in carrying on the negotiations at Washington. Under this suggestion, Chile and Peru renewed diplomatic relations in 1928 in order to see how to make a direct arrangement. This was effectively accomplished on June 3, 1929, when the final treaty ending the old dispute was signed in Lima. Tacna was returned to the sovereignty of Peru and Arica remained in Chile's possession, ceded in perpetuity. In compensation, the latter paid Peru six million dollars in gold. The treaty being ratified by the respective congresses, they immediately proceeded to the demarcation of both provinces. Bolivia's aspirations to have its own port on the Pacific were ignored.[7] The arrangement of 1929 opened a new period of cordiality between Chile and Peru, signalized chiefly by the commercial treaty of 1935 between both republics.

THE AMERICANIST POLICY OF CHILE

Aside from that question nothing has seriously disturbed the good relations of the republic with other countries. If the European war from 1914 to 1918, which reached world-wide proportions, did seriously endanger local commerce and finances, it did not involve the country in the complications of international policy, since Chile declared the most rigorous neutrality and held to it firmly. Therefore its position later in the League of Nations and other international assemblies held in Europe with the assistance of American countries, to settle the new questions aroused by the war, has been profitable and of no little significance for its credit and prestige.[8]

The cordial and friendly foreign policy of Chile has not suffered alteration; and, although the greater part of its mercantile interests and intellectual offerings brought it nearer to the old continent, especially before the conflagration of 1914, America has been its principal field of action. Its American policy, however, has not excelled in practical results. If it has tended to widen its commercial relations and to encourage navigation by cheapening transportation, it has not gained many benefits thereby, because increased customs duties present difficulties to interchange on a large scale.

In the Pan-American congresses—solemn assemblies of all the states of the continent—that have met at Washington, Mexico, Río de Janeiro, Buenos Aires, Santiago, Havana, and Montevideo,

---

[7] For the settlement of the dispute with Peru, see Dennis, *Tacna and Arica,* Chap. XIII, and also his *Documentary History of the Tacna-Arica Dispute.*

[8] For conditions in Chile during the World War, see P. A. Martin, *Latin America and the War* (Baltimore, 1925), pp. 264-347.

Chile's position has had to be at times a contentious one, especially in the one at Mexico, because Peru, with its eyes fixed on Tacna and Arica and counting on the adherence of Argentina, tried to bind the American countries to obligatory arbitration. According to this principle, every international question in which two states find themselves in disagreement must be submitted to arbitration. Chile, which had given so much evidence in favor of optional arbitration, supported the latter formula and triumphed. These conferences have discussed many other interesting points of inter-American policy and already have served to unite the countries of the continent in a common purpose. Mutual discords have frequently broken out among them, but in recent years their animosity has been quieted. Within these conferences the real and efficient leadership of the United States has been clearly brought out. The government of Chile, recognizing that fact, has oriented its external policy toward a close and permanent connection with the great northern republic upon bases of an economic and intellectual type.[9]

No less important has been the increasing closeness of its relations with the Argentine Republic, manifest in practical form in the inauguration of the transandine railroad through Uspallata in 1910, and in the commemorative ceremonies of the centenary of independence of both countries, which took place the same year. That railroad is the first to bind together straight across the great cordillera the capitals of the two republics, and the centenary celebration gave occasion for a reciprocal visit of their presidents and a great demonstration of fraternity. Similar demonstrations, with like purpose, have frequently taken place since then between both countries without any interruption.

Chile has put into practice a similar policy with Peru and Bolivia on the Pacific coast, with Brazil and Uruguay on the Atlantic coast, and with all the other South American countries. Its connections with the more remote republics, from Mexico to Panama, including the Greater Antilles, have not been less cordial, so that no threat of conflict, no misunderstanding has affected the republic in recent years.

---

[9] See D. Y. Thomas, *A Hundred Years of the Monroe Doctrine* (New York, 1923), *passim;* Alejandro Alvarez, *The Monroe Doctrine* (New York, 1924), *passim.* The press of Santiago during the winter of 1936-1937 frequently commended the attitude of President Franklin D. Roosevelt in connection with the Buenos Aires Conference. A recent mass meeting in Santiago expressed a wholehearted support of the northern executive's humanitarian policy in favor of the Jews and purposed to foster Jewish immigration into Chile. See *New York Times,* November 22, 1938.

CHAPTER XXI

CONTEMPORARY SOCIAL DEVELOPMENT

POPULATION AND WEALTH

In the last twenty years of the nineteenth century, two events chiefly influenced Chilean society: the War of the Pacific and the Revolution of 1891. The war extended the frontiers of the country into the deserts of the north between 18° and 24° of latitude, and placed under Chile's sovereignty the exploitation of the abundant natural wealth of that zone: nitrate, guano, copper, sulphur, and other products. The revolution drew out the civic spirit, stressed democratic forms in the government, and brought with it a parliamentary regime as unmethodical as it was costly. Under this regime, class differentation was emphasized and the proletariat began its struggle for the betterment of living conditions. Foreign events and above all the special attention to the wage-earning classes, which resulted from the World War of 1914-1918, gave greater impetus to that struggle; and it has not ceased up to the present time. Such a politico-social attitude has produced disturbances and other consequences in the actual economy of the country, an economy characterized by a constant increase in productive sources.

The population, nevertheless, has increased only very slowly. The Census of 1907 computed it at 3,231,496 inhabitants; that of 1920 stated that it had reached 3,731,573 that year; and that of 1930 (which is the last) brought the level up to 4,287,445. Statistical calculations for 1938 indicate the figure of 4,700,000. The annual percentage of increase is one of the lowest in America. Approximately half of this population is distributed among towns of more than one thousand inhabitants, and half in the smaller villages and in the country. But if one were to consider as forming urban population only those who live in cities of more than five thousand inhabitants, its total will not average above 43 per cent. In any case, it is an actual fact that the urban population has increased in proportion to the rural since the middle of the preceding century and this is even more the case in the present century.[1]

---

[1] The population on September 30, 1937, was estimated at 4,583,003 in *Estadística chilena* (September, 1937), p. 529. Owing to the relatively high death

If the well-being of that population were to be measured by the income which it produces for the State, it would be considered highly satisfactory. In 1910 the national exchequer disposed of five hundred and forty million pesos of six pennies. In 1940 it will dispose of more than two billion pesos in current money, not counting payments on the foreign debt. The treasury obtains its greatest receipts from indirect taxes, among which for a long time was that of customs on imported articles and on the exportation of nitrate and other mineral products. Added to that tax are those which are levied upon the manufacture and sale of alcohol, upon sealed paper and postage stamps, those connected with banking and insurance firms, and those providing for the construction of roads, paving, and other improvements. Also in recent years there have been introduced special taxes, whose proceeds are ample, on commercial sales (2.5 per cent) and industrial production (5 per cent).

Direct imposts bring in heavy receipts. The tax upon inheritances and gifts, which is one of them, means very little compared with the income tax, which is the principal one. This latter is proportional and progressive on the annual returns of real estate, on business of any kind in all spheres of activity, on salaries and pensions that exceed a certain sum, and, without any exception, on the practice of lucrative professions. It is at the same time fiscal and municipal; the State and the municipalities receive their quota of the tax—and it has come to replace with great advantage to the treasury the former property tax.

Prosperity which shows itself in the increase of fiscal receipts is a positive fact, proof of which is made evident in all orders of national activity. Without taking into account internal commerce —by land and sea—which amounts to a great deal, or commerce in transit, likewise great, one needs only to consider the development of foreign commerce in order to prove it. Reducing figures to legal money of six pence gold it is noted that in 1890 foreign trade amounted to 406,000,000 pesos, an exceptional figure. In the following years it kept fluctuating between 2,400,000 and 3,200,-000. But from 1931 on there was a restriction of foreign markets and with it a drop during the next few years to less than a billion, a figure at which importation and exportation are still maintained.

The products of greatest importance in the export trade have been fertilizing substances, principally nitrate; metallic bullion,

---

rate, the annual increase in population is comparatively small. The death rate, however, seems to be slowly decreasing.

above all, copper; cereals, especially wheat; and some animal products, mainly wool. The articles in the import trade that have required the greatest expenditures are textiles, manufactured articles, iron, coal, and machinery of all kinds. Among the most important foreign markets in Europe are England, Germany, France, Italy, and Holland; in America, the United States, Peru, Ecuador, Argentina, and Bolivia; in Asia, China, Japan, and India; in Oceania, Australia.[2]

This mercantile growth is an expression of the industry of the entire body politic in national production. Agriculture, cattle raising, lumbering, fishing, mining, the many industries derived from these commodities or necessary to their exploitation—in short, all the agencies of wealth scattered throughout the territory—have felt the influence of a powerful current of labor that has made a great display of energy, especially in the last thirty years.

The considerable losses and disturbances caused in private business by the revolution of 1891, also the alarms of external war during the agitated debate with Argentina for a long time restrained the initiative and activities of labor. But scarcely were the wounds of the revolution healed and those fears allayed than activity was renewed, with the force of uncontrolled expansion. Money flowed into Chile from all quarters, and hundreds of very different kinds of enterprises sprang up suddenly in the form of joint stock corporations (*sociedades anónimas*); that is, associations of capital to compete with each other for gain from one end of the country to the other. The gold washings of Magallanes, the stock farms of Chilean Patagonia, colonization in vacant state lands, lumbering in the southern forests of the central valley, metals, nitrate, guano, and iodine in the northern zone were the principal objects of these enterprises. Industrial activity overflowed also into the territory of Bolivia, where it introduced Chilean energy, as in its own land. Although all this feverish enterprise resulted in a major catastrophe in 1907, it left behind, in every case, much of its initiative, which in these later years has become more active and fruitful.

The government has interested itself in this movement and has desired to emphasize it and give it state protection. First it has exercised in its favor an indirect protection by expending part of the public income on the opening of new roads, on the construction of bridges and new railroads, on the extension of telegraph lines,

---

[2] For Chile's foreign trade during the first nine months of 1937, see *ibid.* (September, 1937), p. 494.

on the improvement of harbors, on the increasing of maritime communications, on the creation of new police service, and on other public services. Its action in such matters, however, has not given all the advantage that might be hoped for, if one considers the increased expense that it imposes on the treasury.

For many years the railroads, particularly, have been more impaired than any other service, but lately their improvement has been rapid. The Trans-Andine Railway of central Chile, which unites Buenos Aires and Santiago, is finished. The great project of the "Longitudinal Railroad" from Tacna to Puerto Montt, connecting the partial lines that crossed that territory, has also been almost completed since the time when its construction was begun under a law of the republic (1908).[3]

In spite of these efforts, the traffic capacity of the roads in operation has not increased in proportion to the quantity of cargo it has been necessary to move; for this reason the national treasury has lost profits, producers have limited their business, and individuals have frequently had to pay advanced prices caused by the scarcity of products of general consumption in the large centers of population. However this may be, the country is crossed already by more than ten thousand kilometers of steel rails. The auto bus and commercial aviation complete the lines of communication.

But if the government protection to these economic interests has not had all the effects desired, it has afforded, on the other hand, direct encouragement through the establishment of a systematic protective policy. Various laws, the greater part of which have originated in congress, have gradually been passed in favor of agriculture, among them the surcharge of the customs tariffs which tax the introduction of some of its products and industries, and the irrigation, with governmental coöperation, of a good part of the territory. Customs duties on animals imported into the territory favor cattle raising. For many industrial products manufactured in Chile—sugar, shoes, matches, and other articles—the same economic policy has been planned, reacting in an effective way against the old "free trade" system or competition, which the governments of the conservative and liberal regimes have almost uniformly put into practice with regard to articles of necessary consumption. The result has been from the very beginning an obvious benefit for the protected industries. Thus the government has succeeded in giving stability and energy to national manufacturing, a source of production whose future in almost all its activities now

---

[3] See p. 367.

seems assured. The expositions that their promoters have for some time been holding show concretely its rapid and certain progress.[4]

The system of paper money has for a long period been firmly established as a complement to protectionism. The bank note, forced into circulation as legal tender, has always been considered as a last resort in a passing crisis. In 1895 the country had already survived nearly twenty years of paper money. The credit of the State was affected by it; on the faith or confidence given to it rested the acceptance of such values as are called "fiduciary."

On that date, the government of Jorge Montt thought the moment had come to substitute money of real value for paper money and finally issued the law of metallic conversion on a basis of eighteen pence per peso, in place of the forty-eight that it had formerly been valued at. The State was directed to exchange bills for "solid pesos" of silver and "condors" and "escudos" of gold, and at the same time a limit was placed on the quantity of bills that the banks of emission could issue to the public. But in less than three years the unforeseen happened. The alarms of war with Argentina, the abuse that had formerly been made of banking credit, and the excess of imports determined the lowering of international exchange to fourteen pence. The paper issued by the banks depreciated. Metallic coinage acquired a premium and began to be exported as merchandise—which it was because of its real value— or to be hoarded by its large holders, who hoped thereby to obtain a better premium. The banks, on their part, restricted credits; there was fear of bankruptcy; their clientele did not pay. The depositors hurried to withdraw their deposits. The banking crisis was then announced with the prospect of an "economic crisis."[5] There was general restlessness.

Thus the situation at the middle of 1898 constituted a real "run on the banks," until their vaults were almost exhausted. The government came to their aid and issued the law of moratorium, by virtue of which the adjustment of all payments was suspended for a month. When the moratorium was ended there appeared a new issue of paper money, of enforced circulation, and with the guarantee of the State. From that date the conversions announced were indefinitely postponed and further emissions have been issued. After each one, international exchange fell; paper money was worth less; property, leases, merchandise—all rose in unaccustomed pro-

---

[4] See Wilhelm Mann, *Chile luchando por nuevas formas de vida*, II, 102-105.
[5] See Martner, *Estudio de política comercial chilena*, II, 532-535.

portions; and proprietors, agriculturists, industrialists, with abundant banking credit and with profits and secure markets, have kept increasing their gains in greater proportion.

In that way paper money was the principal cause of the increasing cost of living. Its proportion in circulation has expanded sixfold in thirty years (1895-1925). All those who live on fixed incomes, including employees, and all those who live on day wages, including labor in general, have felt the effects of this situation. They have demanded—now of their employers if they were private employees, now of the government, if they were public employees — an increase in their salaries in order to be able to meet the costs imposed on them by the new order of things. All have obtained it. The laborers, in turn, demanded an increase in their wages. Some employers accorded it to them voluntarily; more did not. Against these the laborers have with great frequency employed the urgent method of strikes, which have assumed, on occasions, bloody characteristics through the clash of workmen with police, particularly in Santiago, in Antofagasta, in Valparaiso, in Arauco, and in Tarapacá. But in this manner they have recently succeeded in obtaining the desired increase.

The order of things sketched above was considerably modified in 1926 with the opening of the Central Bank of Chile, the only institution authorized by the State to issue paper money with a sufficient guarantee in gold. The convertible gold bill "at sight and to bearer" in that way brought about the stabilization of the value of money at the figure of six pence per peso; and the fluctuations of exchange, carrying with them instability in prices and increasing cost of living, ceased for a time.

But this conversion was put into practice only half way, so accustomed was the country to the monetary regime of paper. And as we stated before, in 1932 it returned to incontrovertibility. New bank notes were issued and the value of the peso dropped to one and one-half pence.

In spite of the vicissitudes indicated, the economic situation of the country has shown assured stability. The earthquake of August, 1906, whose damages were reckoned in hundreds of millions of pesos, did not affect it, at least immediately, in such a profound way as was feared. Along with an increase in the cost of living, caused by a new depreciation in coinage, came a rise in laborers' wages, due to the demand for hands for the reconstruction of Valparaiso and other cities destroyed by the catastrophe. Years later, in 1920, more than forty thousand laborers were thrown out of work because operations were paralyzed in the nitrate plants. The government had to open feeding places for them and spend on them many millions of pesos. A year after, however, the unemployed population was absorbed by other productive activities.[6]

In 1928 an earthquake destroyed Talca, just as that of 1906 had destroyed Valparaiso. The economic consequences were similar and in the next year were aggravated with the crisis in agriculture and mining. This produced in the following years a new condition of unemployment among day laborers and artisans which affected two hundred thousand individuals. Only in 1935 was the country able to absorb almost all its idle population, thanks to the re-establishment and increase in productive activities.

From the animosities following the numerous conflicts between capital and labor, there has arisen in Chile the "labor question," which is the same as the one called here, and still more frequently in the European countries, the "social question." In Chile this question has seldom taken on revolutionary characteristics. It has not been anything more than the confused, almost unconscious, aspiration, natural in all men, to better their material and moral condition by increasing their incomes, gaining instruction, and procuring comfort and well-being. The diffusion of education now tends to define this aspiration more exactly and cause the State to give preferential attention to it.

Nevertheless, there was a time when it was thought that the question might take on the characteristics of a violent and aggressive social struggle. This was in October, 1905, when, after a meeting to ask for the abolition of the tax on Argentine cattle, bloody strikes broke out in Santiago and for two consecutive days kept the imprisoned populace in the most lively alarm and the workmen on a general strike. Since these events strikes have not been rare, but have not taken such a serious turn, although some, like that at Iquique in 1907, and later those at Lota, have given rise to bloody measures of repression. On the other hand, there have been developed workmen's protective associations, among which the "Labor Federation of Chile" with its multiple "federal councils," and the "Union of Workmen of the World" (the IWW) and the Confederation of Laborers of Chile (CTCH) have played

---

[6] Fluctuation in employment marked the years 1925, 1926. Conditions improved thereafter until 1930, after which date the situation became steadily worse until 1933. Since then there has been marked improvement due to the rise of local industries and the resort to gold washings. See Thomson, *op cit.*, pp. 286, 287. An interesting proposal, with respect to Chile's economic and social conditions, is presented by Carlos Keller R., *Un país al garete* (Santiago, 1932).

Above: A ship of the Chilean desert with its crew of nitrate workers.
Below: Chilean nitrate prepared for export. Courtesy Grace Line.

Above: Gathering the grape crop of Chile, February-March. *Below:* A Chilean copper mining center, July. Courtesy Grace Line.

a most important rôle. The union movement has grown rapidly in the last few years and has spread from the working classes to the guilds of private and public employees for the special purpose of mutual aid.[7] The syndicates, which legislation in behalf of private and public employees has created, have unified and strengthened the action of the laboring classes for bettering their living conditions.

On the other hand the intimate relation between population and wealth has been frequently observed in Chile. Greater abundance in production has brought with it a greater proportion of marriages and births. Population in general has increased, although slowly, together with public and private wealth. Formerly the emigration of workers and of Chilean peons to neighboring countries in search of well-paid jobs was a common practice. In an earlier period, Peru, Bolivia, and Argentina profited from the energy of these workmen much more than they do now. Nearly an entire region of the last named republic, the territory of Neuquén, was populated by emigrants from Chile. Thus the Chilean population increased less than it should. But for some years things have been changing. That emigration has stopped and now it is the neighboring countries and Europe that discharge their excess population into Chile.

Immigration and colonization, always scant, have brought into the country in recent years a small number of immigrants and European colonists, principally Swiss, Germans, Italians, and Spaniards. Some have been sent by colonizing agents whom the government of Chile maintains in Europe; others have come under contract to industrialists for their labor, and others of their own free will, attracted by the high daily wage. The immigrant has settled down like any other laborer. The colonist has not; he has received his plot in the unsettled lands of the State, either directly from it or through a concessionaire, individual or collective, that under certain conditions has become possessed of a portion of public land. Besides foreign colonies, national colonies have also been established, composed of individual Chileans, to whom the State grants plots of land to cultivate and to live on with their families. Indian colonies have also been formed, composed of Araucanians indigenous to a certain region—the last descendants of an ancient race which has frequently had to suffer from the plundering of reckless speculators.

But the material progress of Chile has not only been shown in the increase of its wealth and its population; it has also become

---

[7] See "Chile," *Encyclopædia Britannica* (14th edition), V, 489-490.

apparent in the development of its cities. Santiago is now a capital of more than six hundred thousand inhabitants; it is well lighted and clean, with rapid transit lines. Its drainage, with a complete network of sewers, has been finished and is being extended to the outlying suburbs. It has spread out in all directions, and its buildings have gained rapidly in solidity and splendor. The abundant fiscal income has permitted the construction of magnificent public buildings, and the accumulation of a number of palaces which have transformed the appearances of the city. Valparaiso was traveling on the same prosperous road when destroyed by the earthquake, after which it rallied in a short time and was rebuilt cleaner and better than before, with public parks and new broad avenues, making it an attractive modern city. Like these two central cities, Concepción, Temuco, Valdivia, and Osorno, in the south, have in turn developed an extraordinary vitality; and in the north Antofagasta and Iquique, despite fluctuations in mineral wealth, for which they serve as centers, have been beautified and have prospered to the point of having a life of their own and being considered among the most important cities of Chile.

CULTURE AND EDUCATION

Intellectual progress has for the last thirty years run parallel to economic progress. None of the elements that make up the culture of the country has gone backward. All have extended their influence steadily and consistently. The press has enlarged its services and its spheres of action. Each special activity, each political, scientific, or religious school of thought has come to have its organ of expression and a public that supports it. Daily papers and reviews of widely different character have multiplied. The book trade with Europe and America has expanded enormously. The master works of science and literature of the most cultured countries of the world can be read in Chile today at relatively little expense. Thus, reading has become customary among people of some education as a habit fostered more and more by their intellectual desires.

This does not mean that the benefits of education have penetrated equally the different social strata; the countryman and the laborer, because of the little leisure their tasks leave them; the business man and the politician, because of their belief that they have nothing to learn; the casual wanderer and the ordinary clipper of coupons, because of their systematic disdain of study, have not yet succeeded in adapting themselves to the new form of culture. This condition simply shows that there is an increasing intellectual group in the country, which, after developing itself by means of European culture and the observation of the very society in which it lives, supports the daily, the review, and the book in order to have a medium through which to express its ideas.

The intellectual nucleus has been slowly forming by means of the continually more active development of public education, above all in the primary branches. Statistics have shown that in 1920 there were about 3,500 schools of primary grade in the republic which gave instruction to about 300,000 children of both sexes. Since then the number of schools as well as the attendance has increased until the latter exceeds 450,000 children in 1937. The great majority of those schools are supported by the State. But at the same time that many are subsidized by it, others are municipal or else belong to parishes and religious communities. The governments have paid special attention to them. In spite of this, the service has been imperfect in its administrative organization and in pedagogical efficiency and is still very far from satisfying the increasing needs of a growing population. The number of pupils in school is not even half of the population of school age who should be receiving education. Night schools and Sunday classes for adults help to extend the benefits of primary education to the mass of the people.

In 1920, after a long, tiresome struggle in the government, in congress, and in the press, the law of compulsory primary instruction was passed for all children over seven years of age, and this was to take effect in February, 1921. The application of the law has had to take place slowly, however, and it still will require many years to establish effectively the compulsory school attendance for all children included under it, for the lack of the most necessary elements, including buildings, furniture, material for teaching—in short, money—and a personnel prepared in sufficient numbers for such a vast work. But, however that may be, the quality and development of this national service has undergone far-reaching changes in a relatively short time.

If the school of today were compared to what it was even in the middle of the past century, so great a progress would be noted that almost no point of contact could be found between them. The colonial method of "reading by spelling," the brutal punishments of "glove" and "ferrule," the dark, unventilated rooms, the almost total lack of books, benches, blackboards, pictures, and maps, the ignorance and the servile position of the teachers—all this has been ended, never to return. In some provincial villages, however, far from the more populous centers, the old type of school has survived, although modified by the very atmosphere created by general culture. In the sphere of primary education, the most serious problem now is that of the needy child who will have to be fed and clothed in order to enforce his attendance at school.

But what has obviously been raised to a much higher level than formerly is the personnel of primary instruction. From the normal schools for men and women have gone out, year after year, a multitude of teachers, destined for service, with a regular technical and practical preparation; the greater part of the primary schools of the State are under their direction. Private organizations, among which the oldest is the "Society for Primary Instruction," cooperate effectively in the enlargement and perfection of this service, with their own schools established without regard to cost and serving as models of their kind.[8]

Secondary education has been developed along with primary instruction. More than ninety government *lycées* (*liceos fiscales*) for boys and girls distributed throughout the republic receive at least fifty thousand pupils. They have as their task the scientific instruction and moral education of youth and accomplish their ends by following a very different course from the old school. On the basis of the gradual and progressive system of concentration, in accordance with the intellectual development of the pupil, they have tried to banish forever mechanical learning by rote, replacing it with an objective, experimental study of the principal branches of knowledge, made as practical as possible.

As there are normal schools for preparing the personnel of primary teaching, so there is the Pedagogical Institute (*Instituto pedagógico*) for preparing the personnel of secondary instruction. During a full half century (it was established in 1889), it has already graduated many hundreds of men and women teachers. In this way teaching has become a stable profession. The teaching body engaged in Germany to serve in that institution has effectively fulfilled its mission. The reform of the *lycées*, then, has been carried out in accordance with German methods. From the Institute of Physical and Technical Education created in 1906 have come the professors of the branches which its name indicates.

On the other hand private initiative has encouraged the growth of numerous private colleges, either subsidized by the State or wholly independent. The Catholic Church, also, with the object of extending its creed by means of the education of the new generations, has established several private colleges distinct from the

---

[8] See Rippy, Martin, and Cox, *Argentina, Brazil, and Chile since Independence*, pp. 399-401. See also Mann, *op. cit.*, II, 265-274; and *New International Year Book, 1937*, p. 148.

seminaries of each diocese. These, together with the colleges of the religious orders that have been functioning for a long time in the country, contribute powerfully to general knowledge. Even more, a private institution, the "League of Poor Students" (*Liga de estudiantes pobres*) which has had many years of existence, co-operates to the same end, procuring funds for promising students who would lack the means for study without such assistance.

But all this vast work of education, intended especially to prepare cultivated people for society, has been giving way to the advance, more vigorous every day, of a new branch of education; namely, technical and practical instruction, tending especially to develop workers prepared to earn a living in the fields of industry and commerce. For a long time there was only one school of arts and crafts in the country. During recent years the government determined to found others, and subsidized several private institutions of the kind. Progress in this direction is still slight, but there has been some advance.[9] It means much that there is recognition of the urgent need of giving the Chilean foremen and the Chilean workers such technical preparation as will put them in a position to compete advantageously with the foreign foremen and workers.

Furthermore, a field for woman has been opened, where she can apply her talents freely, honestly, and profitably. For this purpose professional schools for girls have recently multiplied. Their development has been such that a normal course has had to be founded, designed to prepare teachers for these schools. The schools for agriculture, mining, and drawing as applied to industry have attained a similar development.

Commercial institutes (business schools) have also been created. Their number is sufficient and their work is guaranteed and given standing through the employment of their graduates by mercantile organizations. In this way some of the young men who would have sought a field for study and means of livelihood in the liberal professions have changed their course; they have gone directly into the occupations that create wealth for individual and collective profit.

On this account one might think that there has been a reduction in the university courses which prepare for liberal professions, but it has not been so. Higher education has continued to receive in its halls even more students in law, engineering, and medicine than before, in spite of the fact that there is evidently a diminishing

---

[9] See Mann, *op. cit.*, II, 289, 300; also Charles E. Chapman, "The Chilean Educational System with Especial Attention to the Position of the University," in *Hisp. Amer. Hist. Rev.*, III (August, 1920), 395-402.—J. A. R.

expectation of profit in these "careers." In the higher, as in the secondary, education courses have been revised and improved. Thus the schools of medicine and of engineering have won an excellent reputation, while the school of law, more conservative in reforming its teaching system, has also begun to employ new methods of instruction and has broadened its scope to include economic and social studies. In 1928 there was created the Faculty of Agricultural Theory and Veterinary Science; in the following year, the Faculty of Fine Arts; and, in 1934, the Faculty of Industrial Commerce and Economy. With these the field of the University of Chile was considerably enlarged. About the same year (1934) the Faculty of Philosophy and Education (formerly called Philosophy and Humanities) created a Superior Institute with general or nonprofessional studies in sciences and letters, in addition to the Pedagogical Institute which was already in existence. Private institutions of higher learning have contributed to the growth and perfection of this grade of teaching. They are the Catholic University, which dates from 1888; the University of Concepción, created in 1915; and the Santa María Foundation, a sort of technical university which has been functioning in Valparaiso for six years.[10]

In general, the greatest efforts of intelligent men of the country have been devoted to the extension and improvement of public education. There are many, in recent years, who have excelled in its service. Among the primary instructors, one of the most reputable figures was Abelardo Núñez, who died in 1910. With constant devotion to primary studies he combined the reputation of having been one of the most influential directors of the review in this field with that of having composed the first "readers," in which several generations have learned at one and the same time how to read, together with the rudiments of science. Another public servant, no less fit for this kind of teaching, is Claudio Matte, who has earned the gratitude of his fellow citizens with his advice and his tireless efforts in behalf of schools. Neither can the name of Dario Salas be ignored, a schoolmaster himself, afterward raised to the highest offices in the field of education, who, with his book, *El problema nacional*, gave a decided impetus to the passing of the law for compulsory primary education.

An outstanding figure in secondary and higher instruction is the professor and rector of the state university, Valentín Letelier, whose splendid works, *Filosofía de la educación, La evolución de*

---

[10] For an article on the Instituto Santa María, see *Chile,* Vol. V, No. 28 (July, 1928), p. 251.

la historia, Génesis del derecho (Genesis of the Law) and *Génesis del estado (Genesis of the State)*[11] are numbered among the few publications of sociological literature in Chile. He died in 1919 at sixty-seven years of age, when much was still hoped for from his untiring labor. Other competent teachers of this century are Joaquín Cabezas, creator and supporter of the Institute of Physical and Technical Education; and Enrique Molina, to whose initiative and constancy we owe the University of Concepción.

In 1902 a general educational assembly was held in Santiago, in which the most experienced professors discussed all matters of this kind. The national secondary educational assembly held in Santiago in 1912 had a like theoretical importance, although it was not of much immediate benefit. A whole vast plan of reform arose from these two assemblies, and, in accordance with it, improvements have been gradually made in these fields.

Another characteristic sign of the development of national instruction is the revision of all textbooks. Educational literature has been enriched in recent years by many new books, written by members of the Chilean teaching profession, in accordance with the most modern tendencies of education. In the higher branches of instruction there has been so little material of this nature that textbooks have constituted almost all the scientific literature of the country. Among the foreigners who performed the most scientific work in Chile during the last third of the past century, Rudolfo Amando Philippi merits special mention. He was an erudite German who died in 1904 when past ninety years of age, after a residence of more than half a century in the country. During this time he was professor, director of the National Museum, explorer of deserts, and, above all, a naturalist whose works form a very rich collection of original observations.

LETTERS AND ART

In the present century, Chilean literature acquired characteristics of its own that set it apart from that of the rest of the continent. This prevailing tendency is continually strengthened by the study and observation of the country's past and present condition, and all the manifestations of national life.

History continues to be the field most cultivated. The three founders of national historical literature during the time of the

---

[11] Letelier's *Filosofía* was published in Santiago in 1892; his *Evolución,* in 1900; his *Génesis del derecho,* in Santiago in 1919; and his *Génesis del estado,* in Buenos Aires in 1917.

republic—Amunátegui, Vicuña Mackenna, and Barros Arana—
have died. Barros Arana's life extended into the present century,
for he died in 1907 at seventy-seven years of age. When he finished
his great *Historia jeneral de Chile* he did not rest, although he was
already seventy-five years old, but wrote and published his final
work, *Un decenio* [*Decade*] *de la historia de Chile* (*1841-1851*).
This book, together with the *Historia de la administración del General Prieto, 1831-1841,* by Ramón Sotomayor Valdés, cited above,
and the *Historia jeneral* of Barros Arana himself, complete the
methodical presentation of the development of the country up to
the middle of the nineteenth century,[12] although principally from
a political, biographical, and military point of view.

Investigation in the above aspects, although scarcely begun, has
advanced some thirty years more with the works of Alberto Edwards, *El gobierno de don Manuel Montt* (*The Government of
Manuel Montt*); Agustín Edwards, *Cuatro presidentes de Chile*
(*Four Chilean Presidents*); and Gonzalo Bulnes, *Historia de la
guerra del Pacífico* (*History of the War of the Pacific*). But at
the same time investigation delved more deeply into earlier times
with the publication of special histories and collections of historical
documents. Among the men who figure as the chief authors of such
works are Domingo Amunátegui Solar, who, with his books on
*El instituto nacional, La sociedad chilena del siglo xviii. Los
mayorazgos y títulos de Castilla* (*The Society of the Eighteenth
Century. The Entailed Estates and Titles of Castile*), and *Las
encomiendas de indíjenas en Chile* (*Native Encomiendas in Chile*),
besides several other works, has made important contributions to
the history of educational and social institutions;[13] Alejandro
Fuenzalida Grandón, who with three other books of great interest—
Lastarria i su tiempo (*Lastarria and his Time*), *Historia del
desarrollo intelectual de Chile* (*History of the Intellectual Development of Chile*), and *La evolución social de Chile*[14]—has pushed
forward in the same direction as Amunátegui Solar; Tomás
Thayer Ojeda, with his works on the conquerors and the first cities
of Chile; Tomás Guevara, who died in 1935, whose regional his-

---

[12] Barros Arana finished his *Historia jeneral* (16 vols.) in 1902. A revised
edition appeared in 1930. His *Decenio* was published in Santiago in 1905-1906.
The second edition of Sotomayor Valdés, *Historia de Chile bajo el gobierno del
General D. Joaquín Prieto* (4 vols.) was published in Santiago (1900-1903).

[13] *El instituto nacional* was published in Santiago in 1891; the *Mayorazgos*
(3 vols.) in Santiago, 1901-1904; and the *Encomiendas,* in Santiago in 1909.

[14] The *Lastarria* was published in Santiago in 1893; the *Historia del desarrollo
intelectual de Chile* came out in Santiago in 1903; and the *Evolución social,* in
Santiago, in 1906.

tories—*Provincia de Curicó* (*The Province of Curicó*), and *Civilización de la Araucanía* (*The Civilization of Araucania*), and his studies on the *Psicología del pueblo araucano* (*Psychology of the Araucanian People*)[15]—have also greatly increased the knowledge of the nation's past; Crescente Errázuriz, who has not rested in his task of furthering knowledge of the period of the conquest in the light of the latest documents available, and who, in a series of volumes, has reflected the history of the times of Pedro de Valdivia, Francisco Villagra, and other conquerors; Gonzalo Bulnes, who with his *Historia de la guerra del Pacífico*[16] has completed his labor as historiographer of the crises through which Chile passed in its relations with Peru; and Agusto Orrego Luco, distinguished physician and writer, who in a work published after his death in 1933 has given a picture of the "old country" which is not lacking in originality.[17]

The publication of historical documents was started more than half a century ago with a "Colección de historiadores de Chile" ("Collection of the Historians of Chile"). The principal part in this task has been taken by Luis Montt, author of several bibliographical works, who died in 1909, and José Toribio Medina, who likewise died in 1930, who to that collection has added another—Collección de documentos inéditos para la historia de Chile (Collection of Unpublished Documents for the History of Chile). Both publications have reached a hundred volumes and refer entirely to the colonial period.[18] Furthermore, Medina is the author of a hundred other bibliographies which make him one of the most prolific investigators on record.

On the other hand, at government cost or by private initiative, there have also been published the "Colección de historiadores i de documentos [inéditos] relativos a la independencia de Chile (Collection of Historians and of Unpublished Documents relative to the Independence of Chile") begun by Enrique Matte Vial, who died in 1922, and another collection of *Sesiones de los cuerpos legislativos, 1810-1846* (*Sessions of the Legislative Bodies*). These two collections,[19] however, like the two above, have reached another

---

[15] Tomás Guevara's *Civilización* (7 vols. in 8) was published in Santiago in 1898-1913; his *Psicología*, in Santiago, in 1908.

[16] Bulnes died in 1936.

[17] Orrego Luco's name does not appear in the available bibliographies.

[18] The "Colección de historiadores de Chile" dates from 1861.

[19] "Colección de historiadores de documentos relativos a la independencia de Chile," 1900; *Sesiones de los cuerpos legislativos, 1811-1845* (28 vols. Santiago, 1886-1906).

hundred volumes; and their principal object consists in furnishing to future historians the sources for investigation.

Light literature has in its turn attained an appreciable development. From Paris, until his death there in 1920, Alberto Blest Gana continued to write novels. His last productions were *Durante la reconquista* (*During the Reconquest*), *Los trasplantados* (*The Transplated*), and *El loco estero* (*The "Madcap"*).[20] A goodly number of young literary men are still attempting to make a name for themselves in this field; the future will have something to say about them. The same is true in poetry. Three of the most notable poets of the present generation are gone: Ricardo Fernández Montalva, Pedro Antonio González, and Carlos Pezoa Véliz. The first, a man of deep feeling, with a strong sense of rhythm, has left a body of poetry very much enjoyed by those of like temperament. González, in spite of the small amount of his work, has exercised an influence that should endure. He was the poet of human ideals, who sang of the conquests of science and the great struggles of the spirit. Pezoa Véliz, lost in the prime of young manhood, left a quantity of original and delicate verses. The three lived unfortunate lives, always at the mercy of their own temperaments. Today Samuel Lillo, Víctor Domingo Silva, Pedro Prado, Gabriela Mistral, and Pablo Neruda hold the sceptre of Chilean poetry with distinct merits and tendencies.[21]

Artistic culture has made progress even more worthy of attention. The annual expositions in the Salon of Fine Arts are more largely attended each year, and the criticism of works exhibited there has recorded a high degree of excellence. So numerous have been the young artists of these last years and so great their rivalry that since 1906 one group of them, considering the salon too restricted and the jury, charged with admissions and the conferring of prizes, futile, has established free salons for the exhibition of their works.[22]

The painters mentioned above, Lira and Correa, have given place to a brilliant multitude of landscape painters, realists, colorists, impressionists, portrait painters, futurists, cubists—all

---

[20] His *Durante la reconquista* appeared in Paris, 1897, Santiago, 1933; *Los trasplantados,* Paris, 1911? and *El loco estero* in Paris in 1909.

[21] Consult Sturgis E. Leavitt, "Chilean Literature, a Bibliography of Literary Criticism, Biography, and Literary Controversy," in *Hisp. Amer. Hist. Rev.,* V (1922), Feb.-Aug., 116-143, 274-297, 531-534.

[22] *Hoy* for June 9, 1933, reports the semiannual exhibition of the National Society of Fine Arts as being very successful.

young men, industrious and ambitious for glory.[23] Several of them have gone to Europe to finish their studies, either pensioned by the government, or through private aid, or at their own expense.

Plaza and Arias, masters of Chilean sculpture, produced in this period their last and most notable works. Plaza carved in Paris his admirable "Quimera," which has given him a world-wide reputation. Arias carved there also his "Descensión," representing the death of Christ, which has given him a place among the best sculptors. To these names are now added those of many young artists who are on the way to fame.[24]

THE CHURCH AND RELIGIOUS EVOLUTION

The Chilean Church has prospered in these latter days both in the splendor of its service and the learning of its priests. Its relations with the State have been maintained in perfect harmony, and with the help of the latter it has multiplied its buildings and extended its social influence. Directed by the prelate, Mariano Casanova, until 1908, the date of his death, and afterward by Juan Ignacio González Eyzaguirre and Crescente Errázuriz, three cultivated and earnest men of its priesthood, it has not had to suffer the violent collisions with the civil authority that at times so embittered the spirit of the philanthropic and warlike archbishop, Rafael Valentín Valdivieso. Separation from the State in conformity with the Constitution of 1925, far from damaging its position, has given it a place of much greater security under the present direction of Monseñor Horacio Campillo.

A marked religious evolution, however, is to be noted throughout the country. It is not that the people are leaving the Church; at least three fourths of the national population continue to be as sincerely Catholic as during former times. Nor does it experience hostility from those who are not Catholic: the Protestants in the republic are almost entirely foreigners, English, North Americans, or Germans, and respectful toward all beliefs; the freethinkers do not constitute a group organized against the Church; they are simply private persons who feel themselves free from the necessity of complying with the precepts of any religion whatsoever. The evolution noted presents other manifestations—religious tolerance and religious indifference.

---

[23] The names of recent painters are listed with some criticism of their work by Mann, *op. cit.*, II, 180-192.

[24] For a brief reference to contemporary sculpture in Chile, see *ibid.*, pp. 192-196.

Today it is not a mark of honor in a believer to hate all other faiths except his own, or the men who support or embody such faiths. In judging an individual, one does not ask what religion he practices or what he believes. It is also obvious that most people do not now pay attention to, or practice with the former diligence, the commands prescribing abstinence, fast, and confession at certain periods of the year. Those persons who of old were afflicted by the devil have completely disappeared and the *penitentes* and even the *cucuruchos* (paper cones) are disappearing. The solemn sacrifice of the mass, processions, and other celebrations of the Church show a slim attendance of men. Even the political influence of the clergy has diminished. The type of electoral priest, aggressive and troublesome, who is remembered from the times of the theological contests, has become rare, and this has redounded to the benefit of religion itself. It is respected the more as it mixes less in the quarrels of men. The republic has thus attained religious peace and an absolute liberty of worship that is founded in the customs of society and the very soul of the people. The separation of Church and State, once so bitterly opposed, aroused in 1925 no protests or recriminations among religious authorities or believers; neither has the spread of Protestant beliefs stirred up resistance. Among them, the Evangelical Church has achieved comparative prosperity.

Ecclesiastical dignitaries have shown themselves prepared for this situation and have developed a religious propaganda as persistent as it is energetic, in order to restore to the Church its one-time social predominance. When it has been possible, they have increased the celebrations and exercises of worship. They have preached everywhere against religious indifference. They have excommunicated more than one newspaper that encouraged it. They have not missed any opportunity to stimulate the piety and faith of the people.

In 1895 Archbishop Casanova celebrated a diocesan synod in which the internal regime of the national church was completely reorganized. It had been more than a century since Bishop Alday had called together the preceding synod, and already the rules established at that time were not in keeping with the modern needs of the Catholic system of the country. Ten years later there was also held a solemn eucharistic congress, in which religious dogmas were established with greater firmness and splendor. Assemblies of this kind have been called together more recently, and because of them the public celebrations of thanksgiving have achieved large proportions.

Because of the earthquake of 1906, acts of piety were repeated which, on similar occasions, the national church had offered to the faithful, occasions as numerous as the seismic catastrophes in the country. In a pastoral that Monsignor Casanova directed to all Chilean Catholics, he declared that this terrible phenomenon had been a manifestation of the wrath of God for their sins; and, reviewing one by one the evils from which Chilean society suffered, he declared that it also meant a threat of greater punishment to follow, if they persisted in continuing in such a deplorable course. The prelate pointed out, among these evils, the insatiable thirst for wealth, the excess of luxury, the indifference toward the destitute, and, above all, the State education which did not inculcate religious sentiment in the child. Forgetfulness of God and the idolatry of money, he said, were the two gangrenes which were eating into society at the beginning of the twentieth century.

These utterances are the exact reflection of two dominating and well-defined purposes, which for a long time have been giving vitality to the Catholic Church: that of attracting the working classes, offering them protection in the name of the Christian socialism which Pope Leo XIII proclaimed to the world in one of his most famous encyclicals;[25] and that of attracting the young men who are able to study by means of religious education. To attain the first object, it has developed associations of the proletariat, directed by their priests, and has created other new associations dedicated to different saints. To attain the second object, it has founded the Catholic University and numerous seminaries and schools, which it supports. Almost all congregations in Chile devote themselves to teaching, and thus coöperate to those ends with admirable success. These are, then, the two most effective forms of propaganda of the Church and it must be recognized that, whatever may be the end they pursue, at least they are civilizing forms of propaganda. The Church has likewise reorganized its internal system in recent years. It has increased the number of bishoprics to eleven and has set up precise rules to be observed by the faithful in the different regions of the country. With the aid of its own press, with the moral and material coöperation of its principal members, with the indoctrination of numerous brotherhoods of men and women through the constant preaching of its priests, it has succeeded in acquiring over conscience a great power. This power is

[25] The encyclical "Rerum Novarum," on May 18, 1891, set forth Christian principles dealing with relations between capital and labor. This bull and others growing out of it are mentioned in the *Catholic Encyclopedia,* IX, 172.

freely tolerated. It may not be superior to what it enjoyed prior to its separation from the State, but at least it seems more efficient.

In the arduous campaign against what it is customary to call the "spirit of the age," that is to say, religious indifference, the Chilean clergy has shown vigorous intellectual force. Brilliant orators are found among them, such as Ramón Angel Jara; theologians, like Rafael Fernández Concha, among whose works the *Filosofía del derecho* (*Philosophy of Law*) and the treatise *Del hombre* (*On Man*) merit special attention; writers, such as Rodolfo Vergara Antúñez, whose texts on literature are especially esteemed as well as many others of his books; historians, such as the prelate himself, Crescente Errázuriz; and, finally, poets such as Esteban Múñoz Donoso, author of *La Colombia*, which, although not very smooth metrically, and perhaps too fantastic, is the only epic poem written by a Chilean during the republic. Among the present clergy vigorous personalities likewise stand out, such as the presbyter Carlos Casanueva, to whose rectorship the Catholic University owes so much.

HEALTH AND SOCIAL WELFARE

In the midst of its great economic and intellectual progress, Chile has also shown signs of backwardness. Although enjoying a healthy climate, extraordinarily mild in the regions most inhabited, its people seem to be decimated by numerous endemic and epidemic diseases, which enormously weaken Chilean productive forces. Smallpox, tuberculosis, and typhus, which attack all classes of people, and scarlet fever and whooping cough, which especially attack children, have been sadly frequent. In the last epidemic of smallpox that attacked the country, it is estimated that five to ten thousand persons died annually. Furthermore, the bubonic plague sometimes causes ravages in the northern regions, where the climate favors its development. In recent years, typhus fever has been the most stubborn and most widespread epidemic. It is encouraged by the filth and malnutrition resulting from the widespread unemployment of the proletariat.[26]

But there is no need for the mortality record among the mass of the population in these epidemic scourges to be so high. Infant mortality, above all, is somewhat heartbreaking in the Chilean home,

---

[26] *Hoy*, in its issue for December 25, 1931, reports 130,000 workers out of employment. In the following March the number was given as over 60,000, and in April, 1933, as 54,000. The same periodical during the years 1933-1937 frequently refers to the prevalence of typus in the country. See also Thomson, *op. cit.*, p. 287.

particularly in the homes of the poor. The large family of the nation loses today, just as it did formerly, the greater part of its children at an early age. More than to any other cause, the evil is chargeable to the very bad hygienic condition of the people. Their dwellings, damp, restricted, unhealthy; their incurable uncleanliness; their great ignorance of the most elemental rules for preserving health; their unconquerable alcoholism, which ruins their descendants—these are the determining causes of the high mortality.

Foreigners who have traveled for some time through the important cities of Chile cannot but feel depressed in the presence of the deplorable situation of the laboring classes. One of them has graphically characterized it by calling it "the worst side of Chile." Among other observations relative to it, this foreigner states:

Hundreds and hundreds of the holes in which those human beings are lodged present an indescribable appearance of low civilization. Walls and floors of mud, frequently without windows, having gaps opened in the wall for doors, a lot of rags for the family and most of the time not enough for all; once in a while a small brazier with lighted coal or a heap of firebrands, around which the members of the family group themselves like Indians, because it must be remembered that the common people are almost all of Araucanian origin; filthy insects that one sees the mothers gathering from the heads of their little children, and above all, an aversion against washing themselves because they consider water harmful: these are the characteristics of the quarters inhabited by the poor. Often one hears it said that those unfortunates need nothing better. In reality, the authorities live luxuriously, and do very little to spread knowledge of better conditions of existence; enjoying themselves to all appearances, while leaving the poor to the privations to which they are accustomed. It is admitted with greatest frankness and is evident to every one, that the dominating vice in the lower classes is chronic alcoholism. Many workers labor on an average four and at times [only] three days a week.[27]

However exaggerated much of this criticism may be and however much it may also be applied in an equal degree to other countries of higher civilization, it is certain that it ought to teach Chileans not to regard with their usual apathy the affliction of so many of their fellow creatures; especially if one considers that to their efforts the republic owes much of its prosperity and glory. Naturally it is not true that the public agencies of Chile have manifested such indifference to the welfare of the people. The sanitary organization has been completely made over during the past twenty

---

[27] See Edward A. Ross, *South of Panama* (New York, 1915), p. 94-113, and other foreign commentators.

years, and its services have constantly been extended in a more satisfactory and efficient manner. For some time the Ministry of Health, Social Welfare, and Assistance has been at the head of those services.[28] The principal office of these boards is located in Santiago and each district has its respective departmental sections. The Superior Council is the technical institution that studies and advises the government as to sanitary methods. The boards are the administrative institutions that dispense the funds devoted to public charity and supervise the establishments devoted to the same ends. There is also a permanent service of vaccination to prevent smallpox by means of inoculation with animal virus. The cities also have in charge several services of the same kind, but their most effective work is seen in the support of dispensaries for administering medical aid to the sick who lack funds.

In 1918 the sanitary code was passed, by which was created the general sanitation office under the immediate supervision of which come all the other institutions, and which gives permanence and legal enforcement to all hygienic regulations. Later, in 1925, the Ministry of Hygiene and Social Supervision, later called the "Ministry of Social Welfare," has undertaken a most active work, that of making the workingman's dwelling sanitary as shown by the recent "decree law on dwellings";[29] and a no less active propaganda for fighting epidemic and endemic diseases which reach serious proportions in the country. The Mortgage Loan Bank,[30] too, which is a state institution, has erected in Santiago and in other cities entire districts of hygienic dwellings for workers and employees. The hogsty of the infamous tenement (*conventillo*)[31] has almost disappeared in the important cities.

Public beneficence is also served by numerous hospitals and asylums, which the State maintains with general and special funds, composed of "charitable legacies" and other revenues; by various houses for foundlings and two insane asylumns, one in Santiago and the other in Concepción. More than two hundred thousand persons enter these institutions every year—an entire population of poor unfortunate people with which society must burden itself, not only

---

[28] Under Law No. 5802 matters of public health are under the control of the National Council of Public Health, presided over by the minister of that department. See *El mercurio*, February 21, 1936.

[29] *Ibid.*, August 1, 1935, mentions a proposed expenditure by the government of a half-million pesos for inexpensive houses. See also Mann, *op. cit.*, I, 190-193.

[30] See p. 291.

[31] See n. 29, *supra*.

because charity is a Christian duty, but principally because it is a social duty to assist the destitute.

Much has been said of the obligation of the State to secure cheap and hygienic houses for the workingman. Little, however, has been accomplished along this line. Only in recent years has congress voted appreciable sums for constructing workingmen's houses. Much has also been said about the necessity of legislation on behalf of labor, in order to relieve the manual laborer from excessive toil and secure indemnity for him in case of accident, to regulate the occupations of women and the employment of children, to establish compulsory weekly rest periods, and to insure the working man against unemployment and invalidism, and in case of death. In all these fields something has been accomplished.

If the law of "Sunday rest" is not yet always complied with, it is generally respected; the law relating to "labor accidents" is applied under ordinary conditions; and the hygiene of industrial establishments is now an object of effective administration. Under the influence of the military movements of 1924 and 1925, the labor code, the insurance of workers and employees, and other laws have resulted in more effective government protection to individuals of the social labor groups. This legislation has come to be the most complete and perfect of any on the continent. It has included all the resolutions of the Labor Office at Geneva under control of the League of Nations, and, even if it has not been applied or carried out with the rigor which would be desirable, it is certain that it promotes greater social justice in keeping with the rising culture of the proletarian masses.[32]

Public Welfare banks for the employees of all classes—general, municipal, and private—established since 1925 have contributed especially to the well-being of the middle classes. Among the effective benefits which they offer are the acquisition of property, health and retirement pensions, even the pawnshop for the family needs. On the other hand the shareholding movement, in the form of Consumers Coöperatives, at the same time has extended and tends to lighten the cost of living for the same classes. Moreover deposits in the individual banks have considerably increased.

DELINQUENCY AND JUDICIAL PROCEDURE

Age-old misery and ignorance have rested upon the country. To these have been due the deplorable sanitary condition of the

---

[32] Moisés Poblete Troncoso, who for several years has served on the staff of the International Labor Office at Geneva, has important articles on labor legisla-

national population which recently has tended to remedy itself and the abandonment in which, thanks to individualistic egoism, the laboring population was maintained up to recent times.

Nor is their moral laxity owing to any other cause.[33] The increase of delinquency, especially of bloody crimes such as assassinations, wounds, and injuries of all kinds, has been shown by the statistics on criminology to be one of the standing evils of Chile. Crimes against property, whether robberies, thefts, or frauds, also add greatly to the general delinquency. But two facts especially stand out in this antisocial life—alcoholism is the principal factor causing crime, and crimes against property are committed in great part by children under sixteen years of age. It is this that is called "delinquent precocity," and its proportion is greater in Chile than in most other civilized countries.

The State has had to organize rigidly the defense of society; that is, penal repression. It has been obliged to increase periodically the urban and rural police force, organized recently into a national body of *carabineros*, and criminal judges have had continually to exercise greater severity. Even the penalty of lashing, which humiliates without correcting the individual, and which has fallen into disuse, has been reëstablished. Numerous penal institutions must be maintained in order to imprison delinquents, including schools of correction for children; houses of correction for women; and jails, prisons, and penitentiaries for adults, according to the term of punishment. For some time there was a penal colony on the larger island of Juan Fernández, a colony that was soon suppressed, where there were many married criminals who could there carry on normal work and home life. More than one hundred thousand individuals, accused or condemned for different crimes, pass annually through these institutions. Such is the delinquent population of the country.

The State has to assume the charge of providing shelter and food for this population. In these institutions the criminals perform the kind of work which they already know, or they are taught a trade. According to law, they must indemnify the State for their sustenance by the product of their labor, pay their victims the damages caused by the crime, and form a reserve fund for their

---

tion in Latin America in *International Labor Review*, XXX (Geneva, July, 1932), 58-80; *ibid.*, XXXII (November, 1935), 637-664. See also *Legislación social obrera chilena* (Santiago, 1924), and his *Labor Organzation in Chile* (Washington, 1928); and Thomson, *op. cit.*, pp. 285, 286.

[33] *Hoy* for July 14, 1933, emphasizes alcoholism as being responsible for the increase in mortality and crime among the Chilean population.

return to freedom. As a matter of fact the State has done nothing as yet to indemnify itself or the victims. Criminals generally earn very small wages, because the workshops in which they labor are run by private contractors who exploit them. As most of the prisoners do not know how to read or write, the State also provides schools for them, and even affords them a special religious service; but it has been observed that more than half of those who complete sentences in such institutions return again to a life of crime, and again are sent back to the cell. They are not reformed and relapse again into crime as often as eight or ten times. The stigma attached to criminals hinders them from procuring good remunerative employment and, finding themselves alone and repelled by all society, they can only return to their former life.[34]

Next to the increase of delinquency, one must note the excessive increase in judicial litigation, another form of moral degredation. New courts, new judges, new officers have had to be created to take care of the daily increasing needs of litigants. The passion for gain and gambling, characterized by the enormous revival of games of chance among all social classes, has undoubtedly contributed to this development. But, at the same time, the administration of justice has gained in rapidity and seriousness. The last organic codes, those of civil procedure and of penal procedure prepared many years ago and passed during the government of Germán Riesco, due in large measure to his initiative, have marked effective progress in the judicial practices of the country. With them national legislation is completed, and the ancient legislation of the colony, which still ruled procedure, after nearly a century of independence, has been reformed. Public morality has not gained so much by this change as has correct procedure in the enforcement of all laws.

THE CHILEAN PEOPLE AND THEIR EVOLUTION

From what we have just set forth, one can see that the morality and the health of the great masses of the people do not correspond to the prosperous state of other phases of national life. Men have not been wanting who, basing their opinion on this fact, have de-

---

[34] *Ibid.*, on September 29, 1933, states that the inmates of prisons are forced to live in frightful conditions. *El mercurio*, on July 17, 23, 1935, states that thirty million pesos are to be used in prison construction, a half million of which is for a penal colony. The same paper, on March 21, 1936, reports the prisons of the country as being in a deplorable state, and on April 8 of that year mentions that prison conditions are similar to those of twenty years before. See also Mann, *op. cit.*, I, 261-278.

clared that Chilean nationality is decadent. But this decadence does not exist. Here are four centuries of history to belie that idea. Before talking about the decadence of Chile, its social evolution should be mentioned, and then its progress will be evident. Four hundred years have barely passed since the first Spaniards stepped upon Chilean soil and engrafted European civilization upon native barbarism. They founded its cities, explored its territory, cultivated its fields, and exploited its mines. They did even more— they constituted a new society. The native race, although despoiled and maltreated, was the basis of this society. On that race was grafted the Spanish, and there resulted a third race, with common vices and virtues. In this way the native element did not disappear; it kept on living and will always live in the blood and spirit of the nation; it forms the people.

When the struggle for independence began, this people had hardly risen a degree above its primitive barbarism. More than a hundred years have passed since then; and can one say that the race is the same as when, still barbarian, it eagerly and fiercely threaded the forests of Arauco? the same as when every natural phenomenon was viewed as an omen of disaster? the same as when, in the encomienda and the *mita*, it bled under the whip of its masters? The power, tenacity, and bravery that it inherited from the native and from the Castilian adventurer has been seen developing everywhere. This has been the race that formed the soldiery in the wars of emancipation and then during the periods of civil agitation filled the ranks of those fighting for liberty. This has been the race that, three times, carried the flag of the republic across seas and deserts as far as the territory of Peru; and its hands are the hands which have built cities, confined the rivers in canals, laid rails for the locomotive, and hoisted the sails and fired the guns of Chilean vessels.

The fusion of both races, it is true, has not been completely accomplished; but it is advancing rapidly, favored by the democratic atmosphere of political institutions, by the development of public education, and by the very expansion of national wealth. The facility of land and sea communications, the industrial growth of the country, which dates from a recent period, and the greater daily expansion of the urban centers have also been factors of primary importance in giving representation and unity to this abundant Hispanic-native admixture, which now works freely, attends schools, is organized into society, hears about public institutions, and is the driving force in all the stir of civic life.

Its vices and defects form part of the inheritance from its ancestors. If it cannot yet strip itself of that heritage, it is because it is carried in the blood and because the intellectual and economic evolution of the republic does not reach it in the same degree that it reaches the leading classes. But these same classes, now comprehending their obligations toward the mass of the population, daily tend to establish greater solidarity with it; and, whether as governing elements or as forces of private initiative, many of their members devote part of their time to the advancement of that evolution.

Whoever, then, observes the development of this people and compares what it was with what it is, cannot say that it has decayed; and whoever keeps in mind the great qualities of vigor and energy that it has always displayed will not fear whatever fate the future has to offer it. At most one will be able only to regret that it may suffer critical moments from exhaustion or from debauchery.

MODERN

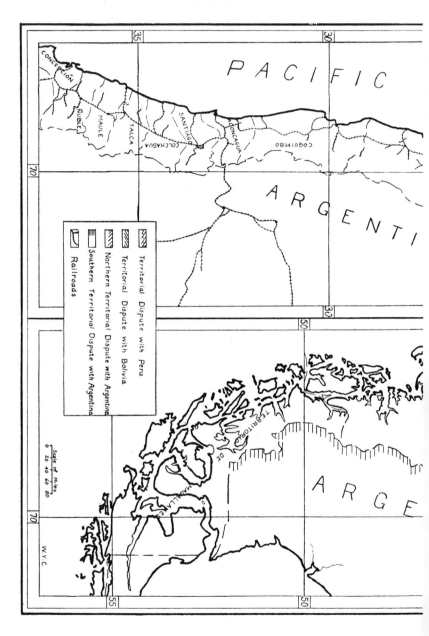

Legend:
- Territorial Dispute with Peru
- Territorial Dispute with Bolivia
- Northern Territorial Dispute with Argentina
- Southern Territorial Dispute with Argentina
- Railroads

Scale of Miles
0 20 40 60 80

W.Y.C.

CHILE

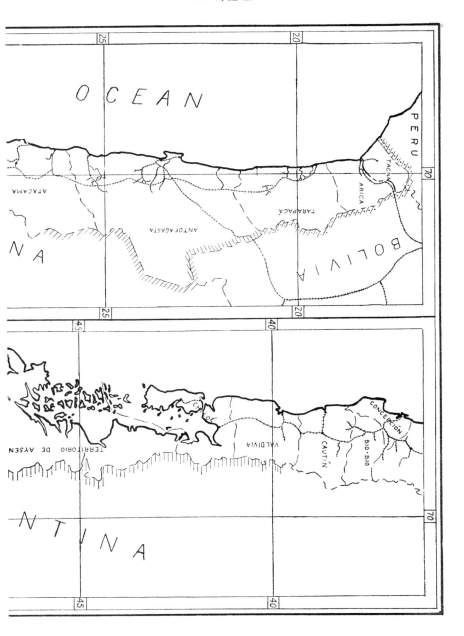

IN PREPARING the sketches that follow, the editor and translator found Virgilio Figueroa's *Diccionario histórico y biográfico de Chile* peculiarly useful. It covers much the same ground and largely supercedes the older work of Pedro Pablo Figueroa, *Diccionario biográfico de Chile*. P. P. Figueroa is not a relative of Virgilio. Both writers are charged with numerous minor errors and often show a partisan bias, but they give us details that can be found nowhere else. An attempt has been made to check their accounts with those of other writers but in many cases, particularly for recent events, their statements have had to be accepted in lieu of more authoritative ones. For the colonial period the scholarly work of José Toribio Medina, *Diccionario biográfico colonial de Chile*, is essential. All three of these compilations have been supplemented by José Espasa's *Enciclopedia universal ilustrada, Europeo-Americana*.

In order to simplify the references to these three authorities, the editor has adopted the following abbreviations: Espasa, "E"; Figueroa, "F"; Medina, "M." Because of his numerous references to *Historia jeneral de Chile* (see p. 354) of Diego Barros Arana, he has also made use of the initial "B" for that writer. Use has also been made of *Who's Who in Latin America*, edited by Percy Alvin Martin (Stanford, 1935). All other references in the Biographical Notes are given in full.

José Fernando ABASCAL y Souza (1743-1827), Marqués de la Concordia, a native of Oviedo, entered the army in 1762, fought in Morocco and at Rousillon, and became a general in the war against France, 1793-1795. In 1804, after service in Cuba and Mexico, he was appointed viceroy of Peru. Captured by the English while on his way to that post, he eventually escaped and assumed command there. During the invasion of Spain by Napoleon's forces, he exerted himself to send supplies and munitions to the mother country. He introduced many reforms in the viceroyalty, such as establishing schools and abolishing the Inquisition, and especially strove to maintain harmonious relations between the Spaniards and Creoles—hence his title. After the revolutionary outbreak in Buenos Aires on May 25, 1810, he proceeded to reincorporate the neighboring provinces of Córdoba, Potosí, La Paz, and Charcas with his viceroyalty. He formed within his jurisdiction a royalist party that did much to suppress insurrection. Neverthless, Ferdinand VII replaced him in 1816 with his subordinate, Palezuela.—E, I, 181.

Antonio de Acuña y Cabrera (d. 1662) had seen military service in Piedmont and Lombardy before coming to Peru, where he enjoyed some prestige through the influence of his relatives rather than through his own merits. Appointed to the presidency of Chile by the viceroy of Peru, he took possession of the office in May, 1650, and his appointment was confirmed by the sovereign some two years later. His term of office was then extended to eight years, but he was deposed on February 20, 1655, as shown in the text. Although he was ordered back to his post by the *audiencia* in Santiago, the viceroy summoned him to Peru and sent four hundred soldiers to enforce the order. In Lima, through family influence, he escaped the consequences of his folly, but died in that city.—M, p. 11.

Francisco de Aguirre (*ca.* 1507-1580?) was born in Talavera de la Reina and first saw military service in Italy, being present at the sack of Rome in 1527. Arriving in Peru about 1536, he fought against Almagro. He campaigned in Upper Peru with Gonzalo Pizarro and Diego de Rojas, accompanied Valdivia to Chile, filled various municipal offices in Santiago, and, reoccupying the valley of Coquimbo, first settled by Juan Bohón, established there the city of La Serena. Furthermore, he was designated by Valdivia as lieutenant-governor and in that capacity began to dispute with another Spaniard, Juan Núñez del Prado, for possession of the city of El Barco, east of the Andes, where he founded Santiago del Estero. While engaged in subduing the neighboring Indians, he learned of the death of Valdivia and recrossed the Andes to assume the government of the province. Recognized as governor in the north, he found himself opposed by Francisco de Villagra, who obtained equal recognition in the south. Ultimately both claimants were taken prisoner and banished to Lima by Hurtado de Mendoza. In 1569 Aguirre became governor of Tucumán but, owing to charges brought by his enemies before the Inquisition, he retired to La Serena where he died.—E, III, 647; M, pp. 18-30.

Pedro Aguirre Cerda (1879-   ), born in Los Andes, was educated in the local schools and in the Liceo of San Felipe. In 1897 he entered the Instituto pedagógico where he prepared himself to teach Spanish, at the same time taking up the study of law in the National University. He received his title as advocate in 1904, when professor of Spanish in the National Institute. In 1910 he went to Europe to study public finance and pedagogy and on his return took an active part in educational and financial reform. He became deputy for his native town of Los Andes, was minister of justice and public instruction in 1918, assisted in organizing Alessandri's campaign for the presidency, served as minister of the interior in three of Alessandri's cabinets and as senator from Concepción, and shared Alessandri's exile. He is justly famed for his eloquence, his mental energy, his skill in political manipulation, and his social outlook. Later as president of the radical party he favored a liberal-progressive policy rather than a radical one. A successful lawyer and man of business, proprietor of a considerable estate, and a skillful party leader, he was made president in 1938 by the Popular front.—F, I, 186-192.

Manuel de ALDAY y Axpe (1712-1788) was born in Concepción. His earlier studies were carried on in his native city at the seminary of San José. He obtained his doctorate in both theology and jurisprudence at the University of San Marcos in Lima in 1739. Nominated by the king as bishop of Santiago on September 8, 1753, he took possession of his office on August 24, 1755, amid universal expressions of satisfaction. He fulfilled his duties with "notable moderation, prudence, and virtue." He presided over a diocesan synod at Santiago in 1763, twice visited all portions of his province, and issued to the faithful therein notable pastoral letters. His most significant task was the rebuilding of the Cathedral of Santiago, to which he contributed from his private fortune.—M, pp. 43-44; Vicente Carvallo y Goyeneche, *Descripción histórico-jeográfica del reino de Chile,* in "Colección de historiadores de Chile," Vol. IX, chap. xcii.

Juan de Dios ALDEA (1853-1879) was the son of a schoolmaster residing in Chillán. He received some education in the Franciscan school of his native city, entered the marine artillery when still very young, and by his industry and good conduct had become second sergeant at the time of his glorious death. He was buried along with his fellow heroes in Iquique, where their remains were later identified and transferred to Valparaiso. In that city a worthy monument commemorates their valor.—F, I, 302-304.

Jerónimo de ALDERETE y Mercado (1518-1556) was a native of Olmedo. He arrived in Peru in 1535 and gained his first experience in fighting the Indians of Upper Peru. Joining Valdivia in northern Chile, he took part in the founding of Santiago and was selected as one of the first *regidores* of that city. His survey of the coast to the Biobío, his campaigns against the Indians and against Gonzalo Pizarro, and his part in the founding of cities led Valdivia to regard him as one of his best officers. He was given a substantial encomienda and was selected by that leader to report conditions in Chile at the Spanish court. Alderete had to journey to England, where Philip II was then sojourning with his wife, Queen Mary. His report, backed up by a substantial supply of Chilean gold, produced a good impression on the Spanish ministers, and, when they learned of Valdivia's death, Alderete was appointed governor of Chile. He was destined never to fill the office, for while on his way back he died at the island of Tobago near Panama—of fever, according to one account; of injuries received from a fire on shipboard, which drove him insane, according to another.—E, IV, 352; M, pp. 44-49.

Arturo ALESSANDRI Palma (1868-   ) was born in Linares, educated in the *colegio* of the French fathers, and obtained his license as advocate in 1893. His law thesis dealt with a social subject. He became prominent among the young men of the liberal party, assisted in the candidacy of the younger Errázuriz, became deputy in 1897, and in the following year was minister of industry and public works. In 1913 he was in charge of the treasury and for a time in 1918 held the ministry of the interior, a position which enabled him to begin his own campaign for the presidency. Early recognized as an incomparable orator, he distinguished himself in the speech he pronounced before the Argentine congress at the centennial celebration of 1910 and again in 1915 at the inauguration of the railroad from Arica to La Paz. In addition, during these earlier years, he served as attorney for foreign and domestic corporations and was looked upon as a sort of liberal conservative, although displaying on occasion interest in measures of social welfare.

Urged on by his presidential aspirations, Alessandri, as the election year of 1920 approached, completely changed his political philosophy. Voicing popular discontent at existing economic and social conditions, he inaugurated a whirlwind campaign which at the close resulted in a disputed election. This election was resolved by the appointment of a tribunal of honor which determined that, while frauds were committed on both sides, fewer marked the course of Alessandri's followers, and hence they awarded him the presidency over his competitor, Luis Barros Borgoño. The events of his troubled administration are detailed in the text. His withdrawal from the presidency, his exile, and his triumphant return in 1925 paved the way for the constitution of that year, a document on which Alessandri exerted great influence. Failing to complete his term in office because of the dispute over his successor, Alessandri remained in the country for a time as a private but influential citizen, as was shown by his speech on the Tacna-Arica question in July, 1926. Suffering exile under Ibáñez, he returned after 1931 and in the following year was triumphantly reëlected president, an office which he held until the end of his constitutional period in 1938.—F, I, 350-365.

Diego de ALMAGRO (1475-1538) was supposedly an abandoned infant found in Almagro, a small town near Ciudad Real. He is reported to have passed some time in the Spanish army and then to have fled from Spain because he had killed a man. In Panama he became so intimate with Pizarro that the historian Oviedo characterizes the twain as "one soul with two bodies." If so, it was an unlettered friendship in which Almagro's more trustful nature was no match for the other. He lost an eye in the first attempt of the two against Peru and drew only the position of commandant at Túmbez, with a modest salary, in the grant which Pizarro obtained at court. It needed all the tact and persuasion of Fernando de Luque to keep these untutored soul mates from blows. Nor did the presence of Pizarro's half brothers, particularly Hernando, prove agreeable to the overreached Almagro. For the time being they patched up their friendship. Almagro shared in the spoil guilefully won from Atahualpa, although taking no part in the Inca's capture and betrayal, and later helped in persuading Alvarado to desist from his projected conquest of Quito and leave the field to the Pizarros and himself. Almagro's part in the first expedition to Chile and in the bloody strife around Cuzco is described in the text. He left a son, child of an Indian woman of Panama, who avenged his father's death by devising the assassination of Francisco Pizarro. Later, after being defeated at Chupas, the younger Almagro met death at the hands of the hangman who had executed his father.—Manuel de Mendiburu, *Diccionario histórico-biográfico del Perú* (8 vols. Lima, 1874-1890), I, 102-166; E, IV, 787.

Eulogio ALTAMIRANO Aracena (1836-1905) was born in San Felipe, educated in the National Institute, and obtained his degree as advocate in 1860. After acquiring prestige as a lawyer, he entered politics. In 1870 he became minister of justice, worship, and public instruction under Pérez and continued in office under Errázuriz as minister of the interior—a post held by him during the entire administration. He held other cabinet posts during succeeding administrations and was also a deputy or senator from Concepción, serving likewise on the *comisión conservadora* as counselor of state and as intendant of Valparaiso. During the War of the Pacific, he was special envoy in the conferences at Arica (see p. 333) and later fought in the battles before Lima. He opposed the administration of Balmaceda and in his later years held subordinate judicial positions.—E, IV, 953; F, I, 401-403.

Luis ALTAMIRANO Talavera (?-?) had a military career dating from the Civil War of 1891 upon which he entered as captain. Afterward he passed through the usual military grades and took part in various commissions to Europe and other American countries and was lieutenant general at the beginning of the revolutionary movement in 1924. Elevated by the discontented militarists to the junta which replaced President Alessandri, he headed that body until the following January when a second military overturn sent him into private life. Altamirano was supposedly becoming too partial to the aristocratic element and unmindful of his duty to the group that had brought him to political distinction. His high character and patriotic action together with his long and honorable service saved him from becoming a sacrifice to the second military revolution.—F, I, 403-406.

Manuel de AMAT y Junient (1704-1790) was the second son of the Marqués de Castebell, member of a family of considerable repute for learning. After lengthy military service in Spain, Italy, and Africa, during which he gained knighthood in the Order of St. John and the rank of field marshal, he was appointed governor and captain-general of Chile in 1754. Intelligent and energetic in fulfilling his duties, he affected to believe the appointment below his merits and displayed little sympathy toward those he governed. Nevertheless his career in Chile led to promotion in 1761 to the viceroyalty of Peru. The creation of a police force for Santiago was due to a mutiny among the city prisoners which he in person repressed with severity.—B, VI, 195-218; M, pp. 73-74.

Miguel Luis AMUNÁTEGUI Aldunate (1828-1888) was born in Santiago and received his first instruction from his parents. The early death of his father forced him to help in the support of the family, while pursuing his course at the National Institute. Entering his alma mater at the age of fourteen, he distinguished himself as a student, tutored others for examinations, and at the age of nineteen, through special dispensation and the influence of his constant mentor, Andrés Bello, received the chair of humanities in the institute. The salary from this position, supplemented by his income from private classes, enabled him to support his mother and sister and educate his two brothers. He was aided in these family tasks by Don Gregorio Víctor (1830-1898), and this association in early privation and training made the two brothers inseparable companions. Don Miguel Luis entered journalism and public office in 1848 and at the same time joined the liberal party. In addition to their joint historical work, Miguel Luis essayed various biographies and in 1853 presented to the ministry an important memoir upon the right of Chile to the Strait of Magellan, to be followed shortly by *La dictatura de O'Higgins*. Thenceforward he continued his active political and administrative career, of which the pages of the present work bear frequent witness. The high spots of his career were his service as minister of the interior in 1868 and as unsuccessful candidate for the presidential nomination in 1875 (see pp. 313 and 320). In 1857 he published an important memoir on public instruction in Chile and as minister of public instruction under Pinto opened professional instruction in the University of Chile to women. Had he survived, his moderating tendencies might have made him the presidential candidate of 1891 and thus have prevented the civil strife of that year.

Miguel Luis was the more prominent of the two brothers, but Gregorio

Víctor, modest and retiring, was his silent helper in many activities for which the other derives credit. The latter likewise engaged in newspaper work and after 1862 published important biographies and studies of the colonial period under his own name. From 1868 on, he devoted himself to a judicial career, including membership in the court of appeals in 1875 and in the supreme court in 1889. At the same time he collaborated with his brother until the latter's death. A statue to the two brothers in Santiago fittingly commemorates their public career.—F, I, 478-482. For a critical study of the elder Amunátegui's work see Cruz, *Estudios sobre la literatura chilena*, I, 215-285. See also C. Norla Vicuña, *Don Luis Amunátegui (1828-1888)* (Paris, 1889?). Of the volumes mentioned (p. 353), *El descubrimento* appeared in 1862; and *Los precursores*, in 1870-1872.

Domingo AMUNÁTEGUI Solar (1860-   ), born in Santiago, was the son of Don Miguel Luis Amunátegui. He was educated in the National Institute and the National University and became an advocate in 1881. In 1887 he became subsecretary of justice and in 1889, professor of constitutional law in the Pedagogical Institute, professor of history in the National Institute, and dean of the faculty of humanities. He has served in several ministries from 1907 to date, was twice rector of the university, and has been honored by membership in learned societies at home and abroad. In addition to numerous articles of a political and educational character, he has contributed important studies upon the literary, political, and social conditions of Chile, especially during the colonial epoch. His *Historia de Chile*, a school text, appeared in 1933.— F, I, 490-491.

George ANSON (1697-1762) entered the British navy in 1712. From June to November in 1741 he was on the coast of South America. In 1739 Anson was appointed commodore of a fleet to sail to the Pacific. Setting out on September 18, 1740, in six ill-fitted and ill-manned vessels, the expedition rounded Cape Horn. In spite of the loss of three of these ships, they captured the Philippine galleon. He returned in the *Centurion* by way of the Cape of Good Hope on June 15, 1744, bringing a treasure worth £500,000. He was then appointed a member of the admiralty and was influential in securing the passage of several naval construction bills in parliament. He became an admiral two years prior to his death.—*Dictionary of National Biography* (London, 1885-), II, 31-36. For an account of his expedition see the work written by his companion, Richard Walter, *A Voyage Round the World* (London, 1748). The latest biography was written by M. V. Anson, *Life of Admiral Anson* (London, 1912).

José Gregorio ARGOMEDO Montero (1767-1830) was born in San

Fernando. During the colonial period, he occupied minor municipal posts, and after the deposition of García Carrasco became secretary of the general government, minister of the court of appeals, councilor of state, member of congress, vice president and president of the supreme court, and rector of the University of San Felipe. After joining the revolution of 1810, he proposed the calling of a general American congress in which all nations of the new world were to have representation. He edited the most important documents of the revolution.—F, I, 573-576.

Virginio Árias Cruz (1855-   ) was born in Ranquil, near Concepción. Son of a modest farmer, who died when Virginio was eight years old, the future sculptor owed much of his inspiration to his mother and his early training to practical work in ornamenting and repairing churches. He later joined a class in sculpture at the University of Chile and accompanied his instructor, Nicanor Plaza, to Paris. In 1875 he was admitted to the *salon* of that city and to the School of Fine Arts. In 1882 he gained recognition with his statue "El roto chileno," and thereafter frequently received honorable mention or medals at Paris, at Buffalo, and in Chile. In 1900 he became director of the Escuela de bellas artes in Santiago, and during his term as director reorganized its curriculum. His list of works includes statues of the leading public men of Chile, some of whose figures ornament the plazas of Santiago, the Palace of Fine Arts, and the National Library. The monument to Baquedano is a notable example of his recent work.—F, I, 578-581.

Justo Arteaga Alemparte (1834-1882) and Domingo Arteaga Alemparte (1835-1880) were both born in Concepción, the sons of Justo Arteaga Cuevas, a notable Chilean general—F, I, 626-628. Both pursued studies in the National Institute, where they came under the influence of the notable journalist, Manuel Blanco Cuartín, who was also their French teacher. Both derived from this early training many characteristics of style, which later appear in their writings—exact and striking phrasing, good taste, robust expression. They inherited the fighting instinct but they fought with the pen and not the sword and they fought fairly and with grace. Their daily contributions to the press form meritorious literary products and at the same time afford charming sketches of noteworthy contemporaries.—F, I, 623-625.

Justo Arteaga early entered journalism in a goodly company, speedily proving its most conspicuous exemplar. Prone to ally himself with the opposition, he accomplished more for liberal ideas by his sketches and editorials than did thousands of speeches uttered in congress yet he "never soiled his gloves, when he grasped the axe. He alone knew how to wound with courtesy." His brother was more of the poet than was Justo, but on occasion could himself wield a facile editorial pen. Often the two worked together and the careful critic frequently finds himself at a loss to determine the part of each in their joint productions.

The early works of Justo appeared in *El país, La actualidad,* and *La discusión.* Later during two considerable periods he wrote for *El ferro-carril* and still later for *Los tiempos.* His brother spent the years from 1851 to 1857 in exile with their father, learned through necessity some-thing of business, wrote his early poems, and on his return to Chile joined his brother in publishing a short-lived but provocative paper, *La semana.* Domingo, for some years after 1860, headed a section of the foreign office. The two were also associated after 1866 in bringing out *La libertad,* a paper which just suited their genius. At the same time they published numerous political pamphlets and likewise held seats in congress. In 1870 appeared their most significant joint product, *Los constituyentes chilenos de 1870.* The edition edited by Robert Huneeus (Santiago, 1910) proved extremely useful for the notes of the present volume. Both died prematurely but left behind a flattering legacy of prose and poesy for the enrichment of Chilean literature. See the in-troductory sketch by Robert Huneeus in *Los constituyentes chilenos de 1870,* pp. vii-lxii. See also F, I, 623-625.

ATAHUALPA (d. 1533), the fourteenth and last of the Inca rulers of Peru, was the illegitimate son of Huaina Capac, greatest of the Inca line. His father divided his conquests, leaving the southern portion to Huascar and the northern portion with headquarters at Quito to Atahualpa. Dissatisfied with this division, the latter had fought with and captured and imprisoned his half brother shortly before Pizarro landed to begin his conquest. The usual story that Atahualpa was be-trayed and captured at the famous parley near Cajamarca, through the device of proffering a copy of the Bible for his consideration, is matched by another to the effect that Pizarro, foreseeing an attempt on the part of the Inca to entrap him, simply arranged a more successful trap for the unlucky Atahualpa. This pretext for the captive ruler's death is simply in keeping with the bloody and treacherous tale of this con-quest.—Mendiburu, *op. cit.,* I, 370-404; E, VI, 840-842.

José Manuel BALMACEDA Fernández (1840-1891) was born in Santi-ago. His grandfather came to Chile from Old Castile and his father held the offices of senator and counselor of state. José Manuel pursued his studies at the Conciliar Seminary, in preparation for the Church, but he soon forsook a religious career and faith and became a consistent opponent of ecclesiastical privilege. He began his public life at the age of twenty-four by serving Don Manuel Montt as private secretary at the "American Congress" held in Lima. His wealth, his distinguished personal appearance, and his grace and brilliance as an orator assured for him a successful political career. In 1866 he joined the Arteaga Alemparte brothers in publishing *La libertad*. His editorial experience and his work in the Reform Club brought him into the congress that became known through its political reforms as *La asamblea constituyente* (see p. 298). During the succeeding decade he continued his labors in the press and in congress, taking a prominent part in the debates of the latter body, and in 1878 he was sent as minister to Buenos Aires. Here his diplomacy did much to keep Argentina from joining Peru and Bolivia in the War of the Pacific. He returned to Chile to support with tongue and pen measures to carry on the war and to secure the results of conquest. In the cabinet of Santa María he became minister of foreign relations and thus took charge of the measures to liquidate the war. Then as minister of the interior he took the lead in pushing the various "ecclesiastical" reforms of the Santa María administration and in promoting public works. His part in these reforms added to his reputation as an orator, but not to his general popularity. Nevertheless President Santa María, who had not at first favored him as a candidate, finally accepted him as his successor and secured his election as first magistrate. The text gives us the chief events of his administration, which despite continued partisan strife was marked by substantial progress. At the close of his administration, following the disastrous civil war, he put an end to his own life in order to save his associates from further persecution and to give point to his last political manifesto. For this purpose his spectacular death proved a fruitful sacrifice. A favorable but partisan sketch of Balmaceda appears in Justo and Domingo Arteaga Alemparte, *Los constituyentes*, pp. 147-152. See also M. H. Hervey, *Dark Days in Chile;* R. Salas Edwards, *Balmaceda y el parliamentarismo en Chile, passim;* F, II, 80-85.

Manuel BAQUEDANO (1826-1897) was born in Santiago. Son of a notable soldier, he ran away from home to his first military experience and was commissioned lieutenant at the age of thirteen. In the battle of Loncamilla he fought against his own father, but rendered aid to his wounded parent after the battle and also saved the poet, Eusebio Lillo, from imprisonment. Retiring from the army for political reasons in 1854, he became a farmer, but reëntered the service in 1859, and also served against the Araucanians in 1868. As brigadier general he began the campaign in Antofagasta in 1879 and, replacing Escala, emerged from the War of the Pacific as generalissimo. After the war he served as senator and counselor of state but took no active part in the civil war of 1891. His course as military commander of Santiago, after the abdication of Balmaceda, gave rise to considerable controversy.—E, VII, 604; F, II, 105-106.

Orozimbo BARBOZA Puga (1838-1891) was born in Chillán and educated in his native city. Descended from a family of soldiers, he joined the army in 1856 and for the next twenty years saw service in the Araucanian country. He became colonel in 1876. In 1880 and 1881 he was highly commended for his bravery and skill in the fighting around Tacna and Arica and later in the vicinity of Lima. After the War of the Pacific he served as intendant of the province of Valdivia and remained true to President Balmaceda during the civil war, serving that executive as general in chief. In the final battle of Placilla he was killed while personally fighting against a superior force of the enemy's cavalry.— F, II, 110-113.

Eduardo de la BARRA Lastarria (1839-1900) was born in Santiago, spent his early days in La Serena, and graduated as civil engineer from the National Institute in 1860. As a student of this institution he obtained prizes for his verse and after graduation continued there as teacher of literature, mathematics, and history. In 1864 he became popular through his first book of poems and was led into radical journalism. In 1872 he became a subordinate in the ministry of finance and later published important pamphlets in behalf of the radical party. In 1876 he became rector of the *liceo* at Valparaiso. Endowed with all-inclusive talent and restless energy, he kept himself immersed in political disputes, condemned the revolution of 1891, and suffered exile in Uruguay and Argentina. His reputation as educator and poet led the Argentine government to bestow numerous commissions upon him, but his bitter experience abroad hastened his death. His frankness and skill in polemics made him a persistent defender of truth as he interpreted it.— F, II, 124-126.

Diego BARROS ARANA (1830-1907) was born in Santiago. Son of a prominent merchant and political leader who operated in Chile and Argentina, young Barros Arana early acquired a liking for public affairs. His education, begun in the National Institute, was continued in the university, but ill-health forced him to give up the law and devote himself to literature and history. His first essay, appearing in 1850, proclaimed him the future historian of Chile—a prophecy which he abundantly justified by his devotion to research, his fecund production, and his ability to organize his material rapidly and present it in monographic form. Much of this he later incorporated in voluminous general works. He wrote as a narrator and annalist, rather than in a critical philosophical spirit, but occasionally displayed severity and passion in his judgments. From the beginning of his literary labors he was connected with contemporary newspapers and reviews. In 1855 he became a member of the faculty of philosophy and humanities of the University of Chile, and with some interruptions continued to teach and write textbooks in history, literature, and geography, which were used throughout Hispanic America. His biting and incisive articles attacking the administration of Manuel Montt led to his exile—a period which he utilized in gathering documentary material in Argentina, Brazil, Spain, and other European centers. He was twice rector of the university, frequently a deputy in congress, although no orator, and served as adviser to the commission discussing boundaries with Argentina. His writings, covering the colonial period, the wars of independence, the early national period, and contemporary happenings, run into scores of titles. To his outstanding work, *Historia jeneral de Chile,* the author of the present work and all other recent historians of Chile are greatly indebted.—E, VII, 957-958; F, II, 139-141. For a less favorable view see Cruz, *op. cit.,* I, 145-213. A series of tributes to Don Diego and bibliographic data are published in *Revista chilena de historia y geografía,* LXVI (July-September, 1930), 6-346; also *ibid.,* LXXI (January-April, 1932), 54-69.

Luis BARROS Borgoño (1858-   ), son of the historian Barros Arana, was born in Santiago and studied in the National Institute and the University of Chile. He received his law degree in 1880 and while still a student taught history in the institute. In 1883, while holding a subordinate post in the foreign ministry, he participated in the final negotiations that closed the war with Peru. Later he assisted in bringing about peace with Bolivia. Under Jorge Montt he was minister of war and did much to preserve peace with Argentina. In addition he helped direct the *Caja de crédito hipotecario* (Mortgage Loan Bank) and published several works on education, history, and public finance. While heading the department of foreign relations under Sanfuentes, he brought Chile into the League of Nations. He was defeated for the presidency in 1920 but in 1925 was called upon by his successful rival to complete the latter's administration and to usher in the government of Emiliano Figueroa. Retiring to private life, he resumed his banking and cultural activities.—E, I, 1355 (App.); F, II, 142-145.

Daniel BARROS Grez (1834-1904), a prominent engineer and mathematician, is best known as a novelist and writer of fables. He also attempted the drama. Most of his literary work emanated from Talca, where the family lived after the death of his father, who was convicted in 1837 of conspiring against the intendant of Curicó. Varied judgments have been pronounced upon the work of Barros Grez, but his

Pipiolos y pelucones (see p. 355) is accepted as one of the outstanding interpretations of Chilean life.—F, II, 148.

Ramón BARROS Luco (1835-1919) was born and educated in Santiago and gained the degree of advocate in 1858. Devoted to agriculture, he published notable financial articles which at once gave him a secure position in the liberal party. He headed the treasury under the first Errázuriz and also during part of the administration of Santa María. He served eight times as minister of the interior. As president of the chamber of deputies he signed the manifesto deposing Balmaceda. Later he served as president of the senate, headed several charitable and financial bodies, and was author of various juridicial works. In 1897 he was made special envoy to France and in 1903, during the illness of Germán Riesco, acted as vice president. His work as minister was characterized by faithful but seemingly careless attention to detail rather than by brilliant execution. He was distinguished for his sleepy, taciturn manner, his ironic smile, and his apparent lack of attention; but somehow he created the impression that he thus solved more problems than his more energetic associates. At any rate, all parties turned to him as president in the crisis of 1910. His great preoccupation during his presidency was the construction of the National Library. An important monument to his charity is the hospital that bears his name. After his presidency he held the title and emoluments of vice-admiral of the navy.—E, VII, 958; F, II, 152-155.

Emilio BELLO Codecido (1869-   ) was licensed as advocate in 1889 and immediately entered upon a notable administrative and congressional career. As grandson of Andrés Bello he has continued the family tradition for learning and effective public service by active membership in the liberal democratic party and by filling notable cabinet and diplomatic posts. Since the political overturn of 1924-1925 he has spent some time in exile but in 1936 was called to assume the war portfolio in the second administration of Alessandri.—F, II, 169-172.

Andrés BELLO López (1781-1865) was a native of Caracas. He had already gained outstanding reputation in Venezuelan letters and politics when he took up his residence in England in 1810. Although holding important diplomatic posts, he gained his living largely from his work as teacher and translator, while devoting his energies to reading and to writing for literary reviews. He was on intimate terms with James Mill, Bentham, and other advanced thinkers. In 1829 he came to Chile, where he spent the remainder of his life. The pages of Galdames abundantly attest to his manifold activities. He was poet, literary critic, and educator, and his monuments to fame are his *Princi-*

pios del derecho internacional and his *Gramática de la lengua castellana.*
His poetry is not spontaneous but he was very successful in imitating
the *Georgics* of Virgil and in his *Silvas americanas* he presents striking
descriptions of life in the tropical forests.—F, II, 172, 173. See also
M. L. Amunátegui, *Vida de Don Andrés Bello* (Santiago, 1882), and
Ensayos biográficos, II, 5-242; E. C. Hills, *The Odes of Bello, Olmedo,
and Heredia* (New York, 1920), pp. 3-9; Eugenio Orrego Vicuña, *Don
Andrés Bello* (Santiago, 1935).

Bello's advice on the best method of studying history is worth noting:
"Learn to judge for yourselves. Aspire to independence of thought.
Drink in the sources—at least in the torrents (*caudales*) nearest to
them. The very language of the original historians, their ideas, even
their prejudices and their fabulous legends, are a part of history and
not the least instructive and true. Would you, for instance, know what
the discovery and conquest of America was? Read the Journal of
Columbus, the letters of Pedro de Valdivia, those of Hernán Cortés.
Bernal Díaz will tell you much more than Solís or Robertson. Interro-
gate each civilization through its works. Demand of each historian that
he give his warrants."—Domingo Amunátegui Solar, *Bosquejo histórico de la literatura chilena,* p. 80.

Diego José BENAVENTE Bustamante (1789-1867) was born in Concepción and early entered upon the struggle for independence. Emigrat-
ing to Argentina with Carrera after the battle of Rancagua, he remained in that country until 1823. On his return to Chile, he reorganized
the treasury department and served as counselor and minister of state,
minister plenipotentiary, director of the Banco hipotecario, and member of the university faculty. He opposed Portales with energy but was
absolved from participation in his death. His *Ensayo sobre la
hacienda pública de Chile* (Santiago, 1842) and his *Memorias de las
primeras campañas de independencia* (Santiago, 1844) attracted considerable public attention.—E, VIII, 23; F, II, 178.

Ambrosio de BENAVIDES (1720-1787), born in Granada, was after
more than twenty years of service only a lieutenant colonel when in
1760 he was appointed governor of Puerto Rico. Relieved of that office in 1766, he was two years later transferred to Peru, as president of
the *audiencia* of Charcas. He arrived in Santiago as governor on December 12, 1780. Although then an old and sickly military man and
not brilliant, he proved a prudent and discreet administrator, bringing
about many reforms and local improvements.—B, VI, 402; M, pp.
126-127.

Antonio Alejandro BERNEY, or Vergne, came to Chile in 1776. A man
of less practical ability than Gramusset (*q.v.*), but no less influenced

by illusory political and social ideas, he gained a precarious living as a teacher of Latin and mathematics. At the time of his arrest, he had formulated a bizarre manifesto with which the conspirators were to launch their revolution. They sought to bring Rojas into their plot, but he gave them his sympathy rather than his coöperation.—M, p. 133. See also Bernard Moses, *Spain's Declining Power in South America, 1730-1806,* pp. 228-239.

Francisco BILBAO Barquín (1823-1865) was born in Santiago. Accompanying his father into exile at the age of eleven, he was destined to spend the greater part of his mature years outside of Chile. His great-grandfather was compromised in a conspiracy in 1780. Hence he came naturally by his radical temperament and early determined to aid the oppressed, to know the truth, and to declare it openly. Five years among the Chilean exiles in Lima gave a permanent bent to his revolutionary spirit. In 1839, he returned with his father to Santiago and entered the National Institute. Bello, Lastarria, and Vicente Fidel López (see p. 275) contributed to his education but the last-named alone could satisfy his inquiring mind. The mental awakening that was then expressing itself in renewed political contests, in short-lived but stimulating periodicals, and in the founding of the university affected the none-too-steady intellect of Bilbao. When barely past his twenty-first birthday, he attracted public attention by his dramatic apostrophe to José Miguel Infante, who had steadfastly refused, in his last moments, to receive the sacraments of the Church that he had opposed during his life. This youthful act, more spectacular than convincing, was shortly followed by the publication of *La sociabilidad chilena* (see p. 286), characterized by the courts as blasphemous, immoral, and seditious. The author was fined and in lieu of payment condemned to prison, but his admirers paid the fine and threatened to mob the judges. Life in Santiago, however, proved insupportable for the daring author. An article of his was burned; he was expelled from the institute and went into voluntary exile to France, where for five years he still further immersed himself in revolutionary ideas as well as in contemporary science. On his return he organized along with Eusebio Lillo (see p. 487) the *Sociedad de la igualidad*—an act which led to the outbreak of 1851, and a second and permanent exile. Meeting with further persecution in Peru he went to Europe in 1854 and in 1856 to Buenos Aires, where he died. In his last years he devoted himself to the task of unifying Argentina and the whole American continent without abating his opposition to the influence of the Church. He especially sought to arouse his fellow Americans to the danger revealed in the invasion of Mexico and Santo Domingo. His final book, *El evanjelio americano* (Buenos Aires, 1864), reverts to the theme of his *Sociabilidad chilena.* His death by tuberculosis was hastened by his efforts to save a woman from drowning.—F, II, 201-202. See also Cruz, *op. cit.*, I, 7-58.

Bartolomé BLANCHÉ Espejo (1879-   ), on finishing his course in the Military School (1895), began his service in the cavalry. He continued his military training in Germany (1904) and later served on the general staff from 1912-1914, besides exploring the Río Negro and other points in Chile. After taking part in organizing the military junta of 1924, he served as subsecretary of war and opposed the civilian junta, presided over by Alcibíades Roldán. He supported the military junta of 1925 and helped to suppress some of the early revolts against Ibáñez. He has frequently represented his government abroad and has received numerous decorations from his own and from foreign governments.—F, II, 211-216; *Hoy,* May 20, 1937, p. 19.

Manuel BLANCO Cuartín (1822-1890), born in Santiago, was the son of the notable Argentinian poet and littérateur, Ventura Blanco Encalada, at one time dean of the faculty of philosophy and humanities of the University of Chile. He received some early impressions from the Spanish poet and publicist, José Joaquín de Mora (see p. 250). Educated at the National Institute, he at first planned a career in medicine, but because of deafness turned to journalism and literature. His first work in 1845 attracted attention because of his easy style and elegant concepts. After preliminary work in minor periodicals, of which *El mosaico* was his favorite, and collaboration with the Arteaga Alemparte brothers on *La semana,* he became editor in 1866 of *El mercurio* and in the course of twenty years' service published numerous articles and poems that attracted wide attention outside the country and made the paper famous. In 1876 he joined the faculty of philosophy and humanities of the University of Chile, where his advent, marked by a notable address, "Lo que queda de Voltaire" (What Remains of Voltaire), provoked a notable newspaper controversy. Affiliated with the conservative party, Blanco Cuartín was Catholic in the best sense, a man of independent judgment, and modern in his outlook. Notwithstanding his literary fame, his death passed almost unnoticed by contemporary writers.—F, II, 216.

Manuel BLANCO Encalada (1790-1876) was born in Buenos Aires, but was sent to Spain to complete his education and then served in the Spanish navy against the French. Twice sent to America on the outbreak of revolt there, in 1813 he joined the revolutionists of Chile, was taken prisoner after Rancagua, and exiled to Juan Fernández. On his return he served in the artillery at Cancha Rayada and Maipú, later began the organization of the Chilean navy (see p. 210), and continued in that branch of the service under Cochrane. For a brief period in 1826 he held the presidency ad interim. After Paucarpata, he retired to private life until 1847. In 1852 he took over the Chilean embassy in Paris and in 1865 directed naval operations against the Spanish fleet.— E, VIII, 1084; F, II, 216-218.

William BLEST (1800-1884) was the father of the novelist Alberto Blest Gana and of the poet William Blest Gana. Of Irish birth, the elder Blest came to Chile in 1827 and married there. In 1828 he wrote an important brochure on the common diseases of Chile, which was published by the government. As physician and surgeon he acquired an immediate reputation, which a long and laborious practice abundantly justified. He also frequently served as deputy and senator.—F, II, 226.

Alberto BLEST Gana (1831-1920) was the son of the Irish Chilean physician, William Blest (see above). Together with his famous brothers, Guillermo and Joaquín (see F, II, 226-229), he received his early training from his father, later entered the Military Academy of Santiago, and finished his engineering course in Paris. For a time he taught in the War Academy, headed a section in the ministry of war, and later was intendant of Colchagua. In 1870 he entered the Chamber of Deputies, but in 1871 he began a diplomatic career which included work in the United States, Great Britain, and France. Remaining in the latter post twenty years, he rendered important service to Chile in the purchase of arms during the wars of 1879 and 1891. He never returned to his native land after 1886, but his numerous novels, headed by *Martín Rivas* (Santiago, 1862), present the best character- izations of Chilean life and justify the Chilean claim that he is the leading novelist of Spanish America.—F, II, 227; Alfred Coester, *The Literary History of Spanish America,* pp. 224-228.

Guillermo BLEST Gana (1829-1905), distinguished as a poet and journalist, also wrote dramas and novels. Exiled for his opposition to the government of Manuel Montt, he visited Europe and on his return entered the diplomatic service, first as minister to Ecuador and later to Argentina, where he is credited with the discovery of the secret treaty between Peru and Bolivia (see p. 324). During the War of the Pacific he served as *jefe político* at Lima. Later he held the office of intendant at Tarapacá and Linares, and other subordinate positions. His later years were embittered by a sense of being passed over in popular favor.—F, II, 228.

Jorge BOONEN Rivera (1858-1921), born in Valparaiso, was the son of a Flemish settler who located in Chile in 1851. He was educated in part in Belgium, graduated from the military school of Santiago in 1879, became captain in 1881, a colonel ten years later, brigadier in

1898, and general of division in 1903. He took part in the campaign against Peru, was military attaché in Spain, and became chief of staff under Emilio Körner. In the battle of Placilla, he commanded the third division and his action in that battle later led to a bitter controversy and duel with Estanislao del Canto. Boonen survived despite a direct wound in the forehead and the affair caused a great sensation in the country. Boonen retired from the army in April, 1921. His *Ensayo sobre la geografía militar de Chile* appeared in 1897.—F, II, 233-235.

William I. BUCHANAN (1852-1909) was appointed minister to Argentina by President Cleveland in 1894. Afterward he served as director-general of the Pan-American Exposition at Buffalo in 1901 and later was a member of several special missions to Hispanic America. In the dispute over the Atacama region, Mr. Buchanan was able to bring about a prompt settlement by siding in turn with the Chilean or the Argentinian representative, when his vote would give either the decision upon a specific point. See *Dictionary of American Biography*, III, 219; W. A. Hirst, *Argentina* (London, 1910), p. 109.

Gonzalo BULNES Pinto (1851-1936), son of President Manuel Bulnes, was born in Santiago and educated in the *liceo* of the Padres Franciscanos and at the National Institute. He then spent three years in Europe, whence he returned to Chile and devoted himself to business and agriculture, varied by periods of political and diplomatic activity. At times, he was closely associated with nitrate and insurance enterprises and was a frequent contributor to the daily press and to historical publications. The two volumes mentioned in the text appeared in 1878 and were shortly followed by a three-volume *Historia de la guerra del Pacífico* (Valparaiso, 1912-1919). He was minister to Germany and Italy and, as special envoy to Ecuador in 1923, settled an unpleasant incident with that country. Later he served acceptably as special and regular ambassador to Argentina. The celebration in 1935 of the sixtieth anniversary of his marriage to Señora Carmela Correa was an occasion for public congratulations in the Santiago press.—F, II, 276-278.

Manuel BULNES Prieto (1799-1866) was born in Concepción and early entered upon his military career in that city. His espousal of the cause of the revolution forced him into exile, from which he escaped to join San Martín. He participated in the later battles which secured independence and then was sent to fight the Araucanians and outlaws in the south, with success, as noted above. His successful campaign against the Peru-Bolivian Confederation (see p. 270) made him president of Chile from 1841-1851. Moderate rather than liberal in his views, he consistently pursued a conservative course in government.—E, IX, 1388; F, II, 281-282.

Joaquín CABEZAS García (1867-   ), a graduate of the men's normal school of Santiago (1886), was sent abroad three years later to study the Swedish system of physical and manual education, and continued his studies in Belgium in psychology and pedagogy. In 1893 he was made professor of manual training in the normal school and also taught gymnastics in the National Institute. He created the School of Physical Education in 1906 and reorganized it in 1919, thus making it peculiarly his institution. He is the author of numerous textbooks and has played an important part in all educational activities.—F, II, 304; *Hoy*, August 27, 1936, p. 16.

Andrés Avelino CÁCERES (1833-1924) was born at Ayacucho, Peru. As a youth he served under Ramón Castilla and from 1857 to 1860 he was military attaché at Paris. During the war against Chile he became a general and after the fall of Lima he was provisional president. In 1886 he became regular president and after an interval was again suggested for the office but declined because of intense opposition. He held diplomatic posts in France, Great Britain, and Italy.—E, X, 256.

Narciso CAMPERO (1815-1896) was born in Valle de Tojo, Bolivia, and studied law in Argentina, but he returned to his native country to fight against Chile. He completed his law studies in the University of Chuquisaca (now Sucre), pursued military studies in Europe, and took an active part in the uprisings against the dictators, Córdoba and Melgarejo. By successive stages he rose to the rank of general of division, minister of war, and supreme commander of the Bolivian army. During the war with Chile, in which he gave a good account of himself, he became president of Bolivia and in that capacity he had to accept the Treaty of 1884. He then retired to private life.—E, X, 1265.

Enrique CAMPINO (1794-1877?), who was picked out by the conspirators to head the revolt, was himself a member of congress and came from a prominent family. His military record, however, was bad and his name inspired no confidence. He was later implicated in the conspiracy of Quillota but was saved from execution (see p. 269). He held the office of senator in 1863.—B, XV, 131-144; F, II, 320-323.

Estanislao del CANTO Arteaga (1840-1923) was born in Quillota and educated in the Military School, which he entered in 1856. Beginning his service in 1859, the year of the second uprising against Montt, he took part in the battle of Cerro Grande (see p. 299) and engaged in numerous campaigns against the Araucanians. As colonel he participated in the Peruvian campaigns and in 1889 he was prefect of police in Santiago. Relegated to Tacna by President Balmaceda, he was in an excellent position to aid the revolutionists against that executive. He became general of division in 1891, was sent on a military mission to Europe in 1892, and forced to retire from the army in 1897. His later years were embittered by jealousy of his associates.—F, II, 343-344.

Ignacio de la CARRERA (1747-1818) was born in Santiago, his mother being the daughter of a member of the *audiencia* of Chile. He had a restless disposition, and his father sent him to Peru where he passed some seven years in Lima; and then to Spain, where he lived for a year and a half in Cádiz, devoted to business. His wealth and aristocratic connections made him a valuable adherent of the patriotic cause to which his three sons were martyrs. See Miguel Luis Amunátegui, *Camilo Henríquez* (2 vols. Santiago, 1889), I, 5-7; J. T. Medina, "Bibliografía de Don José Miguel Carrera," in *Rev. chil. de hist. y geog.*, XL, 326-371; F, II, 364.

José Miguel CARRERA (1785-1821), the first president of Chile, was born in Santiago and executed in Mendoza. His parents wished him to have a literary career, but, having decided military tastes, he entered the cavalry regiment of Farnesio in Spain and distinguished himself during the war against the French, rising to the rank of captain. On learning of the outbreak of the revolution he returned to Chile and after the fall of Martínez de Rozas took the conspicuous part detailed in the preceding pages. As a consequence of the rivalry with O'Higgins, he did not support the latter in the battle of Rancagua. After this reverse he went to Buenos Aires and thence to the United States. He returned to Buenos Aires in 1816 and later organized a plan to seize the supreme power in Chile, but was captured and shot. A monument was erected to him in Santiago in 1864.—E, XI, 1324; B, VIII, 392. See Collier and Cruz, *La primera misión de los Estados Unidos de América en Chile, passim;* Luis Galdames, *La evolución constitucional de Chile, 1810-192[6]*, I, 189-191; Vicuña Mackenna, *El ostracismo de los Carreras;* for the *Diario militar* of Carrera see "Colección de historiadores i de; documentos relativos a la independencia de Chile," Vol. I. A description of Carreras' *Diario militar* is to be found in B, IX, 634-637, especially n. 9 on p. 636. See also *ibid.*, n. 14, on pp. 610-615; Agusto Iglesias, *José Miguel Carrera. La rebelión armada en América* (Santiago, 1934).

Mariano CASANOVA Casanova (1833-1906) was born in Santiago, began his studies in the National Institute, and finished them in the Conciliar Seminary. He early displayed talents that justified his receiving orders as presbyter and being chosen professor in the seminary and member of the faculty of sacred sciences and theology in the University of Chile. In 1861 he received the degree of attorney from the university. In 1865 he journeyed to Europe and then took up parish duties in Valparaiso, where he was distinguished for his pulpit eloquence and for a polemical controversy with the Protestant, David Trumbull. In 1888 he founded the Catholic University of Santiago. In 1886 he became archbishop of Santiago and four years later tried to harmonize congress and Balmaceda. Remaining neutral during the civil war, he added to his prestige by a second visit to Europe in 1894, during which he had an audience with the pope. In 1895 he completed a code of laws for the Chilean church; in 1896, made a spectacular fraternal visit to Argentina; and, in 1899, brought about a meeting of all the higher clergy of South America.—F, II, 377-378.

Carlos CASANUEVA Opazo (18 -   ) received his degree in law in 1896 but, preferring the Church, he was ordained as presbyter in 1900. Although holding a few parish charges, his main efforts have been in the field of religious education and journalism and in behalf of the unprivileged classes. In 1920 he became rector in the Catholic University where he improved and broadened its scientific courses. He opened its classes to women in 1924, to adults in 1926, and at various times has organized conferences on topics of general business interest. Modest, industrious, and talented, he has done much to make his institution deservedly popular.—F, II, 381.

CAUPOLICÁN (d. 1558), the Araucanian chief, was probably born near Palmaiquén in the early part of the sixteenth century. After defeating Valdivia and Villagra, as narrated in the text, he himself suffered three disastrous routs, was taken prisoner, and barbarously executed. It is claimed that he tried without success to save Valdivia from torture and death and that he on his part offered to return Valdivia's skull, sword, and gold chain if he were spared. The failure of his messenger to bring back these articles meant his own death at Cañete. His fame apparently is due more to the verses of Ercilla than to his own skill and valor, although he possessed those qualities to a remarkable degree. Nicanor Plaza (q. v.) has made a famous statue of this chieftain.— E, XII, 645.

Thomas CAVENDISH (1555?-1592) was a native of Trimley St. Martin, Suffolk, England. Like many of his contemporaries he early took to piracy. His first considerable voyage was in 1585 in the company of Sir Richard Grenville, who sailed under the direction of Sir Walter Raleigh to attempt the first settlement of Virginia. After returning to England, he sought to imitate the exploit of Sir Francis Drake and in July, 1586, set out with a fleet of three ships on what proved to be the second English circumnavigation of the globe. Later in that year he discovered and named Port Desire, near the Strait of Magellan. On March 30, 1586, he reached the Bay of Quintero on the Chilean coast; at Arica, some time later, he plundered and burned several Spanish ships; and, continuing his plundering, burning course along the entire South American coast and across the Pacific, he finally reached Plymouth on September 16, 1588. His arrival aroused great enthusiasm among his fellow countrymen. He attempted to repeat his exploit but died at sea on this voyage. See *Dictionary of National Biography,* IX, 358-363.

José Ignacio CIENFUEGOS Astorga (1762-1845) was born and educated in Santiago and became curate in Talca in 1790. He became active in the movement for independence and suffered exile on the island of Juan Fernández. On his return he served as archdeacon of the cathedral at Santiago, was proprietary senator under O'Higgins, was a member of various congresses, and was interested in promoting education. In 1827 he founded the Instituto literario of Talca, which afterwards became the *liceo* of that city. In addition to the journey to Rome mentioned in the text, he was later, because of charges made by the papal delegate, forced to go to Rome to clear himself. This he did successfully and later became bishop of Concepción. Retiring from this charge in 1837, he spent the rest of his life in Talca. Barros Arana gives an account of his mission to Rome.—B, XIII, 568-577; F, II, 400.

Abdón CIFUENTES Espinosa (1836-1928) was born in San Felipe, province of Aconcagua. Coming from a family of moderate means it was necessary for him to struggle hard for professional and political position. He was educated in the *liceo* of San Felipe and in the National Institute at which in 1862 he became professor of history. He early showed marked literary aptitude as well as ultramontane tendencies and was soon regarded as the ready scribe and fiery orator of the conservative party. He was one of the founders and a long-time contributing editor of *El independente,* a conservative organ. He helped organize the Unión católica de Chile, a charitable and cultural society of the Catholic Church and was one of the founders of the Catholic University of Santiago. In 1889 he was made professor of public constitutional law on its staff. In 1867 he became subsecretary in the ministry which carried through the legislation noted in the text (see p. 313). He was elected deputy from Rancagua and in congress at once became the chief orator of the conservative party, a leadership that he maintained to the end of a long political career. In the revolution of 1891 he espoused the side of congress and with the success of the revolutionists became senator. His literary output was largely polemic in character and much of it has not survived the papers in which it was published. Characterized in his early years as the spoiled child of his party, he lived to become its grand old man, honored and respected even by those who disagreed with his political and religious views.—

E, XIII, 191; F, II, 402-405; Justo and Domingo Arteaga Alemparte, *Los constituyentes chilenos de 1870* in "Biblioteca de escritores de Chile," II, 422-425. His addresses have been collected in three volumes, *Colección de discursos de Abdón Cifuentes* (Santiago, 1916). The *Diario ilustrado* of Santiago, of Sunday, May 16, 1926, published a two-page sketch of his life, on the occasion of his ninetieth birthday.

Thomas COCHRANE (1775-1860), Earl of Dundonald, was a native of Anesfield, Lanarkshire, Scotland. He lived a varied and tumultuous life. Entering the British navy in 1795, he filled the years of his early service with brilliant exploits at sea and continual wrangling with his associates and superiors, varied by equally stormy political experiences. Despite his popularity with the masses, he failed to gain due promotion and was unjustly accused of fraud, fined, and imprisoned. This punishment, it seemed, was due more to his independent course in parliament than to any real guilt. Hence he was in a mood to enter the Chilean service in 1818. He soon made Chile the mistress of the southern Pacific, but received no compensation for this service. He even lost his share of the prize money for the daring capture of Valdivia. Nor did he fare better in the Brazilian or Grecian service, although the former bestowed a marquisate on him. Later he was restored to rank and partial compensation in the British navy, in which service he became vice-admiral in 1842 and admiral in 1854. In his later years he distinguished himself by his mechanical inventions. As a commander he prevailed in personal combat, in which he was able to do much with small means. His career presents an injudicious admixture of political independence and bad temper, of honesty, skill, and daring, of insubordination, and popular appeal.—F, II, 416. His own account of his life appears in *Narrative of Services in the Liberation of Chile, Peru, and Brazil*. See B, XII, 173, *et seq.;* Pilling, *The Emancipation of South America*, chap. xxii; and *Dictionary of National Biography*, XI, 165-175.

Carlos CONDELL de la Haza (1843-1887), born in Valparaiso, was partly of Scotch ancestry. After studying in the *colegio* of the French Fathers and in England, he entered the Naval School at Valparaiso in 1858. In 1865 he showed his qualities as fighter as well as seaman by capturing the Spanish vessel *Covadonga*. The same qualities gave him a victory over the Peruvian cruiser *Independencia*, in the battle of Iquique (see p. 327). He died at Quilpué, with the rank of vice-admiral.—E, XIV, 1066; F, II, 428-429.

Simón de CORDES (d. *ca.* 1600), mariner, was born in Antwerp. As a young merchant, he resided for a year in Lisbon and married there.

Acting as vice-admiral in the Dutch navy, in 1598 he was sent with a fleet to attack the Spaniards in the South Seas, and was later reinforced by two other Dutch expeditions. One report represents him as having been killed by natives on the island of Santa María, near Concepción; another states that he disappeared en route to Japan.—E, XV, 554; B, III, 305-320; IV, 102-114.

Rafael CORREA Muñoz (1863-   ), born in Santiago, was a pupil of Pedro Lira and has attracted attention because of his animal pictures. His paintings have been exhibited in Paris, in Buffalo, and in Argentina. His exhibition in Santiago in 1924 attracted wide attention. In 1926 he was elected president of the Sociedad de Bellas Artes of Chile.— F, II, 449.

Jean Gustave COURCELLE-SENEUIL (1813-1892) was born in Seneuil, France. In youth and early manhood he combined work in metallurgy with his studies in economics. After 1848 he served as subordinate in the treasury office, but with the establishment of the empire he went to South America and for ten years (1853-1863) taught political economy in the law school of the University of Chile. After his return to France he served on the Council of State in 1879 and in 1882 entered the Academy of Moral and Political Science. While in Chile he edited the Ley de Bancos (Banking Law). Original in his concepts, he sought to give a scientific background to economics and to separate theory from practice. He strongly defended free trade and favored decentralization in government. He died in Paris.—E, XV, 1358; F, II, 467-468.

Miguel CRUCHAGA Tocornal (1867-   ) became an advocate in 1889 and took the part of congress in the revolution of 1891. He began to teach law in the Catholic University in 1892 and in the University of Chile four years later. He was deputy from Melipilla (1900-1906) and as such became prominent in matters of finance and foreign affairs. He became minister of the treasury in 1903 and of the interior in 1905. He served continuously as minister and ambassador abroad from 1908 to 1927, when, having failed to settle the long-standing dispute with Peru, he temporarily withdrew in favor of Carlos Dávila (see p. 410), until Alessandri again brought him into office. In the course of his diplomatic activities he was frequently called to serve upon mixed commissions where other countries were involved. His textbook on international law has been deservedly popular in Chile. He has also written numerous pamphlets on diplomatic and financial questions and has been a member of important international gatherings.— F, II, 484-486; *Hoy,* December 23, 1932, p. 8; August 30, 1935, p. 3; January 14, 1937, p. 35.

José María de la CRUZ Prieto (1801-1875) was born in Concepción,

saw service under Carrera, and after the disaster at Rancagua (see
p. 184) emigrated to Mendoza with other fugitive revolutionists, and
there joined San Martín. After the battles of Chacabuco and Maipú,
in which he fought bravely, he assisted as secretary of the committee
that organized the first Peruvian expedition, and occupied numerous
subordinate military posts. He was twice in the cabinet as minister of
war and marine, served as governor of Valparaiso and intendant of
Concepción, and deputy and senator. He was general in chief of the
army in south Chile, when he was put forward as presidential candidate
against Montt, but after the battle at Loncomilla he retired to private
life.—E, XVI, 643; F, II, 493-495.

William DAMPIER (1652-1711) cruised along the coast of California
in 1685 and afterward sailed to the Philippines and the coast of China,
arriving in England on September 16, 1691. Dampier made another
voyage in 1704, returning in 1707, and in the following year was commissioned as pilot on an expedition with Woodes Rogers around the
world, returning in 1711. His own writings form the best source for
his expeditions. Also see *Early Voyages to Australia* (R. H. Major,
ed. London, 1859), Hakluyt Society Publications, 1st Series, Vol. XXV,
pp. 99-111, 134-164. Dampier's career connects him with earlier filibustering enterprises and the more regular naval and scientific work of
the eighteenth century. Moreover, he was able to write of his adventures
in a clear, entertaining, and convincing style. His voyages embraced the
East Indies, the China coast, Australia, the West Indies, and the coasts
of both Americas, where he had already made two extensive forays before undertaking the more regular voyages during the War of Spanish
Succession, in which Selkirk (*q. v.*) figures. See Willard Hallam Bonner,
Captain William Dampier: Buccaneer-Author (Stanford University,
1934).

Carlos DÁVILA (1884-   ), native of Los Angeles, known especially
as editor and director of *La nación* (1917-1927) and of *Los tiempos,*
has through these publications revolutionized the press of Chile. As
ambassador to the United States (1927-1931) he made his country and
its resources better known and increased the nitrate sales. After his
short and troubled presidency he took up newspaper work in New
York. He was noted for his moderate socialistic ideas.—F, II, 541; *Hoy,*
July 8, 1932, p. 4; September 16, 1932, p. 8.

Hilarión DAZA (*né* Grasolé. 1840-1894) was born in Sucre and
adopted his maternal name of Daza. His uncle gave him a rudimentary
education, after which the nephew entered the army. In 1864 he gained
the confidence of the Bolivian tyrant Melgarejo, and in 1870 gained
popularity by starting a revolt against his patron. In 1873 he took

over the government and initiated some beneficial reforms. In the early stages of the war with Chile, showing himself inept, his soldiers deposed him. He ranks as a close second to Bolivia's worst president, Malgarejo. —E, XXVI, 1378; Dennis, *Tacna and Arica, passim.*

Sebastián Díaz, O. P. (1741—*ca.* 1813), a native of Santiago and a graduate in 1763 of the University of San Felipe, was a well-known Dominican friar, the second prior of his order in Chile, and one of the most learned teachers of the University of San Felipe. His principal work, noted in the text, was probably published in Lima in 1782 but failed to present the ideas of the author clearly or in agreeable form; hence it was superseded when better books came in from the outside.— M, p. 240. See also J. T. Medina, *Historia de la literatura colonial de Chile,* II, 533-547.

Juan Díaz de Solís (d. 1516) was born at Lebrija near Seville. He had already served in the Casa da India of Portugal before he was selected by the Spanish government in 1508, together with Vicente Yáñez Pinzón, to course the American Atlantic coast from Honduras to the fortieth parallel of south latitude. In 1512 he was made pilot major of Spain to succeed Amerigo Vespucci. In 1513 he began preparations for a western voyage to the Spice Islands but did not leave until the end of 1515 and early in the following year discovered La Plata River where he met his death.—E, XVIII, 895.

Ignacio Domeyko (1802-1889) was born in Lithuania. As a boy he beheld the march of Napoleon's forces against Russia; as a youth he and his intimate friend Adam Mickiewicz attended the University of Wilna, where with other students they frequently clashed with the Russian authorities. He also studied in Vienna. In 1831 he joined in the futile revolt that still further enslaved his native Poland and forced him into a Paris exile. In 1837 he left Paris for Chile under contract to teach chemistry, minerology, and other natural sciences in the *liceo* of La Serena. In 1856 he took up his professional work in the capital, and in 1876 became rector of the University of Chile. He was at one and the same time a scientist, a sincere Christian, and a poet.—F, II, 585. See also M. L. Amunátegui, *Ensayos biográficos,* I, 185-415.

Francis Drake (*ca.* 1545-1596) had, strictly speaking, begun his expeditions—whether piratical or not—long before 1578. In 1565, at the age of twenty, he had made a voyage to the coast of Guinea under Sir John Hawkins, his kinsman and mentor. He likewise accompanied Hawkins to the West Indies on the ill-fated voyage of 1567-1568, in the course of which the principals lost all the vessels of their small fleet at Vera Cruz except the ones they personally commanded. In 1570 Drake obtained a privateering commission from Queen Elizabeth under which he made two profitable raids in the West Indies and the Caribbean area before starting out in 1577 on his famous voyage to the Pacific. From September, 1578, until near the end of that year, he continued his seizure of ships along the coast of Chile. See Sir Julian S. Corbett, *Drake and the Tudor Navy* (New York, London [etc.], 1899), and William Wood, *Elizabethan Sea Dogs* (New Haven, 1921), pp. 95-195, 221-229. See also Henry Raup Wagner, *Sir Francis Drake's Voyage Around the World, its Aims and its Achievements* (San Francisco, 1926).

Alberto Edwards Vives (1874-1934) was born in Valparaiso. He held a minor official position in the revolution of 1891, became an attorney in 1896, was elected as deputy in 1909, and became chief of the statistical office ten years later. As such he was in charge of the Census of 1920, and at different dates—1914, 1915, 1926—was minister of the treasury. He edited the writings of J. J. Vallejo (see p. 275). For a sketch of his life and outstanding contributions see *Rev. chil. de hist. y geog.*, LXXIV (Jan.-April, 1933), 5-64. See also F, III, 33.

Mariano Egaña Fabres (1793-1846) was born in Santiago, finished his study of law at the age of eighteen, and shortly thereafter was made secretary of the *junta representativa* of the sovereignty of Chile. After Rancagua he went into captivity with his father to Juan Fernández. After his return he became fiscal agent of the court of appeals and held other offices under the government. During the years 1824-1829 he was minister plenipotentiary in various European countries. In 1830 he was made minister of the interior but refused the office, preferring to act as fiscal agent of the supreme court. In 1831 he was elected to the chamber of deputies, became its president in 1836, and in addition was plenipotentiary to Peru. He later acted as minister of justice until 1841. He played a leading part in framing the Constitution of 1833.— E, XIX, 170; F, III, 39-41.

Juan Egaña Riesco (1769-1860) was born in Lima of a Chilean father and a Peruvian mother. He was graduated in jurisprudence from the University of San Marcos in Lima, and took up his residence in Chile near the end of the century. He became the chief legislator of the early years of the republic; and he also devoted considerable attention to the education of youth, being one of the founders of the National Institute. His son, Mariano Egaña, collaborated with him in various important matters of legislation.—F, III, 36-37. See also Amunátegui Solar, *Bosquejo histórico*, pp. 10, 11.

Juan Sebastián de Elcano (1476-1526) was a native of Guetaria (Guipúzcoa). Accustomed from his youth to a seafaring life, he embarked with Magellan in 1519, and during the early part of the voyage alternately opposed and supported his chieftain. After Magellan's death, Elcano took charge of the two remaining ships of the squadron and conducted one successfully back to Spain, thus completing the first circumnavigation of the globe. For this feat and for its probable value in the spice trade, he was rewarded by a coat of arms representing a globe, set off by two clove buds and the inscription *Primus Circumdediste Me*. He was one of the commissioners appointed by Spain to settle the dispute with Portugal over the Spice Islands. In 1525, as second in command, he joined the expedition of García Jofre de Loaisa, bound for the Spice Islands but, separating from his leader at the Strait of Magellan, he claimed to have discovered the open sea below the tip of the continent. He rejoined Loaisa, and after a stormy passage of fifty-one days the two passed through the strait into an equally stormy Pacific. Loaisa perished from the hardships of the voyage in July, 1526, and Elcano a month later. The Spanish government never paid to his mother the salary due him, but in 1671 an admirer dedicated a tomb for him in his native town. In 1800 and in 1869 monuments were erected there in his honor.—E, XIX, 496-498.

Alonso de ERCILLA y Zúñiga (1533-1594), born in Madrid, was the son of a noted jurist who died when the poet was barely a year old. His widowed mother became a lady in waiting to Empress Isabella, wife of Charles V. As a boy Ercilla early became a page to Philip II and journeyed with the prospective monarch through Flanders, France, Germany, and England. In Spain he met and conversed with the leading conquerors of Mexico and Peru. He was in London with Philip II when that prince received tidings of Valdivia's death. He accompanied Jerónimo de Alderete (*q. v.*) when that leader started for America and continued on to Lima after his superior's death. He arrived in Chile with Hurtado de Mendoza, in 1557, and was commissioned as captain; but, when in the following year an altercation arose between him and a fellow officer, he was banished from that colony. Despite this rigorous penalty Ercilla, upon his return to Spain, regained the favor of Philip II, to whom he dedicated his famous epic. The first part of *La araucana* appeared in 1569, the second in 1578, and the third in 1590. The work follows Ariosto in spirit and is worthy a place beside *Os Lusiadas* of Camoens. In 1571 the poet became knight of the Order of Santiago and later served as gentleman in waiting to Leopold II of Austria.—M, pp. 254-272; Coester, *The Literary History of Spanish America* (New York, 1916), pp. 6-10.

Fernando ERRÁZURIZ (1771-1841) was a member of the junta that succeeded O'Higgins who, like many other men of the period, suffered persecution after Rancagua. He was a member of the convention of

1822 and for many years senator, becoming president of the senate. He served three different times as president ad interim of the republic.— E, XX, 543.

Federico ERRÁZURIZ Echaurren (1850-1901) became an advocate at the age of twenty-three but never practiced law. He preferred the simple but elegant life of the great Chilean landowner, an occupation which he combined for nearly thirty years with service in congress. Professedly a liberal, he made little of political principles but utilized his knowledge of human nature to advance his personal fortune. He served as minister of war in 1890 and for a few months in 1894 was minister of justice. As deputy in 1891 he exerted himself to amplify the law extending pardon to the Balmacedists. Elected a senator in 1894, he began two years later a vigorous campaign for the presidency. He succeeded in defeating his more austere rival through unlimited promises and the lavish use of funds, but needed the decision of a court of honor to gain the office by the narrow majority of two votes. He was a careful but not distinguished executive. The most important act of his administration was the settlement of boundary disputes with Argentina. He died in office a few weeks before the completion of his term.—F, III, 59-61.

Ladislao ERRÁZURIZ Lazcano (18   -   ) received his title as advocate in 1905 and immediately affiliated with the liberal party. Son of an active revolutionist of 1891 and member of a family that had already given two presidents to the republic, he early aspired to this high office. He became a member of congress in 1915 and a senator in 1920. Already recognized as an orator and skilful politician, in 1920, he became minister of war and was responsible for the mobilization of troops to the northward during prospective trouble with Peru. With the fall of the Alessandri government in 1924, he began to plan his own candidacy for the presidency. He was aided by the National Union and the support of that group aroused the fears of the military clique that had displaced Alessandri and overthrown the junta headed by Altamirano. As a result of this last overturn Errázuriz and others suffered temporary exile. Reëlected senator in 1926, he returned to Chile where he was enthusiastically received by his fellow unionists. An object of attention to the Ibáñez government, he again suffered exile and has since played little part in public affairs.—F, III, 68-70.

Crescente ERRÁZURIZ Valdivieso (1839-1931) was born in Santiago and educated in the seminary of that city, where he was ordained presbyter in 1863. He later served as professor in the seminary and held the chair of canonical law in the University of Chile. In addition to holding many subordinate church offices, he founded *El estandarte católico* in 1874 and entered the Dominician order ten years later. He was favorably known for his historical work. *Los oríjenes de la iglesia chilena, 1540-1603,* was published in 1873 and at once established his reputation as a serious historian. He was called to the archbishopric of Santiago in 1919 and during the course of ten years he reorganized the dioceses of his jurisdiction, encouraged social and religious movements among the laity, sought to regulate extremes in fashions and public exhibitions, and promoted eucharistic congresses. His most substantial contribution to contemporary life was to bring about the peaceful separation of Church and State—long a bitter issue in Chilean politics. His sympathetic character, his simple eloquence, and his forceful and correct literary style added much to his prestige. During his service as archbishop, his birthdays called forth numerous expressions of personal regard in the daily press.—F, III, 74-77; *Rev. chil. de hist. y geog.,* LXXII (May-Aug., 1932), 5-175.

Federico Errázuriz Zañartu (1825-1877), born in Santiago, was a member of an illustrious Chilean family of Navarrese descent. Educated in the Conciliar Seminary, the National Institute, and the University of Chile, he obtained his degree as advocate in 1846. He became a member of the faculty of laws in 1847 and of the faculty of theology in 1848. One of the early members of the Reform Club (see p. 286), he consistently opposed the administration of Montt and along with Lastarria, Bilbao, and others suffered exile under that magistrate because of his part in the outbreak of 1851. Later he pursued a less partisan course. He was noted as a historian, served in congress, filled efficiently two ministerial posts in the administration of Pérez, introducing in each important reforms, and in 1871 became president of the republic. In this office he continued the course of reform and of material progress that characterized his ministries.—E, XX, 544; F, III, 77-80.

Erasmo Escala (1826-1884) was born in Valparaiso, entered the Military School as cadet in 1837, and in the following year joined the army for service in Peru. During the uprisings of 1851, he supported the government and lost his left hand fighting in the streets of Santiago, but continued in the conflict until the decision at Loncomilla (see p. 290). He helped defend Valparaiso during its bombardment by the Spaniards in 1866. After his successful campaigns in Antofogasta and Tarapacá he became general of division. Following the war he became deputy in congress, affiliated with the conservative party.—F, III, 81-82.

Alonso de Escobar Villaroel (1503-1574) came to Peru in 1531, took part in the siege of Cuzco and the pacification of Upper Peru, and later distinguished himself for his gallant and vigorous combats with the Indians of Chile. For six years he was a member of the town council of

Santiago, serving twice as alcalde, and even after his offense against the faith he was given a public commission by that body.—M, p. 280.

Juan Nepomuceno Espejo (1821-1876) was born in Talca. His first public service occurred in connection with the campaign against Santa Cruz (see p.....). After the battle of Yungay he entered the National Institute and began in 1843 his connection with a series of short-lived opposition papers. Lastarria (see p. 275) was his literary mentor and under such tutelage he knew both exile and imprisonment. Freed from prison through the efforts of Manuel Camilo Vial, he supported the policy of that minister for a time, then resigned from the editorial staff of *El progreso,* the paper he then edited, to take part in the gold rush to California. On his return to Chile in 1854 he entered business, but four years later returned to journalism and to the liberal cause. He took part in the "religious" disputes of the sixties and served in parliament from 1864 onward. A journalist by nature, he was also one of the most popular poets of Chile.—E, XXII, 164; F, III, 93; Justo and Domingo Arteaga Alemparte, *Los constituyentes chilenos de 1870,* in "Biblioteca de escritores de Chile," II, 250-256.

Agustín Eyzaguirre Arechavala (1776-1837) was born and died in Santiago. He was elected a member of the first national congress of 1811. In 1813, as a member of the *junta gubernativa,* he exerted himself strongly to arouse public spirit and at the same time to bring about certain liberal reforms. After Rancagua he was confined on the island of Juan Fernández. During the O'Higgins' government, he remained outside Chile looking after his own affairs, being one of the chief promoters and the director of a silk-importing company. After the resignation of O'Higgins in 1823, he returned to Chile and was twice appointed to office, once as a member of the *junta gubernativa* which succeeded O'Higgins and again as vice president of Chile in 1826. After being in office for four months, a military rising compelled his retirement.—E, XXII, 1580; F, III, 115.

José Alejo Eyzaguirre Arechavala (1783-1850) was born in Santiago, educated in the Concilar Seminary and the University of San Felipe, and received his investiture as a priest in 1807. He was absent from the country until 1815 and in 1822 was banished by O'Higgins. Called back by Freire, he served in the congress that adopted the Constitution of 1828 (see p. 232), and in the council of state. In 1844 he was named archbishop of Santiago but resigned the following year.—F, III, 115.

Elías Fernández Albano (1845-1910), after studying in the National Institute and the University of Chile, entered upon the practice of law in 1869 and became deputy in 1884. As a politician he was popular with all factions, was frequently summoned to assist the administration, especially during the frequent cabinet changes of the nineties, and often held important cabinet posts. For some ten years he directed the Caja hipotecaria (Mortgage Bank) and was general adviser of all political factions. His position at the head of the cabinet in 1910 made him the acting president for a few weeks.—F, III, 134.

Rafael FERNÁNDEZ Concha (1832-1912) received his title as advocate in 1855 and in the following year became professor of canonical law. In 1857 he joined the faculty of law and political science and in 1860 was ordained as a priest. He occupied important posts in the archbishop's establishment and gained recognition as an orator and as a writer, especially on ecclesiastical law. He became titular bishop in 1901 and served modestly and simply in many public stations, including that of counselor of state.—F, III, 153, 154.

Ricardo FERNÁNDEZ Montalva (1866-1899) completed the first years of the law course, but thereafter devoted himself to literature, especially poetry, and to bohemian life. He has been called the Musset of Chile. His first novel appeared in 1895, his first drama in 1888, and a volume of poems in 1897. He contributed to various periodicals but not for money. In 1891 he was named secretary of the Chilean legation in Paris, but lost this place with the fall of Balmaceda and returned to find his ancestral home destroyed and his course of life broken.—F, III, 143.

Tomás de FIGUEROA Caravaca (1746-1811) was born in the province of Granada. Obtaining membership in the Royal Guard in 1765 before he was twenty and contracting a fortunate marriage, he faced a brilliant military career, but a love intrigue and the consequent duel, in which he killed his opponent, led to his condemnation for murder— a sentence that was commuted to imprisonment in Valdivia. Escaping to Spain from that prison, he secured a pardon in 1773 on condition that he serve in Valdivia in some military capacity. In the Indian wars of that jurisdiction he showed himself a capable but cruel officer, but for more than twenty years he obtained no substantial promotion. He was located at Concepción when the supreme junta was installed in Santiago and immediately swore fidelity to that body. Martínez de Rozas brought him to Santiago and secured for him a commission as colonel. He seemed sincere in his support of the new government but was led to ally himself with the Spanish malcontents who plotted to overthrow it, and thus became the first conspicuous victim of the revolution in Chile.—B, VIII, 304-332; F, III, 172-174.

Emiliano FIGUEROA Larraín (1866-1931) was a descendant of Tomás Figueroa (see p. 161). Educated in the Colegio of San Ignacio and the National University, he entered upon the profession of law in

1890 and at the same time held a minor office in the *intendencia* of Santiago. He supported the party that continued Balmaceda's policy, became deputy in 1900, and president of the chamber of deputies five years later. He became minister of justice and public instruction in 1907, returned to the same post in 1909, and in 1910, by virtue of being the minister of the cabinet longest in public service, became acting president during the centennial celebrations. Afterward, as minister to Spain and to Argentina, his courtesy, common sense, and industry made him decidedly popular, and in the latter country he was instrumental in bringing about that understanding between Argentina, Brazil, and Chile known as the "A B C Pact." On a second mission to Argentina in 1924 he secured recognition of the temporary government that succeeded President Alessandri. In 1925, as sole candidate of the leading parties, he was elected president of Chile under the new constitution. Unable to meet the problems of a new era and drawn into a conflict between the executive and supreme court, over which his brother presided, Don Emiliano first sought a leave of absence and then resigned the presidency. In 1928, upon renewal of diplomatic relations with Peru, he served acceptably as ambassador to that country. He died as the result of an automobile accident.—F, III, 175-178.

Ramón FREIRE Serrano (1787-1851) was born in Santiago and entered the Chilean army in 1811. He became captain of dragoons in 1814. After the battle of Rancagua he went to Argentina where he enlisted under the famous corsair Brown who operated in the Pacific. Returning to Argentina in 1816, he joined San Martín on his expedition to Chile and with one hundred men captured Talca. After Chacabuco and Maipú he was appointed intendant of Concepción and military chief of that province. In 1820 he defeated Benavides and his army of two thousand men. In 1823 he declared against O'Higgins and after the latter's loss of power was made supreme dictator. His career as chief executive is treated in the present text. After the defeat at Lircay he suffered a second exile, broken by one unsuccessful attempt to regain power (see p. 265). In 1842 he was permitted to return to Chile where he passed the rest of his life in quiet, quite divorced from politics. Superb as a soldier, he was vacillating in political affairs.—E, XXIV, 1189; F, III, 205-212.

Amadeo Francisco FRÉZIER (1682-1773), a member of a family of English origin, was born at Chambéry, France. After pursuing studies in language, literature, theology, and mathematics, he served five years in the army and later carried on engineering work at St. Malo. His visit to Chile and Peru (1712-1714) was to engage in general study and to suggest measures for the military defense of these colonies. His *Re-*

lation du voyage de la mer du sud (Paris, 1716) contains much industrial and commercial data concerning Chile and affords a suggestive contemporary interpretation of existing conditions.—B, V, 525-528.

Alejandro Fuenzalida Grandón (1865-   ) was born in Copiapó, studied in the local *liceo* and the state university, and received his title as advocate in 1889. He began his teaching career as inspector in the National Institute in 1885 and also contributed to the press. In 1894 he became professor of history and geography in the National Institute and in 1900 added to his schedule a course in administrative law at the university. In 1911 he was commissioned to study the system of public instruction in Prussia and to visit various European museums. In 1918 he retired from active teaching. The books mentioned in the text were published between 1899 and 1911. In 1919 he published a historical monograph, *El mineral del teniente.*—F, III, 234.

Gavino Gaínza (1760?-1822?) began his military career at the age of fourteen. After service at Oran and before Gibraltar, he came to Havana in 1750 and saw service in Louisiana and before Pensacola. Later, in 1783, he was transferred to Lima where he served with a brief intermission at Guayaquil, until given command of the royalist forces in Chile. During this time he married a sister of Rocafuerte. Here his conduct of operations brought him before a military court, which reproved but freed him. His next important service was in Central America where he figured in the events of 1821-1822, which brought about independence there. He died in obscurity in Mexico.—E, XXV, 403; F, III, 239.

Pedro León Gallo Goyenechea (1830-1877), native of Copiapó, was educated at the National Institute and entered the national guard at the age of eighteen. His first political articles displayed his versatility and the high quality of his genius. He fought against the insurgents of Santiago in the uprising of April 20, 1851 (see p...) and upon returning to Copiapó engaged with his brothers in developing the nitrate industry of the north, but without losing his devotion to literature. As *regidor* of his native city he agitated for a popular assembly to revise the national constitution and ultimately became chief of the revolutionary movement of 1859. His defeat meant a few years of exile in the United States and Europe where his poetry attracted favorable notice. He was enthusiastically received on his return to Chile in 1863 and later elected to congress where his literary skill, both in verse and prose, his eloquence, his consistent liberalism, his marked sympathy, combined with his wealth, gave him a commanding position. His untimely death called forth universal expressions of grief.—E, XXV, 616; F, III, 255-257; Justo and Domingo Arteaga Alemparte, *op. cit.,* pp. 189-193; Blanco Cuartín, *Artículos escogidos*, pp. 611-617.

Agustín GAMARRA (1785-1840) was born in Cuzco and early entered upon a military career, but left the Spanish army for that of Peru in 1821. He distinguished himself in his early campaigns against Bolivia in 1826, but was later defeated in the war between Peru and Colombia. He contended with Lamar and Obregoso for supremacy in Peru and with the Bolivian, Santa Cruz. After the defeat of the latter, Gamarra became temporary president of Peru, but was killed in the battle of Ingavi in 1840, which determined the final separation of Bolivia from Peru.—E, XXV, 627.

Manuel José GANDARILLAS Guzmán (1790-1842) was born in Santiago. He studied law, joined the revolutionists, and associated with Camilo Henríquez. He was with the Carreras and, like many of his fellows, spent several years in exile in Argentina. Returning to Chile after the fall of O'Higgins, he served as finance minister and as minister of the interior under Freire, making a good record in each office. He also collaborated in editorial work on *El hambriento* (see p. 237), *El araucano*, and other ephemeral publications of the period, including *El philopolita* (see p. 261). His *Polémicas políticas* gave him considerable fame. He served several terms in congress and for a time was a member of the supreme court, and for five years *auditor de guerra*.—E, XXV, 677; F, III, 270-271. See also Sotomayor Valdés, *Historia de Chile durante los cuarenta años*, I, 322, 444.

Francisco GARCÍA CALDERÓN (1834-1905) was born at Arequipa. He entered the Peruvian congress for the first time in 1867 and in the following year became minister of the treasury. Assuming the provisional presidency of Peru after the flight of Piérola, in 1881, he tried to secure the aid of the United States against the invaders but was himself arrested by the Chileans and taken to Valparaiso. On his return to Peru he was president of the senate and through his influence secured the passage of many important acts. He is also known as a writer on law subjects.—E, X, 652. See also Dennis, *Documentary History*, pp. 169, 173, 178, 183, 191, 197; Evans, *Diplomatic Relations*, pp. 105-109.

Francisco Antonio GARCÍA CARRASCO (1743-1811) was born at Ceuta and entered the army at the age of sixteen. After 1785 he continued his military duties in Buenos Aires and in Montevideo. Coming to Chile in 1796, he gained royal approval and a brigadier's commission through the capture of a North American vessel engaged in contraband trade. While inspecting forts on the frontier, he was summoned to the governorship of Chile. Vain and with little education, although represented as a man of agreeable manners; indecisive, while prompt to punish disobedience of royal orders, he hastened the revolution through his muddling. However, he was by no means so monstrous as often represented. In some respects he resembled the governor of Barrataria as portrayed by Cervantes.—B, VIII, 19; F, III, 285-286.

Juan GARCÍA DEL RÍO (1794-1856) was born in Cartagena, Colombia. Because of his interest in public law, he early began a political career, during which he was often called upon to assist Bolívar and his associates in the founding of great Colombia. He opposed, but without success, the separation of Venezuela from the republic, but acquiesced in the inevitable step. He collaborated with Bello in the publishing of *Repertorio americano*. His death occurred in the city of Mexico.— E, XXV, 789; Coester, *op. cit.*, p. 74.

Antonio GARCÍA Reyes (1817-1855) was born in Santiago. Because of his brilliant contributions to *El araucano,* he was given employment in the ministry of the interior. In 1849 he was minister of the treasury for a year. In addition to his legal practice and literary work, he was a member of the faculty and council of the University of Chile, wrote a memoir upon the First National Squadron in 1846, helped edit the code of military law in 1843 and the penal code in 1852, and served as fiscal of the supreme court of justice. He died at Lima while on his way to the United States to assume the post of minister of Chile to that republic.—E, XXV, 821; F, III, 290.

Victorino GARRIDO (d. 1838), a native of Old Castile, came to Chile in 1818 as commissary of the last Spanish reinforcements sent to that country. After being disembarked at Talcahuano, he and numerous other officers, cut off by the capture of the frigate *María Isabel* (see p. 210), embraced the cause of the revolution and were given employment by O'Higgins. Garrido steadily advanced in public service and by his intrigues contributed to the success of the conservatives at Lircay. He was an important adviser in public affairs up to his death.—F, III, 310-311; Sotomayor Valdés, *Historia de Chile,* II, 170, *et seq.*

Pedro de la GASCA (1485-1567) was born in Barco de Avila. After filling important offices in Spain, Charles the Fifth named him president of the *audiencia* of Lima for the purpose of restoring order in that troubled conquest. La Gasca succeeded in enticing from the rebellious Gonzalo Pizarro most of the latter's troops and then easily subdued and executed the rebel himself. He then reëstablished the *audiencia* at Lima, reorganized civil administration, and adopted measures to increase the mineral wealth of Peru. After returning to Spain he served as bishop of Sigüenza and of Palencia and died at Valladolid.—E, XXV, 976.

Claudio GAY (1800-1872) was born at Draguignan, France. From

1828 to 1842 he explored a large part of Chile under the commission mentioned in the text. Later in life he performed similar tasks in northern Africa, Asia Minor, and surrounding regions. In 1856 he became a member of the Paris Academy of Sciences. His *Histórica física y política de Chile* (Paris, 1844-1854) consists of six volumes of history proper, supplemented by two volumes of documents, together with eight volumes devoted to the zoology of the country and eight volumes devoted to its botany, and an atlas.—F, III, 312-313.

Alonso de GÓNGORA Marmolejo (1524-1576) was born in Carmona, Spain. For some forty years he shared in the gains and losses of the Araucanian wars, occasionally filling some minor civil office and subject to minor lawsuits, without much personal profit. His chronicle, *Historia de Chile desde su descubrimiento hasta el año del 1575 compuesta por el Capitán Alonso de Góngora Marmolejo y seguida de varios documentos,* is published in the second volume of "Colección de historiadores de Chile," p. xiii.—B, II, 436, n. 47; M, p. 368.

Gil GONZÁLEZ de Ávila (15 ? -   ) was one of the two Dominicans who in 1557 accompanied García Hurtado de Mendoza to Chile and began the foundation of a convent in Santiago. These Dominicans were under the influence of Friar Tomás de San Martín, bishop of Charcas, who evolved the theory that those who received encomiendas because of their services in suppressing the rebellion of Gonzalo Pizarro and who observed the royal regulations respecting the treatment of Indians could conscientiously hold Indians in servitude while the first conquerors could not. The latter, in achieving their conquest, supposedly did not observe any law, "natural, divine, human, canonical, or civil." Barros Arana characterizes this simply as putting theology and the confessional at the service of the king and of the new encomenderos.—B, II, 305-310. The quotation from this paragraph occurs in B, II, 307, and is from Góngora Marmolejo, *op. cit.,* p. 95.

Juan Ignacio GONZÁLEZ Eyzaguirre (1844-1918), the fourth archbishop of Santiago, was born in that city and ordained as presbyter in 1867. He served as vice-rector in the seminary of Santiago, rector of the seminary of Valparaiso, and vicar-general of the archbishop of Santiago before he was invested with the last-named office. As a counselor of state and contributor to the secular and religious press, he made a reputation for himself which he greatly increased during his term as archbishop, because of his charitable work and his patronage of religious education.—F, III, 348.

Rodrigo GONZÁLEZ Marmolejo (1487-1564) was a native of Constantina, near Seville. After participating in a disastrous campaign against the Indians of Upper Peru, he accompanied Valdivia to Chile, where he combined the breeding of horses and other practical tasks with his duties as parish priest. Notwithstanding his advanced years, he journeyed to Concepción after it was founded, to inspire the troops there with his own zeal for the conquest. Valdivia, who greatly praised his services, early urged the appointment of his associate as the first bishop of Santiago. When the bishopric of Charcas was created in 1551, Santiago was part of that diocese, and González Marmolejo, who had looked after the property interests of the Church in Chile, was in 1555 made its vicar-general. Two years later, in response to repeated petitions from Valdivia and the local *cabildo,* he was named suffragan bishop of Santiago, under the jurisdiction of the bishop of Lima, but hostilities between the king and the pope prevented official action until 1563, when the creation of the diocese was duly solemnized. The aged and infirm appointee was unable to participate in the formal installation and died the following year.—B, II, 353-355; M, pp. 372-374. See also Errázuriz, *Los oríjenes de la iglesia chilena,* chaps. x, xiv.

Pedro Antonio GONZÁLEZ Valenzuela (1863-1903) was born in the province of Talca. Early an orphan, he was brought up by a clerical uncle. He pursued desultory courses in the *liceo* of Valparaiso and elsewhere, supporting himself by teaching literature and history in private institutions, and casually attended some law courses in the university. His first verse, presented in the Radical Club, was received with enthusiasm. He fell into an unfortunate love affair which drove him still more rapidly along his Bohemian course. While recognized for his poetic ability during his lifetime, he achieved his greatest fame after death.— F, III, 357.

Andrés Antonio GORBEA (1792-1852) was a native of Viscaya and noted for the application of mathematics to engineering. He came to Chile in 1826 and taught in the Liceo de Mora, the National Institute, and the Military Academy. He trained a full generation of Chilean mathematical engineers.—E, XXVI, 695; F, III, 363.

Manuel Julián GRAJALES (d. 1855) was still a medical student when, in 1803, he was attached to the commission sent to America to combat smallpox. He came to Chile in 1807 after vaccine had already been introduced into the country. He immediately organized local juntas to assist him in extending the use of it. In each of the cities of Valparaiso and Santiago he personally vaccinated more than eight thousand persons. He returned to Peru in 1808, but in 1813 he was appointed by Viceroy Abascal surgeon of the royalist forces serving in Chile. Captured by the patriots, he was well treated by them because of his former services and his charitable, friendly disposition. He settled in Chile and continued to practice there until 1826, when he returned to

Spain, but the people of Chile never forgot his services.—B, VII, 270-277.

Antonio GRAMUSSET (1740-1785) was born in Premelieu, France, and arrived in Chile in 1764. Lively and mercurial in temperament, he saw service in the militia and attempted to enter the priesthood before he failed in agriculture. He was experimenting on a hydraulic machine for pumping water from mines when he was arrested in January, 1781, along with Berney (or Vergne) for conspiring against the government.—M, pp. 379-380; B, VI, 404.

Miguel GRAU (1834-1879) was a son of a Colombian officer who was residing in Piura at the time of Grau's birth. From the age of ten Grau followed the sea and at the age of eighteen he obtained an appointment as midshipman in the Peruvian navy. After taking part in subduing a rebellion in 1858, Grau was in the merchant service for two years. In this practical school he acquired a reputation for ability, resourcefulness, and courage, and, what was more unusual, for his kind disposition. He rejoined the navy in 1860, became captain in 1868, and in 1875, as a deputy in congress, supported the government of Manuel Pardo. He was given command of the *Huáscar* at the outbreak of the war with Chile and was blown to pieces by a shell from the *Cochrane* in the battle described in the text. See Markham, *History of Peru*, pp. 387-392.

Marmaduke GROVE Vallejos (1878-   ) was born in Copiapó. He began an active life of varied adventure in 1898 as second lieutenant of artillery. From the beginning he was distinguished for his energetic and resolute character. As early as 1910 he began to contribute articles to the press. In 1920 he became subdirector of the Military School where he distinguished himself as a teacher. He defended the revolution of 1924 in the press, although not taking an active part in it, but was associated with Ibáñez in the overturn of 1925. He was then put in charge of aviation and in 1926 was sent to Europe for further study. While in London two years later, he was expelled from the service, but was later permitted to return to Chile, only to be banished in 1931 to the island of Pascua, because of an unsuccessful attempt to overthrow the government of Ibáñez, who, in turn, was forced to flee from Chile. Grove, who meanwhile had escaped to France, was permitted to return and once more placed in command of the air forces. This position enabled him to assist in the overthrow of Montero—an event that preceded by only a few weeks his second banishment to Pascua, but he speedily returned to his native land to contest the presidency, in October, 1932, with Alessandri. His activity as prospective candidate of the Workers' party in 1933 led to further ostracism, but on his election as senator from Santiago in 1935, while still absent, he was allowed to take his seat and to continue his revolutionary activity. Disturbances in 1936 led his enemies to propose another exile for the inquiet but popular revolutionist. He was proposed as the presidential candidate of the extreme left in 1938, but withdrew in favor of Aguirre Cerda (see p. 399).—F, III, 380; *Hoy*, November 5, 1936, p. 21; *ibid.*, November 26, 1936, pp. 16-22.

Tomás GUEVARA Silva (1865-   ) was born in Curicó and educated in the local *liceo* and in the National Institute. He fought against Peru and on his return began, but did not complete, the study of law. In 1894 he was appointed professor in the *liceo* of Curicó, at the same time filling the post of alcalde and other local municipal offices. He performed similar services in various centers of southern Chile and in 1913 founded and became rector of the *liceo* in Santiago which bears Lastarria's name. He has represented Chile abroad in various historical and educational missions. His most important writings are those relating to the Araucanian Indians. In 1927 he retired from active educational work.—F, III, 394.

Camilo HENRÍQUEZ González (1769-1825) assumed the pen name Quirino Lemáchez late in life, but within a few years he had become editor in turn of ten different newspapers in Santiago, as well as in Buenos Aires, where he took refuge after the defeat of Rancagua. While in exile, he devoted himself to the study of mathematics and the study and practice of medicine. In 1822 he was recalled to Santiago by O'Higgins, where he devoted himself to newspaper work. He became a member of congress in 1824 but died in the following year. Among his writings are numerous patriotic hymns and two essays—one of the latter in favor of independence in America, and the other in favor of liberty of thought.—F, III, 439-440. See also Amunátegui Solar, *Bosquejo histórico*, pp. 7-8.

Juan HENRÍQUEZ (b. 1630) was a native of Lima but was taken as a child to Spain. He studied at Salamanca and at the age of nineteen entered upon a meritorious military career which included campaigns before Bordeaux and Milan and on the Portuguese border. For four years he was a military prisoner—an experience which afforded him time for further scholarly reading. Invested in the same year with the Order of the Knights of Santiago and the governorship of Chile, his previous career gave promise of an honorable administration.—B, V, 122, *et seq.*; M, pp. 396-403.

Sir James HILLYAR (1769-1849) entered the British navy early enough to take part in the American Revolution. During the French wars, he saw fighting with the Channel fleet and in the Mediterranean, and in 1810-1811 helped reduce the Dutch possessions in the East

Indies. He was on his way to destroy the American fur establishments in the north Pacific when he blockaded and finally captured the American frigate *Essex*, under Commodore David Porter, in the harbor of Valparaiso.—*Dict. Nat. Biog.*, XXVI, 432.

Mateo Arnaldo HOEVEL (b. 1773), born in Gothenburg, Sweden, went to the United States at the age of twenty and engaged in trade. He was serving as supercargo of the frigate *Grampus* when on November 11, 1803, the vessel was seized in Talcahuano and its cargo confiscated. Upon his protest he received an indemnity of some forty-two thousand dollars. In 1811 he became naturalized in Chile, married into a prominent family, and immediately became influential among the revolutionists. The press, together with three printers, was introduced into Chile in November, 1811, along with merchandise consigned to Hoevel. Although designated by Poinsett as vice-consul of the United States, Hoevel suffered exile to Juan Fernández during the Spanish reconquest, along with other Chilean patriots. Shortly after his return, he retired permanently to private life.—F, III, 467.

García HURTADO DE MENDOZA (1535-1609), second son of the Marqués de Cañete, was born in Cuenca, Spain. Appointed governor of Chile after the death of Valdivia, he took possession of his post at Coquimbo on April 15, 1557. Of active mind and body, he fought against the Indians with marked success, carried on explorations and founded new settlements. Although condemned to certain penalties in his *residencia* in 1562, he was pardoned by Philip II. In 1588 he was appointed viceroy of Peru, whence he returned to Spain in 1596. He died in almost complete oblivion. Under his auspices the Jesuit, Bartolomé de Escobar, wrote his *Crónica del reino de Chile,* and Pedro de Oña wrote his epic poem, *El Arauco domado.* He is also mentioned in the pages of Ercilla and in the *Historia de Chile* by Góngora Marmolejo (see p. 87, n. 1). Other literary productions contain material relating to him, among them a play by Lope de Vega, entitled *Arauco domado.*— E, XXVIII, 756. See also Medina, *Historia de la literatura colonial de Chile,* II, 199-215.

Carlos IBÁÑEZ del Campo (1877-   ) was born in Chillán, educated at the *liceo* of Linares and at the Military School which he entered in 1896, and became a lieutenant in 1900. In 1903 he was permitted to help organize the army of Salvador. He returned to Chile in 1909 as captain and served in various military posts as cavalry officer. In 1922 he represented Chile at the Brazilian centennial. As major he took a minor part in the revolution of 1924, but assumed leadership in that of the following January. As a result of this revolution, he became minister of war and continued in that position after the return of

Alessandri and in the government of Barros Borgoño and of Emiliano Figueroa. Under the latter he became minister of the interior and directed the policy of the administration without relinquishing his control of the army. When President Figueroa resigned, Ibáñez became vice-president and as such in 1927 dictated measures for his own election as president. His administration was severely autocratic. He imprisoned or exiled many of his prominent opponents, after the fashion of dictatorships already established in Spain and Italy, but his acts were generally directed, as he himself claims, in the best interests of the under-privileged classes. While conditions continued prosperous, he was successful in maintaining order and in furthering the educational and material progress of the country. He curtailed the powers of congress, changed the municipal organizations, and repressed the activities of political factions. The depression of 1929 undermined his government and led to his overthrow and exile in 1931. His fall was due in part to his own unwillingness to shed blood in maintaining his authority. During his exile he lived the greater part of the time in Argentina, but in 1932 he made one abortive attempt to return and later was permitted to do so for a time. He was a fascist candidate for president in 1938 but was arrested and then threw his strength to Aguirre Cerda (q.v.). He compares his aim in government to that of Balmaceda and avers that like that executive he was a sacrifice to the resentment of the Chilean aristocracy.—F, III, 499-512; E, VI (App.), 142.

Miguel IGLESIAS (1822-1901) pursued a law course and subsequently managed his family estates until 1861, when he was elected a member of the Peruvian congress. During the War of the Pacific he distinguished himself both in the field and in the ministry of war. He kept up resistance against the Chilean army after the fall of Lima and was elected president in 1883. He ended the war and began the process of recovery, but in 1885 a revolt forced him to leave Peru and he continued to live in Spain until his death.—E, XXVIII, 938.

José Miguel INFANTE (1778-1844) was born in Santiago. At the University of San Felipe he studied law and received his degree in 1806. He was the first to recommend the convocation of a congress elected by popular vote. He presided over the new *junta de gobierno* called in 1813. In that year he was sent to replace General Pinto in Buenos Aires and, on his return to Chile in 1818, he was appointed minister of finance by O'Higgins. He joined the insurrection against his chief and after the latter's forced resignation was the most important member of the *junta de gobierno*. In 1823 General Freire called upon Infante to organize the senate which was created at that time. One of his measures was the abolition of slavery in July 24, 1823. He favored a federal republic patterned after the United States of North America (see p. 230). In 1831 he retired from public life.—E, XXVIII, 1400; F, III, 527-530. See also Domingo Santa María, *Vida de Don José Miguel Infante* (Santiago, 1902).

Antonio José de Irisarri (1786-1868) was born in Guatemala and trained both in his native land and in Europe. As executor of his father's extensive business, he visited Mexico and Peru and in 1809 came to Chile, where he married and speedily became enmeshed in the revolutionary movement. In addition to his literary activity he held such posts as commander of the civil guard, supreme director of state, and minister of the interior and of foreign relations, and served on important missions to American and European countries. He founded newspapers in Santiago, Curaçao, London, and New York and wrote a definite account of the assassination of Sucre. At the time of his death he was minister of Guatemala and El Salvador in the United States. See Antonio Batres Jauregui, *Irisarri* (Guatemala, 1896); also Miguel Luis Amunátegui, *Camilo Henríquez*, Vol. I, chap. xii; Sotomayor Valdés, *Historia de Chile*, Vol. II, chap. xxvi; *Anales de la Universidad de Chile*, CXVII (Santiago, 1911), 129, *et seq.*

Ramón Angel Jara (1852-1917) first studied for the law, then prepared himself for an ecclesiastical career. As a student, and after his ordination, he acquired a wide reputation throughout Chile and in neighboring countries as a notable orator before becoming bishop of Ancud in 1896. He became chaplain to President Balmaceda and associated his name with the founding of important charitable and educational institutions, including the Catholic University of Santiago. In 1910 he was transferred to the diocese of La Serena where he continued until his death.—F, III, 560.

Jorge Juan y Santacilla (1713-1773) was a native of Alicante, Spain. After studying at Salamanca and taking part in extensive military campaigns against the Moors, he was sent to America in 1734, along with Antonio de Ulloa, and spent the next eleven years in the combined task of making astronomical observations, attempting to protect the west coast ports of South America against British expeditions (see p. 94), and noting infractions of the royal ordinances. The literary results of this voyage will be mentioned under Ulloa. On his return to Spain he spent the remainder of his life in scientific work and routine naval tasks, varied by a brief but successful diplomatic mission to Morocco. He was the author of numerous technical naval treatises.—E, XXVIII, 3028.

Emilio Körner (1846-1920) was born in Saxony, obtained his bachelor's degree in 1866, and in the same year took part in the campaign against Austria. In 1885 he was professor of tactics and military history in the School of Artillery and Engineers of Berlin with the rank of captain, when he came to Chile under contract as instructor in the Military School at Santiago. He founded the Academy of War for higher military courses, participated in the revolution of 1891, and continued in the military service as major general and later chief of staff, retiring in 1910. To his persistence was due the adoption in 1900 of a law for obligatory military service. He died in Germany, but his remains were brought to Santiago in 1924.—F, III, 602-603.

Juan LADRILLERO (*ca.* 1550) is identified by some writers with Juan Fernández Ladrillero, a native of Moguer in Huelva and a resident of Colima in New Spain. He espoused the royal cause against the rebellious Gonzalo Pizarro and came to Chile with Hurtado de Mendoza, who sent him to explore the Strait of Magellan. He held an encomienda of Indians in the province of Viacha, Peru. His widow is represented as a resident of La Paz in 1582. There is scant mention of his fortunate achievement in contemporary chronicles, but the Spanish historian, Juan B. Múñoz, published the documents in question near the close of the eighteenth century. These reports were used by Miguel Luis Amunátegui in his *Cuestión de límites entre Chile i la república arjentina* (3 vols. Santiago, 1879-80), I, 388-456.—B, II, 200, n. 8, 206, n. 13; M, p. 443.

Pedro LAGOS Marchant (1832-1884) was born in Chillán some three years before its destruction by an earthquake left his family homeless and destitute. His early education, therefore, was on a farm, supplemented by private instruction and by a course in the Military School. Because of absence from Santiago he escaped the uprising of his regiment in 1851 when Colonel Pedro Urriola lost his life (see p. 288). He supported the government during the disturbances that occurred under President Montt and in the following decade rendered a good account of himself in the wars with the Araucanians. Absent from the army for a time, he was recalled in 1875 and in the War of the Pacific gained reputation and promotion in the campaign of Tacna-Arica and before Lima. After the taking of this city, he was made brigadier and later military commander of Santiago. He died three years later in Concepción.—F, III, 620-622.

Jean François Galaup de LA PÉROUSE (1741-1788?) was a French naval officer who won a brilliant record in the war ending in 1783. On August 1, 1785, he left Brest on his famous voyage, doubled Cape Horn without the loss of a man, and entered Concepción Bay on February 23, 1786. Although cordially received by the local authorities in accordance with royal orders from Spain, O'Higgins, who was then in charge of the *intendencia,* would not permit the French naturalists accompanying La Pérouse to visit a volcano in the interior. The expedition spent a month in the vicinity and its members recorded many interesting observations of contemporary life. The vessel of the expedition was wrecked in 1788, near the New Hebrides, with the loss of all on board. The reports and maps casually sent home beforehand were incorporated in four sumptuous volumes, issued at Paris in 1797.—B, VII, 129-132.

Juan Gregorio LAS HERAS (1780-1866) was born in Buenos Aires and served in the campaigns against the English before that city in 1806-1807. He came to Chile in 1813 and took part in the battle of El Membrillar (see p. 180). He joined San Martín in 1816, was present at Chacabuco, and from 1824 to 1826 occupied the posts of governor and captain-general at Buenos Aires. He then resigned and retired to Chile, where he continued to live until his death.—E, XXIX, 920. See also Pilling, *The Emancipation of South America,* pp. 102, *et seq.*

José Victorino LASTARRIA Santander (1817-1888) was born at Rancagua, in a family of reduced fortune but already distinguished for its literary and commercial activities. Educated in the College of Mora (p. 98) and the National Institute, and later under the tutelage of Bello, he received his degree as attorney at law in 1839 and early began to teach, preparing his own textbooks. He also wrote for the newspapers, especially for those opposed to the conservative government, for his temperament made him a fighter both in the forum and the press. His career in congress was long, active, and honorable, but he rarely filled ministerial posts or associated closely with contemporary executives. From the beginning he gained recognition as lawyer and jurisconsult. His *Elementos de derecho público constitucional* appeared in 1844, based in considerable measure on the *Cours de droit naturel* of Henri Ahrens (Brussels, 1837), and long served as a text for Chilean youth. This was followed by several constitutional and political studies, influenced by the positive philosophy of the time. For a brief period in 1863 he filled the post of minister to Peru, and in the following year the same post in Brazil. He was a member of literary and scientific societies in Chile and abroad. In addition to his numerous textbooks, his constitutional studies, and his journalistic ventures, Lastarria won a secure place as "master" in the academic world, as orator in parliament, as philosophical historian, as critic and littérateur, and as raconteur of Chilean folk tales. His *Obras completas* in thirteen volumes appeared under the editorship of Alejandro Fuenzalida Grandón, who also published in two volumes *Lastarria i su tiempo.*—F, III, 653-655. For a brief critique of his life in mid-activity, see Justo y Domingo

Arteaga Alemparte, *Los constituyentes chilenos de 1870*, pp. 26-50. See also Joaquín Rodríguez Bravo, *Don José Victorino Lastarria*; and Coester, *op. cit.*, p. 200.

General Francisco de la LASTRA (1777-1852) was a member of one of the most distinguished families of Chile. After studying in Spain and serving in the Spanish navy, in 1811, he embraced the cause of independence in Chile, where he organized the naval and military forces. In 1814 he was appointed supreme director of the state and took part in the Treaty of Lircay. After Rancagua he was imprisoned on the island of Juan Fernández. Returning after Chacabuco he was made colonel and given command of the forces of Valparaiso. He served in a number of important military and naval offices and was appointed minister of war and marine. After some years in retirement, he re-entered politics in 1839 and in 1841 was appointed minister of the *cámara* of appeals relating to military matters.—E, XXIX, 954; B, IX, 436, *et seq.*; F, III, 657-660.

Juan José LATORRE Benevente (1846-1912), born in Santiago, was the son of the Bolivian minister to Chile. After preliminary studies in the private schools of Valparaiso, he entered the Naval School and in 1861 began his career in the navy. He participated in the war with Spain and carried on hydrographic work in the southern part of the country. In the War of the Pacific, after participating in preliminary engagements, he gave a significant demonstration of modern naval methods in the sea fight at Point Angamos (see p. 330). His bravery and skill in that encounter gained recognition abroad, particularly in France. He was in that country on a special mission when the Civil War of 1891 broke out. Because he remained faithful to the existing government, he tarried abroad for three years as an exile, after the fall of Balmaceda. On his return he served as senator, counselor of state, and cabinet officer.—F, III, 663-666.

LAUTARO (b. *ca.* 1535) was captured by Valdivia when fifteen years old. From his captors he learned much that enabled him to lead his people successfully, when he returned to them in 1553. Ercilla (see p. 84) devotes a number of cantos to him and his name later (see p. 207) became synonymous with Chilean independence.—B, II, 101-102; *Rev. chil. de hist. y geog.*, LXXI (Jan.-April, 1932), 70, 117.

Ventura LAVALLE González was the son of a prominent officeholder in Buenos Aires and brother of the prominent Argentinian general, but was naturalized in Chile. In addition to the incident mentioned in the text, Lavalle, as minister to Peru in 1842, helped to make peace between that country and Bolivia after the battle of Ingavi.—F, III, 670. See also Sotomayor Valdés, *Historia de Chile*, II, 173.

Valentín LETELIER Madariaga (1852-1919) was born in Linares and educated in the *liceo* of Talca and in the National Institute. He obtained his degree of advocate in 1875. While taking his law course, he conducted classes in history in private schools and published a monograph on O'Higgins. He began teaching in 1877 at Copiapó and along with his teaching published numerous articles on philosophical and pedagogical subjects. In 1878 he returned to Santiago in a subordinate judicial post and in the following year became deputy and later secretary of the Chilean legation in Berlin. While there he published *Chile en 1883* which did much to attract emigration to his native land. After returning to Santiago in 1885, he compiled and edited *Cuerpos legislativos desde 1811 hasta 1845,* a work of twenty-five volumes containing the proceedings of congress for those years. He opposed Balmaceda and on the triumph of the revolutionists became professor of administrative law in the university and was also fiscal of the tribunal of accounts. He contributed sociological and philosophical articles to periodicals and later was elected rector of the university. He served as president of the Pan-American Scientific Congress in 1909.—F, IV, 40.

Jacob L'HERMITE (d. 1624) was a Dutch navigator who went to the Dutch East Indies in 1605 and prepared a memoir on the commerce of those regions, returning to Holland in 1623. In the following year he was placed in command of a large squadron which was ordered to attack the Spanish colonies in the Pacific but he died June 2, 1624, after an unsuccessful attack on Callao. An account of his voyages was published in Amsterdam in 1843.—E, XXVII, 1213; B, IV, 188. See also René Augustin Constantin de Renneville (ed.), *Recueil des voyages qui ont servi et l'establissement de la compagnie des Indes orientales* (5 vols. Amsterdam, 1702-1706), Vol. V.

Eusebio LILLO Robles (1826-1910) early abandoned his studies to take up a literary and revolutionary career. His first poetic work appeared in 1844 and his output of verse continued steadily throughout his life. He edited opposition journals during conservative control and took an active part in the outbreaks of the fifties—a part that forced him into exile for some years. He refused a chair in the University of Chile in 1870 but organized and directed for some years the Banco de Bolivia in La Paz. For a brief time in 1886 he was in the cabinet of Balmaceda, and after the latter's death acted as his literary executor. He is known as a poet of elegant and correct form.—E, XXX, 731; F, IV, 51-54; Coester, *op. cit.,* p. 210.

Pedro LIRA Rencoret (1846-1912), born in Santiago, early showed remarkable talent for painting. Nevertheless, in keeping with his father's wishes, he received a solid course at the National Institute and later at the university, where he obtained his law degree in 1869. Thereafter he devoted himself to his art. From 1872 to 1882 he resided in Paris, where he studied under Delaunay and Lepage. His own work shows the results of their training, results which he capitalized in annual exhibits at Paris and which won for him immediate recognition as artist and instructor when he returned to his native Chile. Here, in the course of three decades, he greatly increased the artistic output of the country, organized its productive groups, published a *Diccionario artístico* and gained recognition in neighboring countries. His work as a portrait painter was distinctly notable.—F, IV, 75-76.

Francisco López de Zúñiga (1599-1656), of illustrious family, entered upon a military career at the age of seventeen, and became a captain after a campaign in Flanders. In 1635 he returned to Spain and was appointed governor of Santa Cruz de la Sierra in Alto Peru; but, before he could reach his post he was offered the governorship of Chile and took over the office at Concepción on May 1, 1639. He sought in accordance with his instructions to introduce the *alcabala* into Chile; but, this innovation arousing much animosity, he shortly petitioned that the tax be abolished. Instead, it was considerably reduced. He advised a vigorous campaign against the Araucanians and took the field himself in January, 1640, with seventeen hundred men. Aided by the Jesuits, he began negotiations for a peace which resulted in the Pact of Quillín on January 9, 1641, by which the complete independence of the natives was recognized. It was not a real pacification and the governor was obliged to take the field once more in January, 1643, with all the troops he could raise, including some from Buenos Aires. He rescued a number of prisoners held by the Indians and took some captives and considerable booty. The Dutch under Brouwer (*q. v.*) invaded Chile in May, 1643, but after his death returned to Brazil. To prevent another invasion, the governor strengthened the fortifications at Valdivia. On May 8, 1646, he relinquished his post and after a favorable *residencia* lived for ten years in Peru. While returning to the Peninsula in 1656 he and his family perished during an attack on his vessel by the English. He left a good record as governor. From his father he inherited the title of Marqués de Baides.—M, pp. 477-478; E, XXXI, 161; B, IV, 349-408.

Vicente Fidel López (1815-1903) was born in Buenos Aires. Fleeing from the tyranny of Rosas, he remained in Chile from 1847 to 1852, when he returned to his native country and in 1874 became rector of its national university. He was novelist and littérateur and his most important work is *Historia de la república argentina, su origen, su revolución y su desarrollo político.*—E, XXXI, 122; F, IV, 112; and Coester, *op. cit.,* pp. 121, 161.

Fernando de LUQUE (d. 1532) was of Andalusian birth. He came to Darien with Pedrarias in 1514 and later resided in Panama, where he was associated with Pizarro and Almagro as capitalist of the Peruvian triumvirate. He was to contribute or borrow the costs of the expedition, computed at 30,000 pesos, while the others achieved the conquest. Under a new agreement made in 1529, after Pizarro had gained his direct grant from the king, Luque was to be bishop of Túmbez and protector of the Indians of Peru, but he died before entering upon his charge. His death removed the peacemaker of the triumvirate and thus opened the way to the tragic quarrels that arose between the two survivors.—Mendiburu, *op. cit.,* V, 100-103.

Patricio LYNCH Zaldívar (1826-1886) was born in Santiago, educated in the Military School, and in 1838 entered the marines. After taking part in the war against the Peru-Bolivian Confederation, he entered the British service and participated in Chinese campaigns. In 1847 he returned to Chile and performed routine duties in the army and the marine. In the war against Peru and Bolivia he conducted a memorable naval expedition along the northern coast of Peru, for which he was severely censured by neutral nations; and later he served brilliantly in the battles before Lima and acted as military governor of Lima until 1884. In that same year he was appointed minister to Spain and died at Tenerife on his return homeward.—F, IV, 130-132. E, XXXI, 952, gives slightly different data. See also Hancock's *History of Chile,* p. 305.

Juan MACKENNA O'Reilly (1771-1814) was of Irish extraction. Sent to Spain at the age of thirteen under the patronage of his maternal uncle, Count O'Reilly, he entered the engineer corps in 1787. He saw service in Peru, while the elder O'Higgins was viceroy. He came to Santiago in 1808, and his plan of defense for that city attracted prompt preferment. He became governor ad interim of Valparaiso in 1811, but was later banished on the order of the Carreras, whose jealousy he had aroused. He coöperated with O'Higgins in the campaigns of 1813-1814 and after Rancagua took refuge in the Argentine. He was killed at Buenos Aires in a duel with Luis Carrera (see p. 193).—E, XXXI, 1202; F, IV, 153-154.

Fernando de MAGALLANES (*ca.* 1480-1521) is commonly known in English as Ferdinand Magellan. The Portuguese form of his name is Fernão Magalhães. He was of lesser noble blood, and his birthplace is unknown. After early service at the court of Portugal, he accompanied Almeida to India and continued to serve there under Albuquerque. He made a second voyage to the Far East in 1509. On both occasions marked differences occurred between him and his commanders. He returned to Portugal in 1512 to vindicate himself, but, being denied justice, he fled to Spain and proposed to undertake a westward voyage to the Spice Islands with Ruy Falero. After a year of preparation, marked by jealous opposition on the part of Spanish rivals, he started in August, 1519, on his world-encircling voyage. After a winter of mutiny and privation, in the Bay of San Julián on the Argentine coast, on October 21, 1520, he discovered the strait that bears his name and, after a stormy passage of thirty-six days, entered the Pacific Ocean. He touched the Ladrone Islands on March 6, 1521, and on April 27 he was killed in an encounter with the natives of the Philippines. These dates simply set off chapters in an unparalleled struggle to overcome distance, disaffection, famine, superstition, and nature in its worst phases. Juan Sebastián de Elcano (*q. v.*) brought the surviving vessel of the expedition back to Spain.—E, XXXII, 55-59. See also James Alexander Robertson (ed.), *Magellan's Voyage Around the World, by Antonio Pigafetta* (Cleveland, 1906); F. H. H. Guillemard, *Life of Ferdinand Magellan, and the First Circumnavigation of the Globe, 1480-1521* (London, 1890); and Stefan Zweig, *Conqueror of the Seas: The Story of Magellan* (New York, 1938).

José Antonio Manso de Velasco (b. 1688) was born in Logroño. After extensive military experience in Spain and Italy, he came to Chile in 1737, where he served as lieutenant-governor, captain-general, and president. In 1738 he assembled the principal Chilean caciques in Tapihue and ratified the peace already agreed upon. He founded seven cities in Chile and in 1744, after acquiring the rank of field marshal, became viceroy of Peru. He also wrote a narrative of the principal events of his term of office. As a result of his long service in Peru, he gained the title of Conde de Superunda. On returning to Spain he had the misfortune to be among those who were at Havana when it was surrendered to the English in 1762.—M, pp. 496-498; E, XXXII, 1004; B, VI, 95.

Francisco Casimiro Marcó del Pont (1770-1819) was born in Vigo. Fourteen years later he became a cadet in the infantry of Saragoza, where he later distinguished himself in the siege of 1808, and where he was taken prisoner by the French and remained in captivity until the restoration of Ferdinand VII, who in 1815 sent him to Chile with the rank of brigadier and field marshal. He spent the rest of his life in Chile.—E, XXXII, 1368.

José Gaspar Esquivel Marín (1772-1839) was born in La Serena and educated in the College of San Carlos. He became a doctor of canon and civil law, and obtained a professorship of law by competition. He acquired considerable renown as a jurisconsult and was legal adviser of the *consulado* and of Mateo del Toro Zambrano, Conde de la Conquista. After Rancagua he went to Buenos Aires and upon his return to Chile, disapproving of the policy of O'Higgins, he kept out of politics for a time and devoted himself to the practice of law. In 1823 he was appointed minister of the supreme court and in 1825 was elected to congress from San Fernando. He signed the liberal constitution of 1828 and also the constitution of 1833. For some time he was president of the Academia de Abogados.—F, IV, 191-192.

Tomás Marín de Poveda (1650-1703) was a native of Lucar in Granada. As a boy he accompanied his uncle, Bartolomé González de Poveda to Charcas, where the latter served as president of the *audiencia* and later as archbishop of the diocese. The boy embraced the career of arms in the new world, serving without distinction first in Peru and later in 1670, in Chile. Such was the decadence of the home government that, on his return to Spain, he purchased a commission as lieutenant-general of cavalry and it is said that he also bought the governorship of Chile. On January 5, 1692, he entered Santiago with great pomp and during the next two years undertook campaigns against the pirates and the Indians. The first noteworthy dramatic representations in Chile were given at Concepción in 1693, in connection with his marriage. He founded the towns of Buena Esperanza, Itata, Rere, Talca, and Chimborazo, but Rere and Talca were the only ones to survive. His governorship, which lasted until 1700, was not regarded with favor. In 1702 he was given the title of Marqués de Cañada Hermosa.—M, pp. 500-502; E, XXXIII, 130; B, V, 254.

Ventura Marín Recabarren (1806-1877) devoted his youth to the study of science, and early gained repute as a lawyer and philosopher. His *Elementos de la filosofía del espíritu humano* (Santiago, 1834) long served in Chile as a textbook. Ascetic by nature, he finally retired to a convent, but without assuming any religious profession.—E, XXXIII, 129; F, IV, 192.

Rafael Maroto (1783-1847) was born in the town of Lorca, Spain. He distinguished himself in the wars against Napoleon by his part in the siege of Zaragoza. He was taken prisoner by the French but escaped. In December, 1813, he sailed for Peru at the head of the regiment of Talavera, and was sent to reconquer Chile. After the victory of the patriots Maroto returned to Spain in 1825, where he took part in the Carlist wars and, on the failure of other leaders, commanded the forces of Don Carlos. Despite opposition he maintained his position and finally made with Espartero the treaty that ended the seven years of conflict. He died in Chile, where he had gone to arrange some business affairs.—E, XXXIII, 284; F, V, 198.

Fernando Márquez de la Plata y Orozco (1740-1818) was born in Seville, the son of an *oidor* of that city. His services in America began in 1775 and, after holding minor positions in the Peruvian and the Platine provinces, he became in turn a member of the *audiencias* of Lima and Quito and in 1803 a member of the *audiencia* of Santiago. A consistent supporter of the revolution, he suffered exile in Mendoza, but returned to die in Santiago.—M, pp. 506-508.

Juan Martínez de Rozas Correa (1759-1813) was born in Mendoza and began his studies at the University of Córdoba. Completing his higher education at the University of San Felipe, he became attorney in 1784 and for five years filled the chair of philosophy in the royal college of San Carlos. He obtained his doctorate in canon and civil law in 1786, and during the later colonial period he filled various legal and military posts in Chile, which brought him into relations with royal officials, especially García Carrasco. At the same time he was gradually being influenced by the revolutionary ideas that made him the philosopher of independence. After the break with García Carrasco he retired to Concepción and began a vigorous correspondence with prospective insurgents in Chile and in the Platine provinces. He was formerly given credit for composing the *Catecismo político-cristiano,* the authorship of which is now attributed to Irisarri. He died shortly after his exile to Mendoza (see p. 172), his birthplace. In view of his cultural and official background and his services in behalf of independence, he has been called the founder and teacher of the Chilean nation.—E, XXXIII, 547-548; F, IV, 209-211. See also Domingo Amunátegui Solar, "Noticias inéditas sobre Don Juan Martínez de Rozas," in *Anales de la Universidad de Chile,* CXXVII (Santiago, 1910), 27-106.

José Antonio Martínez Garcés de Aldunate (1730-1811) was born in Santiago. Studying theology and law, he was graduated from the University of San Felipe with the degree of doctor in 1755. He filled many ecclesiastical posts and was thrice rector of his alma mater. In 1805 he was made bishop of Guamanga, Peru. Before departing for his see, he divided his property among his relatives and the poor, endowed various institutions, and performed other charitable works. He became bishop of Santiago in 1810.—E, XXXIII, 530; F, I, 320-321.

Guillermo Matta Goyenechea (1829-1899) was born in Copiapó and educated at the National Institute and in Germany. He published his first poems in 1847 and later developed an original philosophic type of verse that involved him in furious controversies with his fellows. In addition, in the radical press he opposed the Montt administration so vigorously that he suffered three years of exile, during which he visited different European countries and continued his literary tasks in Madrid. His return to Chile in 1862 did not free him from polemic strife, for he served one prison sentence for his revolutionary propaganda. Nevertheless his verse assumed a patriotic note in the contest against Spain and Peru and after 1870 he served as deputy in congress, as intendant of Atacama, and, after 1882, as minister to Germany and Italy. He returned to Chile in 1887 to be hailed as the Victor Hugo of America. His ministry to Buenos Aires was interrupted by civil war, during which he espoused the cause of congress. He returned to Chile to fill the office of intendant at Concepción and at Atacama and to add to his reputation as a patriotic poet. He was a prominent mason. One of the leading public schools of Santiago, endowed by his wife, bears his name.—F, IV, 217-218.

Manuel Antonio MATTA Goyenechea (1828-1892) was born at Copiapó. He pursued his studies at the Conciliar Seminary at Santiago, at the National Institute, and later in the universities of Germany. In the latter he gained an unusual cultural equipment, especially in philosophy and political science, and so perfected himself for later translations from the German language. As orator and writer, both in prose and verse, he was reserved to the point of coldness, often prolix, sometimes vague, and apt to give an impression of philosophic calm that bordered on indecision. As the years wore on, however, he overcame many of these earlier handicaps and finished his course as the undisputed leader of the radical party. He began to contribute to liberal papers immediately upon his return from Europe, became a deputy from Copiapó in 1855, joined with his brother Guillermo (see p. 298), Benjamín Vicuña Mackenna, and other men in publishing a reform paper called *La asamblea constituyente*, and with his associates speedily found himself in prison, where he uttered a memorable oration to encourage his fellow prisoners. Condemned with two companions to death, he was instead exiled to England, whereupon he spent two years in European travel and after some delay in Lima was permitted to return to his native land. The remaining years of his life were divided between literary work and politics. For more than twenty years he continued as deputy from Copiapó, holding an occasional cabinet office, but devoting himself primarily to party leadership and reform. He espoused the congressional side in the civil war of 1891, and later became minister of foreign relations and public worship. This phase of his career was not in keeping with his life-long anticlerical attitude, but he warmly defended the cause of Chile in the *Baltimore* affair (see p. 403), and, when the administration neglected to support him, resigned from the ministry and died shortly thereafter.—F, IV, 218-219; Justo and Domingo Arteaga Alemparte, *Los constituyentes chilenos de 1870*, pp. 56-63.

Claudio MATTE Pérez (1852-   ) was born in Santiago and obtained his license as lawyer in 1879. After travel abroad, he devoted himself to educational administration and to the writing of textbooks. During the revolution of 1891, he acted as confidential agent of the revolutionists at Berlin, later became a deputy, and served in one ministry under President Jorge Montt. He retired from politics and devoted himself to work for the primary schools. In 1926 he became rector of the University of Chile, but his attempts at reform led to serious strikes among the students and to his own resignation in 1927. He has since, from his own funds, constructed one of the model schools of the city.—F, IV, 224.

José MAZA (1889-   ), born in Los Angeles, was noted from student days as a political organizer and public speaker. He gained his degree as attorney in 1913, was elected as deputy in 1921, became minister of justice and public instruction in 1925, and a year later was chosen as senator from Valdivia. He opposed the method of selecting parliament in 1930 (see p. 384), was charged with conspiracy, but escaped sentence by voluntary exile. Returning from exile, he was again elected to the senate and in 1936 became its presiding officer. He is regarded as a shrewd, conciliatory politician.—F, IV, 234; *Hoy*, March 10, 1936, p. 25, and June 12, 1936, p. 10.

Diego de MEDELLÍN (1496-1593) was born in 1496 in the Estremaduran city of that name and entered the Franciscan order in the province of Salamanca. Coming to Peru in the early years of the conquest, he taught philosophy, theology, and jurisprudence in the University of San Marcos, was nominated as third bishop of Santiago in 1573, and arrived in Chile in 1576. Some irregularity clouded the beginning of his administration, because for months he lacked the necessary papal confirmation and hence assumed office solely by royal order. For seventeen years he performed the duties of his office with "rare skill and singular energy" and died at the advanced age of seventy-seven years.—Errázuriz, *Los oríjenes de la iglesia chilena, 1540-1603*, chaps. xxi-xxxv.

José Toribio MEDINA Zavala (1852-1930) was born in Santiago and educated at the National Institute and the University of Chile, where he obtained his degree as advocate in 1873. After practicing law for two years, he held a minor diplomatic post in Peru, meanwhile devoting himself to bibliographic and historical work, which thenceforth became his sole occupation, except during the war with Bolivia and Peru. Even in the midst of military service he collaborated on a biography of Arturo Prat (see p. 327). Long voyages to Europe permitted him to gather the multitudinous documents which in the course of a half-century bore fruit in more than three hundred titles. His first pioneer work mentioned in the text appeared in 1878 and the second, in 1884. His writings upon the colonial press and the Inquisition alone fill a score of volumes. He was a recognized authority on the coins and maps of the colonial period and on its bibliography, a prolific biographer, a tireless editor of documents—varied tasks which have lightened all research in the field and greatly helped to enrich the early chapters of the present work. In 1923 the University of Chile held a special session in honor of Señor Medina on his completing fifty years of unusually productive work, a celebration in which learned societies outside of Chile also participated. He was spared for seven more active years, during which, as he expressed it, he "worked much and wearied little."—F, IV, 238-240; *Revista chilean de historia y geografía*, XLVII (July-Sept., 1923), 7-453. Pages 333-452 of this article are devoted to a catalogue of his writings and to biographical data.

Casto MÉNDEZ Núñez (1824-1869) was a native of Vigo, a province of Galicia. After preliminary studies for his profession, Méndez Núñez began his career as sailor—a career which included the Carlist wars in Spain, service on the African coast, in the La Plata region, the Philippines, and finally in the Spanish intervention on the west coast of South America. His most disagreeable duty—the bombardment of Valparaiso—is noted in the text (p. 309). He was wounded in a later bombardment of Callao, relinquished command of the fleet to another, and returned to Spain. Despite the inglorious ending of this campaign further honors awaited him, but he did not long survive to enjoy them. —E, XXXIV, 588-590.

Francisco de MENESES, or Menezes (1614-1679), member of a noble Portuguese family, was born at Cádiz. Entering the Spanish army as a mere youth, he gained reputation through his skill as a horseman and as a bullfighter rather than on the battlefield. He served for twenty-five years in Milan, Flanders, Portugal, and Catalonia and was in constant difficulty with his companions and superiors, but escaped punishment, although once condemned to death through the influence of Don Juan of Austria, natural son of Philip IV. In 1663, as general of artillery, he was appointed governor of Chile. He had no qualifications for the office and his appointment shows the decadence then prevalent in the Spanish service. On reaching Buenos Aires, where he first landed, he was put under arrest because of quarrels with his companions and on his arrival at Santiago entered upon a dispute with the bishop, which resulted in his prompt excommunication. The bellicose governor in turn tried unsuccessfully to exile the bishop. The term of Meneses was marked by all sorts of disorders while his services amounted to little. On being finally dismissed, he sought safety in flight, but was arrested, imprisoned, and fined heavily. He died in prison, leaving a large fortune. —E, XXXIV, 663-664. For a more favorable sketch see M, pp. 529-531; B, V, 39, et seq.

Juan Ignacio MOLINA (1737-1829) was born near the banks of the Maule River. An orphan from early childhood, he was educated by the Jesuits at Talca and Concepción, where he took his first vows. Distinguished as a student, he was early put in charge of the library of the principal Jesuit house in Santiago. He was still a simple "brother" of the order when with his fellow Jesuits he was exiled from Chile in 1768, and about two years later settled in Bologna. In this city, in 1776, he published anonymously his *Compendio de la historia geográfica, natural, i civil del reino de Chile* and in 1782 his *Compendio sobre la historia natural de Chile*, which established his literary and scientific reputation. His *Historia civil* appeared in 1787 and was translated and published in Madrid in 1795. While his work is not scientific in the modern sense, it is characterized by keen observation and clear expression. He was obliged to write most of it from memory. Linguist, philosopher, and man of science, he was also distinguished for love of Chile, to which he always hoped to return. His most fervent wish, during his last illness, was for a drink of water from the Cordillera. A monument to his memory stands in front of the university in Santiago.— M, pp. 541-544; B, VII, 531-540. See also Medina, *Historia de la literatura colonial de Chile*, II, 420-421, 523-533; *Rev. chil. de hist. y geog.*, LXXIII (Sept.-Dec., 1932), 71-82.

Enrique MOLINA Garmendía (1871-   ) was born in La Serena and received the customary law degree. After preliminary work as teacher of history and philosophy in the *liceos* of Chillán and Concepción, he became rector of the *liceo* of Talca, where for ten years he made a remarkable record as instructor and writer upon educational topics. In 1916 he was again transferred to Concepción and in the following year expanded the local *liceo* into the "free" University of Concepción, became its president in 1919, and speedily made it a powerful force in contemporary education. He fitted himself for its leadership by travel and study in Europe and in the United States and on his return through his energy, ability, and practical management made the university in methods, equipment, and curriculum the leading institution of higher learning in Chile. His success in Concepción led to his being summoned in 1927 to head the University of Chile in Santiago and to take over the new post of superintendent of public instruction. Differences arising between him and the minister of education soon led to his resignation. He returned to Concepción, after a brief journey to Europe, and in 1930 contracted a loan that enabled him to house the university more effectively than any similar institution in the country. It is maintained in large part by a general lottery.—F, IV, 287.

Juan Esteban MONTERO Rodríguez (1879-   ) was born in Santiago. He became advocate in 1901 and thereafter devoted himself almost exclusively to the teaching and practice of his profession. He served as counsel for the state railways and for the Council of Fiscal Defense, represented prominent nitrate interests, and gave instruction in civil law at the University of Chile. He had held no prominent political office before the events of 1931 called him to high executive responsibilities. During the troublous days of July, 1931, he was twice minister of the interior for a few days each time. Since his brief administration as president he has lived in retirement.—F, IV, 309; *Hoy,* November 20, 1931, p. 9.

Jorge MONTT Álvarez (1845-1922) was born in Casablanca, entered the Naval School in 1858, and three years later began his active service on the *Independencia.* During the war with Spain, he participated in the capture of the *Covadonga* (see p. 308). Both before and after that conflict, he filled routine naval offices with distinction. During the war with Peru, he served with like distinction as commander of the *O'Higgins.* In 1884 he discharged an important naval mission to Europe and in 1887 was named maritime governor at Valparaiso. This position enabled him to further the designs of the revolutionary party in 1891. His services on this occasion made him president of the republic—a position for which he possessed few qualifications. His efforts, therefore, were largely directed to routine tasks. More skillful hands determined the course of political development, but the president employed his personal honesty and good sense to correct obvious mistakes. After retiring from the presidency, he filled minor posts which afforded him a comfortable livelihood but permitted him to leave little to his family aside from an honorable name. Obviously he did not belong to the family of the great Manuel Montt, but he helped bridge an important period in Chilean politics.—E, XXXVI, 810; F, IV, 311-312.

Luis MONTT Montt (1848-1909) became deputy in 1876, gained his title as advocate in 1880, and in the same year became professor of literature in the National Institute. From 1886 until his death he was director of the National Library. His publications were largely historical but he also published one volume of poems.—F, IV, 316.

Pedro MONTT Montt (1848-1910), son of President Manuel Montt (see p. 289), was born in Santiago and trained for a life-long public career in the National Institute and the University of Chile. He became advocate in 1870 and four years later entered the chamber of deputies. An accomplished linguist and an orator of torrential caliber, he became a successful champion of educational and charitable causes and, as the recognized chief of the nationalist Montt-Varista party, gained both hearty friends and active enemies. In 1886, as president of the chamber of deputies, he brought to an end the bitter debate over the budget (see p. 341), and thus ensured the succession of Balmaceda. In the latter's first cabinet he served as minister of justice and public instruction. In 1887 he headed the newly created ministry of industry and public works, and in 1889 held the portfolio of the treasury. In 1891 he was one of the leading opponents of Balmaceda and represented the insurgent government at Washington, where he was obliged to defend Chile in the unfortunate *Baltimore* affair. He served as minister in the cabinets of Don Jorge Montt, became senator in 1901, and president in 1906. Through his election, with the prestige of his father's name and of his own meritorious career, the Chilean public expected a moral regeneration of the country. In this they were disappointed; the disruptive tendencies in politics and public finance were too strong for him. He repressed the strikes of 1907 with the armed forces of the republic, but he could not turn the tide of corruption which then permeated national life and hampered his most notable undertakings. Wearied with his losing fight against general corruption and the unceasing round of festivities to which public life and family tradition subjected him, he died during the fourth year of his presidency while on a voyage to Europe for medical treatment.—F, IV, 317-318; E, XXXVI, 811.

Manuel MONTT Torres (1809-1880) was born in Petorca of a distinguished Catalonian family that had been impoverished by espousing the revolutionary cause. The poverty of his childhood permitted only casual instruction but in 1822 he was fortunate enough to secure a scholarship in the National Institute, where his character and ability at once attracted favorable notice. He received the degree of bachelor in 1830. He spent some time in the law office of Manuel José Gandarillas and in 1831 gained the rank of attorney. In swift succession, he became vice rector of the institute, professor of Roman and civil law, deputy ad interim in congress and rector of the institute, displaying in the last-named post that energy and insistence on orderly progress, discipline, and conformity to law which characterized him through life. He became subsecretary in the ministry of the interior in time to help suppress the revolt of Quillota (see p. 269) and to organize the expedition against Peru (see p. 270); at the same time he was ad interim member and attorney of the supreme court. In 1840 he was elected as regular deputy to congress. That same year he became minister of the interior and again held this office in 1845, serving also the ministry of war and marine, and after 1841 he took over the post of minister of justice, worship, and public instruction. In all these tasks he displayed conspicuous organizing and administrative ability. His efforts in behalf of education were especially fruitful. Under his direction the university and the normal school for men were organized and the entire system of public instruction given new impetus. The astronomical observatory, the school for deaf-mutes, and various charitable and correctional institutions date from his ministry. He stimulated scientific exploration, organized new provinces, negotiated new commercial treaties, introduced railroads, modified taxes, and projected new fiscal establishments. His manifold activities marked him, in the estimation of some, as the true organizer of the government of Chile, but he is rather to be regarded as the one who most definitely continued the work of Portales, rather than as the one who supplanted that great leader. His efficiency was measurably counteracted by his severity and inflexibility, and for that reason his administration was a tempestuous one. His personal following became prominent as a political party. After leaving the presidential office, he continued in the supreme court, where he provoked an attempt in 1868 to impeach him (see p. 313). He was then elected senator, and served as counselor of state and as envoy to Peru. Few Chileans have equaled him in public usefulness, none has surpassed him.—E, XXXVI, 810; F, IV, 318-321. See also Galdames, *El decenio de Montt;* Blanco Cuartín, *Artículos escogidos,* pp. 537-542; Alberto Edwards, *El gobierno de Don Manuel Montt, 1851-1861* (Santiago, 1932).

José Joaquín de MORA (1783-1864) was born in Cádiz and studied law in Granada, but took up arms during the French invasion of Spain. During this conflict, he was taken prisoner and on his return to Spain became known for his work as a journalist, poet, translator of dramas, and politician. His liberal views forced him into exile after 1823. Going first to London, he was there brought into sympathy with the American struggle for independence and in 1827 came to Buenos Aires, on the invitation of Rivadavia. In succession he resided in Chile, Peru, and Bolivia, engaging in each country in newspaper and general literary and educational work and holding in each many important political posts. In 1839 he returned to Spain, still keeping up his literary and educational activities, and for some years served as Spanish consul general in London.—E, XXXVI, 864-865; B, XV, 222, 223, 304, and XVI, 28-30; F, IV, 324.

Luiz Múñoz de Guzmán (1735-1808), born in Seville, was a well-known Spanish naval officer and a magistrate. He served in many parts of the world, including Hispanic America and, because of his excellent record, was appointed president of the *audiencia* of Quito from 1791 to 1796, being succeeded in that office by the Baron de Carondelet. In 1802 he was commissioned lieutenant general and appointed governor and captain general of Chile.—E, XXXVII, 423-424.

Esteban Múñoz Donoso (1844-1907) was born in Curicó, studied in the seminary of Santiago, became presbyter in 1868, and for the next quarter-century served as professor in the seminary and later combined with his professorship the editorial work of *El estandarte católico*. His most significant poem bears the title *La colombia.*—F, IV, 341.

Francisco Núñez de Pineda y Bascuñan (1607-1680), born in Chillan, belonged to one of the most distinguished families of Chile. For more than forty years his father had fought the Indians on the frontier and the son, after some preliminary training under the Jesuits, also entered the army and became a captain. In 1629 he was captured by the Indians in the battle of Cangrejeras. The seven months that followed gave him the experiences which, as an old man, he incorporated in *Cautiverio feliz* (see Coester, *op. cit.*, p. 14). Although he filled other important stations in the Spanish service, including the command of Valdivia, his reputation rests upon this work, "the most popular and widely read book of colonial times in Chile." The volume offers a valuable picture of the social and economic life of the Araucanians and affords the author a chance to condemn the encomienda system and the rapacity of the traders. It was published in 1863 as the third volume of "Colección de historiadores de Chile."—M, pp. 577-586.

José Abelardo Núñez Murúa (1840-1910) was born in Santiago, studied in the National Institute and the University of Chile, and gained the title of advocate in 1866. In that same year, after serving in the secretariat of the chamber of deputies, he entered upon his life work as teacher and administrator in the system of primary instruction. In 1869 he served as intendant of Ñuble. He was general secretary of the National Society of Agriculture and in 1875 directed the agricultural exposition in Santiago. In 1879 he was commissioned to study systems of education abroad and on his return contributed educational articles to the press and directed the *Revista de instrucción primaria*. As administrator, he introduced many reforms before his retirement in 1897 and after that date he prepared a famous text, *El lector americano,* which long served for classes in primary reading. The Normal School of Santiago bears his name.—F, IV, 377.

Ambrosio O'Higgins (*ca.* 1720-1801) or "Higgins," as he wrote it, father of the better-known Bernardo O'Higgins, was born in Ballinary (or Vallenar, as it appears later in his Spanish title), county of Sligo, Ireland. As a youth he was sent to Spain, where an uncle was a member of a religious order. This connection may have afforded young Higgins some education, but he early connected himself with a firm of Irish merchants in Cádiz. Under their protection he undertook a disastrous trading venture to Peru, and went from there to Chile in 1761. Here he spent some time in engineering work and in constructing huts along the Andean trail to Mendoza. A trip to Spain in 1766 enabled him to prove his talent to the colonial authorities, and with his return to Chile his promotion was rapid. Successful in his campaigns against the Araucanians, he became a brigadier in 1783 and in 1786 was made intendant at Concepción. Three years later he was commissioned field marshal and also appointed governor of Chile. He carried on the duties of the latter post with his accustomed skill and energy and as a result was advanced in 1796 to the post of viceroy at Lima—the most distinguished office in the Spanish colonies. He died in office on March 18, 1801, the first conspicuous Irishman in American politics!—M, pp. 592-596; B, VII, 5-104.

Bernardo O'Higgins y Riquelme (1778-1842) was permitted by fate to surpass his father (see above) in reputation, if not in solid worth. Born out of wedlock and unrecognized by his father during his childhood, he was later taken into his father's household and educated in Lima, Peru, and in Spain, and England, where he came in contact with Miranda and other leaders in the struggle for independence. He inherited part, at least, of his father's estate and, after that parent's death, returned to Chile and to the life of a farmer and local officeholder. He was already plotting an insurrection against Spain, when the events of 1810 brought him openly into the conflict. His subsequent career may be followed in the text. Exile was to him an inevitable but bitter experience. He was but half Chilean, hence he never commended himself to the Santiago aristocracy; on the other hand, after his banishment, he continually longed to return to his childhood home and the scenes of his stirring career.—F, IV, 389-393.

Pedro de Oña (b. 1570), the son of a Spanish captain, was a native of Angol. At the age of twenty he was enrolled in the University of San Marcos in Lima. Presumably he completed the law course there, as he always uses the title *Licenciado* in his published works, and also the course in theology, for his works show a deep religious strain. He may have taken part in suppressing an uprising in Quito. If so, he was doubly prepared to undertake an indigenous epic. His *Arauco domado* appeared in Lima in 1596. In this he showed himself to be a pious and energetic narrator, the first native literary light of Chile. His last known poem appeared in 1643.—M, pp. 605-610. See also Medina, *Historia de la literatura colonial de Chile*, Vol. I, chaps. vi-ix; Coester, *op. cit.*, pp. 10-12.

Martín García Óñez de Loyola (1549-1598), a renowned member of a noble Guipuzcoan family, came to Peru in 1568 and served as captain of his guard for Viceroy Francisco de Toledo. He won great fame in 1572 by capturing Tupac Amaru, whose niece he subsequently married. He served as corregidor at various points in Peru and was recommended as governor for Paraguay, but before taking office there he received word of his appointment to Chile. He served in the latter colony from 1592 until his death in battle.—B, III, 187-189.

Pedro Opazo Letelier (1876-   ) received his early training in the *liceo* of Talca and prepared to study medicine but was forced instead into agriculture. A member of the liberal-democratic party, he became deputy from Talca in 1921 and three years later, senator. In 1920 he held the war office for a brief period and in 1930 was president of the senate. Throughout his active career he has kept closely in touch with banking and railroad interests.—F, IV, 402.

Domingo Ortiz de Rozas (1683-1756) belonged to an Asturian family of considerable prestige. He took part in the War of Spanish Succession and later served in Italy and Africa, winning the rank of *mariscal de campo*. He was appointed governor of Buenos Aires in 1742. He gave considerable attention to uprooting smuggling and to fortifying the port of Montevideo, and to conducting suits against certain employees of the government, including his own predecessor. Promoted to the rank of lieutenant general, he was entrusted in 1745 with the governorship of Chile where he founded many towns, and for which he received his title. He died on shipboard in the vicinity of Cape Horn.—M, p. 624; E, XL, 735; B, VI, 164.

Mariano Osorio (1722-1818) was born in Seville. Connected with a leading family of the region, he was permitted to enter the artillery school at Segovia and after completing his course received regular promotion in the artillery. In 1808 as captain he took part in the two sieges of Zaragoza. He was sent to Lima as commandant general of artillery in 1812, where his skill in military affairs and his gracious personality gained for him the favor of the viceroy, who sent him to replace Gaínza. He died at Panama while on his way to Spain after his defeat at Maipú.—F, IV, 422; B, IX, 516.

José Tomás Ovalle Bezanilla (1788-1831) was born in Santiago. After completing his legal studies he entered upon a public career. In 1828 he was presiding officer of the *junta gubernativa* in Santiago (B, XV, 474), which attempted to deal with the disorder created by the struggle for supremacy between Freire and Prieto and in February, 1830, was elected vice president of the republic by the congress of plenipotentiaries called to give legal status to existing conditions. When Ruiz Tagle gave up the presidency thus conferred, Ovalle, for a few months, exercised the powers of chief executive until his death. He it was who called his friend Portales to the ministry.—B, Vol. XV, chaps. xxxi, xxxii; Sotomayor Valdés, *Historia de Chile,* I, 75; F, IV, 440.

Abraham Oyanedel (1874-   ), a native of Copiapó, became attorney in 1397. He served in the army of congress in 1891 and then passed to the local courts as prosecutor, and later judge. He was minister (justice) of the supreme court of Chile in 1927 and its president in 1932—a position that automatically made him the vice-president ad interim from October to December of that year.—*Hoy,* October 7, 1932, p. 5.

Antonio Pareja (1758-1813), a native of the province of Córdoba, Spain, was a sailor rather than a soldier. He had gained steady promotion in the Spanish navy, which he entered in 1771, and was especially noted for his conduct in the battle of Trafalgar, during which he fought obstinately, although wounded in action and suffering heavy losses among his crew. He withdrew his vessel, the *Argonauta,* from the fight, but it was so badly shattered that it sank the next day. Pareja bore an excellent reputation among his contemporaries for his bravery, enthusiasm, and humane qualities, but his appointment by Abascal to command an army was a mistake.—B, IX, 9.

José Manuel Pareja Septien (1813-1865) entered the Spanish marine at Cádiz in 1827. In a long career, which included many extensive voyages, campaigns against the Carlists, and service in Cuba, he received many marks of distinction and proofs of royal favor. Sent as commander of the Spanish squadron that intervened in Peru in 1864, he conducted early negotiations with that republic so successfully that in April, 1865, he was promoted to the rank of lieutenant general. He failed, however, to settle affairs with Chile and, while maintaining a blockade of Chilean ports, committed suicide as described in the text. —E, XLII, 24.

Juan Bautista Pastene (1507-ca. 1580) was a native of Genoa. He may be the Juan Bautista who served under Alvarado in Guatemala. If so, like many of his contemporaries, he linked his career with both Americas. In 1534 he reached Venezuela with the fleet sent out by the

German Welsers. His course there commended him to Francisco Pizarro and he served that leader and the royal cause in the conquest of Peru and the civil wars that followed. He was sent south by Vaca de Castro, viceroy of Peru, who during the wars between Charles V and Francis I feared French intrusion in the Pacific. The vessel commanded by Pastene had once formed part of the fleet that bore Pedro de Alvarado from Central America to modern Ecuador. Valdivia did not fear French intruders, but made use of the vessel and of its commander to explore territory that he hoped to add to his government and continued to use Pastene as his chief navigator, as did his successor.—M, pp. 646-656; B, I, 262-267, 420.

José Joaquín PÉREZ Moscayano (1800-1889) was born in Santiago, attended the Royal Caroline College, and completed his studies at the University of San Felipe (see p. 110). After preliminary service as secretary of the Chilean legation in the United States, he acted as chargé in Paris, helped float a loan in London, and filled the post of minister to Argentina. In 1845 he became minister of the treasury and four years later, minister of the interior and of foreign relations. He was senator and counselor of state under Montt. He was a clever politician who knew how to hold the allegiance of his subordinates and the confidence of the people at large. After retiring from the presidency, he still served for some years as senator and counselor.—E, XLIII, 653; F, IV, 495-497.

Carlos PEZOA Véliz (1879-1908), like González, achieved posthumous success. After a youth of sharp privation marked by little formal study, he took up quarters in Viña del Mar as a subordinate municipal laborer. He was driven from this miserable existence by the earthquake of 1906 and returned to Santiago where he published some of his compositions in the current reviews and followed the Bohemian life which brought him to his early and solitary end in the hospital of San Vicente.—F, IV, 503.

Rudolfo Amando PHILIPPI (1808-1904) was born at Charlottenburg, Prussia, and died in Santiago. After studies in medicine and the natural sciences he was made professor in 1835 and in 1849, director of the industrial school of Cassel. Coming to Chile in 1851, he occupied the chair of botany and zoology in the university and directed the museum of natural history. During this period he established the study of the natural sciences in the superior schools of Chile and began an important series of scientific expeditions. He founded the botanical garden of Santiago and identified and named thousands of native plants. His scientific work was the most important undertaken in South America. His *Elementos de historia natural* long served as a textbook in

Chile.—E, XLIV, 383; F, IV, 505, 506; M. L. Amunátegui, *Ensayos biográficos*, IV, 155-191.

Nicolás de PIÉROLA (1839-1913) was born in Camaná, Peru, the son of a naturalist. He studied and practiced law in Lima and also held a professorship at the Colegio Seminar de Lima. When thirty years of age, he was offered the ministry of the treasury but had to decline it and leave the country. In the war with Chile he commanded a battalion under President Prado, but with the defeat of the president again had to flee from the country. By a *coup d'état* in 1879 he assumed the title of chief of the republic but was unable to defend Lima against the Chilean invaders and retreated into the interior and later took refuge in the United States. A successful revolt in 1895 elevated him a second time to the chief magistracy and enabled him to bring about numerous reforms in administration.—E, XLIV, 784.

The PINCHEIRA brothers, Pablo (17?-1832) and José Antonio (17-), acquired their undesirable notoriety during the first third of the nineteenth century. Supposedly aiding the Spaniards, they had for their main purpose the raiding and indiscriminate plundering of the people of southern Chile and the neighboring Argentine territory. General Bulnes defeated their forces in January, 1832, when Pablo met his death. His brother then surrendered, released his captives, including about a thousand women and children, and continued to live in the province of Concepción for more than a half-century.—E, XLIV, 992; also B, XVI, 97-112, especially n. 15; and Sotomayor Valdés, *Historia de Chile*, I, 162-168.

Francisco Antonio PINTO Díaz (1785-1858) was descended from one of the most illustrious families of Santiago. He became a lawyer in 1806. Four years later he joined the revolutionary forces and was sent as minister to Buenos Aires in order to cement friendly relations between the revolutionary governments and to provide Chile with news from Brazil and Europe. In 1813 he was sent to England for the same purpose. He returned to Chile in 1817, fought against the Spanish armies of Alto Peru, and later joined San Martín. During 1822 and 1823, he served as second chief and made the disgraceful campaign of Southern Peru, but in 1824, with new forces, he carried through a new campaign with success. The same year he was appointed minister of the interior and of foreign relations for Chile. Retiring from these offices he served for a time as intendant at Coquimbo. In the beginning of 1827 he was elected vice-president of Chile and, when General Freire resigned the supreme command, became his successor. Being unable to control the revolutionary movements, he retired to private life. In 1841 he became leader of the liberals. He was both a distinguished soldier and a notable littérateur, speaking English and French fluently and writing in a very correct and elegant style. He was a member of the faculty of law in the university.—E, XLIV, 1091. The details of his tempestuous administration are given in B, Vol. XV, chaps. xxv-xxx. See also F, IV, 518.

Aníbal PINTO Garmendia (1825-1884), son of Francisco Antonio Pinto (see p. 170), was born in Santiago and studied at the National Institute, and under Andrés Bello. He defended in the press the views of Bello and also those of Francisco Bilbao (see p. 286). His first diplomatic service was at Rome—a service which opened to him opportunities to study the political and social institutions of Europe. On his return to Chile he became a member of the university faculty of philosophy and letters and renewed his contributions to the local press. In 1862 he was appointed intendant of the province of Concepción, where he contributed greatly to its progress, served in the chamber of deputies, was elected senator in 1870, and in 1871 entered the cabinet of President Errázuriz. This proved the steppingstone to the presidency. Moderate in opinion and conciliatory in disposition, it was his misfortune to encounter two grave problems—the financial crisis and the war against Peru and Bolivia. He survived the presidency only three years.—E, XLIV, 1090; F, IV, 521-522.

Amando PISSIS (1812-1889) was born in Brionde, France, and died in Santiago. He studied in the School of Mines at Paris and early became coeditor of the *Annales* of the French geological society. After a mission to study the mineral resources of Brazil, in 1849 he was given charge of the geographical work being conducted by the Chilean government. He also served as a member of the faculty of physical sciences and mathematics in the University of Chile. His principal work was *Geografía física de la república de Chile* (Paris, 1871), but he produced other technical works on the Andes and the desert of Atacama.—E, XLV, 62; F, IV, 526.

Francisco PIZARRO (*ca.* 1475-1541) was born in Trujillo, the illegitimate son of an officer who had served under the Great Captain. During a neglected and unlettered childhood, he is reputed to have been a swineherd. After military experience in Europe, he went to Santo Domingo in 1509, went with Alonso de Ojeda to Tierra Firma, accompanied Balboa to the Pacific, took part with Pedrarias in planting a colony at Panama, and was residing there when he and his associates entered upon the Peruvian project. From this first expedition, begun in 1524, he was forced to return for help. On his second expedition, he and his men were forced to undergo extreme hardships on the island of Gallo, yet he touched at Túmbez and Paita and surveyed some two hundred leagues along the coast of Peru before returning to Panama and passing to

Spain in 1528 where he met with a favorable reception from Charles V and obtained a personal grant to conquer the region which he had explored. On his return he brought with him his four half-brothers, of whom only one was legitimate. The lurid story of his conquest of Peru, marked by treachery and the double-crossing of his associates, and by his own assassination, belongs to the history of Peru which, as the text indicates, also serves, through Almagro and Valdivia, as an introduction to the history of Chile.—E, XLV, 173-181; Mendiburu, *op. cit.*, VI, 388-506. See also Stella R. Clemence, *Calendar of Spanish Manuscripts concerning Peru, 1531-1651* (Washington, 1932), and *Documents from Early Peru: The Pizarros and the Almagros, 1531-1578* (Washington, 1936).

Nicanor PLAZA (1844-1918) was one of the first students in the university course of fine arts (see p. 356). His early display of artistic talent led the government to send him to Europe for further study. He taught sculpture long and successfully in the School of Fine Arts in Santiago. His "Caupolicán" attracted attention in Paris. His most beautiful work, "La quimera" (Chimera) is one of the masterpieces of the Museum of Fine Arts in Santiago. Plaza died in Florence, Italy.—F, IV, 528.

Diego José Víctor PORTALES Plazazuelos (1793-1837) was born in Santiago. His father intended him for the law, and for a time he studied at the Colegio de San Carlos, but he chose instead to become a merchant and by 1824 had built up one of the most important commercial firms of Chile. He entered politics through the monopoly described in the text, which was designed to meet the service of the debt of five million pesos contracted in England in 1821. Portales soon became known as one of the most powerful politicians in Chile. He knew men profoundly, had good common sense, was energetic, and a capital organizer. He devoted himself to the conservative and aristocratic elements, emphasizing commerce rather than politics and just before the decisive battle of Lircay became the virtual dictator of the country, under both Ovalle and Prieto. He corrected public abuses with an iron hand and paid salaries promptly, but was inflexible when any employee committed the slightest fault. He reorganized the civil guard, established the military academy in Santiago, and gave wide publicity to governmental acts, especially those of the treasury. When he thought the government could carry on, he retired to private life, refusing to become president, but continued to influence public affairs through the minister of the interior, Joaquín Tocornal. In December, 1832, he was appointed governor of Valparaiso and during the few months he exercised that office he made many reforms. Because of his withdrawal from power, his influence began to decline and he was soon charged with enjoying the fruits of government without sharing its responsibility. Finally, he was appointed minister of war by Prieto and in large part the government once more revolved around him. But political disturbances came, one after the other, and he was finally assassinated. His career suggests comparisons with Alexander Hamilton. In 1860 a monument was erected to him. —E, XLVI, 598-600. A judicious sketch, "Portales," was published by a competent critic, Jorge Blest Gana, in *Revista chilena*, VI (November, 1918), 187-202; VII (December, 1918), 24-46. For a brief word on *El hambriento* (p. 237), see *ibid*, p. 33, n. 3. Vicuña Mackenna and the Brazilian diplomat, Joaquín Nabuco, have also written extended sketches of Portales. See also F, IV, 535-538; Galdames, *Evolución constitucional*, I, 832-853; and Francisco A. Encina, *Portales; introducción a la historia de la época de Diego Portales (1830-1891)* (2 vols. Santiago, 1934).

Mariano Ignacio PRADO (1826-1901) was born in Huanuco, Peru. He supported Ramón Castilla in his second campaign for the presidency and gained thereby a colonel's commission. When the Spanish admiral Pinzón made his insulting attack on the Chincha Islands in 1864, Prado seized the occasion to elevate himself to the presidency and hastened to bring Peru into an alliance with Chile and the other west coast republics against Spain. His later attempt to put the public finances in order led to his downfall. During the War of the Pacific he went to Europe to buy arms, but otherwise remained inactive. He died in Paris.—E, XLVI, 1208.

Arturo PRAT Chacón (1848-1879), born near Quirihue, department of Itata, was of Catalonian descent. After a few years in a private school at Santiago, he entered the recently founded Naval School at Valparaiso and shortly thereafter began service at sea that was associated at frequent stages with the *Esmeralda*. He took part in the war with Spain in 1865 and became captain in 1873. Throughout his career he pursued studies in astronomy, mathematics, and other sciences associated with naval operations, obtained a degree in law, and on at least one occasion showed himself to be no mean diplomat. His martyrdom at Iquique made him the naval hero of the war.—E, XLVI, 1275; F, IV, 546-549.

Joaquín PRIETO Vial (1786-1854) was a native of Concepción. In 1805 he became a volunteer in the militia and a few months later took part in an expedition sent to explore the southern Andes (B, VII, 262, n. 10). He performed various services in the patriot ranks between 1811 and 1814, participated in the battles of Chacabuco and Maipú, defeated the outlaw Benavides in 1824 (see p. 208), and between 1823 and 1828 served in various congresses. As an intimate friend and supporter, he contributed much to the success of Portales, who in turn supported him as president. After his two terms in the presidency, Prieto continued in the public service as counselor of state, senator, intendant, and captain general of Valparaiso. Naturally cold and cautious, although polite and diplomatic in manner, Prieto aroused little popular enthusiasm.— E, XLVII, 382; Sotomayor Valdés, *Historia de Chile,* I, 134-141; F, IV, 566-568.

Arturo PUGA Osorio (1879-) was born in Santiago and became a second lieutenant of the Chilean army in 1898 but held no political office until 1927 when he became subsecretary of war. He had supported the revolutions of 1924 and served in the attempted Tacna-Arica plebiscite. In 1928 he became intendant of Tarapacá and from 1929 to 1931 was Chilean minister to Colombia. He is known as a careful and painstaking student of military affairs.—F, IV, 577; *Hoy,* June 10, 1932, p. 7.

Rodrigo de QUIROGA (d. 1580) was a member of a noble Galician family. He came to Peru in 1535 and distinguished himself by his humane conduct in expeditions against the Indians. After joining Valdivia in Chile he filled various municipal offices in Santiago and became Valdivia's lieutenant and later the lieutenant of Hurtado de Mendoza. After Valdivia's death he was helpful in settling the dispute between Villagra (*q. v.*) and his chief rival. Enrolled as knight of the Order of Santiago, he was appointed governor of Chile in 1573 and served until 1578.—M, pp. 716-719.

Pablo RAMÍREZ Rodríguez (1886-) received his training in private schools and at the Catholic University and became advocate in 1908. As a member of the radical party he held a seat as deputy (1912-1921) and became minister of justice and instruction (1919), and of the treasury (1927) while also serving (1928-29) as ad interim in the ministries of agriculture and of education. His attempted reforms in education and finance and his efforts in connection with COSACH (see p. 383 n.) aroused much opposition.—F, V, 602-605.

Alonso de REINOSO (1515-156?) was born in the province of Toledo and in 1535 embarked for America. His earlier services took place in Central America and Yucatan with Montejo and Alvarado, and he accompanied the latter in his last campaigns in Mexico. He joined La Gasca in his campaigns against Hernando Pizarro and came to Chile with Villagra before the death of Valdivia. Assisting the latter in his southern campaigns, he helped found various cities, including Concepción, Valdivia, and Imperial and under Hurtado de Mendoza executed Caupolicán, as described in the text, "with more rigor and haste than forethought." Villagra made him lieutenant in Concepción.—M, pp. 729-737.

Manuel RENGIFO Cárdenas (1793-1845) was born in Santiago. He early acquired an honorable reputation as a merchant in Chile and Peru and as such was employed by Bolívar at Lima to determine Peru's indebtedness to Chile. Becoming minister of the treasury in 1830, he performed laudable work in organizing that ministry and in meeting the existing deficit. By making Valparaiso a port of deposit for foreign merchandise, he greatly increased its importance and enlarged the national revenue. As minister in 1834 and in 1837, he prepared notable memoirs during his incumbency and also served as senator and plenipotentiary to Peru, with which republic he negotiated an important commercial treaty.—E, I, 851; F, V, 614-615; Sotomayor Valdés, *Historia de Chile*, I, 36-39, 201-225, 276, 447.

Vicente REYES Palazuelos (1835-1918) received his title as advocate in 1858 and immediately connected himself with *El ferrocarril* and other papers associated with the liberal party. In 1861 he entered the chamber of deputies, where he was immediately recognized as an accurate and forceful debater. He participated in the reform movement of the early seventies, headed a cabinet for some months in 1877 and 1878, was elected to the senate in 1888, and served as its presiding officer. He condemned the revolutionary movement of 1891 but remained strictly neutral during that contest. In 1894 he was returned without opposition to the senate and remained a member of that body until his death—a tribute to his personal integrity and high principles. In his later public life his sterling character, free from pecuniary scandal or crooked political practice, contrasted clearly with that of most of his contemporaries.—F, V, 624-625.

Rafael de RIEGO y Núñez (1785-1823) was a native of the Asturias and was educated in part at Oviedo. He enrolled in the Royal Guard in 1807 and distinguished himself in opposing the French invasion of the Peninsula until he was taken prisoner. During his captivity in France, he absorbed the revolutionary principles that later made him prominent in resisting the autocratic rule of Ferdinand VII. Certain indiscretions subjected him to the charge of disloyalty on which he was ultimately convicted and executed.—E, LI, 513-514.

Germán RIESCO Errázuriz (1854-1916) was born in Rancagua in a notable Chilean family of Leonese descent. His mother was a sister of the elder President Errázuriz. He gained the title of advocate in 1875, served in a minor capacity in the ministry of justice for five years and then for ten years in the court of appeals as relator and seven years as fiscal (prosecutor), and then passed to the same office in the supreme court. In 1899 he became liberal senator from Talca. Discreet and reserved in manner, he spoke little. His nomination for the presidency in 1901 by the liberal alliance came as a surprise to the country, for he was lacking in political experience and virtually unknown. As nephew of the elder Errázuriz and brother-in-law of the recently deceased president, Riesco did not lack political insight and his character led each faction to support him in the hope of being able to profit from his family influence. His first ministry was of high caliber but speedily dissolved, to be followed by the usual ever-changing combinations that characterized the so-called "parliamentary régime." Despite the prevalent party indiscipline and the president's own ill-health, the Riesco administration fared well in its treaties with Bolivia and Argentina and effected some improvement in public service. In later years public opinion rendered Riesco tardy justice.—F, V, 630-632.

Catalina de los Ríos (d. 1665) was connected with the Lisperguer family through her mother. The founder of that family came to Chile from Worms in 1557 with García Hurtado de Mendoza. Barros Arana (B, IV, 400-401) characterizes as doubtful many of the accusations against the earlier members of this family, although noting that some later seemed to flout the laws and the authorities with impunity. Señora Catalina was charged with poisoning her father, with murdering her lover (a member of the Order of St. John), and with other assassinations, fourteen in all. Brought before the royal *audiencia* in 1660, she escaped the consequences of her crimes through delay and bribery— methods which involved Governor Meneses.—B, III, 400-402; M, pp. 464, 747.

Conrado Ríos Gallardo (1896-   ) has held a prominent place in the liberal party since 1921. His reputation, however, rests largely upon his work as journalist, especially in connection with *La nación,* of which he became managing editor in 1926. As minister of foreign affairs and commerce (1927-1929), he reorganized the ministry, and later served as special envoy to Spain and Peru. He was largely instrumental in bringing about better relations with Bolivia and Peru. He was one of the founders of *Hoy* in 1931.—F, V, 647-649.

Manuel Rivas Vicuña (1880-   ) entered congress as deputy in 1909 and became minister of the treasury in 1912. He was later a member of cabinets in 1922 and 1926, and headed the ministry that was displaced by Ibáñez in 1927. Popularly known as the "Great Rabbi of Liberalism," he has had a long and honorable career as journalist, law professor, and diplomat and is recognized as one of the most skillful politicians and debaters of the country. Most of his writings have appeared in the contemporary press. In politics he has been more successful in defeating ministries than in building up successful cabinets. While an exile in Constantinople, he arbitrated a dispute between the Turks and the Greeks. Later he was the ambassador of Chile at Rome and a delegate at Geneva.—F, IV, 663; *Hoy*, October 1, 1936, p. 23.

Galvarino RIVEROS Cárdenas (1833-1892) was born in the province of Chiloé, educated in the old Military Academy, and began his naval service in 1848. He served well in minor positions, particularly in explorations, and became captain in 1870. As a result of the encounter at Angamos during which he coöperated with Latorre, he was promoted to vice-admiral, but his course provoked much controversy, and as a result he was forced to retire. Later his comrades rendered him justice and, in 1931 a monument was erected to his memory in Cunaco de Véliz.—F, V, 666.

Julio A. ROCA (1843-1914) was born in Tucumán, of a distinguished Argentine family. He was a student in the Colegio Nacional of Uruguay, when at the age of fifteen he volunteered in the struggle between Buenos Aires and the confederation. He became lieutenant colonel in the war against Paraguay. In 1878 he took charge of the campaign against Patagonia which added many leagues of fertile land to the Argentine Republic and made Roca president in 1880. As chief executive he strove to improve communications and reorganize the army. After a mission to Europe, following his administration, he reëntered politics in 1890, later became minister of the interior, and in 1898 was elected president for a second term. He retired to private life in 1904, and his only other public service was as special embassy to Brazil in 1913.—E, LI, 1083.

Manuel RODRÍGUEZ Ardoiza (1785-1818) received the title of advocate in 1809 and was one of the first to take part in the revolutionary movement. He served Carrera loyally as secretary, but after the defeat at Rancagua he temporarily sought refuge in Argentina. He was one of the most faithful supporters of San Martín while there, but saw that his presence was more necessary in Chile. He soon left Argentina for his own country, in spite of the dangers to which his enterprises would subject him. He immediately brought together a goodly number of followers, and with them carried on a guerrilla warfare in the province of Colchagua, thus paving the way for San Martín. After Cancha Rayada, his presence of mind and his forceful character, with his example of energy and enthusiasm, reacted on the people and he was able to form a nucleus of resistance which contributed to the triumph of the Chilean forces at Maipú. In this battle he led a troop called the "Hussars of Death." Other military leaders, jealous of his popularity and prestige, charged him with adhesion to Carrera. He was arrested and was being conducted to trial when he was assassinated by members of his guard, supposedly under secret orders from the government.— E, LI, 1268; F, V, 686.

Zoróbabel Rodríguez Benavides (1839-1901) was born in Quillota and educated in the church schools of Valparaiso and Santiago. He carried on his law studies in the university section of the National Institute, receiving his degree in 1864, but began writing for the press the preceding year and also published his first novel, an imitation of Cervantes. In 1864 he joined with the Amunátegui brothers and Abdón Cifuentes in publishing *El independente,* which soon became the leading conservative paper, and in 1867 Rodríguez assumed sole charge of it. In addition to twenty years' service as editor of that publication, he served as many years as deputy in congress, closely associated with the conservative leader Manuel José Irarrázaval (see p. 362n). In 1872 he published a study of Bilbao which aroused bitter controversy. Domingo Arteaga Alemparte characterized him as a true journalist, but one censurable for his vindictive and ironical tendency. He published a notable *Diccionario de chilenismos* (Santiago, 1875), and *Tratado de economía política* (Valparaiso, 1894), much used both in Chile and in other republics, and other economic works.—F, V, 680; Justo and Domingo Arteaga Alemparte, *op. cit.,* pp. 121-126.

Luis Rodríguez Velasco (1839-1919) was the son of José Antonio Rodríguez (F, V, 676-677). Educated at the National Institute, he began his literary career in 1859 as collaborator on the review *La semana* (see p. 350). In 1865 he engaged in editorial work in Peru against the aggressions of Spain and on his return to Chile published his first book of poems. He edited numerous satirical and radical publications in association with the Arteaga Alemparte brothers (see p. 350) and produced plays that were well received. In 1888 he was elected senator. His version of Victor Hugo's *Ruy Blas* is considered one of the best in Spanish. He composed several stirring songs during the war with Peru, and has indeed been proclaimed one of the best poets of Hispanic America.—F, V, 678.

José Santiago Rodríguez Zorrilla (1752-1832) was born at Santiago. After completing his eccelesiastical studies and holding minor church and educational offices, he became bishop in 1816. Because of his strong attachment to the Spanish government, he was twice exiled and died in Madrid before he could return to Chile, but his ashes were taken to Santiago twenty years after his death.—E, LI, 1322; F, V, 693; M, pp. 756-759.

José Antonio Rojas Uturguren (1732-1817) was born in Santiago and educated in the University of San Felipe, where his scientific bent early manifested itself. As heir to an entailed estate he was early given military rank and served with distinction on the frontiers of Chile. When President Amat was transferred to Peru as viceroy, Rojas accompanied him as adviser and also filled subordinate military and civil offices. In 1770 he went to Spain to obtain royal permission to wed the daughter of a Peruvian officeholder. He achieved his purpose after eight years but the mortifying experience with official corruption and delay destroyed his loyalty to the king. He returned to Chile in 1780, bringing with him a library and modest scientific equipment that gained for him a doubtful reputation among his contemporaries. Becoming imbued with liberal ideas, he took part in the conspiracy planned by the Frenchmen, Berney and Gramusset. Although on detection his two companions were seized and punished, Rojas was not molested, doubtless because the authorities hesitated to proceed against one of so high a social position. His part in the preliminaries of independence sent him into exile on Juan Fernández Island and the hardships suffered there hastened his death.—E, LI, 1397; M, p. 759; F, V, 703.

Diego de Rosales (1601-1677), born in Madrid, was already filling a university chair by 1626. Coming to Peru about that time, he went to Chile in 1629 and shortly thereafter took part in battles with the Indians. He then devoted himself to peaceful but dangerous missionary work and accompanied the Marqués de Baides in the negotiations that resulted in the Pact of Quillín (see p. 90). He continued his missionary work until it was broken up by the infamous Salazar brothers (see p. 112). He also did heroic work at Concepción in the earthquake of 1657 and headed the Jesuit college there. From 1666 to 1674 he was writing his most famous work, *Historia general del reíno de Chile,* which was not published until two centuries after (Valparaiso, 1878), when the manuscript came into the possession of Benjamín Vicuña Mackenna. Another work of his, *La conquista espiritual de Chile,* relating to the lives and work of the Jesuits, has far less merit. From 1666 to 1672 he was rector of the Colegio Máximo at Santiago. Even old age and infirmity could not diminish his zeal in converting the Indians. His historical work is his greatest monument.—B, LII, 340; M, pp. 764-767. See also Medina, *Historia de la literatura colonial de Chile,* Vol. II, chap. vii.

Juan Enrique Rosales Fuentes (17? -1825) was the son of a Spanish merchant; but his mother was a Chilean, Margarita Fuentes y Solar. Through his own marriage he was connected with the powerful Larraín clan. As a youth he spent several years on the Peninsula. By 1801 he was established in Santiago and in July, 1808, he was elected to the *cabildo* of Santiago as one of the twelve representatives of the colonial aristocracy. When named as a member of the junta in 1810, his knowledge of politics and of human nature, coupled with his experience in Spain, probably made him its most brilliant member. He was a member of the tribunal that condemned Lieutenant Colonel Tomás de Figueroa and was exiled to Juan Fernández.—B, VIII, 29, 317; F, V, 713.

Juan Manuel de Rosas (1793-1877), the Argentine dictator, received a mediocre education and hence always distrusted men of learning. He volunteered for service against the English during their second attack on Buenos Aires and then entered upon a training in ranch life which gave him the characteristic qualities of the Gaucho—strength, agility, and cleverness. In the welter of party strife which marked the decade of the twenties, Rosas, who had now become a leader among the plainsmen, at first followed Dorrego. After the latter's death he turned his arms against Lavalle and after defeating him became governor of the province of Buenos Aires. At first regarded with favor by those who hoped for a moderate but orderly government, he adopted a despotic course that alienated the better classes of the population. Secure in the support of the masses, he was granted the exercise of all the powers of government and, aided by his force of assassins known as the *mazorca*, he carried on his tyrannous regime for twenty-three years, until a combination of domestic foes, aided by contingents from Uruguay and Brazil, overthrew him in the battle of Monte Caseros on February 3, 1852. He spent the remainder of his life in England. Despite his tyranny, he must be given credit for establishing the federal system of government in Argentina.—E, LII, 377. See also E. Quesada, *La época de Rosas* (Buenos Aires, 1898); and W. S. Robertson, "Foreign Estimates of the Argentine Dictator, Juan Manuel Rosas" in *Hisp. Amer. Hist. Rev.*, X (May, 1930), 125-137.

Gustavo Ross Santa María (1879-   ) was born in Valparaiso. He is of Scotch Chilean descent and related to the Edwards family. In business from his youth, especially coal mining, he has also acquired a reputation as a speculator. He was an unsuccessful candidate for the senate in 1924 and was banished in 1927. In 1932 his appointment as minister of the treasury aroused both hope and distrust. His friends strongly supported his financial policy and it must be said that he did much to reëstablish the credit of the country. In 1936 he resigned his office and went to Paris, ostensibly to push the sales of Chilean nitrate, but really to await the political campaign of 1938. In this contest he failed to gain the coveted presidency.—F, V, 717; *Hoy*, December 23, 1932, p. 8; August 13, 1936, p. 12.

Martín Ruiz de Gamboa (b. 1531) came to America after service in the Levant and in 1552 went to Chile. He served with varying success in the Araucanian wars, was made lieutenant by Governor Rodrigo de Quiroga, and in that capacity founded the town of Castro on the island of Chiloé. His patron in 1577 left him as governor ad interim and the king, four years later, confirmed him in that post. He acquired a reputation as "a good soldier, a careful administrator, a diligent warrior," notable for his gallantry, courtesy, and liberality, feared by malefactors and beloved by men of good repute. The ordinance that bears his name was adopted upon the insistence of the king and provided for a personal tribute of nine pesos annually from each Indian in the bishopric of Santiago and seven pesos in the bishopric of Imperial. The greater part of this tribute was to be paid to the encomenderos. The ordinance aroused so much opposition that church penalties were necessary to enforce it, and the Indians, unable to pay in money, had their tribute reduced to a labor basis.—B, III, 8-11; M, pp. 774-776.

Francisco RUIZ Tagle Portales (d. 1860), proprietor of an entailed estate in Los Andes, was deputy from that community in the congress of 1811 and an active participant in the program of that body. Nevertheless he was not proscribed during the Spanish reconquest, but held municipal offices in Santiago under the restored regime and as governor ad interim delivered the city to the patriots after Chacabuco. After Maipú (and a forced contribution to the cause), he again became an avowed patriot, holding various local and congressional offices during the disturbed years that followed the abdication of O'Higgins. On the eve of Lircay (see p. 236) he was selected by Portales as president ad interim, but soon resigned. Thereafter, he was not active politically. Barros Arana (B, XV, 374, et seq.) discusses at some length the constitutional question involved in the election of 1828. See also F, V, 730.

José Santos SALAS (18 -) was a military surgeon who had had some practical experience in Spain before 1920. He took a prominent part in the revolution of 1925 and after the return of Alessandri served as minister of hygiene. In this post he gained considerable popularity by favoring better and cheaper dwellings for laborers—a popularity which failed to bring him into the presidency. But his conservative opponent, Emiliano Figueroa Larraín, was then elected. Under Ibáñez in 1927 he again served as minister of hygiene and, as ad interim minister of education and justice, favored educational reforms that could not be carried out because of lack of funds. He was forced out of office in 1928 and has since resided in Italy.—Hoy, February 19, 1936, p. 21.

Manuel de SALAS Corvalán (1755-1841), Chilean politician and economist, was born in Santiago. He early filled municipal and other local offices and as a member of the tribunal de consulado prepared in

1796 a valuable memorial on the economic state of Chile, based on the views of Adam Smith. This was published for the first time in 1843. Salas was well known as a sincere patriot and philanthropist of advanced ideas and of untiring activity. He worked unceasingly to encourage agriculture, mining, industry, and education, and was largely instrumental in the founding of the Hospicio (orphanage), the Academia de San Luis, the National Institute, and the National Library.—M, p. 794; E, LIII, 163; B, VII, 369, n. 9. A portrait of him appears in B, facing p. 224.

Dario Enrique SALAS Díaz (1881-   ) was born in Imperial and educated in the normal schools of Chillán and in the Pedagogic Institute in Santiago. In 1907 he received the doctor's degree in pedagogy from Columbia University, where his daughter later obtained the same degree. The father became professor of pedagogy in 1908 in the Normal School of Santiago and later in the Pedagogic Institute, and translated educational books. In 1918 he became director-general of primary education, and as such was largely instrumental in securing the adoption of a law of compulsory instruction. Under his direction there was a great improvement in the quality of teaching and marked increase in enrollment in primary schools, and in the number and quality of school buildings. He was especially interested in matters of health and in the pay and training of teachers. He carried through these betterments in spite of much opposition. In 1927 he sent twenty-four teachers abroad on special missions to the United States and Europe in order to make a general survey of all aspects of education. In 1929 he was sent on a special tour of study to the United States and Europe, and in 1931 he was elected dean of the faculty of philosophy and social sciences of the University of Chile, but later resigned. At present (1940) he is teaching in the Pedagogic Institute.—F, V, 746-748.

Juan Francisco SÁNCHEZ (1757-?   ) was a native of Galicia. He began his military career at the age of sixteen. Twenty years later he was sent to Concepción, with the rank of captain. He was noted for his extreme fidelity to the royalist cause, and this quality, rather than his technical military knowledge or his general culture, led Pareja to designate him as his successor.—B, IX, 126.

Eulogio SÁNCHEZ Errázuriz (? -   ) came into prominence in 1932 as head of the Republican Militia. A year after the dissolution of this force he sought to unite its elements under a new designation, *Acción nacional*, opposing traditional party methods and the course of President Alessandri.—*Hoy*, October 29, 1936, p. 24.

Pedro SANCHO de Hoz (d. 1547) shared in the capture and despoiling of Atahualpa, wrote an account of that event, as secretary to

Pizarro, and then returned to his municipal post and a lucrative marriage in Toledo, Spain. In 1539 he obtained permission to make discoveries in the region below the grants to Pizarro and Almagro, which enabled him to thrust himself upon Valdivia and plot against his associate, thereby bringing about his own execution (see p. 431).—M, p. 803.

Enrique Salvador SANFUENTES Andonaegui (1848-   ), son of the illustrious poet, Salvador Sanfuentes (see below), was born in Santiago, studied in the National Institute and the university, and received his degree in law in 1870. He practiced his profession, amassed a fortune in business, interested himself in educational problems, and in 1888 entered congress as deputy from Rancagua. As minister under Balmaceda he furthered many notable works of that administration. His nomination as minister of the interior inaugurated the chain of events that brought on the civil war of 1891. Nevertheless he later parted company with Balmaceda and failed to support that chief in the struggle with congress. After the war he headed the liberal-democratic party that continued Balmaceda's policy and later served as minister to France.—F, V, 766-768.

Juan Luis SANFUENTES Andonaegui (1858-   ), of a distinguished Santiago family, was educated in the University of Chile and received his license as advocate in 1879. After brief service in the navy during the war with Peru and Bolivia, he engaged in business and became deputy in 1888. A friend of Balmaceda, after the death of that leader he carried on fortunate speculations in the Santiago stock exchange, reëntered politics in 1900, became senator in 1903, and minister of the treasury during the Riesco administration. He was also counselor of the Caja de crédito hipotecario (Mortgage Loan Bank) and the Savings Bank. An expert in financial affairs, he was also a skillful political manager, making and unmaking ministers almost at will. As president he was to take many a dose of his own medicine. Yet he succeeded in reducing materially the public debt, and in pushing through a program of useful public works. In the election of his successor, he maintained a strict neutrality. Never popular, despite his unaffected manners and skill in controlling others, he passed out of office with fewer friends than when he entered.—F, V, 762-765; Cabero, *Chile y los chilenos*, p. 244.

Salvador SANFUENTES Torres (1817-1860) was the son of a Santiago merchant of Spanish connection. Educated at the National Institute and under the tutelage of Andrés Bello (see p. 453), he received his law degree in 1842. From his youth he studied languages and literature and early became favorably known for his translations from Latin,

English, and French. A painter of some note, he published texts on geography and drawing and wrote a critical analysis of Ercilla's *Araucana*. As an associate of Lastarria he published in *El seminario de Santiago* in 1842 a versified legend, *El campanario,* which marked a new departure in Chilean literature. As secretary of the university (1842-1852), he edited its memorials, twice served as minister of public instruction, during which time he strove to improve the system of public schools, and in 1856 was elected dean of the faculty of philosophy and humanities in the university. In addition he held various diplomatic and judicial offices, including membership in the supreme court of justice, and collaborated on various scientific and literary reviews. His poetry and prose have merited high praise.—E, LIII, 1325; F, V, 765-766; M. L. Amunátegui, *Biografía de D. Salvador Sanfuentes* (Santiago, 1892).

Andrés SANTA CRUZ (1792-1865), member of an illustrious Spanish family of Villavicencio, and reputed descendant of the Incas, was born in La Paz. After serving in the royalist ranks until 1820, he joined the revolutionists under San Martín, took part in the battle of Pichincha under Sucre, and in 1823 was made a general of division in Peru. As chief of the general staff of Bolívar, he participated in the battles of Junín and Ayacucho. Entrusted with a diplomatic mission to Chile, he was quickly recalled to military service in Peru and for a time served as president ad interim (1826). In 1829 he succeeded Sucre as president of Bolivia and devoted himself with energy and enthusiasm to the task of rehabilitating his native country, and later of incorporating it with Peru in a powerful confederation. Unfortunately his intrigues had stirred up powerful enemies as well as friends and, although he initiated important measures to improve the industries, the educational system, and the public finance of Bolivia, his opponents in Peru, aided by Chile, defeated him and forced him into exile. After an attempt to recover power in 1843, he spent his remaining days in a kind of diplomatic exile in Europe. In 1861 he negotiated the concordat between Bolivia and the papacy and in 1863, a commercial treaty with France, in which country he died. Documents relating to his career, collected by his son, were published at La Paz in 1925 under the title, *El General Santa Cruz, gran mariscal de Zepita y del gran Perú.*—E, XLIV, 180. For an unfavorable account of Santa Cruz, see Sotomayor Valdés, *Historia de Chile,* Vol. II, chaps. xix, xxiii, *passim.*

Domingo SANTA MARÍA González (1825-1889) was born in Santiago, in a family of distinguished Spanish and colonial lineage. Educated in the National Institute and later in the University of Chile, he first taught in the former, at the same time pursuing his legal studies and serving as subordinate in the ministry of justice and public instruction. He received his degree as attorney at law in 1847, presenting as his thesis, *Reforma de la ley electoral de 1833* (*Reform of the Electoral Law of 1833*). He supported the reëlection of General Bulnes with tongue and pen and as a reward was appointed, although under legal age, intendant of Colchagua. Success crowned the efforts of the precocious administrator, who thus early displayed his ability to arouse and overcome opposition and to gain popularity, but not to keep it. A liberal by nature, he sought to maintain orderly progress but was inclined to change his course; his moderation, however, did not save him from proscription under Montt. During this decade, he served on the university faculty of philosophy and humanities, wrote his memoirs of O'Higgins and Infante (see p. 230), gained reputation as an orator, and while in exile visited Europe and pleaded the cause of a fellow countryman in the English courts. Recalled to Chile during the administration of Pérez, he became minister of hacienda and later minister of the court of appeals. In 1865 he was entrusted with a diplomatic mission to Europe during the war with Spain, and also helped organize the plan of defense agreed upon with Peru. Pérez appointed him to the supreme court. During the War of the Pacific he held three important cabinet posts, including that of war and marine. In the last capacity he effected important changes in the commanding posts and paved the way for his own accession to the presidency. As chief magistrate he helped to liquidate the war and to push to a conclusion certain "theological" questions (see p. 339), as well as to stir up numerous other political controversies. Thus his administration was the most stormy since that of Montt. After his retirement he edited the *Código de enjuiciamiento civil* (*Code of Civil Procedure*). As a politician he was energetic, approachable, adept in management, and one who could wait patiently his turn for preferment.—F, V, 780-782.

Hernando de SANTILLÁN (1519-1574) was a member of the *audiencia* of Lima in 1548 and served Hurtado de Mendoza as *justicia mayor* and deputy in 1557. Four years later he resumed his duties as *oidor* in Lima. In 1564 he was deputized to establish the *audiencia* at Quito where he ruled tyrannically and was subjected to a heavy fine, subsequently reduced at court. In 1571 he was designated bishop of Charcas (Upper Peru) but died at Lima before he could take possession of his see.— Medina, *Dic. biog.*, p. 812. The ordinance mentioned in the text does not exist in its original form but in summaries given by the chronicler Diego de Rosales and Suárez de Figueroa.—B, II, 223, n. 19; L. B. Simpson, *The Encomienda in New Spain.* It established the principle of laboring in succession, the quota from a tribe being one sixth for work in the mines and one fifth for work in the fields. The master must furnish the laborers with meat three times a week and might require limited service only from women and minors. He must furnish medical care and religious instruction for the laborers and their families. The system failed because the masters opposed it and because the Indians were naturally lazy.—B, II, 223-225.

Domingo Faustino SARMIENTO (1811-1888) was born at San Juan de la Frontera, Argentina, but was taken to Chile by his parents in the wake of San Martín. His earlier life alternated between Argentina and Chile, where for a time he engaged in trade and mining. His business experience, supplemented by his early training, his classroom activities, and his newspaper work gave him a reputation for vast learning—a reputation that was increased by enforced exile and wide travel. He spent two periods of exile in Chile, where he was instrumental in founding and directing the first normal school for men and in writing for *El mercurio*. His interest in politics brought him into difficulty even in his adopted country. He returned to Argentina in 1852 to take up arms against Rosas and later to assist in developing the political and educational systems of his native country, serving as senator, minister of state, and minister plenipotentiary in Paris and Washington. Horace Mann was an intimate friend who greatly influenced Sarmiento's educational policy and Mrs. Mann translated his chief novel, *Facundo*. In 1868 Sarmiento became president of Argentina, and during his administration his chief work was still in the educational field. He died in Asunción, Paraguay, where he had gone to regain his health.—E, LIV, 605-607; Coester, *op. cit.*, pp. 125-135, 198-199.

Lorenzo SAZIE (1807-1865) was born at Monpezat, France. After completing his medical studies and hospital training at Paris, where he acquired a brilliant reputation as a surgeon, he was invited in 1833 to become professor of medicine in Chile. Here he became famous not only for his skill in diagnosis and in surgery, but for his preference to minister to the poorer classes. He was more renowned as a teacher than as a medical writer. His son, Carlos Sazie Heredia, was a noted specialist in nervous diseases and another son, an electrical engineer, did much to advance radio telephony in Chile.—F, V, 789-790.

Alexander SELKIRK (1672-1721), the prototype of Robinson Crusoe, was rescued on January 31, 1709, from Juan Fernández Island. In 1703 he had joined Dampier's expedition to the South Seas as sailing captain under Thomas Stradling. A quarrel between them resulted in Selkirk's remaining on Juan Fernández, from which he was rescued by an English vessel under command of Dampier. After returning to England and relating his experiences, Captain Woodes Rogers wrote *A*

Cruising Voyage round the World (London, 1712), the second edition of which inspired Daniel Defoe to write *Robinson Crusoe*. The fullest account of his adventures, based on contemporary narratives, was written by John Howell, *The Life and Adventures of Alexander Selkirk* (Edinburgh, 1829).

Ignacio SERRANO Montaner (d. 1879) was a native of Melipilla. In 1865 he entered the Naval School, where he proved an alert and distinguished pupil. Within a few years after completing his course, he became a lieutenant and served as instructor on the *Esmeralda*. In 1879 he was serving on another vessel but was transferred to the *Esmeralda* in time for his glorious sacrifice. Even when mortally wounded he is credited with an attempt in his last moments to set fire to the *Huáscar*. His remains rest under the same monument as those of Prat. —F, V, 812-813.

Bartholomew SHARPE had started on his expedition in 1679 and, upon his return to England in 1682, he was tried for piracy in connection with the capture of a Spanish vessel, the *Rosario*. He was acquitted on the ground that the Spaniards had fired first and he had therefore acted in self defense. The best account of his expeditions was written by his companion, Basil Ringrose, in his *Dangerous Voyage and Bold Attempts of Capt. Bartholomew Sharpe, 1684,* which is reprinted in John Esquemeling, *The Buccaneers of America* (London, 1893), Pt. IV, pp. 275-502. A summarized account of the operations of these pirates in the West Indies is given by Clarence H. Haring in *The Buccaneers in the West Indies in the 17th Century* (London, 1910). Haring also lists the different editions of Esquemeling.

Waldo SILVA Algüe (1820-1892) was born in Santiago. He studied in the National Institute and in the university, where he obtained his law degree in 1843. From 1856 to 1867 he served as minister of public instruction and during his ministry formed the library of the institute, organized instruction in sculpture and drawing, replaced the course in Spanish civil law with one in the civil code of Chile, and established various *liceos* and popular libraries. After 1860 he was a member of the court of appeals in Concepción. In 1891 as president of the senate he helped head the revolt against Balmaceda (see p. 346).—F, V, 817-818.

Jorge Gustavo SILVA Endeiza (1881-   ) was trained in the lyceums of La Serena and Valparaiso and completed his law studies in 1921. He became advocate in 1929. From his earliest years he had been engaged in newspaper work and later was connected with public administration, principally concerned with labor issues. While residing and working in Santiago, he contributed to the press of Valparaiso and

Concepción. His articles were generally of a sociological character. By inheritance and training he has been closely allied with the literary interests of the country.—F, V, 827.

José Antonio SOFFIA Agromedo (1843-1886) was born in Santiago and educated at the National Institute. One of the most brilliant pupils of Andrés Bello, he published his first poems in 1863 and thereafter continued to produce verse that gained recognition both in Chile and in Colombia, where he served as minister for six years, contributing widely to the press of that country, as well as his own, and influencing profoundly the literary expression of both countries. Like other contemporary South American poets he published many translations from Victor Hugo. His swift, critical, yet kindly genius captivated any social circle with which he was connected. His early promise gained for him six years in the directorship of the National Library. Later he served in congress, and as school inspector, as *oficial mayor* in the ministry of the interior, as intendant of Aconcagua, and as minister to Colombia, where diplomatically and socially he made a favorable impression. He died suddenly just as he was designated minister to Argentina.—F, V, 848-849.

Emilio SOTOMAYOR Baeza (1823-1894) was born in Melipilla, educated in the Military School, and entered the artillery in 1845. He supported the government in the uprisings against Manuel Montt, wrote widely on military topics, and before the War of the Pacific was sent to Europe to obtain better equipment for the army. In that conflict he contributed to Chilean success, particularly in the battle of Dolores (November 19, 1879) and in the fighting around Lima. He was political chief of that city while the Chilean army occupied it.—F, V, 856-857.

Ramón SOTOMAYOR Valdés (1830-1903) was born in Santiago and educated in the National Institute. In 1853 he began contributing articles to *El ferrocarril* and other newspapers. In 1863 he became minister to Mexico and, on his return in 1866, joined the faculty of philosophy and humanities of the University of Chile. From 1867 to 1872 he filled with success the post of minister to Bolivia, of which country he later published an interesting historical study. In 1875 he published the first volume of what was to be a detailed history of Chile beginning with the year 1831 but completed two volumes only, covering the years up to 1837. His service as *official mayor* in the ministry of the treasury showed high financial ability. He made notable contributions to *La revista del Pacífico*, *La revista chilena*, and other literary reviews.—F, V, 860.

Francisco de Paula TAFORÓ Zamora (1816-1889) was born in Valparaiso and completed his studies in the Conciliar Seminary of Santiago. He early attracted attention through his ability as a preacher. Because of his close relationship with Archbishop Manuel Vicuña, he became vicar and curate at Copiapó, where he interested himself in education and in doing away with parochial fees for baptisms, marriages, and funerals. He was favorably known for his liberal attitude in politics and for his moral writings and sermons, and served the university as a member of the faculty of theology and sacred science. During the stormy decade of Manuel Montt, he spent some years in Peru, where he gained reputation because of his sermons and his efforts in behalf of peace among contending political factions. After his return he served the cathedral at Santiago in minor offices, finally reaching that of archdeacon—a position which he held when refused confirmation as archbishop. Nevertheless, he sought to avoid the break between the government and the papal legate (see p. 339). He served as senator and councilor of state, helped organize the first company of firemen, assisted personally in epidemics of smallpox, and willed his private property to establish an asylum for poor priests.—F, V, 875.

Indalicio TÉLLEZ Cárcamo (18 ? -   ) graduated from the Military School in 1894 and served three years in the German army, and then in Spain. In addition to his services in the army and his historical and military narratives, he studied law and became an advocate in 1918. He also contributed military articles to the press and acted as professor of military tactics and law in the Military School and the War Academy. He was a general in division when he left the latter institution and served for a year as intendant at Tacna. He retired in 1929. His *Historia de Chile, historia militar (1520-1885)*, Vols. I-III, appeared in 1925.—F, V, 884.

Manuel Antonio TOCORNAL Grez (1817-1867), son of Joaquín Tocornal (see below), was born in Santiago and received in his native city an education much above the average. Completing his law course at the age of twenty-two, in 1846 he became a member of the chamber of deputies. He was encouraged by Bello to produce, in 1847, a memoir upon the first national government, which did much to clarify the order of events after 1810. He acquired a reputation both in law and in oratory. "His mouth," states his biographer, "never pronounced and his hand never wrote a slovenly word." He succeeded Bello as rector of the University of Chile.—E, LXII, 328; F, V, 893. See also M. L. Amunátegui, *Ensayos biográficos*, III, 5-107.

Joaquín TOCORNAL Jiménez (1788-1865) was born in Santiago and served his native city in numerous municipal offices, both before and after the universal flight to Argentina in 1814. He was one of the youngest present at the assemblage in the *consulado* (see p. 156), at which the first step toward independence was taken, and was a member and presiding officer of the chamber of deputies when called to a ministerial post. He also presided over the convention that prepared the constitution of 1833 (see p. 240). After 1831 he served in both the ministry of the interior and the ministry of foreign relations and, at the time of the assassination of Portales, temporarily filled all the cabinet offices. In 1841 he was a candidate for the presidency and shortly afterward became superintendent of the Casa de Moneda (mint).— F, V, 892; E, LXII, 327. Of Tocornal a contemporary publication states, "He was probity, information, devotion to public welfare, firmness of character, good judgment, and good friend, and throughout his whole life there has not fallen on his reputation a spot which might tarnish so many and such precious qualities."—Sotomayor Valdés, *Historia de Chile*, I, 179-180.

Mateo del Toro Zambrano (1727-1811) was a native of Santiago. A man of considerable fortune and character, he had held commercial and political offices of high trust, including those of alcalde and corregidor of Santiago and governor ad interim, when he received on March 6, 1771, the title of Conde de la Conquista. During the same year he bought at public sale one of the largest of the confiscated Jesuit estates and thus set up a valuable entail. In 1809 when the French invaded Spain, the central junta at Seville made him brigadier—a promotion that had earlier been denied him—and in 1810 he was given command of Chile (see p. 150). He was the first president of the first *junta de gobierno* in Chile.—B, VIII, 168; E, LXII, 1159; M, pp. 869-870.

José Antonio Torres Arce (1828-1864) was born in Valdivia. His mother was the niece of Camilo Henríquez (see p. 160); his father, a physician of Portuguese descent. Educated at the National Institute, he began his journalistic work on *El mercurio* of Valparaiso. He early showed a gift for humorous and satirical verse, which displayed itself so strongly in opposition to the government of Montt as to force the young poet into a brief exile. He wrote also upon educational topics, took part in current religious controversies, and even prepared a study on the perennial boundary question with Bolivia. Popular culture was his ideal.—F, V, 913.

Manuel Trucco Franzani (1874-   ) was born in Cauquenes and educated there and at the National Institute in Santiago. He received the degree of civil engineer in 1899 and for a time taught mathematics in the institute. From 1901 to 1911 he was connected with the state railway and at the same time continued to teach mathematics. He founded the Institute of Engineers for Chile. From 1911 to 1918 he was dean of the mathematical faculty of the University of Chile and director of the school of engineering. He organized the first national railroad congress (1921) and was active in the electrification of the railway from Valparaiso to Santiago. He retired from his railroad activities in 1924 and in 1926 became senator and later vice-president under Montero. He was ambassador to the United States from 1933 to 1939.—F, V, 917.

Antonio de ULLOA (1716-1795) was a native of Seville. After preliminary instruction in his native city and a cruise at his own expense to the West Indies and the Spanish Main, he joined the Guarda marina (Marine Guard) in 1733 and in the following year, at the age of nineteen, entered upon the task which gave him his best claim to fame, the survey of a segment of the earth's circumference, undertaken by a company of French scientists with the permission of the Spanish government. Ulloa and Jorge Juan were the Spanish representatives, chosen through special favor to accompany this expedition, take part in its operations, and record carefully all sorts of administrative and scientific data concerning the regions and peoples that they might visit. Their main work was carried on in the vicinity of Quito and there they labored from 1735 to 1741, being called off twice to assist in repelling threatened British attacks and to visit Juan Fernández Island and the coast of Chile in a futile pursuit of Anson (see p. 94). They were also involved in a serious quarrel over a point of etiquette with the president of the *audiencia* at Quito, but were saved from the consequences of this quarrel through the viceroy of Peru. Their stay in South America gave them a chance to make a careful study of the Peruvian viceroyalty and of Chile, to which region Ulloa made two voyages. They both proved to be keen and accurate observers and supplemented their own observations by data from official channels. On the return voyage to Spain the two scientists separated. Ulloa was captured by the British and detained for some time in London. His experiences brought him into intimate contact with local scientists and an election to the Royal Society. Moreover, he was permitted to retain the scientific data captured with him and to return to Spain in 1746. These unusual courtesies enabled him and his associate to prepare for publication the five volumes of his *Relación histórica* (see note on Jorge Juan), which appeared in 1748. The four volumes of the narrative are the work of Ulloa, and drew favorable comment for the author from scientific bodies throughout all Europe—a result equally flattering to national pride and to his own reputation. He and his associate also prepared the manuscript report, which was finally published as *Noticias secretas de América* (London, 1826) and is an important source for contemporary conditions in Spanish colonial administration. In 1757 Ulloa was made governor of Huancavelica, Peru—perhaps to correct in a key position the abuses he had so ably described. If so, the fight against corruption and inefficiency proved too much for him. Relieved from an impossible situation he was next sent with an inadequate force in 1765 to take over the province of Louisiana from the French. Again he failed but was not held responsible for the result. Resuming his career in the navy in 1778, he brought back from Vera Cruz the last of the Spanish treasure fleets. In the following year, during the war with Great Britain, he tried without success to capture a fleet of the enemy merchantmen, but his ships were in no condition for the task. In 1772 appeared his *Noticias americanas* in which he summed up much of the information appearing in his earlier work and supplemented this résumé with data acquired during his later colonial experience. In the second part of his *Relación histórica del viaje a la América meridional* (5 Vols. Madrid, 1748), Bk. VIII, chaps. iv-xi, one finds some description of Chile.— B, VI, 122-125; E, LXV, 921. For recent studies of Ulloa see A. P. Whitaker, "Antonio de Ulloa," in *Hisp. Amer. Hist. Rev.*, XV (May, 1935), 155-194; and Lewis Hanke, *"Dos Palabras* on Antonio Ulloa," in *ibid.*, XVI (November, 1936), 479-514.

Luis URIBE Orrego (1848-1914) was born in Copiapó. His mother was a noted poet and with the coöperation of her son founded in 1873 *La revista de Valparaíso.* Uribe was educated in the Naval School of that city, along with Arturo Prat, both under the personal direction of Juan Williams Rebolledo. In the sea fight before Iquique, he preferred to sink his ship rather than surrender to the enemy, as he might have done. Later in *Los combates navales del Pacífico,* he modestly described the combat in which he participated, wrote much on naval topics, served on commissions to Europe, and gained the title of vice-admiral.—P. P. Figueroa, *Diccionario biográfico de Chile,* III, 340.

Pedro Alcántara URRIOLA Balbontín (1797-1851) was born in Santiago. He spent his youth in a period of warfare and naturally took to a career of arms. Playing his part in the events that preceded Rancagua, he remained in Chile to fight with Manuel Rodríguez (see p. 190) and to be taken prisoner by the royalists. After independence he retired to his farm but resumed his military career in 1828 and, after participating in the war against Peru and performing other routine service, became colonel of the Chacabuco Regiment in 1849. Mixing in the political disturbances of 1850, he headed the revolt of the following year and became its most conspicuous victim.—F, V, 939-940.

Gregorio URRUTIA Venegas (1830-1897) was born in San Carlos. Entering the army in 1856, he supported the government of Montt in

1859 and was later active in campaigns against the Araucanians, against the Spanish intervention of 1865, and in the struggle before Lima in 1881. He commanded the congressional forces against Balmaceda in 1891 and held important staff appointments.—F, V, 946.

Luis de VALDIVIA (1560-1642) was born in Granada and entered the Jesuit order in 1581. Shortly afterwards he went to Peru and then came to Chile in 1593 with the first Jesuits to arrive there. While serving as rector of the college in Santiago, he prepared a grammar of the ordinary language spoken in the colony by the Indians and the children of the Spaniards. This was published in 1606. Believing that much of the difficulty with the Indians arose from the ill-treatment they received, he strove earnestly, as related in the text, to suppress the system of personal service to which they were subjected. In order to enforce the king's orders given him, he was given the spiritual government of the diocese of Imperial, where most of the Indians lived. His well-planned efforts were neutralized by the death of his fellow Jesuits at the hands of the Indians (see p. 89) and by continual petty opposition on the part of local officials, civil, military, and ecclesiastical. This opposition forced his return to Spain after eight years, but he did not lose royal favor because of his lack of success in Chile. He was offered a post as counselor of the Indies, but preferred to serve his order as teacher and writer and as general adviser on difficult questions of conscience and on Indian affairs. He thus acquired wide fame for his learning and piety.— B, III, 445, n. 2; E, LXVI, 530; M, pp. 895-904.

Pedro de VALDIVIA (ca. 1500-1554) was born at La Serena, Estremadura, and had already fought in Flanders and at Pavia and had taken part in the conquest of Venezuela when in 1532 he joined Pizarro in Peru. Two years later he started on the conquest of Chile as detailed in this volume. A true colonial pioneer, he showed both the cruelty of the worst and the constructive ability of the best of his contemporaries. For further characterization and a discussion of the sources of information concerning him, see B, I, 206-209, 438-443. Chapters iv-xi of the same volume are devoted to Valdivia's career as conqueror and founder of Chile. See also E, LXVI, 530-532, and Graham, *Pedro de Valdivia*.

Rafael Valentín VALDIVIESO y Zañartu (1804-1878), son of a subordinate magistrate of Santiago, received his early instruction under a private tutor and in the convent of Santo Domingo. Later he studied at the National Institute, where he pursued law courses under Mariano Egaña (see p. 467) and José Santiago Iñiguez, an eminent churchman. Receiving his degree in 1825, he practiced law for eight years, serving during this period as defender of minors before the court of appeals, as *regidor* in the city council of Santiago, and as a member of the chamber of deputies, and gained respect in all these activities because of his industry, ability, and independence. In 1834 he was ordained priest, but continued to act as deputy in congress. A few years in mission work both in southern and in northern Chile established his reputation as an orator, as a warm defender of the Church, and as a ready friend of the poor. He was offered the rectorship of the National Institute, but declined to accept the office and for ten years directed the charity hospital. He was one of the founders of *La revista católica,* and in 1842 became a member of the theological faculty of the new University of Chile. In 1848 he was consecrated archbishop of Santiago—a position that enabled him to found still other educational and charitable institutions. He was an illustrious prelate, but his preliminary work in law and his continual efforts in behalf of charity did not prevent his banishment under Montt. —E, LXVI, 534; F, V, 980-981.

José Joaquín VALLEJO Borkoski (1811-1858) was born at Vallenar, near Copiapó. Left an orphan, he carried on his early studies at La Serena. Later the authorities of that municipality sent him to Santiago to complete his education, first at the *liceo* of Mora (see p. 250) and later in the National Institute. Engaging at first in commerce, he received a minor political appointment in 1835 and three years later began to publish articles in *El mercurio* of Valparaiso. He wielded a caustic pen which he did not hesitate to turn against those in authority or the too-critical foreigner. He signed certain articles satirizing Sarmiento, Mitre, and other Argentines with the pseudonym "Jotabeche," the initial letters of the witty Argentine writer, Juan Bautista Chenao, thus apparently meeting the gibes of critical guests with their own weapons, and thereafter adopted that pen name as his own. Besides contributing to various papers in Santiago and Valparaiso, he founded *El copiapino* in his native province. In this appeared his best productions, called by some critics imitations of the Spaniard Larra, but based on careful studies of the customs and manners of his fellow countrymen. They appeared in book form as *Colección de artículos de Jotabeche . . .* (Santiago, 1847). In 1849 he entered congress from his native Vallenar, where he distinguished himself for his graceful diction. For a brief period before his death he also filled the post of chargé in Bolivia. His fellow countrymen have acclaimed him their most talented exponent of Chilean customs, while the Colombian writer José María Torres y Caicedo pays him merited respect in his *Ensayos biográficos y de critica literaria . . .* (3 vols. Paris, 1863-1868).—F, V, 995.

George VANCOUVER (1758-1798) had been sent by his government to repossess the British establishments at Nootka Sound and to explore the northwest coast of North America. He reached Valparaiso on March

25, 1795, on his return voyage, was cordially received there as a representative of an allied power, and was permitted to journey to Santiago. His narrative describes these two cities, but he indulged in no mapping because unwilling to arouse Spanish sensibilities. The results of his voyage are recorded in *A Voyage of Discovery to the North Pacific Ocean and round the World* (London, 1798).—B, VII, 153-156.

Antonio VARAS de la Barra (1817-1886) was born in Cauquenes. Trained as both surveyor and lawyer, he distinguished himself as instructor and rector of the National Institute. Elected to the chamber of deputies in 1845, he continued in that body almost uninterruptedly until his death, varying the first sixteen years of his congressional career, however, by service in ministerial posts. He was also first president of the Caja del crédito hipotecario (Mortgage Loan Bank). Intelligent, disinterested, and active, he was an orator of rare persuasive power.— E, LXVI, 1498; F, V, 996-999.

Bernardo VERA Pintado (1780-1827), an inhabitant of Santa Fé, was born in Mexico, brought up in the Platine provinces, and came to Chile in 1799, with the captain general. He received his early training in the universities of Córdova and Santiago and then entered upon the practice of law. A cousin of the Argentine patriot, Rivadavia, he maintained a close correspondence with prospective insurgents there that led him to favor similar activities in Santiago. His leadership in congress under the "old country" forced him into exile after Rancagua. In Mendoza he joined the Army of the Andes under San Martín, as auditor-general, took part in the battle of Chacabuco, and two years later composed the early national hymn. He took little part in the political events that followed independence but did much to stimulate early literary expression in Chile.—M. L. Amunátegui, *Ensayos biográficos,* IV, 333-362; F, V, 1018.

Rodolfo VERGARA Antúñez (1847-1914) was born in Talca, became presbyter in 1871, and continued as professor in the seminary of Santiago until 1875. After filling minor posts in the archbishopric, he became rector of the seminary in 1896 and two years later rector of the Catholic University. Distinguished as an educator, he became renowned chiefly for his writings for the religious press.—F, V, 1019.

Claudio VICUÑA Guerrero (1833-1908) was born in Santiago. Left an orphan in his early years, he was brought up by an uncle and studied at the National Institute. He soon devoted himself to agriculture, by which he acquired the means for foreign travel. He became deputy in 1873 and senator in 1879 and contended for public rights and popular suffrage. In the revolt of congress against President Balmaceda, he loyally supported the president and during that conflict was nominated and elected to the presidency to succeed his chief but was deprived of office by Balmaceda's defeat. He spent several years in exile, during which he wrote a defense of his superior, and on his return received a widespread ovation. He headed the liberal-democratic party, founded a newspaper in support of its principles, and in 1901 was the choice of the liberal alliance (see p. 366) for the presidency but led his followers to the support of Don Germán Riesco.—F, V, 1043.

Joaquín VICUÑA Larraín (d. 1857) belonged to a prominent Coquimbo family. He had held minor military offices before achieving temporary fame in this election. He was founder of the city which bears the family name. He is not to be confused with his brother, Francisco Ramón Vicuña, who was then temporarily acting as chief executive of Chile.—F, V, 1047.

Manuel VICUÑA Larraín (1777-1843) was born in Santiago. He was descended from a distinguished Navarrese family that was intimately connected with other wealthy Chilean families of the colonial period, although his own parents were in reduced circumstances. His education was obtained in the Convictorio de San Carlos (see p. 122) and in the University of San Felipe (see p. 110). Ordained as a priest in 1803, he promptly gained a reputation for eloquence and administrative ability. In 1830 he was elevated to the bishopric of Santiago and exerted himself to aid those who suffered from the political persecutions of the period. Having inherited a large fortune, he was able to undertake many works of charity. He became the first archbishop of Chile in 1840. As head of the Church he was distinguished for his mild rule over subordinates. He also served as senator and counselor of state. A statue in his honor erected in 1877 stands in the park of Santa Lucía. —F, V, 1049-1050.

Benjamín VICUÑA MACKENNA (1831-1886) was born at Santiago. Among his progenitors he counted members of the leading families of Chile, but none gave more honor to the connection than Don Benjamín himself. After preliminary instruction in the Colegio of Cueto, where he displayed more fondness for general literature than for the prescribed Latin and arithmetic, he spent a year in the National Institute where he received the degree of bachelor at the age of eighteen. Eight years passed, however, before he received his diploma as counselor at law. His life as a student was varied by clerical tasks and by opportunities to share the social life of Santiago's leading public characters. His first literary article appeared in 1849 and immediately attracted the attention of Andrés Bello. In the following year he joined the Sociedad de la Igualdad, which brought him into intimate contact with Bilbao and into the prevailing current of opposition (see p. 487) and ultimately to prison. Condemned to death, he managed to escape, fled to California, and then spent the next few years in leisure travel in Mexico, the United States, and Europe, where he unearthed much manuscript material relating to early Chile. Incidentally, during these years of turmoil and exile he laid the foundation of his reputation as a historian and publicist. Returning in 1856, he began to publish the results of his studies and travels in contemporary newspapers, especially in *El ferrocarril,* and also lent a pen to opposition sheets. This latter practice forced him once more into exile. In 1863 he became editor of *El mercurio* of Valparaiso, entered congress, and served as special envoy to the United States in 1865, and to Europe in 1870. As a diplomat, he proved a collector of historical documents. As a historian, he is credited with ample imagination, and ability to link documents together and thus to fill innumerable volumes—more than one hundred—but little else. Later critics speak of his vivacity, his infantile ingenuity, and his frivolity. All agree that he was untiring in investigation and in compiling facts, but deny that he made progress in literary art or that he cared to make progress. He produced what the people wanted, when they wanted it, and in terms that they could comprehend. He was a man of astonishing activity, of great personal charm, and of assured social position. His most enduring monument is the famous Cerro de Santa Lucía, a favorite playground of his childhood, transformed during his administration as intendant of Santiago into an attractive park. In settling the accounts incurred in its construction he was forced to part with most of his property and that of his wife. Too independent and outspoken to attain the presidency of the republic, he led an enthusiastic following as a third candidate for that office in 1876, and loyally supported and recorded the cause of Chile in the War of the Pacific, of which he was a voluminous chronicler. His premature death called forth expressions of grief throughout the entire country.—*Rev. chil. de hist. y geog.,* LXX (July-Dec., 1931), 5-177; Ricardo Donoso, *Don Benjamín Vicuña Mackenna, su vida, sus escritos y su tiempo, 1831-1886* (Santiago, 1925); E, LXVIII, 647; F, V, 1050-1053. For a less favorable sketch see Cruz, *Estudios sobre la literatura chilena,* I, 373-391.

Francisco VIDAL Górmaz (1837-   ) studied in the Military School and in 1854 joined the navy where he attracted attention because of his explorations in Chiloé and Magallanes. In 1862 he took charge of the nautical school at Ancud. He took part in military expeditions against Spain in 1865 and proposed in 1874 the creation of a hydrographic office of which he became first director. In that same year he began the publication of the *Anuario hidrográfico.* He did important work in this office during the war with Bolivia. In addition he was the author of numerous other hydrographic works, the result largely of his own personal surveys. An Andean peak bears his name.—F, V, 1057.

José Antonio VIDAURRE Garretón (1798-1837), native of Concepción, belonged to a good family but one of reduced fortune. He began his military career in 1813 but was distinguished for intrigue during the period of political anarchy. In 1829 he organized the battalion of infantry known as the Cazadores de Maipú. His services at Lircay won for him the commission of colonel; and his battalion became noted for its discipline and devotion to its commander. Apparently, while enjoying the confidence of Portales, he was suspected of conspiring with Freire. As a result of complicity in the death of Portales, Vidaurre was executed on July 4, 1837, and his head was exposed in the principal plaza of Quillota, near which place Portales was assassinated. His action has given rise to much controversy, but evidently he did not intend the death of Portales.—F, V, 1058; Sotomayor Valdés, *Historia de Chile,* II, 385, *et seq.*

Francisco de VILLAGRA (*ca.* 1511-1563) was born in Astorga, and arrived in America in 1537. He may have taken part in the campaign against Almagro. Soon after, he came to Chile, where he distinguished himself in minor offices, including that of corregidor of Santiago. He hoped to succeed Valdivia after the latter's death but did not receive the coveted appointment until 1561. A man of abounding energy, he wore himself out through excessive campaigning.—B, II, 297-330.

Gaspar de VILLARROEL (1587-1665) was born at Quito in an impoverished but noble family. His father was a native of Guatemala and his mother of Venezuela. Educated at Lima, he entered the Augustinian order in 1607 and acquired fame as a pulpit orator. In 1622 he visited Spain where, in the course of the next ten years, he published numerous theological works and commentaries. Called to preach before the king and the Council of the Indies by his patron, García de Haro, he received royal appointment as bishop of Santiago in 1637 and took possession of his see a year later. He was injured in the earthquake of May 13, 1647, but continued to minister to those stricken in that terrible catastrophe. He rebuilt the cathedral at Santiago with his own funds. Modest and sincere in manner, he sought to avoid all appearances of rivalry but showed himself a forceful and notable writer. His works form twelve folio volumes. His most famous work, *Gobierno eclesiástico pacífico,* published about 1656, is a vast arsenal of legal knowledge of the colonial period. In 1635 he was transferred to the see of Arequipa and later to Chuquisaca, where he died in poverty.—B, IV, 427; E, LXVIII, 1511; M, pp. 968-973.

Carlos WALKER MARTÍNEZ (1842-1905) was born in Vallenar, the son of an English industrialist. His early studies took place in the Colegio of San Ignacio, and the influence of his early Jesuit instructors doubtless determined his later conservatism. He received his degree in law from the national university in 1866. A few months earlier he had produced in the municipal theater his first, and for a long time his most significant, literary work, the historic drama, *Manuel Rodríguez*. Precocious rather than productive both as poet and politician, he early identified himself with the Sociedad de Amigos del País (Society of the Friends of the Country), an organization formed to fight liberalism, and continued this fight to the end of his life. He held minor posts in the ministry of the interior and the ministry of foreign affairs, visited the United States and Europe, held the post of minister to Bolivia, was elected deputy to congress and to the senate, and in 1891 took part secretly in the opposition to Balmaceda and helped punish the latter's followers. His most distinguishing characteristic was impetuosity. In addition to his ardent Catholicism, he sought, as president of the Sociedad protectora, an institution founded by Vicuña Mackenna, to support the widows and orphans created by the War of the Pacific. As minister of foreign relations in 1899, he defended his country with vigor against the claims of Argentina.—F, V, 1080-1082; Justo and Domingo Arteaga Alemparte, *op. cit.*, pp. 328-331.

William WHEELWRIGHT (1798-1873) was born in Newburyport, Massachusetts. He early engaged in trade with South America, was shipwrecked at Buenos Aires in 1822, and came to Chile in 1824. He served as consul of the United States at Guayaquil, Ecuador, from 1824 to 1829, when he removed to Valparaiso and, encouraged by Portales, established a line of passenger vessels in 1840 to serve the west coast of South America. In addition to his interest in steam navigation, he promoted railroads, telegraph lines, coal mines, and general public utilities, largely with the aid of British capital. He was a true poet of business who conceived great projects and had the energy to carry them out. —*New International Encyclopedia*, XXIII, 587.

Juan WILLIAMS Rebolledo (1826-1910), son of John Williams, companion of Lord Cochrane, was born in the province of Valparaiso. Entering the naval service in 1844, he took part in numerous explorations, especially in the southern part of Chile, and carried out many naval improvements. With the *Esmeralda* he performed notable exploits against the Spanish fleet during the intervention of Spain on the west coast of South America, gained the victory of Papudo (see p. 308), and commanded the combined Peruvian and Chilean fleets. To him was due the efficiency of the Chilean navy at the outbreak of the War of the Pacific. Because of earlier reverses suffered by Chile, he resigned his high command but later published a defense of his course, attributing his lack of success to government orders that hampered his movements. He continued in naval administration after the war and also took part in politics.—F, V, 1095-1096.

Luis de Zañartu (d. 1782), a native of Vizcaya, held many minor offices in Chile. While corregidor he constructed other notable public works, aside from the prison, and also patronized the nunnery of the Carmelites at San Rafael, of which his two daughters became members. Although a conscientious and efficient public servant, he was detested and feared by the populace.—M, p. 995.

José Ignacio Zenteno del Pozo y Silva (1786-1847) was born in Santiago. He entered the college of San Carlos at an early age, and in 1813 began to serve the patriot government as military secretary. After the battle of Rancagua, he emigrated to Mendoza where he soon became secretary to San Martín. Under O'Higgins he assumed charge of the war office and, among other notable services, designed the Chilean flag. He also devoted attention to the navy, a trust that he continued to exercise after he became military and political governor of Valparaiso in 1821. After five years of service in that office he retired from public life, but in 1831 he resumed his military activities, represented the departments of Santiago and La Victoria in congress, and became vice-president of the chamber of deputies. He was the founder and first director of *El mercurio* of Valparaiso. His son Ignacio was also a journalist and collaborated on *El ferrocarril*.—E, LXX, 1180; F, V, 1131.

In ARRANGING the bibliography on Chile, it has seemed best to follow in general the chronological order. Its divisions will thus correspond more closely to the chapters of the present work. The reader should bear in mind that the following lists of books make no attempt to be complete. The aim of the editor has been to suggest the principal sources and most significant works under each heading. From these, the interested reader can readily branch out for himself into any special field.

GENERAL BIBLIOGRAPHIES

There is no general bibliography covering the whole field of Chilean history. The former subdirector of the National Library, Luis Montt, made a beginning in his *Bibliografía chilena; precedada de un bosquejo histórico sobre los primeros años de la prensa en el país* (Vol. I, 1780-1811. Santiago, 1918; Vol. II, 1812-1817. Santiago, 1904). A similar work, but on a more extensive scale, was begun some years later by Emilio Vaisse, entitled *Bibliografía general de Chile. Primera parte, diccionario de autores y obras* (Santiago, 1915). This work stopped at the beginning of the alphabet with the first volume. A work dealing with the literature of Chile is Raúl Silva Castro's *Fuentes bibliográficos para el estudio de la literatura chilena* (Santiago, 1933). An earlier book in English compiled for the International Bureau of American Republics is Philip Lee Phillip's *List of Books, Magazine Articles, and Maps Relating to Chile* (Government Printing Office, Washington, 1903). One may also consult with profit the bibliographic section of the *Hispanic American Historical Review* (IV [February, 1921], 128-141) and other bibliographic sections of this periodical.

PHYSICAL FEATURES

There is no adequate general description of Chile as a whole, but one will find much of value in Fred H. Carlson's, *Geography of Latin America* (chaps. ii, v. New York, 1936); C. F. Jones' *South America* (chap. iv. New York, 1930); and R. H. Whitbeck's *Economic Geography of South America* (chaps. vii, viii. New York, 1930). One may also consult with profit the article on Chile to be found in the fourteenth edition of the *Encyclopædia Britannica*. Isaiah Bowman's *Desert Trails of Atacama* (New York, 1924) is valuable for its description of the nitrate regions of the north. George M. McBride, in *Chile: Land and Society* ("American Geographical Society, Research Series," No. 19. New York, 1936), gives an excellent summary of the geographical

background and shows its effects upon the population as a whole.
Agustín Edwards, in *My Native Land* (London, 1928), gives a brief
popular description of the country. Thomas H. Holdich's *The Countries
of the King's Award* (London, 1904) gives in detail the leading features of southern Chile. Carlos Keller R., in *Sinopsis geográfico-esta-
dística de Chile* (Santiago, 1933), presents in tabulated form the results
of physical as well as human agencies in the country's development.
Claudio Gay (see p. 476), in *Historia física y política de Chile* (26 vols.
Paris, 1844-1854), presents a complete picture of Chile during the
mid-nineteenth century in its varied physical and political aspects.

GENERAL HISTORIES

There is no extensive general history covering the whole period of
Chilean development. The brief text of which the present work is a
translation, Luis Galdames' *Estudio de la historia de Chile* (8th ed.
Santiago, 1938), will serve the purpose of the general reader. Domingo
Amunátegui Solar in still briefer form reviews the same period in his
Historia de Chile (2 vols. Santiago, 1933). A. U. Hancock's *History of
Chile* (Chicago, 1893) presents a narrative covering the story to the date
of publication, but this is more significant for the colonial than for the
national period. Thomas C. Dawson, in his *South American Republics*
(II, 135-231. 2 vols. New York and London, 1903-1904), also sum-
marizes the development of Chile to the end of the nineteenth century.
George F. Scott Elliot's *Chile: Its History and Development* (London,
1907) combines a brief narrative with general description.

COLONIAL PERIOD

The great source for the history of Chile during this period is "Collección de historiadores de Chile y documentos relativos a la historia
nacional" (45 vols. Santiago, 1861-1923). This is made up of narratives
dealing with the sixteenth and seventeenth centuries, references to
some of which may be seen on pp. 87 and 129. Somewhat similar works
of the eighteenth century are those of Friar Juan Ignacio Molina (see
pp. 122, 130). The leading annalist of Chile, Diego Barros Arana, in his
Historia jeneral de Chile (16 vols. Santiago, 1884-1902, revised ed.,
1930), has covered this period in minute detail in the first seven volumes
of his voluminous work. Descriptions of the prehistoric people of Chile
appear in the popular account of Agustín Edwards entitled *Peoples of
Old* (London, [1929]) and in the more scholarly work of Tomás Gueva-
ara, *Historia de Chile: Chile prehispaño* (2 vols. Santiago, 1925-1927),
and of Ricardo E. Latcham, *La prehistoria chilena* (Santiago, 1928).
Robert B. Cunninghame Graham's *Pedro de Valdivia, Conqueror of
Chile* (London, 1926) is a spritely and scholarly narrative of the con-

quest. The early development of the Church is treated at length by Monsignor Crescente Errázuriz in *Los oríjenes de la iglesia chilena, 1530-1603* (Santiago, 1873). The cultural history of the colony is reviewed at length in two works of José Toribio Medina, *Historia de la literatura colonial de Chile* (Vols. I-III. Santiago, 1878) and *La instrucción pública en Chile* (2 vols. Santiago, 1905). The same author also presents the chief colonial characters in *Diccionario biográfico colonial de Chile* (Santiago, 1906). Alejandro Fuenzalida Grandón's *La evolución social de Chile, 1541-1810* (Santiago, 1906) offers valuable data concerning the early families in Chile.

WARS OF INDEPENDENCE

The main source material for this period is to be found in "Colección de historiadores i de documentos relativos a la independencia de Chile" (28 vols. Santiago, 1900-1930). For material which relates primarily to intercourse with the United States, consult W. R. Manning's *Diplomatic Correspondence of the United States Concerning the Independence of the Latin American Nations* (3 vols. New York, 1925). An interesting phase of the diplomatic relations of the period is presented by W. M. Collier and Guillermo Feliú Cruz in *La primera misión de los Estados Unidos de América en Chile* (Santiago, 1926). Sketches of the early revolutionists and their plans appear in Miguel Luis Amunátegui's *Los precursores de la independencia de Chile* (3 vols. Santiago, 1870-1872). Barros Arana's *Historia jeneral* (Vols. VIII-XVI) covers the period of independence and early nationality to 1833. Political activities of the period are narrated at length by Alcibíades Roldán y Álvarez in *Las primeras asambleas nacionales, años de 1811 a 1814* (Santiago, 1890). Bartolomé Mitre's *Historia de San Martín y de la emancipación sud-americana* (3 vols. Buenos Aires, 1890) gives in detail the relation of Chile to Argentina during this period—details which are summarized in *The Emancipation of South America* (London, 1893) by William Pilling. This account of San Martín's connection with Chile is paralleled briefly in Thomas Cochrane's *Narrative of Services in the Liberation of Chile, Peru, and Brazil* (2 vols. London, 1859). The whole story of the period is summed up in A. S. M. Chisholm's *Independence of Chile* (Boston, 1911). John J. Mehegan, in *O'Higgins of Chile* (London, 1913), presents in brief and popular form the life of the Chilean patriot, preceded by a short reference to the career of the elder O'Higgins.

NATIONAL PERIOD

This period of Chilean history lacks an extended narrative. Hancock continues his study to 1893. The brief accounts by Dawson and

Elliot also cover the same period. One may also consult especially for recent years the coöperative work, *Argentina, Brazil, and Chile since Independence* by J. Fred Rippy, P. A. Martin, and I. J. Cox (ed., A. C. Wilgus. Washington, 1935). Chilean writers have produced a large number of monographs dealing with specific periods or events, but no one has attempted to synthesize these data as did Barros Arana for the colonial and revolutionary periods. Alberto Edwards early prepared a brief monograph on the party history of the country during the nineteenth century in his *Bosquejo histórico de los partidos políticos chilenos* (Santiago, 1903). Henry Clay Evans reviews its diplomatic relations and incidentally affords some light on local developments in *Chile and its Relations with the United States* (Durham, N. C., 1927). W. S. Robertson, in *History of the Latin American Nations* (chap. xi. 2nd ed. New York, 1932); Mary W. Williams, in *People and Politics of Latin America* (chap. xxvi. Boston, 1930); and Charles E. Chapman, in *Republican Hispanic America. A History* (pp. 353-371. New York, 1937), summarize the development of Chile since independence. Ramón Sotomayor Valdés started out to write four decades of Chilean history, but his *Historia de Chile durante los cuarenta años trascurridos desde 1831 hasta 1871* (2 vols. Santiago, 1875-1876) proved to be only a detailed description of the administration of Joaquín Prieto (see pp. 255-272). Toward the end of his active life, Barros Arana added to his scholarly reputation by publishing *Un decenio de la historia de Chile (1841-1851)* (in "Obras completas de Barros Arana" (Vols. XIV, XV. Santiago, 1913). Years after his father's presidency (see p. 272) Gonzalo Bulnes brought out as a filial offering his *Historia de la campaña del Perú en 1838* (Santiago, 1878). The first important contribution of Luis Galdames was *El decenio de Montt* (Santiago, 1904). A more recent work and a thoroughly sympathetic one—the last by its gifted writer—is Alberto Edwards' *El gobierno de Don Manuel Montt, 1851-1861* (Santiago, 1932). Sir Clements R. Markham, in *The War between Peru and Chile, 1879-1882* (London, 1882), presents the causes of the War of the Pacific with a strong bias against Chile and continues the story of the war up to the date of publication. Similar in character is the volume by Victor Manuel Maúrtua entitled *The Question of the Pacific* (Rev. ed. New York, 192?). For the Chilean side, Benjamín Vicuña Mackenna, Gonzalo Bulnes, and Diego Barros Arana have produced narratives that naturally are more patriotic than critical. Up to the present, no Chilean writer has ventured to summarize their weighty tomes. The arbitration of the Tacna-Arica question between Chile and Peru in 1921-1925 gave a chance for each contestant to submit unlimited documents in support of its contentions. A few of these are edited by W. J.

BIBLIOGRAPHICAL NOTES 541

Dennis in *Documentary History of the Tacna-Arica Dispute* (Iowa City, 1927), while a summary of the nitrate war and subsequent diplomacy is given by the same author in *Tacna and Arica* (New Haven, 1931). Carlos Walker Martínez in *Historia de la administración de Santa María* (2 vols. in 1. Valparaiso, 1889) not only pays his respects to the subject but introduces readers to political issues that led to the overthrow of Balmaceda. The administration of that executive is treated favorably by his friend, J. Bañados Espinosa, in *Balmaceda, su gobierno y la revolución de 1891* (Paris, 1894); and in a more scholarly manner by Fanor Velasco, *Revolución de 1891* (Santiago, 1925). A contemporary account by an English newspaper correspondent is to be found in M. H. Hervey's *Dark Days in Chile* (London, 1891). The story of the revolutionary changes in 1924-1925 which affected important constitutional reforms is detailed in Enrique Monreal's *Historia completa y documentada del período revolucionario, 1824-1825* (Santiago, 1927). This account is more extensive than the personal explanation afforded by Juan Bennett A. in *La revolución del 5 de setiembre de 1924* (Santiago, [1925]). More recent revolutionary accounts are still too scattered and partisan to give a fair picture of developments.

In many respects the biographies that follow supplement the regular historical accounts. Among useful compilations one may cite Miguel Luis Amunátegui's *Ensayos biográficos* (4 vols. Santiago, 1893-1896), Pedro Pablo Figueroa's *Diccionario biográfico de Chile* (4th ed. Vols. I-III. Santiago, 1897-1901), and Virgilio Figueroa's *Diccionario histórico y biográfico de Chile, 1800-1925* (5 vols. in 4. Santiago, 1925-1931). The two Figueroas are not related. The first has covered the nineteenth century and the second repeats much of this material and continues his work to 1930. In these two productions, and especially in the latter, one finds much of recent Chilean history. The conclusions of these compilers often need, however, to be carefully examined. They are both prejudiced and their works contain many minor mistakes. To a large extent, however, the outsider must depend upon them for a knowledge of recent events. The biographers of Chilean statesmen were frequently their political opponents. Hence it is necessary to discount their opinions. This is particularly true of outstanding characters such as Portales, Montt, Balmaceda, and Alessandri. With respect to Portales, we may mention the unfavorable narratives of B. Vicuña Mackenna, *Don Diego Portales* (Valparaiso, 1863) and of J. V. Lastarria, *Don Diego Portales* (Santiago, 1896). A more scholarly and more reliable account of the great founder is to be found in Francisco

A. Encina's *Portales, introducción a la historia de la época de Diego Portales* (Vols. I, II. Santiago, 1934). Some of the leading characterizations of Manuel Montt have already been mentioned in the history of his decade (see pp. 289-304). The cultural history of the mid-century is fittingly presented in the work of Ricardo Donoso entitled *Barros Arana, educador, historiador, y hombre público* (Santiago, 1931); in Joaquín Rodríguez Bravo's *Don José Victorino Lastarria* (Santiago, 1892); and in Alejandro Fuenzalida Grandón's *Lastarria i su tiempo (1817-1888), su vida, obras e influencia en el desarrollo político e intelectual de Chile* (2 vols. Santiago, 1911). An important movement in the constitutional history of Chile is biographically summarized by Justo and Domingo Arteaga Alemparte in *Los constituyentes chilenos de 1870* (Vol. II of "Biblioteca de escritores de Chile." Santiago, 1910). The career of Balmaceda mentioned in the bibliographic section devoted to national history is skillfully sketched by an outsider in Joaquín Nabuco's *Balmaceda* (Santiago, 1914). He is discussed more critically and at greater length in Ricardo Salas Edwards' *Balmaceda y el parlamentarismo en Chile* (Vols. I, II, 2nd ed. Santiago, 1916). Arturo Alessandri has provoked numerous monographs, favorable and unfavorable, but as yet no adequate biography. The same may be said of Carlos Ibáñez although the work of Aquiles Vergara Vicuña entitled *Ibáñez, César Criollo* (Vols. I, II. Santiago, 1931) offers a doubtful interpretation of his meteoric career.

CONSTITUTIONAL HISTORY

Chile has been prolific in constitutional historians. Among the first to review the numerous experiments in forms of government was Ramón Briseño in his *Memoria histórico-crítica del derecho público chileno, desde 1810 hasta nuestros días* (Santiago, 1849). Few of its leading men from the mid-century on have refrained from discussing its constitutional development. Bello, Lastarria, and numerous others combine such discussions with their literary and educational productions. Among important contributions we may mention that of Julio Bañados Espinosa, *Constituciones de Chile, Francia, Estados Unidos, etc.* (Santiago, 1889), and the work of Joaquín Rodríguez Bravo entitled *Estudios constitucionales* (Santiago, 1888). The standard work in this field, widely used as a text in university courses, is Alcibíades Roldán's *Elementos de derecho constitucional de Chile, 1810-1925* (Vol. I. Santiago, 1925). The leading commentary on the new constitution of 1925 is José Guillermo Guerra's *Constitución de 1925* (Santiago, 1929). For the source materials used by these writers, one must have recourse to *Sesiones de los cuerpos legislativos, 1811-1845* (28 vols. Santiago, 1886-

1906), and to Ricardo Anguita, *Leyes promulgadas en Chile* (11 vols. Santiago, 1912-1918), as well as to the files of *El diario oficial* and the collected speeches of the leading public men.

SOCIAL HISTORY

Many works of a social character afford considerable data. Nicolás Palacios' *Raza chilena* (2 vols. 2nd ed. Santiago, 1918) discusses the development of the Chilean people with special reference to conditions among the lower classes. Domingo Amunátegui Solar in *Historia social de Chile* (Santiago, 1932) traces the origin of the leading families of the country. The same author's *La sociedad chilena del siglo xviii. Mayorazgos i títulos de Castilla* (3 vols. Santiago, 1901-1904) describes the background of the landholding aristocracy. Alberto Cabero in *Chile y los chilenos* (Santiago, 1926) combines social, political, and industrial features of Chilean life from the standpoint of modern social principles, while Alberto Edwards' *Fronda aristocrática en Chile* (Santiago, 1928) seemingly devotes itself to a social class while really presenting the views of a political philosopher. Some attempt at applying social principles to present-day problems appears in Jorge Gustavo Silva's *Nuestra evolución político-social* (Santiago, 1931). Carlos Keller's *Eterna crisis chilena* (Santiago, 1931) touches upon social as well as economic phases. In *Chile luchando por nuevas formas de vida* (2 vols. Santiago, 1936), Wilhelm Mann, an adopted Chilean, discusses with sympathy various phases of the country's development.

LITERARY HISTORY

Colonial literature receives its most adequate treatment at the hands of José Toribio Medina in *Historia de la literatura colonial de Chile* (2 vols. Santiago, 1878). Other significant studies covering both the colonial and national periods are Domingo Amunátegui Solar's *Bosquejo histórico de la literatura chilena* (Santiago, 1918) and Jorge Huneeus Gana's *Cuadro histórico de la producción intelectual de Chile*, in "Biblioteca de escritores de Chile" (Vol. I. Santiago, 1910). J. V. Lastarria presents an interesting personal summary, covering the years 1836-1877, in *Recuerdos literarios* (2nd ed. Santiago, 1885). Alfred Coester, in *The Literary History of Spanish America* (2nd ed. New York, 1928), has an interesting chapter dealing with Chile. For a critical estimate by Raúl Silva Castro of this portion of Coester's work, see *Rev. chil. de hist. y geog.*, LXX (July-Dec., 1931), 260-275. An ambitious attempt to cover this phase of Chilean life, but one still incomplete, is to be found in Pedro N. Cruz's *Estudios sobre la literatura chilena* (Santiago, 1926). The works of many leading writers of the nineteenth century are included in "Biblioteca de escritores de Chile" (11 vols. Santiago, 1910-1913). One of the most thorough discussions of the educational situation in the country is the work of Dario E. Salas, entitled *El problema nacional, bases para la reconstrucción de nuestro sistema escolar primario* (Santiago, 1917). Much of the intellectual output of the country is polemic rather than literary in content, but Andrés Bello's *Obras completas* (15 vols. Santiago, 1881-1893) edited under the direction of the council of public instruction, and José Victorino Lastarria's *Obras completas* edited by Alejandro Fuenzalida Grandón (13 vols. Santiago, 1906-1913), not to mention others, attest the wide variety of Chile's cultural life.

FISCAL AFFAIRS

The most pretentious study of the monetary and commercial problems of Chile is that of the university professor, Daniel Martner, entitled *Estudio de política comercial chilena e historia económica nacional* (2 vols. Santiago, 1923). The Department of Commerce presents the work of Charles A. McQueen, entitled *Chilean Public Finance,* "Special Agent Series," No. 224 (Washington, 1924), as one of its monographs. A scholarly treatise on a leading fiscal problem of the country is that of Frank Whitson Fetter, *Monetary Inflation in Chile* (Princeton, 1931).

REVIEWS

Valuable interpretative articles, as well as source material, are brought out in *Revista chilena,* of which an earlier series was published from 1875 to 1880. The present series began publication in 1917. Another publication of outstanding significance is *Revista chilena de historia y geografía* (Santiago, 1911—). Occasional articles relating to the country appear in *The Hispanic American Historical Review* (Baltimore and Durham, 1918-1922, 1926-   ). Other articles of popular interest appear in contemporary publications such as *Chile* (New York, 1926-1931) and *Current History* (New York, 1915-   ).

INDEX

Pezuela, Joaquín de la, viceroy of Peru, 213

Philip II, of Spain, 468; attitude towards colonies, 61, 82; orders occupation of Strait of Magellan, 92

Philip III, of Spain, expels Moriscos, 96 n.

Philip V, of Spain, Bourbon line of, 103; patron of University of San Felipe, 110

Philippi, Bernardo de, colonizer, 282

Philippi, Rudolfo Amando, naturalist, 282, 293; biog., 504

Philippine Islands, 24

Picón-Salas, Mariano, 17 n.

Piérola, Nicolás de, 337; president of Peru, revolt of, 331; defends Lima, 334; biog., 505

Pigafetta, Antonio, author of The First Voyage of the World by Magellan, quoted, 23 n.

Pilcomayo, Peruvian sloop, 330

Pilling, W., works of, 186 n., 539

Pincheira brothers, bandits, 209, 253, 270; biog., 505

Pintado. See Vera Pintado, Bernardo

Pinto Díaz, Gen. Francisco Antonio, 238, 319; representative in Buenos Aires, 170; reorganizes government, 231, 235; biog., 505

Pinto Garmendia, President Aníbal, character and career of, 319; candidacy of, 320; administration of, 320-25; retires, 336; biog., 506

Pinzón, Vicente Yáñez, 466

Pirates, English, 91, 93, 94, 96

Pisagua, occupation of, 331

Pisco, occupation of, 213, 333

Pissis, Amando, geologist, 293; biog., 506

"Piuquenes, gate of the," 194

Pizarro, Francisco, 41, 444, 445, 504, 518, 528; conqueror of Peru, 25; commissions Valdivia, 37; murdered, 42; biog., 506

Pizarro, Gonzalo, 442, 443, 477, 484; revolt of, 43

Pizarro, Hernando, 445; executes Almagro, 29

Placilla, battle of, 347, 451

Planchón Pass, 194

Plaza, Nicanor, sculptor, 356, 429, 448, 461; biog., 507

Plaza de Armas, Santiago, 40, 100, 114, 253

Plutarch's Parallel Lives, 128-29

Poblete Troncoso, Moisés, 435-36 n.

Poets, of Chile, 355-56, 428

Poinsett, Joel R., U. S. agent, 173, 481

Police, creation of, 110; reorganized, 217, 282; character and methods of, 436. See also Serenos; "Vigilantes"; Carabineros

Political Christian Catechism, quoted, 152-54. See also Irisarri

Political parties, early groups, 145, 147, 164; personal, of Carrera and O'Higgins, 205, 232; federal, 232; pelucones ("bigwigs") and pipiolos, 232-33, 235-236, 238; pelucón supremacy, 255-56; filipolitas, 261-63, 265; revival of party strife, 285-88; liberal-conservative fusion against Montt-Varistas, 296-99, 300; commercial influence on party activities, 301, 302; party shifts and rise of radicals, 305-6, 313, 317; party conventions, 314, 320, 346, 367, 389; disorganization of the liberals and rise of the democrats, 340-42, 344, 361; new parties and "moral principles," 364-66; coalitions and alliances, 366-67, 369; under the Constitution of 1925, 379-80; under Ibáñez, 384; Civic Union elects Montero, 389; partisanship of the right and of the left, 398-401

Pont. See Marcó del Pont

"Poor Clares," 66 n. See also Church

Popular Credit Bank, 391

Population, elements and categories of, colonial period, 77, 79, 101; character of, in eighteenth century, 202; increase in, 244, 301, 356-57; present status and distribution, 412, 438-39

Portales Plazazuelos, Diego José Víctor, 262-63, 354, 454, 509, 516, 525, 533, 534, 541; commercial connections of, 226, 236; character and training of, 236-37; policy and methods of, 238-40, 255, 256; second dictatorship of, 265-66; forces war on Peru, 267-69; assassination of, 269-70; biog., 507-8

Porter, Commodore David, 481

Portobelo, 71, 105

Portugal, 62, 97, 144; pioneer activity of, 19

Postal service, established, 103, 106-7; expansion of, 282, 310

Poveda, Tomás. See Marín de Poveda, Governor Tomás

Poverty. See Social conditions and customs

Prado, Colonel Mariano Ignacio, Peruvian president, 307, 326, 331; biog., 508

Prat Chacón, Captain Arturo, naval officer, 327; biog., 508

Precursores de la independencia de Chile, Los. See Amunátegui Aldunate, Miguel Luis

President, national, powers of, 242, 255, 264; "extraordinary powers" of, 296; reëlection of, 313, 314; in-